Innovations, Standards, and Practices of Web Services:

Emerging Research Topics

Liang-Jie Zhang
Kingdee International Software Group Company Limited, China

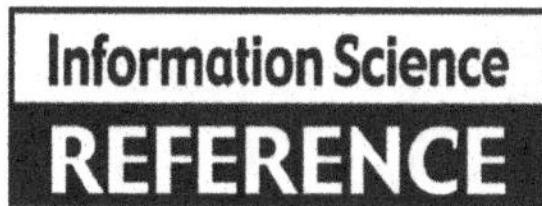

Managing Director: Lindsay Johnston
Book Production Manager: Sean Woznicki
Development Manager: Joel Gamon
Development Editor: Hannah Abelbeck
Acquisitions Editor: Erika Carter
Typesetters: Adrienne Freeland and Mackenzie Snader
Print Coordinator: Jamie Snavely
Cover Design: Nick Newcomer

Published in the United States of America by
Information Science Reference (an imprint of IGI Global)
701 E. Chocolate Avenue
Hershey PA 17033
Tel: 717-533-8845
Fax: 717-533-8661
E-mail: cust@igi-global.com
Web site: http://www.igi-global.com

Library of Congress Cataloging-in-Publication Data

Innovations, standards, and practices of Web services: emerging research topics / Liang-Jie Zhang, editor.
p. cm.
Includes bibliographical references and index.
ISBN 978-1-61350-104-7 (hardcover) -- ISBN 978-1-61350-105-4 (ebook) -- ISBN 978-1-61350-106-1 (print & perpetual access) 1. Web services. I. Zhang, Liang-Jie.
TK5105.88813.I55 2012
384.3'3--dc23

2011034867

British Cataloguing in Publication Data
A Cataloguing in Publication record for this book is available from the British Library.

All work contributed to this book is new, previously-unpublished material. The views expressed in this book are those of the authors, but not necessarily of the publisher.

Table of Contents

Preface

W3C defines a Web service as a software system designed to use standard protocols to support interoperable machine-to-machine interactions (publication, discovery, access, and orchestration) over a network. As Web services technology has matured in recent years, a new scalable Service-Oriented Architecture (SOA) is emerging as the basis for distributed computing and large networks of collaborating applications. To keep with the burgeoning field of web services and information technology, emerging and future research directions like the ones chronicled in this volume are the vital pulse that will keep researchers abreast of the latest and cutting edge.

Innovations, Standards and Practices of Web Services: Emerging Research Topics, edited by Liang-Jie Zhang, offers 17 contributions from authors from around the world, serving as experts in the vast and ever-expanding field of web services. This book has a thematic focus beyond the scope of the technology and language of computer mediated communication and interoperability, reaching instead to the topics of best practices, standards, and new ideas.

In Chapter 1, "*Complex Network Theory Based Web Services Composition Benchmark Toolkit,*" Seog-Chan Oh and Dongwon Lee present a novel benchmark toolkit, WSBen, that is capable of generating synthetic web services data with diverse scenarios and configurations using complex network theory. Web services researchers therefore can evaluate their web services discovery and composition algorithms in a more systematic fashion. The development of WSBen is inspired by their preliminary study on real-world web services crawled from the Web.

Chapter 2 is titled "*USDL: A Service-Semantics Description Language for Automatic Service Discovery and Composition,*" and it was written by Srividya Kona, Ajay Bansal, Luke Simon, Ajay Mallya, Gopal Gupta, and Thomas D. Hite. The authors present an infrastructure using USDL (Universal Service-Semantics Description Language), a language for formally describing the semantics of Web services. USDL is based on the Web Ontology Language (OWL) and employs WordNet as a common basis for understanding the meaning of services. USDL can be regarded as formal service documentation that will allow sophisticated conceptual modeling and searching of available Web services, automated service composition, and other forms of automated service integration.

Chapter 3, "*Privacy-Preserving Trust Establishment with Web Service Enhancements,*" by Zhengping Wu and Alfred C. Weaver, proposes a mechanism whereby the service requester discovers the service provider's requirements from a web service policy document, then formulates a trust primitive by associating a set of attributes in a pre-packaged credential with a semantic name, signed with the requester's digital signature, to negotiate a trust relationship. Thus the service requester's privacy is preserved because only those attributes required to build a trust relationship are revealed.

In Chapter 4, "*Web Services Discovery with Rough Sets*," by Maozhen Li, Bin Yu, Vijay Sahota, and Man Qi, the authors present ROSSE, a Rough Sets based Search Engine for Web service discovery. One salient feature of ROSSE lies in its capability to deal with uncertainty of service properties when matching services. A use case is presented to demonstrate the use of ROSSE for discovery of car services. ROSSE is evaluated in terms of its accuracy and efficiency in service discovery.

Chapter 5, "*A Model-Based Approach for Diagnosing Fault in Web Service Processes*," by Yuhong Yan, Philippe Dague, Yannick Pencolé, and Marie-Odile Cordier proposes a model-based approach to diagnose the faults in a Web service-composed business process. The authors convert a Web service orchestration language, more specifically BPEL4WS, into synchronized automata, to produce a formal description of the topology and variable dependency of the business process. After an exception is thrown, the diagnoser can calculate the business process execution trajectory based on the formal model and the observed evolution of the business process. The faulty Web services are deduced from the variable dependency on the execution trajectory.

Chapter 6, "*Autonomous Web Services Migration in Mobile and Wireless Environments*," by Yeon-Seok Kim, Myung-Woo Park, , and Kyong-Ho Lee, proposes an efficient method for migrating and replicating Web services among mobile devices. Specifically, the proposed method splits the source code of a Web service into subcodes depending on users' preferences for its constituent operations. For the seamless provisioning of services, a subcode with a higher preference is migrated earlier than others. To evaluate the performance of the proposed method, the effect of the code splitting on migration was analyzed.

Chapter 7, "*Estimating the Privacy Protection Capability of a Web Service Provider*," by George O.M. Yee, suggests that users would benefit from being able to choose (assuming that such estimates were made public) the service that has the greatest ability to protect their privacy (this would in turn encourage Web service providers to pay more attention to privacy). Web service providers would benefit by being able to adjust their provisions for protecting privacy until certain target capability levels of privacy protection are reached. This article presents an approach for estimating the privacy protection capability of a Web service provider and illustrates the approach with an example.

Chapter 8, "*Issues on the Compatibility of Web Service Contracts*," by Surya Nepal and John Zic, categorizes compatibility issues in Web service contracts into two broad categories: (a) between contracts of different services (defined as a composability problem), and (b) a service contract and its implementation (defined as a conformance problem). This chapter examines and addresses these problems, first by identifying and specifying contract compatibility conditions, and second, through the use of compatibility checking tools that enable application developers to perform checks at design time.

Chapter 9, "*High Performance Approach for Server Side SOAP Processing*," by Lei Li, Chunlei Niu, Ningjiang Chen, Jun Wei, and Tao Huang, proposes a new approach to improve Web services performance. Focusing on avoiding traditional XML parsing and Java reflection at runtime, this article presents a service-specific simple object access protocol (SOAP) processor to accelerate the execution of Web services. Moreover, the SOAP processor embeds several cache implementations and uses a novel adaptive cache mechanism, which can choose an optimized cache implementation dynamically. Through the experiments in this article, it is to be observed that the proposed approach can achieve a significant performance gain by incorporating the SOAP processor into the SOAP engine.

In Chapter 10, "*A Framework and Protocols for Service Contract Agreements Based on International Contract Law*," by Michael Parkin, Dean Kuo, and John Brooke, a framework and a domain-independent negotiation protocol for creating legally binding contracts for service usage in a distributed, asynchronous service-oriented architecture is presented. The negotiation protocol, which builds on a simple agreement protocol to form a multiround "symmetric" negotiation protocol, is based on an internationally recognized contract law convention. By basing our protocol on this convention and taking into account the limitations of an asynchronous messaging environment, we can form contracts between autonomous services across national and juridical boundaries, necessary in a loosely coupled, widely geographically distributed environment such as the Grid.

Chapter 11, "*XML Data Binding for C++ Using Metadata*," by Szabolcs Payrits, Péter Dornbach, and István Zólyomi presents a novel way to map XML data to the C++ programming language. The proposed solution offers more flexibility and more compact code that makes it ideal for embedded environments. The article describes the concept and the architecture of the solution and compares it with existing solutions. This article is an extended version of the paper from ICWS 2006. The authors include a broader comparison with existing tools on Symbian and Linux platforms and evaluate the code size and performance.

Chapter 12, "*The Assurance Point Model for Consistency and Recovery in Service Composition*," by Susan D. Urban, Le Gao, Rajiv Shrestha, Yang Xiao, Zev Friedman, and Jonathan Rodriguez, displays how their research has defined an abstract execution model for establishing user-defined correctness and recovery in a service composition environment. The service composition model defines a hierarchical service composition structure, where a service is composed of atomic and/or composite groups. The model provides multi-level protection against service execution failure by using compensation and contingency at different composition granularity levels. The model is enhanced with the concept of assurance points (APS) and integration rules, where APs serve as logical and physical checkpoints for user-defined consistency checking, invoking integration rules that check pre and post conditions at different points in the execution process.

Chapter 13, "*Early Capacity Testing of an Enterprise Service Bus*," was written by Ken Ueno and Michiaki Tatsubori. This article proposes a capacity planning methodology and performance evaluation techniques for ESBs, to be used in the early stages of the system development life cycle. The authors actually run the ESB on a real machine while providing a pseudo-environment around it. In order to simplify setting up the environment we provide ultra-light service requestors and service providers for the ESB under test. They show that the proposed mock environment can be set up with practical hardware resources available at the time of hardware resource assessment. The experimental results showed that the testing results with the mock environment correspond well with the results in the real environment.

Chapter 14, "*An Integrated Framework for Web Services Orchestration*," by C. Boutrous Saab, D. Coulibaly, S. Haddad, T. Melliti, P. Moreaux, and S. Rampacek, focuses on two features of Web services. The first one concerns the interaction problem: given the interaction protocol of a Web service described in BPEL, how to generate the appropriate client? Their approach is based on a formal semantics for BPEL via process algebra and yields an algorithm which decides whether such a client exists and synthetize the description of this client as a (timed) automaton. The second one concerns the design process of a service. They propose a method which proceeds by two successive refinements: first the service is described via UML, then refined in a BPEL model and finally enlarged with JAVA code using JCSWL, a new language that we introduce here. Their solutions are integrated in a service development framework that will be presented in a synthetic way.

Chapter 15, "*Security for Web Services: Standards and Research Issues*," by Lorenzo D. Martino, and Elisa Bertino, discusses the main security requirements for Web services and it describes how such security requirements are addressed by standards for Web services security recently developed or under development by various standardizations bodies. Standards are reviewed according to a conceptual framework that groups them by the main functionalities they provide. Covered standards include most of the standards encompassed by the original Web Service Security roadmap proposed by Microsoft and IBM in 2002 (Microsoft and IBM 2002). They range from the ones geared toward message and conversation security and reliability to those developed for providing interoperable Single Sign On and Identity Management functions in federated organizations. The latter include Security Assertion Markup Language (SAML), WS-Policy, XACML, that is related to access control and has been recently extended with a profile for Web services access control; XKMS and WS-Trust; WS-Federation, LibertyAlliance and Shibboleth, that address the important problem of identity management in federated organizations.The chapter also discusses the issues related to the use of the standards and open research issues in the area of access control for Web services and innovative digital identity management techniques are outlined.

Chapter 16, "*Web Service Enabled Online Laboratory*," by Yuhong Yan, Yong Liang, Abhijeet Roy, and Xinge Du, benchmarks the performance of the system when SOAP is used as the wire format for communication and propose solutions to optimize performance. In order to avoid any installation at the client side, the authors develop Web 2.0 based techniques to display the virtual instrument panel and real time signals with just a standard Web browser. The technique developed in this paper can be widely used for different real laboratories, such as microelectronics, chemical engineering, polymer crystallization, structural engineering, and signal processing.

Chapter 17, "*An Efficient Service Discovery Method and its Application*," by Shuiguang Deng, Zhaohui Wu, and Jian Wu proposes an information model for registered services. Based on the model, it brings forward a two-phase semantic-based service discovery method which supports both the operation matchmaking and operation-composition matchmaking. Th authors import the bipartite graph matching to improve the efficiency of matchmaking. An implementation of the proposed method is presented. A series of experiments show that the method gains better performance on both discovery recall rate and precision than a traditional matchmaker and it also scales well with the number of services being accessed.

These 17 chapters present the latest research, perspectives, trends, and emerging issues in the field of web service research. They combine to become an essential reference for practitioners, academics, and students alike, serving as both a reference book and research manual.

Liang-Jie Zhang
Kingdee International Software Group Company Limited, China

Chapter 1
Complex Network Theory Based Web Services Composition Benchmark Toolkit

Seog-Chan Oh
General Motors R&D Center, USA

Dongwon Lee
The Pennsylvania State University, USA

ABSTRACT

In recent years, while many research proposals have been made toward novel algorithmic solutions of a myriad of web services composition problems, their validation has been less than satisfactory. One of the reasons for this problem is the lack of real benchmark web services data with which researchers can test and verify their proposals. In this chapter, to remedy this challenge, we present a novel benchmark toolkit, WSBen, which is capable of generating synthetic web services data with diverse scenarios and configurations using complex network theory. Web services researchers therefore can evaluate their web services discovery and composition algorithms in a more systematic fashion. The development of WSBen is inspired by our preliminary study on real-world web services crawled from the Web. The proposed WSBen can: (1) generate a collection of synthetic web services files in the WSDL format conforming to diverse complex network characteristics; (2) generate queries and ground truth sets for testing discovery and composition algorithms; (3) prepare auxiliary files to help further statistical analysis; (4) convert WSDL test sets to the formats that conventional AI planners can read; and (5) provide a graphical interface to control all these functions. To illustrate the application of the WSBen, in addition, we present case studies selected from three domains: (1) web services composition; (2) AI planning; and (3) the laws of networks in Physics community. The WSBen toolkit is available at: http://pike.psu.edu/sw/wsben/. This chapter is an invited extension of authors' previous publication (Oh & Lee, 2009).

DOI: 10.4018/978-1-61350-104-7.ch001

INTRODUCTION

A *Web Service* is a set of related functionalities that can be loosely coupled with other (web) services on the Web. As long as a web application exposes its functionalities using standard-based web service API such as the XML-based WSDL, it can be used as a web service by other web applications. This openness, platform-independence, and reusability of web services therefore pose tremendous opportunities for web commerce and businesses, enabling web services framework the de facto standard for "accessing" applications and "sharing" data on the Web. Together with the recent surge of interest on the Cloud Computing, the popularity of web services in industries will become even stronger in the near future since virtually all applications in the Cloud Computing can be treated as web services applications.

As a growing number of web services are available on the Web and in organizations, finding and composing the right set of web services for certain tasks become an increasingly important problem. As a result, in recent years, a plethora of research work and products on web services discovery and composition problems have appeared. As of November 2010, according to the estimation of Google Scholar, there are about 1,870,000 scholarly articles mentioning "Web Services Composition". In addition, the web service research community has hosted several open competition programs to solicit algorithms and software to discover pertinent web services and compose them to make value-added functionality as follows:

- EEE 2007: http://ws-challenge.georgetown.edu/wsc07/
- CEC 2008: http://cec2008.cs.georgetown.edu/wsc08/
- CEC 2009: http://ws-challenge.georgetown.edu/wsc09/
- CEC 2010: http://ws-challenge.georgetown.edu/wsc10/

Despite all this attention, however, there have been very few test environments available for evaluating such algorithms and software. The lack of such a testing environment with flexible features hinders the development of new composition algorithms and validation of the proposed ones. Therefore, the need for a benchmark arises naturally to evaluate and compare algorithms and software for the web services discovery and composition problems. As desiderata for such a benchmark, it must have (a large number of) web services in the standard-based WSDL files and test queries that can represent diverse scenarios and situations that emphasize different aspects of various web services application domains. Often, however, test environments used in research and evaluation have skewed test cases that do not necessarily capture real scenarios. Consider the following example.

Example 1 (Motivating) *Let us use the following notations: A web service* $w \in W$*, specified in a WSDL file, can be viewed as a collection of operations, each of which in turn consists of input and output parameters. When an operation op has input parameters* $op^i=\{p_1, ..., p_n\}$ *and output parameters* $op^o=\{q_1, ..., q_n\}$*, we denote the operation by* $op(op^i, op^o)$*. Furthermore, each parameter is viewed as a pair of (name, type). We denote the name and type of a parameter p by p.name and ptype, respectively. For establishing our motivation, we first downloaded 1,544 raw WSDL files that Fan et al. (Fan & Kambhampati, 2005) gathered from real-world web services registries such as XMethods or BindingPoint. We refer to the data set as PUB06. For the purpose of preprocessing PUB06, first, we conducted WSDL validation according to WSDL standard, where 874 invalid WSDL files are removed and 670 files are left out. Second, we removed 101 duplicated WSDL files at operation level, yielding 569 valid WSDL files. Finally, we conducted type flattening and data cleaning processes subsequently. The type flattening process is to extract atomic types from user-defined complex types using type hierarchy of*

Figure 1. #(p.name) distributions. (left) PUB05. (right) ICEBE05.

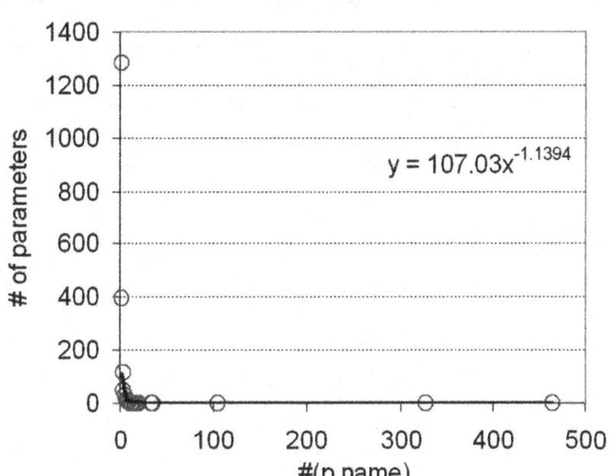

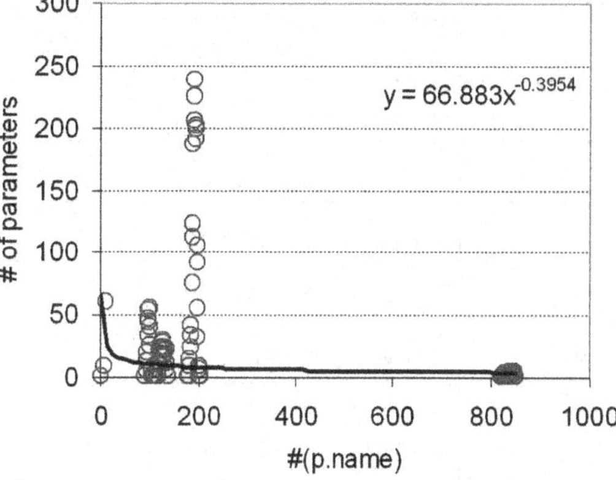

XML schema. This process helps find more compatible parameter faster. Details are found in (Kil et al., 2006). The final step is the data cleansing to improve the quality of parameters. For instance, substantial number of output parameters (16%) was named as "return", "result", or "response" which is too ambiguous for clients. However, often, their more precise underline meaning can be derived from contexts. For instance, if the output parameter named as "result" belongs to the operation named as "getAddress'", then the "result" is in fact "Address". In addition, often, naming follows apparent patterns such as getFooFromBar or searchFooByBar. Therefore, to replace names of parameters or operations by more meaningful ones, we removed spam tokens like "get" or "by" as much as we could.

We measured how many distinct parameters each WSDL file contained. Suppose that given a parameter p∈ P, we denote the number of occurrences of p.name as #(p.name). That is, #("pwd") indicates the number of occurrences of the parameter with name of "pwd". Figure 1 illustrates #(p.name) distributions of PUB06 and the ICEBE05 test set, where the x-axis is #(p.name) and the y-axis is the number of parameters with the same #(p.name) value. The distribution of PUB06 has no humps. We also plotted a power-function, over the #(p.name) distribution, and found that the exponent is 1.1394. Although 1.1394 does not suffice the requirement to be the power law (Denning, 2004), the distribution is skewed enough to be seen as the Zipf-like distribution. Indeed, the parameters such as "license key", "start date", "end date," or "password" have a large #(p.name) value, while most parameters appear just once. This observation also implies the existence of hub parameters, which appear in web services frequently, and serve important roles on the inter-connections between web services. On the contrary, the distribution of ICEBE05 test set has four humps equally at around 1, 100, 200, and 800 with the highest value at third hump. This distribution shape differs considerably from PUB06, the real public web services. This implies that the test environments of ICEBE05 do not necessarily capture characteristics of real web services.

In conclusion, as demonstrated in the example, our claim is that *any web services discovery and composition solutions must be evaluated under diverse configurations of web services networks* including two cases of Figure 1. However, to our best knowledge, there have been no publicly available benchmark tools satisfying such constraints. To address these needs and shortcomings, therefore, we developed the *WSBen*—Web Services discovery and composition Benchmark tool. The main contribution of WSBen is the

Table 1. Summary of notation

Notation	*Meaning*
w, W	Web service, set of web services
p, P	Parameter, set of parameters
r, r^i, r^o	Request, initial and goal parameter sets of r
$G_p(V_p, E_p)$	Parameter node network
$G_{op}(V_{op}, E_{op})$	Operation node network
$G_{ws}(V_{ws}, E_{ws})$	Web service node network
$G^f_{op}(V^f_{op}, E^f_{op})$	Full-matching operation node network
$G_{cl}(V_{cl}, E_{cl})$	Parameter cluster network
$g_{r^i}(p)$	Minimum cost of achieving $p \in P$ from r^i in G_p
xTS	WSBen's 5-tuple input framework (e.g., *baTS*, *erTS* and *nwsTS* are instances)

capability to provide diverse web service test sets based on three network models such as "random", "small-world", and "scale-free" types. These three network models have been shown to be able to model many real-world networks sufficiently correct (Albert & Barabasi, 2002). We also present three use cases in different communities to demonstrate the application of WSBen. In addition, we propose a flexible framework, by which one can study real web service networks, and establish the design foundation of WSBen. Table 1 summarizes important notations used throughout this chapter.

This chapter is organized as follows. First, in the background section, we review concepts and techniques required for the WSBen development, especially focusing on the complex network theory. Second, in the related works section, we discuss related studies in the literature as well as surveying existing world-wide challenges with regard to web services and Semantic Web. Third, in the overview of WSBen section, we present WSBen with its design concept, test set generation mechanism, key functions and characteristics. Fourth, in the use cases of WSBen section, we illustrate how WSBen can be exploited to obtain research benefits, especially by demonstrating three use cases. We expect three use cases enough to provide vigorous experiments and evaluation of our WSBen. Finally, conclusions are provided.

BACKGROUND

In this section, we review prerequisite techniques and concepts required to build WSBen. First, we revisit the definition and complexity of web services discovery and composition problems. Second, we introduce three complex network topologies based on which WSBen is designed to populate WSDL test files. Finally, we explain our conceptual methodology to project a bipartite web service network consisting of three distinct nodes (parameter, operation, and web service) and heterogeneous arc types into three distinct web service networks, each of which consists of single node and uniform arc. The main benefit of projecting web service networks is that it can allow for straightforward analysis on referred network's characteristics. Throughout this chapter, we will use our conceptual web service network concept in order to analyze real public web service networks as well as WSDL test file sets generated by WSBen.

Web Services Discovery and Composition

Suppose that a web service w has one operation so that a web service can be considered as an operation, and input and output parameter sets of w are denoted by w^i and w^0, respectively. When one has a request r that has initial input parameters r^i and desired output parameters r^0, one needs to find a web service w that can fulfill such that (1) $r^i \supseteq w^i$ and (2) $r^o \subseteq w^o$. Finding a web service that can fulfill r alone is referred to as *Web-service discovery* (WSD) problem. When it is impossible for one web service to fully satisfy r, on the other hand, one has to compose multiple web services $\{w_1, w_2, \ldots, w_n\}$, such that (1) for all $w_k \in \{w_1, w_2, \ldots, w_n\}$, w_k^i can be applicable when w_k^i is required at a particular stage in composition, and (2) $(r^i \cup w_1^o \cup w_2^o \cup \ldots \cup w_n^o) \supseteq r^o$. This problem is often called as *web services composition* (WSC) problem. In addition, one can also consider different matching schemes from the operation perspective–"partial" and "full" matching. In general, given w_1 and w_2, if w_1 can be invoked at the current information state and $w_1^o \supseteq w_2^i$, then w_1 can "fully" match w_2. On the other hand, if w_1 cannot fully match w_2, but w_1 can match a subset of w_2, then w_1 can "partially" match w_2. When only full matching is considered in the WSC problem, it can be seen as a single-source shortest path problem whose computational complexity is known as polynomial (Bertsekas, 2000). On the other hand, when both full and partial matching must be considered concurrently, the problem becomes a decision problem to determine the existence of a solution of k operators or less for propositional STRIPS planning, with restrictions on negation in pre- and post-conditions (Nilsson, 2001). Its computational complexity is proved to be NP-complete (Bylander, 1994). Therefore, when the number of web services to search is not small, finding an optimal solution to the WSC problem (i.e., a chain of web services to invoke) is prohibitively expensive, leading to approximate algorithms instead.

Complex Network Models

There are many empirical systems to form complex networks such as the scale-free network and the small-world network, in which nodes signify the elements of the system and edges represent the interactions between them.

Definition 1 (Random network) *A network is defined as the random network on N nodes, if each pair of nodes is connected with probability p. As a result, edges are randomly placed among a fixed set of nodes. The random network can be constructed by means of the Erdos-Renyi's random-graph model* (Erdos, 1996)

Definition 2 (Regular network) $Rg_{(N,k)}$ *is defined as the regular network on N nodes, if node i is adjacent to nodes* $[(i+j) \bmod N]$ *and* $[(i-j) \bmod N]$ *for* $1 \leq j \leq k$*, where k is the number of valid edge of each node. If k=N-1,* $Rg_{(N,k)}$ *becomes the complete N-nodes graph, where every node is adjacent to all the other N-1 nodes.*

We can define some metrics to quantify the characteristic properties of the complex networks as follows:

- L: The average shortest distance between reachable pairs of nodes, where the distance between nodes refers to the number of hops between the nodes. $L(p)$ is defined as L of the randomly rewired Watts-Strogatz graph (Watts & Strogatz, 2002) with probability p:L_{random} is identical to $L(1)$.
- C: The average clustering coefficient. Suppose that for a node i with v_i neighbor,

$C_i = \frac{2E_i}{v_i(v_i - 1)}$, where E_i is the number of edges between v_i neighbors of *i*. *C* is the average clustering coefficient C_i for a network. *C(p)* is defined as *C* of the randomly rewired Watts-Strogatz graph with probability *p*. C_{random} is identical to *C*(1).

Definition 3 (Small-world network) *Small-world networks are characterized by a highly clustered topology like regular lattices and the small network diameter, where the network diameter suggests the longest shortest distance between nodes. Specifically, small-world networks are* $C >> C_{random}$ *and* $L \approx L_{random}$ (Delgado, 2002).

By using the Watts-Strogatz model (Watts, 1999; Watts & Strogatz, 2002), we can construct networks that have the small-world properties. The model depends on two parameters, connectivity (*k*) and randomness (*p*), given the desired size of the graph (*N*). The Watts-Strogatz model starts with a $Rg_{(N,k)}$ and then every edge is rewired at random with probability *p*; for every edge (*i,j*), we decide whether we change *j* node (the destination node of (*i,j*)) with probability *p*. The Watts-Strogatz model leads to different graphs according to the different *p* as follows:

- When *p*=0, an $Rg_{(N,k)}$ is built.
- When *p*=1, a completely random network is built.

Otherwise, with 0<*p*<1, each edge (*i,j*) is reconnected with probability *p* to a new node *k* that is chosen at random (no self-links allowed). If the new edge (*i,k*) is added, the (*i,j*) is removed from the graph. The long-range connections (short-cuts) generated by this process decrease the distance between the nodes. For intermediate values of *p*, there is the "small-world" region, where the graph is highly clustered yet has a small average path length.

Definition 4 (Scale-free network) *Networks are called scale-free networks if the number of nodes that have v number of neighbor nodes is proportional to* $P_w(v) \propto v^{(-\gamma)}$*, where* γ *is typically greater than two with no humps.*

Barabasi and Albert provided several extended models (Albert et al., 1999; Delgado, 2002) to provide the scale-free properties. The extended model uses an algorithm to build graphs that depend on four parameters: m_0 (initial number of nodes), *m* (number of links added and/or rewired at every step of the algorithm), *p* (probability of adding links), *q* (probability of edge rewiring). The procedure starts with m_0 isolated nodes and performs one of the following three actions at every step:

With the probability of *p*, $m \leq m_0$ new links are added. The two nodes are picked randomly. The starting point of the link is chosen uniformly, and the end point of the new link is chosen according to the following probability distribution:

$$\prod_i = \frac{v_i + 1}{\sum_j (v_j + 1)} \quad (1)$$

where $\prod_i$ is the probability of selecting the *i* node, and v_i is the number of edges of node *i*.

The process is repeated *m* times.

- With the probability of *q,m* edges are rewired. For this purpose, *i* node and its link l_{ij} are chosen at random. The link is deleted. Instead, another node *z* is selected according to the probabilities of Equation (1), and the new link l_{iz} is added.
- With the probability of 1-*p*-*q*, a new node with *m* links is added. These new links connect the new node to *m* other nodes chosen according to the probabilities of Equation (1).
- Once the desired number *N* nodes are obtained, the algorithm stops. The graphs generated by this algorithm are scale-

free graphs, and the edges of the graphs are constructed such that the correlations among edges do not form. When $p=q$, the algorithm results in a graph, whose connectivity distribution can be approximated by

$$P(v) \propto (v+1)^{-\frac{2m(1-p)+1-2p}{m}+1} \quad (2)$$

where v is the number of edges.

Diverse Web Service Network Models

A set of web services form a network (or graph). Depending on the policy to determine nodes and edges of the network, there are varieties: web service level (i.e., coarse granularity), operation level, and parameter level (i.e., fine granularity) models. The graph at the middle of Figure 2 has a bipartite graph structure and consists of three distinct kinds of vertices (i.e., parameter, operation, and web-service node) and directed arcs between bipartite nodes (i.e., operation nodes and parameter nodes). An edge incident from a parameter node to an operation node means that the parameter is one of the inputs of the corresponding operation. Reversely, an edge incident from an operation node to a parameter means that the parameter is one of the outputs of the corresponding operation. The graph has two web services, labeled WS1 and WS2. WS1 has two operations Op11 and Op12, and WS2 has one operation, Op21, respectively. There are seven parameters, labeled P1 to P7. According to the node granularity, we can project the upper graph into three different web service networks.

- **Parameter-Node Network:** A graph $G_p(V_p,E_p)$, where V_p is a set of all parameter nodes and E_p is a set of edges. An edge (p_i,p_j) is directly incident from input parameters $p_i \in V_p$ to output parameters $p_j \in V_p$, where there is an operation that has an input parameter matching p_i and an output parameter matching p_j For example, P1→Op11→P3 in the upper graph is projected into P1→P3 in the parameter node network. Figure 3 shows the parameter node network for PUB06 and the ICEBE05 test set.
- **Operation-Node Network:** A graph $G_{op}(V_{op},E_{op})$, where V_{op} is a set of all operation nodes, and E_{op} is a set of edges. An edge (op_i,op_j) is incident from operation $op_i \in V_{op}$ to operation $op_j \in V_{op}$, here op_i can fully or partially match op_j. For example, Op11 partially matches Op12 which, in turn, fully matches Op21 in the upper graph. Therefore, Op11→Op12→Op21 can be shown in the operation node network. In particular, the fully matching operation node network, G^f_{op} has only Op12→Op21.
- **Web service Node Network:** A graph $G_{ws}(V_{ws},E_{ws})$, where V_{ws} is a set of all web-service nodes, and E_{ws} is a set of edges. An edge (ws_i,ws_j) is incident from web-service node $ws_i \in V_{ws}$, to $ws_j \in V_{ws}$, where there is at least one edge between any operation in ws_i and any operation in ws_j. For example, since WS1 possesses Op12 and WS2 possesses Op21 in the upper graph, WS1→WS2 appears in the web service node network.

RELATED WORKS

Constantinescu et al. (2004) proposed a scalable syntactic test bed called "Large-Scale Test Bed" where web services are generated as transformation between sets of terms in two application domains. For doing that, they first defined parameter sets corresponding to application

Figure 2. Web services networks: (a) WSDLs, (b) Conceptual web service network, (c) web service networks from diverse models, (d) Parameter node network, G_p, (e) Operation node network, G_{op}, (f) Fully invocable operation node network, G^f_{op}, and (g) web service node network, G_{ws}.

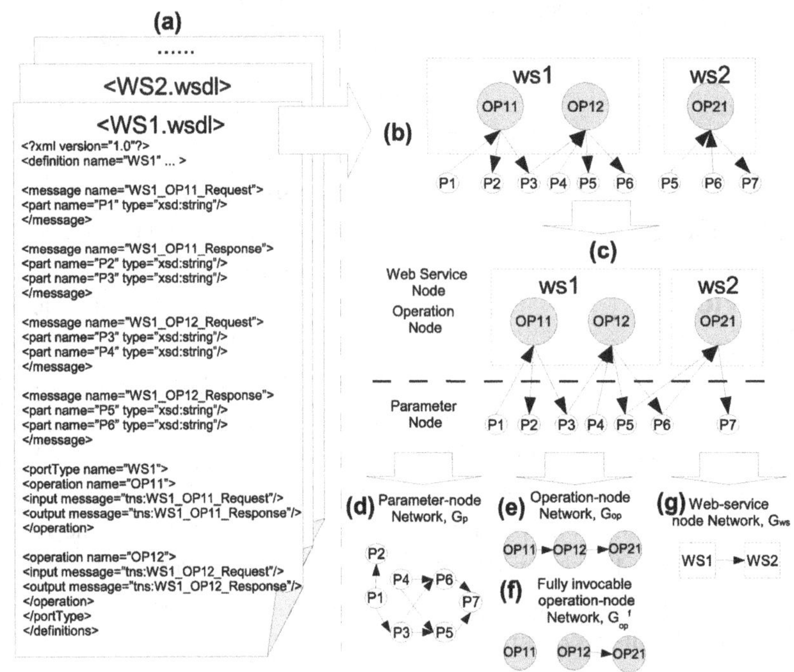

Figure 3. Diverse parameter networks. (left) PUB05. (right) ICEBE05.

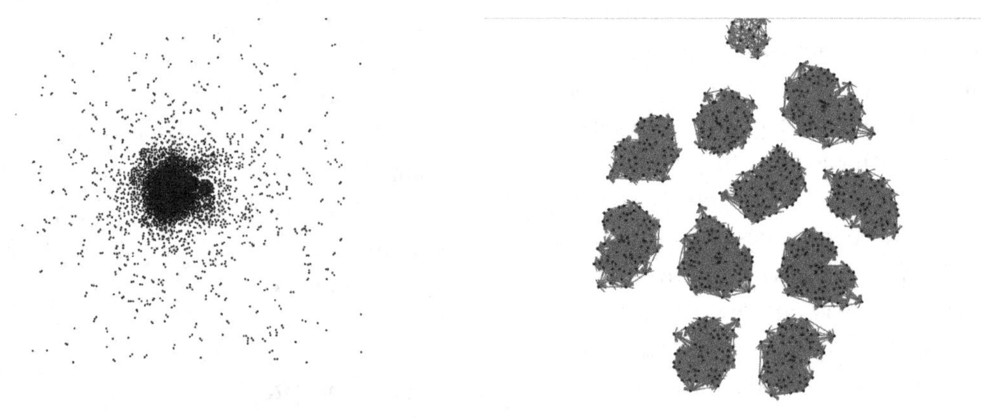

Table 2. Comparison of web services generator

Approach	Service Graph Model	WSDL Web Services Description	Semantic Web Services Description	Visualization Support	Other characteristics
2009 WSC	Random	Yes	Yes	Yes	User can specify the number of concepts, and the solution depth
Services Generator Toolkit (SGT)	Random	Yes	Yes	Yes	JAVA RPC implementation
Large-Scale Test Bed	Random	No	No	No	
WSBen	Complex networks (random, small-world, scale-free)	Yes	No	Yes	Designed to represent realistic network structures. Compatible to AI planning algorithms by generating PDDL or STRIPS files

domains and then, connected those parameter sets randomly and constructed a service graph which structure (i.e., nodes and arcs) is similar to the parameter cluster network of WSBen. However, WSBen takes a significant different approach to construct its parameter cluster networks in that WSBen does not simply connect parameter sets at random but simulates topologies of real web service networks. 2009 web service challenge (http://www.ws-challenge.org/wsc09) (Bleul et al., 2009) gave out a test set generator. This generator has three input parameters: the number of concepts, the number of services and the solution-depth. This test sets have no "predefined structure", so there is no "trick" which can be used by the composition algorithms as they are purely random generated. Cho et al. (2009) proposed "Service Generator Toolkit (SGT)" which provides main components such as: a graph model generator called Random Graph generator, a representation of the graph model called Graph Model, and several graph model exporters such as Java Remote Procedure Call (RPC) Service Unit Test Exporter, Java RPC Service Exporter, Ontology Web language – Services (OWL-S) Semantic Web Service Exporter, and Graph Visualization Exporter. SGT is kind of an enhanced version of Large-Scale Test Bed. The main difference between WSBen and these web services generation toolkits is that WSBen is inspired by extensive studies on real web services, and therefore is designed to support various web service network topologies and distributions. As a result, WSBen can present more realistic testing situation for researchers who want to test their web service discovery or composition algorithms than those of other works. Table 2 summaries the comparison of web services generation toolkits.

XMark (XMark, 2006) is an XML benchmark suite that can help identify the list of functions which an ideal benchmark should support. WSBen uses XMark as a reference model to identify necessary functions to simplify the testing process. One feature that is offered by XMark but not by WSBen is the provision of solutions to queries. In other words, XMark provides queries and their corresponding solutions but WSBen gives requests only because the optimal solution to a web services composition problem may not be obtained in the reasonable time window due to the problem's inherently high complexity. Regarding the latest real web services investigation, Al-Masri and Qusay (2008) conducted a thorough analytical investigation on the plurality of Web service interfaces that exist on the Web today and fetched 2,507 new web services in a database.

There are three unique challenges that have been established to investigate research issues with regard to web services and Semantic Web. First is the Semantic Web Services Challenge (http://sws-challenge.org/wiki/index.php/Main_Page). This venue invites application submissions for demonstrating practical progress towards achieving the vision of the Semantic Web. According to the event, it has the overall goal to advance our understanding of how semantic technologies can be exploited to produce useful applications for the Web. Second is the Web Services Challenge (http://www.ws-challenge.org/wsc09). This venue solicits approaches, methods, and algorithms in the domain of web services discovery and composition. This event evaluates participants' approaches based on their quantitative and qualitative performance results on discovery and composition problems. The Web Services Challenge is more driven by common problems, but the Semantic Web Challenge concentrates more on the environment. As such, the Semantic Web Challenge places more focus on semantics while the Web Services Challenges favors applied and short-term solutions (Brian et al., 2007). Third is the Service Oriented Architecture Contest (http://iscc.servicescomputing.org/2007/) which asks participants to openly choose particular domain-specific problems and show their best approaches for them. There are unique characteristics for each venue so that they have undoubtedly contributed to advance the state-of-art technologies in web services and Semantic Web. Among these challenges, WSBen can be exploited especially for the Web Services Challenge to provide various benchmark environments, discovery and composition problems by varying web services network topologies.

As for WSC, there are a lot of works on service composition and various systems or prototypes being proposed as Service Oriented Computing paradigm becomes the main development and deployment. For example, SELF-SERV (Benatallah et al., 2002), eFlow (Casati et al., 2000), METEOR-S (Sivashanmugam et al., 2003), LLAMA (Patil et al., 2004), Sword (Ponnekanti & Fox, 2002), LLAMA (Panahi et al., 2008) and WSPR (Oh et al., 2006 & 2007). Since it is too much costly to compose results manually when large number of services should be considered, automatic service composition is proposed to enable automatic search of work plans for given requests. Even though, there are many variations, the approaches for automatic service composition can be grouped into two categories: AI planning and graph search. The approaches in (McIlraith & Son, 2002; Sirin et al., 2004; Ponnekanti & Fox, 2002; McDermott, 2002; Zhovtobryukh, 2007) formulate the problem as an AI Planning problem. In other words, given an initial state, a goal, and a set of actions, the planning problem is to find a feasible plan by searching through the states generated by actions from the initial state to the goal state. Some other researches (Hashemian & Mavaddat, 2006; Liang & Su, 2005; Milanovic & Malek, 2006) consider the problem as a graph search problem and try to solve it with technologies like shortest path, A*, etc. Besides, a distributed approach is also suggested (Hu et al., 2008), which improves system performance by utilizing distributed computing capabilities.

We believe that the proposed WSBen is complementary for both AI Planning and graph search approaches. We further demonstrate how one can use WSBen to compare the performance of AI planners for the WSC problems in the illustrative use-cases section.

OVERVIEW OF WSBEN

In this section, we present a novel benchmark tool titled WSBen, which provides a set of functions to simplify the generation of test environments for WSD and WSC problems.

At a higher level, a web service can be assumed as a transformation between two different application domains, and each can be represented by a cluster. This assumption was the basis in developing WSBen. From the perspective of graph theory, WSBen builds *Parameter Cluster Network*, which consists of clusters and directed

Figure 4. Overview of WSBen

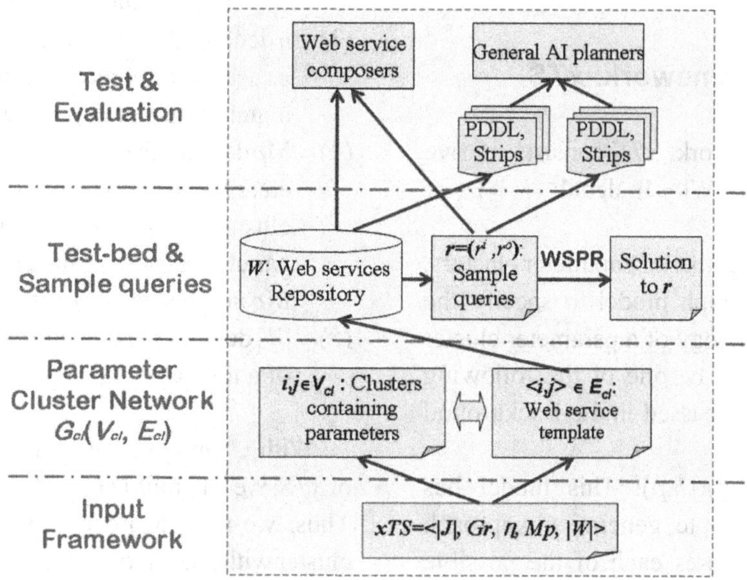

edges connecting two different clusters. These directed edges become web service templates from which WSBen generates web services as users specify. Formally, the parameter cluster network is defined as follows:

Definition 5 (Parameter Cluster Network) *A directed graph $G_{cl}(V_{cl}, E_{cl})$, where V_{cl} is a set of clusters and E_{cl} is a set of directed edges that are incident from input clusters $i \in V_{cl}$ to output clusters $j \in V_{cl}$. Here, cluster i and j contain a set of non-overlapping parameters denoted by Pa_i and Pa_j, respectively, where $Pa_i \cap Pa_j = \varphi$. Each directed edge is also called a web service template, from which WSDL files are generated.*

Figure 4 shows the overview of WSBen. In detail, WSBen consists of the following functionalities:

- **Input framework:** Users can specify and control the generated synthetic WSDL files and their characteristics. For this purpose, WSBen provides an input framework xTS=<|J|,G_r, η ,$Mp_{,}$ |W|>. x*TS* applies existing complex and random network models to specify G*r* Each element of x*TS* will be discussed in more detail below.
- **Parameter cluster network,** $G_{cl}(V_{cl}, E_{cl})$: If *xTS* is given by users, based on the first four elements, WSBen generates G_{cl}. Each cluster of G_{cl} is filled with some number of atomic parameters. In this network, web services are defined as transformations between two different clusters. That is, <*i,j*>∈E_{cl} becomes web service templates. The role of web service templates in the test set generation will be illustrated.
- **Test set and sample requests:** By randomly selecting the web service templates (arcs of the parameter cluster network), WSDL files are generated. Once a test set is generated, users can generate sample test requests *r*=<*r^i*,*r^o*>. The generation process of test sets and test requests will be illustrated.
- **Test and evaluation:** WSBen can export both the web service WSDL files and test requests into files in PDDL (McDermott, 1996) and STRIPS format, enabling con-

current comparison with state-of-the-art AI planners.

WSBen Input Framework: *xTS*

WSBen input framework, *xTS* consists of five tuples, <$|J|$,G_r, η, Mp, $|W|$>. In detail:

(1) $|J|$ is the total number of parameter clusters.

(2) G_r denotes a graph model to specify the underlying topology of a parameter cluster network. G_r can be one of the following three models discussed in the Background section:
   - *Erdos-Renyi*($|J|$,p): This model has such a simple generation approach that it chooses each of the possible $\frac{|J|(|J|)-1)}{2}$ edges in the graph with $|J|$ nodes with probability p. The resulting graph becomes the same as the binomial graph.
   - *Newman-Watts-Strogatz*($|J|$,k,p): The initialization is a regular ring graph with k neighbors. During the generation process, new edges (shortcuts) are added randomly with probability p for each edge. Note that no edges are removed, differing from Watts-Strogatz model.
   - *Barabasi-Albert*($|J|$, m): This graph model is generated by adding new nodes with m edges that are preferentially attached to existing nodes with a high degree. The initialization is a graph with m nodes and no edges. Note that the current implementation of WSBen is limited because it can only generate the simplified version of the extended Barabai-Albert model, by setting p=q=0 and m_0=m, resulting in graphs with γ=2.0±0.1, where γ is the exponent of a power function $P_w(v)$ defined over connectivity v range in the form of $P_w(v) \propto v^{-\gamma}$.

(3) η denotes the parameter condense rate. With η, users can control the density of partial-matching cases in produced web services.

(4) Mp denotes the minimum number of parameters a cluster can contain. In other words, clusters may have a different number of parameters but all clusters must have at least Mp number of parameters.

(5) $|W|$ denotes the total number of web services of a test set.

With $|J|$ and G_r, the first two input elements of *xTS*, we can build G_{cl} with each empty cluster. Thus, we need a procedure to fill each empty cluster with parameters. For this purpose, WSBen uses the following procedure:

(1) A parameter cluster network G_{cl} with empty clusters is built by specifying $|J|$ and G_r.

(2) Co-occurrence probability of each cluster is measured by the following probability:

$$\Delta_j = \frac{k_j}{\max_{j \in V_{cl}} k_j} \eta \tag{3}$$

where Δ_j is the co-occurrence probability of cluster j, and k_j is the edge degree of cluster j.

η is the parameter condense rate which is given by users.

(3) $|Pa_j|$ is measured based on the following equation.

$$|Pa_j| = \frac{Mp}{\Delta_j} \tag{4}$$

where Pa_j is the set of parameters contained in cluster j.

Figure 5. Test set generation with <8, Barbasi-Albert(8,2), 0.8,1.5,100>

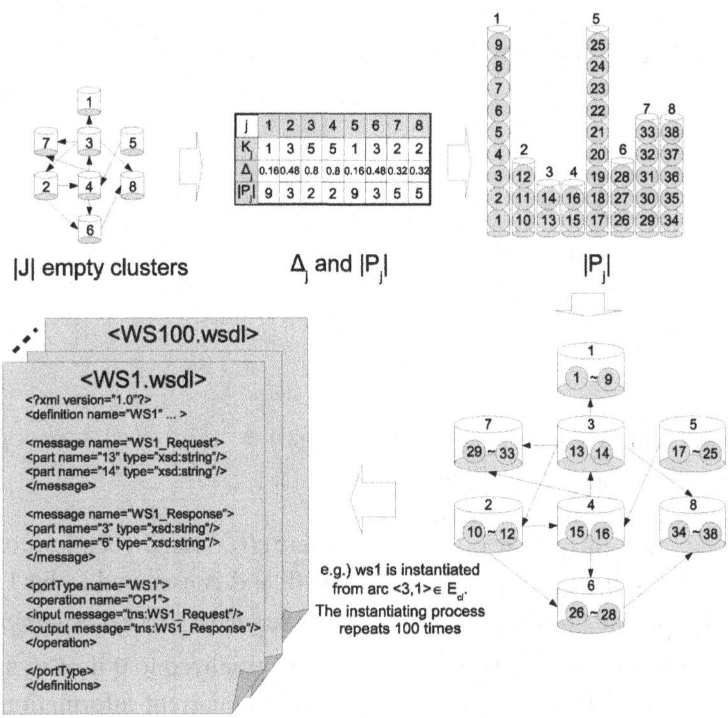
|J| empty clusters
Δ_j and $|P_j|$
$|P_j|$
<WS100.wsdl>
<WS1.wsdl>
<?xml version="1.0"?>
<definition name="WS1" ... >
<message name="WS1_Request">
<part name="13" type="xsd:string"/>
<part name="14" type="xsd:string"/>
</message>
<message name="WS1_Response">
<part name="3" type="xsd:string"/>
<part name="6" type="xsd:string"/>
</message>
<portType name="WS1">
<operation name="OP1">
<input message="tns:WS1_Request"/>
<output message="tns:WS1_Response"/>
</operation>
</portType>
</definitions>
e.g.) ws1 is instantiated from arc <3,1>∈ E_{cl}.
The instantiating process repeats 100 times

(4) For each j cluster, atomic parameters are generated up to $|Pa_j|$, with duplicated parameters forbidden (i.e., $\forall i, j \in V_{cl}$, $Pa_i \cap Pa_j = \varphi$).

Once a complete parameter cluster network, $G_{cl}(V_{cl}, E_{cl})$ is built, WSBen repeats the following procedure until $|W|$ number of web services are generated:

(1) A web service template $<i,j>$ is chosen at random from E_{cl}.
(2) WSBen generates a WSDL file, in which each input parameter is selected from i cluster with probability Δ_i, and each output parameter is selected from j cluster with probability Δ_j.

Figure 5 illustrates how WSBen builds G_{cl} and generates WSDL files based on the G_{cl}. Suppose that xTS=<8, *Barbasi-Albert*(8,2), 0.8,1.5,100> is given. Then, the generation steps are as follows:

(1) WSBen generates a graph of *Barabasi-Albert*(8,2). The direction of each edge is determined at random.
(2) Δ_j and $|Pa_j|$ are specified. For example, Cluster 5 has nine parameters as shown in Figure 5. That is, $|Pa_j|$=9, as $\Delta_5 = \dfrac{k_j}{\max_{j \in V_{cl}} k_j} \eta = \dfrac{1}{5} \times 0.8 = 0.16$, resulting in $|Pa_5| = \dfrac{M_p}{\Delta_5} \approx 9$
(3) Pa_j is specified. For example Pa_5={17,18, 19,20,21,22,23,24,25} as shown in Figure 5 because $|Pa_5|$=9 and for $\forall j \in V_{cl}$, $Pa_5 \cap Pa_j = \varphi$. Note that the parameter names are automatically generated, and thus do not contain any semantics.

Algorithm 1. Forward searching algorithm of WSBen

```
Input: r^i
Output: g_{r^i}(p) for all p reachable from r^i
1: s=r^i, C=φ; d=1;
2: while (δ≠φ) do
3:          δ={w| w∈Ω(s), w∉C};
4:          for p in w^o(w∈δ) do
5:                    if g_{r^i}(p)=∞ then
6:                              g_{r^i}(p)=d; s=s∪{p};
7:          C=C∪δ; d++;
```

(4) Finally, G_{cl} is built and WSBen generates $|W|$ web services. For example, in Figure 5, WS1 is instanced from a web service template <3,1>∈E_{cl}. Note that Δ_1=0.16 and Δ_3=0.8. Δ_1=0.16 suggests that the occurrence probability of each parameter in Cluster 1 has 0.16. Due to the low probability, only "1" and "9" are selected from Cluster 1. Similarly, Δ_3=0.8 means that the occurrence probability of each parameter in Cluster 3 has 0.8. Due to the high probability, all parameters in Cluster 3 that are "13" and "14" are selected. In the case where no parameter is generated, dummy parameters "S" and "T" are filled in the input and output parameters, respectively.

Test Request Generation

The state, $s\in S$ is a collection of parameters in $|P|$. Therefore, r^i and r^o are states. The test request r is constructed such that r^o is farthest away from r^i in a parameter space in terms of $g_{r^i}(p)$ - the cost of achieving $p\in P$ from a state r^i. To obtain $g_{r^i}(p)$, we propose following *Forward Searching* algorithm.

Forward Searching: $g_{r^i}(p)$ can be characterized by the solution of a recursive equation as follows:

$$g_{r^i}(p) = \min_{w\in Ow(p)} [c(w) + \max_{p'\in w^i} g_{r^i}(p')] \qquad (5)$$

where $c(w)$ is an invocation cost of a web service, $w\in W$ and is assumed to be 1. $Ow(p)$ is a set of web services: $Ow(p)=\{w\in W|p\in w^o\}$. At first, $g_{r^i}(p)$ is initialized to 0 if $p\in r^i$, and to ∞ otherwise. Then, the current information state s is set to r^i (Line 1 in Algorithm 1). We denote $\Omega(s)$ by a set of web services $w\in W$ such that $w{\subseteq}^i{\subseteq}s$. That is, w can be invoked or applicable in the state s.

Every time for $\forall w \in \Omega(s)$, each parameter $p\in w^o$ is added to s, and $g_{r^i}(p)$ is updated until $\Omega(s)$ stops to increase, meaning that this process ends with finding $g_{r^i}(p)$ for all parameters reachable from r^i (Lines 2-6 in Algorithm 1).

We can use Equation (5) to drive the lower bound of the optimal cost of WSC solutions. Note that the invocation cost of a web service is assumed to be 1. Thus, the optimal cost of a WSC problem coincides with the minimum number of web services required to solve the WSC problem. For a set of parameters A, we can regard the following cost function:

$$g_{r^i}^{\max}(A) = \max_{p\in A} g_{r^i}(p) \qquad (6)$$

The cost of achieving a set of parameters cannot be lower than the cost of achieving each of

Figure 6. WSBen user interface

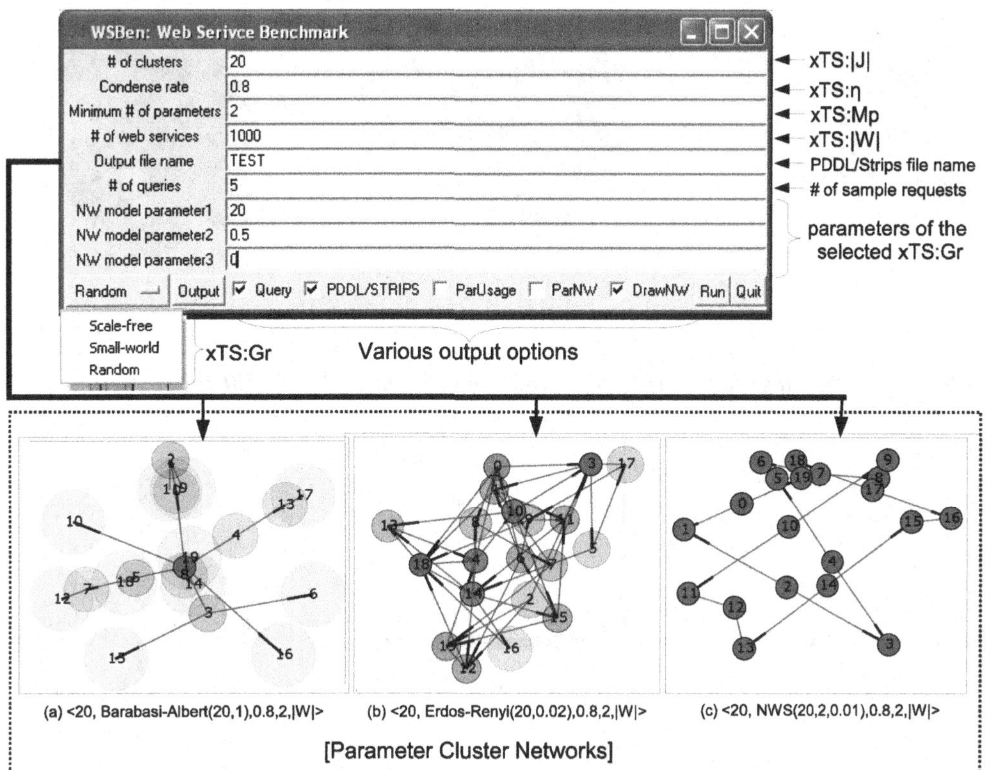

the parameters in the set. Thus, $g_{r^i}^{\max}(A)$ is the lower bound of the optimal cost of achieving r^o from r^i.

Based on the forward searching algorithm, WSBen create a test request r, as follows:

(1) WSBen selects a Cluster $j \in G_{cl}$ at random.
(2) WSBen copies all parameters in the Cluster j (i.e., Pa_j) into r^i, and then r^o is constructed so that it consists of the first five largest parameters in terms of $g_{r^i}(p)$. Consequently, parameters in r^o are farthest away from parameters in r^i in a parameter space.

As a default, WSBen repeats the above procedure five times, generating five request sets for each test set.

Implementation

As shown in Figure 6, WSBen provides user interfaces to specify *xTS* and several parameters, which are required to form a parameter cluster network and generate WSDL files. WSBen is implemented in Python, and run on Python 2.3 or later. It runs on Unix and Windows. For the creation, manipulation, and functions of complex networks, we used a Python package called NetworkX[1]. Current implementation of WSBen is limited as follows: (1) it supports only the exact matching without type compatibility check, and (2) each web service contains only one operation so that a web service can be viewed as equivalent to an operation. Therefore, w^i and w^o indicate the input and output parameter set of a web service, w.

Figure 6 also shows three sample parameter cluster networks, where each circular node rep-

Figure 7. G_p of baTS, erTS, and nwsTS when |W|=1,000

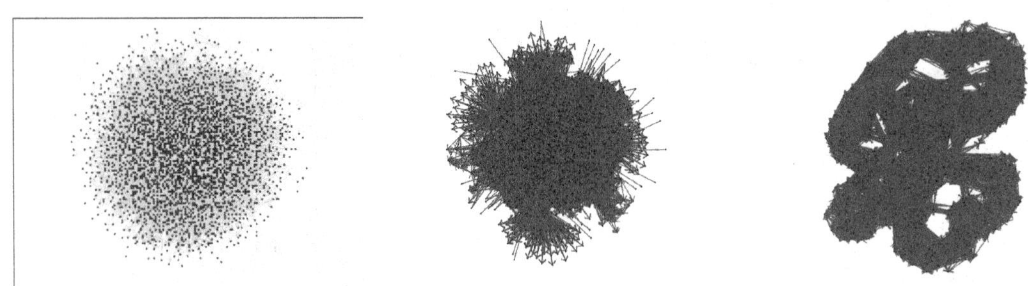

Figure 8. Outgoing edge degree of baTS, erTS, and nwsTS when |W|=1,000

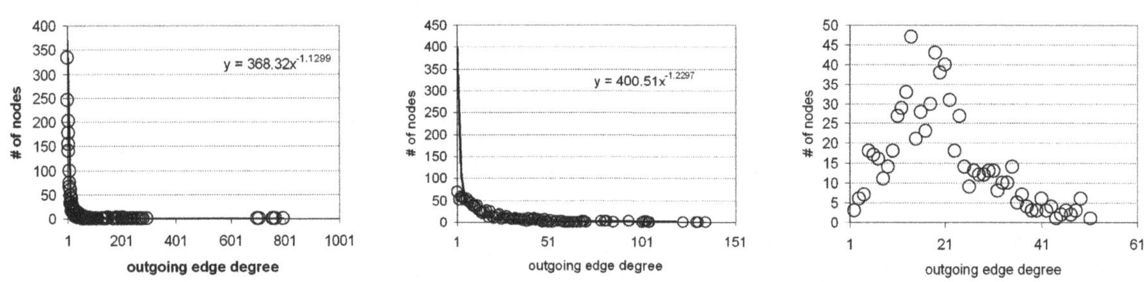

resents a cluster and edges with heads denote the web service template, from which web services are instanced. The size of node is proportional to the number of parameters in the node, while the transparency level of a node's color is inversely proportional to the degree of the node. For example, in the left cluster network, Cluster 18 can be considered a hub cluster in that it has the high degree. Therefore, it is presented by a small circle with denser color.

Following the mechanism of WSBen explained so far, we can build three illustrative test set frameworks by specifying *xTS* as follows:

(1) *baTS*=<100, *Barabasi – Albert*(100,6),0.8,5,|*W*|>
(2) *nwsTS*=<100, *Newman – Watts – Strogatz*(100,6,0.1),0.8,5,|W|>
(3) *erTS*=<100, *Erdos* – R*enyi*(100,0.06),0.8,5, |*W*|>

Figures 7 and 8 show that there are distinctive differences between *baTS*, *nwsTS*, and *erTS* in terms of G_p and outgoing edge degree distribution.

ILLUSTRATIVE USE CASES OF WSBEN

In this section, we present three use cases to demonstrate the capabilities of WSBen: (1) evaluating web services composition algorithms; (2) comparing performance of AI planners; and (3) estimating the size of giant component. These use cases are prepared to provide vigorous experiments and evaluation for assessing the usage of WSBen. For each use case, we will provide three web services test sets by varying *xTS* with three parameter cluster networks such as "random", "small-world", and "scale-free" types. Note that these three network models have the expression power enough to model many real-world networks sufficiently (Albert & Barabasi, 2002). This implies that our generated test cases can be appropriate for representing diverse real-world web service networks. Furthermore, these three web service test sets are significantly distinctive from each other in terms of their web service network topologies and degree distributions as we have shown in the previous section. This indicates that we have sufficient reason to investigate how different network topologies can affect the performance of web service applications or environments.

Evaluating Web Services Composition Algorithms

Recently, many WSC researches have been reported in the web service community. In this chapter, we choose WSPR as a testing WSC algorithm (Oh et al., 2007 & 2008), which was proved effective and efficient in the recent WSC contests, in order to demonstrate WSBen.

In this case, we use three test sets generated by WSBen: (1) *baTS* with $|W|$=5,000; (2) *erTS* with $|W|$=5,000; and (3) *nwsTS* with $|W|$=5,000. The resultant composed services generated by WSPR are shown in Figure 9, where WSPR addressed a request for each of the three test sets. Note that WSBen can automatically create sample requests for a given test set. In the graph, each composed solution has nodes such as "*Ri*" and "R_O", which represent the initial condition and goal state, respectively. Other nodes represent web services. The directed arcs indicate the invocation flow, where a solid edge means full-matching invocation and a dotted edge represents partial-matching invocation. From the experiments based on diverse test sets such as *baTS*, *erTS*, and *nwsTS*, we can understand how different network models of G_{cl} influences the performance of WSC algorithms. In general, given the same number of clusters, the *Barabasi-Albert* model generates G_{cl} with a greater number of parameters, and a larger variance of the number of parameters between clusters than the *Newman-Watts-Strogatz* and *Erdos-Renyi* models do. Due to the greater number of parameters and larger variance, *baTS* needs more partial-matching web services to fulfill the given requests than others. The increasing need for partial-matching web services leads to increasing number of web services in the composed service. This is the reason that the *baTS* case has more web services to create a resultant composed service as shown in Figure 9 (left).

Figure 9. Composed services using WSPR for three test sets. (left) baTS with $|W|$=5,000. (center) erTS with $|W|$=5,000. (right) nwsTS with $|W|$=5,000.

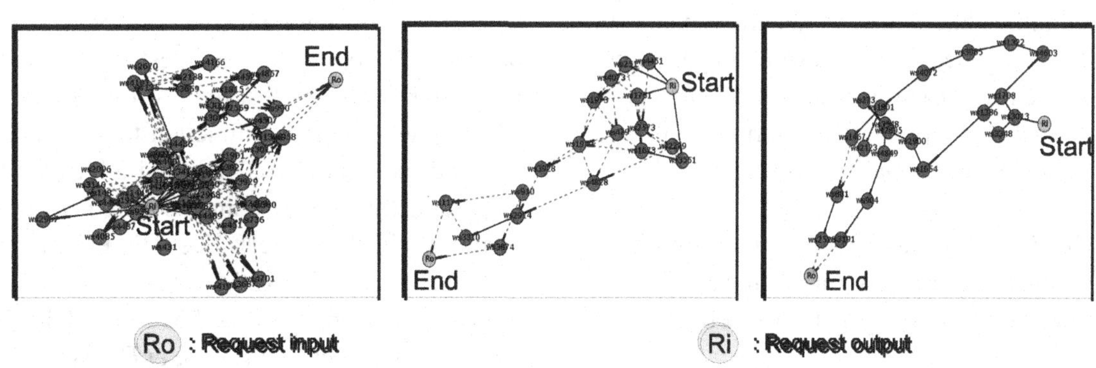

Table 3. Results over baTS with |W|=3,000

Requests	BlackBox		GraphPlan		IPP	
	#W	τ	*#W*	τ	*#W*	τ
r_1	61	478.69	-	-	-	-
r_2	-	-	-	-	-	-
r_3	5	5	5	0.09	5	26.22
r_4	9	27.78	9	0.11	9	28.56
r_5	4	1.4	4	0.04	4	23.97

Table 4. Results over erTS with |W|=3,000

Requests	BlackBox		GraphPlan		IPP	
	#W		*#W*		*#W*	
r_1	75	38.09	-	-	-	-
r_2	50	16.02	-	-	-	-
r_3	22	18.68	-	-	22	24.78
r_4	23	4.38	-	-	23	21.06
r_5	38	4.01	-	-	38	21

Comparing Performance of AI Planners

We can also demonstrate how WSBen can be used to compare the performance of AI planners. For this purpose, we choose three prominent AI planners–Graphplan (Blum & Furst, 1997), Blackbox (Kautz, 1996), and IPP (http://www.informatik.uni-freiburg.de/~koehler/ipp.html). Blackbox and IPP are extended planning systems that originated from Graphplan. In particular, Blackbox is extended to be able to map a plan graph into a set of clauses for checking the satisfiability problem. Consequently, it can run even in large number of operators. For comparing the performance of three planners, we use two evaluation metrics as follows:

(1) τ(Time): It measures how long an algorithm takes to find a right solution, in seconds. This is a measure of computational efficiency.

(2) *#W*: The number of web services in a right solution. This is a measure of effectiveness QoS (Quality of Service)

All AI planners run with their default options, except that the maximum number of nodes for Blackbox and Graphplan was set to 32,768 and 10,000, respectively. Commonly, the time to read operator and fact files is not included in τ. Blackbox and IPP accept only the PDDL format, while Graphplan accepts only the STRIPS format for their operator and fact files. Note that an operator file corresponds to a test set, and a fact file corresponds to a test request file. Also note that WSBen provides a function to convert test sets and requests into PDDL and STRIPS files automatically. The experiments were performed on Linux with three Intel® Xeon™ CPU, running at 2.4GHz with 8GB RAM.

Tables 3, 4, and 5 shows the results of the five test requests for each of *baTS*, *erTS*, and *nwsTS* with |*W*|=3,000. Graphplan ran out of memory

Table 5. Results over nwsTS with |W|=3,000

Requests	BlackBox		GraphPlan		IPP	
	#W		#W		#W	
r_1	48	571.63	-	-	48	29.52
r_2	35	114.67	-	-	35	28.57
r_3	24	192.99	-	-	24	30.19
r_4	26	11.88	-	-	26	28.39
r_5	31	111.21	-	-	-	-

Figure 10. Comparison of real and theoretical size of giant components: (A) random, (B) scale-free, and (C) NWS models

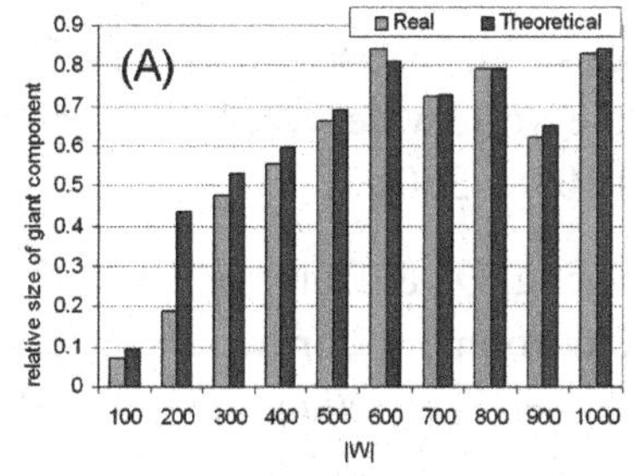

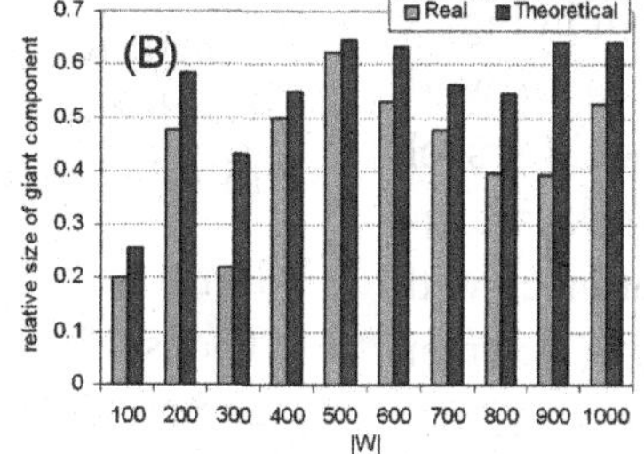

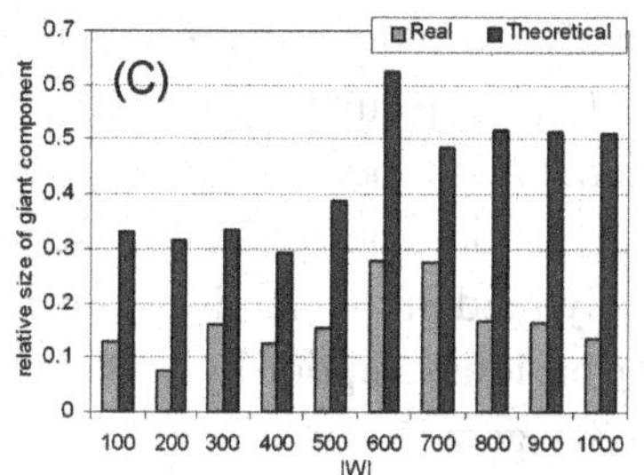

in many cases. IPP also failed to solve the some requests. As a whole, Blackbox showed better performance than others, meaning that it can solve more requests than others. It is because Blackbox uses the local-search SAT solver, Walksat, for the satisfiability problem, so that Blackbox can run relatively well even with a large number of operators.

Estimating the Size of Giant Component

We can estimate the size of giant component in a service network using random graph theory. Often it is believed to be important to have a large and dense giant component in a service network. Otherwise, the isolated services will never have a chance to provide any services to clients. Newman et al. (Newman & Strogatz, 2001) suggested the theoretical framework in order to estimate the giant component size in networks by using random graph theory. In order to see if their theoretical framework works, we generated the g_{op}^{f} with different network size for each of following cases:

(1) *Random model:* <50, *Erdos – Renyi*(100,0.06),0.8,5,|*W*|>
(2) *Scale-free model*: <50, *Barabasi – Albert*(100,6),0.8,5,|W|>
(3) *NWS model*: <50, *Newman – Watts – Strogatz*(100,6,0.1),0.8,5, |*W*|>

For each of these networks, we measured the real size of giant components. Then, we calculated the theoretical size of giant components according to the estimation model of Newman et al. The comparisons between real and theoretical sizes are summarized in Figure 10. For g_{op}^{f} based on the random parameter cluster network in Figure 10(A), the theoretical value of the giant component size is very close to the measured one for each synthetic network. This implies that even a simple random model may be very helpful to estimate the inter-operable portion of such networks with random topology without even analyzing the available network beyond its degree distribution. However, Figure 10(B) shows that the estimation model is not a good model for Scale-free type. There is a considerable gap between theory and real value for many of the synthetic networks in this type. The deviation between theory and actual networks becomes more dramatic for the *NWS* (small world phenomenon and highly clustered property) type shown in Figure 10(C). The results show that the random network model might be good generative model for such web services networks if these networks are entirely random, which is also in accordance with the basic assumption by Newman et al. (Newman & Strogatz, 2001).

CONCLUSION

A novel web service benchmark toolkit, WSBen, is presented with three use cases in different application domains. The WSBen development is inspired by the study on real-world web services, and is designed to provide diverse scenarios and configurations which users can fine-tune easily. As a result, using WSBen, users can conduct extensive experimental validation on their web services discovery and composition algorithms. It is our hope that WSBen will provide useful insights to the design and development of web services discovery and composition solutions and software. The latest version of WSBen is available at: http://pike.psu.edu/sw/wsben/. Further research is needed to extend WSBen to support approximate and semantic matching among web services. Also, we plan to discover additional application areas where the WSBen can be used.

REFERENCES

Al-Masri, E., & Qusay, M. H. (2008). Investigating web services on the World Wide Web. In *Proceedings of WWW*, (pp.795-804). Beijing, China.

Albert, R., & Barabasi, A.-L. (2000). Topology of evolving networks. *Physical Review Letters*, *85*, 5234–5237. doi:10.1103/PhysRevLett.85.5234

Albert, R., & Barabasi, A.-L. (2002). Statistical mechanics of complex networks. *Reviews of Modern Physics*, *74*(1), 47–95. doi:10.1103/RevModPhys.74.47

Albert, R., Jeong, H., & Barabasi, A.-L. (1999). The diameter of the world wide web. *Nature*, *401*, 130–131. doi:10.1038/43601

Benatallah, B., Sheng, Q., & Dumas, M. (2003). The self-serv environment for web services composition. *Internet Computing*, *7*(1), 40–48. doi:10.1109/MIC.2003.1167338

Bertsekas, D. (2000). *Dynamic programming and optimal control* (2nd ed., *Vol. 1*). Boston, MA: Athena Scientific.

Bleul, T., Weise, T., & Geihs, K. (2009). The web service challenge – A review on semantic web service composition. In *Proc. of 2009 Service Oriented Computing*.

Blum, A., & Furst, M. (1997). Fast planning through planning graph analysis. *Artificial Intelligence*, *90*, 281–300. doi:10.1016/S0004-3702(96)00047-1

Brian, B., William, C., Michael, J., & Andreas, W. (2007). WSC-07: Evolving the web services challenge. In *Proc. of 9th IEEE International Conference on E-Commerce Technology and 4th IEEE International Conference on Enterprise Computing, E-Commerce, and E-Services* (CEC-EEE 2007), (pp. 505-508). Tokyo, Japan.

Bylander, T. (1994). The computational complexity of propositional STRIPS planning. *Artificial Intelligence, 69*(1-2), 165–204. doi:10.1016/0004-3702(94)90081-7

Casati, F., Ilnicki, S., Jin, L.-J., Krishnamoorthy, V., & Shan, M.-C. (2000). Eflow: A platform for developing and managing composite e-services. In *Proc. of AIWORC'00*, Washington, DC, USA.

Cho, E., Chung, S., & Zimmerman, D. (2009). Automatic Web services generation. In *Proc. of the 42nd Hawaii International Conference on System Sciences.*

Constantinescu, I., Faltings, B., & Binder, W. (2004). Large scale testbed for type compatible service composition. In *Proc. of 14th International Conference on Automated Planning and Scheduling* (ICAPS), (pp. 23-28). Whistler, British Columbia, Canada.

Delgado, J. (2002). Emergence of social conventions in complex networks. *Artificial Intelligence, 141*, 171–185. doi:10.1016/S0004-3702(02)00262-X

Denning, J. P. (2004). Network laws. *Communications of the ACM, 47*(11), 15–20. doi:10.1145/1029496.1029510

Erdos, P., Graham, R., & Nesetril, J. (1996). *The mathematics of Paul Erdos*. Berlin, Germany: Springer-Verlag.

Fan, J., & Kambhampati, S. (2005). A snapshot of public Web services. *SIGMOD Record, 34*(1), 24–32. doi:10.1145/1058150.1058156

Hashemian, S. V., & Mavaddat, F. (2006). A graph-based framework for composition of stateless web services. In *Proc. of ECOWS 2006*, (pp. 75-86).

Hu, S., Muthusamy, V., Li, G., & Jacobsen, H.-A. (2008). Distributed automatic service composition in large-scale systems. In *Proc. of the Second International Conference on Distributed Event-Based Systems*, Rome, Italy.

Kautz, H., & Selman, B. (1996). Unifying SAT-based and graph-based planning. In *Proc. of the 16th International Joint Conference on Artificial Intelligence* (IJCAI), (pp. 318-325). Stockholm, Sweden.

Kil, H., Oh, S.-C., & Lee, D. (2006). On the topological landscape of semantic web services matchmaking. In *Proc. of 1st International Workshop on Semantic Matchmaking and Resource Retrieval* (SMR2006), (pp. 19-34). Seoul, Korea.

Liang, Q. A., & Su, S. Y. W. (2005). AND/OR graph and search algorithm for discovering composite web services. [IJWSR]. *International Journal of Web Services Research, 2*(4), 48–67. doi:10.4018/jwsr.2005100103

McDermott, D. (1996). A heuristic estimator for means-ends analysis in planning. In *Proc. of the Third International Conference on Artificial Intelligence Planning Systems* (AIPS), (pp. 142-149). Edinburgh, Scotland.

McDermott, D. (2002). Estimated-regression planning for interactions with Web services. In *Proc. of the sixth International Conference on Artificial Intelligence Planning and Scheduling Systems (AIPS)*, (pp. 67-73). Toulouse, France.

McIlraith, S., & Son, T. (2002). Adapting golog for composition of semantic web services. In *Proc. of KR2002*, (pp. 482-493). Toulouse, France

Milanovic, N., & Malek, M. (2006). Search strategies for automatic web service composition. [IJWSR]. *International Journal of Web Services Research, 3*(2), 1–32. doi:10.4018/jwsr.2006040101

Newman, M. E. J., Strogatz, S. H., & Watts, D. J. (2001). Random graphs with arbitrary degree distributions and their applications. *Physical Review E: Statistical, Nonlinear, and Soft Matter Physics, 64*(026118).

Nilsson, J. (2001). *Artificial Intelligence: A new synthesis*. San Francisco, CA: Morgan Kaufmann.

Oh, S.-C., Kil, H., Lee, D., & Kumara, S. (2006). WSBen: A Web-services discovery and composition benchmark. In *Proc. of the Fourth International IEEE Conference on Web Service* (ICWS), (pp. 239-246). Chicago, USA.

Oh, S.-C., & Lee, D. (2009). WSBen: A Web service discovery and composition benchmark. [IJWSR]. *International Journal of Web Services Research*, *6*(1), 1–19. doi:10.4018/jwsr.2009092301

Oh, S.-C., Lee, D., & Kumara, S. (2007). WSPR: A heuristic algorithm for Web-service composition. [IJWSR]. *International Journal of Web Services Research*, *4*(1), 1–22. doi:10.4018/jwsr.2007010101

Oh, S.-C., Lee, D., & Kumara, S. (2008). Effective Web service composition in diverse and large-scale service networks. *IEEE Transaction on Service Computing*, *1*(1), 15–32. doi:10.1109/TSC.2008.1

Panahi, M., Lin, K.-J., Zhang, Y., Chang, S.-H., Zhang, J., & Varela, L. (2009). The LLAMA middleware support for accountable service oriented architecture. In *Proc. of ICSOC'08*, (pp. 180-194). Berlin, Germany: Springer-Verlag.

Ponnekanti, S. R., & Fox, A. (2002). Sword: A developer toolkit for web service composition. In *Proc. of WWW 2002.*

Sirin, E., Parsia, B., Wu, D., Hendler, J., & Nau, D. (2004). HTN planning for web service composition using shop2. *Web Semantics: Science. Services and Agents on the World Wide Web*, *1*(4), 377–396. doi:10.1016/j.websem.2004.06.005

Sivashanmugam, K., Verma, K., Sheth, A., & Miller, J. (2003). Adding semantics to Web services standards. In *Proc. of the first IEEE International Conference on Web services* (ICWS), (pp. 395-401). Las Vegas, NV, USA.

Watts, D. J. (1999). *The dynamics of networks between order and randomness*. Princeton, NJ: Princeton Univ. Press.

Watts, D. J., & Strogatz, S. H. (1998). Collective dynamics of small-world networks. *Nature*, *393*(4), 440–442. doi:10.1038/30918

XMark. (n.d.). *An XML benchmark project*. Retrieved September 17, 2006, from http://monetdb.cwi.nl/xml/

Zhovtobryukh, D. (2007). A petri net-based approach for automated goal-driven web service composition. *Simulation*, *83*(1), 33–63. doi:10.1177/0037549707079226

ENDNOTE

1 https://networkx.lanl.gov/

This work was previously published in International Journal of Web Services Research, Volume 6, Issue 1, edited by Liang-Jie Zhang, pp. 1-19, copyright 2009 by IGI Publishing (an imprint of IGI Global).

Chapter 2
USDL:
A Service-Semantics Description Language for Automatic Service Discovery and Composition[1]

Srividya Kona
The University of Texas at Dallas, USA

Ajay Bansal
The University of Texas at Dallas, USA

Luke Simon
The University of Texas at Dallas, USA

Ajay Mallya
The University of Texas at Dallas, USA

Gopal Gupta
The University of Texas at Dallas, USA

Thomas D. Hite
Metallect Corp., USA

ABSTRACT

Web services and Service-Oriented Computing is being widely adopted. In order to effectively reuse existing services, we need an infrastructure that allows users and applications to discover, deploy, compose, and synthesize services automatically. This automation can take place only if a formal description of the Web services is available. In this article we present an infrastructure using USDL (Universal Service-Semantics Description Language), a language for formally describing the semantics of Web services. USDL is based on the Web Ontology Language (OWL) and employs WordNet as a common basis for understanding the meaning of services. USDL can be regarded as formal service documentation that will allow sophisticated conceptual modeling and searching of available Web services, automated service composition, and other forms of automated service integration. A theory of service substitution using USDL is presented. The rationale behind the design of USDL along with its formal specification in OWL is presented with examples. We also compare USDL with other approaches like OWL-S, WSDL-S, and WSML and show that USDL is complementary to these approaches.

DOI: 10.4018/978-1-61350-104-7.ch002

INTRODUCTION

A Web service is a program available on a web-site that "effects some action or change" in the world (i.e., causes a side-effect). Examples of such side effects include a web-base being updated because of a plane reservation made over the Internet, a device being controlled, and so forth. The next milestone in the Web's evolution is making *services* ubiquitously available. As automation increases, these Web services will be accessed directly by the applications themselves rather than by humans. In this context, a Web service can be regarded as a "programmatic interface" that makes application to application communication possible. An infrastructure that allows users to discover, deploy, synthesize and compose services automatically needs to be supported in order to make Web services more practical.

To make services ubiquitously available we need a semantics-based approach such that applications can reason about a service's capability to a level of detail that permits their discovery, deployment, composition and synthesis. Several efforts are underway to build such an infrastructure. These efforts include approaches based on the semantic web (such as OWL-S (OWL-S, 2003)) as well as those based on XML, such as Web Services Description Language (WSDL (WSDL, 2001)). Approaches such as WSDL are purely syntactic in nature, that is, they merely specify the format of the service. In this article we present an approach that is based on semantics. Our approach can be regarded as providing semantics to WSDL statements. We present the design of a language called Universal Service-Semantics Description Language (USDL) which service developers can use to specify formal semantics of Web services (Bansal et al., 2005; Simon, Bansal, Mallya, Kona, Gupta, & Hite, 2005). Thus, if WSDL can be regarded as a language for formally specifying the syntax of Web services, USDL can be regarded as a language for formally specifying their semantics. USDL can be thought of as *formal service documentation* that will allow sophisticated conceptual modeling and searching of available Web services, automated composition, and other forms of automated service integration. For example, the WSDL syntax and USDL semantics of Web services can be published in a directory which applications can access to automatically discover services. That is, given a formal description of the context in which a service is needed, the service(s) that will precisely fulfill that need can be determined. The directory can then be searched for the exact service, or two or more services that can be composed to synthesize the required service.

To provide formal semantics, a common denominator must be agreed upon that everybody can use as a basis of understanding the meaning of services. This common conceptual ground must also be somewhat coarse-grained so as to be tractable for use by both engineers and computers. That is, semantics of services should not be given in terms of low-level concepts such as Turing machines, first-order logic and their variants, since service description, discovery, and synthesis then become tasks that are practically intractable and theoretically undecidable. Additionally, the semantics should be given at a conceptual level that captures common real world concepts. Furthermore, it is too impractical to expect disparate companies to standardize on application (or domain) specific ontologies to formally define semantics of Web services, and instead a common universal ontology must be agreed upon with additional constructors. Also, application specific ontologies will be an impediment to automatic discovery of services since the application developer will have to be aware of the specific ontology that has been used to describe the semantics of the service in order to frame the query that will search for the service. The danger is that the service may not be defined using the particular domain-specific ontology that the application developer uses to frame the query, however, it may be defined using some other domain-specific ontology, and so the application developer will be prevented from discovering the service even though it exists. These reasons make an ontology based on OWL WordNet (OWL WordNet, 2003; WordNet, 1998) a suitable candidate for a universal ontology of basic concepts upon which arbitrary meets and joins can be added in order to gain tractable flexibility.

We describe the meaning of conceptual modeling and how it could be obtained via a common universal ontology based on WordNet in the next section. Then we give a brief overview of how USDL attempts to semantically describe Web services. Then we present the design of USDL, where we discuss precisely how a WSDL document can be prescribed meaning in terms of WordNet ontology followed by a complete USDL annotation for a Hotel-Reservation service. Theory of service substitution is discussed where we present the theoretical foundations of service description and substitution in USDL. Automatic discovery of Web services using USDL is discussed in the service discovery section. Composition of Web services using USDL is discussed in the service composition section followed by the implementation of a discovery and composition engine. Comparison of USDL with other approaches like OWL-S, WSDL-S, and WSML is presented. Finally, related work, conclusions and future work are addressed.

A UNIVERSAL ONTOLOGY

To describe service semantics, we should agree on a common ground to model our concepts. We can describe what any given Web service does from first principles using approaches based on logic. This is the approach taken by frameworks such as dependent type systems and programming logics prevalent in the field of software verification where a "formal understanding" of the service/software is needed in order to verify it. However, such solutions are low-level, tedious, and undecidable to be of practical use. Instead, we are interested in modeling higher-level concepts. That is, we are more interested in answering questions such as, what does a service do from the end user's or service integrator's perspective, as opposed to the far more difficult questions, such as, what does the service do from a computational view? We care more about real world concepts such as "customer", "bank account", and "flight itinerary" as opposed to the data structures and algorithms used by a service to model these concepts. The distinction is subtle, but is a distinction of granularity as well as a distinction of scope.

In order to allow interoperability and machine-readability of our documents, a common conceptual ground must be agreed upon. The first step towards this common ground is standard languages such as WSDL and OWL. However, these do not go far enough, as for any given type of service there are numerous distinct representations in WSDL and for high-level concepts (e.g., a ternary predicate), there are numerous disparate representations in terms of OWL, representations that are distinct in terms of OWL's formal semantics, yet equal in the actual concepts they model. This is known as the semantic aliasing problem: distinct syntactic representations with distinct formal semantics yet equal conceptual semantics. For the semantics to equate things that are conceptually equal, we need to standardize a sufficiently comprehensive set of basic concepts, that is, a universal ontology, along with a restricted set of connectives.

Industry specific ontologies along with OWL can also be used to formally describe Web services.

This is the approach taken by the OWL-S language (OWL-S, 2003). The problem with this approach is that it requires standardization and undue foresight. Standardization is a slow, bitter process, and industry specific ontologies would require this process to be iterated for each specific industry. Furthermore, reaching an industry specific standard ontology that is comprehensive and free of semantic aliasing is even more difficult. Undue foresight is required because many useful Web services will address innovative applications and industries that don't currently exist. Standardizing ontology for travel and finances is easy, as these industries are well established, but new innovative services in new upcoming industries also need to be ascribed formal meaning. A universal ontology will have no difficulty in describing such new services.

We need an ontology that is somewhat coarse-grained yet universal, and at a similar conceptual level to common real world concepts. WordNet (WordNet, 1998) is a sufficiently comprehensive ontology that meets these criteria. As stated, part of the common ground involves standardized languages such as OWL. For this reason, WordNet cannot be used directly, and instead we make use of an encoding of WordNet as an OWL base ontology (OWL WordNet, 2003). Using OWL WordNet ontology allows our solution to use a universal, complete, and tractable framework, which lacks the semantic aliasing problem, to which we map Web service messages and operations. As long as this mapping is precise and sufficiently expressive, reasoning can be done within the realm of OWL by using automated inference systems (such as, one based on description logic), and we automatically reap the wealth of semantic information embodied in the OWL WordNet ontology that describes relationships between ontological concepts, especially subsumption (hyponym-hypernym) and equivalence (synonym) relationships.

USDL: AN OVERVIEW

As mentioned earlier, USDL can be regarded as a language to formally specify the semantics of Web services. It is perhaps the first attempt to capture the semantics of Web services in a universal, yet decidable manner. It is quite distinct from previous approaches such as WSDL and OWL-S (OWL-S, 2003). As mentioned earlier, WSDL only defines syntax of the service; USDL provides the missing semantic component. USDL can be thought of as a formal language for service documentation. Thus, instead of documenting the function of a service as comments in English, one can write USDL statements that describe the function of that service. USDL is quite distinct from OWL-S, which is designed for a similar purpose, and as we shall see the two are in fact complementary. OWL-S primarily describes the states that exist before and after the service and how a service is composed of other smaller sub-services (if any). Description of atomic services is left under-specified in OWL-S. They have to be specified using domain-specific ontologies; in contrast, atomic services are completely specified in USDL, and USDL relies on a universal ontology (OWL WordNet Ontology) to specify the semantics of atomic services. USDL and OWL-S are complementary in that OWL-S's strength lies in describing the structure of composite services, that is, how various atomic services are algorithmically combined to produce a new service, while USDL is good for fully describing atomic services. Thus, OWL-S can be used for describing the structure of composite services that combine atomic services described using USDL.

USDL describes a service in terms of portType and messages, similar to WSDL. The semantics of a service is given using the OWL WordNet ontology: portType (operations provided by the service) and messages (operation parameters) are mapped to disjunctions of conjunctions of (possibly negated) concepts in the OWL WordNet ontology. The semantics is given in terms of how a service *affects* the external world. The present design of USDL assumes that each side-effect is one of the following four operations: *create, update, delete,* or *find.* A generic *affects* side-effect is used when none of the four apply. An application that wishes to make use of a service automatically should be able to reason with WordNet atoms using the OWL WordNet ontology.

We also define the formal semantics of USDL. As stated earlier, the syntactic terms describing portType and messages are mapped to disjunctions of conjunctions of (possibly negated) OWL WordNet ontological terms. A service is then formally defined as a function, labeled by the side-effect.

The main contribution of our work is the design of a Universal Service-Semantics Description Language (USDL), along with its formal semantics, and a theory of service substitution using it.

DESIGN OF USDL

The design of USDL rests on two formal languages: Web Services Description Language (WSDL) (WSDL, 2001) and Web Ontology Language (OWL) (OWL, 2003). The Web services Description language (WSDL) (WSDL, 2001) is used to give a syntactic description of the name and parameters of a service. The description is syntactic in the sense that it describes the formatting of services on a syntactic level of method signatures, but is incapable of describing what concepts are involved in a service and what a service actually does, that is, the conceptual semantics of the service. Likewise, the Web Ontology Language (OWL) (OWL, 2003), was developed as an extension to the Resource Description Framework (RDF) (RDF, 2003), both standards are designed to allow formal conceptual modeling via logical ontologies, and these languages also allow for the markup of existing web resources with semantic information from the conceptual models. USDL employs WSDL and OWL in order to describe the syntax and semantics of Web services. WSDL is used to describe message formats, types, and method prototypes, while a specialized universal OWL ontology is used to formally describe what these messages and methods mean, on a conceptual level.

USDL can be regarded as the semantic counterpart to the syntactic WSDL description. WSDL documents contain two main constructs to which we want to ascribe conceptual meaning: messages and portType. These constructs are aggregates of service components which will be directly ascribed meaning. Messages consist of typed parts and portType consists of operations parameterized on messages. USDL defines OWL surrogates or proxies of these constructs in the form of classes, which have properties with values in the OWL WordNet ontology. USDL also defines a new class called *Concept* that is used to represent any real-world concept used in the description of a Web service. *Concept* class has many subclasses to categorize different kind of real-world concepts. USDL introduces a *Condition* class to semantically describe pre-conditions and post-conditions of a Web service. The *affects* property describes the side-effects of a Web service. In this section we present the OWL classes and properties for all the USDL constructs.

Concept

USDL defines a generic class called *Concept* which is used to define the semantics of *parts* of *messages*. See Box 1.

The USDL *Concept* class denotes the conceptual objects constructed from the OWL WordNet ontology. For most purposes, message parts and other WSDL constructs will be mapped to a subclass of USDL *Concept* so that useful concepts can be modeled as set theoretic formulas of union, intersection, and negation of basic concepts. These subclasses of *Concept* are *BasicConcept*, *QualifiedConcept*, *InvertedConcept*, *ConjunctiveConcept*, and *DisjunctiveConcept*.

Basic Concept

A *BasicConcept* is the actual contact point between USDL and WordNet. This class acts as proxy for WordNet lexical entities. The property cardinality restrictions require all USDL *BasicConcepts* to have exactly one defining value for the *isA* property. An instance of *BasicConcept* is considered to be equated with a WordNet lexical concept given by the *isA* property. See Box 2.

Box 1.

```
<owl:Class rdf:ID="Concept">
    <rdfs:comment> Generic class of USDL Concept </rdfs:comment>
    <owl:unionOf rdf:parseType="Collection">
      <owl:Class rdf:about="#BasicConcept"/>
      <owl:Class rdf:about="#QualifiedConcept"/>
      <owl:Class rdf:about="#InvertedConcept"/>
      <owl:Class rdf:about="#ConjunctiveConcept"/>
      <owl:Class rdf:about="#DisjunctiveConcept"/>
    </owl:unionOf>
  </owl:Class>
```

Box 2.

```
<owl:Class rdf:about="#BasicConcept">
  <rdfs:subClassOf rdf:resource="#Concept"/>
    <rdfs:subClassOf>
      <owl:Restriction>
        <owl:onProperty rdf:resource="#isA"/>
        <owl:cardinality rdf:datatype="&xsd;nonNegativeInteger"> 1 </
owl:cardinality>
      </owl:Restriction>
    </rdfs:subClassOf>
</owl:Class>
```

The *isA* property is defined in as follows:

```
<owl:ObjectProperty rdf:ID="isA">
    <rdfs:domain
rdf:resource="#BasicConcept"/>
    <rdfs:range rdf:resource="&wn;Lex
icalConcept"/>
  </owl:ObjectProperty>
```

Qualified Concept

A *QualifiedConcept* is a concept classified by another lexical concept. The property cardinality restrictions require all USDL *QualifiedConcepts* to have exactly one defining value for the *isA* property, and exactly one value for the *ofKind* property. An instance of *QualifiedConcept* is considered to be equated with a lexical concept given by the *isA* property and classified by a lexical concept given by the optional *ofKind* property. See Box 3.

Inverted Concept

In case of *InvertedConcept* the corresponding semantics are the complement of USDL concepts. See Box 4.

Conjunctive and Disjunctive Concept

The *ConjunctiveConcept* and *DisjunctiveConcept* respectively denote the intersection and union of USDL *Concepts*. The property cardinality restrictions on *ConjunctiveConcept* and *DisjunctiveConcept* allow for *n*-ary intersections and unions (where $n \geq 2$) of USDL concepts. For generality, these concepts are *BasicConcepts*, *QualifiedConcepts*, *ConjunctiveConcepts*, *DisjunctiveConcepts*, or *InvertedConcepts*. See Box 5.

Box 3.

```
<owl:Class rdf:about="#QualifiedConcept">
    <rdfs:subClassOf rdf:resource="#Concept"/>
    <rdfs:subClassOf>
      <owl:Restriction>
        <owl:onProperty rdf:resource="#isA"/>
        <owl:cardinality rdf:datatype="&xsd;nonNegativeInteger"> 1 </
owl:cardinality>
      </owl:Restriction>
    </rdfs:subClassOf>
    <rdfs:subClassOf>
      <owl:Restriction>
        <owl:onProperty rdf:resource="#ofKind"/>
        <owl:cardinality rdf:datatype="&xsd;nonNegativeInteger"> 1 </
owl:cardinality>
      </owl:Restriction>
    </rdfs:subClassOf>
  </owl:Class>
  <owl:ObjectProperty rdf:ID="isA">
    <rdfs:domain rdf:resource="#QualifiedConcept"/>
    <rdfs:range rdf:resource="#Concept"/>
  </owl:ObjectProperty>

  <owl:ObjectProperty rdf:ID="ofKind">
    <rdfs:domain rdf:resource="#QualifiedConcept"/>
    <rdfs:range rdf:resource="#Concept"/>
  </owl:ObjectProperty>
```

Box 4.

```
<owl:Class rdf:about="#InvertedConcept">
    <rdfs:subClassOf rdf:resource="#Concept"/>
    <rdfs:subClassOf>
      <owl:Restriction>
        <owl:onProperty rdf:resource="#hasConcept"/>
        <owl:cardinality rdf:datatype="&xsd;nonNegativeInteger"> 1 </
owl:cardinality>
      </owl:Restriction>
    </rdfs:subClassOf>
</owl:Class>

<owl:ObjectProperty rdf:ID="hasConcept">
    <rdfs:domain rdf:resource="#Concept"/>
    <rdfs:range rdf:resource="#Concept"/>
</owl:ObjectProperty>
```

Box 5.

```
<owl:Class rdf:about="#ConjunctiveConcept">
    <rdfs:subClassOf rdf:resource="#Concept"/>
    <rdfs:subClassOf>
      <owl:Restriction>
        <owl:onProperty rdf:resource="#hasConcept"/>
        <owl:minCardinality rdf:datatype="&xsd;nonNegativeInteger">2</
owl:minCardinality>
      </owl:Restriction>
    </rdfs:subClassOf>
  </owl:Class>
  <owl:Class rdf:about="#DisjunctiveConcept">
    <rdfs:subClassOf rdf:resource="#Concept"/>
    <rdfs:subClassOf>
      <owl:Restriction>
        <owl:onProperty rdf:resource="#hasConcept"/>
        <owl:minCardinality rdf:datatype="&xsd;nonNegativeInteger">2</
owl:minCardinality>
        </owl:Restriction>
    </rdfs:subClassOf>
  </owl:Class>
```

Box 6.

```
<owl:ObjectProperty rdf:ID="affects">
    <rdfs:comment>Generic class of USDL Affects</rdfs:comment>
    <rdfs:domain rdf:resource="#Operation"/>
    <rdfs:range rdf:resource="#Concept"/>
 </owl:ObjectProperty>
```

Affects

The *affects* property is specialized into four types of actions common to enterprise services: *creates*, *updates*, *deletes*, and *finds*. See Box 6.

Note that each of these specializations inherits the domain and range of the *affects* property. Most services can be described using one of these types of effects. For those services that cannot be described in terms of these specializations, the parent *affects* property can be used instead which is described as an USDL concept. See Box 7.

Conditions and Constraints

Services may have some external conditions (pre-conditions and post-conditions) specified on the input or output parameters. *Condition* class is used to describe all such constraints. Conditions are represented as conjunction or disjunction of binary predicates. Predicate is a trait or aspect of the resource being described. See Box 8.

A condition has exactly one value for the *onPart* property and at most one value for the *hasValue* property, each of which is of type USDL *Concept*. See Box 9.

Box 7.

```
<owl:ObjectProperty rdf:about="#creates">
  <rdfs:subPropertyOf rdf:resource="#affects"/>
</owl:ObjectProperty>
<owl:ObjectProperty rdf:about="#updates">
  <rdfs:subPropertyOf rdf:resource="#affects"/>
</owl:ObjectProperty>
<owl:ObjectProperty rdf:about="#deletes">
  <rdfs:subPropertyOf rdf:resource="#affects"/>
</owl:ObjectProperty>
<owl:ObjectProperty rdf:about="#finds">
  <rdfs:subPropertyOf rdf:resource="#affects"/>
</owl:ObjectProperty>
```

Box 8.

```
<owl:Class rdf:ID="Condition">
    <rdfs:comment>Generic class of USDL Condition</rdfs:comment>
    <owl:unionOf rdf:parseType="Collection">
       <owl:Class rdf:about="#AtomicCondition"/>
       <owl:Class rdf:about="#ConjunctiveCondition"/>
       <owl:Class rdf:about="#DisjunctiveCondition"/>
    </owl:unionOf>
 </owl:Class>
```

Conjunctive and Disjunctive Conditions

The *ConjunctiveCondition* and *DisjunctiveCondition* respectively denote the conjunction and disjunction of USDL *Conditions*. The property cardinality restrictions on *ConjunctiveCondition* and *DisjunctiveCondition* allow for *n*-ary conjunctions and disjunctions (where $n \geq 2$) of USDL conditions. In general any *n*-ary condition can be written as a combination of conjunctions and disjunctions of binary conditions. See Box 10.

Messages

Services communicate by exchanging messages. As mentioned, messages are simple tuples of actual data, called *parts*. Take for example, a flight reservation service similar to the SAP ABAP Workbench Interface Repository for flight reservations (SAP, 2001), which makes use of the following message. See Box 11.

The USDL surrogate for a WSDL message is the *Message* class, which is a composite entity with zero or more parts. Note that for generality, messages are allowed to contain zero parts. Each part of a message is simply a USDL Concept, as defined by the *hasPart* property. Semantically messages are treated as tuples of concepts. See Box 12.

Continuing our example - flight reservation service, the *ReserveFlightRequest* message is given semantics using USDL as follows, where *&wn;customer* and *&wn;name* are valid XML references to WordNet lexical concepts. See Box 13.

Box 9.

```
<owl:Class rdf:about="#AtomicCondition">
    <rdfs:subClassOf>
      <owl:Restriction>
        <owl:onProperty rdf:resource="#hasConcept"/>
        <owl:cardinality rdf:datatype="&xsd;nonNegativeInteger">1</
owl:cardinality>
      </owl:Restriction>
    </rdfs:subClassOf>
    <rdfs:subClassOf>
      <owl:Restriction>
        <owl:onProperty rdf:resource="#onPart"/>
        <owl:cardinality rdf:datatype="&xsd;nonNegativeInteger">1</
owl:cardinality>
      </owl:Restriction>
    </rdfs:subClassOf>
    <rdfs:subClassOf>
      <owl:Restriction>
        <owl:onProperty rdf:resource="#hasValue"/>
        <owl:maxCardinality rdf:datatype="&xsd;nonNegativeInteger">1</
owl:maxCardinality>
      </owl:Restriction>
    </rdfs:subClassOf>
 </owl:Class>
<owl:ObjectProperty rdf:ID="onPart">
    <rdfs:domain rdf:resource="#AtomicCondition"/>
    <rdfs:range rdf:resource="#Concept"/>
 </owl:ObjectProperty>
<owl:ObjectProperty rdf:ID="hasValue">
    <rdfs:domain rdf:resource="#AtomicCondition"/>
    <rdfs:range rdf:resource="#Concept"/>
 </owl:ObjectProperty>
```

PortType

A service consists of portType, which is a collection of procedures or operations that are parametric on messages. Our example flight reservation service might contain a *portType* definition for a flight reservation service that takes as input an itinerary and outputs a reservation receipt. See Box 14.

The USDL surrogate is defined as the class *portType* which contains zero or more *Operation*s as values of the *hasOperation* property. See Box 15.

As with the case of *messages*, *portType*s are not directly assigned meaning via the OWL WordNet ontology. Instead the individual *Operation*s are described by their side-effects via an *affects* property. Note that the parameters of an operation are already given meaning by ascribing meaning to the messages that constitute the parameters. See Box 16.

An operation can have one or more values for the *affects* property, all of which are of type USDL Concept, which is the target of the effect. The *hasInput*, *hasOutput*, *and affects* properties are defined in Box 17.

The complete USDL specification, that is, the formal definitions of the classes and properties in OWL are presented in (USDL, 2006).

Box 10.

```
<owl:Class rdf:about="#ConjunctiveCondition">
    <rdfs:subClassOf rdf:resource="#Condition"/>
    <rdfs:subClassOf>
      <owl:Restriction>
        <owl:onProperty rdf:resource="#hasCondition"/>
        <owl:minCardinality rdf:datatype= "&xsd;nonNegativeInteger">2</
owl:minCardinality>
      </owl:Restriction>
    </rdfs:subClassOf>
</owl:Class>

<owl:Class rdf:about="#DisjunctiveCondition">
    <rdfs:subClassOf rdf:resource="#Condition"/>
    <rdfs:subClassOf>
      <owl:Restriction>
        <owl:onProperty rdf:resource="#hasCondition"/>
        <owl:minCardinalityrdf:datatype= "&xsd;nonNegativeInteger">2</
owl:minCardinality>
      </owl:Restriction>
    </rdfs:subClassOf>
</owl:Class>
<owl:ObjectProperty rdf:ID="hasCondition">
    <rdfs:domain rdf:resource="#Concept"/>
    <rdfs:range rdf:resource="#Condition"/>
</owl:ObjectProperty>
```

Box 11.

```
  <message name="#ReserveFlight_Request">
    <part name="#CustomerName" type="xsd:string">
    <part name="#FlightNumber" type="xsd:string">
    <part name="#DepartureDate" type="xsd:date">
  ...
  </message>
```

SEMANTIC DESCRIPTION OF A SERVICE

This section shows an example syntactic description of a Web service using WSDL and its corresponding semantic description using USDL.

Hotel Reservation Service

The service described here is a simplified hotel-reservation service published in a Web service registry. This service can be treated as atomic: that is, no interactions between buying and selling agents are required, apart from invocation of the service and receipt of its outputs by the buyer. Given certain inputs and pre-conditions, the service provides certain outputs and has specific side-effects. This service takes in a *HotelChain*, *StartDate*, *NumNights*, *NumPersons*, *NumRooms*, *FirstName*, and *LastName* as input parameters. It has a few input pre-conditions that *NumNights* and *NumRooms* must be greater than zero and

Box 12.

```
<owl:Class rdf:ID="Message">
    <rdfs:comment> Generic class of USDL Message  </rdfs:comment>
    <owl:unionOf rdf:parseType="Collection">
      <owl:Class rdf:about="#Input"/>
      <owl:Class rdf:about="#Output"/>
    </owl:unionOf>
    <rdfs:subClassOf>
      <owl:Restriction>
      <owl:onProperty rdf:resource="#hasPart"/>
      <owl:minCardinality rdf:datatype="&xsd;nonNegativeInteger">0</
owl:minCardinality>
      </owl:Restriction>
    </rdfs:subClassOf>
</owl:Class>

<owl:Class rdf:about="#Input">
    <rdfs:subClassOf rdf:resource="#Message"/>
</owl:Class>
<owl:Class rdf:about="#Output">
    <rdfs:subClassOf rdf:resource="#Message"/>
</owl:Class>
<owl:ObjectProperty rdf:ID="hasPart">
    <rdfs:domain rdf:resource="#Message"/>
    <rdfs:range rdf:resource="#Concept"/>
</owl:ObjectProperty>
```

Box 13.

```
<Message rdf:about="#ReserveFlight_Request">
    <hasPart rdf:resource="#CustomerName"/>
    <hasPart rdf:resource="#FlightNumber"/>
    <hasPart rdf:resource="#DepartureDate"/>
</Message>
<QualifiedConcept rdf:about="#CustomerName">
    <isA rdf:resource="#Name"/>
    <ofKind rdf:resource="#Customer"/>
</QualifiedConcept>
<BasicConcept rdf:about="#Name">
    <isA rdf:resource="&wn;name"/>
</BasicConcept>
<BasicConcept rdf:about="#Customer">
    <isA rdf:resource="&wn;customer"/>
</BasicConcept>
<!-- Similarly concepts FlightNumber and DepartureDate are defined -->
```

Box 14.

```
  <portType rdf:about="#Flight_Reservation">
    <hasOperation rdf:resource="#ReserveFlight">
  </portType>
  <operation rdf:about="#ReserveFlight">
    <hasInput rdf:resource="#ReserveFlight_Request"/>
    <hasOutput rdf:resource="#ReserveFlight_Response"/>
    <creates rdf:resource="#FlightReservation" />
  </operation>
```

Box 15.

```
<owl:Class rdf:about="#portType">
    <rdfs:subClassOf>
      <owl:Restriction>
      <owl:onProperty rdf:resource=#hasOperation"/>
      <owl:minCardinality rdf:datatype="&xsd;nonNegativeInteger">0</
owl:minCardinality>
      </owl:Restriction>
    </rdfs:subClassOf>
</owl:Class>
<owl:ObjectProperty rdf:ID="hasOperation">
    <rdfs:domain rdf:resource="#portType"/>
    <rdfs:range rdf:resource="#Operation"/>
 </owl:ObjectProperty>
```

Box 16.

```
<owl:Class rdf:about="#Operation">
    <rdfs:subClassOf>
      <owl:Restriction>
        <owl:onProperty rdf:resource="#hasInput"/>
        <owl:minCardinality rdf:datatype="&xsd;nonNegativeInteger"> 0</
owl:minCardinality>
      </owl:Restriction>
    </rdfs:subClassOf>

    <rdfs:subClassOf>
      <owl:Restriction>
         <owl:onProperty rdf:resource="#hasOutput"/>
         <owl:minCardinality rdf:datatype="&xsd;nonNegativeInteger">0</
owl:minCardinality>
      </owl:Restriction>
    </rdfs:subClassOf>
    <rdfs:subClassOf>
      <owl:Restriction>
        <owl:onProperty rdf:resource="#affects"/>
        <owl:minCardinality rdf:datatype="&xsd;nonNegativeInteger">1</
owl:minCardinality>
      </owl:Restriction>
    </rdfs:subClassOf>
</owl:Class>
```

Box 17.

```
<owl:ObjectProperty rdf:ID="hasInput">
  <rdfs:domain rdf:resource="#Operation"/>
  <rdfs:range rdf:resource="#Input"/>
</owl:ObjectProperty>
<owl:ObjectProperty rdf:ID="hasOutput">
  <rdfs:domain rdf:resource="#Operation"/>
  <rdfs:range rdf:resource="#Output"/>
</owl:ObjectProperty>
<owl:ObjectProperty rdf:ID="affects">
  <rdfs:domain rdf:resource="#Operation"/>
  <rdfs:range rdf:resource="#Concept"/>
</owl:ObjectProperty>
```

StartDate must be greater than today. This service outputs a *Reservation* at the end of transaction.

WSDL Annotation

The following is WSDL definition of the service. This service provides a single operation called *ReserveHotel*. The input and output messages are defined below. The conditions on the service cannot be described using WSDL. See Box 18.

USDL Annotation

The following is the complete USDL annotation corresponding to the above mentioned WSDL description. The input pre-condition and the global constraint on the service are also described semantically. See Box 19.

A Book-Buying Service example is presented in (Bansal et al., 2005).

A THEORY OF SUBSTITUTION OF SERVICES

Next, we will investigate the theoretical aspects of USDL. This involves concepts from set theory. From a systems integration perspective, an engineer is interested in finding (discovering) a service that accomplishes some necessary task. Of course, such a service may not be present in any service directory. In such a case the discovery software should return a set of services that can be used in a context expecting a service that meets that description (of course, this set may be empty). To find services that can be substituted for a given service that is not present in the directory, we need to develop a theory of *service substitutability*. We develop such a theory in this section. Our theory relates service substitutability to WordNet's semantic relations. In order to develop this theory, we must first formally define constructs such as USDL-described concepts, affects, conditions and services, which we will also call concepts, affects, conditions and services for short. While it is possible to work directly with the XML USDL syntax, doing so is cumbersome and so we will instead opt for set theoretic notation.

Definition 1 (Set of WordNet Lexemes)

Let Ω be the set of WordNet lexemes. The following semantic relations exist on elements of Ω:

1. **Synonym:** A pair of WordNet Lexemes having the same or nearly the same meaning have the synonym relation. Example, 'purchase' is a synonym of 'buy'.

Box 18.

```
<definitions...>
    <portType name="ReserveHotel_Service">
      <operation name="ReserveHotel">
        <input message="ReserveHotel_Request"/>
        <output message="ReserveHotel_Response"/>
      </operation>
    </portType>
    <message name="ReserveHotel_Request">
      <part name="HotelChain" type="xsd:string"/>
      <part name="StartDate" type="xsd:date"/>
      <part name="NumNights" type="xsd:integer"/>
      <part name="NumPersons" type="xsd:integer"/>
      <part name="NumRooms" type="xsd:integer"/>
      <part name="FirstName" type="xsd:integer"/>
      <part name="LastName" type="xsd:integer"/>
    </message>
    <message name="ReserveHotel_Response">
      <part name="Reservation" type="xsd:string"/>
    </message>
  </definitions>
```

Box 19.

```
<definitions>
    <portType rdf:about="#ReserveHotel_Service">
      <hasOperation rdf:resource="#ReserveHotel"/>
    </portType>
    <operation rdf:about="#ReserveHotel">
      <hasInput  rdf:resource="#ReserveHotel_Request"/>
      <hasOutput rdf:resource="#ReserveHotel_Response"/>
      <creates rdf:resource="#HotelReservation"/>
    </operation>
    <Message rdf:about="#ReserveHotel_Request">
      <hasPart rdf:resource="#HotelChain"/>
      <hasPart rdf:resource="#StartDate"/>
      <hasPart rdf:resource="#NumNights"/>
      <hasPart rdf:resource="#NumPersons"/>
      <hasPart rdf:resource="#NumRooms"/>
      <hasPart rdf:resource="#FirstName"/>
      <hasPart rdf:resource="#LastName"/>
    </Message>
<Message rdf:about="#ReserveHotel_Response">
      <hasPart rdf:resource="#HotelReservation"/>
</Message>
<Condition rdf:about="#greaterThanToday">
  <hasConcept rdf:resource="#greaterThan"/>
  <onPart rdf:resource="#StartDate"/>
  <hasValue rdf:resource="#TodaysDate"/>
</Condition>
```

continued on following page

Box 19. Continued

```
<!-- Similarly we can define Condition
       #greaterThanZero on parts #NumRooms
       and #NumNights -->

<QualifiedConcept rdf:about="#HotelChain">
   <isA rdf:resource="#Chain"/>
   <ofKind rdf:resource="#Hotel"/>
</QualifiedConcept>

<QualifiedConcept rdf:about="#StartDate">
   <isA rdf:resource="#Date"/>
   <ofKind rdf:resource="#Start"/>
</QualifiedConcept>
<QualifiedConcept rdf:about="#TodaysDate">
  <isA rdf:resource="#Date"/>
  <ofKind rdf:resource="#Today"/>
</QualifiedConcept>

<!-- Similarly we can define Qualified
       Concepts for #NumNights, #NumPersons,
       #NumRooms, #FirstName, #LastName -->

<BasicConcept rdf:about="#Chain">
   <isA rdf:resource="&wn;chain"/>
</BasicConcept>
<BasicConcept rdf:about="#Hotel">
  <isA rdf:resource="&wn;hotel"/>
</BasicConcept>
<BasicConcept rdf:about="#Start">
   <isA rdf:resource="&wn;start"/>
</BasicConcept>

<BasicConcept rdf:about="#Date">
   <isA rdf:resource="&wn;date"/>
</BasicConcept>
<BasicConcept
   rdf:about="#greaterThan">
   <isA rdf:resource
   ="&wn;greater_than"/>
</BasicConcept>
<BasicConcept rdf:about="#Date">
   <isA rdf:resource="&wn;date"/>
</BasicConcept>
<BasicConcept rdf:about="#Today">
   <isA rdf:resource="&wn;today"/>
</BasicConcept>
<BasicConcept
    rdf:about="#Reservation">
    <isA   rdf:resource
     ="&wn;reservation"/>
</BasicConcept>
```

continued on following page

Box 19. Continued

```
<!-- Similarly we can define Basic
      Concepts for #nights, #rooms,
      #number, #persons, #name, etc. -->
</definitions>
```

2. **Antonym:** A pair of WordNet Lexemes having the opposite meaning have the antonym relation. Example, 'start' is an antonym of 'end'.
3. **Hyponym:** A word that is more specific than a given word is called the subordinate or hyponym of the other. Example, 'car' is a hyponym of 'vehicle'.
4. **Hypernym:** A word that is more generic than a given word is called the super-ordinate or hypernym of the other. Example, 'vehicle' is a hypernym of 'car'.
5. **Meronym:** A word that names a part of a larger whole is a meronym of the whole. Example, 'roof' and 'door' are meronyms of 'house'.
6. **Holonym:** A word that names the whole of which a given word is a part is a holonym of the part. Example, 'house' is a holonym for 'roof' and 'door'.

Definition 2 (Representation of USDL Concepts)

1. A Basic Concept $c = x$, where x is a WordNet lexeme, defines the values of *isA* property. Example, *customer* is a Basic Concept and a WordNet lexeme.
2. A Qualified Concept $c = (X, Y)$, where X, Y are USDL concepts, defines the values of *isA* and *ofKind* properties. Example, concept *FlightNumber* is a *number ofkind flight* represented as (*number*, *flight*).
3. An Inverted Concept c is represented as $\neg X$ where X is an USDL concept. Example, concept *not a customer name* can be represented as ¬ (*name*, *customer*).
4. Let X, Y be USDL Concepts.
   i. Conjunctive Concept c is represented as $X \wedge Y$. Example, concept *EvenRationalNumber* is represented as (*number*, *even*) ∧ (*number*, *rational*).
   ii. Disjunctive Concept c is represented as $X \vee Y$. Example, concept *OrderNumber/Availability-Message* is represented as (*number*, *order*) ∨ (*message*, *availability*).

Definition 3 (Universe of USDL Concepts)

Let Θ be the set of USDL concepts. Θ can be inductively constructed as follows:

1. $x \in \Omega$ implies $x \in \Theta$
2. $X, Y \in \Theta$ implies $(X, Y) \in \Theta$
3. $X \in \Theta$ implies $\neg X \in \Theta$
4. $X, Y \in \Theta$ implies $X \vee Y \in \Theta$
5. $X, Y \in \Theta$ implies $X \wedge Y \in \Theta$

Definition 4 (Semantic relations of Basic Concepts)

Semantic relations hold between two Basic concepts if their corresponding WordNet lexemes have the same semantic relation in Ω. For example, Basic Concept *Purchase* is a synonym of Basic Concept *Buy*.

Definition 5 (Synonym and Antonym Relation of Qualified Concepts)

Let C_1 and C_2 are Qualified Concepts where $C_1 = (X_1, Y_1)$, $C_2 = (X_2, Y_2)$ and $X_1, X_2, Y_1, Y_2 \in \Theta$.

1. C_1 is synonym of C_2 if X_1 is recursively a synonym of X_2 and Y_1 is recursively a synonym of Y_2.
2. If $X_1 = w_1$ and $X_2 = w_2$ where $w_1, w_2 \in \Omega$, then X_1 is synonym of X_2 if w_1 and w_2 have the synonym relation in Ω.

For example, Qualified Concept (*date, begin*) is a synonym of Qualified Concept (*date, start*). Similarly we can determine the antonym relation between Qualified Concepts. For example, Qualified Concept (*date, begin*) is a antonym of Qualified Concept (*date, end*).

Definition 6 (Hyponym and Hypernym Relation of Qualified Concepts)

Let C_1 and C_2 are Qualified Concepts where $C_1 =(X_1, Y_1)$, $C_2 =(X_2, Y_2)$ and $X_1, X_2, Y_1, Y_2 \in \Theta$.

1. C_1 is hypernym of C_2 if any one of the following holds:
   i. X_1 is recursively a hypernym of X_2 and Y_1 is recursively a hypernym of Y_2.
   ii. X_1 is recursively a hypernym of X_2 and Y_1 is recursively a synonym of Y_2.
   iii. X_1 is recursively a synonym of X_2 and Y_1 is recursively a hypernym of Y_2.
2. If $X_1 = w_1$ and $X_2 = w_2$ where $w_1, w_2 \in \Omega$, then X_1 is hypernym of X_2 if w_1 and w_2 have the hypernym relation in Ω.

For example, Qualified Concept (*number, vehicle*) is a hypernym of Qualified Concept (*number, car*). Similarly we can determine the hyponym relation of Qualified Concepts. For example, Concept (*number, car*) is a hyponym of (*number, vehicle*).

Definition 7 (Holonym and Meronym Relation of Qualified Concepts)

Let C_1 and C_2 are Qualified Concepts where $C_1 = (X_1, Y_1)$, $C_2 =(X_2, Y_2)$ and $X_1, X_2, Y_1, Y_2 \in \Theta$.

1. C_1 is meronym of C_2 if any one of the following holds:
   i. X_1 is recursively a meronym of X_2 and Y_1 is recursively a meronym of Y_2.
   ii. X_1 is recursively a meronym of X_2 and Y_1 is recursively a synonym of Y_2.
   iii. X_1 is recursively a synonym of X_2 and Y_1 is recursively a meronym of Y_2.
2. If $X_1 = w_1$ and $X_2 = w_2$ where $w_1, w_2 \in \Omega$, then X_1 is meronym of X_2 if w_1 and w_2 have the meronym relation in Ω.

For example, Qualified Concept (*door, brown*) is a meronym of Qualified Concept (*house, brown*). Similarly we can determine the holonym relation of Qualified Concepts. For example, Qualified Concept (*house, brown*) is a holonym of Qualified Concept (*door, brown*).

Definition 8 (Semantic Relations between Inverted Concepts)

Let C_1 and C_2 be two Inverted concepts where $C_1 = \neg X_1$ and $C_2 = \neg X_2$.

1. C_1 is a synonym of C_2 if X_1 and X_2 are synonyms.
2. C_1 is an antonym of C_2 if X_1 and X_2 are antonyms.
3. C_1 is a hypernym of C_2 if X_1 and X_2 are hyponyms and vice versa.
4. C_1 is a meronym of C_2 if X_1 and X_2 are holonyms and vice versa.

For example, Inverted Concept ¬ (*date, begin*) is a synonym of Inverted Concept ¬ (*date, start*). The synonym-antonym relation, hyponym-hypernym relation and meronym-holonym relation can be extended to Conjunctive and Disjunctive concepts.

Definition 9 (Semantic Relations between Conjunctive (resp., Disjunctive) Concepts)

Let C_1 and C_2 be two Conjunctive (resp., Disjunctive) concepts where $C_1 = X_1 \wedge Y_1$ and $C_2 = X_2 \wedge Y_2$.

1. C_1 is a synonym of C_2 if X_1 is a synonym of X_2 and Y_1 is a synonym of Y_2 OR X_1 is a synonym of Y_2 and Y_1 is a synonym of X_2.
2. C_1 is a hypernym of C_2 if one of the following holds:
   i. X_1 is a hypernym of X_2 and Y_1 is a hypernym/synonym of Y_2
   ii. X_1 is a hypernym/synonym of X_2 and Y_1 is a hypernym of Y_2
   iii. X_1 is a hypernym of Y_2 and Y_1 is a hypernym/synonym of X_2.
   iv. X_1 is a hypernym/synonym of Y_2 and Y_1 is a hypernym of X_2.

For example, Conjunctive Concept (*vehicle, blue*) Λ (*vehicle, automatic*) is a hypernym of (*car, blue*) Λ (*car, automatic*). Similar to the above defined hypernym relation, we can define the antonym, hyponym, meronym, and holonym relations between Conjunctive (resp., Disjunctive) Concepts.

Definition 10 (Substitution of Concepts)

1. **Exact Substitution:** For any concepts *C, C'* ∈ Θ, if *C* is a synonym of *C'*, then *C* is the exact substitutable of *C'* and *C* can safely be used in a context expecting concept *C'*. Example, concept *Purchase* is an exact substitutable of concept *Buy*.
2. **Generic Substitution:** For any concepts *C, C'* ∈ Θ, if *C* is a hypernym of *C'*, then *C* is the generic substitutable of *C'* and *C* can safely be used in a context expecting concept *C'* or a super-ordinate of *C'*. Example, concept (*number, vehicle*) is a generic substitutable of concept (*number, car*).
3. **Specific Substitution:** For any concepts *C, C'* ∈ Θ, if *C* is a hyponym of *C'*, then *C* is the specific substitutable of *C'* and *C* can safely be used in a context expecting concept *C'* or a sub-ordinate of *C'*. Example, concept (*number, car*) is a specific substitutable of concept (*number, vehicle*).
4. **Part Substitution:** For any concepts *C, C'* ∈ Θ, if *C* is a meronym of *C'*, then *C* is the part substitutable of *C'* and *C* can safely be used in a context expecting a concept that is a part of *C'*. Example, concept *Roof* is a part substitutable of concept *House*.
5. **Whole Substitution:** For any concepts *C, C'* ∈ Θ, if *C* is a holonym of *C'*, then *C* is the whole substitutable of *C'* and *C* can safely be used in a context expecting a concept that is a whole of *C'*. Example, concept *House* is a whole substitutable of concept *Roof*.

Definition 11 (Representation of Affects)

Let $\Gamma = \{(L, E) \mid L \in (\Psi \cup \Theta), E \in \Theta\}$ be the set of USDL side-effects, where Ψ = {*creates, updates, deletes, finds*}, *L* is the affect type and *E* is the affected object. The affect type could be one of the pre-defined affects from Ψ or a generic effect which is described as a concept.

Definition 12 (Substitution of Affects)

USDL *affect* is represented as a pair where the first element is the affect type and second element is the affected object. Both affect type and the affected object are described as USDL concepts.

Let A_1 and A_2 be two affects where $A_1 = (L_1, E_1)$ and $A_2 = (L_2, E_2)$. A_1 can safely be used in a context expecting affect A_2 if all of the following hold:

1. Concept L_1 is substitutable for L_2
2. Concept E_1 is substitutable for E_2.

These substitutables can be of kind Exact, Generic, Specific, Part, or Whole which also determines the kind of substitution of the affect A_1 in a context expecting A_2. Example, affect (*finds*, *VehicleNumber*) is a generic substitution of affect (*lookup*, *CarNumber*) as concept *finds* is an exact substitutable of *lookup* and concept *VehicleNumber* is a generic substitutable of concept *CarNumber*.

Definition 13 (Representation of Conditions)

Let $\Phi = \{(P, Arg_1, Arg_2) \mid P, Arg_1, Arg_2 \in \Theta\}$ be the set of USDL conditions. P is the constraint which is either a binary or a unary predicate. Arg_1 is the concept on which the predicate acts and Arg_2 is the concept which represents a value. Arg_2 is an optional parameter.

Definition 14 (Substitution of Conditions)

USDL condition is represented as a tuple made up of the constraint or predicate and two arguments. The constraint and the arguments are described as USDL concepts.

Let C_1 and C_2 be two conditions where $C_1 = (P_1, FirstArg_1, SecondArg_1)$ and $C_2 = (P_2, FirstArg_2, SecondArg_2)$. C_1 can safely be used in a context expecting condition C_2 if all of the following hold:

1. Concept P_1 is substitutable for P_2
2. Concept $FirstArg_1$ is substitutable $FirstArg_2$
3. Concept $SecondArg_1$ is substitutable for $SecondArg_2$

These substitutables can be of kind Exact, Generic, Specific, Part, or Whole which also determines the kind of substitution of the condition C_1 in a context expecting C_2. Example, condition (*greaterThan*, *NumberOfNights*, 0) is an exact substitution of condition (*moreThan*, *NumberOfNights*, 0).

Definition 15 (Representation of a Web Service)

For any set S, let $S^* = \{\varepsilon \mid \varepsilon \text{ not in } S\} \cup \{(x,y) \mid x \in S, y \in S^*\}$ be the set of lists over S. Let Σ be the set of USDL service descriptions represented in the form of terms. The USDL description of a Web service consists of:

1. A list of Inputs, $I \in \Theta^*$
2. A list of Outputs, $O \in \Theta^*$
3. A list of Pre-Conditions, *Pre-Condition* $\in \Phi^*$
4. A list of Post-Conditions, *Post-Condition* $\in \Phi^*$
5. Side-effects, (*affect-type, affected-object*) $\in \Gamma$

USDL service description can be treated as a term of first-order logic (Lloyd, 1987). The side-effect of a service comprises of an affect type and the affected object. The service can be converted into a triple as follows:

(Pre-Conditions, affect-type(affected-object, I, O), Post-Conditions)

The function symbol *affect-type* is the side-effect of the service and *affected object* is the object that changed due to the side-effect. I is the list of inputs and O is the list of outputs. *Pre-Conditions* are the conditions on the input parameters and *Post-Conditions* are the conditions on the output parameters of the service. We represent services as triples so that they can be treated as terms in first-order logic. The first-order logic unification algorithm (Lloyd, 1987) then can be extended to specialized unifications for exact, generic, specific, part and whole substitutions.

Now that the formal definitions of concept, affects, conditions and service descriptions are given, we would like to extend the theory of substitutability over Σ so that we can reason about substitutability of services.

Definition 16 (Substitution of a Web service)

Let σ and σ' be two services where

σ is represented as *(Pre-Condition, affect-type(affected-object, I, O), Post-Condition)* and

σ' is represented as *(Pre-Condition', affect-type'(affected-object', I', O'), Post-Condition')*.

σ can safely be used in a context expecting service σ' if all of the following hold:

1. *Pre-Condition* is substitutable for *Pre-Condition'*.
2. If the terms *affect-type(affected-object, I, O)* and *affect-type'(affected-object', I', O')* can be unified by applying an extended unification algorithm. The unification mechanism applied is different based on the kind of substitution needed.
3. *Post-Condition* is substitutable for *Post-Condition'*.

Definition 17

For any services S_1, $S_2 \in \Sigma$, we say $S_1 \leq S_2$ if S_1 is a substitutable of S_2 based on one of the WordNet semantic relations. Thus far our notions of service substitutability are based on the six WordNet semantic relations discussed earlier. However, one can define the notion of service substitutability independently using the actual semantics (e.g., denotational semantics) of the program that realizes this service. Consider a service S_1 with inputs I_1 and outputs O_1, and another service S_2 with inputs I_2 and outputs O_2; we ignore the side-effects of these services for the moment. The ideal conditions under which service S_1 can be substituted for service S_2 is the following: $I_1 \subseteq I_2$ and $O_2 \subseteq O_1$. Essentially, the inputs needed by S_1 must be present in the inputs being provided in anticipation of availability of S_2. Likewise, the outputs produced by service S_1 should contain the outputs anticipated from service S_2. In such a case, S_1 can be directly substituted for S_2. There can be other types of general substitution relation defined. However, for these other types of substitutions, the code of the service being used for substitution may have to be modified or wrappers placed around it.

One can, however, develop a more general notion of substitutability based on denotational semantics (Schmidt, 1986). Let $[|S_1|]$ and $[|S_2|]$ be the semantic denotations of programs that implement services S_1 and S_2 respectively (note that the side-effects of these services will be captured as the state that becomes an argument in a denotational definition). Note that $[|S_1|]$ and $[|S_2|]$ can be regarded as points in a complete partial order (Schmidt, 1986) that represents the space of all functions. Service $[|S_1|]$ can be substituted for $[|S_2|]$ if $[|S_1|]$ and $[|S_2|]$ lie in the same chain in the complete partial order (i.e., either $[|S_1|] \subseteq [|S_2|]$ or $[|S_2|] \subseteq [|S_1|]$ where $\subseteq$ is the relation that induces the complete partial order among denotations of the services).

Given the definition of substitutability based on denotational semantics, one can prove the soundness and completeness of our notion of substitutability based on the WordNet semantic relations, that is,

$S_1 \leq S_2 \Rightarrow [|S_1|] \subseteq [|S_2|]$ (soundness)

$[|S_1|] \subseteq [|S_2|] \Rightarrow S_1 \leq S_2$ (completeness)

Intuitively, one can see that these relationships hold, since the $\leq$ relation is defined in terms of subsumption of terms describing the service's inputs and outputs and its effect (create, update, delete, find and the generic affects). These soundness and completeness proofs are not included here due to lack of space.

SERVICE DISCOVERY

Now that our theory of service substitutability has been developed, it can be used to build tools for automatically discovering services as well as for automatically composing them. It can also be used to build a service search engine that discovers matching services and ranks them.

We assume that a directory of services has already been compiled, and that this directory includes a USDL description document for each service. Inclusion of the USDL description makes service directly "semantically" searchable. However, we still need a query language to search this directory, that is, we need a language to frame the requirements on the service that an application developer is seeking. USDL itself can be used as such a query language. A USDL description of the desired service can be written, a query processor can then search the service directory to look for a "matching" service.

A discovery engine gets USDL descriptions from a service directory and converts them into terms of logic. The terms corresponding to the USDL query can be compared with the terms from the directory using an extended/special unification algorithm. Depending on the type of match required, the unification mechanism could be different. That is, the matching or unification algorithm used can look for an *exact*, *generic*, *specific*, *part* or a *whole* match depending on the desire of the user. Part and Whole substitutions are not useful while looking for matching services, but are very useful while selecting services for service composition. Also using Part or Whole substitutions for discovery may produce undesired side-effects. The discovery engine can also rank the various services discovered. In this scenario, the discovery engine returns a list of substitutable services after applying ranking based on the kind of match obtained. Exact substitutables are assigned the highest rank among the different kind of substitutables. The following is the default ranking order used for the different substitutions.

1. Exact Substitution: The matching service obtained is equivalent to the service in the query.
2. Generic Substitution: The matching service obtained subsumes the service in the query.
3. Specific Substitution: The matching service obtained is subsumed by the service in the query.
4. Whole Substitution: The matching service obtained is a composite service of the service in the query and some other services.
5. Part Substitution: The matching service obtained is a part of a composite service that the query describes.

The implementation of the service discovery engine is presented in the later part of the article.

With the USDL descriptions and query language in place, numerous applications become possible ranging from querying a database of services to rapid application development via automated integration tools and even real-time service composition (Hite, 2005). Take our flight reservation service example. Assume that somebody wants to find a travel reservation service and that they query a USDL database containing general purpose flight reservation services, bus reservation services, and so forth. One could then form a USDL query consisting of a description of a travel reservation service and the database could respond with a set of travel reservation services whether it is via flight, bus, or some other means of travel. This flexibility of generalization and specialization is gained from semantic information provided by USDL.

SERVICE COMPOSITION

For service composition, the first step is finding the set of composable services. USDL itself can be used to specify the requirements of the composed service that an application developer is seeking. Using the discovery engine, individual services that make up the composed service can be selected. Part substitution technique can be used to find the different parts of a whole task and the selected services can be composed into one by applying the correct sequence of their execution. The correct sequence of execution can be determined by the pre-conditions and post-conditions of the individual services. That is, if a subservice S_1 is composed with subservice S_2, then the postconditions of S_1 must imply the preconditions of S_2.

In fact, the WordNet Universal ontology can also be helpful in automatically discovering services that can be composed together to satisfy a service discovery query. To achieve this, the discovery engine looks at the USDL concepts that describe the service in the query. It then searches the WordNet ontology to find out the meronymous components of that concept. The services that exactly match the meronymous components are then discovered using the standard discovery mechanism. Preconditions and postcondition consistency is then used to find the order in which the meronymous components should be stitched together to produce the desired service.

The formal definition of the Composition problem is presented in (Kona, Bansal, & Gupta, 2007). The implementation of such a service composition engine is presented later in the Implementation section. Such an engine can aid a systems integrator in rapidly creating composite services, that is, services consisting of the composition of already existing services. In fact, such an engine can also be extended to automatically generate boilerplate code to manage the composite service, as well as menial inter-service data format conversions needed to glue the meronymous components together.

IMPLEMENTATION

Our discovery and composition engine is implemented using Prolog (Sterling & Shapiro, 1994) with Constraint Logic Programming over finite domain (Marriott & Stuckey, 1998), referred to as CLP(FD) hereafter. The repository of services contains one USDL description document for each service. USDL itself is used to specify the requirements of the service that an application developer is seeking. In this section, we present a high-level description of our implementation along with experimental results and the details are presented in (Kona, Bansa, Gupta, & Hite, 2006). The software system is made up of the following components.

Triple Generator

The triple generator module converts each service description into a triple.

In this case, USDL descriptions are converted to triples like:

(Pre-Conditions, affect-type(affected-object, I, O), Post-Conditions)

The function symbol *affect-type* is the side-effect of the service and *affected object* is the object that changed due to the side-effect. *I* is the list of inputs and *O* is the list of outputs. *Pre-Conditions* are the conditions on the input parameters and *Post-Conditions* are the conditions on the output parameters. Services are converted to triples so that they can be treated as terms in first-order logic and specialized unification algorithms can be applied to obtain exact, generic, specific, part and whole substitutions. In case conditions on a service are not provided, the *Pre-Conditions* and *Post-Conditions* in the triple will be null. Similarly if the affect-type is not available, this module assigns a generic affect to the service.

Query Reader

This module reads the query file and passes it on to the Triple Generator. We use USDL itself as the query language. A USDL description of the desired service can be written, which is read by the query reader and converted to a triple. This module can be easily extended to read descriptions written in other languages.

Semantic Relations Generator

We obtain the semantic relations from the OWL WordNet ontology. OWL WordNet ontology provides a number of useful semantic relations like synonyms, antonyms, hyponyms, hypernyms, meronyms, holonyms and many more. USDL descriptions point to OWL WordNet for the meanings of concepts. A theory of service substitution is described in detail which uses the semantic relations between basic concepts of WordNet, to derive the semantic relations between services. This module extracts all the semantic relations and creates a list of Prolog facts. We can also use any other domain-specific ontology to obtain semantic relations of concepts. We are currently looking into making the parser in this module more generic to handle any other ontology written in OWL.

Discovery Query Processor

This module compares the discovery query with all the services in the repository. The processor works as follows:

1. On the output parameters of a service, the processor first looks for an *exact* substitutable. If it does not find one, then it looks for a parameter with hyponym relation, that is, a *specific* substitutable.
2. On the input parameters of a service, the processor first looks for an *exact* substitutable. If it does not find one, then it looks for a parameter with hypernym relation, that is, a *generic* substitutable.

The discovery engine, written using Prolog with CLP (FD) library, uses a repository of facts, which contains a list of all services, their input and output parameters and semantic relations between parameters. The following is the code snippet of our engine. See Box 20.

The query is parsed and converted into a Prolog query that looks as follows:

discovery (sol (queryService, ListOfSolutionServices).

The engine will try to find a list of *SolutionServices* that match the *queryService*.

Composition Query Processor

The composition engine is written using Prolog with CLP (FD) library. It uses a repository of facts, which contains all the services, their input and output parameters and the semantic relations between the parameters. The query is converted into a Prolog query that looks as follows:

Composition (queryService, ListOfServices).

The engine will try to find a *ListOfServices* that can be composed into the requested queryService. Our engine uses the built-in, higher order predicate 'bagof' to return all possible *ListOfServices* that can be composed to get the requested *queryService*. The following is the code snippet of our composition engine. See Box 21.

Box 20.

```
discovery        (sol (Qname, A)):-  dQuery (Qname, I, O), encodeParam (O,
OL),
          /* narrow candidate services(S) using output list (OL)*/
          narrowO (OL, S),
         fd_set(S, FDs), fdset_to_list (FDs, SL),
          /* expand InputList (I) using semantic relations */
          getExtInpList (I, ExtInpList),
         encodeParam (ExtInpList, IL),
          /* Narrow candidate services(SL) using input list (IL)*/
          narrowI (IL, SL, SA),
         decodeS (SA, A).
```

Box 21.

```
composition(sol(Qname, Result)):-
          dQuery(Qname, QueryInputs, QueryOutputs),
          encodeParam(QueryOutputs, QO),
          getExtInpList(QueryInputs, InpList),
          encodeParam(InpList, QI),
          performForwardTask(QI, QO, LF),
          performBackwardTask(LF, QO, LR),
          getMinSolution(LR, QI, QO, A), reverse(A, RevA),
          confirmSolution(RevA, QI, QO), decodeSL(RevA, Result).
```

Output Generator

After the Composition engine finds a matching service, or the list of atomic services for a composed service, the results are sent to the output generator in the form of triples. This module generates the output files in any desired XML format.

Experimental Results

In order to test the performance of our engine, we needed a huge repository with Web service descriptions. Currently, only repositories with WSDL descriptions are available. So we tested our engine for performance using repositories from WS-Challenge website (WSC, 2006), slightly modified to fit into the USDL framework. The performance on USDL files should be similar. The repositories are of various sizes (thousands of services) and they contain their WSDL descriptions of services. The queries and solutions are provided in an XML format. The semantic relations between various parameters are provided in an XML Schema file. We evaluated our approach on different size repositories and tabulated Preprocessing and Query Execution time. Table 1 shows performance results of our algorithm on discovery queries and table 2 shows the results of our algorithm on composition queries. The tables show the repository size, the number of input-output parameters in each repository, the time taken to pre-process the repository, the query execution time, and the time taken to add or update a service into an already pre-processed repository. The times shown in the tables are the wall clock times. The actual CPU time to pre-process the repository and execute the query should be less than or equal to the wall clock time. We found that after the pre-processing of the repositories is completed, the query processing time is negligible

Table 1. Performance on discovery queries

Repository Size (number of services)	Number of I/O parameters	Pre-Processing Time in seconds	Query Execution Time in milli-seconds	Incremental Update time in milli-seconds
2000	4-8	36.5	1	8
2000	16-20	45.8	1	23
2000	32-36	57.8	2	28
2500	4-8	47.7	1	19
2500	16-20	58.7	1	23
2500	32-36	71.6	2	29
3000	4-8	56.8	1	19
3000	16-20	77.1	1	26
3000	32-36	88.2	3	29

(just 1 to 3 milli-secs.) even for complex queries with large repositories.

COMPARISON WITH OWL-S, WSDL-S, AND WSML

In this section we present a comparison of USDL with other popular approaches such as OWL-S (OWL-S, 2003), WSML (Comparison, 2005), and WSDL-S (WSDL-S, 2005). Our goal is to identify the similarities and differences of USDL with these approaches. OWL-S is a service description language which attempts to address the problem of semantic description via highly detailed service ontology. But OWL-S also allows for complicated combining forms, which seem to defeat the tractability and practicality of OWL-S. The focus in the design of OWL-S is to describe the structure of a service in terms of how it combines other sub-services (if any used). The description of atomic services in OWL-S is left under-specified (Balzer, Liebig, & Wagner, 2004). OWL-S includes the tags *presents* to describe the *service profile*, and the tag *describedBy* to describe the *service model*. The profile describes the (possibly conditional) states that exist before and after the service is executed. The service model describes how the service is (algorithmically) constructed from other simpler services. What the service actually accomplishes has to be inferred from these two descriptions in OWL-S. Given that OWL-S uses complicated combining forms, inferring the task that a service actually performs is, in general, undecidable. In contrast, in USDL, what the service actually *does* is directly described (via the verb *affects* and its refinements *create, update, delete*, and *find*).

OWL-S recommends that atomic services be defined using domain-specific ontologies. Thus, OWL-S needs users describing the services and users using the services to know, understand and agree on domain-specific ontologies in which the services are described. Hence, annotating services with OWL-S is a very time consuming, cumbersome, and invasive process. The complicated nature of OWL-S's combining forms, especially conditions and control constructs, seems to allow for the aforementioned semantic aliasing problem (Balzer et al., 2004). Other recent approaches such as WSMO, WSML, WSDL-S, and so forth, suffer from the same limitation (Comparison, 2005). In contrast, USDL uses the universal WordNet ontology to solve this problem.

Note that USDL and OWL-S can be used together. A USDL description can be placed under the *describedBy* tag for atomic processes, while OWL-S can be used to compose atomic USDL services. Thus, USDL along with WordNet can be

Table 2. Performance on composition queries

Repository Size (number of services)	Number of I/O parameters	Pre-Processing Time in seconds	Query Execution Time in milli-seconds	Incremental Update time in milli-seconds
2000	4-8	36.1	1	18
2000	16-20	47.1	1	23
2000	32-36	60.2	1	30
2500	4-8	58.4	1	19
2500	16-20	60.1	1	20
2500	32-36	102.1	1	34
3000	4-8	71.2	1	18
3000	16-20	87.9	1	22
3000	32-36	129.2	1	32

treated as the universal ontology that can make an OWL-S description complete. USDL documents can be used to describe the semantics of atomic services that OWL-S assumes will be described by domain-specific ontologies and pointed to by the OWL-S *describedBy* tag. In this respect, USDL and OWL-S are complementary: USDL can be treated as an extension to OWL-S which makes OWL-S description easy to write and semantically more complete. OWL-S can also be regarded as the composition language for USDL. If a new service can be built by composing a few already existing services, then this new service can be described in OWL-S using the USDL descriptions of the existing services. Next, this new service can be automatically generated from its OWL-S description. The control constructs like *Sequence* and *If-Then-Else* of OWL-S allows us to achieve this. Note once a composite service has been defined using OWL-S that uses atomic services described in USDL, a new USDL description must be written for this composite service (automatic generation of this description is currently being investigated). This USDL description is the formal documentation of the new composite service and will make it automatically searchable once the new service is placed in the directory service. It also allows this composite service to be treated as an atomic service by some other application. See Box 22.

For example, the aforementioned *ReserveFlight* service which creates a flight reservation can be viewed as a composite process of first getting the flight details, then checking the flight availability and then booking the flight (creating the reservation). If we have these three atomic services namely *GetFlightDetails*, *CheckFlightAvailability* and *BookFlight* then we can create our *ReserveFlight* service by composing these three services in sequence using the OWL-S *Sequence* construct. The following is the OWL-S description of the composed *ReserveFlight* service.

We can generate this composed *ReserveFlight* service automatically. The component services can be discovered from existing services using their USDL descriptions. Once we have the component services, the OWL-S description can be used to generate the new composed service.

RELATED WORK

Discovery and composition of Web services has been active area of research recently (McIlraith, Son, & Zeng, 2001; McIlraith et al., 2002; Picinielli, Emmerich, Zirpins, & Schutt, 2002;

Box 22.

```
<rdf:RDF xmlns:rdf=http://www.w3.org/1999/02/22-rdf-syntax-ns#...
  <process:CompositeProcess rdf:ID="ReserveFlight">
      <process:composedOf>
        <process:Sequence>
            <process:components rdf:parseType="Collection">
                <process:AtomicProcess rdf:about="#GetFlightDetails"/>
                <process:AtomicProcess rdf:about="#CheckFlightAvailability"/>
                <process:AtomicProcess rdf:about="#BookFlight"/>
            </process:components>
        </process:Sequence>
      </process:composedOf>
  </process:CompositeProcess>
  </rdf:RDF>
```

Srivastava, 2002; Srivastava & Koehler, 2003). Most of these approaches are based on capturing the formal semantics of the service using an action description languages or some kind of logic (e.g., description logic). The service composition problem is reduced to a planning problem where the sub-services constitute atomic actions and the overall service desired is represented by the goal to be achieved using some combination of atomic actions. A planner is then used to determine the combination of actions needed to reach the goal. In contrast, we rely more on WordNet (which we use as a universal ontology) and the meronymous relationships of WordNet lexemes to achieve automatic composition. The approaches proposed by others also rely on a domain-specific ontology (specified on OWL/DAML), and thus suffer from the problem mentioned earlier, namely, to discover/compose such services the discovery/composition engine has to be aware of the domain specific ontology. Thus, completely general discovery and composition engines cannot be built. Additionally, the domain-specific ontology has to be quite extensive in that any relationship that can possibly exist between two terms in the ontology must be included in the ontology. In contrast, in our approach, the complex relationships (USDL concepts) that might be used to describe services or their inputs and outputs are part of USDL descriptions and not the ontology. Note that our approach is quite general and it will work for domain-specific ontologies as well, as long as the synonym, antonym, hyponym, hypernym, meronym, and holonym relations are defined between the various terms of the domain specific ontology.

Another related area of research involves message conversation constraints, also known as behavioral signatures (Hull & Su, 2004). Behavior signature models do not stray far from the explicit description of the lexical form of messages, they expect the messages to be lexically and semantically correct prior to verification via model checking. Hence, behavior signatures deal with low-level functional implementation constraints, while USDL deals with higher-level real world concepts. However, USDL and behavioral signatures can be regarded as complementary concepts when taken in the context of real world service composition and both technologies are currently being used in the development of a commercial services integration tool (Hite, 2005).

CONCLUSION AND FUTURE WORK

To reliably catalogue, search and compose services in a semi-automatic to fully-automatic manner we need standards to publish and document services.

This requires language standards for specifying not just the syntax, that is, prototypes of service procedures and messages, but it also necessitates a standard formal, yet high-level means for specifying the semantics of service procedures and messages. We have addressed these issues by proposing a Universal Service-Semantics Description Language (USDL), its semantics, and we have proved some useful properties about this language. The current version of USDL incorporates current standards in a way to further aid markup of IT services by allowing constructs to be given meaning in terms of an OWL based WordNet ontology. This approach is more practical and tractable than other approaches because description documents are more easily created by humans and more easily processed by computers. USDL is currently being used to formally describe Web services related to emergency response functions (Bansal et al., 2005). These semantic descriptions of Web services can be used to build tools for automatically discovering services as well as for automatically composing them. It can also be used to build a service search engine that discovers matching services and ranks them. Our semantics-based approach uses semantic description of Web services (i.e., USDL descriptions) to perform Web service Discovery and Composition tasks. The composition engine finds substitutable and composite services that best match the desired service. The composition flow is determined automatically without the need for any manual intervention. The engine finds any sequential or non-sequential composition that is possible for a given query. Many optimization techniques can be applied to the system so that it works efficiently even on large repositories. Use of Constraint Logic Programming helped greatly in obtaining an efficient implementation of this system. The built-in predicates in CLP provided support for efficient searching and indexing.

Our current and future work involves the application of USDL to formally describing commercial service repositories (for example SAP Interface Repository and services listed in UDDI), as well as to service discovery and rapid application development (RAD) in commercial environments (Hite, 2005). Current and future work also includes automatically generating USDL description from the code/documentation of a service as well developing tools that will allow automatic generation of new services based on combining USDL descriptions of existing atomic services. The interesting problem that arises then: can USDL description of such automatically generated services be also automatically generated? This problem is also part of our current/future work. The Composition engine can be extended to support an external database to save off preprocessed data. This will be particularly useful when service repositories grow extremely large in size which can easily be the case in future. Also, the engine can be extended to find other kinds of compositions with loops such as repeat-until and iterations and generate their OWL-S description. Analyzing the choice of the composition language and exploring other language possibilities is also part of the future work. The engine can be extended to perform a diagnosis and suggest missing services when a composition solution is not found, that is, suggesting those services that would have completed the composition and would have produced a composite service by meeting all the query requirements.

REFERENCES

Balzer, S., Liebig, T., & Wagner, M. (2004). Pitfalls of OWL-S—a practical semantic web use case, *International Conference on Service-Oriented Computing*, pp. 289-298.

Bansal, A., Kona, S., Simon, L., Mallya, A., Gupta, G., & Hite, T. (2005). A Universal Service-Semantics Description Language, *European Conference On Web services*, pp. 214-225.

Bansal, A., Patel, K., Gupta, G., Raghavachari, B., Harris, E. D., & Staves, J. C. (2005). Towards Intelligent Services: A case study in chemical emergency response, *International Conference on Web services*, pp. 751-758.

ChallengeW. S. (2006) http://insel.flp.cs.tu-berlin.de/ wsc06

Comparison: A conceptual comparison between WSMO and OWL-S (2005) www.wsmo.org/TR/d4/d4.1/v0.1

Hite, T. (2005). *Service Composition and Ranking: A strategic overview*. Internal Report, Metallect Inc.

Hull, R., & Su, J. (2004). Tools for design of composite Web services, *International Conference on Management of Data*, pp. 958-961.

Kona, S., Bansal, A., & Gupta, G. (2007). Automatic Composition of Semantic Web Services, *International Conference on Web services*, pp. 150-158.

Kona, S., Bansal, A., Gupta, G., & Hite, T. D. (2006). Efficient Web Service Discovery and Composition using Constraint Logic Programming, *Applications of Logic Programming in Semantic Web and Semantic Web Services (AL-SPWS) Workshop at FLoC 2006.*

Lloyd, J. W. (1987). *Foundations of Logic Programming*. Springer-Verlag.

Marriott, K., & Stuckey, P. (1998). *Programming with Constraints: An Introduction*. MIT Press.

McIlraith, S., & Narayanan, S. (2002). Simulation, verification and automated composition of Web services, *World Wide Web Conference*, pp. 77-88.

McIlraith, S., & Son, T. C. (2002). Adapting golog for composition of semantic Web services, *International Conference on Principles of Knowledge Representation*, pp. 482-493.

McIlraith, S., Son, T. C., & Zeng, H. (2001). Semantic Web services. *IEEE Intelligent Systems, 16*(2), 46–53. doi:10.1109/5254.920599

OWL. Web Ontology Language Reference (2003) www.w3.org/TR/owl-ref

OWL-S. Semantic markup for Web services (2003) www.daml.org/services/owl-s/1.0/owl-s.html

OWL WordNet. Ontology-based information management system, WordNet OWL-ontology (2003) http://taurus.unine.ch/ knowler/ wordnet.html

Picinielli, G., Emmerich, W., Zirpins, C., & Schutt, K. (2002). Web service interfaces for inter-organizational business processes - an infrastructure for automated reconciliation, *International Enterprise Distributed Object Computing Conference*, pp. 285-292.

RDF. Resource Description Framework (2003) www.w3.org/RDF

SAP. Interface Repository (2001) http://ifr.sap.com/ catalog/query.asp

Schmidt, D. (1986). *Denotational Semantics: A Methodology for Language Development*. McGraw-Hill.

Simon, L., Bansal, A., Mallya, A., Kona, S., Gupta, G., & Hite, T. (2005). Towards a Universal Service Description Language, *Next Generation Web services Practices*, pp. 175-180.

Srivastava, B. (2002). Automatic Web services Composition using planning, *International Conference on Knowledge based Computer Systems*, pp. 467-477.

Srivastava, B., & Koehler, J. (2003). Web services Composition - Current Solutions and Open Problems, *International Conference on Automated Planning and Scheduling.*

Sterling, L., & Shapiro, E. (1994). *The Art of Prolog*. MIT Press.

USDL - Formal Definitions in OWL, Internal Report, The University of Texas, Dallas. (2006) www.utdallas.edu/~srividya.kona/USDLFormal-Definitions.pdf

WordNet. A Lexical Database for the English Language (1998) www.cogsci.princeton.edu/~wn

WSDL. Web services Description Language (2001) www.w3.org/TR/wsdl

WSDL-S. Web service Semantics (2005) www.w3.org/ Submission/WSDL-S

ENDNOTE

1 This is an expanded version of the article "A Universal Service-Semantics Description Language" that appeared in European Conference on Web services, 2005 (Bansal et al., 2005) and received its best article award.

This work was previously published in International Journal of Web Services Research, Volume 6, Issue 1, edited by Liang-Jie Zhang, pp. 20-48, copyright 2009 by IGI Publishing (an imprint of IGI Global).

Chapter 3
Privacy-Preserving Trust Establishment with Web Service Enhancements

Zhengping Wu
University of Bridgeport, USA

Alfred C. Weaver
University of Virginia, USA

ABSTRACT

Web services are increasingly utilized in people's daily lives to achieve various functionalities. Trustworthiness has become a critical factor for service provision and governance. The lack of effective trust establishment mechanisms impedes the deployment of diverse trust models for web services. One important issue is that collaborating organizations need mechanisms to bridge extant relationships among cooperating parties. Meanwhile, a trust establishment mechanism for web services must ensure privacy and owner control at all times due to the subjectivity of trust relationships. As an alternative and complementary approach to direct trust establishment, we describe an indirect trust establishment mechanism to bridge and build new trust relationships from extant trust relationships with privacy protection. Another issue is the lack of mechanisms that can directly establish trust relationships with privacy-preserving capabilities for web services. Current web service technologies encourage a service requester to reveal all its private attributes in a pre-packaged digital credential to the service provider to fulfill the requirements for verification. This may lead to privacy leakage. We propose a mechanism whereby the service requester discovers the service provider's requirements from a web service policy document, then formulates a trust primitive by associating a set of attributes in a pre-packaged credential with a semantic name, signed with the requester's digital signature, to negotiate a trust relationship. Thus the service requester's privacy is preserved because only those attributes required to build a trust relationship are revealed.

DOI: 10.4018/978-1-61350-104-7.ch003

INTRODUCTION

Web services facilitate collaborations and interoperations between business partners, software agents, service providers and consumers, which promote loosely coupled and dynamic service-oriented architectures. But they do not address the business aspects of interactions such as security, access control, business partner selection, service level agreement monitoring, and auditing – the activities that build trust between a consumer and a provider of a web service and that will ultimately determine which services are used and which are not. The issues of trustworthiness are tightly bound in the minds of consumers. For example, a consumer would generally trust the Citibank online services to conduct online banking in a secure and responsible manner, because Citibank has a massive physical network of banks and has been in the financial market over one hundred years. On the other hand, a consumer probably wouldn't entrust his/her savings to a newly launched financial institution with no obvious connections to any legitimate business. The point here is that as web services begin to gain a foothold in electronic business, critical services will probably be limited to extensions of pre-existing business relationships with already trusted companies.

How can a business service provider engender new trust or transfer trust to a new consumer via an existing agent? And how can two companies establish a trust relationship in order to provide and consume business services or share information over web services? They have to negotiate in order to establish a conventional business trust relationship, and so they would almost certainly want to do the same for a trust relationship using web services. Web service standards UDDI (Clement, 2004), WSDL (Chinnici, 2007), and SOAP (Gudgin, 2007) say nothing about this. Thus, although it would be possible to find a web service to use just by examining a UDDI registry, it is unlikely to be used prior to investigation of its reputation and reliability. To establish a trust relationship, the consumer and the service provider require a negotiation process. The negotiation process needs to exchange trust-related information between the two parties. The parties can exchange private attributes to build the trust relationship directly, or they can use pre-established relationships to build a new one via a trusted third party. Exchange of private attributes may put the privacy of the consumer and the service provider at risk. For example, a hacker may pretend to be a consumer to access useful information from the service provider. More seriously, a hacker can pretend to be a service provider to gather private attributes from consumers for malicious usage. We need to reduce that risk. As an alternative, using pre-established relationships may be a more convenient and more secure way.

To provide additional functionalities for security, privacy and many other purposes, "web service enhancements" appear. Web service enhancements are a series of specifications describing security, privacy and other contexts applied to web services by several industrial practitioners. In this paper we describe an indirect trust establishment mechanism using web service enhancements for bridging extant trust relationships to produce new trust relationships. Using an exchange of privileges obtained from a commonly trusted third party (who has established trust relationships with both parties) avoids disclosure of any private attributes. Meanwhile this mechanism still allows free negotiation and trust agreement selection between the involved parties when subjective judgments have to be made. We also propose a privacy-preserving mechanism that reveals the minimal number of attributes necessary to build the desired trust relationship for the web service environment. Using this mechanism, a set of attributes signed by the service requester's digital signature is associated with a trust primitive element. This element is used to negotiate a trust relationship. Any changes of policy requirements associated with this trust relationship are dynamically enforced using a trust group element. The second section provides an overview of related work. The third section describes how to use web service enhancements to bridge extant trust relationships. The fourth section introduces the proposed privacy-preserving mechanism in the proposed indirect trust establishment. The fifth section describes a parallel privacy-preserving mechanism for direct trust establishment. The sixth section illustrates an implementation of these mechanisms in a context of healthcare applications. The seventh section discusses the performance of the proposed mechanisms and a case study. The last section concludes with contributions and future work.

RELATED WORK

Several types of trust establishment mechanisms have been described in the literature for service-oriented computing and cross-domain applications. The most basic way is to map the identity of the service requester (or one identity in the service requester's security domain) to one identity in the service provider security domain. Other extant trust management systems build trust relationships between different security domains using the requester's role as a basis for mapping. More recently, group-based mechanisms have been proposed to build trust relationships.

While "role" is an abstract concept, in a complex organizational setting such as a healthcare environment one might assign differing roles, and hence differing access permissions, to physicians, technicians, and patients. In Sandhu et al.'s paper on role-based access control (Sandhu, 1996), role-based trust establishment process is implied by setting a mapping between local roles and roles within remote domains, which we call a role-to-role mapping. In Chadwick et al.'s paper (Chadwick, 2003), the authors propose using X.509 certificates to manage trust relationships. This trust establishment process also employs a manual configuration of static role-to-role mappings to form a trust relationship before an actual access occurs. In the mechanism proposed by Freudenthal et al. (Freudenthal, 2002), predefined trust relationships are used to complete the trust establishment process for dynamic cross-domain environments. The common approach of (Sandhu, 1996), (Chadwick, 2003), and (Freudenthal, 2002) is that the authors try to decide whether to grant access at run-time by deciding what permissions each requester has according to the assigned role and the predefined trust relationship associated with that role. The use of role as a basis for trust establishment creates a problem in domain-to-domain interactions, which is the potential misalignment of the precise definition of roles from one domain to another. One consequence could be that the domain whose users are requesting access might legitimately need to create special roles that map more precisely to the agreed intent of the requested operation. In that case, the users would be enabled by the policies of the domain they are accessing to take actions beyond those allowed them by their own domains' policies. A more general problem with roles is that their use generally does not conform to the principle of least privilege, as promoted by Schneider (Schneider, 2003), which limits the security privileges to actual needs.

Vandenwauver et al. (Vandenwauver, 1997) use group-based mechanisms to describe a collection of security requirements agreed to by the administrators for a group of domains. This group-based mechanism reduces the administrator's burden of creating an explicit policy to manage each trust relationship. The authors also assume that a recognized consortium of group members has created a trust group with predefined membership requirements. The service provider has to verify some non-identity attribute information about each service request. This trust group mechanism lacks the process of negotiation before building a trust relationship. Li et al. (Li, 2002) proposes an entire trust management framework that can group logically related objects so that permissions about them can be assigned in one operation. These logical groups are defined by an authority, not via a negotiation process. Both group-based mechanisms mentioned above require some superior authority to create or predefine group information, and thus the resulting trust establishment mechanisms are not fully dynamic; they may not keep pace with the changing policies and requirements of the service providers.

Using indirect mechanisms to bridge extant trust relationships is a convenient and efficient method to produce new trust relationships, but very few indirect trust establishment mechanisms have been designed for a web services environment. However, several types of indirect trust models and the corresponding trust establishment mechanisms have been proposed for service-oriented computing (Papazoglou, 2003), which are the foundations of web services. The trust relationships involved in the interactions between web services are enabled by separate authorities issuing security tokens (A Joint White Paper, 2002), which certify the identities or other non-identity attributes for the requesters or providers of web services. There are two major types of trust models for these trust relationships. One type is the centralized model and the other type is the distributed model.

In centralized trust models, a common trusted intermediary, called the "Trust Authority," is used for establishing trust relationships between any two entities. However, it may be difficult to find an ideal central authority if the community of trustees is large and heterogeneous. If a trust authority is determined, token recipients are typically able to ascribe a sufficient level of trust to a security token because they can be confident of its origin. For example, they know and trust the authority that issued the token and can verify the token's origin through cryptographic means. It is through the existing trust they have in the third party security token issuer that they are able to derive indirect trust for the holder of a security token created by the same issuer. The Privacy Enhanced Mail (PEM) certification (Kent, 1993) assumes that everyone in the world trusts one ultimate authority to verify the identities of other certificate senders (an assumption we find unrealistic). The PEM model does not allow for multiple levels of trust within its certification hierarchy. Unlike PEM, the X.509 authentication framework and its variant for web services (Lawrence, 2006) follows a multiple trust authority structure. It postulates that everyone will obtain certificates from an official certifying authority (CA). The CAs are organized into a global hierarchy of certifying authorities. All users within a "community of interest" have keys that have been signed by CAs with a common ancestor in this global hierarchy, which forms a tree structure.

In distributed trust models, a static or dynamic web of trust is woven with less structured logical interactions between networks (Dimmock, 2004) compared with the centralized trust models. It is assumed that trust is transitive under certain contexts, because trust-related information can be propagated through one or more chains of trusted intermediaries in the networks. In the Pretty Good Privacy (PGP) system (Zimmermann, 1995), an entity generates a public/private key pair. Each entity is responsible for acquiring the public key certificates needed and for assigning degrees of trust to their source. There is no common ancestor to act as the trust server for grouping the users within a community of interest. Instead, trust is propagated through chained structures formed by individual entities. When comparing X.509 with PGP, it has been pointed out that the most apparent difference is the architecture (Josang, 1996) (Ellison, 1999). X.509 has hierarchic structures for professional or government organizations with liabilities, whereas PGP has anarchic structure based on informal relationships and undefined roles. Like the logic-based systems described in (Rangan, 1992) (Abadi, 2003) (Pimlott, 2006), there is no partial trust (degree of trust) in this kind of system; trust is either complete or nonexistent. In the solution proposed by Tarah et al. in (Tarah, 1992), the degrees of trust from different entities could have conflicts, and the final degree of trust needs to be composed from different trust values (Damiani, 2005).

Yet none of the above frameworks or systems can accommodate all trust models. However, all the trust models co-exist in the real world and all the trust models are used in daily life. So a flexible framework to accommodate all these trust models is desirable. Other associated questions remain open, e.g., the actual meaning of a trust value and how different trust values can be combined to yield a composite value. Users generally prefer to control their own private information. But none of the above mechanisms address privacy issues, which could lead to information leakage during the propagation of trust-related information in direct and indirect trust establishment processes. To solve these issues, we introduce an indirect trust establishment mechanism using a bridging protocol to augment direct negotiation and establishment of trust. We use an alternative method to supplement indirect trust establishment with lightweight negotiation to provide owner control in the process of bridging extant trust relationships. At the same time, to guarantee privacy protection, we use privileges granted by a common third party as a substitute for exchanging private attributes during the trust negotiation. Parallel in direct trust establishment, all the identity-based, role-based and group-based mechanisms do not address privacy issues, which could lead to superfluous information disclosure during the trust establishment process. We propose a privacy-preserving mechanism for trust establishment, which maintains the idea of negotiation but without inadvertent disclosure of unnecessary information.

BRIDGING TRUST RELATIONSHIPS WITH WEB SERVICE ENHANCEMENTS

Web Service Enhancements

Web services use SOAP to exchange information over the network. SOAP is a lightweight method for exchanging structured information in a decentralized environment. XML (eXtensible Markup Language) is used in SOAP to define a flexible messaging framework that can exchange a message over a variety of underlying protocols. Although SOAP is the basic infrastructure for information exchange between web services, it does not provide any privacy and security mechanisms for the information exchanged. To provide privacy, security, trust, and other functionalities for web services, web service enhancements are proposed.

Among this set of enhancements, the web service security specification requires that an incoming access request message prove a set of claims such as name, public key, permission, capability, or an existing trust relationship to guarantee security. A web service indicates its requirements and other security related information in its policy document together with the privileges to be granted for the entities satisfying these requirements (e.g., a WS-Policy file). If an access request arrives without having the required proof of claims, the service provider ignores or rejects the request. These claims are contained in security tokens. A security token is a representation of security-related information conveyed within the format of a SOAP message (Vedamuthu, 2007). If an issuer cryptographically endorses a security token, the token is called a signed security token. A security token service (STS) is a web service that issues security tokens (Rangan, 1992). That is, it makes assertions based on evidence that it trusts to whomever trusts it. To communicate trust, a security token service requires proof, such as a security token or a set of security tokens, and issues a new security token

Figure 1. Workflow of the bridging protocol

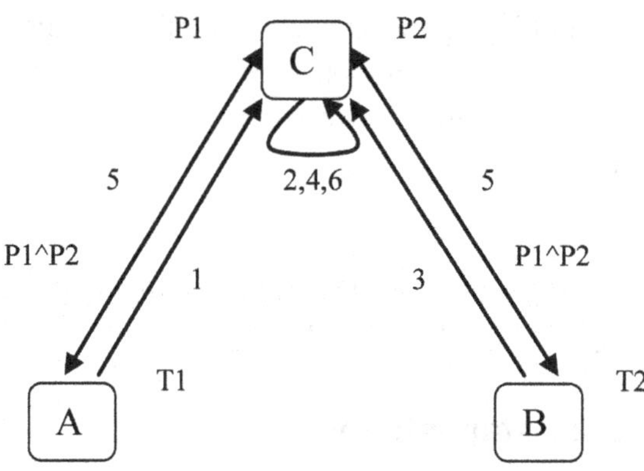

with its own trust statement (note that for some security token formats this can be just a re-issuance or co-signature). Another important related service is the attribute service. An attribute service is a web service that maintains attribute information about entities within a security domain.

With these services one entity can rely upon a second entity to execute a set of actions or to make a set of assertions about a set of subjects or scopes (Lawrence, 2008), which is called trust establishment. Trust relationships can be established by exchanging private attributes or bridging existing trust relationships; these techniques focus on owner control and utilizing extant trust relationships respectively. We propose a new indirect trust establishment mechanism to incorporate owner control into the process of bridging extant trust relationships.

A Bridging Protocol

The proposed indirect trust establishment mechanism uses a common third party as the anchor to bridge two extant trust relationships. The central part of this mechanism is a bridging protocol. An extant trust relationship is represented as a trust group element, which includes a trust relationship name (T), a list of participants involved in this relationship, and a list of privileges (P) granted for that relationship. This trust relationship can be established via an on-line trust negotiation or a contract written on paper. In the bridging protocol, the common third party needs to discover any difference in privileges granted to the two participants in order to provide the two participants equal standing and the opportunity to make their own subjective decisions for the new trust relationship. Figure 1 shows the workflow of the protocol to establish a new trust relationship between A and B using extant trust relationships between A and C, and B and C. The step numbers of the protocol correspond to the numbered arrows in Figure 1.

1. A sends to C a request to establish a trust relationship with B, using an extant trust relationship (T1) with C.
2. After C receives A's request, C waits for a similar request from B. If a time limit expires, C sends a fail message to A and exits its waiting state.
3. B sends to C a request to establish a trust relationship with A, utilizing its trust relationship (T2) with C.
4. After receiving the requests from both A and B, C compares its granted privileges P1 and P2 for T1 and T2, and calculates the intersection of P1 and P2 (P1^P2).
5. C sends P1^P2 to A and B, and asks whether they agree to build the new trust relationship based upon common privileges P1^P2.
6. *If both A and B respond with a positive answer, C sends confirmations to both A and B. Both A and B produce corresponding new policies for the newly established trust relationship, and create a new trust group element to represent this trust relationship. If either A or B rejects the privileges represented by P1^P2, C asks A and B to establish a trust relationship directly by mutual identity verification or private information exchange. The new trust group element contains a name for the new relationship, a list of participants within this trust relationship*

(here A and B), and a trust level decided by each participant. So the copies of the trust group element kept by A and B contain the same name and participant list, but have their own trust levels associated with this trust relationship.

This protocol resolves two problems introduced in section 1. First, it introduces a lightweight negotiation process into the indirect trust establishment (bridging extant trust relationships), which assumes that every participant has the right to make its own decisions. Second, it prevents privacy leakage by exchanging privileges granted by the common third party instead of exchanging private attributes.

The Common Third Party

How to find an appropriate common third party is also an issue. The participants A and B need to exchange partner information to find out which one is appropriate for a common third party. As with most companies, A and B's partner lists should be expected to represent private information. Companies are generally unwilling to reveal their business partner lists to companies who have not already established a trust relationship. To solve this problem, we propose a complimentary protocol below to find all common third parties.

1. A and B send requests to all their trusted partners respectively, to ask if they are willing to act as the common third party.
2. Only participants who are both A and B's trusted partner receive requests from both A and B. If a participant agrees to act as the common third party, it sends a message indicating its willingness to A and B.
3. From all the candidates who send back their willingness, A and B choose one as the common third party.

Either A or B can express its willingness to use one of the commonly trusted parties. The potential partner either agrees or starts a brief negotiation to establish the common third party before the trust establishment process with indirect privacy enhancement.

PRIVACY-PRESERVING INDIRECT TRUST ESTABLISHMENT

Trust Establishment

Trust establishment is the initial step towards trust management over multiple security domains. Its importance has been addressed since 1994 (Beth, 1994). To establish a trust relationship among multiple parties effectively and efficiently, a dynamic and flexible trust establishment mechanism must be developed (Reiter, 1999). Most existing trust management systems establish trust relationships via a trusted third party and they are based on public key certificates in which the trusted third party signs a specially formed message certifying the identity associated with a public key. The two best-known certificate systems are those of PGP and X.509. They attempt to solve part of the trust management problem of finding a suitably trustworthy copy of the public key of someone with whom one wants to communicate. This common trusted third party solution may result in a tree structure of all involved parties.

Some other existing systems try to weave a web of trust instead of a tree structure. In this case, the direct trust establishment mechanism becomes the most basic building block. The simplest way is to map one identity in a security domain to one identity in another security domain. Some other extant trust management systems also establish trust relationships with other domains using roles as a basis for mapping. And more recently, group-based mechanisms have been proposed to establish trust relationships. We will identify issues related to privacy-preserving trust establishment for direct and indirect trust relationships, and provide solutions for privacy protection using web service enhancements in an interconnected and federated network environment.

Privacy Protection

Privacy-preserving technology consists of various tools for various applications, which includes cryptographically secured protocols for on-line critical information transmission, digital certificates, cookie management software, privacy policy languages, etc. Meanwhile, various anonymity protection techniques are being developed such as mix cascades and anonymous authentication for peer-to-peer networks. There are also privacy-preserving techniques proposed for data mining and database queries, as well as enterprise privacy auditing and enforcement tools for user privacy preferences. Privacy-preserving trust establishment has particular relevance to the provision of owner control, pseudonymity or anonymity, and proof of knowledge.

- **Owner control:** *Control over identity, credential, and private attribute information must be given to the owner, and users can modify or erase information if desired. Also, the security domain administrator does not endorse any disclosure of any piece of the user's private information. The choice of attributes to be disclosed is entirely under the owner's control.*
- **Pseudonyms and anonymity:** *The holder of the pseudonym can prove ownership by forming a digital signature using the corresponding private key. Such keys could be bound to attributes within digital certificates to form attribute certificates. One can also uses of a trusted third party to act as a mediator, vouching for the user or his/her computing device but removing any information identifying the user.*
- **Proof of knowledge:** *Inspection of a user's credential can prove the holder's entitlement to the credential without revealing any persistent information.*

Active and Passive Models

For all the information exchange in trust establishment for federated networks, participating entities in that interconnected environment may be either passive or active. Passive entities wait to be contacted by active entities, while active entities are capable of initiating interactions or communications with passive entities or active entities. The distinction between active entities and passive entities allows for flexible deployment of entities for trust related activities over multiple security domains, such that some entities may only actively interact with a trusted set of partners, while others may passively listen for one or more interactions or service requests from strangers. With these different types of entities, several privacy control models are possible.

- **Active model:** *From the point of view of active entities, the requirements of privacy control can be 'pushed' or 'advertised' first, and then potential partners can follow corresponding policies for subsequent trust related activities.*
- **Passive model:** *From the point of view of passive entities, private information and attributes are always kept as secrets; privacy control is applied to those kinds of information when that information has to be disclosed or released.*
- **Hybrid model:** *Active and passive entities keep their roles while they work together to provide privacy enhancement in the interactions for trusted related activities.*

We will apply a hybrid model that takes advantage of both active and passive entities to construct privacy-preserving trust establishment using web service enhancements. A flexible but effective privacy-preserving mechanism is possible by designing and implementing a comprehensive framework that incorporates all these different models and facilities.

Privacy-Preserving Indirect Trust Establishment

Owner control is embedded in our proposed bridging protocol for indirect trust establishment. Any participating parties can decide which subset of privileges granted by the common third party will be used as the foundation for new trust relationships. Anonymity and proof of knowledge are also achieved by subsets of privileges, because different subsets of privileges imply different levels of trustworthiness for different new relationships. In indirect trust establishment, A and B choose an active model, and C (the common third party) chooses the passive model in order to keep A's and B's privileges as secrets until they are willing to disclose them as the foundations for a new trust relationship. Privacy is also protected by using commonly granted privileges instead of private attributes to negotiate a new relationship using the bridging protocol.

PRIVACY-PRESERVING DIRECT TRUST ESTABLISHMENT

Since privacy protection is also a concern in direct trust establishment, which involves direct negotiation between participating parties, we propose another privacy-preserving mechanism for direct trust establishment. We introduce two new elements, trust primitive and trust group, to facilitate privacy protection in this process.

Trust Primitive and Owner Control

Definition 1: A trust primitive is defined as the minimal subset of attributes in a pre-packaged digital credential, which has a complete semantic meaning according to a set of policy requirements. A trust primitive is signed by the credential holder, which is either an individual user or a security domain.

In the proposed privacy-preserving direct trust establishment for web service environments, a trust primitive is represented as a subset of attributes in the attribute service and conveyed as an XML element when it is exchanged between securities domains. As illustrated in Figure 2, trust primitive 1 corresponds to an electronic library access rule with three required attributes (4, 6, and 7). The holder of the digital credential can form this trust primitive element and will be allowed to use the electronic library if the server can verify that its three attributes are valid (that is, if the token has been issued by an acceptable authority, the token is not expired, and the holder operates in the role of student, faculty or staff). Since neither the name nor ID number is part of the set of attributes associated with this trust primitive, anonymous access is permitted. Trust primitive 2 is for library checkout. It contains the same three attributes in trust primitive 1 plus attribute 2, ID number, which is needed for library accounting. Trust primitive 3, consisting of attributes 3, 6 and 7, might be used to verify same-sex gender before granting entrance to a dorm floor, or by substituting attributes 1 or 2 for attribute 3 it might be used to verify a specific individual's residence on the dorm floor before granting entrance.

A credential holder forms a trust primitive voluntarily. Every request for retrieving a trust primitive from an outside domain will be verified by the attribute service to selectively disclose the subset of attributes associated with the trust primitive. Another merit of trust primitives is that they prevent initiation of selective disclosure from anyone except the credential holder. Thus owner control is achieved. Figure 3 shows the workflow of the proposed protocol working with trust primitives for privacy-preserving direct trust establishment.

Figure 2. Attributes and three possible trust primitives

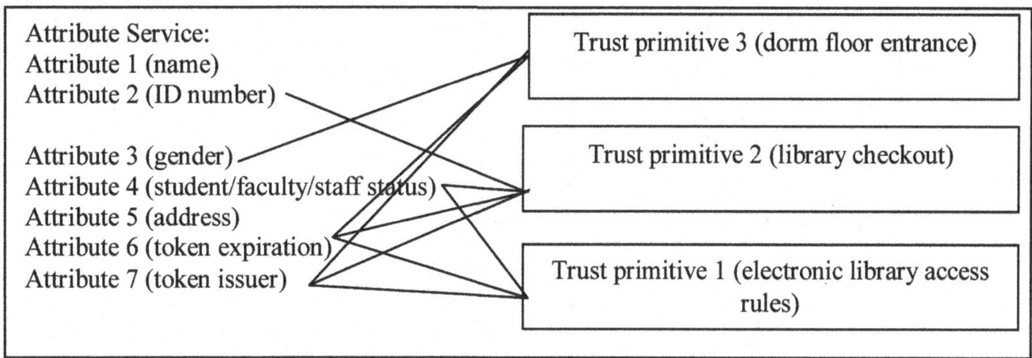

In this protocol, a service requester and a service provider (two principals) from different security domains are assumed. Before the beginning of this privacy-preserving enhanced trust establishment workflow, the attributes of the service requester are stored at the attribute service of the service requester's security domain. The requester is also assumed to hold a security token containing its identity and other security related information. The workflow is initiated by a need for the requester to disclose some of its attributes to the service provider for negotiation. This need could be triggered by the access policy of the service provider's security domain, which is publicly accessible via a policy document, or by the service provider's direct request for the requester to provide one or more attributes. Thus a hybrid model is accommodated in this privacy-preserving protocol. Then the workflow executes from step one through step ten to finish a round of information exchange for trust establishment process. Step numbers below correspond to the numbered arrows in Figure 3.

1. After reading the service provider's access policy or receiving a request for proving some attributes to obtain access, the requester initiates a service request, which contains the trust primitive corresponding to the policy or request for attributes from the service provider, to the STS in its own security domain. The security token held by the requester is also embedded in this service request message for proof of identity.
2. When the STS receives the service request, the STS extracts the security token from the message, verifies the legitimacy of the security token, and registers the trust primitive at the attribute service in its own security domain.
3. Then the STS adds this trust primitive to the requester's security token, re-signs the security token, and sends it back to the requester.
4. When the requester gets the newly signed security token, the requester embeds the security token in the access request and sends the request.
5. After receiving the requester's access request, the service provider asks its own STS to check whether the request complies with the service's access policy.
6. The STS of the service provider sends a request for attribute verification to the STS of the requester. The newly signed security token of the requester is sent together with the request.
7. The STS of the requester extracts the trust primitive, which corresponds to the access policy of the service provider, and uses this

Figure 3. Workflow of privacy-preserving direct trust establishment

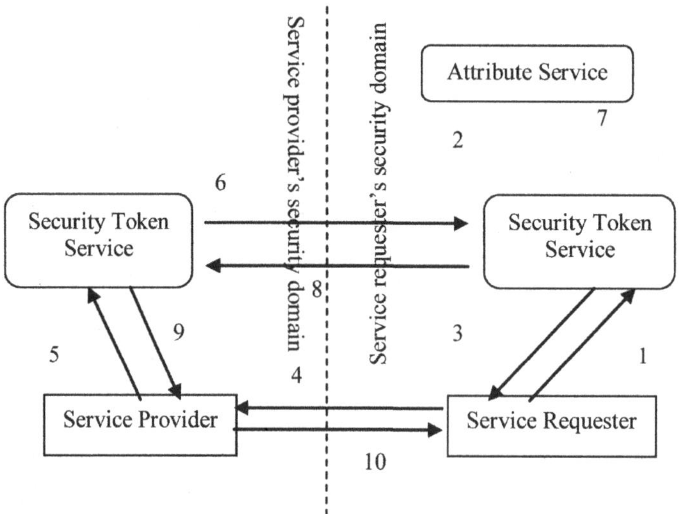

trust primitive as the query keyword to search the attributes disclosed by the requester at its attribute service.

8. The STS of the requester returns the attributes retrieved from the attribute service.
9. The STS of the service provider performs verification and sends its decision regarding the access request (granted/denied) to the service provider.
10. If access is granted, the service provider performs the requested operation and returns information to the requester; otherwise the provider issues a denial.

Sometimes the requester also needs to verify some of the service provider's attributes to negotiate a trust relationship, so the roles of the requester and the service provider can be interchanged. Several rounds of exchange form the negotiation needed to build a trust relationship between the two principals.

Trust Group and Partial Disclosure

Definition 2: A trust group represents a group of partners who comply with the same set of policy requirements. The partners here are entities who have direct trust relationships with the policyholder.

A trust group name is associated with a set of policy requirements. For example, if the service provider creates a set of policy requirements in the form of a WS-Policy file for negotiation of a trust relationship, the trust group name will be attached at the end of the file. Every partner complying with this set of policy requirements will use this trust group name to represent the corresponding trust relationship. A WS-Policy file containing a trust group looks like the example in Box 1.

After negotiation, a new trust group element is added to the requester's security token, and the security token is signed by the requester's STS again. Alternatively, the security token is replaced by a new security token issued by the service provider's STS, which contains the corresponding trust group element representing the new trust relationship. A trust group element is represented by three XML tags (trust group name and two domain/individual identities). Every policy holder also needs to record all the trust group elements with which the holder is involved, and

Box 1. WS-Policy file containing a trust group

```
<?xml version="1.0" encoding="utf-8" ?>
<policyDocument xmlns="http://schemas.microsoft.com/wse/2003/06/Policy">
<policies
xmlns:wssp="http://schemas.xmlsoap.org/ws/2002/12/secext" xmlns:wsp="http://
schemas.xmlsoap.org/ws/2004/09/policy">
<wsp:Policy wsu:Id="trustlevelsec-token">
<wssp:SecurityToken wsp:Usage="wsp:Required">
<wssp:TokenType>http://www.contoso.com/tokens/customXml#TrustLevelSecToken
</wssp:TokenType>
<wssp:TokenIssuer>http://www.cs.virginia.edu/TrustLevelSTS.ashx/
wssp:TokenIssuer>
</wssp:SecurityToken>
<wssp:SecurityToken wsp:Usage="wsp:Required"></wssp:SecurityToken>
</wsp:Policy>
</policies>
<trustGroup>TG001</trustGroup>
</policyDocument>
```

so do the partners. The trust group element looks like the example given in Box 2.

Access requests after the negotiation are granted by a verification of the trust group element in security tokens. If the access requirement for a trust group element changes in a service provider's policy, then the service provider needs to revalidate the previous trust relationship by invalidating the old trust group element, asking for the requester's trust primitives again, and then verifying whether the new trust primitives meet the requirements of the changed policy. If access is granted, a new trust group element will replace the old one for future use.

PROTOTYPE SYSTEM

Implementation of Privacy-Preserving Indirect Trust Establishment

We have implemented the whole trust establishment system using the Microsoft.Net platform. The.Net framework together with the Web Service Enhancement (WSE) 2.0 SDK (Microsoft, 2006), which supports the WS-Security (Lawrence, 2006) and WS-Trust standards (Lawrence, 2008), provides a complete platform for our system implementation. All the building blocks in our system architecture use web services as internal interfaces. Figure 4 illustrates the system architecture for privacy-preserving indirect trust establishment. With the help of the proposed bridging protocol, trust domains can establish new trust relationships by extending current trust boundaries more smoothly and more securely. In this system architecture, the STSs are the main portals for interactions across trust domains. The STS is in charge of issuing and exchanging security tokens, which contain critical information such as identities, privileges and trust-related information. A policy repository is used to store and retrieve policy requirements and the corresponding privilege information used by the bridging protocol. The negotiation engine controls the whole process of information exchange and negotiation step by step. Each trust domain has an entire deployment of this system. But according to the bridging protocol and indirect trust establishment process, the functionalities used by participants A, B and the common third party C are different.

Box 2. Trust group element

```
<trustGroup>
<trustGroupName>TG001</trustGroupName>
<domain1>http://abc.com/localSTS.asmx/domain1>
<domain2>http://def.com/localSTS.asmx/domain2>
</trustGroup>
```

In an indirect trust establishment mechanism, we use the trust group element to represent an established trust relationship. In a security token, the trust group element contains a name for the relationship together with information from the two domains between which the trust relationship is established. In the policy repository, every trust group element is associated with a set of privileges granted by another party. Figure 5 illustrates the different formats of a trust group element in a security token and in the policy repository.

Implementation of Privacy-Preserving Direct Trust Establishment

Meanwhile, this privacy-preserving enhanced trust establishment system is a subsystem of a federated cyber trust system (Weaver, 2003). It provides the functionality of negotiating, building, and managing trust for a web service environment. When the federated cyber trust system is applied to a healthcare environment with hospital, pharmacy, insurance and billing security domains, the shaded boxes shown in Figure 6 are the modules involved in the trust establishment system. Boxes with dashed border lines represent different security domains; boxes with solid border lines represent modules in the hospital domain; arrows represent information flows or interactions. All the modules use web services as interfaces for their interactions.

We also have a graphic user interface to assist users to define and sign their trust primitives for privacy protection, which is shown in Figure 7.

Another concern is token formats. Among all the interactions between modules, there are two different types of interactions. One is the interaction between modules within a security domain. The other is the interaction between security domains. Two types of security tokens are used with different purposes to convey identities, credentials, trust group elements and other trust related information between service modules. We use username tokens to facilitate the interactions between service modules within the same security domain since it has little overhead and is easy to extend; we use SAML (Lockhart, 2008) tokens to enable interactions between security domains since SAML is a recognized standard for interoperability among different platforms. Figure 8 gives examples of two token formats before being embedding into SOAP messages.

The architecture of our privacy-preserving enhanced direct trust establishment is illustrated in Figure 9. The web service requester and web service provider build a dynamic trust relationship via negotiation engines and security token services in both security domains. The security token service in our implementation also includes a set of web services to interpret and exchange security tokens. At the same time, the security token service uses an attribute service to register trust primitives for the requester. Negotiation engines control the overall workflow to build trust relationships dynamically, which include the implementation of the protocol described in section 5 for a single round of negotiation.

Figure 4. The architecture of the indirect trust establishment mechanism

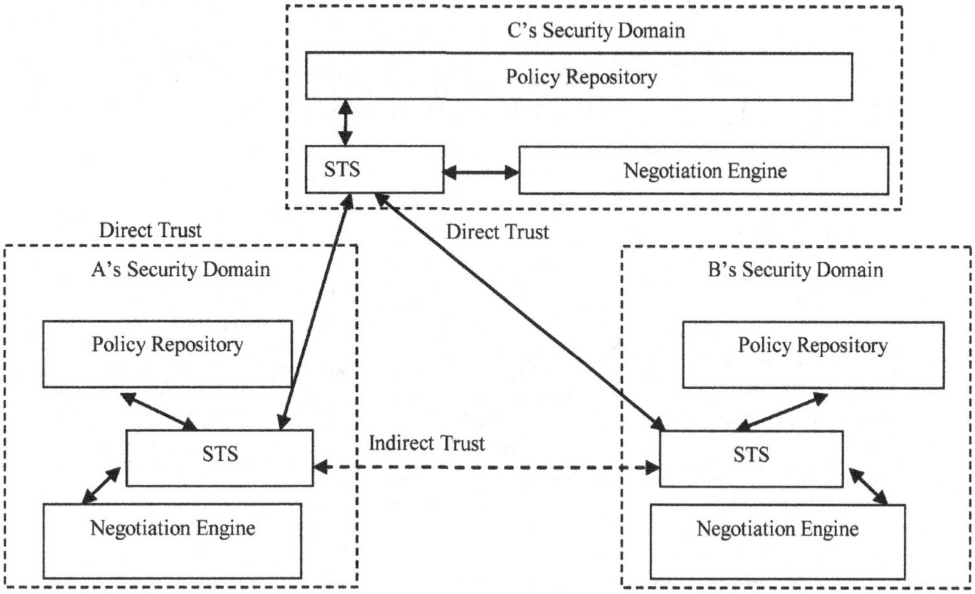

Figure 5. A trust group element in a security token and in the policy repository

```
<trustGroup>
<trustGroupName
>TG001
</trustGroupName
>
<domain1>
http://www.cs.virg
inia.edu/localSTS.
asmx
</domain1>
<domain2>
http://www.ee.virg
inia.edu/localSTS.
asmx
</domain2>
</trustGroup>
```

In a Security Token

```
<?xml version="1.0" encoding="utf-8" ?>
<policyDocument
xmlns="http://schemas.microsoft.com/wse/2003/06/Policy">
<policies
mlns:wssp="http://schemas.xmlsoap.org/ws/2002/12/secext"
xmlns:wsp="http://schemas.xmlsoap.org/ws/2004/09/policy">
<wsp:Policy wsu:Id="trustlevelsec-token">
<wssp:SecurityToken wsp:Usage="wsp:Required">
<wssp:TokenType>
http://www.contoso.com/tokens/customXml#TrustLevelSecToken
</wssp:TokenType>
<wssp:TokenIssuer>
http://www.cs.virginia.edu/TrustLevelSTS.ashx
</wssp:TokenIssuer>
</wssp:SecurityToken>
<wssp:SecurityToken wsp:Usage="wsp:Required">
</wssp:SecurityToken>
</wsp:Policy>
</policies>
<trustGroup>
TG001
</trustGroup>
<privileges>
read&write
</privileges>
</policyDocument>
```

In the Policy Repository

Figure 6. Federated cyber trust system for a healthcare application

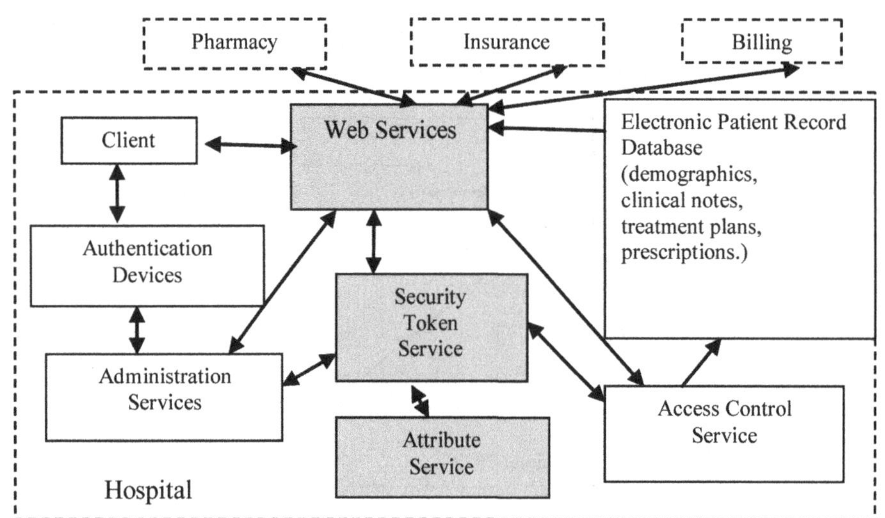

Figure 7. Graphic user interface for trust primitive definition

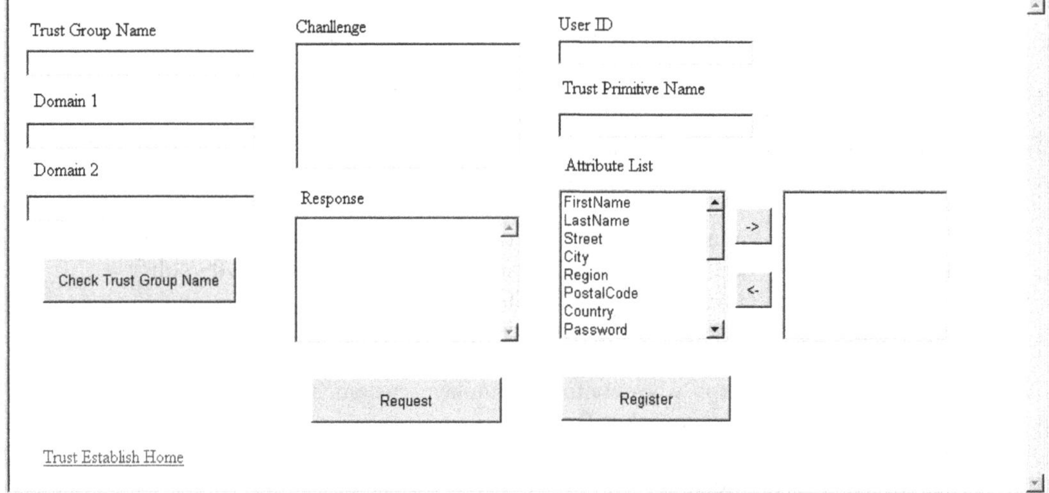

DISCUSSION

A Case Study for Healthcare Applications

As we know, paper-based operations are still dominant in the healthcare industry, because trust relationships in healthcare applications are still based on paper contracts and certificates. And third-party-issued paper certificates can still lead to privacy leakage. With new legislation such as HIPAA and Sarbanes-Oxley, strict privacy protection is imposed on healthcare applications. We describe a detailed case study to illustrate how the proposed mechanisms and architecture can be applied to real healthcare applications to perform privacy-preserving trust establishment using web services. Figure 10 illustrates the real workflows to build a new trust relationship when a patient needs to fill a prescription at a new pharmacy us-

Figure 8. Token formats

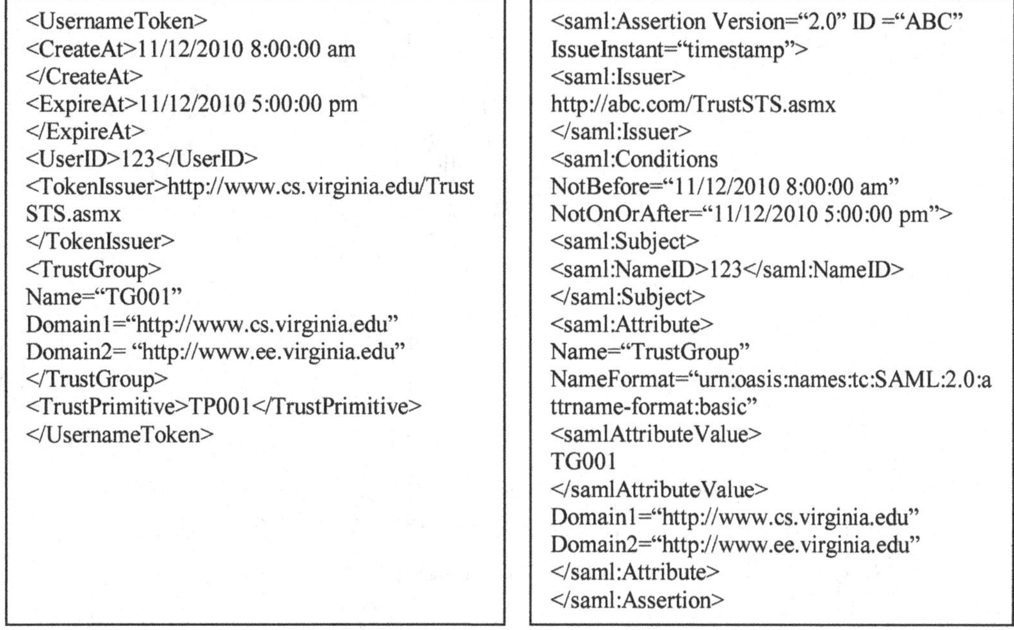

```
<UsernameToken>
<CreateAt>11/12/2010 8:00:00 am
</CreateAt>
<ExpireAt>11/12/2010 5:00:00 pm
</ExpireAt>
<UserID>123</UserID>
<TokenIssuer>http://www.cs.virginia.edu/Trust
STS.asmx
</TokenIssuer>
<TrustGroup>
Name="TG001"
Domain1="http://www.cs.virginia.edu"
Domain2= "http://www.ee.virginia.edu"
</TrustGroup>
<TrustPrimitive>TP001</TrustPrimitive>
</UsernameToken>
```

UserName Token

```
<saml:Assertion Version="2.0" ID ="ABC"
IssueInstant="timestamp">
<saml:Issuer>
http://abc.com/TrustSTS.asmx
</saml:Issuer>
<saml:Conditions
NotBefore="11/12/2010 8:00:00 am"
NotOnOrAfter="11/12/2010 5:00:00 pm">
<saml:Subject>
<saml:NameID>123</saml:NameID>
</saml:Subject>
<saml:Attribute>
Name="TrustGroup"
NameFormat="urn:oasis:names:tc:SAML:2.0:a
ttrname-format:basic"
<samlAttributeValue>
TG001
</samlAttributeValue>
Domain1="http://www.cs.virginia.edu"
Domain2="http://www.ee.virginia.edu"
</saml:Attribute>
</saml:Assertion>
```

SAML Token

Figure 9. The architecture of privacy-preserving enhanced direct trust establishment

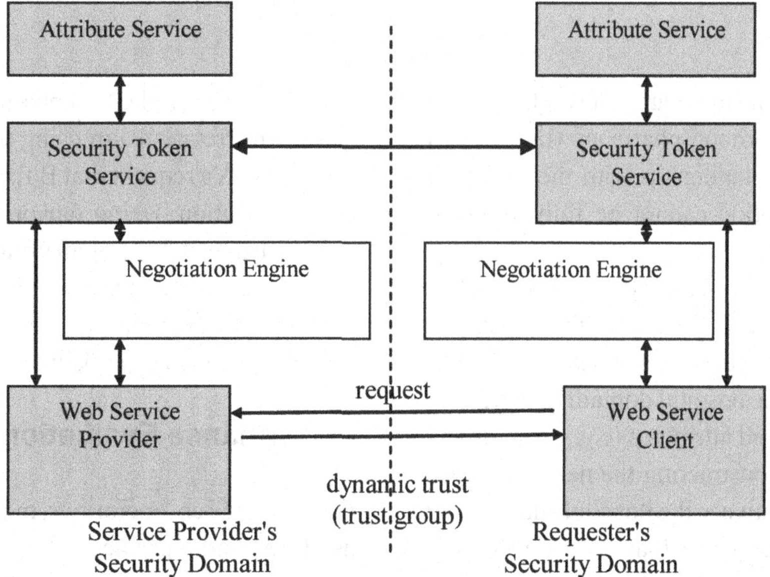

Figure 10. A case study with interactions between a hospital and two pharmacies

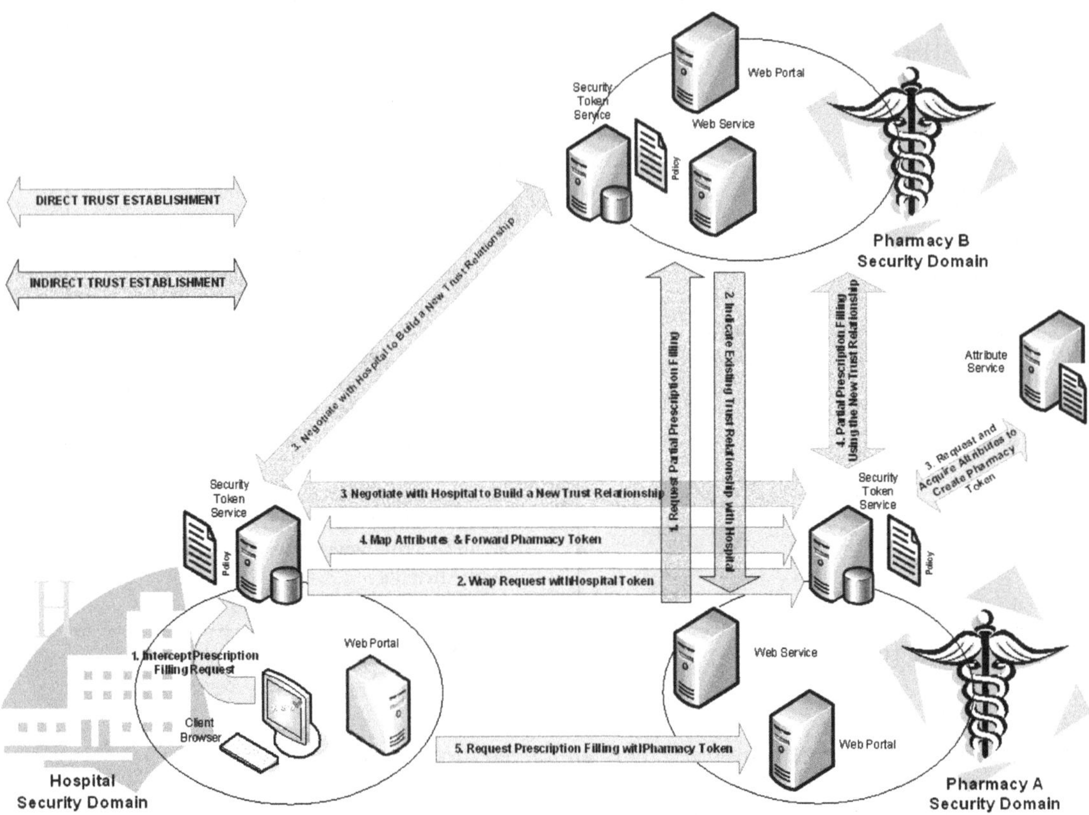

ing web services, and to bridge a trust relationship to another neighborhood pharmacy (that has an established trust relationship with the hospital) when the prescription cannot be fully filled at that new pharmacy.

First, a patient at the hospital tries to fill a prescription at a new pharmacy (pharmacy A). Then the direct trust establishment protocol is applied to allow the hospital domain to verify the pharmacy's required attributes (e.g., a pharmacy license) prior to constructing the new trust relationship needed between the hospital and the new pharmacy. Then suppose that a portion of the prescription cannot be filled by the new pharmacy, so it forwards a request for filling the remainder of the prescription to a neighborhood pharmacy (pharmacy B). Assuming the neighborhood pharmacy has an existing trust relationship with the hospital, the two pharmacies can bridge a new trust relationship using the hospital as the anchor for A's request that B fill the remainder of the prescription. Using our proposed direct and indirect trust establishment protocols can not only fulfill the required trust relationship constructions but can also provide privacy protections in the trust relationship establishment processes.

Performance Evaluation

For federated co-operations, management of trust needs to handle privacy protections within these co-operations. We achieve privacy-preserving trust establishment via two protocols using web service enhancements. The proposed privacy-preserving mechanisms do not change the structure of other daily operations, such as user enrollment,

Figure 11. Comparison of direct trust establishment protocols' performance (with and without privacy-preserving enhancement)

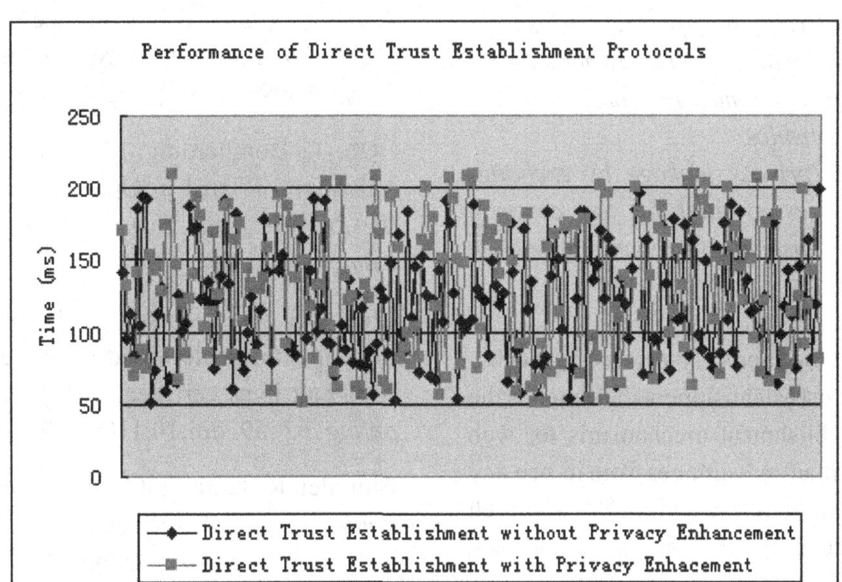

user authentication, and verification. And the privacy-enhanced indirect trust establishment is achieved via a whole new protocol design using existing trust relationships, which avoids direct exchange of sensitive information. The privacy-enhanced direct trust establishment only enhances a few additional steps in federated co-operations using available features in WS-Policy, security tokens, and attribute services. These mechanisms can also be easily embedded into other trust establishment protocols with certain modifications.

We compared the performance of the direct trust establishment without privacy enhancement, which shows all the credentials available in attributes upon request, and the proposed privacy-enhanced trust establishment protocol described in section 5.1. We randomly choose trust establishment processes conducted by patients and hospital staff when new trust relationships need to be built with a new domain. We measured the time used for two trust establishment processes (see Figure 11). The blue (black) series is the direct trust establishment with privacy enhancement; the red (grey) series is without privacy enhancement. Although the difference of the time used for a single direct trust establishment process varies from 50ms to 198ms, the mean value of the direct trust establishment time with privacy enhancement is 128.08ms and the mean value of the direct trust establishment process without privacy enhancement is 123.51ms (a 3.70% difference). We found that the performace cost of using these privacy-preserving mechanisms was negligible.

CONCLUSION

In this paper we described an indirect trust establishment augmented with lightweight negotiation to achieve owner control and privacy protection simultaneously. Our research motivation comes from the inadequacy of binary trust and the difficulty of using subjective formulas combining multiple (even conflicting) trust values. Our new privacy-preserving mechanism in indirect trust establishment is an alternative method with these advantages:

- *It introduces the negotiation process into the indirect trust establishment (bridging extant trust relationships), which assures that every participant has owner control over the decision-making process for new trust relationships.*
- *It prevents privacy leakage by exchanging privileges granted by the common third party instead of exchanging private attributes.*

Also we described a privacy-preserving mechanism for direct trust establishment that extends the extant trust establishment mechanisms for web services to gain many advantages from its privacy control and dynamic capabilities. Our research motivation comes from the complicated privacy requirements inherent to current healthcare data management and similar sensitive information management. Our new trust establishment mechanism is dynamic with these advantages:

- *It allows only the requester to choose what attributes may be viewed by the service provider. Therefore, it is capable of enforcing the requester's privacy.*
- *It allows only the chosen attributes to be viewed by the service provider. Therefore, it is capable of disclosing private attributes selectively.*
- *It allows any trust relationships to be renewed whenever the service provider's policy is updated. Therefore, it is inherently dynamic.*

Our future research will focus on the topological impact of privacy-preserving mechanisms and their applications to privilege delegation and enforcement of trust relationships.

REFERENCES

Abadi, M. (2003). Logic in access control. *Proc. of the 18th Annual IEEE Symposium on Logic in Computer Science*, (pp. 228-233).

Beth, T., Borcherding, M., & Klein, B. (1994), Valuation of Trust in Open Networks, *Proc. of the 3rd European Symposium on Research in Computer Security*, 3-18.

Chadwick, D., Otenko, A., & Ball, E. (2003). Implementing role based access controls using X.509 attribute certificates. *IEEE Internet Computing*, 62–69. doi:10.1109/MIC.2003.1189190

Chinnici, R., et al. (2007). *Web services description language (WSDL) version 2.0 part 1: Core language*. Retrived from http://www.w3.org/TR/2007/REC-wsdl20-20070626

Clement, L., et al. (2004). *UDDI version 3.0.2*. Retrieved from http://uddi.org/pubs/ uddi-v3.0.2-20041019.htm

Damiani, E., Vimercati, S., Samarati, P., & Viviani, M. (2005), A WOWA-based aggregation technique on trust values connected to metadata. *Proc. of International Workshop on Security and Trust Management*, (pp. 131-142).

Dimmock, N. (2004). Using trust and risk in role-based access control policies. *Proc. 2004 Symposium on Access Control Models and Technologies*, (pp. 156-162).

Ellison, C., et al. (1999). *SPKI certificate theory*. (Internet Report, RFC 2693).

Freudenthal, E., Pesin, T., Port, L., Keenan, E., & Karamcheti, V. (2002). dRBAC: Distributed role-based access control for dynamic coalition environments. *Proc. of 22nd International Conference on Distributed Computing Systems*, (pp. 411-420).

Gudgin, M., et al. (2007). *SOAP version 1.2 part 1: Messaging framework* (2nd ed.). Retrieved from http://www.w3.org/TR/2007/ REC-soap12-part1-20070427/

IBM Corporation & Microsoft Corporation. (2002). *Security in a Web services world: A proposed architecture and roadmap*. Retrieved from http://www.ibm.com/developerworks/ library/ specification/ ws-secmap/

Josang, A. (1996). The right type of trust for distributed systems. *Proc. 1996 New Security Paradigms Workshops*, (pp. 119-131).

Kent, S. (1993). *Privacy enhancement for internet electronic mail: Part II: Certificate-based key management*. (Internet Report, RFC 1422).

Lawrence, K., et al. (2006). *Web services security X.509 certificate token profile 1.1*. Retrieved from http://docs.oasis-open.org/ wss/v1.1/ wss-v1.1-spec-os-x509TokenProfile.pdf

Lawrence, K., et al. (2006). Web services security: SOAP message security 1.1. Retrieved from http:// www.oasis-open.org/ committees/download.php/ 16790/wss-v1.1-spec-os-SOAPMessageSecurity.pdf

Lawrence, K., et al. (2008). *WS-Trust 1.4*. Retrieved from http://docs.oasis-open.org/ ws-sx/ ws-trust/ 200802/ ws-trust-1.4-ed-01.pdf

Li, N., Mitchell, J., & Winsborough, W. (2002), Design of a Role-Based Trust-Management Framework, *Proc. of the 2002 IEEE Symposium on Security and Privacy*, 114-130.

Lockhart, H., et al. (2008). *Security assertion markup language (SAML) V2.0 technical overview*. Retrieved from http://www.oasis-open.org/ committees/download.php/ 27819/ sstc-saml-tech-overview-2.0-cd-02.pdf

Microsoft. (2006). *Major features of the web services enhancements*. Retrieved from http://msdn.microsoft.com/ en-us/ library/ ms819965.aspx

Papazoglou, M., & Georgakopoulos, D. (2003). Service-oriented computing. *Communications of the ACM, 46*(10), 25–28.

Pimlott, A., & Kiselyov, O. (2006). Soutei, a logic-based trust-management system. *Proc. of 8th International Symposium on Functional and Logic Programming*, (pp. 130-145).

Rangan, P. (1992). An axiomatic theory of trust in secure communication protocols. *Computers & Security, 11*, 163–172. doi:10.1016/0167-4048(92)90043-Q

Reiter, M. (1999). Authentication metric analysis and design. *ACM Transactions on Information and System Security, 2*(2), 138–158. doi:10.1145/317087.317088

Sandhu, R., Coyne, E., Feinstein, H., & Youman, C. (1996). Role-based access control models. *IEEE Computer, 20*(2), 38–47.

Schneider, F. (2003). Least privilege and more. *IEEE Security and Privacy, 1*(3), 55–59.

Tarah, A., & Huitema, C. (1992). Associating metrics to certification paths. *Proc. 2nd European Symposium on Research in Computer Security*, (pp. 175-189).

Vandenwauver, M., Govaerts, R., & Vandewalle, J. (1997). Role based access control in distributed systems. *Communications and Multimedia Security, 3*, 169–177.

Vedamuthu, A., et al. (2007). *Web services policy 1.5 - Framework*. Retrieved from http://www.w3.org/ TR/2007/ REC-ws-policy-20070904

Weaver, A., Dwyer, S., Snyder, A., Van Dyke, J., Hu, J., Chen, X., & Mulholland, T. (2003). Federated, secure trust networks for distributed healthcare IT services. *Proc. of IEEE International Conference on Industrial Informatics*, (pp. 162-169).

Zimmermann, P. (1995). *The official PGP user's guide*. MIT Press.

Chapter 4
Web Services Discovery with Rough Sets

Maozhen Li
Brunel University, UK

Bin Yu
Level E Limited, UK

Vijay Sahota
Brunel University, UK

Man Qi
Canterbury Christ Church University, UK

ABSTRACT

Web services are emerging as a major technology for building service-oriented distributed systems. Potentially, various resources on the Internet can be virtualized as Web services for a wider use by their communities. Service discovery becomes an issue of vital importance for Web services applications. This paper presents ROSSE, a Rough Sets based Search Engine for Web service discovery. One salient feature of ROSSE lies in its capability to deal with uncertainty of service properties when matching services. A use case is presented to demonstrate the use of ROSSE for discovery of car services. ROSSE is evaluated in terms of its accuracy and efficiency in service discovery.

INTRODUCTION

Web services are emerging as a major technology for developing service-oriented distributed systems. Potentially, many resources on the Internet or the World Wide Web can be virtualized as services for a wider use by their communities. Service discovery becomes an issue of vital importance for Web service applications. As shown in Figure 1, discovered services can either be used by Web service applications or they can be composed into composite services using workflow languages such as BPEL4WS (Andrews et al, 2003). UDDI (Universal Description, Discovery and Integration, http://www.uddi.org) has been proposed and used for Web service publication and discovery. However, the search mechanism supported by UDDI is limited to keyword matches. With the

DOI: 10.4018/978-1-61350-104-7.ch004

Figure 1. A layered structure for service-oriented systems

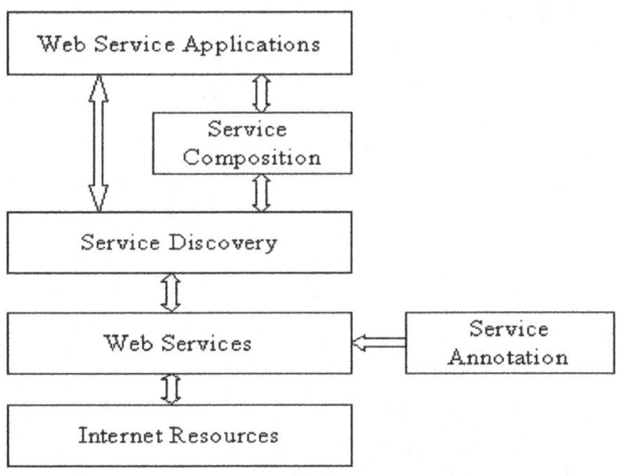

development of the Semantic Web (Berners-Lee et al, 2001), services can be annotated with metadata for enhancement of service discovery. The complexity of this metadata can range from simple annotations, to the representation of more complex relationships between services based on first order logic.

One key technology to facilitate this semantic annotation of services is OWL-S (Martin et al, 2004), an OWL (Web Ontology Language, http://www.w3.org/TR/owl-features/Reference) based ontology for encoding properties of Web services. OWL-S ontology defines a service profile for encoding a service description, a service model for specifying the behavior of a service, and a service grounding for invoking the service. Typically, a service discovery process involves a matching between the profile of a service advertisement and the profile of a service request using domain ontologies described in OWL. The service profile not only describes the functional properties of a service such as its inputs, outputs, pre-conditions, and effects (IOPEs), but also non-functional features including service name, service category, and aspects related to the quality of a service. In addition to OWL-S, another prominent effort on Semantic Web services is WSMO (Roman et al, 2005) which is built on four key concepts

Table 1. Two service advertisements with uncertain service properties

Service advertisements	Property	Property	Property
S_1	P_1	P_2	
S_2		P_2	P_3

– ontologies, standard WSDL based Web services, goals, and mediators. WSMO stresses the role of a mediator in order to support interoperation between Web services.

However, one challenging work in service discovery is that service matchmaking should be able to deal with uncertainty in service properties when matching service advertisements with service requests. This is because in a large-scale heterogeneous system, service publishers and requestors may use their pre-defined properties to describe services, e.g. in the form of OWL-S or WSMO. For a property explicitly used in one service advertisement, it may not be explicitly used by another service advertisement within the same service category. As can be seen from Table 1, the property P_1 used by the service advertisement S_1 does not appear in the service advertisement S_2. When services S_1 and S_2 are matched with a query using properties P_1, P_2 and P_3, the property P_1 becomes an uncertain property when matching S_2. Similarly, the property P_3 becomes an uncertain property when matching S_1. Consequently, both S_1 and S_2 may not be discovered because of the existence of uncertainty of properties even though the two services are relevant to the query.

It is worth noting that properties used in service advertisements may have dependencies, e.g. both P_1 and P_3 may be dependent properties of P_2 when describing services S_1 and S_2 respectively. Both S_1 and S_2 can be discovered if P_1 and P_3 (which are uncertain properties in terms of the user query) can be dynamically identified and reduced in the matching process. To increase the accuracy of service discovery, a search engine should be

Figure 2. ROSSE components

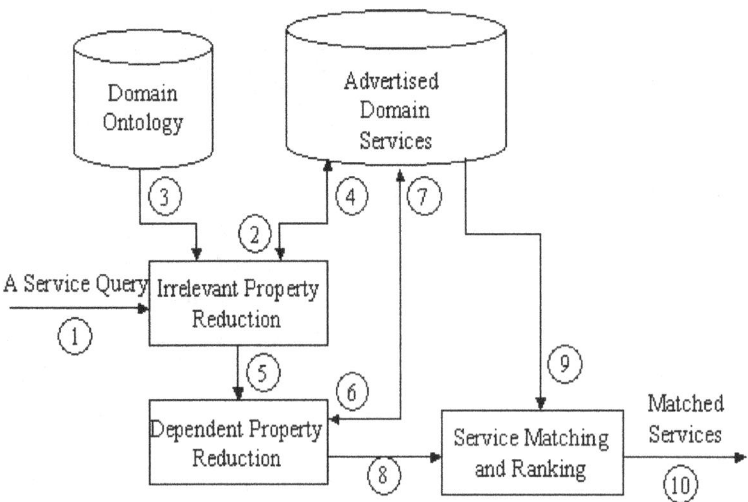

able to deal with uncertainty of properties when matching services.

In this paper, we present ROSSE, a Rough Sets (Pawlak, 1982) based Search Engine for Web service discovery. One salient feature of ROSSE lies in its capability to deal with uncertainty in service properties (attributes) when matching service advertisements with service requests. Experiment results show that ROSSE is more effective in service discovery than existing mechanisms such as UDDI keyword matching and OWL-S matchmaking.

The remainder of this paper is organized as follows. Section 2 presents the design details of ROSSE. Section 3 gives a case study to demonstrate the use of ROSSE for discovery of car services. Section 4 evaluates ROSSE from the aspects of accuracy and efficiency in service discovery. Section 5 discusses some related work, and Section 6 concludes the paper.

ROSSE DESIGN

ROSSE considers input and output properties individually when matching services. For the simplicity of expression, input and output properties used in a service request are generally referred to as service request properties. The same goes to service advertisements.

Figure 2 shows ROSSE components. The Irrelevant Property Reduction component takes a service request as an input (step 1), and then it accesses a set of advertised domain services (step 2) to remove irrelevant service properties using the domain ontology (step 3). Reduced properties will be marked in the set of advertised domain services (step 4). Once invoked (step 5), the Dependent Property Reduction component accesses the advertised domain services (step 6) to discover and reduce indecisive properties which will be marked in advertised domain services (step 7). Invoked by the Dependent Property Reduction component (step 8), the Service Matching and Ranking component accesses the advertised domain services for service matching and ranking (step 9), and finally it produces a list of matched services (step 10).

In the following sections, we describe in depth the design of ROSSE components for service matchmaking and discovery. Firstly, we introduce Rough sets for service discovery.

Figure 3. Approximation in rough sets

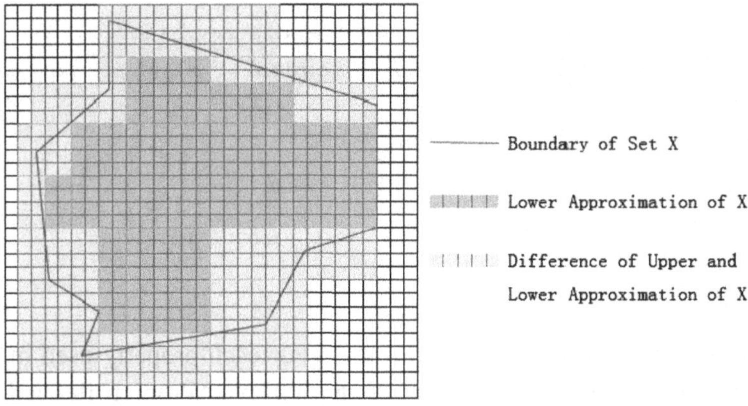

Rough Sets for Service Discovery

Rough sets method is a mathematic tool that can deal with uncertainty in knowledge discovery. It is based on the concept of an upper and a lower approximation of a set as shown in Figure 3. For a given set X, the yellow grids (lighter shading) represent its upper approximation, and the green grids (darker shading) represent its lower approximation. We introduce Rough sets for service discovery in the following way.

Let:

- Ω be a domain ontology.
- U be a set of N service advertisements, $U = \{s_1, s_2, \ldots, s_N\}$, $N \geq 1$.
- P be a set of K properties used in the N service advertisements, $P = \{p_1, p_2, \ldots, p_K\}$, $K \geq 2$.
- P_A be a set of M properties used in service advertisements which are relevant to a service request R within the domain ontology Ω,
- $P_A = \{p_{A1}, p_{A2}, \ldots, p_{AM}\}$, $P_A \subseteq P$, $M \geq 1$.
- X be a set of service advertisements relevant to the service request R, $X \subseteq U$.
- $\underline{X}$ be the lower approximation of the set X.
- $\overline{X}$ be the upper approximation of the set X.

According to the Rough sets theory, we have

$$\underline{X} = \{x \in U : [x]_{P_A} \subseteq X\} \quad (1)$$

$$\overline{X} = \{x \in U : [x]_{P_A} \cap X \neq \varnothing\} \quad (2)$$

For a property used by a service request $p \in P_A$, we have

- $\forall x \in \underline{X}$, x definitely has property p.
- $\forall x \in \overline{X}$, x possibly has property p.
- $\forall x \in U - \overline{X}$, x absolutely does not have property p.

The use of "definitely", "possibly" and "absolutely" are used to encode properties that cannot be specified in a more exact way. This is a significant addition to existing work, where discovery of services needs to be encoded in a precise way, making it difficult to find services which have an approximate match to a query.

Advertised domain service properties may be irrelevant (having no effect on service matching) or relevant (having an impact on service matching). Certain properties used by advertised services may be redundant which can be reduced without losing essential classificatory information. The concept of the reduct is fundamental for Rough sets theory

Algorithm 1. Reducing irrelevant properties from service advertisements

```
for each property  pA used in service advertisements
  for all properties used in a service request
      if  pA is nomatch with any  pR
         then pA is marked with nomatch;
      end if
   end for
end for
```

(Winiarski, 2001). Service property reduction can be considered as a process of finding a smaller (than the original one) set of properties with the same or close classificatory power as the original set. For a service query, the most relevant properties of advertised services can be determined after property reduction.

Reducing Irrelevant Properties

When searching for a service, a service request may employ some properties which are irrelevant to the properties used in a service advertisement within one domain ontology. These irrelevant properties used in service advertisements should be removed before the service matchmaking process is performed.

Let

- p_R be a property used in a service request.
- p_A be a property used in a service advertisement.

Following the work proposed in (Paolucci et al, 2002), we define the following relationships between p_R and p_A:

- **exact** match, p_R and p_A are equivalent or p_R is a subclass of p_A.
- **plug-in** match, p_A subsumes p_R.
- **subsume** match, p_R subsumes p_A.
- **nomatch**, no subsumption between p_R and p_A.

For each property used in a service request, the Irrelevant Property Reduction component uses Algorithm 1 to remove irrelevant properties from advertised services. For those properties used in service advertisements that have a nomatch result, they will be treated as irrelevant properties. Service advertisements are organised as service records in a database. Properties are organised in such a way that each property uses one column to ensure the correctness in the following reduction of dependent properties. As a property used in one service advertisement might not be used in another one, some properties may have empty values. For a service request, a property with an empty value in a service record becomes an uncertain property. If a property in an advertised service record is marked as nomatch, the column associated with the property will be marked as nomatch. As a result, all properties within the column including uncertain properties (i.e. properties with empty values) will not be considered in service matchmaking.

Reducing Dependent Properties

Properties used by service advertisements may have dependencies. Dependent properties are indecisive properties which have no effect on service matching. Building on the work proposed in (Jensen et al, 2005), we designed Algorithm 2 to reduce dependent properties from advertised services.

Let

- Ω, U, P, P_A be defined as in Section 2.1.
- P_A^D be a set of L_D decisive properties for identifying service advertisements relevant to the service request R in terms of Ω,
- $P_A^D = \{p_{A1}^D, p_{A2}^D, \ldots, p_{AL_D}^D\}, P_A^D \subseteq P_A, L_D \geq 1$.
- P_A^{IND} be a set of L_{IND} indecisive properties for identifying service advertisements relevant to the service request R in terms of Ω,
- $P_A^{IND} = \{p_{A1}^{IND}, p_{A2}^{IND}, \ldots, p_{AL_{IND}}^{IND}\}$, $P_A^{IND} \subseteq P_A, L_{IND} \geq 1$.
- $IND()$ be an indiscernibility relation.
- f be a mapping function from a property to a service advertisement.

Then

$$IND\,(P_A^{IND}) = \{(x, y) \in U : \forall p_{Ai}^{IND} \in P_A^{IND}, f(x, p_{Ai}^{IND}) = f(y, p_{Ai}^{IND})\} \quad (3)$$

$$P_A^D = P_A - P_A^{IND} \quad (4)$$

For a service request, the Dependent Property Reduction component uses Algorithm 2 to find the decisive properties in service advertisements. Specifically, service advertisements with the maximum number of nonempty property values are used in the algorithm as targets to find indecisive properties. The targeted services can still be uniquely identified without using these indecisive properties. All possible combinations of individual indecisive properties are checked with an aim to maximally remove indecisive properties which may include uncertain properties whose values are empty. In the mean time, the following service discovery process is speeded up due to the reduction of dependent properties.

Computing Match Degrees

The Service Matching and Ranking component uses the decisive properties to compute the match degrees of advertised services related to a service request.

Let

- Ω, U, P, P_A be defined as in Section 2.1.
- P_R be a set of M properties used in a service request R. $P_R = \{p_{R1}, p_{R2}, \ldots, p_{RM}\}$, $M \geq 1$.
- P_A^D be a set of L_D decisive properties for identifying service advertisements relevant to the service request R in terms of Ω,
- $P_A^D = \{p_{A1}^D, p_{A2}^D, \ldots, p_{AL_D}^D\}, L_D \geq 1$.
- $m(p_{Ri}, p_{Aj})$ be a match degree between a property P_{Ri} and a property P_{Aj} in terms of Ω, $p_{Ri} \in P_R, 1 \leq i \leq M, p_{Aj} \in P_A^D, 1 \leq j \leq L_D$.
- $v(p_{Aj})$ be a value of the property p_{Aj}, $p_{Aj} \in P_A^D, 1 \leq j \leq L_D$.
- $S(R, s)$ be a similarity degree between a service advertisement s and the service request R, $s \in U$.

Algorithm 3 shows the rules for calculating a match degree between a property used in a service request and a property used in a service advertisement. A decisive property with an empty value has a match degree of 50% when matching each property used in a service request. A property used in a service advertisement will be given a match degree of 100% if it has an exact match relationship with a property used in a service request. A match degree of 50% will be given if it has a plug-in relationship with a service request property and the relationship is out of five generations. Similarly, a property used in a service advertisement will be given a match degree of 50% if it has a subsume relationship with a service request property and the relationship is out of three generations.

Algorithm 2. Reducing dependent properties from advertised services.

```
S is a set of service advertisements with the maximum number of nonempty prop-
erty values relevant to a service request;
      P_A is a set of properties used by the S set of service advertisements;
      P_A^D is a set of decisive properties, P_A^D ⊆ P_A;

      P_A^IND is a set of individual indecisive properties, P_A^IND ⊆ P_A
 ;
      P_A^IND_Core is a set of combined indecisive properties,
         P_A^IND_Core ⊆ P_A^IND;
      P_A^D = Ø; P_A^IND = Ø; P_A^IND_Core = Ø;
      for each property p∈ P_A
         if p is an indecisive property for identifying the S set of services
            then
           add p into P_A^IND;
          P_A^IND_Core = Ø;
          add p into P_A^IND_Core;
         end if
      end for
      for i=2 to sizeof(P_A^IND)-1
         calculate all possible i combinations of the properties in P_A^IND;
         if any combined i properties are indecisive properties for identify-
ing
                     the S set of services
              then
           P_A^IND_Core = Ø;
           add the i properties into P_A^IND_Core;
           continue;
            else if any combined i properties are decisive properties
               then break;
         end if
       end for
       P_A^D = P_A-P_A^IND_Core;
       return P_A^D;
```

Each decisive property used for identifying service advertisements has a maximum match degree when matching all the properties used in a service request. $S(R, s)$ can be calculated using formula (5).

$$S(R,s) = \sum_{j=1}^{L_D} \sum_{i=1}^{M} \max(m(p_{Ri}, p_{Aj})) \Big/ L_D \tag{5}$$

Using the formula (5), ROSSE calculates a matching degree for each service advertisement related to a service request. The similarity degrees

Algorithm 3. The rules for calculating match degrees between properties used in service requests and service advertisements respectively

```
for each property p_Aj ∈ P_A^D, v(p_Aj) ≠ NULL
   for each property p_Ri ∈ P_R
         if   p_Aj is an exact match with p_Ri
              then   m(p_Ri, p_Aj) = 1;
         else if p_Aj is a plug-in match with p_Ri
                          then if p_Ri is the kth subclass of p_Aj and 2≤k≤5
                         then m(p_Ri, p_Aj) = 1-(k-1)×10%;
                            else if p_Ri is the kth subclass of p_Aj and k>5
                                   then m(p_Ri, p_Aj) = 0.5;
               end if
       else if p_Aj is a subsume match with p_Ri
                then   if p_Aj is the kth subclass of p_Ri and 1≤k≤3
                                    then m(p_Ri, p_Aj) = 0.8-(k-1)×10%;
                             else if p_Aj is the kth subclass of p_Ri and k>3
              then m(p_Ri, p_Aj) = 0.5;
                   end if
         end if
   end for
 end for
 for each property p_Aj ∈ P_A^D, v(p_Aj) = NULL
    for each property p_Ri ∈ P_R
         m(p_Ri, p_Aj) = 0.5;
    end for
 end for
```

are used to produce a lower and an upper approximation sets of discovered services.

ROSSE CASE STUDY

In this section, we present a use case of ROSSE to discover vehicle services. Figure 4 shows the ontologies used in this scenario defining the classifications of *vehicles, objects, exhausts, locations, configurations, brands* respectively. Two ontologies are used to classify configurations of vehicles represented respectively by *e1-e5* and *g1-g4*. Relevant vehicle services are registered with ROSSE. In the following sections, we describe how services are matched in terms of the following query to search for car services that sell red BMW mini coopers that have an exhaust of 1.0, and are configured with ABS, manufactured in the UK. Price information is also provided by the car services.

Query: Car, mini cooper, ABS, UK, BMW, Exhaust 1.0, Price, Red

Building a Decision Table

A service decision table is used to compute dependent properties among services. As the number of services registered with ROSSE can

Figure 4. Ontolgogies used in the search scenario

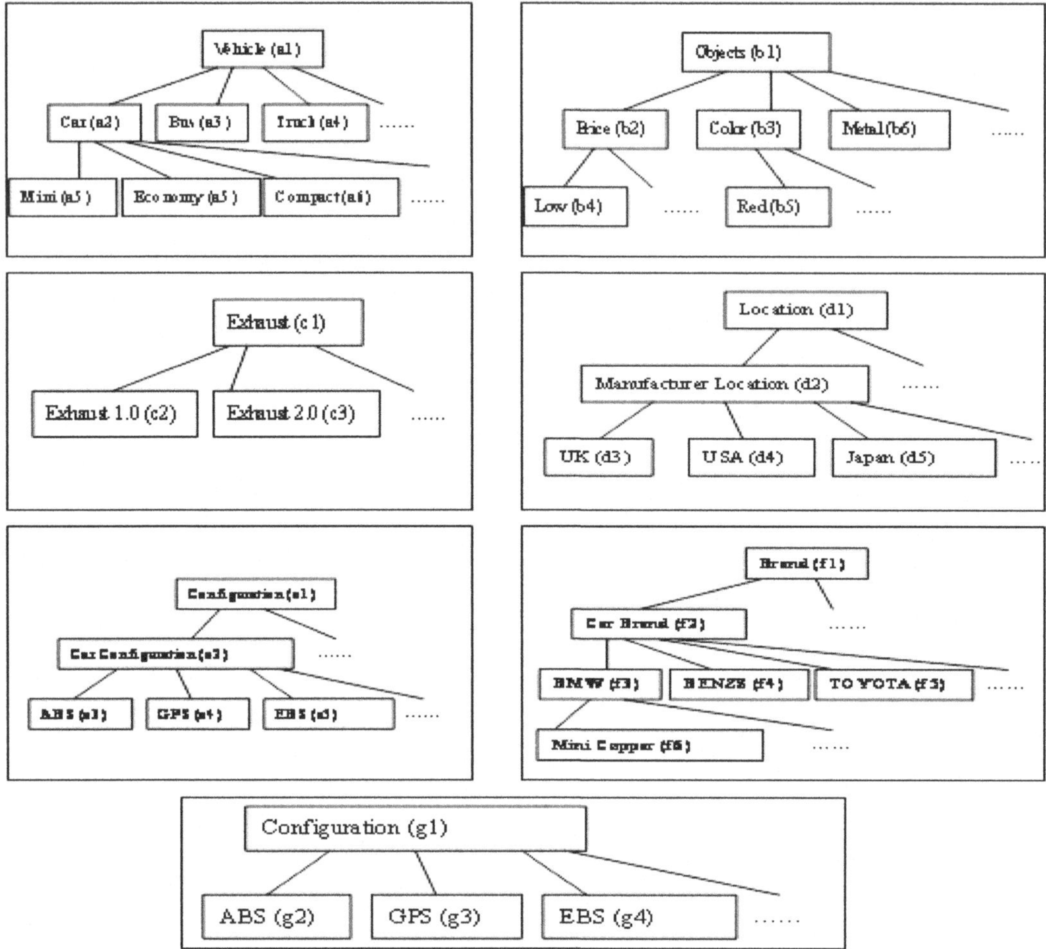

be tremendous, the decision table is constructed by sampling registered services. For a specific query, ROSSE randomly selects a certain number of services records. A service record is selected as long as one of its properties has a valid relationship with a property used in a service query. The relationship can be *exact*, *plug-in* or *subsume* as defined in algorithm 1 which is described in the Section 2.2.

Table 2 shows a segment of the decision table with 13 service records for discovery of car services. As can be seen from Table 2, properties of advertised services that are relevant to the car service query are *f6*, *g2*, *d3*, *f3*, *c2*, *b2*, *b3*, *d2*, *c1*, *e1/g1*, *d1*, *b6*. If a property in a service record is marked with *1*, this means that the property is used by the service in its advertisement. For example, the service S_1 has properties of *f6*, *g2*, *d3*, *f3*, *c2*, *d1*, and *b6* in its advertisement. A property marked with *0* in a service record means that the service does not have the corresponding property in its advertisement, e.g. properties such as *b2*, *b2*, *d2*, *c1*, and *e1/g1* are not used by the service S_1 for advertisement. However, it should be noted that a property marked with 0 in a service record does not necessarily mean this property is not relevant to the service. Such a property might be an inherent property of the service. ROSSE deals with properties marked with 0 as uncertain properties when matching services.

Table 2. A segment of the decision table used for discovery of car services

services \ properties	f6	g2	d3	f3	c2	b2	b3	d2	c1	e1/g1	d1	b6
S_1	1	1	1	1	1	0	0	0	0	0	1	1
S_2	0	1	0	1	0	0	0	0	0	0	1	1
S_3	0	1	0	1	0	0	1	1	1	1	0	0
S_4	0	1	0	0	0	1	1	1	0	1	0	0
S_5	0	1	1	0	1	0	0	0	0	1	0	0
S_6	1	1	1	1	1	1	0	0	0	0	0	0
S_7	0	1	0	0	0	0	1	1	1	0	0	0
S_8	1	1	1	1	1	0	0	0	0	1	0	0
S_9	0	1	0	1	0	0	0	1	0	0	1	1
S_{10}	0	1	0	0	0	0	0	0	1	0	1	0
S_{11}	0	1	0	0	1	0	0	1	0	0	0	0
S_{12}	0	1	0	1	0	0	0	0	1	0	1	1
S_{13}	1	1	1	1	1	1	1	0	0	1	0	0

Computing Dependent Properties

Once a service decision table is constructed, the next step is to compute dependent properties. Using the algorithm 2 presented in Section 2.3, properties *g2*, *d3*, *f3*, and *c2* are indecisive properties which are reduced from the decision table in matching services as shown in Table 3. Table 4 shows the segment of the decision table without dependent properties.

Computing Match Degrees

Decisive properties are used for computing the similarities between an advertised service and a service request. For each decisive property used in a service advertisement and a property used in the service query, a maximum matching degree can be computed using ontologies defined in Figure 4. Table 5 shows the matching degrees of the decisive properties used in the exemplified 13 service records. It should be noted that both *e1* and *g1* refers to the same property *Configuration*, but they use different ontology definitions as shown in Figure 4. The matching degree of *Configuration* to the *ABS* property used in the query is computed in such way that a mean of two matching degrees using the two ontology definitions (i.e. 100% and 90%) is computed which is 95%.

It is worth noting that for an uncertain property which is marked with the number of 0 in a box of Table, a matching degree of 50% is given. Based on the formula (5) presented in Section 2.4, the similarity degree between an advertised service and a service query can be computed. In the car service query case, for example, service S_1 has a similarity degree of 66.25% and service S_{13} has a similarity degree of 74.375%.

ROSSE IMPLEMENTATION AND EVALUATION

ROSSE is implemented with Java on a Pentium IIII 2.6G with 512M RAM running Red Hat Fedora Linux 3. Figure 5 shows the homepage of ROSSE. It has two registries for service registration, a UDDI registry and an OWL registry. The

Table 3. Computed dependent properties

services \ properties	f6	g2	d3	f3	c2	b2	b3	d2	c1	e1/g1	d1	b6
S_1	1	1	1	1	1	0	0	0	0	0	1	1
S_2	0	1	0	1	0	0	0	0	0	0	1	1
S_3	0	1	0	1	0	0	1	1	1	1	0	0
S_4	0	1	0	0	0	1	1	1	0	1	0	0
S_5	0	1	1	0	1	0	0	0	0	1	0	0
S_6	1	1	1	1	1	1	0	0	0	0	0	0
S_7	0	1	0	0	0	0	1	1	1	0	0	0
S_8	1	1	1	1	1	0	0	0	0	1	0	0
S_9	0	1	0	1	0	0	0	1	0	0	1	1
S_{10}	0	1	0	0	0	0	0	0	1	0	1	0
S_{11}	0	1	0	0	1	0	0	1	0	0	0	0
S_{12}	0	1	0	1	0	0	0	0	1	0	1	1
S_{13}	1	1	1	1	1	1	1	0	0	1	0	0

Table 4. The segment of the decision table without dependent properties

services \ properties	f6	b2	b3	d2	c1	e1/g1	d1	b6
S_1	1	0	0	0	0	0	1	1
S_2	0	0	0	0	0	0	1	1
S_3	0	0	1	1	1	1	0	0
S_4	0	1	1	1	0	1	0	0
S_5	0	0	0	0	0	1	0	0
S_6	1	1	0	0	0	0	0	0
S_7	0	0	1	1	1	0	0	0
S_8	1	0	0	0	0	1	0	0
S_9	0	0	0	1	0	0	1	1
S_{10}	0	0	0	0	1	0	1	0
S_{11}	0	0	0	1	0	0	0	0
S_{12}	0	0	0	0	1	0	1	1
S_{13}	1	1	1	0	0	1	0	0

UDDI registry is used to register services with WSDL interfaces, and the OWL-S registry is used to register services with OWL-S interfaces. The UUID of a WSDL service registered with the UDDI registry is used to uniquely identify semantic annotation records of the registered service. In this way, WSDL services registered with ROSSE can be matched with semantic inferences instead of

Table 5. Computation of matching degrees

Match Degrees	100%					95%	90%	
properties / services	f6	b2	b3	d2	c1	e1/g1	d1	b6
S_1	1	0	0	0	0	0	1	1
S_2	0	0	0	0	0	0	1	1
S_3	0	0	1	1	1	1	0	0
S_4	0	1	1	1	0	1	0	0
S_5	0	0	0	0	0	1	0	0
S_6	1	1	0	0	0	0	0	0
S_7	0	0	1	1	1	0	0	0
S_8	1	0	0	0	0	1	0	0
S_9	0	0	0	1	0	0	1	1
S_{10}	0	0	0	0	1	0	1	0
S_{11}	0	0	0	1	0	0	0	0
S_{12}	0	0	0	0	1	0	1	1
S_{13}	1	1	1	0	0	1	0	0

using keywords only. jUDDI (http://ws.apache.org/juddi) and mySQL (http://www.mysql.com) are used to build the UDDI registry and UDDI4J (http://uddi4j.sourceforge.net/) is used to query the registry. OWL-S API (http://www.mindswap.org/2004/owl-s/api) is used to parse OWL-S documents to register services with OWL-S interfaces with the OWL-S registry in ROSSE.

ROSSE provides graphical user interfaces to register services. Figure 6 shows a page to register a *vehicle* service that has a WSDL Interface, and Figure 7 shows the four steps used to semantically annotate the *vehicle* service. Figure 8 shows the registration of a zip code finding service with an OWL-S interface in ROSSE.

For a service request, ROSSE computes a matching degree for each service advertisement in terms of its functional input and output properties using formula (5). As shown in Figure 5, ROSSE can discover services with WSDL interfaces or OWL-S interfaces. It can also discover the best service from service advertisements which

Figure 5. ROSSE user interface

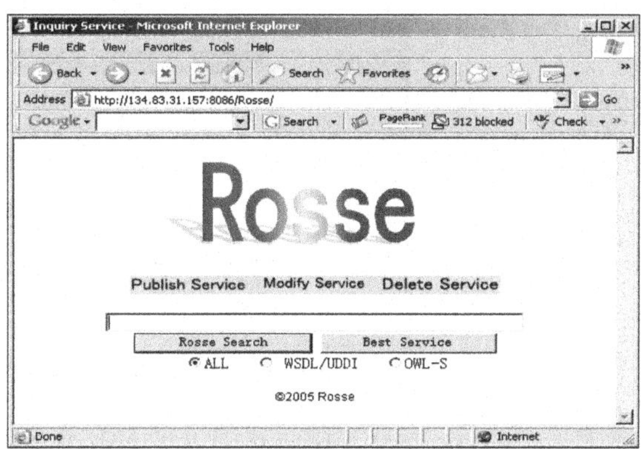

has the highest matching degree related to a service request.

In this section, we evaluate the accuracy and efficiency of ROSSE in service discovery. We compare ROSSE with UDDI and OWL-S respectively. RACER (Haarslev et al, 2001) was used by OWL-S to infer the relationships between properties used in service queries and service advertisements. We implemented a light

Figure 6. Registering a service that has a WSDL interface

Publish Service - Opera Preview
File Edit View Bookmarks Tools Help
http://brunel-huang:8086/Rosse/publish4.jsp
Add DETAILS of the Service :
Service Name Tanker seller
Service Description A test Service of Vehicle
Service Leasing Time From 00 00 00 To 23 59 59 (e.g. From 00:00:00 To 23:59:59)
Service Leasing Price Peaktime 600 99 Offpeak 300 30 (e.g. Peaktime 9.99 Offpeak 0.00)
Service Required CPU 350 MHz
Service Required Memory 100 M
Service Access Point1 http://brunel-huang:8086/tanker
Overview Document1 http://brunel-huang:8086/tanker?wsdl
Service Access Point2 http://localhost:8086/vehicle
Overview Document2 http://localhost:8086/vehicle?wsdl
Service Access Point3 http://brunel-huang:8080/HC
Overview Document3 http://brunel-huang:8080/HC?wsdl

Figure 7. Annotating a vehicle service with semantic information

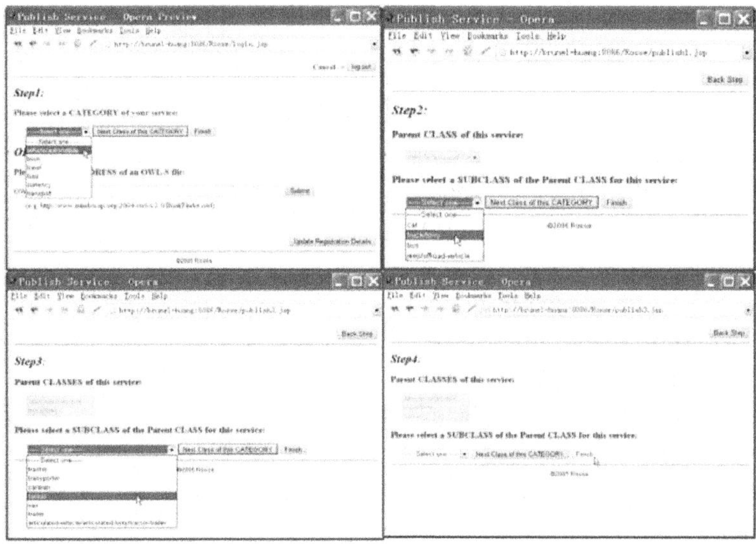

Figure 8. Registering OWL-S services with ROSSE

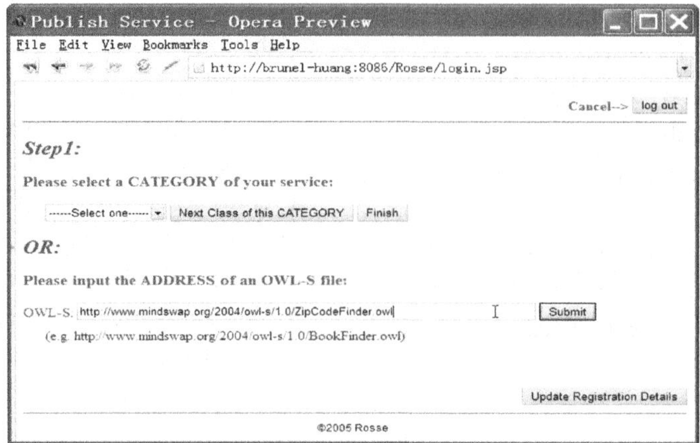

Figure 9. Pizza ontology structure

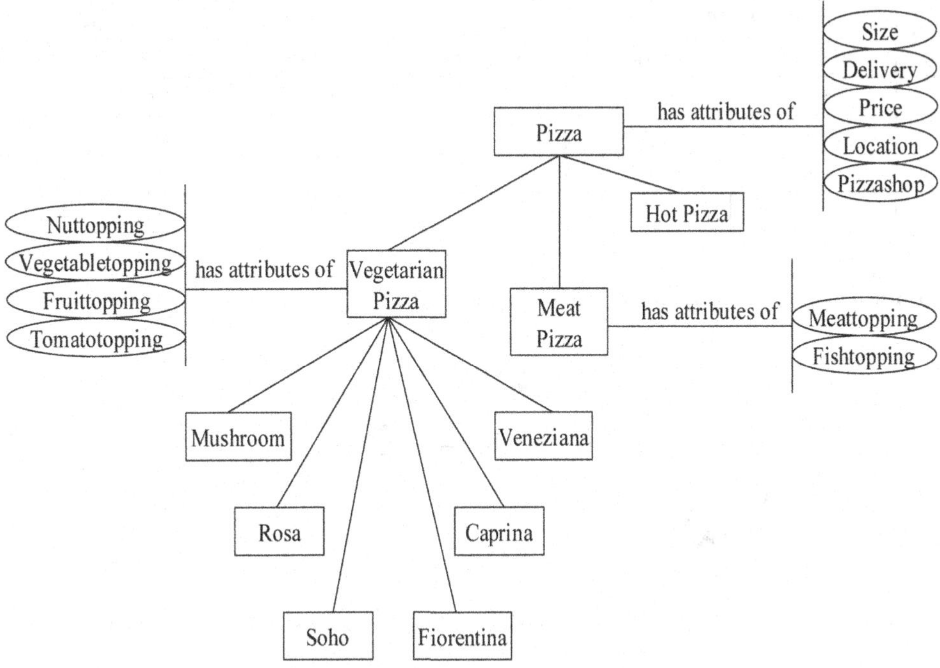

weighted reasoning component in ROSSE to overcome a high overhead incurred by RACER. The component uses the Protégé OWLAPI (http://protege.stanford.edu/plugins/owl/api/) to parse OWL documents.

We designed Pizza services for the tests using the Pizza ontology defined by http://www.co-ode.org/ontologies/pizza/pizza_20041007.owl. Figure 9 shows the Pizza ontology structure. The approach adopted here can be applied to other domains – where a specific ontology can be specified. The use of service properties needs to be related to a particular application-specific ontology.

ROSSE Accuracy in Service Discovery

Precision and recall are standard measures that have been used in information retrieval for measuring the accuracy of a search method or a search engine (Rijsbergen, 1979). We performed 4 groups of tests to evaluate the precision and recall of ROSSE in service discovery using 10 service records in each group. Each service had 5 properties of which 2 properties were dependent properties. For a service query, each group had 3 relevant services. The 10 services in group 1 did not have uncertain properties, but group 2 had 3 services with uncertain properties, group 3 had 5 services with uncertain properties and group 4 had 7 services with uncertain properties. Properties such as *Size, Price, Nuttoping, Vegetariantopping,* and *Fruittopping* were used by the advertised services. Table 6 shows the evaluation results.

In the tests conducted for group 1, both OWL-S and ROSSE have a precision of 100%. This is because all service advertisements in this group do not have uncertain properties (i.e. properties with empty values). UDDI discovered 4 services, but only 2 services were relevant to the service query with a precision of 50%, and a recall of 66.7%. In the tests of the last 3 groups where advertised services have uncertain properties, OWL-S cannot discover any services producing a precision of 0 and a recall of 0. Although UDDI can still discover some services in these tests, the

Table 6. ROSSE accuracy in service discovery.

Service Property Certainty Rate	UDDI		OWL-S		ROSSE	
	Precision	Recall	Precision	Recall	Precision	Recall
100%	50%	66.7%	100%	100%	100%	100%
70%	33.3%	33.3%	0	0	100%	33.3%
50%	0	0	0	0	100%	33.3%
30%	0	0	0	0	100%	33.3%

Figure 10. ROSSE efficiency in service matchmaking

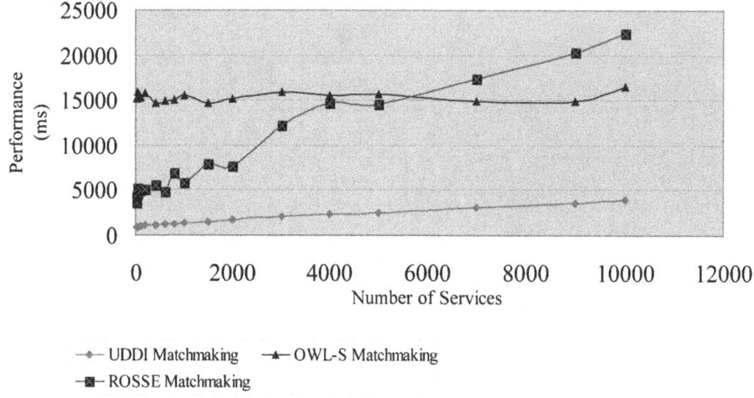

precision of each group is low. For example, in the tests of group 3 and group 4 where the service property certainty rates are 50% and 30% respectively, UDDI cannot discover any relevant services. ROSSE is more effective than both UDDI and OWL-S in dealing with uncertain properties when matching services. For example, ROSSE is still able to produce a precision of 100% in the tests of the last 3 groups albeit with a low recall which is 33.3%.

ROSSE Efficiency in Service Discovery

We have registered 10,000 Pizza service records with ROSSE for testing its efficiency in service discovery. Service discovery involves two processes, one is service matchmaking and the other is service accessing (i.e. accessing matched services). We compared the efficiency of ROSSE in matching services with that of UDDI and OWL-S respectively, and the evaluation results are plotted in Figure 10. We also compared their efficiency in accessing matched services, and the results are plotted in Figure 11.

From Figure 10 we can see that UDDI has the least overhead in matching services. This is because UDDI only supports keyword based exact matching. UDDI does not support the inference of the relationships between requested service properties and advertised service properties which is a time consuming process. We also observe that ROSSE has a better performance in service matchmaking than OWL-S when the number of advertised services is less than 5500. This is because ROSSE used a simpler reasoning component than RACER which was used by OWL-S for matching services. However, the overhead of ROSSE in service matchmaking increases when the number of services gets larger. This is due to

Figure 11. ROSSE efficiency in accessing matched services

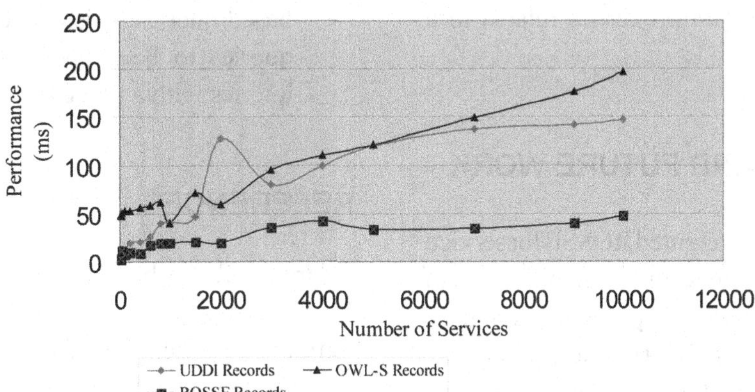

the overhead caused by a reduction of dependent properties. The major overhead of OWL-S in matching services is caused by RACER which is sensitive to the number of service properties instead of the number of services.

From Figure 11 we can see that the ROSSE matchmaking algorithm is most efficient in accessing matched services due to its reduction of dependent properties. The OWL-S has a similar performance to UDDI in this process.

RELATED WORK

Service matchmaking is becoming an issue of vital importance in service-oriented systems. UDDI has been proposed to support service publication and discovery. However, the search mechanism supported by UDDI is limited to keyword matches and does not support any inference based on the taxonomies referred to by the tModels. Various extensions (ShaikhAli et al 2003, Powles et al 2005, Miles et al 2003) have been proposed to complement UDDI with rich descriptions and powerful match mechanisms in support of service discovery.

Among the extensions, the UDDI-M approach (Miles et al, 2003) is flexible in attaching metadata to various entities associated with a service, but this approach assumes the properties used in service advertisements and in service requests are consistent. Semantic Web service technologies such as OWL-S and WSMO have been proposed to enhance service discovery with semantic annotations. However, the classical OWL-S matching algorithm (Paolucci et al, 2002) cannot deal with uncertainty in service properties when matching service advertisements with service requests. This work has been extended in various way in applying Semantic Web services for service discovery. For example, Jaeger et al. (2005) introduce "contravariance" in matching inputs and outputs between service advertisements and service requests using OWL-S. Li et al. (2004) introduce a "intersection" relationship between a service advertisement and a service request. Majithia et al. (2004) introduce reputation metrics in matching services. However, these OWL-S based methods still cannot deal with missing (uncertain) properties.

WSMO introduces mediators trying to support distinct ontologies employed by service requests and service advertisements. However, the discovery mechanism (Keller et al, 2004) proposed in WSMO requires that properties used by both the goals and services should be consistent.

Compared with the work mentioned above, ROSSE matchmaking can deal with uncertain properties in matching services. It takes all service advertisements belonging to one service category into one search space to dynamically identify and reduce irrelevant and dependent properties which may be uncertain properties related to a service request.

CONCLUSION AND FUTURE WORK

In this paper we have presented ROSSE for service discovery. ROSSE is novel in its capability to deal with uncertainty of service properties for high accuracy in service discovery. The preliminary experimental results achieved so far are encouraging. However, the following issues need to be considered for ROSSE enhancement:

- It has been shown that finding a minimal reduct in Rough set is a problem of NP-hard when the number of attributes gets large (Skowron et al, 1992). Heuristic methods need to be investigated to speed up the process in service property reduction.
- Services registered with ROSSE could be tremendous. Scalability is one the issues that need to be tackled. UDDI Version 3 (http://uddi.org/pubs/uddi_v3.htm) provides larger support for multiple registries, but the specification does not specify how these registries should be structured for enhanced scalability in service registration. Distributed Hash Table (DHT) based Peer-to-Peer (P2P) systems such as Chord (Stoica et al. 2003) and Pastry (Rowstron et al. 2001) have shown their efficiency and scalability in content lookup. Scalability in ROSSE can be improved with DHT structured P2P systems.
- Advertised services may be further described in terms of their non-functional properties related to QoS such as reliability and cost. One challenge is how to model such QoS data so that functionally matched services can be evaluated in terms of their QoS properties.
- Currently ROSSE only supports keyword-based queries. It is expected that complex queries to be supported in ROSSE, e.g. queries with a range or fuzzy queries.

REFERENCES

Andrews, T., Curbera, F., Dholakia, H., Goland, Y., Klein, J., Leymann, F., Liu, K., Roller, D., Smith, D., Thatte, S., Trickovic, I., Weerawarana, S., (2003), Business Process Execution Language for Web Services version 1.1.

Berners-Lee, T., Hendler, J., & Lassila, O. (2001). The Semantic Web. *Scientific American, 284*(4), 34–43. doi:10.1038/scientificamerican0501-34

Haarslev, V., & Möller, R. (2001), Description of the RACER System and its Applications, *Proc. of 2001 International Workshop on Description Logics (DL-2001)*, Stanford, USA.

Jaeger, M., Rojec-Goldmann, G., Mühl, G., Liebetruth, C., & Geihs, K. (2005), Ranked Matching for Service Descriptions using OWL-S, Proc. of Communication in Distributed Systems (KiVS) 2005, Kaiserslautern, Germany. Keller, U., Lara, R., Polleres, A., Toma, I., Kifer, M. and Fensel, D., WSMO Web Service Discovery, http://www.wsmo.org/2004/d5/d5.1/v0.1/20041112/d5.1v0.1_20041112.pdf

Jensen, R., Shen, Q., & Tuson, A. (2005), Finding Rough Set Reducts with SAT, *Proceedings of the 10th International Conference on Rough Sets, Fuzzy Sets, Data Mining, and Granular Computing (RSFDGrC)*, pp.194-203, Lecture Notes in Computer Science, Springer, Regina, Canada.

Li, L., & Horrocks, I. (2004). A software framework for matchmaking based on semantic web technology. *International Journal of Electronic Commerce, 8*(4), 39–60.

Majithia, S., Ali, A., Rana, O., & Walker, D. (2004), Reputation-Based Semantic Service Discovery, *Proceedings of WETICE 2004*, Italy.

Martin, D., Paolucci, M., McIlraith, S., Burstein, M., McDermott, D., McGuinness, D., et al. (2004), Bringing Semantics to Web Services: The OWL-S Approach, *Proceedings of the First International Workshop on Semantic Web Services and Web Process Composition (SWSWPC 2004)*, San Diego, California, USA.

Miles, S., Papay, J., Dialani, D., Luck, M., Decker, K., Payne, T., & Moreau, L. (2003). Personalised Grid Service Discovery. *IEE Proceedings Software: Special Issue on Performance Engineering, 150*(4), 252–256.

Paolucci, M., Kawamura, T., Payne, T., & Sycara, K. (2002), Semantic Matching of Web Service Capabilities, *Proceedings of the 1st International Semantic Web Conference (ISWC)*, Berlin.

Pawlak, Z., Rough sets, (1982), *International Journal of Computer and Information Science, 11*(5), 341-356. doi:10.1007/BF01001956

Powles, A., & Krishnaswamy, S. (2005), Extending UDDI with Recommendations: An Association Analysis Approach, *Proceedings of WSMDEIS 2005*, Miami, USA.

Rijsbergen, C. (1979). *Information Retrieval, 1979*. London: Butterworths.

Roman, D., Keller, U., Lausen, H., Bruijn, J., Lara, R., & Stollberg, M. (2005). Web Service Modeling Ontology. *Applied Ontology, 1*(1), 77–106.

Rowstron, A., & Druschel, P. (2001). *Pastry: Scalable, distributed object location and routing for large-scale peer-to-peer systems, Proceedings of Middleware* (pp. 329–350). Lecture Notes in Computer Science, Springer.

ShaikhAli. A., Rana, O., Al-Ali, R., Walker, D., UDDIe: An Extended Registry for Web Service, Proceedings of SAINT Workshops, Orlando, Florida, USA, 2003.

Skowron, A., & Rauszer, C. (1992). In Slowinski, R. (Ed.), *The discernibility matrices and functions in information systems, Decision Support by Experience - Application of the Rough Sets Theory* (pp. 331–362). Kluwer Academic Publishers.

Stoica, I., Morris, R., Liben-Nowell, D., Karger, D., Kaashoek, M., Dabek, F., & Balakrishnan, H. (2003). Chord: A Scalable Peer-to-Peer Lookup Protocol for Internet Applications. *IEEE/ACM Transactions on Networking, 11*(1), 17–32. doi:10.1109/TNET.2002.808407

Winiarski, R. (2001). Rough sets methods in Feature Reduction and Classification. *International Journal of Applied Mathematics and Computer Science, 11*(3), 565–582.

This work was previously published in International Journal of Web Services Research, Volume 6, Issue 1, edited by Liang-Jie Zhang, pp. 69-86, copyright 2009 by IGI Publishing (an imprint of IGI Global).

Chapter 5
A Model-Based Approach for Diagnosing Fault in Web Service Processes

Yuhong Yan
Concordia University, Canada

Philippe Dague
University Paris-Sud 11, France

Yannick Pencolé
LAAS-CNRS, France

Marie-Odile Cordier
IRISA, France

ABSTRACT

Web services based on a service-oriented architecture framework provide a suitable technical foundation for business process management and integration. A business process can be composed of a set of Web services that belong to different companies and interact with each other by sending messages. Web service orchestration languages are defined by standard organizations to describe business processes composed of Web services. A business process can fail for many reasons, such as faulty Web services or mismatching messages. It is important to find out which Web services are responsible for a failed business process because we could penalize these Web services and exclude them from the business process in the future. In this paper, we propose a model-based approach to diagnose the faults in a Web service-composed business process. We convert a Web service orchestration language, more specifically BPEL4WS, into synchronized automata, so that we have a formal description of the topology and variable dependency of the business process. After an exception is thrown, the diagnoser can calculate the business process execution trajectory based on the formal model and the observed evolution of the business process. The faulty Web services are deduced from the variable dependency on the execution trajectory. We demonstrate our diagnosis technique with an example.

DOI: 10.4018/978-1-61350-104-7.ch005

1 INTRODUCTION

Web services not only function as middleware for application invocation and integration, but also function as a modeling and management tool for business processes. In a Service Oriented Architecture paradigm, a business process can be composed of Web services distributed over the Internet. This kind of business processes can be flexible and optimal by using the best services from multiple companies. Various Web service process description languages are designed by standard bodies and companies. Among them, Business Process Execution Language for Web Service (BPEL4WS, denoted as BPEL after) (Andrews, Curbera, Dholakia, Goland, & *et.al.,* 2003) is the de facto standard used to describe an executable Web service process. In this paper, we study the behavior of a business process described in BPEL.

As any other systems, a business process can fail. For a Web service process, the symptom of a failure is that exceptions are thrown and the process halts. As the process is composed of multiple Web services, it is important to find out which Web services are responsible for the failure. If we could diagnose the faulty Web services, we could penalize these Web services and exclude them from the business process in the future. The current throw-and-catch mechanism is very preliminary for diagnosing faults. It relies on the developer associating the faults with exceptions at design time. When an exception is thrown, we say certain faults occur. But this mechanism does not guarantee the soundness and the completeness of diagnosis.

In this paper, we propose a model-based approach to diagnose faults in Web service processes. We convert the basic BPEL activities and constructs into synchronized automata whose *states* are presented by the values of the *variables*. The process changes from one state to another by executing an *action*, e.g. assigning variables, receiving or emitting messages in BPEL. The emitting messages can be a triggering *event* for another service to take an action. The diagnosing mechanism is triggered when exceptions are thrown. Using the formal model and the runtime observations from the execution of the process, we can reconstruct the unobservable trajectories of the Web service process. Then the faulty Web services are deduced based on the variable dependency on the trajectories. Studying the fault diagnosis in Web service processes serves the ultimate goal of building self-manageable and self-healing business processes.

This paper is organized as follows: section 2 analyzes the fault management tasks in Web service processes and motivates the use of Model-based Diagnosis (MBD) for Web services monitoring and diagnosis; section 3 presents the principles for MBD; section 4 formally defines the way to generate an automaton model from a BPEL description; section 5 extends the existing MBD techniques for Web service monitoring and diagnosis; section 6 is the related work, and section 7 is the conclusion.

2 ADVANCED FAULT MANAGEMENT FOR WEB SERVICE PROCESSES

A Web service process can run down for many reasons. For example, a composed Web service may be faulty, an incoming message mismatches the interface, or the Internet is down. The *symptom*[1] of a failed Web service process is that *exceptions* are thrown and the process is halted. The current fault handling mechanism is throw-and-catch, similar to programming languages. The *exceptions* are thrown at the places where the process cannot be executed. The *catch* clauses process the exceptions, normally to recover the failure effects by executing predefined actions.

The throw-and-catch mechanism is very preliminary for fault diagnosis. The exception reports where it happened and returns some fault information. The exceptions can be regarded as associated with certain faults. When an exception is thrown, we deduce that its associated fault occurred. Customized exceptions are especially defined for this purpose. This kind of association relations rely on the empirical knowledge of the developer. It may not be a real cause of the exceptions. In addition, there may exist multiple causes of an exception which are unknown to the developer. Therefore, the current throw-and-catch mechanism does not provide sound and complete diagnosis. For example, when a Web service throws an exception about a value in a customer order, not only the one that throws the exception may be faulty, but the one that generates these data may also be faulty. But a Web service exception can only report the Web service where the exception happens with no way to know who generated these data. In addition, all the services that modified the data should be also suspected. Not all of this kind of reasoning is included in the current fault handling mechanism. *A systematic diagnosis mechanism which is based on the model of the Web service process and a solid theoretical foundation needs to be developed.* This is the objective of this paper.

The diagnosis task is to determine the Web services responsible for the exceptions. These Web services will be diagnosed faulty. During the execution of a BPEL process, the exceptions come from the BPEL engine or the infrastructure below, e.g. Apache Tomcat, and Internet. We classify the exceptions into *time-out* exceptions and *business logic* exceptions.

The *time-out* exceptions are due to either a disrupted network or unavailable Web services. If there is a lack of response, we cannot distinguish whether the fault is in the network or at the remote Web service, except if information is transmitted by the network fault management in the first case. Since we cannot diagnose which kind of faults prevent a Web service from responding, we can do little with *time-o*ut exceptions. Indeed what can be done is more statistics at the level of process classes (and not process instances) that will be used by experts to improve the QoS.

The *business logic* exceptions occur while invoking an external Web service and executing BPEL internal activities. For example, mismatching messages (including the type of parameters and the number of parameters mismatching) cause the exceptions to be thrown when the parameters are passed to the remote method. BPEL can throw exceptions indicating the input data is wrong. During execution, the remote service may stop if it cannot process the request. The most common scenarios are the invalid format of the parameters, e.g. the data is not in a valid format, and the data is out of the range. The causes of the exceptions are various and cannot be enumerated. The common thread is that a business logic exception brings back information on the variables that cause the problem. In this paper, our major effort is on diagnosing business logic-related exceptions at the process instances level.

The advanced fault management mechanism serves the ultimate goal to build self-manageable Web service processes. Fault management mechanisms can be among other self-manageable functions. Some functions related to fault management are:

- **Monitoring** the execution of Web service process, and record necessary and sufficient information for online/offline diagnosis. Insufficient information cannot produce correct diagnosis. In Web service processes, we need to keep a chronological record for some of the variables.
- **Detecting** faulty behavior. In other physical tasks, detecting needs to compare the observations with the predictions from the system description to discover the discrepancies. For Web service processes, this task is a trivial one to observe exceptions. But we can imagine building new detectors in order to detect symptoms earlier and "closer" to the causes.

- **Diagnosing** the causes of exceptions. This is the major focus of this paper. See Section 5 for detail.
- **Recovering** from the failure effects. BPEL uses predefined compensation handlers and fault handlers to eliminate failure effects. As failure effects cannot be revealed by the empirical diagnosis mechanism in BPEL, the predefined compensation actions may not be sufficient. A more advanced recovery mechanism has to be defined, based on the model-based diagnosis developed in this paper, although it is not covered in this paper.

3 THE PRINCIPLE OF MODEL-BASED DIAGNOSIS FOR DISCRETE EVENT SYSTEMS

MBD is used to monitor and diagnose both static and dynamic systems. It is an active topic in both Artificial Intelligence (AI) and Control Theory communities. Automated diagnosis has been applied to all kinds of systems, such as communication systems, plant processes and automobiles. The early results in MBD are collected in (Hamscher, Console, & de Kleer, 1992). Let us briefly recall the terminology and notations adopted by the model-based reasoning community.

- **SD:** system description. In the AI-rooted diagnostic techniques, SD is symbolically modeled, e.g. in first-order logic sentences, and in DES as used in this paper.
- **COMPS:** a finite set of constants to represent the components in a system.
- **System:** a pair (*SD*, *COMPS*).
- **D:** a mode assignment to each component in the system. An assignment to a component is a unary predicate. For example, for a component $c_i \in COMPS$, $\neg ab(c_i)$ means c_i working properly, and $ab(c_i)$ means c_i is in an abnormal mode. Obviously a component has different behavior for different modes.
- **Observables:** the variables that can be observed/measured. For a physical system, the observables are the variables measured by sensors, or events reported by alarms, etc.
- **OBS:** a set of observations. They are the values of the *Observables*. They can be a finite set of first-order sentences, e.g. value assignments to some variables.
- **Observed system:** (*SD*, *COMPS*, *OBS*).

Diagnosis is a procedure to determine which components are correct and which components are faulty in order to be consistent with the observations and the system description. Therefore, logically, a consistency-based diagnosis is:

Definition 1. *D is a consistency-based diagnosis for the observed system ⟨SD, COMPS, OBS⟩, if and only if it is a mode assignment and* $SD \cup D \cup OBS \not\models \bot$.

From Definition 1, diagnosis is a mode assignment *D* that makes the union of *SD*, *D* and *OBS* logically consistent. *D* can be partitioned into two parts:

- D_{ok} which is the set of components which are assigned to the $\neg ab$ mode;
- D_f which is the set of components which are assigned to the *ab* mode.

Usually we are interested in those diagnoses which involve a minimal set of faults, i.e., the diagnoses for which D_f is minimal for set inclusion.

Definition 2. *A diagnosis D is minimal if and only if there is no other diagnosis D' for ⟨SD, COMPS, OBS⟩ such that* $D_f' \subset D_f$

The dual concept of a diagnosis is a conflict.

Definition 3. *A set $CO \subseteq COMPS$ is a conflict for $\langle SD, COMPS, OBS\rangle$, if and only if $SD \cup OBS \cup \{\neg ab(C) | C \in CO\} \models \perp$.*

Similarly a minimal conflict is a conflict that is minimal for set inclusion. In (Reiter, 1987), Reiter introduces the hitting set algorithm for computing minimal diagnoses using the set of conflicts.

Definition 4. *(Reiter, 1987) Let C be a collection of sets. A hitting set for C is a set $H \subseteq \cup \cup S_{\in C} S$ such that $H \cap S \neq \emptyset$ for each $S \in C$. A hitting set is minimal if no proper subset of it is a hitting set.*

Theorem 1. *(Reiter, 1987) A set $D \subseteq COMPS$ is a minimal diagnosis for $\langle SD, COMPS, OBS\rangle$ if and only if D is a minimal hitting set for the collection of conflicts (or equivalently for the collection of minimal conflicts).*

When the system description is in first order logic, the computation of all diagnoses is more generally rooted in automated reasoning, relying on prime implicates of SD ∪OBS in the form of disjuncts of *ab*-literals, and on their prime implicants in the form of conjuncts of *ab*-literals (Hamscher *et al.*, 1992).

When applying MBD, a formal system description is needed. Therefore, we need to study the proper formal model for Web service processes. As the interactions between Web services are driven by message passing, and message passing can be seen as discrete events, we consider the Discrete Event Systems (DES) suitable to model Web service processes. Many discrete event models, such as Petri nets, process algebras and automata, can be used for Web service process modeling. These models were invented for different purposes, but now they share many common techniques, such as symbolic representation (in addition to graph representation in some models) and similar symbolic operations. In this paper, we present a method to represent Web service processes described in BPEL as automata in Section 4. Here we introduce MBD techniques for automata. A classic definition of deterministic automaton is as below:

Definition 5. *An automaton Γ is a tuple $\Gamma = \langle X, \Sigma, T, I, F\rangle$ where:*

- *X is a finite set of states;*
- *Σ is a finite set of events;*
- *$T \subseteq X \times \Sigma \rightarrow X$ is a finite set of transitions;*
- *$I \subseteq X$ is a finite set of initial states;*
- *$F \subseteq X$ is a finite set of final states.*

Definitions 6, 7 and 8 are some basic concepts and operations about automata.

Definition 6. *Synchronization between two automata $\Gamma_1 = \langle X_1, \Sigma_1, T_1, I_1, F_1\rangle$ and $\Gamma_2 = \langle X_2, \Sigma_2, T_2, I_2, F_2\rangle$, with $\Sigma_1 \cap \Sigma_2 \neq \emptyset$, produces an automaton $\Gamma = \Gamma_1 || \Gamma_2$, where $\Gamma = \langle X_1 \times X_2, \Sigma_1 \cup \Sigma_2, T, I_1 \times I_2, F_1 \times F_2\rangle$, with:*

$T((x_1, x_2), e) = (T_1(x_1, e), T_2(x_2, e))$, *if* $e \in \Sigma_1 \cap \Sigma_2$,
$T((x_1, x_2), e) = (T_1(x_1, e), x_2)$, *if* $e \in \Sigma_1 \backslash \Sigma_2$
$T((x_1, x_2), e) = (x_1, T_2(x_2, e))$, *if* $e \in \Sigma_2 \backslash \Sigma_1$

Assume $s = \Sigma_1 \cap \Sigma_2$ is the joint event set of Γ_1 and Γ_2, Γ can also be written as $\Gamma = \Gamma_1 ||_s \Gamma_2$.

Example 1. *In Figure 1, Γ_1 and Γ_2 are two automata. The third one Γ_3 is produced by synchronizing Γ_1 and Γ_2.*

Definition 7. *A trajectory of an automaton is a path of contiguous states and transitions in the automaton that begins at an initial state and ends at a final state of the automaton.*

Example 2. *The trajectories in the automaton Γ_3 in Figure 1 can be represented as the two formulas below, in which []* means the content in [] repeated 0 or more times:*

Figure 1. An example of synchronization

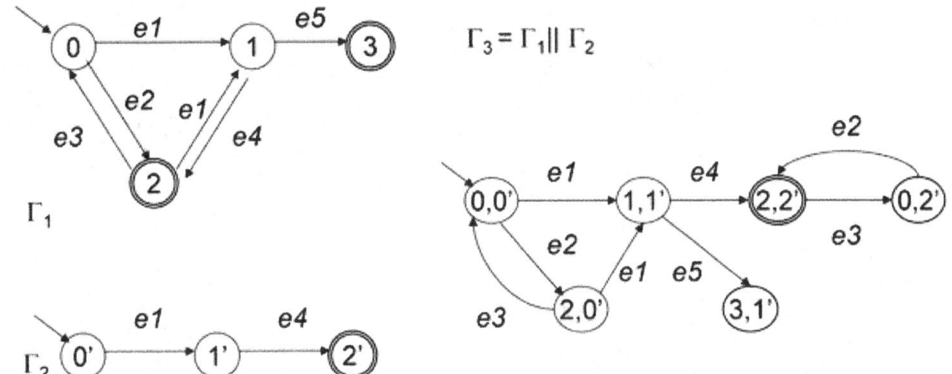

$[(0,\ 0') \xrightarrow{e2} (2,\ 0') \xrightarrow{e3}]^*[(0,\ 0') \xrightarrow{e1} (1, 1') \xrightarrow{e4} (2, 2')][\xrightarrow{e3} (0, 2') \xrightarrow{e_2} (2, 2')]^*$,

$[(0,\ 0') \xrightarrow{e2} (2,\ 0') \xrightarrow{e3}]^*[(0,\ 0') \xrightarrow{e2} (2, 0') \xrightarrow{e1} (1, 1') \xrightarrow{e4} (2, 2')][\xrightarrow{e3} (0, 2') \xrightarrow{e2} (2, 2')]^*$.

Definition 8. *Concatenation between two automata* $\Gamma_1 = \langle X_1, \Sigma_1, T_1, I_1, F_1\rangle$ *and* $\Gamma 2 = \langle X_2, \Sigma_2, T_2, I_2, F_2\rangle$, *with* $\Sigma_1 \cap \Sigma_2 = \varnothing$ *and* $F_1 \cap I_2 \neq \varnothing$, *produces an automaton* $\Gamma = \Gamma_1 \circ \Gamma_2$, *where* $\Gamma = \langle X_1 \cup X_2, \Sigma_1 \cup \Sigma_2, T_1 \cup T_2, I_1, F_2 \cup (F_1 \backslash I_2)\rangle$.

The principle of diagnosis using DES models was founded by (Sampath, Sengupta, Lafortune, Sinnamohideen, & Teneketzis, 1995) and (Cordier & Thiébaux, 1994). System description *SD* models both correct and faulty behavior of a system. Assume system description *SD* is an automaton Γ, and observed events in chronological order are represented as another automaton *OBS*. Assume the joint event set of Γ and *OBS* is s. In this context, we call Diagnosis the automaton produced by synchronizing Γ and *OBS*:

$$\text{Diagnosis} = \Gamma \|_s \text{OBS} \quad (1)$$

From the definition of synchronization, it is easy to prove that each trajectory in Diagnosis explains the sequence of observations in the sense that observable events in the trajectory occur in the identical chronological order as in *OBS*, i.e.:

$$\text{Diagnosis} \models OBS \quad (2)$$

Therefore, Diagnosis for DES is what is called an *abductive diagnosis* in MBD theory.

Example 3. *In Figure 1,* Γ_1 *is a system description in which* e_2 *and* e_3 *represent occurrences of faults which are not observable directly (otherwise, the diagnosis would be trivial).* Γ_2 *is an observation in which two events* e_1 *and* e_4 *are observed sequentially. The Diagnosis is* Γ_3.

It is not so easy to compute the trajectories of Diagnosis because there are several possibilities for trajectory expansion that can arise from partial observations. We need to get all the possible trajectories. For trajectory expansion, people basically use search algorithms. Other algorithms, rooted from search algorithms, can also be used. For example, planning tools and model checking tools are used for trajectory expansion. Of course, these tools have to be modified in order to get complete trajectories.

Diagnostic process is almost achieved when Diagnosis is obtained, because Diagnosis explains the observations based on SD (as an automaton Γ).

Figure 2. An example of Diagnosis

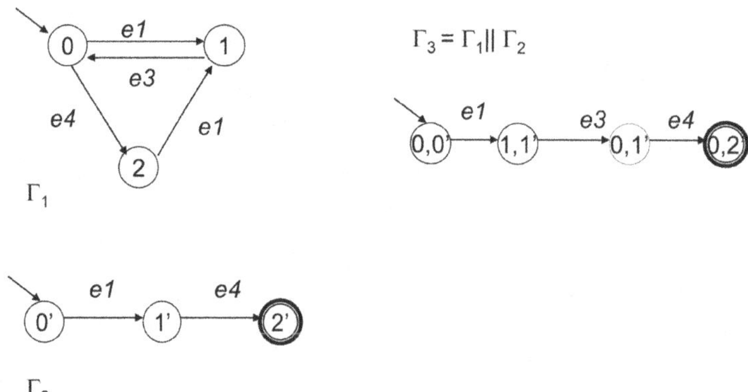

If we want to obtain diagnoses {D} as mode assignments as in the consistency-based framework, we need a mapping function *f*: Diagnosis → {*D*}. Each trajectory *t* in Diagnosis is mapped into a *D*, i.e. $t \rightarrow D$. As domain knowledge, a faulty event e_f is known to be associated with a fault mode $F(c_i)$ of some component c_i, i.e. $e_f \leftrightarrow F(c_i)^2$. If e_f is included in a trajectory *t*, we deduce that the correspondent fault $F(c_i)$ occurs. Formally,

Proposition 1. *Assume t is a trajectory in Diagnosis, then* $t \rightarrow D$ *where mode assignment D is defined by* $D_f = \{c_j \mid e_f \leftrightarrow F(c_j) \text{ and } e_f \in t\}$ *(and thus* $D_{ok} = \{c_j \mid c_j \in COMPS \backslash D_f\}$*).*

As each fault event maps to a fault, practically we need only to know the set of faulty events in a trajectory:

$$t \rightarrow \{e_f \mid e_f \in t\} \quad (3)$$

From (3), if we know $\{e_f\}$, we can easily get D_f and thus *D*. In the following, we use $\{e_f\}$ to represent a D_f. As there are often multiple trajectories $\{t^i\}$ in Diagnosis, the diagnoses $\{D^i\}$ are also multiple:

Proposition 2. *Assume* $\{t_i\}$ *is the set of all trajectories in Diagnosis, then* $\{t^i\} \rightarrow \{D^i\}$*, where* $D_f^i = \{c_j \mid e_f^i \leftrightarrow F(c_j) \text{ and } e_f^i \in t^i\} \subseteq D^i$.

In general, we are interested only in minimal diagnoses, i.e. in Proposition 2 we keep only those D_f^i which are minimal.

Example 4. *From Diagnosis* Γ_3 *inFigure 1, we get 2 kinds of possible sequences of faulty events:*

{[e2, e3], [e3, e2]*}, {[e2, e3]*, e2, [e3, e2]*}. From the above sequences, we can get three diagnoses: {}, {e2}, {e2, e3}. The minimal diagnosis is {}, which means no fault.*

In Example 4, different trajectories give us different diagnoses. It can be no faults, or *e*2 (mapped to its fault), or both *e*2 and *e*3. They are all sound. Adding more observables is a way to clarify the ambiguity. To determine the observables for diagnosing a certain fault is the problem of diagnosability which is not covered in this paper. Below is another example without ambiguity:

Example 5. *InFigure 2,* Γ_1*is SD and* Γ_2*is OBS.* Γ_3*is Diagnosis. Since e3 is within the only trajectory, we can deduce that a fault represented by e3 occurred.*

We need to point out that the existing diagnosis methods for physical systems modeled as DES are not in general suitable for Web service processes. First, we cannot enumerate faults in Web service environments because we do not know how a Web service can be faulty if it belongs to another company. Second, it is relatively easy to keep a record for how the software is executed by recording any selected variables. In contrast, it is more difficult to insert a sensor in a physical system. Therefore it is very difficult to reconstruct the trajectories for a physical system, but it is not a key issue for diagnosing a Web service process. We will discuss the diagnosis of Web services in Section 5.

Several advances have recently been made: the decentralized diagnoser approach (Pencolé & Cordier, 2005) (a diagnosis system based on several interacting DESs); the incremental diagnosis approach (Grastien, Cordier, & Largouët, 2005) (a monitoring system that online updates diagnosis over time given new observations); active system approaches (Baroni, Lamperti, Pogliano, & Zanella, 1999) (approaches that deal with hierarchical and asynchronized DESs); and diagnosis on reconfigurable systems (Grastien, Cordier, & Largouët, 2004). The existing techniques, such as the diagnoser approach (Pencolé, Cordier, & Rozé 2002) or the silent closure (Baroni *et a*l., 1999), reconstruct the unobservable behavior of the system that are required to compute diagnoses.

4 MODELING WEB SERVICE PROCESSES WITH DISCRETE-EVENT SYSTEMS

4.1 Description of the Web Service Processes

BPEL is an XML-based orchestration language developed by IBM and recognized by OASIS (Andrews et al., 2003). BPEL is a so-called executable language because it defines the internal behavior of a Web service process, as compared to choreography languages that define only the interactions among the Web services and are not executable.

BPEL defines fifteen activity types. Some of them are *basic activities*; the others are *structured activities*. Among the basic activities, the most important are the following:

1. the ⟨receive⟩ activity is for accepting the triggering message from another Web service;
2. the ⟨reply⟩ activity is for returning the response to its requestor;
3. the ⟨invoke⟩ activity is for invoking another Web service.

The structured activities define the execution orders of the activities inside their scopes. For example:

- Ordinary sequential control between activities is provided by ⟨sequence⟩.
- Concurrency and synchronization between activities is provided by ⟨flow⟩.
- Loop is provided by ⟨while⟩.
- Nondeterministic choice based on external events is provided by ⟨pick⟩ and ⟨switch⟩.

Execution orders are also modified by defining the synchronization links between two activities (cf. Section 4.3.3). Normally, BPEL has one entry point to start the process and one point to exit, though multiple entry points are allowed. The variables in BPEL are actually the Simple Object Access Protocol (SOAP) messages defined in Web Service Description Language (WSDL). Therefore, the variables in BPEL are objects that have several attributes (called "parts" in WSDL).

4.2 An Example: the Loan Approval Process

Example 6. *The loan approval process is an example described in the BPEL Specification 1.1 (Andrews et al., 2003). It is diagrammed in Figure 3.*

Figure 3. A loan approval process. Activities are represented in shaded boxes. The inVar and outVar are respectively the input and output variables of an activity

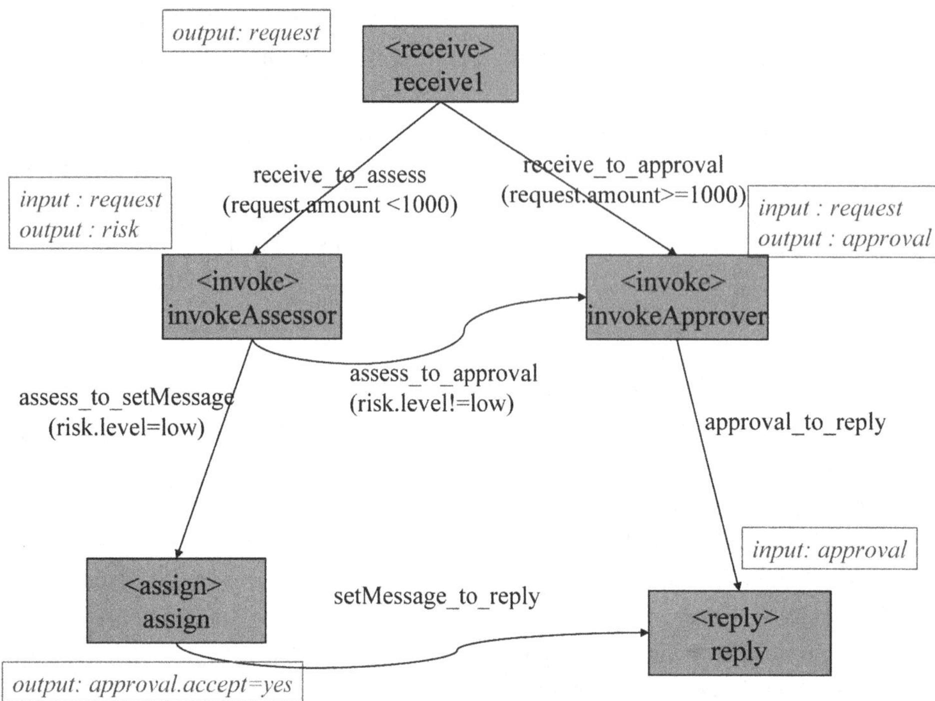

This process contains five activities (big shaded blocks). An activity involves a set of input and output variables (dotted box besides each activity). All the variables are of composite type. The edges show the execution order of the activities. When two edges are issued from the same activity, only one edge that satisfies a triggering condition (shown on the edge) will be activated. In this example, the process is triggered when a ⟨receive⟩ activity named *receive1* receives a message of a predefined type. First, *receive1* initializes a variable *request*. Then, *receive1* dispatches the request to two ⟨invoke⟩ activities, *invokeAssessor* and *invokeApprover*, depending on the amount of the loan. In the case where the amount is large (*request.amount* >= 1000), *invokeApprover* is called for a decision. In the case where the amount is small (*request.amount* < 1000), *invokeAssessor* is called for risk assessment. If *invokeAssessor* returns with an assessment that the risk level is low (*risk.level* = *low*), a reply is prepared by an ⟨assign⟩ activity and later sent out by a ⟨reply⟩ activity. If the risk level is not low, *invokeApprover* is invoked for a final decision. The result from *invokeApprover* is sent to the client by the ⟨reply⟩ activity.

4.3 Modeling Web Services Process with Discrete-Event Systems

A Web service process defined in BPEL is a composition of activities. We are going to model a BPEL activity as an automaton. A BPEL code has a finite set of variables and a BPEL state is associated with an assignment of these variables. A BPEL activity is triggered when its initial state satisfies a finite set of triggering conditions which is a certain assignment of variables. After an activity is executed, the values of the state variables are changed. We need to extend the classic automaton definition to include the operations on state variables.

Assume a BPEL process has a finite set of variables $V = \{v_1,..., v_n\}$, and the domain $D = \{D_1,..., D_n\}$ for V is real values R or arbitrary strings. $C = \{c_1,..., c_m\}$ is a finite set of constraints. A constraint c_j of some arity k is defined as a subset of the cartesian product over variables $\{v_{ji},..., v_{jk}\} \subseteq V$, i.e. $c_j \subseteq D_{jl} \times \cdots \times D_{jk}$, or a first order formula over $\{v_{ji},..., v_{jk}\}$. A constraint restricts the possible values of the k variables.

A BPEL state s is defined as an assignment of variables. A BPEL transition t is an operation on the state s_i, i.e., $(s_j, post(V_2)) = t(s_i, e, pre(V_1))$, where $V_1 \subseteq V$, $V_2 \subseteq V$, $pre(V_1) \subseteq C$ is a set of preconditions that s_i has to satisfy and $post(V_2) \subseteq C$ is a set of post-conditions that the successor state s_j will satisfy. In another word, the transition t is triggered only when the starting state satisfies the preconditions, and the operation of this transition results in a state that satisfies the post-conditions. If a state s satisfies a constraint c, we annotate as c ∧ s. Then, the semantics of transition t is also represented as:

$$t{:}(s_i \wedge pre(V_1)) \xrightarrow{e} (s_j \wedge post(V_2)).$$

Definition 9. *A BPEL activity is an automaton* $\langle X, \Sigma, T, I, F, C\rangle$, *where C is a constraint set that defines states X and* $T{:}\ X \times \Sigma \times 2^C \rightarrow X \times 2^C$.

4.3.1 Modeling Basic Activities

In the following, we enumerate the model for each basic activity.

Activity ⟨receive⟩: $\langle\{s_o, s_f\}, \{received\}, \{t\}, \{s_o\}, \{s_f\}, C\rangle$ with $t{:}\ (s_o \wedge SoapMsg.type = MsgType) \xrightarrow{received} (s_f \wedge RecMsg = SoapMsg)$, where *MsgType* is a predefined message type. If the incoming message *SoapMsg* has the predefined type, *RecMsg* is initialized as *SoapMsg*.

Activity ⟨reply⟩: $\langle\{s_o, s_f\}, \{replied\}, \{t\}, \{s_o\}, \{s_f\}, C\rangle$ with $t{:}\ (s_o \wedge exists(RepMsg)) \xrightarrow{replied} (SoapMsg = RepMsg \wedge s_f)$, where *exists(RepMsg)* is the predicate checking that the replay message *RepMsg* is initialized. *SoapMsg* is the message on the wire.

Activity ⟨invoke⟩

Synchronous invocation: $\langle\{s_o, wait, s_f\}, \{invoked, received\}, \{t_1, t_2\}, \{s_o\}, \{s_f\}, C\rangle$ with $t_1{:}\ (s_o \wedge exists(InVar)) \xrightarrow{invoked} (wait)$, and $t_2{:}\ (wait \wedge SoapMsg.type = MsgType) \xrightarrow{received} (s_f \wedge exists(OutVar))$ where *InVar* and *OutVar* are the input and output variables.

Asynchronous invocation: $\langle\{s_o, s_f\}, \{invoked\}, \{t\}, \{s_o\}, \{s_f\}, C\rangle$ with $t{:}\ (s_o \wedge exists(InVar)) \xrightarrow{invoked} (s_f)$, asynchronous invocation does not wait for a return message.

Activity ⟨assign⟩: $\langle\{s_o, s_f\}, \{assigned\}, \{t\}, \{s_o\}, \{s_f\}, C\rangle$ with $t{:}\ (s_o \wedge exists(InVar)) \xrightarrow{assigned} (s_f \wedge OutVar = InVar)$

Activity ⟨throw⟩: $\langle\{s_o, s_f\}, \{thrown\}, \{t\}, \{s_o\}, \{s_f\}, C\rangle$ with $t{:}\ (s_o \wedge Fault.mode = Off) \xrightarrow{thrown} (s_f \wedge Fault.mode = On)$

Activity ⟨wait⟩: $\langle\{s_o, wait, s_f\}, \{waiting, waited\}, \{t_1, t_2\}, \{s_o\}, \{s_f\}, C\rangle$ with $t_1{:}\ (s_o \wedge Wait\_mode = Off) \xrightarrow{waiting} (wait \wedge Wait\_mode = On)$ $t_2{:}\ (wait \wedge Wait\_mode = On) \xrightarrow{waited} (s_f \wedge Wait\_mode = Off)$

Figure 4. The automata for ⟨switch⟩ and ⟨while⟩

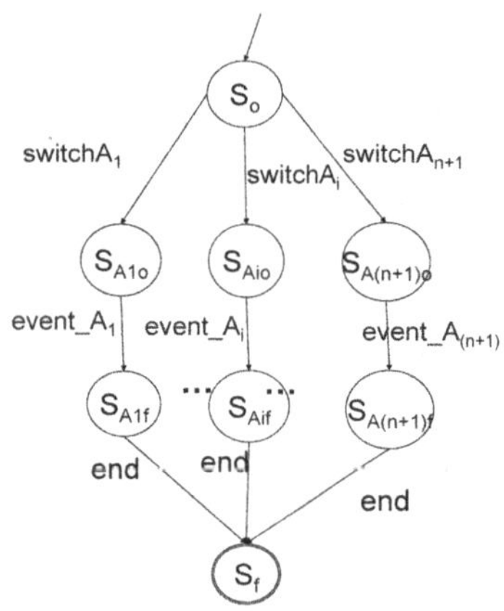

(a)The automaton for ⟨switch⟩

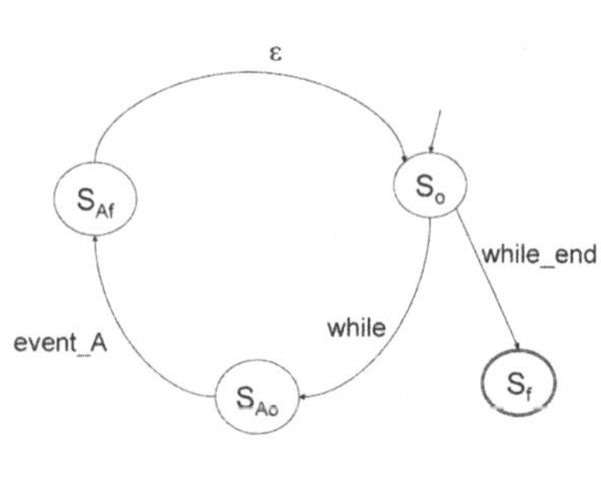

(b)The automaton for ⟨while⟩

This model is not temporal. We do not consider time, so the notion of delay is not considered in this activity.

Activity ⟨empty⟩: $\langle \{s_o, s_f\}, \{empty\}, \{t\}, \{s_o\}, \{s_f\}, C\rangle$

$t{:}\ (s_o) \xrightarrow{empty} (s_f)$

4.3.2 Modeling Structured Activities

Structured activities nest other activities. We can model the structured activities as automata. Note that any automaton modeling a basic activity or a structured activity has only one initial state and one final state. In the following are the automata for the structured activities.

Sequence

A ⟨sequence⟩ can nest *n* activities ⟨A_i⟩ in its scope. These activities are executed in sequential order. Assume ⟨A_i⟩: $\langle S_{Ai}, \Sigma_{Ai}, T_{Ai}, \{s_{Aio}\}, \{s_{Aif}\}, C_{Ai}\rangle$, $i \in \{1,..., n\}$.

Activity ⟨sequence⟩: $\langle \{s_o, s_f\} \cup \bigcup S_{Ai}, \{end\} \cup \bigcup \{callA_i\} \cup \bigcup \Sigma_{Ai}, \{t_i\} \cup \bigcup T_{Ai}, \{s_o\}, \{s_f\}, \bigcup C_{Ai}\rangle$ with

$t_0{:}\ (s_o) \xrightarrow{callA_1} (s_{A1o})$

$t_i{:}\ (s_{Aif}) \xrightarrow{callA_{i+1}} (s_{Ai+1o})$

$t_n{:}\ (s_{Anf}) \xrightarrow{end} (s_f)$

If assume $s_o = s_{A1o}$, $s_f = s_{Anf}$, and $s_{Aif} = s_{Ai+1o}$, for $i = [1,..., n\text{-}1]$, a short representation of ⟨sequence⟩ is the concatenation of the nested activities A1∘A2 ⋯∘An.

Switch

Assume a ⟨switch⟩ has *n* ⟨case⟩ branches and one ⟨otherwise⟩ branch (see Figure 4(a)). Assume ⟨A_i⟩ : $\langle S_{Ai}, \Sigma_{Ai}, T_{Ai}, \{s_{Aio}\}, \{s_{Aif}\}, C_{Ai}\rangle$, $i \in \{1,..., n+1\}$.

Activity ⟨switch⟩: $\langle \{s_o, s_f\} \cup \bigcup S_{Ai}, \{end\} \cup \bigcup \{switchA_i\} \cup \bigcup \Sigma_{Ai}, \bigcup \{t_{io}\} \cup \bigcup \{t_{if}\} \cup \bigcup T_{Ai}, \{s_o\}, \{s_f\}, \bigcup C_{Ai}, \cup \bigcup pre(V_i)\rangle$.

Assume V_1,..., V_n are variable sets on *n* ⟨case⟩ branches, $pre(V_1)$,..., $pre(V_n)$ are the constraints defined by the attributes condition in ⟨case⟩. The transitions are defined as below:

$t_{io}{:}\ (s_o \wedge \neg pre(V_1) \wedge \cdots \wedge pre(V_i) \cdots \wedge \neg pre(V_n)) \xrightarrow{switchA_i} (s_{Aio}),\ \forall i \in \{1, ..., n\}$

$t_{(n+1)o}{:}\ (s_o \wedge \neg\ pre(V_1) \wedge \cdots \wedge \neg\ pre(V_i)$

Figure 5. Build concurrency as synchronized DES pieces

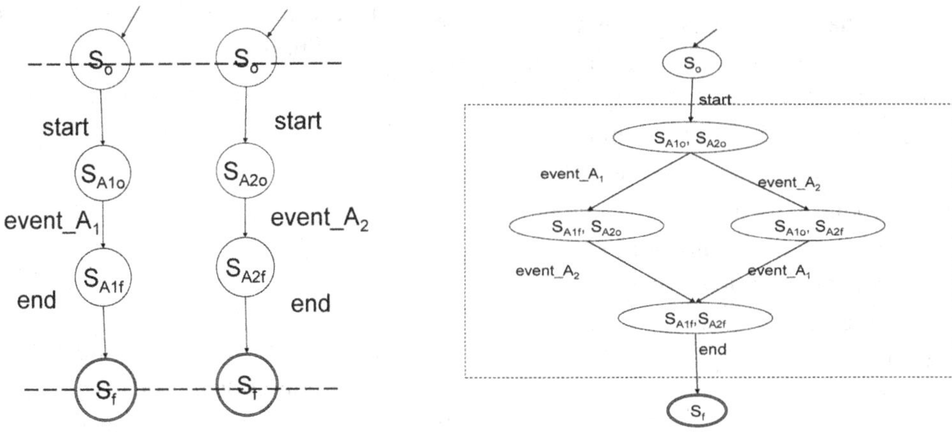

(a) Concurrency branches for DES pieces (b) The joint DES model

$\cdots \wedge \neg pre(V_n)) \xrightarrow{switchA_{n+1}} (s_{A(n+1)o})$

$t_{if}: (s_{Aif}) \xrightarrow{end} (s_f), \forall i \in \{1, \ldots, n+1\}$

While Assume ⟨while⟩ nests an activity ⟨A⟩: $\langle S_A, \Sigma_A, T_A, \{s_{Ao}\}, \{s_{Af}\}, C\rangle$ (see Figure 4(b)).

Activity ⟨while⟩: $\{s_o, s_f\} \cup S_A$, $\{while, while\_end\} \cup \Sigma_A$, $\{t_o, t_f, t\} \cup T_A$, $\{s_o\}$, $\{s_f\}$, $C \cup pre(W)\rangle$.

Assume W is a variable set, and $pre(W)$ is the constraint defined by the attribute condition in ⟨while⟩.

$t_o: (s_o \wedge pre(W)) \xrightarrow{while} (s_{Ao})$

$t_f: (s_o \wedge \neg pre(W)) \xrightarrow{while\_end} (s_f)$

$t: (s_{Af}) \xrightarrow{\varepsilon} (s_o)$

Flow

A ⟨flow⟩ can nest n activities $\langle A_i\rangle$ in its scope. These activities are executed concurrently. Assume $\langle A_i\rangle : \langle S_{Ai}, \Sigma_{Ai}, T_{Ai}, \{s_{Aio}\}, \{s_{Aif}\}, C_{Ai}\rangle$, i $\in \{1,\ldots, n\}$.

Activity ⟨flow⟩: $\langle \{s_o, s_f\} \cup \bigcup S_{Ai}$, $\{start, end\} \cup \bigcup \Sigma_{Ai}$, $\bigcup \{t_{io}, t_{if}\} \cup \bigcup T_{Ai}$, $\{s_o\}$, $\{s_f\}$, $\bigcup C_{Ai}\rangle$ with

$t_{io}: (s_o) \xrightarrow{start} (s_{Aio})$

$t_{if}: (s_{Aif}) \xrightarrow{end} (s_f)$

Notice that the semantic of automata cannot model concurrency. We actually model the n-paralleled branches into n automata and define synchronization events to build their connections. The principle is illustrated in Figure 5. At the left, each branch is modeled as an individual automaton. The entry state s_o and the end state s_f are duplicated in each branch. Events *start* and *end* are the synchronization events. At the right is the automaton resulted by synchronization. More complicated case in joining the paralleled branches is discussed in subsection 4.3.3. The key point in reasoning about decentralized automata is to postpone the synchronization until a synthesis result is needed, in order to avoid the state explosion problem (Pencolé et al., 2002)(Pencolé & Cordier, 2005). In Web service diagnosis, it is the situation (cf. subsection 5.1).

Pick

Assume a ⟨Pick⟩ has n ⟨onMessage⟩ and one ⟨onAlarm⟩ branches. ⟨onMessage⟩ branches are triggered by predefined events. Assume activities $\{A_1,..., A_n\}$ are corresponding to the n branches respectively. ⟨onAlarm⟩ branch is triggered by a time-out event produced by a timer. Assume activity A_{n+1} is corresponding to ⟨onAlarm⟩ branch. Exactly one branch will be selected based on the occurrence of the event associated with before any others. Assume $\langle A_i\rangle$: $\langle S_{Ai}, \Sigma_{Ai}, T_{Ai}, \{s_{Aio}\}, \{s_{Aif}\}, C_{Ai}\rangle$, i ∈ {1,..., n+1}.

Activity ⟨pick⟩: $\langle \{s_o, s_f\} \cup \bigcup S_{Ai}, \bigcup \{start_{Ai}\} \cup \{end\} \cup \bigcup \Sigma_{Ai}, \bigcup \{t_{io}, t_{if}\} \cup \bigcup T_{Ai}, \{s_o\}, \{s_f\}, \bigcup C_{Ai} \cup \bigcup exists(event_{Ai})\rangle$ with

t_{io}: $(s_o \wedge exists(event_{Ai})) \xrightarrow{start_{Ai}} (s_{Aio})$

t_{if}: $(s_{Aif}) \xrightarrow{end} (s_f)$

4.3.3 Synchronization Links of Activities

Each BPEL activity can optionally nest the standard elements ⟨source⟩ and ⟨target⟩. The XML grammar is defined as:

```
<source linkName ="ncname" tran-
sitionCondition = "bool -
expr"?/><target linkName ="ncname"/>
```

A pair of ⟨source⟩ and ⟨target⟩ defines a link which connects two activities. The target activity must wait until the source activity finishes. Therefore, links define the sequential orders of activities. When one ⟨flow⟩ contains two parallel activities which are connected by a link, the two activities become sequentially ordered. An activity may have multiple ⟨source⟩ or ⟨target⟩ elements. Links can express richer logics, but they make the processes more difficult to analyse.

⟨source⟩ can be modeled similarly like an ⟨activity⟩, with "*transitionCondition*" as the triggering condition.

Activity ⟨source⟩: $\langle \{s_o, s_f\}, \{\varepsilon\}, \{t\}, \{s_o\}, \{s_f\}, transitionCondition\rangle$ with

t: $(s_o \wedge transitionCondition) \xrightarrow{\varepsilon} (s_f)$,

When an activity is the ⟨target⟩ of multiple links, a join condition is used to specify how these links can join. The join condition is defined within the activity. BPEL specification defines standard attributes for this activity:

```
<activityName ="ncname", joinCondi-
tion ="bool - expr", suppressJoinF
ailure ="yes|no"/>
```

In this case, the synchronization event end as in Figure 5(a) is removed. If the ending state of ⟨flow⟩ is the starting state s_o' of the next activity, the precondition of s_o' is the *joinCondition*. For example, either of the endings of the two branches can trigger the next activity can be represented as: $s_o' \wedge (exists(s_{A1f}) \vee exists(s_{A2f}))$.

4.4 Modeling the Loan Approval Process

In this section, we present the complete DES model for the process in Example 6.

***Example** 7. The loan approval process in Example 6 contains five activities: ⟨receive1⟩, ⟨invokeAssessor⟩, ⟨invokeApprover⟩, ⟨assign⟩, ⟨reply⟩. The five activities are contained in a ⟨flow⟩. Six links, ⟨receive_to_assess⟩, ⟨receive_to_approval⟩, ⟨assess_to_setMessage⟩, ⟨assess_to_approval⟩, ⟨approval_to_reply⟩, and ⟨setMessage_to_reply⟩, connect the activities and change the concurrent orders to sequential*

Figure 6. Automaton modeling loan approval process

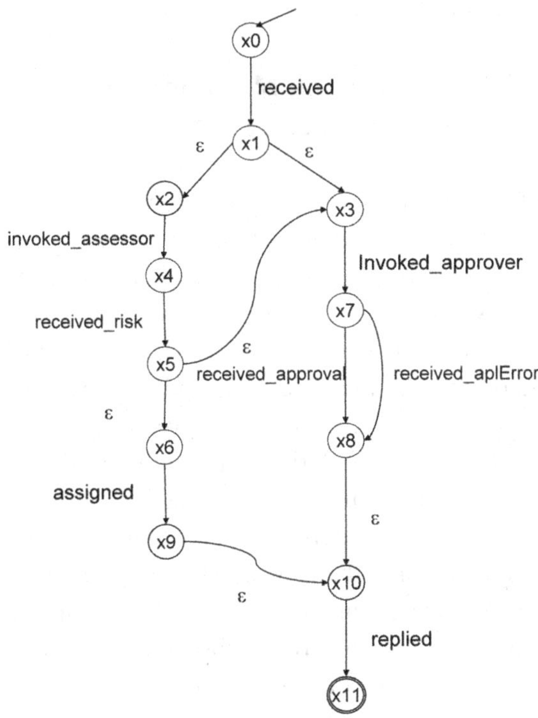

orders between the activities. In this special case, there are actually no concurrent activities. Therefore, for clarity, the event caused by ⟨flow⟩ is not shown. Assume the approver may return an error message due to an unknown error. Below is the formal representation of the process (also reference toFigure 6).

⟨receive1⟩ = $\langle \{x_0, x_1\}, \{received\}, \{t_1\}, \{x_0\}, \{x_1\}, C\rangle$, with t_1: $(x_0 \wedge SoapMsg.type = MsgType) \xrightarrow{received} (x_1 \wedge request = SoapMsg)$, where

MsgType is a predefined message type. If the incoming message *SoapMsg* has the predefined type, request is initialized as *SoapMsg*.

⟨receive_to_assess⟩ = $\langle \{x_1, x_2\}, \{\varepsilon\}, \{t_2\}, \{x_1\}, \{x_2\}, C\rangle$, with t_2: $(x_1 \wedge request.amount < 1000) \xrightarrow{\varepsilon} (x_2)$.

⟨receive_to_approval⟩ = $\langle \{x_1, x_3\}, \{\varepsilon\}, \{t_3\}, \{x_1\}, \{x_3\}, C\rangle$, with t_3: $(x_1 \wedge request.amount \geq 1000) \xrightarrow{\varepsilon} (x_3)$.

⟨invokeAssessor⟩ = $\langle \{x_2, x_4, x_5\}, \{invoked\_assessor, received\_risk\}, \{t_4, t_5\}, \{x_2\}, \{x_5\}, C\rangle$ with t_4: $(x_2 \wedge InVar = request) \xrightarrow{invoked\_assessor} (x_4)$, and t_5: $(x_4) \xrightarrow{received\_risk} (x_5 \wedge OutVar = risk)$ where *InVar* and *OutVar* are the input and output variables.

⟨assess_to_setMessage⟩ = $\langle \{x_5, x_6\}, \{\varepsilon\}, \{t_6\}, \{x_5\}, \{x_6\}, C\rangle$, with t_6: $(x_5 \wedge risk.level = low) \xrightarrow{\varepsilon} (x_6)$.

⟨assess_to_approval⟩ = $\langle \{x_5, x_3\}, \{\varepsilon\}, \{t_7\}, \{x_5\}, \{x_3\}, C\rangle$, with t_7: $(x_5 \wedge risk.level = high) \xrightarrow{\varepsilon} (x_3)$.

⟨invokeApprover⟩ = $\langle \{x_3, x_7, x_8\}, \{invoked\_approver, received\_approval, received\_aplError\}, \{t_8, t_9, t_e\}, \{x_3\}, \{x_8\}, C\rangle$ with t_8: $(x_3 \wedge InVar = request) \xrightarrow{invoke\_approver} (x_7)$, and t_9: $(x_7) \xrightarrow{received\_approval} (x_8 \wedge OutVar = approval)$, and t_e: $(x_7) \xrightarrow{received\_aplError} (x_8 \wedge OutVar = errorMessage)$ where *InVar* and *OutVar* are the input and output variables.

⟨assign⟩: $\langle \{x_6, x_9\}, \{assigned\}, \{t_{10}\}, \{x_6\}, \{x_9\}, C\rangle$ with t_{10}: $(x_6) \xrightarrow{assigned} (x_9 \wedge approval.accept = yes)$

$\langle$setMessage_to_reply$\rangle$ = $\langle\{x_9, x_{10}\}, \{\varepsilon\}, \{t_{11}\}, \{x_9\}, \{x_{10}\}, C\rangle$, with $t_{11}: (x_9) \xrightarrow{\varepsilon} (x_{10})$.

$\langle$approval_to_reply$\rangle$ = $\langle\{x_8, x_{10}\}, \{\varepsilon\}, \{t_{12}\}, \{x_8\}, \{x_{10}\}, C\rangle$, with $t_{12}: (x_8) \xrightarrow{\varepsilon} (x_{10})$.

$\langle$reply$\rangle$: $\langle\{x_{10}, x_{11}\}, \{replied\}, \{t_{13}\}, \{x_{10}\}, \{x_{11}\}, C\rangle$ with $t_{13}: (x_{10} \wedge exists(approval)) \xrightarrow{replied} (x_{11} \wedge SoapMsg = approval)$, where *SoapMsg* is the message on the wire.

5 MODEL-BASED DIAGNOSIS FOR WEB SERVICE PROCESSES

A Web service process can run down for many reasons. For example, a composed Web service may be faulty, an incoming message mismatches the interface, or the Internet is down. The diagnosis task is to determine the Web services responsible for the exceptions. These Web services will be diagnosed faulty. In this paper, our major effort is on diagnosing business logic-related exceptions.

In our framework, *COMPS* is made up of all the basic activities of the Web service process considered, and *OBS* is made up of the exceptions thrown and the events of the executed activities. These events can be obtained by the monitoring function of a BPEL engine. A typical correct model for an activity $\langle A\rangle$ is thus:

$$\neg ab(A) \wedge \neg ab(A.input) \Rightarrow \neg \mathrm{ab(A.output)} \qquad (4)$$

For facilitating diagnosis, the BPEL engine has to be extended for the following tasks: 1) record the events emitted by executed activities; 2) record the input and output SOAP messages; and 3) record the exceptions and trigger the diagnosis function when the first exception is received. *Diagnosing* is triggered on the first occurred exception[3]. The MBD approach developed relies on the following three steps with the techniques we introduced in the content above.

1) A Prior Process Modeling and Variable Dependency Analysis

All the variables in BPEL are global variables, i.e. they are accessible by all the activities. An activity can be regarded as a function that takes input variables and produces output variables. An activity has two kinds of relation to its input and output variables: defining and utilizing. We use *Def(A, V)* and *Util(A, V)* to present the relation that activity *A* defines variable *V* or utilizes *V*. An activity is normally a utilizer of its input variables, and is a definer of its output variables. This is similar to the view point of programming slicing, a technique in software engineering for software debugging (cf. Subsection 6.1). But BPEL can violate this relation by applying some business logic. For example, some variables, such as order ID and customer address, are not changeable after they are initialized in a business process. Therefore, a BPEL activity may be a utilizer of its output variables. In BPEL, it is defined in *correlation sets*. In this case, we use *Util(A, (V1, V2))* to express that output *V2* is correlated to input *V1*. In this case, Formula 4 can be simplified as:

$$\neg ab(A.input) \Rightarrow \neg ab(A.output), \text{ if } Util(A, (A.input, A.output)) \qquad (5)$$

In Example 8, we give a table to summarize the variable dependency for the load approval process. This table can be obtained automatically from BPEL. The approach is not presented due to lack of space.

Example 8. *The variable dependency analysis for the loan approval process is inTable 1.*

Table 1. The variable dependency analysis for the loan approval process.

Variables	Parts	Definer	Utilizer
request	firstname lastname amount	receive1 receive1 receive1	invokeAssessor, invokeApprover invokeAssessor, invokeApprover invokeAssessor, invokeApprover
risk	level	invokeAssessor	
approval	accept	assign, invokeApprover	reply
error	errorCode	invokeApprover	

2) Trajectories Reconstruction from Observations after Exceptions are Detected

As mentioned earlier, the observations are the events and exceptions when a BPEL process is executed. The events can be recovered from the log file in a BPEL engine. The observations are formed in an automaton. The possible trajectories of the process are calculated by synchronizing the automaton of the observations with the automaton of the system description:

trajectories = *trajectories of SD||OBS* (6)

We do not require to record each event during the execution, but just enough to be able to identify the real trajectory of the process. This is very useful when some events are not observable and when there are too many events to record. Reference to Subsection 5.2 for more discussion.

Example 9. *In the loan approval example, assume that OBS={received, invoked_assessor, received_risk, invoked_approver, received_aplErr} (as inFigure 7(a)). Received_aplErr is an exception showing that there is a type mismatch in received parameters. We can build the trajectory of evolution as below, also shown inFigure 7(b).*

$$(x_0) \xrightarrow{received} (x_1) \xrightarrow{\varepsilon} (x_2) \xrightarrow{invoked\_assessor} (x_4) \xrightarrow{received\_risk} (x_5) \xrightarrow{\varepsilon} (x_3) \xrightarrow{invoked\_approver} (x_7) \xrightarrow{received\_aplErr} (x_8)$$

3) Accountability Analysis for Mode Assignment

Not all the activities in a trajectory are responsible for the exception. As a software system, the activities connect to each other by exchanging variables. Only the activities which change the attributes within a variable can be responsible for the exception.

Assume that activity A generates exception e_f, and t is a trajectory ending at A. The responsibility propagation rules are (direct consequences of the contraposition of Formula 4 and 5):

$$e_f \in \Sigma_A \vdash ab(A) \vee \vee\{ab(A.InVar.part) | A.InVar.part \in A.InVar\} \quad (7)$$

$\forall A_i, A_j \in t, A_j \neq A_i, A_j$ is the only activity between A_j and A_i such that $Def(A_j, A_i.InVar.part)$,

$$ab(Ai.InVar.part) \vdash ab(A_j) \vee \vee\{ab(A_j.InVar.part) | A_j.InVar.part \in A_j.InVar\} \quad (8)$$

The first rule in (7) states that if an activity A generates an exception e_f, it is possible that activity A itself is faulty, or any part in its $A.InVar$ is abnormal. Notice a variable is a SOAP message which has several parts. $A.InVar.part$ is a part in $A.InVar$[4]. The second rule in (8) propagates the responsibility backwards in the trajectory. It states

Figure 7. (a) the observations; (b) the loan approval process evolution trajectory up to the exception

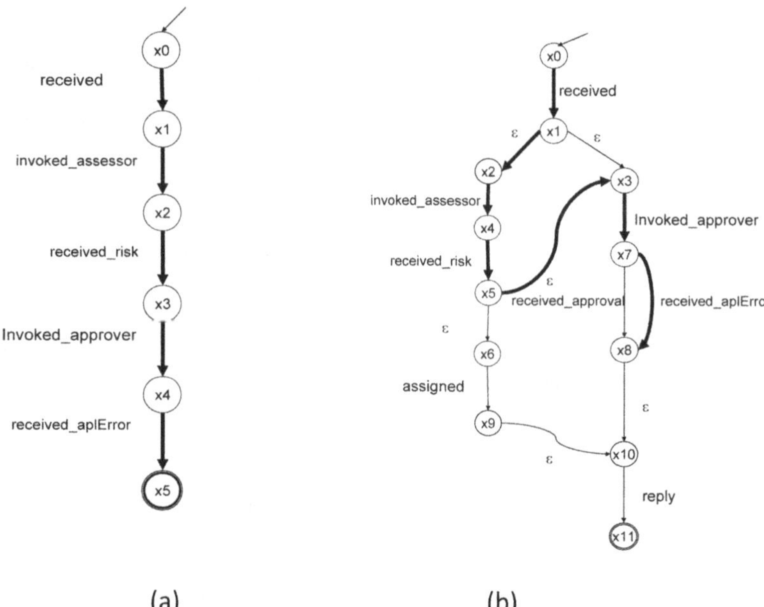

that an activity $A_j \in t$ that defines a part of A_i.*InVar* which is known as faulty could be faulty; and its inputs could also be faulty. If there are several activities that define a part of A_i.*InVar*, only the last one counts, because it overrides the changes made by the other activities, i.e. A_j is the last activity "between" A_j and A_i that defines A_i.*InVar*, as stated in (8). After responsibility propagation, we obtain a *responsible set* of activities $RS = \{A_i\} \subseteq t$.

The set $CO = \{A\} \cup \{A_i | A_i \in RS\}$ is a conflict set, because if all the components in *CO* are correct, there should be no exceptions. Then a diagnosis is any of A or A_i in the responsible set is faulty:

$$\{D_f\} = \{\{A\}\} \cup \{\{A_i\} | A_i \in RS\} \quad (9)$$

Each D_f is a single fault diagnosis and the result is the disjunct of the D_f. The algorithm is as following. Lines 1-2 apply rule (7). Lines 3-8 apply rule (8). This algorithm checks each activity in t. Therefore the complexity of this algorithm is $O(|t|)$.

Example 10. *For the loan approval example, we have the trajectory as in Example 9. We do the responsibility propagation. As invokeApprover generates the exception, according toFormula (7), invokeApprover is possibly faulty. Then its input request is possibly faulty. Among all the activities {receive1, invokeAssessor, invokeApprover} in the trajectory, receive1 defines request, invokeAssessor and invokeApprover utilize request. Therefore, receive1 is possibly faulty, according toFormula (8). receive1 is the first activity in the trajectory. The propagation stops. The diagnosis is:*

$$\{D_f\} = \{\{receive1\}, \{invokeApprover\}\}$$

Example 10 has two single faults {*receive1*} and {*invokeApprover*} for the exception *received_aplErr*, which means either the activity ⟨receive1⟩ or ⟨invokeApprover⟩ is faulty. In an empirical way, an engineer may associate only one fault for an exception. But our approach can find all possibilities. Second, if we want to further identify which activity is indeed responsible for the exception, we can do a further test on the data. For example, if the problem is wrong data format, we can verify

Algorithm 1. Calculate Diagnosis for a Faulty Web Service Process

```
INPUT: A0 - the activity generating the exception.
t - a list of activities in a reserved trajectory ending at A0, taken in re-
verse order with A0 excluded.
Variables: V - a list of faulty variable parts, initialized as {}.
OUTPUT: D - the list of all possible faulty activities, initialized as {A0}.
Notes about the algorithm: 1) list.next() returns the first element of a list;
list.add(element) adds an element at the end of the list; list.remove(element)
removes an element from the list. 2) Activity A has a list of input variables
A.InVars and output variables A.OutVars. 3) a variable var has a list of parts
var.Parts.
for each variable var in A0.InVarsdo
        V.add(var.Parts)
whileA = t.next()! = nulldo
        if ∃p ∈ V, Def(A, p) then
              D.add(A)
              V.remove(v)
              for each variable var in A.InVarsdo
                        V.add(var.Parts)
return D
```

the data format against some specification, and then identify which activity is faulty.

5.1 Multiple Exceptions

There are two scenarios where multiple exceptions can happen. The first scenario is the chained exceptions when one exception causes the others to happen. Normally the software reports this chained relation. We need to diagnose only the first occurred exception, because the causal relations for other exceptions are obvious from the chain.

The second scenario is the case when exceptions occur independently, e.g. two paralleled branches report exceptions. As the exceptions are independent, we diagnose each exception independently, the synthesis diagnoses are the union of all the diagnoses. Assume the minimal diagnoses for exception 1 are $\{D_i^1\}$, where $i \in [1,..., n]$, and the minimal diagnoses for exception 2 are $\{D_j^2\}$, where $j \in [1,..., m]$, the synthesis diagnoses are any combinations of D_i^1 and D_j^2: $\{D_i^1 \cup D_j^2 | i \in [1,..., n], j \in [1,..., m]\}$.

What interests us most is the synthesis of the minimal diagnoses. So, we remove the $D_i^1 \cup D_j^2$ that are supersets of other ones. This happens only if at least one activity is common to $\{D_i^1\}$ and $\{D_j^2\}$, giving rise to a single fault that can be responsible for both exceptions. Such activities are thus most likely to be faulty (single faults being preferred to double faults).

5.2 Without Full Observability

Equation 6 can recover trajectories from *OBS*. Actually if we can record all the events in a model, trajectories are equal to *OBS*. It is a trivial case. The problem occurs when we do not have full observability. For example, a third party BEPL engine does not allow us to record all the events crucial for diagnosis, or the process is too large to record every event. Equation 6 gets all the possible trajectories satisfying *OBS*. Therefore, this method can deal with missing events. At the meantime, if there are multiple trajectories satisfying *OBS*, the diagnoses are the union of the diagnoses obtained from all the trajectories. This can result in a larger number of diagnoses, i.e. diagnosis is not precise.

It is a trade-off between observability and diagnosability. Increasing observability, i.e. observing more events, can result in more precise diagnosis, while increasing the observing cost. It is our future work to study the minimal observables for diagnosing a fault.

5.3 Offline Diagnosability Analysis

Diagnosability analysis is normally conducted offline without executing the processes. We do not touch diagnosability analysis problems in this paper. But diagnosability is related to the method of diagnosis. Assuming an exception at a place in a BPEL process, diagnosability analysis of this exception involves to calculate all the trajectories from the process entry point to the assumed exception and find diagnoses on each trajectory. The method is similar as the three steps in Section 5, just the second step is replaced by a graph traverse algorithm to compute all the trajectories between two nodes on the graph formed by the automaton model.

5.4 Multiple Trajectories

Lack of full observability and offline diagnosability analysis can cause multiple trajectories. Assume trajectories $\{t_1,...,t_n\}$. Using our diagnosis algorithm, each trajectory t_i has conflict set CO_i. But as the trajectories are the possible execution paths, they do not occur at the same time, the conflict sets are not all contradictory at the same time. Indeed only one of these trajectories, even if which one is unknown, really happened. In this case, we do not have to use hitting set algorithm to compute diagnoses. We define simply the synthesis diagnoses as the disjunction of all the diagnoses, $\vee\{D_i\}$, which means diagnoses are in any of $\{D_i\}$.

5.5 Obtaining the Dependency Table

The variable dependency table can be automatically constructed from BPEL. Regard a BPEL activity $\langle A \rangle$ as a function $OutVar=f_A(InVar)$. Then $\langle A \rangle$ is the utilizer of *InVar* and definer of *OutVar*. Before, we have defined $\langle A \rangle$ as an automaton. Then *InVar* is the variables used in so and *Outvar* is the variables used in s_f.

Due to some business logic, some variables, such as order ID and customer address, are not changeable after they are initialized in a business process. BPEL uses correlation set to define that two variables are identical in values. The *correlation set* is referenced by an activity. When an activity has a correlation set within its scope, the correlation indicates if this activity initiates the variables by setting the attribute initiate. If initiate is "yes", this activity is the definer for both of the variables, otherwise, this activity is the utilizer for both of the variables.

5.6 Implementation

There are many BPEL engines in the market. We extended ActiveBPEL (Active Endpoint, 2007), an open source from Active Endpoints, to implement our diagnosis mechanism. ActiveBPEL allows us to record every executed activity and messages in the execution. These activities and messages are the observations during execution and they correspond to a subset of the events and states in our formal model. Therefore, from the synchronization of the observations and the formal model result the execution trajectories. The diagnosis function is a java package that is invoked when an exception is caught. It takes the observations and the dependency table as inputs, calculates the trajectories and uses Algorithm 1 to calculate diagnoses.

6 RELATED WORK AND DISCUSSION

6.1 A Brief Comparison to Program Slicing

Program slicing is a well known technique in software engineering for software debugging (Weise, 1984). If we have a specific program Π, a location within this program *#n (n* is a number given to a line), and a variable x, then a slice is itself a program that is obtained from the original program by removing all statements that have no influence on the given variable at the specified position. Since slices are usually smaller than the original program they focus the user's attention on relevant parts of the program during debugging. Slices can be computed from Program Dependence Graph (PDG) (Ottenstein & Ottenstein, 1984) as a graph reachability problem. A PDG G_Π for a program Π is a direct graph. The vertices of G_Π represent assignment statements and control predicates that occur in program Π. In addition G_Π includes the distinguished *entry* vertex. The edges of the graph represent either control or data dependencies. Given a criterion $\langle n, x\rangle$, the slice is computed in two steps. First, the vertex *v* representing the last program position before n where variable x is defined must be localized. Second, the algorithm collects all vertices that can reach v via a control or flow dependency edge. The statements represented by the collected vertices (including vertex *v*) are equal to the program slice for Π.

Wotawa has discussed the relationship between MBD based debugging and program slicing (Wotawa, 2002). In his work, each statement in a program is viewed as a component with a mode, inputs and outputs. The logic representation of a statement *#n* is $\neg ab(n) \rightarrow out(n)=f(in(n))$, i.e. if *#n* is not faulty, the output *out*(*n*) is a function of the input in(n) according to the syntax of the program. He observed that the strongly connected components in the PDG have an influence one each other. Only if all the components are not faulty, the super component composed by these components is not faulty. He defined a dependency model whose nodes are the strongly connected components in the PDG and added a logic rule to describe the relation between the super component and the components within it. Assume $\{s_1,s_2,\ldots, s_n\}$are strongly connected and the name of the super component is *SC*, then the rule is $\neg ab(s_1) \wedge\ldots \wedge\neg ab(s_n) \rightarrow \neg ab(SC)$. With the additional rule, logic deduction can more precisely identify the faulty components. Under this kind of modeling, slices of a single variable are equivalent to conflicts in MBD. And MBD and program slicing should draw equivalent conclusions on which statements are faulty.

We consider that diagnosing Web service processes is not equivalent to program debugging. First, we are interested in the faults due to the unknown behavior of the external Web services and due to the interaction between Web services. We assume that the Web service processes are described correctly in BPEL or a Web service process description language. This implicitly excludes the structured activities to be faulty. This is equivalent to consider only data dependency in program slice. Second, though Web service process description languages are like programs, they are simpler than programs. For example, they do not use pointers or other complicated data structures as in programs, and they do not use *Goto* and its other restricted forms as in unstructured program. This makes it possible that diagnosing Web service processes can be simpler than diagnosing programs.

The diagnosis method developed in this paper can be compared to dynamic slicing introduced in (Korel & Laski, 1988). Similar to our method, dynamic slicing considers the bugs should be within the statements that actually affect the value of a variable at a program point for a particular execution of the program. Their solution, following after Weiser's static slicing algorithm, solves the problem using data-flow equations, which is also similar to the variable dependency analysis presented in this paper, but not the same.

An external Web service can be seen as a procedure in a program, with unknown behavior. For a procedure, we normally consider the outputs brought back by a procedure are generated according to the inputs. Therefore, in slicing, the outputs are considered in the definition set (the set of the variables modified by the statement). For Web services, we can know some parts in SOAP response back from a Web service should be unchanged, e.g. the name and the address of a client. This relation is defined as correlation set. We should point out that the variable dependency analysis in this paper is different from slicing. As a consequence, the diagnosis obtained from MBD approach in this paper can be different from slicing, and actually more precise.

As MBD approach can integrate more business logic into its model, it is less rigid than slicing. In this sense, MBD is more business oriented, not program oriented, which makes it more suitable for diagnosing Web service processes than slicing.

6.2 MBD in Diagnosing Component-based Software

Besides Wotawa's work mentioned above, some other people have applied MBD on diagnosing component-based software systems. We found that when diagnosing such systems, the modeling is rather at the component level than translating lines of statements into logic representations. Grosclaude in (Grosclaude, 2004) used a formalism based on Petri nets to model the behaviors of component-based systems. It is assumed that only some of the events are monitored. The history of execution is reconstructed from the monitored events by connecting pieces of activities into possible trajectories. Console's group is working towards the same goal of monitoring and diagnosing Web services like us. In their paper (Ardissono *et al.*, 2005), a monitoring and diagnosing method for choreographed Web service processes is developed. Unlike BPEL in our paper, choreographed Web service processes have no central model and central monitoring mechanism. (Ardissono et al., 2005) adopted grey-box models for individual Web services, in which individual Web services expose the dependency relationships between their input and output parameters to public. The dependency relationships are used by the diagnosers to determine the responsibility for exceptions. This abstract view could be not sufficient when dealing with highly interacting components. More specifically, if most of the Web services claim too coarsely that their outputs are dependent on their inputs, which is correct, the method in (Ardissono et al., 2005) could diagnose almost all the Web services as faulty. Yan *et al.* (Yan, Pencolé, Cordier, & Grastien, 2005) is our preliminary work to the present one, focusing on Web service modeling using transition systems. The major work in this paper is to complete the monitoring and diagnosis methods and present the diagnosis algorithm. The syntax of modeling in this paper is improved from (Yan *et al.*, 2005) with simplified representation of states and explicit definition of constraints. As a result, the model for a process can be more readable and a slightly fewer states. This paper is also self-contained with MBD background and discussions on fault management tasks for Web service processes.

6.3 Related Work in Web Service Monitoring, Modeling and Composition

Several groups of researchers work on Web service monitoring frameworks. (Baresi, Ghezzi, & Guinea, 2006) proposes BPEL^2 which is the original BPEL with monitoring rules. Monitoring rules define how the user wants to oversee the execution of BPEL. But (Baresi et al., 2006) does not specify the monitoring tasks. (Mahbub & Spanoudakis, 2004) proposes a framework for monitoring requirements of BPEL-based service compositions. Their approach uses event calculus for specifying the requirements that must be monitored. Requirements can be behavioral properties of the coordination process or assumptions about the atomic or joint behavior of the deployed services. Events, produced by the normal execution of the process, are stored in a database and the runtime checking is done by an algorithm based on integrity constraint checking in temporal deductive databases. These frameworks can be used for recording the events and messages used for diagnosis.

In addition to automata used in this paper, Petri nets and process algebra are also used as formal models for Web service processes. For example, (Salaün, Bordeaux, & Schaerf, 2004; Ferrara, 2004; Viroli, 2004) map BPEL into different Process Algebra; (Ouyang et al., 2005; Schmidt & Stahl, 2004) present different semantics of BEPL in Petri nets; (Fisteus, Fern'andez, & Kloos, 2004; Foster, Uchitel, Magee, & Kramer, 2003; Fu, Bultan, & Su, 2004) use automata to model BPEL for verification. These models have similar expression power and similar reasoning or computing techniques.

Web service composition techniques are relevant to this paper because they generate new Web service processes. AI planning methods are the most commonly used techniques for Web service composition. (Narayanan & McIlraith, 2002) starts from DAML-S descriptions and automatically transforms them into Petri nets. Other works, as (Berardi, Calvanese, De Giacomo, Lenzerini, & Mecella, 2003; Lazovik, Aiello, & Papazoglou, 2003; Pistore, Traverso, Bertoli, & Marconi, 2005), rely on transition rules systems. (Rao & Su, 2004) is a survey paper on automated Web service composition methods. Re-planning is relevant to this paper because it can be used to modify the Web service processes for fault recovery. (Canfora, Penta, Esposito, & Willani, 2005) presents a re-planning technique based on slicing techniques. When the estimated QoS metrics are not satisfied, the re-planning selects other Web services to replace the ones in the process.

7 CONCLUSION

Web services are the emergent technology for business process integration. A business process can be composed of distributed Web services. The interactions among the Web services are based on message passing. To identify the Web services that are responsible for a failed business process is important for e-business applications. Existing throw-and-catch fault handling mechanism is an empirical mechanism that does not provide sound and complete diagnosis. In this paper, we developed a monitoring and diagnosis mechanism based on solid theories in MBD. Automata are used to give a formal modeling of Web service processes described in BPEL. We adapted the existing MBD techniques for DES to diagnose Web service processes. Web service processes have all the features of software systems and do not appear to function abnormally until an exception is thrown and they are stopped, which makes the diagnosis principle different from diagnosing physical systems. The approach developed here reconstructs execution trajectories based on the model of the process and the observations from the execution. The variable dependency relations are utilized to deduce the actual Web services within a trajectory responsible for the thrown exceptions. The approach is sound and complete in the context of modeled behavior. A BPEL engine can be extended for the monitoring and diagnosis approach developed in this paper.

REFERENCES

Active Endpoint. (2007). www.active-endpoints.com/active-bpel-engineoverview.htm.

Andrews, T., Curbera, F., Dholakia, H., Goland, Y., et al. (2003). Business process execution language for web services (bpel4ws) 1.1. (ftp://www6.software.ibm.com/software/developer/library/ws-bpel.pdf, *retrievedApril10, 2005*)

Ardissono, L., Console, L., Goy, A., Petrone, G., Picardi, C., & Segnan, M. (2005). Cooperative model-based diagnosis of web services. *In Proceedings of the 16th international workshop on principles of diagnosis (DX-2005)* (pp. 125–132).

Baresi, L., Ghezzi, C., & Guinea, S. (2006). Towards self-healing compositions of services. In Krämer, B. J., & Halang, W. A. (Eds.), *Contributions to ubiquitous computing* (*Vol. 42*). Springer.

Baroni, P., Lamperti, G., Pogliano, P., & Zanella, M. (1999). Diagnosis of large active systems. *Artificial Intelligence, 110*(1), 135–183. doi:10.1016/S0004-3702(99)00019-3

Berardi, D., Calvanese, D., De Giacomo, G., Lenzerini, M., & Mecella, M. (2003). Automated composition of e-services that export their behavior. In *Proceedings of the 1st int. conf. on service-oriented computing (icsoc'03)* (p. 43-58).

Canfora, G., Penta, M. D., Esposito, R., & Willani, M. L. (2005). Qos-aware replanning of composite web services. In *Proceedings of IEEE international conference on web services.*

Cordier, M.-O., & Thiébaux, S. (1994). Event-based diagnosis for evolutive systems. In *Proceedings of the fifth international workshop on principles of diagnosis (DX'94)* (pp. 64–69).

Ferrara, A. (2004). Web services: a process algebra approach. In *Proceedings of the 2nd international conference on service oriented computing (icsoc)* (p. 242-251). New York, NY, USA: ACM Press.

Fisteus, J., Fernández, L., & Kloos, C. (2004). Formal verification of bpel4ws business collaborations. In K. Bauknecht, M. Bichler, & B. Prll (Eds.), *Proc. of 5th international conference e-commerce and web technologies (ec-web).*

Foster, H., Uchitel, S., Magee, J., & Kramer, J. (2003). Model-based verification of web service compositions. In *Proc. of eighteenth IEEE international conference on automated software engineering (ase03).*

Fu, X., Bultan, T., & Su, J. (2004). Analysis of interacting bpel web services. In *Proc. of the 13th international world wide web conference (www'04).* ACM Press.

Grastien, A., Cordier, M.-O., & Largouët, C. (2004). Extending decentralized discrete-event modelling to diagnose reconfigurable systems. In *Proceedings of the fifteenth international workshop on principles of diagnosis (DX-04)* (pp. 75–80). Carcassonne, France.

Grastien, A., Cordier, M.-O., & Largouët, C. (2005). Incremental diagnosis of discrete-event systems. In *Proceedings of the sixteenth international workshop on principles of diagnosis (DX-05)* (pp. 119–124). Pacific Grove, California, USA.

Grosclaude, I. (2004). Model-based monitoring of software components. In *Proceedings of the 16th European conf. on artificial intelligence (ECAI'04)* (pp. 1025– 1026).

Hamscher, W., Console, L., & de Kleer, J. (Eds.). (1992). *Readings in model-based diagnosis.* Morgan Kaufmann.

Korel, B., & Laski, J. (1988). Dynamic program slicing. *Information Processing Letters, 29*(3), 155–163. doi:10.1016/0020-0190(88)90054-3

Lazovik, A., Aiello, M., & Papazoglou, M. (2003). Planning and monitoring the execution of web service requests. *In Proceedings of the 1st int. conf. on service-oriented computing (ICSOC'03)* (pp. 335–350).

Mahbub, K., & Spanoudakis, G. (2004). A framework for requirements monitoring of service based systems. In *Proceedings of the 2nd international conference on service oriented computing* (p. 84-93).

Narayanan, S., & McIlraith, S. (2002). Simulation, verification and automated composition of web services. In *Proceedings of the eleventh international world wide web conference (www-11)* (p. 77-88).

Ottenstein, K., & Ottenstein, L. (1984). The program dependence graph in software development environment. In *Acm Sigsoft/Sigplan software engineering symposium on practical software development environments* (p. 177-184).

Ouyang, C., van der Aalst, W., Breutel, S., Dumas, M., ter Hofstede, A., & Verbeek, H. (2005). *Formal semantics and analysis of control flow in ws-bpel* (Tech. Rep.). BPM Center Report BPM-05-13. (BPMcenter.org)

Pencolé, Y., & Cordier, M.-O. (2005). A formal framework for the decentralised diagnosis of large scale discrete event systems and its application to telecommunication networks. *Artificial Intelligence Journal, 164*(1-2), 121–170. doi:10.1016/j.artint.2005.01.002

Pencolé, Y., Cordier, M.-O., & Rozé, L. (2002). Incremental decentralized diagnosis approach for the supervision of a telecommunication network. In *Proceedings of 41th IEEE conf. on decision and control (CDC'2002)* (pp. 435–440). Las Vegas, USA.

Pistore, M., Traverso, P., Bertoli, P., & Marconi, A. (2005). Automated composition of web services by planning at the knowledge level. In *Proceedings of the 19th international joint conference on artificial intelligence (ijcai-05)* (p. 1252-1260).

Rao, J., & Su, X. (2004). A survey of automated web service composition methods. In *Proceedings of the first international workshop on semantic web services and web process composition (swswpc)*.

Reiter, R. (1987). A theory of diagnosis from first principle. *Artificial Intelligence, 32*(1), 57–95. doi:10.1016/0004-3702(87)90062-2

Salaün, G., Bordeaux, L., & Schaerf, M. (2004). Describing and reasoning on web services using process algebra. In *Proceedings of the second IEEE int. conf. on web services (ICWS'04)* (pp. 43–51).

Sampath, M., Sengupta, R., Lafortune, S., Sinnamohideen, K., & Teneketzis, D. (1995). Diagnosability of discrete-event systems. *IEEE Transactions on Automatic Control, 40*(9), 1555–1575. doi:10.1109/9.412626

Schmidt, K., & Stahl, C. (2004). A Petri net semantic for bpel: validation and application. In *Proc. of 11th workshop on algorithms and tools for Petri nets (awpn 04)* (p. 1-6).

Viroli, M. (2004). Towards a formal foundation to orchestration languages. [Elsevier.]. *Electronic Notes in Theoretical Computer Science, 105*, 51–71. doi:10.1016/j.entcs.2004.05.008

Weise, M. (1984). Program slicing. *IEEE Transactions on Software Engineering, 10*(4), 352–357. doi:10.1109/TSE.1984.5010248

Wotawa, F. (2002). On the relationship between model-based debugging and program slicing. *Artificial Intelligence, 135*, 125–143. doi:10.1016/S0004-3702(01)00161-8

Yan, Y., Pencolé, Y., Cordier, M.-O., & Grastien, A. (2005). Monitoring web service networks in a model-based approach. In *3rd IEEE European conference on web services (ecows05)*. Växjö, Sweden: IEEE Computer Society.

ENDNOTES

1. In diagnosis concept, symptom is an observed abnormal behavior, while fault is the original cause of a symptom. For example, an alarm from a smoke detector is a symptom. The two possible faults, a fire or a faulty smoke detector, are the causes of the symptom.
2. $F(c_i)$ is a specific fault mode. When we do not know a specific fault mode, we use $ab(c_i)$ to represent c_i is faulty.
3. When a Web service engine supports multiple instances of a process, different instances are identified with a process ID. Therefore, diagnosis is based on the events for one instance of the process.
4. Sometimes, the exception returns the information about the part *A.InVar.part* is faulty. Then this rule is simplified.

This work was previously published in International Journal of Web Services Research, Volume 6, Issue 1, edited by Liang-Jie Zhang, pp. 87-110, copyright 2009 by IGI Publishing (an imprint of IGI Global).

Chapter 6
Autonomous Web Services Migration in Mobile and Wireless Environments

Yeon-Seok Kim
Yonsei University, South Korea

Myung-Woo Park
Yonsei University, South Korea

Kyong-Ho Lee
Yonsei University, South Korea

ABSTRACT

With the emergence of powerful mobile Internet devices such as smartphones, mobile devices are expected to play the role of service providers or even brokers, as well as clients. However, the frequent mobility of devices and the intermittent disconnection of mobile and wireless network may degrade the availability and reliability of services. To resolve these problems, this paper proposes an efficient method for migrating and replicating Web services among mobile devices. Specifically, the proposed method splits the source code of a Web service into subcodes depending on users' preferences for its constituent operations. For the seamless provisioning of services, a subcode with a higher preference is migrated earlier than others. To evaluate the performance of the proposed method, the effect of the code splitting on migration was analyzed.

INTRODUCTION

With the emergence of powerful mobile Internet devices such as smartphones, mobile devices are expected to play the role of service providers or even brokers as well as clients. Web services (Huhns & Singh, 2005; Stal, 2006) are standard-based technologies to implement a service-oriented architecture in an open environment such as Web. As Web services have been designed mainly for wired network and desktop environments, there is a growing interest in devising the mobile adaptation of the conventional Web services technologies like WS4D (Zeeb et al., 2007), which is called as

DOI: 10.4018/978-1-61350-104-7.ch006

mobile Web services (Sirirama et al., 2006; Schall et al., 2006). Meanwhile, it is difficult to provide Web services on mobile devices seamlessly, since wireless and mobile environments still involve unstable connectivity unlike the typical client-server environment.

If Web services autonomously migrate among mobile devices in this unstable wireless environment, seamless provisioning of services would be possible. For example, when a service cannot be provided during the movement of a device, it can be migrated to an appropriate mobile device and provide its functionality continuously. Additionally, requests can be distributed by replicating the service to other devices when the requests are concentrated on one device. Moreover, in the case of a client's request for a service that takes large parameters such as multimedia files, the service itself can be replicated and executed at the client side, resulting in saving resources. Therefore, the migration and replication of services is essential for the availability and reliability of services in mobile and wireless network environments.

A number of researches on Web service migration have been performed. Some of them define a migratable Web service and migrate them to an appropriate host according to contextual changes. For this purpose, Lin et al. (2008) propose migration policies. Depending on the monitoring result of network resources or service requirements, services are migrated or replicated to appropriate host devices. However, most of them target desktop and wired environments or do not consider the constraints of wireless and mobile environments such as low bandwidth. Therefore, their approaches might take much longer time to migrate mobile Web services.

In this paper, we propose a migration method of Web services through splitting their codes. Specifically, an original code of a service, which implements the functionality of a service, is split into subcodes based on users' preferences to its constituent operations. The subcodes of higher preference are migrated earlier to minimize the latency of the operations of high priority and raise the efficiency of Web services migration and replication in wireless and mobile environments. To evaluate the performance of the proposed method, the effect of the code splitting on migration was analyzed. Furthermore, to show the feasibility of the proposed migration method.

Meanwhile, the process of identifying when and where to migrate services is an important issue. For the seamless provisioning of a service, we have to determine which device is the most suitable target host. This process involves a mechanism to describe context models and migration strategies, which are relevant to the migration of Web services in mobile environments. For this purpose, we employ the context model and migration policy proposed by our former research to determine when and where to migrate services in mobile environments (Kim & Lee, 2007). The method determines a target host based on the migration policy of a service as well as the information collected from devices in the neighborhood of the origin host that is hosting the service.

The organization of this paper is as follows. A brief survey of research trends on service migration is presented. Next, the methods of splitting Web services codes, and migrating and replicating them are described. The effect of splitting codes on migration is also analyzed through experiments. Finally, we summarize the conclusions and further studies.

RELATED WORK

This section summarizes research trends on the migration and replication of services as shown in Table 1.

Sheng et al. (2009) replicate services for increasing the availability of Web services. The method periodically monitors the states of hosts and determines the number of services, which will be replicated, deployment time, and target hosts etc. However, this method is not suitable to

Table 1. Previous works on Web service migration

Author	Year	Feature
Sheng et al.	2009	Monitor periodically the states of hosts and determine the number of the services replicated, deployment time, target hosts etc.
Messing & Goscinski	2008	Propose a Service Management Broker (SMB) for supporting the service migration in a Grid environment
Schmidt et al.	2008	Define self-adaptive migratable Web services and migrate the services according to context changes
Lin et al.	2008	Propose two migration policies
Hammerschmidt & Linnemann	2006 2005	Propose a migration framework which supports Web services based on Tomcat-Axis
Ishikawa et al.	2004	Propose the migration of mobile Web services
Pratitha & Zaslavsky	2004	Select a target server based on context information such as network bandwidth
Kern et al.	2005 2004	Propose a more rapid execution of mobile agents through splitting and arranging codes
Bellavista et al.	2004	Propose a middleware for receiving and executing a list of binary files from neighboring devices
Montanari et al.	2004	Propose a middleware framework which can implement migration policies application-independently
Mifsud & Stanski	2002	Monitor context information of available target hosts and migrate Web services to a specific target host

a distributed environment because of a centric registry for recoding the states of hosts and Web services.

Messing & Goscinski (2008) propose a Service Management Broker (SMB) for supporting the service migration in a Grid environment. SMB migrates services to an appropriate host when a host cannot provide services anymore, a user requests service migration, or it is possible to provide effectively services by the appearance of a good host. Specifically, SMB considers various contexts such as prices, reliability, QoS, service requirements, execution environments, and operating system. However, their method is difficult to apply to a distributed environment because they use a centric registry for discovering and publishing services.

Schmidt et al. (2008) propose a Self-Adaptive Migratable Web Service (SAM-WS) for supporting interoperability in ubiquitous environments. SAM-WS means a migratable Web service for supporting the heterogeneity of devices and the adaptability of applications. The infrastructure saves execution state of a service and determines a target host based on context changes. However, this method must register all hosts in a centric registry. Lin et al. (2008) propose job migration policies in P2P Grid systems. The method migrates jobs to an under-loaded host from an overload host for reducing the response time and increasing the availability of resources. Specifically, they use two migration policies such as Load Barrier Policy and Minimal Job Turnaround Time Policy. Load Barrier Policy considers CPU load and Minimal Job Turnaround Time Policy considers the heterogeneity of resources, network bandwidth, job migration price, CPU performance, and length of job queue. This method does not target Web services.

Hammerschmidt & Linnemann (2005) propose a migration framework, which supports Web services based on Tomcat-Axis. Particularly, since instances are supported, connections do not need to be restarted after migration. Ishikawa et al. (2004) propose the migration of mobile Web services, which are defined as composite Web services.

Particularly, agents that execute several services in a composite Web service can migrate to an appropriate host. An endpoint of each service in a composite Web service can be changed; however, the endpoint of a composite Web service does not change. Pratitha & Zaslavsky (2004) propose a framework and strategies for migrating Web services. Based on context information such as network bandwidth, their method selects a target server, to which a service should be migrated. Moreover, their method defines service modules in advance according to context information and selects a proper module to the corresponding context.

Meanwhile, Kern et al. (2004) propose a more rapid execution of mobile agents through splitting and arranging codes which implement the functionality of agents. A shortcoming of this method is that the execution order of agent functions in each host must be fixed. The middleware for an ad-hoc network proposed by Bellavista et al. (2004) can receive and execute a list of binary files from neighboring devices. Montanari et al. (2004) propose a middleware framework which can implement migration policies application independently. The method of Mifsud & Stanski (2002) monitors context information of available target hosts and migrates Web services to a specific target host.

Previous works are mostly based on desktop and wired environments, and therefore the latency of Web services are too long to apply to wireless and mobile environments. Therefore, it is difficult to deal with a service migration efficiently in mobile and wireless environments. In this article, we aim at presenting how to migrate services quickly and to reduce the latency of service requests during migration.

SPLITTING WEB SERVICE CODES

A splitting method of Web service codes is described. For the splitting and migration method, the framework of Figure 1 is proposed.

The code splitter splits a Web service code and saves them in a code repository in a component form. The migration manager encapsulates components and instances in a transportable form, and unpacks the encapsulated form and saves it at the resource space. The service execution manager manages the execution of a service, which stops and restarts the service execution. The context manager collects context information from the current and adjacent mobile devices and decides when and where to migrate services. The channel manager takes charge of the establishment of network connections. The logger records the execution history of the modules of the framework.

How to split a Web service code by the code splitter in the proposed framework is shown in Figure 2. In our method, it is assumed that original source codes of Web services are proportionate to their compiled codes.

Figure 1. The proposed framework

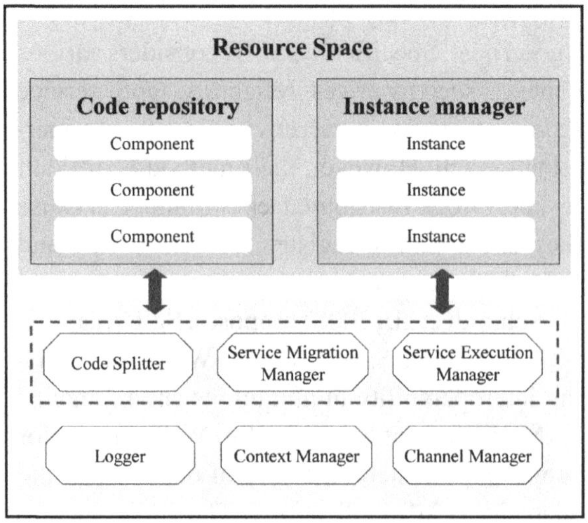

Figure 2. The process of splitting codes

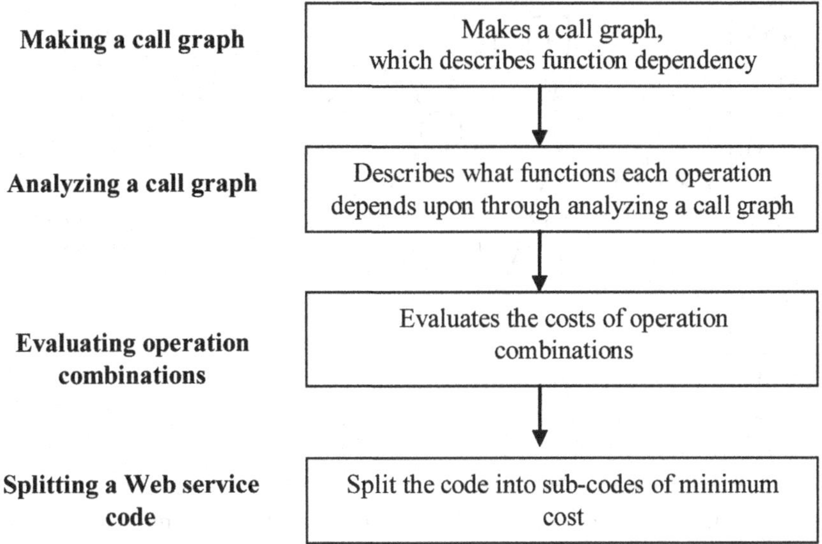

Making and Analyzing a Call Graph

A code that implements a Web service is analyzed and represented with a call graph, and the dependency among functions (or methods) is derived from the call graph. The proposed method for computing the dependency among functions is based on the method of Grove & Chambers (2001). The functions exposed as operations in a WSDL interface are recorded particularly and are used in the next analyzing step. After making the call graph, it is analyzed in order to determine functions, upon which each operation depends. The analysis progresses following nodes, to which each operation node is connected. Figure 3 illustrates making and analyzing a call graph.

Evaluating Operation Combinations and Splitting a Web Service Code

A condition required in code splitting is that each split code should contain at least one operation and exists in a class form so that it can be compiled. The code split must have all the functions, upon which its operations depend. However, if operations depend on functions in common, code splitting is impossible or inefficient. Copying appropriate codes of functions can solve this problem. In the call graph of Figure 3, operations 1, 2 and 3 commonly depend on function E, and therefore disjoint code splitting is impossible. However, if function E is copied, it is possible to split the code as shown in Figure 4.

It is possible but somewhat inefficient to copy all the function codes that are used in common. In Figure 4, functions B, C, D, and E need to be copied in order to split operations 2 and 3, and those four functions are almost a half of all the function code, including operations. Therefore, whether functions would be copied should be determined for efficient code splitting. Alternately, an original code is split based on which operations will exist in a class, and then the combination of operations can decide which functions need to be copied.

The selection of the optimal code split is related to both the total size of the codes split and users' preferences to operations. If a code segment has not arrived in a target server, it is impossible to invoke its operation. In this case, users' dis-

Figure 3. An example of making and analyzing a call graph

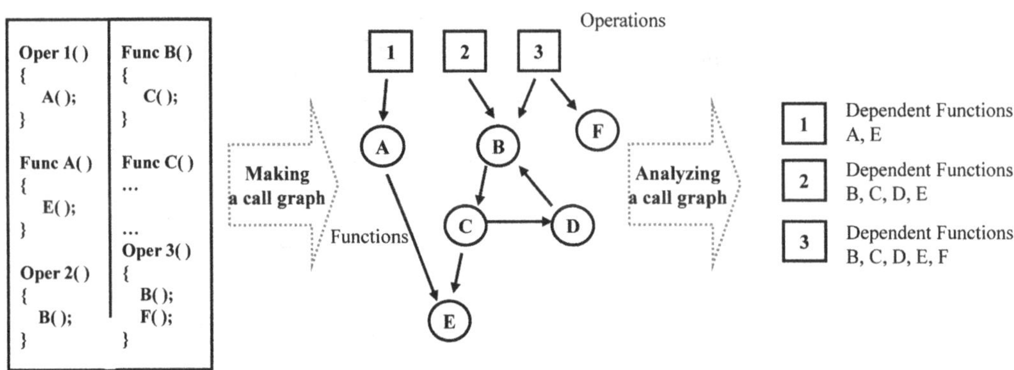

satisfaction with the service would be raised. The proposed method transmits a code segment of higher priority earlier to minimize its service discontinuance. So, the dissatisfaction rate of a code segment at a certain time is proportionate to the time to migrate the total codes that include it and the code segments with a higher priority. The dissatisfaction would be also proportionate to user preferences. User preferences can be statistically calculated from users' previous requests by the logger. In this paper, the dissatisfaction with a service migration is formulated and computed by a cost function as follows:

$$Cost = \sum_{i=1}^{n} (p_i \times \sum_{j=1}^{i} S_j) \qquad (1)$$

Figure 4. An example of copying functions

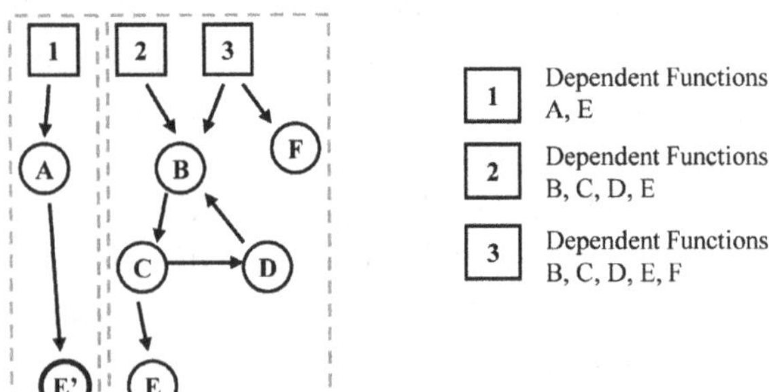

Where $i<j \rightarrow p_i \geq p_j$, $p_i = p_j \rightarrow S_i \leq S_j$, n is the number of partitions, $p_i (0 \leq p_i \leq 1)$ is the sum of user preferences to operations in the ith partition, $S_j (0 \leq S_j \leq 1)$ is the total code size of jth partition.

The proposed method computes the costs of every possible combination of code split. It finds the combination of minimum cost that corresponds to the optimal split of operations. The original service code is split according to the optimal combination. Each partition of operations and their functions is compiled and saved as a component in the code repository.

MIGRATING AND REPLICATING WEB SERVICES

The proposed method handles both migration and replication. The former occurs when an origin server cannot provide a service anymore because of some reasons including battery shortage and non-service area. The replication of a service is done when the service needs to be copied to a different server temporarily to maintain its quality. Example cases are as follows: 1) when network bandwidth becomes more crowded and traffic slows down; 2) when the number of requests from a particular location grows rapidly; 3) when a client wants to use a service with large parameters.

When the migration of a service occurs, its endpoint should be changed as the corresponding endpoint of the target host. In the case of replication, a new endpoint is added to the existing list of endpoints of an origin server. The context manager selects between migration and replication depending on context information.

Migrating Web Services

When the battery level of an origin server becomes very low or a service cannot be provided any more due to the location change of its device into non-service area, the service should be migrated to an appropriate target device. If a target server accepts the migration request, the components and instances in a transportable form are transmitted as shown in Figure 5. Specifically, existing requests on the execution queue of the service execution manager are processed on the server selected between the origin server and the target server for faster execution. This is basically the same with the case of a service request during migration. At the same time, instances and their associated components on the resource space are transmitted in order of the user preference.

Whenever a component and/or its instance arrive, the service execution manager of the target server deploys the operations of the component. As soon as all the components and instances have arrived at the target server, they are deleted on the origin server. If the components and instances of a service have not arrived at the target server due to any reason, the process of migration halts. Additionally, the origin server searches again for a new target server. The former target server maintains the components and instances already arrived for a certain period of time. After the time period, the target server deletes them.

If a service is requested during its migration, the proposed method determines which server between the origin and target servers executes the request faster. Figure 6 describes the control flow of the process. In the case where the component of the operation called has already transmitted to the target server, t_o is the time to receive the instance from the target server, execute it on the origin server, respond its result to a client, and transmit the instance updated to the target server, that is, synchronize two instances between the two servers. t'_n includes the time to notify a client that the request should be made to the target server and the time for the client to request the operation to the target server and receive its response. Figure 7(a) describes the case of Figure 6-①.

Figure 5. An example procedure of Web services migration

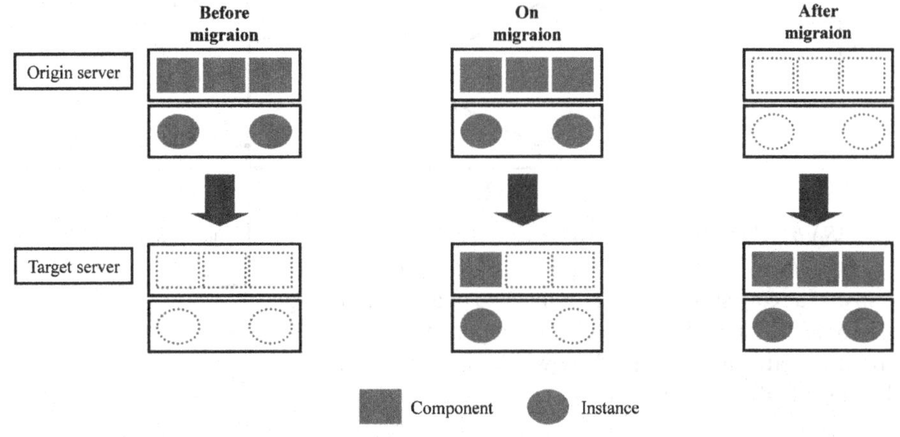

In the case where the code has not been transmitted yet, t'_o corresponds to the time required to respond to the client request and transmit the instance and component of the operation to the target server. t''_n includes the time to forward the component and client request to the target server and execute the operation on the target server. It also contains the time for the origin server to notify a client that the result should be received from the target server and for a client to receive the result from the target server. Figure 7(b) illustrates the case of Figure 6-②.

Replicating Web Services

The replication of a Web service is classified into two cases: the replications of a service to another server, and to the client requesting it.

Replication to Another Server

The method of replication is similar to that of migration. If a target server accepts a replication request, the corresponding components and instances are transmitted. However, all the instances do not need to be transmitted, and after finishing the replication process the components are not deleted from its origin server. The instances that have been transmitted to the target server are deleted on the origin server. When a replication occurs, the origin server records the target servers on the list of replications. Additionally, the origin server may request the target server to delete the replicated service. If a service is requested during replication, the same processes with the case of migration are applied.

Figure 8 is an example of a service replication, where an origin server with three components and five instances communicates with five clients. The

Figure 6. The flow of processing in case of a service call on migration

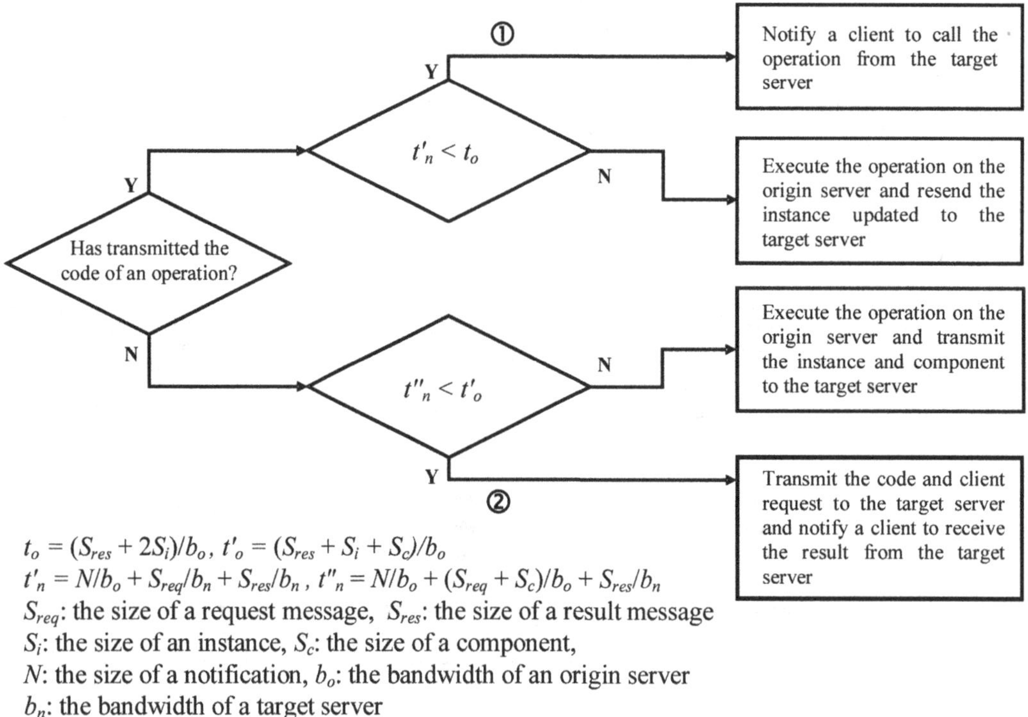

Figure 7. Service requests during the migration process

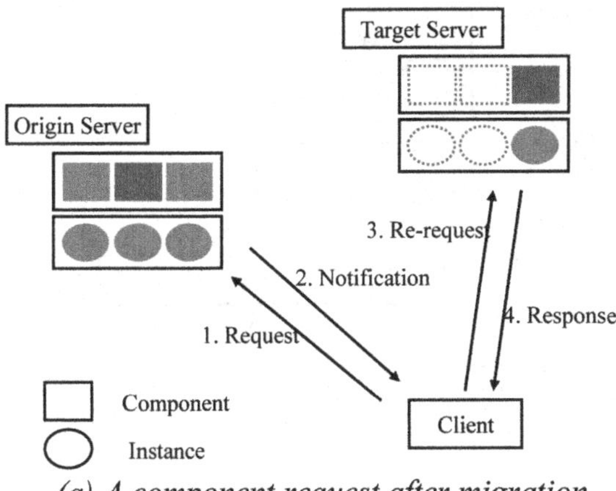

(a) A component request after migration

(b) A component request before migration

context manager decides which server should be selected as the target server and which instances should be migrated. For example, after copying three components and three instances, the target server and three clients would reconfigure their connections. The three instances would be removed from the origin server, resulting in reducing traffic on the origin server.

Replication to a Client

If a service requires a large message as an input parameter, a client may want to download the service code of small size and execute it on his or her device as illustrated in Figure 9.

To do this, a client should examine the component information about an operation and compare the sizes of the parameter and component. If a component were downloaded, an origin server would record the client on the replication list. Likewise, the origin server may request the client to delete the component.

If a replication is requested during migration or replication, a server, from which the component would be downloaded more quickly, should be determined as shown in Figure 10. While t''_o indicates the download time of the component and instance from the origin server, t'''_n corresponds to the time to notify the client that the component and instance would be downloaded from a new server and receive them from the new server.

EXPERIMENTAL RESULTS

We have experimented to evaluate the effect of the proposed code splitting approach on migration.

Performance Analysis

To evaluate the performance of the proposed code splitting method, we measured the time to split codes from three different experiments. First, to investigate how much the method is affected by the dependency among operations, we experimented with a test data, where Web services consist of 10 operations and each operation calls three functions. Second, concerning the number of functions called by an operation, the test was done with services, which contain 10 operations and 20 functions. Here we varied the number of functions, which are called by an operation, from 2 to 20. The third test is about the number of operations in a service. Web services contain operations that call 10 functions. Here the number of operations was varied from 1 to 10. In our experiments, the dependencies

Figure 8. An example of Web services replication

Figure 9. Component replication

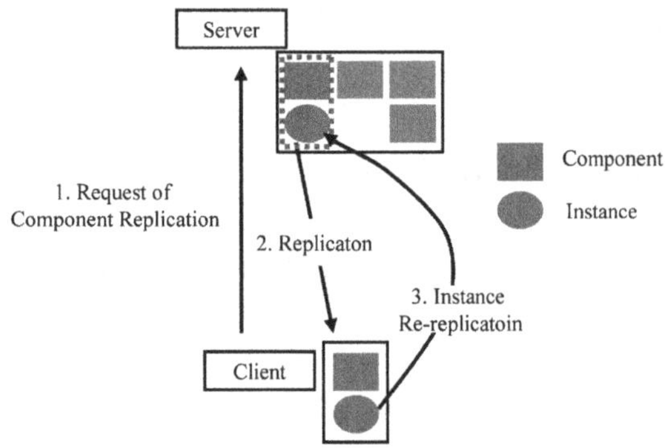

between operations and functions were randomly selected. In each experiment, the size of functions was also varied from 1KB (kilobyte) to 100KB.

Evaluation in Terms of the Dependency between Operations

If operations in a service share functions in common, we can say that they depend on each other. We define the dependency of operation *a* in a service as:

operation_dependency(*a*) = the number of operations sharing functions in common with *a*/ the total number of operations in a service (2)

Figure 11(a) shows the experimental results about the relation between the average value of operation dependencies and the time taken to split codes. The figure shows that operation dependency and splitting time are scarcely related. If a Web service has many functions shared by its operations, the possibility of splitting would be low. Otherwise, the possibility of splitting would be high. Since only the functions shared by operations are copied, the number of copied functions is limited, resulting in increasing a limited amount of time. Consequently, the operation dependency is shown to be unrelated to the splitting time. Moreover, Figure 11(b) shows that the dependency is unrelated to the total size of the codes split. The test was done with services, whose operations and functions have the size of about 10KB.

Evaluation in Terms of the Number of Functions Called by Operations

The experimental result of Figure 12(a) shows that as the number of functions called by operations grows, splitting time increases. Nodes in a call graph represent functions or operations. The number of functions called by operations determines the number of edges among function nodes. As the number of connections among nodes, we need more time to analyze and split the graph.

Figure 10. The flowchart for a replication request during migration or replication

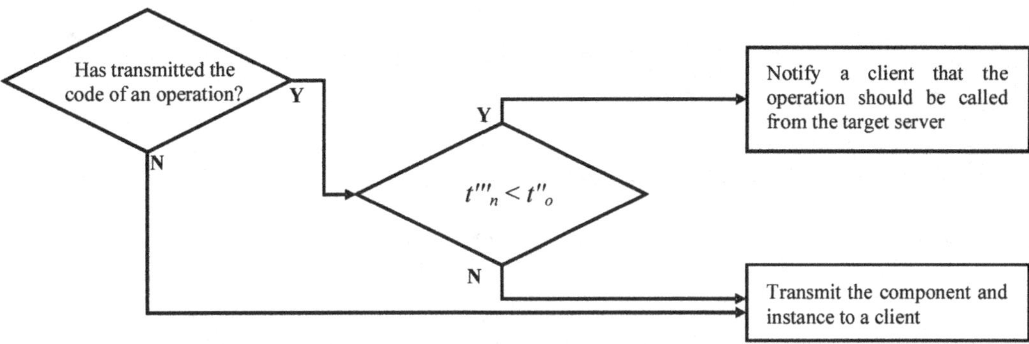

$t''_o = (S_c + S_i)/b_o$
$t'''_n = N/b_o + S_{req}/b_n + (S_c + S_i)/b_n$
S_c: the size of a component, S_i: the size of an instance
N: the size of a notification, S_{req}: the size of a request message
b_o: the bandwidth of an original server, b_n: the bandwidth of a target server

Figure 12(b) shows the relationship between the number of functions called by an operation and the size of the codes split. The test was done with services, whose operations and functions have the size of about 10KB. In the cases where the numbers of the function called are 2 or 4, since the numbers are relatively small and each operation did not share functions, there was no difference in the size of the codes split before and after splitting. While increasing the number of functions called by an operation until it reached 12, no regularities were found. In the case of 14 or more functions, operations called more than 70% of functions in this test. Splitting did not happen since too many functions needed to be copied otherwise.

Evaluation in Terms of the Number of Operations

As shown in Figure 13, there was a close correlation between the number of operations and the splitting time. An increase in the number of operations results in an exponential growth of the splitting time since all possible combinations of operations need to be considered to determine the code splitting of minimum cost.

As a result, we find that the splitting time of a service is related with its code size, the number of functions called by operations, and the number of operations, while the dependency among operations seldom affects the splitting time. In particular, the splitting time grows exponentially as the number of operations increases. We have a plan to consider this matter to enhance the processing time of the proposed method.

Comparison with Previous Works

Table 2 shows the qualitative comparison of the proposed method with previous works. While Schmidt et al. (2008) support the migration of Web services and their instances, they target desktop and wired environments. Hammerschmidt & Linnemann (2005) support the migration of instances to reduce network traffic and resource

Figure 11. An experimental result on operation dependency

(a) Splitting time. *(b) Total size of the codes split (function size 10KB).*

Figure 12. An experimental result on the number of function calls

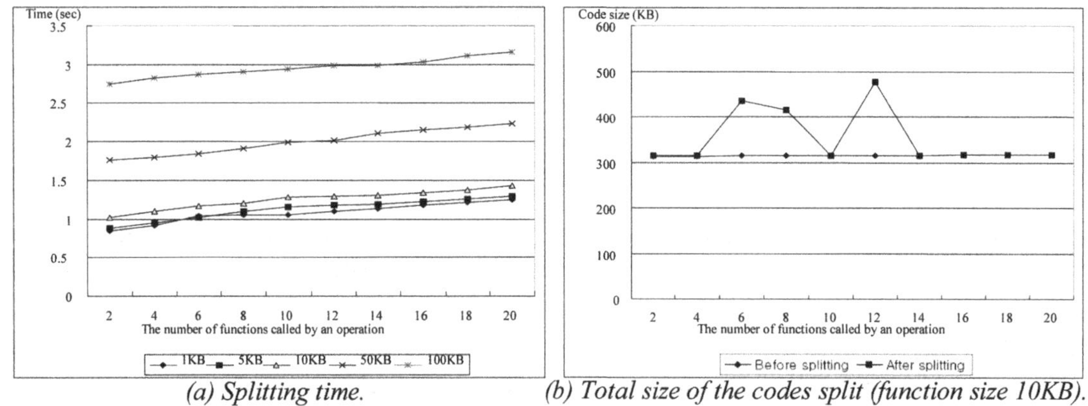

(a) Splitting time. *(b) Total size of the codes split (function size 10KB).*

Table 2. Comparison with previous works

Features Methods	Web services	Instance preservation	Reconfiguration	Supporting mobile and wireless environments	Context-awareness
Sheng et al.	O*	X	X	X	O
Messing & Goscinski	O	X	X	O	O
Schmidt et al.	O	O	X	O	O
Lin et al.	X	X	X	O	O
Hammerschmidt & Linnemann	O	O	X	X	X
Ishikawa et al.	O	X	X	X	X
Pratitha & Zaslavsky	O	X	O	X	O
Kern & Braun	X	O	X	X	X
Bellavista et al.	X	X	X	O	O
Montanari et al.	X	X	X	X	O
Mifsud & Stanski	O	X	X	X	X
The proposed method	O	O	X	O	O

* O: supported, X: not supported

Figure 13. An experimental result on the number of operations

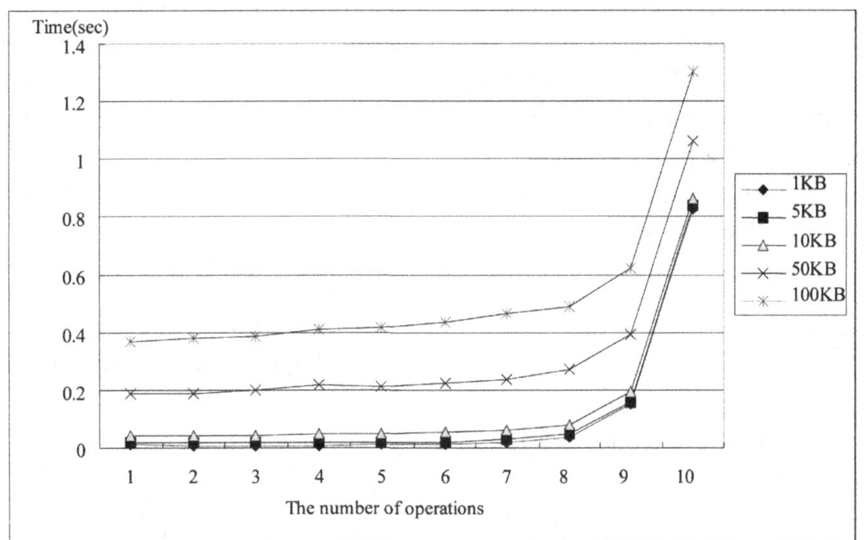

consumption on an origin server. The method of Pratitha & Zaslavsky (2004) migrates services to a target server, which is selected based on context information. Services are composed of service modules, which have been defined in advance depending on context. However, as the size of a service increases, it takes a lot of resources to migrate the service. They do not handle the migration of service instances and the replication of services. Among the methods concerning code mobility, Bellavista et al. (2004) and Montanari et al. (2004) support the migration of binary codes, but do not offer the instance migration.

In this paper, we present a method for migrating and replicating Web services on mobile and wireless environments. Based on the context information of mobile devices, the proposed method selects between migration and replication. Additionally, service instances are preserved during migration and replication. The proposed framework does not consider the reconfiguration of services after migration. The reconfiguration involves increases in code size since it requires codes, which are relevant to each context, to be implemented. Therefore, it may be not suitable for wireless and mobile environments.

CONCLUSION AND FUTURE STUDY

This paper presents an efficient method for migrating and replicating Web services through code splitting. Specifically, a service is split into sub-codes based on users' preferences to its constituent operations. The sub-codes of higher preference are migrated earlier to minimize the discontinuance of the operations of high priority and raise the efficiency of Web services migration and replication in wireless and mobile environments. From experimental results, we found that the proposed splitting method depended on the size of a Web service and the number of functions called by its operations. In particular, as the number of operations increased, the splitting time grew at an exponential rate. Experimental results show that the proposed migration method helps services to be provided continuously.

The proposed method selects an optimal combination of code split, on which the source code is split and compiled into components. However, it may be necessary to merge and split the codes split repeatedly since user preferences may change rapidly and frequently. Therefore, to reflect the changing desires and preferences of users dynamically at runtime, we have a plan to enhance the proposed migration method to make it possible to accommodate user feedback at runtime.

REFERENCES

Bellavista, P., Corradi, A., & Magistretti, E. (2004). Lightweight code mobility for proxy-based service rebinding in MANET. *Proceedings of the 1st Int'l Symp. Wireless Communication Systems*, Port Louis, Mauritius, September 20-22, (pp. 208-214).

Grove, D., & Chambers, C. (2001). A framework for call graph construction algorithms. *ACM Trans. Programming Languages and Systems*, *23*(6), 685–746. doi:10.1145/506315.506316

Grove, D., DeFouw, G., Dean, J., & Chambers, C. (1997). Call graph construction in object-oriented languages. *Proceedings of the ACM SIGPLAN Conf. Object-Oriented Programming Systems Languages and Applications*, Atlanta, USA, October 5-9, (pp. 108-124).

Hammerschmidt, B. C., & Linnemann, V. (2005). Migrating stateful Web services using Apache AXIS and P2P. *Proceedings of the IADIS Int'l Conf. Applied Computing*, Algarve, Portugal, February 22-25, (pp. 433-441).

Hammerschmidt, B. C., & Linnemann, V. (2006). Migratable Web services: Increasing performance and privacy in service oriented architectures. *IADIS International Journal on Computer Science and Information System*, *1*(1), 42–56.

Huhns, M. N., & Singh, M. P. (2005). Service-oriented computing: Key concepts and principles. *IEEE Internet Computing*, *9*(1), 75–81. doi:10.1109/MIC.2005.21

Ishikawa, F., Yoshioka, N., Tahara, Y., & Honiden, S. (2004). Toward synthesis of Web Services and mobile agents. *Proceedings of AAMAS Workshop on Web Services and Agent-based Engineering (WSABE)*, New York, USA, July 19-20, (pp. 227-245).

Kern, S., & Braun, P. (2005). Towards adaptive migration strategies for mobile agents. *Proceedings of the Second GSFC/IEEE Workshop on Radical Agent Concepts (WRAC)*, NASA Goddard Space Flight Center Visitor's Center Greenbelt, MD USA, September 20-22, (pp. 334-345).

Kern, S., Braun, P., Fensch, C., & Rossak, W. (2004). Class splitting as a method to reduce migration overhead of mobile agents. *Proceedings of the Int'l Conf. Ontologies, Databases and Application of Semantics (ODBASE'04)*, Agia Napa, Cyprus, October 25-29, (pp. 1358-1375).

Kim, Y.-S., & Lee, K.-H. (2007). An efficient policy establishment scheme for web services migration. *Proceedings of the Int'l Conf. Convergence Information Technology (ICCIT'07)*, (pp. 595-600).

Lin, S.-J., Huang, M.-C., Lai, K.-C., & Huang, K.-C. (2008). Design and implementation of job migration policies in P2P grid systems. *Proceedings of IEEE Asia-Pacific Services Computing Conf. (APSCC'08)*, Yilan, Taiwan, December 9-12, (pp. 75-80).

Messing, M., & Goscinski, A. (2008). Service migration in autonomic service oriented grids. *Proceedings of the 6th Australasian Workshop on Grid Computing and e-Research (AusGrid'08)*, Wollongong, Australia, January 22-25, (pp. 45-54).

Mifsud, T., & Stanski, P. (2002). Measuring performance of dynamic web service migration using LAMS. *Proceedings of the 10th Int'l Conf. Software, Telecommunications and Computer Networks (SoftCOM)*, Venice, Italy, October 8-11, (pp. 214-218).

Montanari, R., Lupu, E., & Stefanelli, C. (2004). Policy-based dynamic reconfiguration of mobile-code applications. *Computer*, *37*(7), 73–80. doi:10.1109/MC.2004.63

Pratistha, I. M., & Zaslavsky, A. B. (2004). Fluid: Supporting a transportable and adaptive web service. *Proceedings of the 2004 ACM Symp. Applied Computing*, Nicosia, Cyprus, March 14-17, (pp. 1600-1606).

Schall, D., Aiello, M., & Dustdar, S. (2006). Web services on embedded devices. *Web Information System*, *1*(1), 1–6.

Schmidt, H., Kapitza, R., Hauck, F. J., & Reiser, H. P. (2008). Adaptive Web service migration. *Proceedings of the 8th IFIP WG 6.1 Int'l Conf. Distributed Applications and Interoperable Systems (DAIS'08). Lecture Notes in Computer Science*, *5053*, 182–195. doi:10.1007/978-3-540-68642-2_15

Sheng, Q. Z., Maamar, Z., Yu, J., & Ngu, A. H. H. (2009). Robust Web services provisioning through on-demand replication. *Proceedings of the 3th Int'l United Information Systems Conf. (UNISCON'09), Lecture Notes in Business Information Processing, 20*(2), 4-16.

Sirirama, S. N., Jarke, M., & Prinz, W. (2006). Mobile Web services provisioning. *Proceedings of the Advanced Int'l Conf. Telecommunications and Int'l Conf. Internet and Web Application and Services*, Guadeloupe, France, February 19-22, (pp. 120-126).

Stal, M. (2006). Using architectural patterns and blueprints for service-oriented architecture. *IEEE Software*, *23*(2), 54–61. doi:10.1109/MS.2006.60

Zeeb, E., Bobek, A., Bohn, H., Pruter, S., Pohl, A., & Krumm, H. ... Timmermann, D. (2007). WS4D: SOA-Toolkits making embedded systems ready for Web Services. *Proceedings of the 2nd Int'l Workshop on Open Source Software and Product Lines* (OSSPL'07), Limerick, Ireland, June.

Chapter 7
Estimating the Privacy Protection Capability of a Web Service Provider[1]

George O.M. Yee
National Research Council, Canada

ABSTRACT

The growth of the Internet has been accompanied by the growth of Web services (e.g., e-commerce, e-health, etc.), leading to important provisions put in place to protect the privacy of Web service users. However, it is also important to be able to estimate the privacy protection capability of a Web service provider. Such estimates would benefit both users and providers. Users would benefit from being able to choose (assuming that such estimates were made public) the service that has the greatest ability to protect their privacy (this would in turn encourage Web service providers to pay more attention to privacy). Web service providers would benefit by being able to adjust their provisions for protecting privacy until certain target capability levels of privacy protection are reached. This article presents an approach for estimating the privacy protection capability of a Web service provider and illustrates the approach with an example.

DOI: 10.4018/978-1-61350-104-7.ch007

INTRODUCTION

This work considers Web services to be: a) Web-based services that employ Extensible Markup Language (XML), Web service Definition Language (WSDL), Simple Object Access Protocol (SOAP), and Universal Description, Discovery, And Integration (UDDI) in a Service-Oriented Architecture (SOA) (O'Neill, Hallam-Baker, MacCann, Shema, Simon, Watters, et al., 2003); and b) existing and previous generations of Web-based applications that involve Web browsers interacting with Web servers that do not employ XML, WSDL, SOAP, or UDDI. This work applies to all Web services described above.

Numerous Web services targeting consumers have accompanied the rapid growth of the Internet. For example, Web services are available for banking, shopping, learning, healthcare, and government online. However, most of these services require a consumer's personal information in one form or another, leading to concerns over privacy. For Web services to be successful, privacy must be protected. Various approaches have been used to protect personal information, including data anonymization (Iyengar, 2002; Kobsa & Schreck, 2003) and pseudonym technology (Song, Korba, & Yee, 2006). Approaches for privacy protection that are in the research stage include: treating privacy protection as an access problem and then bringing the tools of access control to bear for privacy control (Adams & Barbieri, 2006); treating privacy protection as a privacy rights management problem using the techniques of digital rights management (Kenny & Korba, 2002); and considering privacy protection as a privacy policy compliance problem, verifying compliance with secure logs (Yee & Korba, 2004).

It is also important to estimate the privacy protection capability of a Web service provider. Suppose such estimates for similar Web services A, B, and C are made available to consumers. This leads to the following benefits. If the consumer has to choose one service from among A, B, and C, then the estimates can help the consumer decide which service to select (probably the service that has the highest capability for privacy protection). In addition, the fact that consumers have access to these estimates may encourage service providers to pay more attention to protecting consumer privacy and result in higher levels of consumer trust and acceptance of Web services. Alternatively, Web service providers can use such estimates to implement services that meet predefined goals of privacy protection. Predefined levels of the estimates could be expressed as quality-of-service requirements. The estimates could then be evaluated for incremental versions of a service until the predefined levels are achieved.

The objectives of this article are to a) define estimates of the privacy protection capability of a Web service provider, b) show how the estimates can be calculated, and c) illustrate the calculation of the estimates using a Web service example.

This article extends the work of Yee (2006) by: a) improving the practicality of the approach by refocusing on estimating privacy protection capability rather than measuring how well privacy is protected; b) updating the definition of the estimates; c) updating the method for calculating the estimates; d) updating and extending the application example; e) enlarging the related works section; f) adding an evaluation section; and g) improving the clarity of the writing in all sections.

The rest of this article is organized as follows. Section "Estimates of Privacy Protection Capability" introduces the privacy protection model and defines the estimates. "Calculation of the Estimates" shows how to calculate the estimates. The section called "Application Example" illustrates the calculation of the estimates. A discussion of related work then follows. "Evaluation of Approach" discusses the strengths and weaknesses of the approach. Finally, the article ends with conclusions and directions for future research.

ESTIMATES OF PRIVACY PROTECTION CAPABILITY

Privacy

In order to define estimates of a Web service provider's capability to protect consumer privacy, it is necessary first to examine the nature of personal privacy. As defined by Goldberg, Wagner, and Brewer (1997), privacy refers to the ability of individuals to *control* the collection, retention, and distribution of information about themselves. This leads to the following definitions for this work.

Definition 1: Privacy refers to the ability of individuals to control the collection, use, retention, and distribution of information about themselves.

Definition 2: A provider's protection of user privacy refers to the provider's use of provisions to give a user desired control over the provider's collection, retention, and distribution of information about the user.

Definition 1 is the same as given by Goldberg et al. (1997) except that it also includes "use." To see that "use" is needed, consider, for example, that one may agree to give out one's credit card number (private information) to pay for one's own purchase but not to pay for someone else's purchase. The "provisions" in Definition 2 refer to whatever means or technologies are needed to give the user the required control (uphold the user's privacy); for example, access control mechanisms, policy negotiation mechanisms, and policy compliance mechanisms. These provisions depend on the nature of the control required by the user. For example, if the user specifies that the user's information is not to be kept past a certain date, the provider must have in place a provision to track how long the information has been in its possession.

It follows from Definition 2 that if the service provider is to make provisions to protect the user's privacy, it needs to know how the user wishes to control personal information. Thus, there must be a means of communicating the nature of this control, from the user to the service provider. This communication is normally carried out using a statement of privacy preferences called a *privacy policy*. Figure 1 is an example of a user privacy policy for e-learning from Yee and Korba (2005). In Figure 1, each item of information about the user corresponds to a "privacy rule" that spells out who can collect the information, how the item is to be used (purpose), how long it can be retained, and who it can be disclosed to. For example, the information item "name, address, tel" is to be used for identification; it may be collected by E-Learning Inc., it can be retained by E-Learning Inc. indefinitely, and E-Learning Inc. must not disclose it to any other party. Figure 2 illustrates the use of a privacy policy to express how the user wishes to control private information. The arrows from the user are numbered to show that the privacy policy must come first. The bidirectional arrow between the user and the privacy policy indicates that the user both specifies the policy and complies with it. On the provider side, the provisions for user control (blue box) must comply with the privacy rules in the user's privacy policy, giving the user desired control over the user's personal information. The service provider would have to agree to comply with the user's privacy policy before it can receive any of the user's private information. Where the service provider does not agree to the user's policy, the user can negotiate with the provider (Yee & Korba, 2003a, 2003b) until there is agreement, or the user can try a different provider.

Privacy Policy Violations

Once the provider has agreed to comply with the user's privacy policy and is in possession of the user's private data, the user's privacy is fully protected, provided there are no violations of the user's privacy policy. To define estimates of a provider's capability to protect privacy or to avoid privacy policy violations, it is necessary to look at

Figure 1. Example privacy policy for e-learning

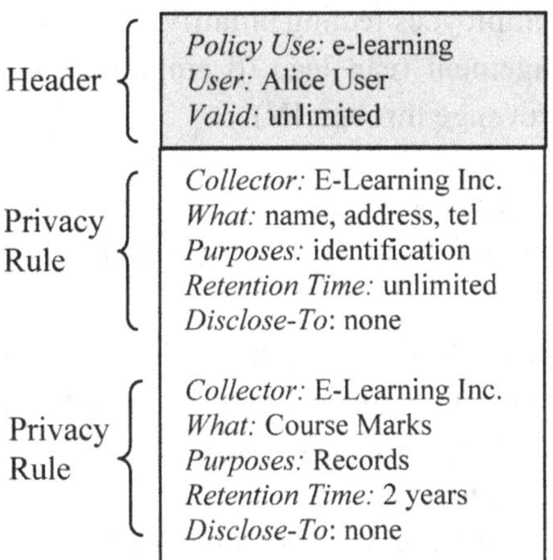

Figure 3. Example PIP; squares indicate storage points, triangles indicate use points

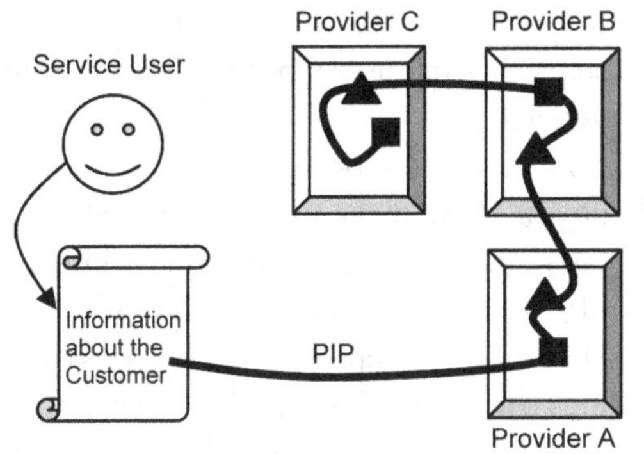

where violations can occur. To see where violations can occur, the flow of the private information is traced, from the point where it leaves the service user to where the information is used and stored. This leads to the next definition.

Definition 3: The private information path (PIP) is the path drawn through all points traversed by the private information, from the point where it leaves the service user to the point(s) where it is stored, possibly traversing points in between where it is used. The PIP can traverse multiple providers where providers disclose the user's private information to other providers.

Figure 2. Using a privacy policy to express user control over private information

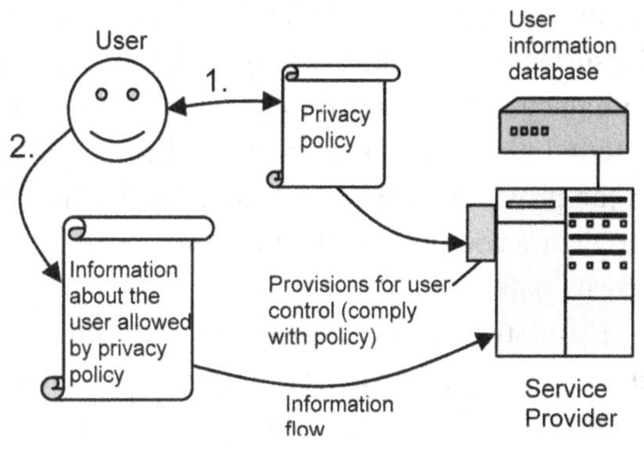

The PIP (see Figure 3) is an informal mechanism to help the security/privacy analyst visualize where attacks on the private information can happen.

Privacy violations can be classified as internal and external violations, as follows:

Definition 4: An internal violation (IV) (or inside attack) of privacy policy is one that is carried out by an insider of the provider organization (i.e., someone who has special data access privileges by virtue of an association with the organization [e.g., employee]), whose access and use of the private information does not comply with the user's privacy policy. An external violation (EV) (or outside attack) of privacy policy is one that is carried out by a noninsider of the provider organization, whose access and use of the private information does not comply with the user's privacy policy.

An example of an internal violation is where an employee secretly copies private information and sells it to the provider's competitors, in violation of privacy policy. Other examples of internal violations are from the category of unintentional or accidental violations, where the user's private information could be leaked (e.g., private data inadvertently sent in an e-mail) or misplaced (e.g., recently, a prominent bank was discovered to be faxing confidential customer records to a farmer) due to poor business processes. Thus, an internal violation may be very difficult to detect since on the surface the employees may appear to comply with the user's privacy policy. An example of an external violation is where an attacker unknown to the provider plants a Trojan horse inside the provider's computer system to steal confidential private data.

Estimating a service provider's capability to protect privacy involves looking at what provisions are in place to prevent IV and EV, that is, prevent attacks that violate the user's privacy policy.

Provisions against IV would have to cover both violations due to poor information management (e.g., lack of suitable tracking mechanisms) and violations that are intentional and malicious. These violations correspond to information management vulnerabilities within the provider organization that allow the violations to occur. Examples of such vulnerabilities are:

- Lack of anyone in the provider organization who is accountable for the private information in the organization's possession.
- Poor business processes that lack mechanisms to track which data are used where or used for what purpose; for example, employees casually providing the names of clients for a survey.
- Poor education and enforcement of company policies regarding the proper care and handling of personal information; for example, employees bringing work home that contains private information in the clear.
- Divulging personal information unwittingly to an attacker who uses social engineering.
- Lack of adequate security provisions to protect private information; for example, private data stored in the clear in data bases.
- Poor working conditions that give rise to employees feeling unfairly treated by management (can lead to employees seeking revenge through IV).

The following provisions aim to prevent IV or lessen the probability of it occurring:

- Educating employees and effectively enforcing company policies regarding the proper care and handling of personal information.
- Training employees on how to recognize and resist social engineering that targets the divulgence of personal information.
- Use of a privacy policy compliance system (PPCS) (Yee & Korba, 2004; Lategan & Olivier, n.d.) that automatically ensures that the user's privacy policy is not violated.
- Use of a monitoring system to monitor how insiders make use of the private data; the monitoring can be done in real time or off-line (users' sessions recorded).
- Use of cryptographically secure logs (these logs can be later inspected to check for policy violations) to record each transaction involving private data on all servers.
- Use of reputation mechanisms to record and indicate the past performance of the provider organization in terms of integrity (e.g., Better Business Bureau).
- Use of seals of approval that attest to the fact that the provider organization has undergone and passed rigorous inspections of its processes; for example, ISO 9001: 2000 (International Organization for Standardization, n.d.).

This list is of course not exhaustive. A provider may employ none, one, or more than one of these provisions.

In the case of provisions against EV, the question to ask is: "What are possible EV violations of a privacy policy?" These violations are carried out by attackers who have not been granted access to the targeted private information. These attackers target a range of security vulnerabilities, from software systems that can be breached to access the private information to simple theft of laptops and other devices used to store private information.

Our estimates of the capability to protect privacy will depend on the provisions that have been put in place against both IV and EV vulnerabilities.

There are situations in which multiple service providers may be involved in a single service. In these situations, a provider may share private information with other providers. For example, an online book store (e.g., Amazon.com) may make use of an online payment service (e.g., Paypal.com) and a shipping service (e.g., fedex.com) in order to sell the consumer a book. For the sake of exposition, the *first* provider is the one with which the user chooses to interact. *Second* providers are providers with which the first provider shares the user's private data in order to complete its purpose (such as selling a book in the example above). *Third* providers are ones with which the second provider shares the original user's private data in order to use the third providers' services. Similarly, it is possible to define *fourth* providers, *fifth* providers, and so on. For convenience, label second, third, fourth, and so forth providers as *chained* providers. In order to evaluate the first provider for its capability to protect privacy, it is necessary to carry out the same evaluation for all chained providers that are linked to the first provider in terms of service usage, as just described, and that receive the original user's private information due to this linkage. In other words, IV and EV would need to be examined not just for the first provider but also for each chained provider in turn. Second providers would be identified in the original user's privacy policy under "Disclose-To" (see Figure 1). Similarly, third providers would be identified in the first provider's privacy policy, fourth providers would be identified in the second provider's privacy policy, and so on. Of course, all second providers have to agree to comply with the first provider's privacy policy (the first provider is the "user" here), all third providers have to agree to comply with the second provider's privacy policy, and so on. Further, the first provider would incorporate into its privacy policy the portions of the original user's privacy policy that relate to the private information to be shared with the second providers, each second provider would incorporate into its privacy policy the portions of the original user's privacy policy that relate to the private information to be shared with the third providers, and so on.

Past Violations

Intuitively, a service provider's record of past privacy violations should impact its future capability of privacy protection. As for a sex offender, one could say that the fact that a service provider has violated privacy in the past means that it is more likely to lack the capability of privacy protection in the future. However, the comparison may not be so clear cut. A service provider may be intensely motivated by profit and public image. In fact, one could argue that a company that has violated privacy in the past is more likely to put measures in place to avoid violating privacy in the future in order to protect its public image and profit, especially if knowledge of the past violation is in the public domain. In this case, the capability of privacy protection in the future is *increased* if it has violated privacy in the past, not decreased. The influence of a provider's past privacy violations on its future capability of protecting privacy can be postulated as depending on at least the following factors:

- The type of service provider, for example, profit-oriented, nonprofit-oriented: A profit-oriented provider will probably want to put measures in place to avoid future privacy violations to protect its profit, increasing its future capability of protecting privacy;

- The severity of the past privacy violation: The type of information violated and the number of people affected by the violation contribute to this severity, for example, a disclosure of credit card numbers affecting 10,000 people would generally be regarded as more severe than a disclosure of personal e-mail addresses affecting 100 people; probably the more severe the violation, the more the service provider is motivated to avoid violations in the future, likely increasing its future capability of protecting privacy;
- The time when new measures against future violations were installed: If the installation occurred after the past violations, this could indicate that the service provider was serious about avoiding future violations, likely increasing its future capability of protecting privacy. Of course, the installation may have been carried out for other reasons (e.g., window dressing to prop up the company's shares); it is difficult to be sure, but in general perhaps the provider can be given the benefit of the doubt.

Given the above discussion, it is suggested that past violation information not be integrated into estimates of future capability of protecting privacy, but rather that it is treated simply as *contextual information*, to be considered in conjunction with the estimates developed below as "support," that is, suggesting an increase in future privacy protection capability. This is primarily due to the imprecise nature of any conclusions that might be drawn from past violations, as discussed. Table 1 shows how the above factors from past violations can, to varying degrees, support the future capability of protecting privacy. To use Table 1, one would first calculate the estimates of future privacy protection capability as presented below. Then these estimates would be supported by the entry in Table 1 that corresponds to the choice of past violation influencing factors down the left side and across the top of the table. If the service provider has no past privacy violations, Table 1 does not apply, and the estimates are not affected by past violations.

Note that the above ideas on provider behavior in response to a privacy violation have not been verified. This is left for future work.

Definition of the Estimates

An estimate of a service provider's capability for protecting the service user's privacy may be defined as follows:

DEFINITION 5: An *estimate* of a provider's capability for protecting user privacy is a numerical rating (e.g., percentage) that indicates the approximate degree to which the provider is capable of avoiding IV and EV.

Table 1. Support for future privacy protection capability based on the service provider's response to past violations

	Nonprofit-Oriented Service Provider		**Profit-Oriented Service provider**	
Severity of Past Violations	**No New Measures Installed Post Violations**	**Some New Measures Installed Post Violations**	**No New Measures Installed Post Violations**	**Some New Measures Installed Post Violations**
Low	Very Low Support	Low Support	Low Support	Medium Support
Medium	Very Low – Low Support	Low-Medium Support	Low-Medium Support	Medium-High Support
High	Low Support	Medium Support	Medium Support	High Support

Exhibit 1.

$$E_1 = (p + q) / (m + n), \quad \text{if } m + n > 0, \quad \text{so that } 0 \le E \le 1 = 1, \quad \text{if } m + n = 0.$$

Exhibit 2.

$$e_i = p/m, \quad \text{if } m > 0, \quad \text{so that } 0 \le e_i \le 1 = 1, \quad \text{if } m=0$$
$$e_e = q/n, \quad \text{if } n > 0, \quad \text{so that } 0 \le e_e \le 1 = 1, \quad \text{if } n=0.$$

In Definition 5, suppose for example that the estimate (rating) of a provider's capability for protecting user privacy is 70%. This means that the provider's installed provisions are *capable* of avoiding violations of user privacy approximately every 7 out of 10 times. This does NOT mean that the provider's installed provisions *actually* avoid the violations approximately every 7 out of 10 times. An estimate as described in Definition 5 only rates capability; rating actual privacy protection performance would be much more complex and is not needed to achieve the benefits claimed for the approach proposed here.

In Definition 5, the capability to avoid IV and EV depends on effective protective provisions (e.g., encrypting the private data, together with careful encryption key management) that the organization has in place to prevent violations. Let E denote an estimate of capability to protect privacy. By Definition 5, E will need to account for the provisions used against IV and EV.

To account for the provisions against IV, we propose that a special privacy impact assessment (PIA) (Treasury Board of Canada, n.d.), explained below—extended to identify vulnerabilities that can lead to malicious IV—be carried out to identify IV vulnerabilities. Suppose that such an assessment identified that m IV vulnerabilities and countermeasures (provisions against IV) are in place for p of these vulnerabilities. To account for provisions against EV, we propose that a special security threat analysis (Salter, Saydjari, Schneier, & Wallner, 1998), explained below, oriented towards discovering EV vulnerabilities be carried out. Suppose that this analysis identified that n security vulnerabilities and countermeasures (provisions against EV) are in place for q of these vulnerabilities. Then, one formulation of E is (See Exhibit 1).

Another formulation of E is:

$$E_2 = (e_i, e_e)$$

where e_i accounts for the provisions used against IV and e_e accounts for the provisions used against EV, and (See Exhibit 2).

E_1 has the advantage of providing a single number for ease of comparison between different providers. A threshold t for E_1 may be predetermined such that for E_1 above t, the provisions installed by the provider against IV and EV are deemed to give it an adequate capability to protect privacy.

E_2 has the advantage of focusing in on where an organization stands in terms of its provisions against IV or EV separately. Thresholds t_i and t_e may be predetermined for e_i and e_e respectively, such that for e_i or e_e above its respective threshold, the corresponding installed provisions against IV or EV are deemed to give the provider an adequate

Figure 4. Region (shaded) in which a service provider's capability to protect privacy is acceptable

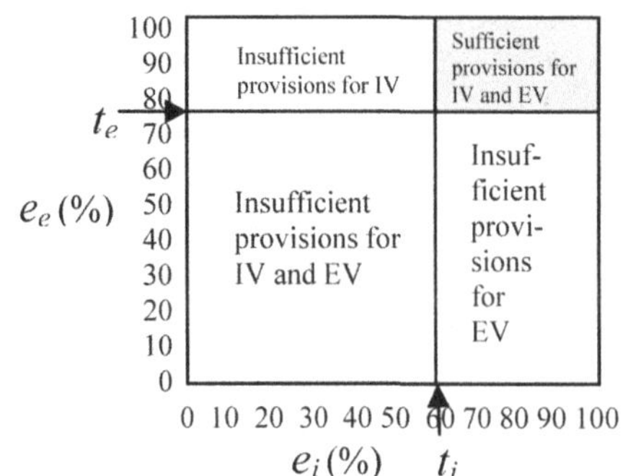

capability to protect against IV or EV. In practice, e_i and e_e may be expressed as percentages that define a region in a 100 x 100 plane in which a provider's capability to avoid privacy policy violations is adequate (acceptable) (shaded region in Figure 4).

We will use both E_1 and E_2. The thresholds t, t_i, and t_e may be set by a privacy authority, such as a privacy commissioner, responsible for ensuring that the public's privacy is protected.

For chained provider situations (see above), the evaluation of E requires special treatment. The following rule is proposed for these situations.

CHAINED RULE: *E evaluation for a service with chained providers:* A first provider passes E evaluation (i.e., each estimate is above or equal to its threshold) if and only if the first provider and each of its chained providers that receives the original user's private information all pass E evaluation.

The chained rule ensures that if at least one chained provider that receives the original user's private data fails E evaluation, the corresponding first provider is also regarded as having failed, even if it itself passes. This outcome seems to agree with personal wishes since the original user would not want private information abused by a chained provider after the user placed trust in the first provider.

CALCULATION OF THE ESTIMATES

Determination of *m* and *p* for IV

This determination requires a special PIA (Treasury Board of Canada, n.d.) in order to identify IV vulnerabilities and provisions against these vulnerabilities. A basic description of how a PIA is carried out, along with an extension to identify vulnerabilities that could lead to malicious IV follows.

A PIA is a comprehensive process designed to assist organizations to determine the impacts of program and service delivery initiatives on individual privacy. It has the following main stages:

a. **Project Initiation:** Define the scope for the PIA, allocate team resources, and adapt PIA tools according to the scope. The team may consist of privacy and security experts, legal experts, program managers, system managers, and so on.
b. **Data Analysis:** Describe proposed business process diagrams and identify clusters of personal information in business processes. Develop detailed data flow charts
c. **Privacy Analysis:** Complete privacy analysis questionnaires. Discuss answers to questions that require further detail. Identify and describe privacy issues and implications

Table 2. Questionnaire to identify vulnerabilities leading to malicious IV

	Question	Rationale
1.	Is the private information of high value to outside agencies or a competitor?	The higher the value, the more a malicious attacker will be tempted to steal and sell the information.
2.	What are some possible ways for an unauthorized insider to gain access to the private information?	This question will identify security weaknesses.
3.	What are some possible ways for an authorized insider to violate the privacy policy?	This question will identify nonsecurity weaknesses (e.g., using the private information for a different purpose).
4.	Does the organization have an employee assistance program that includes counseling and help with financial difficulties?	Such a program may eliminate some financial motivation for a malicious IV.
5.	Does the organization have an ombudsman or other impartial agent to assist employees with their grievances?	Such an impartial agent may eliminate or reduce the motivation to seek revenge by committing a malicious IV.
6.	Does the organization have a history of perceived injustices to employees?	If the answer is "yes," employees may be motivated by revenge to commit a malicious IV.
7.	Does the organization conduct a stringent background and reliability check on a candidate for employment prior to hiring the candidate?	While a background and reliability check is not guaranteed to weed out potential inside attackers, it should eliminate those with criminal backgrounds.
8.	Does the organization require candidates for employment to disclose any potential conflicts of interest they may have with respect to their new employment and any outside interests prior to hire? Does the organization require ongoing disclosure of conflicts of interest after hire?	Eliminating conflicts of interest should reduce related motivations for malicious inside attacks. For example, an inside attacker may secretly compromise private information in favor of an outside interest, believing that the compromise is undetected.

d. **Privacy Impact Assessment Report:** Summarize the privacy risks and evaluate the degree of risk involved. Identify and discuss actions or options to mitigate the risks. End by taking any other considerations into account and describe the path forward.

We are primarily interested in the vulnerabilities identified by the privacy analysis portion of the PIA through a series of questionnaires. The latter are concerned with the management of private information in order to comply with privacy legislation. To identify vulnerabilities that could lead to malicious IV, we propose extending the privacy analysis with an additional questionnaire designed to discover risks that could result in malicious IV, as shown in Table 2, to be used in conjunction with the PIP.

In identifying vulnerabilities, the PIA team may weigh the vulnerabilities in terms of how likely they are to lead to violations, and eliminate the ones that are unlikely to be violated. The weighing process may consider such factors as risk to the violator that the violator could be caught as well as the violator's motivation for the violation.

The total number m of IV vulnerabilities is the sum of the number of vulnerabilities identified using this questionnaire and the number of vulnerabilities identified in the above PIA that are potential internal violations. The number of provisions already in place countering these vulnerabilities gives p. Since an organization may plan to install a certain number of such provisions in the future, it is possible to obtain p, reflecting both provisions in place and planned. However, the author's opinion is that p should count only provisions already in place, since something that is planned may never actually happen.

Determination of *n* and *q* for EV

This determination requires a threat analysis of security vulnerabilities in the organization's systems that could allow EV to happen. An overview of threat analysis follows.

Threat analysis or threat modeling is a method for systematically assessing and documenting the security risks associated with a system (Salter et al., 1998). The results can help development teams identify the strengths and weaknesses of the system and serve as a basis for investigations into vulnerabilities and required mitigation. Threat modeling involves understanding the adversary's goals in attacking the system based on the system's assets of interest. It is predicated on that fact that an adversary cannot attack a system without a way of supplying it with data or otherwise accessing it. In addition, an adversary will only attack a system if it has some assets of interest. The following threat modeling terminology is selected from Salter et al. (1998):

- **Attack path:** A sequence of conditions in a threat tree that must be met for an attack goal (threat) to be achieved. A valid attack path (one with no mitigated conditions) is a vulnerability.
- **Threat:** The adversary's goals, or what an adversary might try to do to a system. Threats to a system always exist, regardless of mitigation.
- **Threat Tree or Attack Tree:** An analysis tool that describes the attack paths for a particular threat. A threat tree is comprised of hierarchical conditions and allows the threat to be characterized. The root of the threat tree is the threat to which the tree corresponds.

The method of threat analysis given by Salter et al. (1998) was intended for external threats to systems. The steps in this method are:

1. Create attack trees for the system.
2. Apply weights to the leaves.
3. Prune the tree so that only exploitable leaves remain.
4. Generate corresponding countermeasures.
5. Optimize countermeasure options.

However, the above steps are oriented towards the development and implementation of systems. In this work, it is not necessary to optimize the countermeasures since we are not concerned with implementation. On the other hand, it is necessary to identify the threats before creating the attack trees. Thus, the above steps are modified to:

1. Identify threats on the user's private data.
2. Create attack trees for the provider's service.
3. Apply weights to the leaves.
4. Prune the tree so that only exploitable leaves remain. Count the number of such leaves or vulnerabilities (this gives the n).
5. Determine if countermeasures are in place for the vulnerabilities found in Step 4. Count the number of these vulnerabilities so mitigated (this gives the q).

A description of each step follows.

Step 1: Identify threats on the user's private data. This step requires experience and imagination and may involve confirming details with management or the developers of the service.

Examine the architecture and all available details of the service and enumerate possible outside threats on the user's private data. Represent the system pictorially to get the big picture. It is useful to identify the main or root threat which includes most if not all other threats, for then only one attack tree needs to be created. Disregard any existing provisions against outside threats; they will be accounted for in Step 5. For example, a possible outside threat for an online banking service is theft of private information from the bank's customer information database.

Step 2: Create attack trees for the provider's service. Corresponding to each treat identified in Step 1, systematically create an attack tree by putting yourself in the adversary's place in finding the weak points in the work processes or the service system and the paths which will lead to realizing the threat. This analysis terminates in a series of vulnerability leaves for each attack tree.

(In this work, each attack tree is represented by hierarchical indented headings rather than pictorially, which can take up too much space and become unwieldy).

Step 3: Apply weights to the leaves. For each leaf, assign qualitative values (e.g., high, medium, low) for adversary risk, impediment to access, cost, and motivation (added for IV but applies to EV too). For example, an adversary sending an e-mail containing a virus attachment has low risk (probability of being identified is low), medium impediment to access (probability of the victim not opening the attachment and unleashing the virus is medium), low cost (cost to the adversary to create the virus e-mail is low), and high motivation (the adversary wants to cause as much disruption as possible). These values can be represented as a 4-tuple (L, M, L, H) where L, M, H stand for low, medium, high respectively, and the left most position in the tuple is risk, followed by impediment to access, followed by cost, and finally motivation. As another example, an adversary who is an insider with authorized access to private information and who wants to steal that information may be weighted as (L, L, L, H), that is, the adversary has low risk (probability of being caught is low), low impediment to access (adversary already has authorized access), low cost (cost to the adversary to make a copy of the information is low), and high motivation (the financial value of the information is very high). The provider with a vulnerability weighting of (L, L, L, H) has to think seriously about adding provisions to mitigate the vulnerability, as this weighting means that there is a very high probability that an attack using this vulnerability will occur.

Step 4: Prune the tree so that only exploitable leaves remain. Count the number of such leaves or vulnerabilities. Prune by deciding what levels (high, medium, low) of risk, impediment to access, cost, and motivation the provider is willing to have associated with the remaining vulnerabilities. These levels will determine which vulnerabilities are exploitable, and therefore add to the provider's cost to install countermeasures (provisions against privacy policy violations). Providers may choose to spend more or less on countermeasures by setting levels that result in less or more, respectively, leaves being pruned. For example, setting a level of (H, M, H, L) would prune all leaves with matching levels as well as all leaves that match (H, H, H, L) since (H, H, H, L) implies an even lower probability of attack than (H, M, H, L).

After pruning the tree, count the number n of exploitable leaves or vulnerabilities that remain.

Step 5: Determine if countermeasures are in place for the vulnerabilities found in Step 4. Count the number of these vulnerabilities so mitigated. Examine what countermeasures are in place for the vulnerabilities found in Step 4 and count the number of vulnerabilities q that have countermeasures. This step requires knowledge and experience of which countermeasures can be applied in a given situation.

Example Calculation of *n* and *q* Using Threat Analysis

Consider the automatic bank teller machine (ATM) that is ubiquitous in most shopping malls. There are many possible threats against an ATM but let us consider one threat: the threat of an adversary obtaining a bank customer's private account information for using an ATM. A possible attack tree for this threat is as follows:

1. Adversary obtaining a customer's account information for using an ATM
    - 1.1. Adversary holds up customer obtaining customer's access card and pin
    - 1.2. Adversary installs an ATM front end that secretly captures the customer's card info and pin
        - 1.2.1. The captured information is stored in the front end
        - 1.2.2. The captured information is transmitted to the adversary

1.3. Adversary finds customer's access card and has a way of discovering the pin
    1.3.1. Adversary guesses the pin based on researching the customer
    1.3.2. Adversary uses a dictionary attack to discover the pin
    1.3.3. Adversary uses social engineering to obtain the pin

It can be seen that the root of this attack tree (1) contains the threat and the branches are attack paths that are alternative ways to realize the threat. For example, the path (1, 1.3, 1.3.3) is a legitimate attack path. The leaves of this tree are the nodes 1.1, 1.2.1, 1.2.2, 1.3.1, 1.3.2, and 1.3.3. As an example of applying weights to this tree, the leaf 1.1 has very high risk to the attacker, the impediments to access is low (customers with ATM cards are plentiful), the cost to the attacker to carry out the attack is low (e.g., fake gun), and the attacker's motivation is high (attacker is desperate for money). Because the risk to the attacker is very high, the path (1, 1.1) may be pruned from the tree. Similarly, the leaf 1.2.1 may be unlikely since the risk to the adversary is high (the front end could be discovered before the captured data could be retrieved). As well, the leaves 1.3.1 and 1.3.2 are infeasible due to the fact that the ATM captures the card and flags the account after a fixed number of pin entries. After pruning the unlikely attack paths from the tree, the tree that remains is as follows:

1. Adversary gaining access to customer's account information for using an ATM
    1.2. Adversary installs an ATM front end that secretly captures the customer's card info and pin
        1.2.2 The captured information is transmitted to the adversary
    1.3. Adversary finds customer's access card and has a way of discovering the pin
        1.3.3 Adversary uses social engineering to obtain the pin

Thus there are two likely attack paths: (1, 1.2, 1.2.2) and (1, 1.3, 1.3.3). A countermeasure for (1, 1.2, 1.2.2) would be to disallow any possibility of a front end being installed to an ATM, perhaps by physically redesigning the ATM or by frequent random inspections and monitoring. Suppose that this countermeasure is not yet in place. A countermeasure for (1, 1.3, 1.3.3) would be to strengthen procedures so that social engineering cannot succeed (e.g., no one is allowed to give out the customer's pin no matter what the circumstance). Suppose that this countermeasure is already in place. Then for this example, $e_e = q/n = 1/2$.

APPLICATION EXAMPLE

Consider a Web service, such as Easy123Drugs.com, that is an online drug store (e.g., Walgreens.com). Easy123Drugs is a multiprovider service that makes use of two business Web services: an online payment service PayAsYouLikeIt.com (e.g., Paypal.com) and an accounting service AccountingAsNeeded.com (e.g., cbiz.com). Suppose Easy123Drugs, PayAsYouLikeIt, and AccountingAsNeeded (all fictitious names with no hits on Google) are all Web services that are based on the service-oriented architecture (SOA) (O'Neill et al., 2003), employing XML-based protocols (not necessarily the case for the real life examples cited here). Due to space limitations in this article, the details regarding UDDI lookup and service binding via SOAP and WSDL (O'Neill et al., 2003) will not be described here. It is assumed that these initialization steps occur as required. Figure 5 shows the network architecture of these services after service lookup and binding have occurred. The dashed lines in Figure 5 indicate logical communication channels.

Table 3 shows the service user's private information required by each provider. The user provides required private information to Easy123Drugs once the user's privacy policy has been agreed to by Easy123Drugs. Easy123Drugs then

Figure 5. Network architecture of Easy123Drugs service

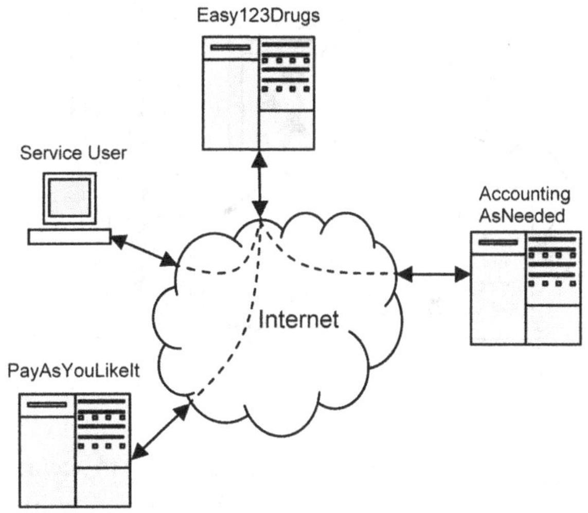

Table 3. Private information required

Web Service Provider	Private Information Required
Easy123Drugs	User's name, drug name and quantity, doctor's name and authorization, user's address
PayAsYouLikeIt	User's name, credit card details
AccountingAsNeeded	User's name, drug name, doctor's name, quantity of drug sold, price paid by user, user's address

discloses the user's private information to PayAsYouLikeIt and AccountingAsNeeded according to the user's privacy policy and after these second providers agreed with Easy123Drug's privacy policy (which contains the user's privacy preferences with regard to the information disclosed).

Easy123Drugs.com decides to hire a privacy auditor, certified to apply the above estimation methods, to estimate its capability of protecting privacy, with the intention of using the results in its advertising (assuming the results are good).

Calculation of *m* and *p*

To determine values for *m* and *p*, the auditor puts together a team to do a PIA for each service. Assume that each service stores the user's private data in a database and that the internal threats to the user's private data are about the same for each service. It is then possible to do one PIA that applies to all three services. However, the countermeasures in place are likely to be different for each service. The PIA team traces the flow of private information as shown by the PIP in Figure 6. In this figure, the customer's private information (Table 3) arrives first at Easy123Drugs where it is received (first triangle), stored (first square), and processed, including forwarding some of the information to PayAsYouLikeIt and AccountingAsNeeded (second triangle). Similarly, selected information (Table 3) is received at PayAsYouLikeIt and AccountingAsNeeded where it is stored and processed.

The PIA team performs the PIA and uncovers IV vulnerabilities that fall under malicious attacks and unintentional disclosures, as follows:

Figure 6. PIP for Easy123Drugs; squares indicate storage points, triangles indicate use

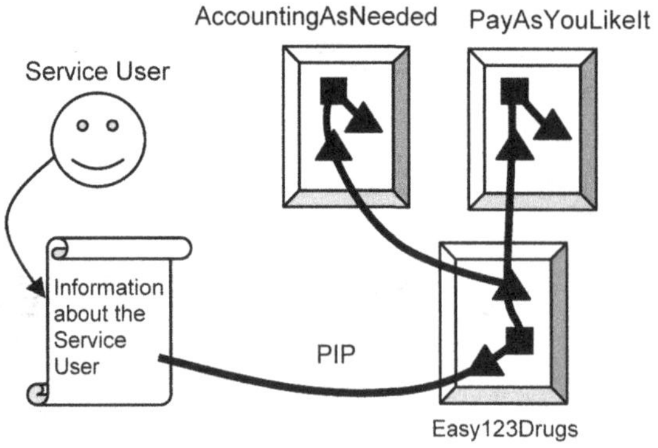

Malicious attacks:

a. Attacker steals the data for sale to an outside interest.
b. Attacker uses the data for social engineering a personal goal.
c. Attacker passes the data to a friend as a favor.
d. Attacker passes the data to a competitor free of charge.

Unintentional disclosure:

e. The data are inadvertently disclosed in an e-mail.
f. The data are inadvertently disclosed in a conversation.
g. A laptop containing the data is stolen.
h. Paper copies of the data are misplaced.
i. Paper copies of the data are left in a public area in plain view.
j. The data's retention time expires unknown to any staff.

For the malicious attacks, the PIA analysis considered the risks to the attacker and the attacker's motivation to carry out the attack. Due to the possibility that the source of the data could be traced, together with the fact that the data themselves are of relative low value (e.g., not military secrets), the risks to the attacker for a) and d) were considered very high and therefore these attacks are unlikely to occur. On the other hand, the risks to the attacker for b) and c) were considered low with the attacker's motivation high to medium since these attacks involve personal goals and relationships. Thus b) and c) were considered serious vulnerabilities that needed attention. Similarly, due to the fact that staff had undergone thorough training in safeguarding their laptops and paper copies, only vulnerabilities e), f), and j) were considered serious, requiring attention. Thus, the PIA identified five IV vulnerabilities that can be assigned to each provider as follows: Easy123Drugs gets the full $m=5$ vulnerabilities, PayAsYouLikeIt gets $m=4$ vulnerabilities since it has a retention time tracking mechanism, and AccountingAsNeeded gets $m=2$ vulnerabilities since it has the retention time tracking and the remaining unintentional vulnerabilities do not apply to accountants because they are trained in safe data handling procedures.

Suppose the PIA found that Easy123Drugs and PayAsYouLikeIt have countermeasures in place against all vulnerabilities except for b) (the exact nature of the countermeasures is not important for this example). Suppose that AccountingAsNeeded has countermeasures in place against both of its vulnerabilities. Therefore, $p=4$ for Easy123Drugs, $p=3$ for PayAsYouLikeIt, and $p=2$ for AccountingAsNeeded. Table 4 contains the values for m and p.

Table 4. Calculation of E_1 and E_2

Service	m	p	n	q	$E_1 = (p + q) / (m + n)$	$e_I = p/m$	$e_e = q/n$	$E_2 = (e_I, e_e)$ (%)
Easy123Drugs	5	4	7	6	.83	.80	.86	(80, 86)
PayAsYouLikeIt	4	3	6	5	.80	.75	.83	(75, 83)
AccountingAsNeeded	2	2	6	5	.88	1.0	.83	(100, 83)

Calculation of *n* and *q*

The threat analysis described above is now applied to calculate *n* and *q* for each provider. Again, assume that each service stores the user's private data in a database. Assume also that the external threats to the user's private data are the same for each service. It is then possible to do one threat analysis that applies to all three services. However, the countermeasures in place are likely to be different for each service. Following the steps mentioned above,

Step 1: Using Figure 5 to visualize possible threats against the user's data, the main EV threat that includes most other EV threats is: "outside attacker compromises the user's private data."

Steps 2 and 3: The attack tree and weights are as follows.

1. Outside attacker compromises the user's private data.
   - 1.1. Attacker steals the user's private data.
     - 1.1.1. Attacker launches a man-in-the-middle attack on a communication channel to eavesdrop. (L, L, L, M)
     - 1.1.2. Attacker launches a Trojan horse attack on a provider's system. (L, L, L, M)
     - 1.1.3. Attacker launches a phishing attack on the user. (L, L, M, H)
     - 1.1.4. Attacker uses social engineering to deceive a provider staff member into giving out the user's data. (M, M, L, M)
     - 1.1.5. Attacker breaks into a provider's premises to steal the user's data. (H, H, M, H)
     - 1.1.6. Attacker mugs a provider employee and steals the employee's access card to enter a provider's premises and steal the user's data. (H, H, L, M)
   - 1.2. Attacker modifies the user's private data.
     - 1.2.1. Attacker launches a man-in-the-middle attack on a communication channel to modify the user's data. (L, L, L, M)
     - 1.2.2. Attacker launches a virus attack on a provider's system. (L, L, L, M)
     - 1.2.3. Attacker uses social engineering to deceive a provider staff member into giving the attacker access to modify the user's data. (M, M, L, M)
     - 1.2.4. Attacker breaks into a provider's premises to modify the user's data. (H, H, M, H)
     - 1.2.5. Attacker mugs a provider employee and steals the employee's access card to enter a provider's premises and modify the user's data. (H, H, L, M)

Some of the reasoning behind the motivation weightings are: vulnerability 1.1.3 has motivation H as phishing is a quick way to obtain private data such as bank account information; vulnerabilities 1.1.5 and 1.2.4 have motivation H because breaking and entering is a serious crime and the attacker must be highly motivated before contemplating such an action.

Step 4: The attack tree can be pruned by removing attack paths that are weighted with at least two Hs other than for motivation. Applying this criterion removes the attack paths (1, 1.1, 1.1.5), (1, 1.1, 1.1.6), (1, 1.2, 1.2.4), and (1, 1.2, 1.2.5). This leaves seven vulnerabilities that can be assigned to each provider as follows: Easy123Drugs gets the full *n=7* vulnerabilities, PayAsYouLikeIt gets *n=6* vulnerabilities since the phishing attack really only applies to Easy123Drugs, and AccountingAsNeeded gets *n=6* vulnerabilities, again because the phishing attack does not apply to it. Note that the man-in-the-middle attack on a channel is double counted when it is considered a vulnerability for the provider at each end of the channel. However, this double counting is remedied by the countermeasure, which removes the vulnerability from both providers.

Step 5: Suppose that Easy123Drugs has countermeasures in place against all vulnerabilities except phishing (again, the exact nature of the countermeasures is not important here). Suppose also that PayAsYouLikeIt and AccountingAsNeeded have countermeasures in place against all vulnerabilities except social engineering. Therefore, *q=6* for Easy123Drugs, *q=5* for PayAsYouLikeIt, and *q=5* for AccountingAsNeeded. Table 4 contains the values for *n* and *q* as well as the calculated results for E_1 and E_2.

Suppose the minimum acceptable threshold for E_1 is *t=85*. Then the results (Table 4) show that AccountingAsNeeded is the only provider that passes E_1 evaluation. The other providers need to add more provisions against IV or EV in order to pass. They may choose to add provisions that are easy to install or that are the least expensive. It can also be observed that AccountingAsNeeded is the most capable of protecting privacy whereas PayAsYouLikeIt is the least capable. However, comparing these providers to select which one to use based on E_1 is not feasible since their services are all different.

Plotting E_2 for minimum acceptable thresholds $t_i=80$ and $t_e=80$ according to Figure 4 gives Figure 7, which shows that each service passes E_2 evaluation except for PayAsYouLikeIt (with $E_2 = (75, 83)$).

PayAsYouLikeIt is deficient in provisions for IV. For Easy123Drugs to pass E_2 evaluation as a first (i.e., multiprovider) service, PayAsYouLikeIt would have to add provisions against IV vulnerability b) above (see the chained rule above). Had thresholds t_i and t_e both been set to 90, no provider would pass. In this case, development would need to install a countermeasure against phishing, employees would need to be trained to resist social engineering, and provisions against IV would need to be added for providers that lacked

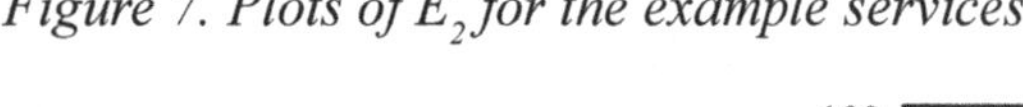

Figure 7. Plots of E_2 for the example services

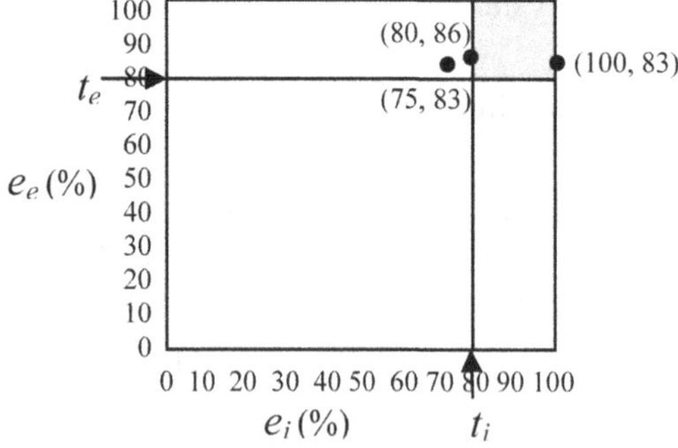

these countermeasures. This shows that estimates of privacy protection capability can be used as a tool by development or management (e.g., to require social engineering training) in order to achieve predefined goals of privacy protection.

To consider the effects of past violations, suppose that Easy123Drugs had a disgruntled employee who 2 years ago passed private information to the news media that a certain famous actress was purchasing cancer drugs. Suppose that this made headlines and as a result, Easy123Drugs was sued by the actress and had to pay her 2 million dollars in damages. Easy123Drugs has since made policy changes to ensure that employees feel that they are treated fairly by the company, including the hiring of an ombudsman and a counselor. This past violation can thus be considered of high severity with some new measures installed post violation in order to avoid such violations in the future. Based on Easy123Drugs' response to this past violation, Table 1 shows *high support* (right-most column under profit-oriented service provider) for the provider's future privacy protection capability. In other words, Easy123Drugs will be highly motivated to make sure that it is capable of protecting privacy.

RELATED WORK

The literature appears empty on works dealing directly with estimates of a service provider's capability to protect privacy. Only works that are indirectly related were found. These refer to the economics of security or the economics of privacy (see http://www.cl.cam.ac.uk/~rja14/econsec.html - available as of May 6, 2006). These authors hold the view that the lack of security or the lack of privacy are not due to the lack of technological solutions but rather are due to other (perhaps perverse) considerations such as economics and profitability. This work differs from that view in that the proposed approach evaluates the capability to protect privacy by counting provisions against privacy violations that ARE in place, NOT WHY they may or may not be in place. Nevertheless, their view is valuable in understanding how to improve privacy protection, and is thus seen as complementary to this work. Another area that is indirectly related to this work concerns privacy audits (Enright, n.d.) and privacy risk (or impact) assessment (or analysis) (Treasury Board of Canada, n.d.). As explained above, the latter consists of methods or guidelines on how to identify vulnerabilities or risks in managing private information in order to comply with privacy legislation. We applied a privacy impact assessment to find IV vulnerabilities. In general, these and other methods in the privacy audit domain can be introduced into this work to better understand risks that lead to IV and EV. For example, they could help identify a new class of privacy vulnerabilities. Alternatively, this work could be used in a privacy audit to obtain more comprehensive results, but further research in this regard is needed. Of course, the area of threat analysis is indirectly related to this work (although we applied threat analysis, it is still only indirectly related as a means to an end). Threat analysis has been used for many years and several forms of it exist. The different forms can differ in how weighting is done (as this work too has introduced motivation into the weighting), how a threat is defined, how many people should be involved in carrying out a threat analysis, how much detail is recorded, and so on. Other authors who have recently written on threat analysis include Karger (2006) and Rippon (2006). An older reference for basic threat analysis is Bauer (2002). Finally, other indirectly related work consists of the entire area of privacy enhancing technologies, some of which were mentioned above as provisions against IV. Also in this category is the work allowing Web sites to specify their privacy policies using platform for privacy preferences (P3P) (W3C, n.d.) to allow for automatic user agent interpretation of a privacy policy, and the machine readable privacy policy languages of

P3P preference exchange language (APPEL) (W3C, 2002) and enterprise privacy authorization language (EPAL) (IBM, 2003).

EVALUATION OF APPROACH

Since, as far as can be determined, this work is new, an evaluation of the proposed approach by direct comparisons to other similar works is not possible. Therefore, this evaluation is conducted by considering how well the approach can accomplish its stated purpose by considering in turn the suitability of each component of the approach or how well a component can perform its function.

The goal of the proposed approach is to evaluate the privacy protection capability of a service provider. This is achieved by considering a provider's installed provisions against violations of privacy policy and the provider's history of past violations, if any. It was postulated that a past violation under the "right" circumstances (i.e., profit-oriented provider, sizable violation known to the public, additional provisions to prevent future violations installed after the past violation) would motivate the provider to improve its capability to protect privacy. The approach consists of three components: i) a model of privacy protection in terms of privacy policy violations, ii) definition of estimates of a provider's capability to protect privacy, and iii) methods for calculating the estimates.

The model of privacy protection is based on preventing internal and external violations against privacy policies. This model requires that personal privacy policies exist in a provider organization and that the provider has agreed to uphold them. This requirement is reasonable since most online organizations today have their own privacy policies. Today, personal privacy policies are in the minority when compared to organizational privacy policies, but personal privacy policies should increase with time, in line with the increasing demand for organizations to respect personal privacy preferences.

The definitions of the estimates appear to be straightforward, and follow the model of privacy protection in terms of counting provisions against violations. Moreover, they provide not only a useful single number (E_1) comparison between different providers of similar services, but also an easy graphical visualization (by plotting E_2) of where a provider stands in terms of its capability to protect against IV and EV separately (Figure 4). The advantage of straight forward estimates should not be underestimated, since they need to be understandable by the general public, and "the simpler, the better."

The proposed methods for calculating the estimates naturally have strengths and weaknesses. Strengths include: a) both PIA and threat analysis are well known and have been practiced for years; b) both are well documented in the literature; and c) PIA is an approach recommended by privacy authorities. Weaknesses include: a) PIA is a rather long and involved procedure requiring management support; b) the questionnaire for identifying vulnerabilities that could lead to malicious IV requires testing to confirm its validity; c) PIA results may depend on the skill and knowledge of the people involved with doing the PIA; d) the results from threat analysis may depend on the skill and knowledge of the threat analyst; and e) in the threat analysis, the subjective weighting of the leaves and the pruning criterion are not as exact as one would like (the pruning criterion depends partly on how much money the organization is willing to spend on countermeasures, and links back to the economics of security related work mentioned above). Despite the weaknesses of the threat analysis, it is an accepted procedure and has been applied in many situations to assess threats. The threat analysis procedure may be improved with further research, or the application of other methods (such as privacy audit methods mentioned above) can be incorporated. To help mitigate weaknesses a), c), d), and to some extent e), we suggest that the methods be applied by a separate, impartial firm specialized in performing

PIA and threat analysis. To go further, guidelines on applying the methods could be standardized by a privacy authority, and only firms certified by the same authority may apply the methods. This would ensure that the calculation of the estimates of capability to protect privacy is done fairly and consistently for each provider. This approach of using certified third parties to evaluate something is not new; it has been applied successfully to determine conformance to the ISO 9000 series of standards (International Organization for Standardization, n.d.) as well as to evaluating ratings relative to the capability maturity model integration (CMMI) (Carnegie Mellon Software Engineering Institute, n.d.) for software producers.

The accuracy of the proposed estimates may be another point of contention. It may be argued that a simple count of provisions against IV or EV is not enough; actual protection of privacy depends on the *effectiveness* of these provisions. The author agrees that if effectiveness could be incorporated into the estimates, the results would be more accurate. However, effectiveness itself depends on many factors, such as the capability of the provision to do what it is supposed to do, how the provision is implemented, the environment in which the provision operates, and so on. The decision was made to avoid these complexities, opting instead for straightforward easy-to-calculate estimates. The author believes that this is reasonable, trusting that providers would not throw money away on ineffective provisions.

The idea that under the "right" circumstances (see second paragraph in this section), past violations would motivate a provider to protect privacy in the future is untested, as noted above under "Past Violations." Nevertheless, the idea seems intuitively reasonable. Testing this idea is left for future work.

Finally, it should be pointed out that a provider that is estimated to have the capability to protect privacy may still not do so in reality. For instance, this may happen if key people responsible for maintaining privacy enhancing technologies leave the provider. Another reason may be that the provider perceives goals other than privacy protection as having more immediate higher priority, such as spending money on new production capabilities rather than hiring people needed to maintain privacy enhancing technologies. Still a third reason may be that the provider has undergone a restructuring (e.g., acquired by another provider) and the new people in charge have different priorities. Incorporating such almost always unforeseeable changes into a method for likelihood estimation of privacy policy compliance would be very complicated and difficult. Nevertheless, it may be assumed that in general, providers that have the capability to protect privacy will do so, especially if failure to protect privacy means stiff legal penalties. Stiff legal penalties for failure to protect privacy have already been implemented (U.S. Government, n.d.).

In summary, the author believes that the approach proposed in this work is a reasonable first attempt at evaluating the capability of a provider to protect user privacy. Key challenges regarding the potentially subjective nature of the threat analysis may be reduced with further research.

CONCLUSION AND FUTURE RESEARCH

This work has proposed estimates for evaluating a provider's capability to protect privacy and illustrated the calculation of the estimates using an example of a multiprovider service. The estimates serve at least four important functions: 1) they make it possible for providers to be challenged if their capability for protecting privacy is perceived to be inadequate; 2) they allow for enforceable privacy protection legislation requiring providers to ensure that they can meet privacy policy compliance requirements; 3) they allow customers to compare providers in terms of their capability to protect privacy when deciding which provider to use for a particular service; and 4) they enable the providers themselves to improve their services by showing them i) where they stand in terms of privacy protection capability against IV and EV and ii) what provisions against IV or EV they need to add in order to improve their standing.

It is envisioned that providers will want to advertise their estimates to show that they exceed standard privacy protection capability thresholds (which could be standardized by an international body) in the same way that they advertise conformance to ISO 9000. This could encourage providers to achieve higher levels of privacy protection, which in turn could lead to greater public trust in Web service providers resulting in increased commerce.

Future research includes improving the methods for calculating the estimates, such as increasing the effectiveness of the procedure for threat analysis by automating it and making it more foolproof, as well as investigating other possible estimates of capability to protect privacy.

ACKNOWLEDGMENT

The author gratefully acknowledges the support of the National Research Council Canada for this work.

REFERENCES

W3C. (2002, April 15). *A P3P preference exchange language 1.0 (APPEL1.0)* (W3C Working Draft). Retrieved November 9, 2006, from http://www.w3.org/ TR/ P3P-preferences/

W3C. (n.d.). *Platform for privacy preferences (P3P) project.* Retrieved November 9, 2006, from http://www.w3.org/P3P/

Adams, C., & Barbieri, K. (2006). Privacy enforcement in e-services environments. In Yee, G. (Ed.), *Privacy protection for e-services*. Hershey, PA: Idea Group, Inc.

Bauer, M. (2002). Practical threat analysis and risk management. *Linux Journal, 2002*(93), 9. Retrieved November 7, 2008, from http://www.linuxjournal.com/ article/5567

Carnegie Mellon Software Engineering Institute. (n.d.). *Welcome to the CMMI Website*. Retrieved November 9, 2006, from http://www.sei.cmu.edu/cmmi/cmmi.html

Enright, K. P. (n.d.). *Privacy audit checklist.* Retrieved May 6, 2006, from http://cyber.law.harvard.edu/ clinical/privacyaudit.html

Goldberg, I., Wagner, D., & Brewer, E. (1997). Privacy-enhancing technologies for the Internet. In. *Proceedings of the IEEE COMPCON, 97*, 103–109.

IBM. (2003, June 12). *The enterprise privacy authorization language (EPAL 1.1)*. Retrieved June 2, 2007, http://www.zurich.ibm.com/ security/ enterprise-privacy/epal/

International Organization for Standardization. (n.d.). *Selection and use of the ISO 9000:2000 family of standards*. Retrieved January 28, 2006, from http://www.iso.org/iso/ en/iso9000-14000/ understand/ selection_use/selection_use.html

Iyengar, V. S. (2002). Transforming data to satisfy privacy constraints. In *Proceedings of the SIGKDD '02*, Edmonton, Alberta (pp. 279-288).

Karger, P. A. (2006, July). Privacy and security threat analysis of the federal employee personal identity verification (PIV) program. In *Proceedings of the Second Symposium on Usable Privacy and Security*, Pittsburgh, Pennsylvania (pp. 114-121).

Kenny, S., & Korba, L. (2002, November). Adapting digital rights management to privacy rights management. *Computers & Security, 21*(7), 648–664. doi:10.1016/S0167-4048(02)01117-3

Kobsa, A., & Schreck, J. (2003, May). Privacy through pseudonymity in user-adaptive systems. *ACM Transactions on Internet Technology*, *3*(2), 149–183. doi:10.1145/767193.767196

Lategan, F., & Olivier, M. (n.d.). *PrivGuard: A model to protect private information based on its usage.* Retrieved December 14, 2005, from http://mo.co.za/ open/privgrd.pdf

O'Neill, M., Hallam-Baker, P., MacCann, S., Shema, M., Simon, E., & Watters, P. A. (2003). *Web services security.* McGraw-Hill/Osborne.

Rippon, W. J. (2006, April). Threat assessment of IP based voice systems. In *Proceedings of the 1st IEEE Workshop on VoIP Management and Security 2006*, Vancouver, B.C., Canada (pp. 19-28).

Salter, C., Saydjari, O. S., Schneier, B., & Wallner, J. (1998, September). Towards a secure system engineering methodology. In *Proceedings of New Security Paradigms Workshop* (pp. 2-10).

Song, R., Korba, L., & Yee, G. (2006). Pseudonym technology for e-services. In Yee, G. (Ed.), *Privacy protection for e-services.* Hershey, PA: Idea Group, Inc.

Treasury Board of Canada. (n.d.). *The privacy impact assessment guidelines: A framework to manage privacy risk.* Retrieved May 6, 2006, from http://www.tbs-sct.gc.ca/ pgol-pged/piatp-pfefvp/ course1/mod2/mod2-5_e.asp

U.S. Government. (n.d.). *General overview of standards for privacy of individually identifiable health information.* Retrieved October 19, 2006, from http://www.hhs.gov/ ocr/hipaa/guidelines/ overview.pdf

Yee, G. (2006, September 18-22). Measuring privacy protection in Web services. In *Proceedings of the 2006 IEEE International Conference on Web Services (ICWS 2006)*, Chicago (pp. 647-654).

Yee, G., & Korba, L. (2003a, May 18-21). *The negotiation of privacy policies in distance education.* Paper presented at the 14th IRMA International Conference, Philadelphia.

Yee, G., & Korba, L. (2003b, January 27-31). Bilateral e-services negotiation under uncertainty. In *Proceedings of the 2003 International Symposium on Applications and the Internet (SAINT2003)*, Orlando, Florida (pp. 352-355).

Yee, G., & Korba, L. (2004, July 6-9). Privacy policy compliance for Web services. In *Proceedings of the 2004 IEEE International Conference on Web Services (ICWS 2004)*, San Diego (pp. 158-165).

Yee, G., & Korba, L. (2005). Semi-automatic derivation and use of personal privacy policies in e-business. [IGI Global, Inc.]. *International Journal of E-Business Research*, *1*(1), 54–69. doi:10.4018/jebr.2005010104

ENDNOTE

1 NRC Paper Number: NRC 50725. This article is a significant extension of Yee (2006).

This work was previously published in International Journal of Web Services Research, Volume 6, Issue 2, edited by Liang-Jie Zhang, pp. 20-41, copyright 2009 by IGI Publishing (an imprint of IGI Global).

Chapter 8
Issues on the Compatibility of Web Service Contracts

Surya Nepal
CSIRO ICT Centre, Australia

John Zic
CSIRO ICT Centre, Australia

ABSTRACT

In the Service Oriented Architecture (SOA) model, a service is characterized by its exchange of asynchronous messages, and a service contract is a desirable composition of a variety of messages. Though this model is simple, implementing large-scale, cross-organizational distributed applications may be difficult to achieve in general, as there is no guarantee that service composition will be possible because of incompatibilities of Web service contracts. We categorize compatibility issues in Web service contracts into two broad categories: (a) between contracts of different services (which we define as a composability problem), and (b) a service contract and its implementation (which we define as a conformance problem). This chapter examines and addresses these problems, first by identifying and specifying contract compatibility conditions, and second, through the use of compatibility checking tools that enable application developers to perform checks at design time.

INTRODUCTION

The Service Oriented Architecture (SOA) model is being promoted for use in the development of the next generation of large scale distributed applications. These applications are comprised of a collection of independent, autonomous, abstract services that are provided by business partners and third party service providers. Though the model is simple, the SOA vision of large-scale, cross-organizational distributed applications may be difficult to achieve due to the issues of incompatibility of service contracts and their respective implementations.

Some of the most significant issues arise because the SOA model is based on an *abstraction*

DOI: 10.4018/978-1-61350-104-7.ch008

paradigm, with internal operations of the service deliberately hidden. The service is defined solely through the sequence of messages communicated. Hoare (Hoare, 1995) and Milner (Milner, 1989) recognized this in their seminal works in process algebra. Such system descriptions that abstract away internal operations may result in composed behaviors that differ from each other despite apparently offering the same message sequence inputs and outputs. Potentially, these differences lead to undesirable behaviors such as deadlocks or starvation. Avoiding these undesirable service behaviors may be achieved by composing this type of system with an "adaptor" that essentially prohibits those undesirable states ever being reached, while still preserving the external communication. This approach is an active area of research within the business process community (Benatallah, Casati, Grigori, Nezhad & Touami,2005). However, these adaptors are typically written by the service providers themselves. Because they are written by and are a part of the provider's service, the provider has had the opportunity to be aware of some of the internal operations of the service. They have "looked inside the box" and realized the operations that lead to undesirable behaviors. In this book chapter, we present an alternative methodology and support tools that allow the rigorous development of service contracts and their implementations. This methodology is able to assure completeness, acceptable consistent state and termination for the service. There is no requirement to "look inside the box" in order to achieve a composed system that behaves as expected, and there is no need to build specialized adaptors.

Problem Statement

Building applications using the SOA model is getting easier with the good support from Web services standards (BPEL4WS, 2002; SSDL, 2005; WS-BA, 2005) and support tools. Because of the availability of these standards and tools, architects are able to specify service-oriented applications, as well as allow developers the capacity to build service-oriented applications. Nonetheless, as with any distributed systems, issues of deadlocks, race conditions, failures and exceptions, concurrency and asynchrony remain, and need careful attention. Previously, similar issues were faced by the distributed transaction community with partial resolutions being based on the use of ACID based technologies (Elmagarmid, 1992; Gray & Reuter, 1992). However, as these solutions are for tightly coupled, short-lived applications, they are inappropriate in the autonomous, loosely coupled, cross-organizational SOA environment.

Figure 1. Composition and conformance relations between service contracts and service implementations

$$\begin{array}{cccccc} & C & \xrightarrow{Compose} & C_1 & \otimes^C & C_2 \\ Conform & \downarrow & & \downarrow & & \downarrow \\ & S & \xrightarrow{Compose} & S_1 & \otimes^S & S_2 \end{array}$$

Analysis of service compatibility issues is highly amenable to model checking and the judicious application of formal methods. A growing body of work is examining the use and application of formal methods and model checking to establishing the compatibility of service-oriented applications. Compatibility issues are studied in two broad categories: (a) between a service contract and its implementation (Nakajima, 2002) and (b) between contracts of different services (Bultan, Fu, Hall & Su, 2003;Foster, Uchitel, Kramer, & Magee, 2004; Greenfield, Kuo, Nepal, & Fekete, 2005; Nararaynan & Mcllraith, 2002). We define the first category as a *composability problem* (Milanovic and Malek, 2004)) and the second category as a *conformance problem*.

Figure 1 shows the distinction between the *conformance* and *composition* relations between service contracts and service implementations used in this chapter. Note that there are two separate composition relations, one at the contract level, which is the focus in this chapter, and one at the service level (which is discussed briefly at a later section). The domain of this service contract composition relation is the set of all (abstract) contracts that are used to specify the behaviors of the composed system. The range of the relation is the set formed from a composition operation $\otimes^{C}$ of individual service contracts that are typically provided by individual service providers. There is a similar relation at the service implementation level, with the domain of the composition relation being the idealized and intended behavior of the system, and the range being the set of composed service implementations (under another operation ($\otimes^{S}$). Conformance, on the other hand is a *refinement* relation (Abrial, 1996) between the set of abstract contract level specifications, and a corresponding set of service implementations that are developed from these specifications. However, it is outside the scope of this paper to prove these relations, and they will be the subject of a future work. This chapter is focused on elaborating a methodology for developing a service oriented system that adheres (as much as possible) to the behaviors implied in Figure 1. To help illustrate the above problem statement, a simple e-procurement example between a service provider (merchant) and a client (customer) of this service is used as a working example throughout this chapter.

First, it is worthwhile noting that ensuring the compatibility (under composition) between participating service contracts is not always straightforward. For example, the merchant and customer services in an e-procurement scenario are said to be compatible (under composition) if they can work with each other and that there are no undesirable or unexpected interactions. The system needs to handle everything from the ideal case, where everything goes smoothly, to service level exceptions (e.g., customer requests for cancellation of the ordering process, late payment, or where there is a delay in delivery of the goods ordered and paid for). Previous work (Greenfield et al., 2005) in service contract compatibility defined three compatibility criteria. The *completeness* criteria can be checked easily using message queues in model checkers and has previously been examined (Greenfield et al., 2005). This book chapter examines the two latter criteria (*termination* and *acceptable consistent state*) further and presents our analysis using an e-procurement example. We briefly summarize it below.

WS-Business Activity (WS-BA) (WS-BA, 2005) can be used to describe termination patterns in service contracts. Our approach enables application programmers to specify termination patterns and check the termination criterion at design time. Fundamentally, we note that services must terminate in a globally acceptable consistent state. For example, in the e-procurement application, an acceptable consistent state is when both the merchant and customer are satisfied; the merchant receives the payment and delivers the goods, and the customer pays for the invoice and receives the goods. One of the ways of specifying these states is to define global constraints over application states of each of the participating autonomous services. However, this is not possible as application states of an autonomous service are, by definition, internal to each service and not accessible by others. Short of the merchant and customer services developing their own dedicated adaptor processes so as to ensure that the systems are compatibility, we propose a way of stating acceptable states in contracts using only message related states. Our approach is based on the assumptions that significant states are reflected in the sequences of messages exchanged, and consequently global acceptable states can be defined by the conjunction of local acceptable states that can be checked at design time.

As mentioned earlier, the second source of incompatibility is the *non-conformance* of business processes with their external behaviors, expressed through service contracts. That is, the external behaviors of the services are not implemented correctly, or alternatively, the external behavior of the service does not reflect the internal behavior of a business process. We address this problem in this chapter by describing the relationship between the business process workflows and Web service contracts through constraints.

Finally, we demonstrate the feasibility of our approach by developing a set of support tools. The important aspect of our tools is that it detects the compatibility errors (described by Bultan et al. (2003), Foster et al. (2004), and Nararaynan and Mcllraith (2002)), as well as classifying errors and provides reasoning for them. This helps developers to understand the reasons behind the incompatibility, and correct them at design time. The main differentiator of our approach from other existing approaches (e.g., Benatallah, Casati, & Toumani, 2004; Bultan et al., 2003; Cheng, Singh, & Vouk, 2002; Foster et al., 2004; Greenfield et al., 2005; Nararaynan & Mcllraith, 2002) is that they work with service contracts expressed in notations that do not deal with acceptable consistent states and termination patterns. This requires access to some internal details of the services, violating their opaque and autonomous properties. Essentially, they allow service contracts to "look inside the box" and use information gained in the contract specification. This chapter presents a proposal to overcome this limitation in four ways. First, we support a definition of termination patterns in contracts based on the WS-BusinessActivity standard. Second, we use the messages exchanged between services to specify application-specific acceptable consistent states. Third, we provide a set of guidelines to application programmers and developers on the use of our proposed solutions. Finally, we show the feasibility of the proposed approach by developing tools that support the methodology.

The organization of the chapter and its contributions can be summarized as follows. The first section examines the composability of service contracts in service-oriented applications. We then move onto describing the design and implementation of a tool to check the compatibility between Web services contracts in the next section. The third section examines the conformance between a service contract and its implementation. The fourth section describes the design and implementation of a conformance checking tool allowing the user to determine whether an implementation conforms to its service contract. The fifth section reviews the related work and the final section concludes the chapter with possible future works.

CONTRACT COMPOSABILITY

We define the compatibility problems between service contracts as a *composability* problem. First, this section provides a motivating example and highlights the composability problems between Web service contracts. Second, the section presents our approach by defining acceptable termination states and the WS-BusinessActivity (WS-BA) based termination protocol in Web services contracts using a rule-based protocol framework. This framework is supported by the simple object access protocol (SOAP) service description language (SSDL) (Parastatidis, Woodman, Webber, Kuo & Greenfield, 2006). Finally, the section then presents guidelines to application developers on how to define termination states and patterns using our approach.

Motivating Example

Consider the e-procurement scenario shown in Figure 2. This scenario shows the interactions between a merchant service and a customer service. The services are loosely coupled to each other and hosted by different businesses. The interactions between the parties are long running and stateful, i.e., each service keeps its own (internal) state reflecting the current state of interactions. The set of interactions between these two parties are categorized into three activities of: (1) placing

Figure 2. A normal exchange of merchant and customer messages for an e-procurement service

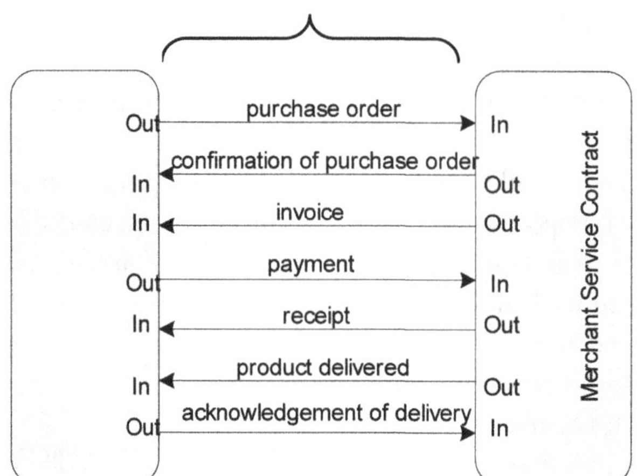

an order, (2) payment and (3) delivery. In turn, these activities are each composed of sequences of customer initiated and merchant initiated messages. For example, the purchase activity is initiated when the customer sends a "purchase order". The merchant may accept or reject the purchase order. The merchant sends "confirmation of purchase order" if it is accepted; otherwise, it sends a reject message.

The compatibility problems (Brogi, Canal, Pimentel, & Vallecillo, 2004) may be illustrated by examining the following example of a merchant service. Figure 3 illustrates the normal workflow for this merchant service and its corresponding normal external behavior. The customer's business process sends a purchase order to the merchant. The merchant then reserves the goods requested; sends the purchase order confirmation to the customer and starts the payment and delivery activities.

The payment process consists of sending an invoice, receiving a payment, and sending a receipt to the customer. The delivery process consists of arranging transportation, shipment of goods, informing the customer that the goods have been dispatched and are in transit, and receiving an acknowledgement from the customer that the goods have been received. The workflows terminate after the delivery and payment processes have both been completed.

Figure 2 shows a normal message exchange between the customer and merchant. A service contract is defined in terms of the externally observable messaging behavior of a single service. Contracts are used to specify the messages that a service can send and receive, as well as the causal relationships between the messages. They typically cannot, however, specify all failures or exception conditions. We define a normal application protocol as the set of all sequences of messages that can be exchanged between the services participating in a distributed application. As the messaging behavior of a service is itself defined by its contract, it follows that the application protocol of a service-based application is the set of all possible message sequences that are allowed by the composition of the participating contracts.

Figure 4 shows a part of an example contract of a merchant payment activity, expressed as a SSDL rule-based protocol. The rule in the

Figure 3. Merchant process with its service contract

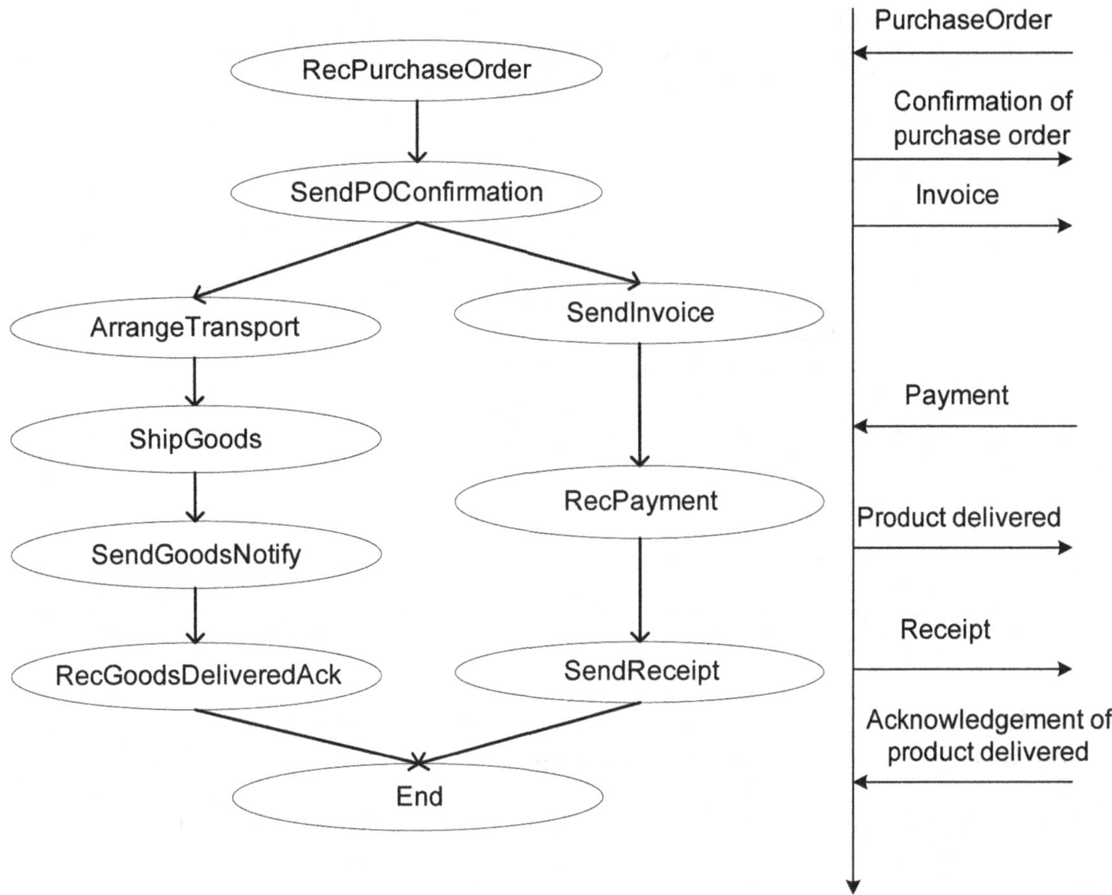

contract defines the causal relationship between the payment message and the invoice message: the invoice can only be sent out if a payment message has been previously received.

Compatibility Problems

It is easy to define and check compatibility between service contracts if no changes and deviations from normal processing occur in the e-procurement scenario. However, many deviations and exceptions from normal behavior do arise in practice, with the result that both parties need to have in place recovery mechanisms to further process messages in order to preserve compatibility.

The compatibility problem due to composition comes from coordinating services provided by independent, stateful services and ensuring that the services always reach acceptable consistent outcomes despite failures and exceptions. For example, in the e-procurement scenario, the customer may fail to pay by a specific date. If the merchant does not receive payment by that date, a payment reminder is sent to the customer. However, the customer payment may be already in transit when the reminder was sent out, and so the customer may have already terminated when a payment reminder arrives following its sending of the payment. This results in service incompatibility as shown in Figure 5 (a). We note that the

Figure 4. Example merchant contract in SSDL rule-based protocol

```
<ssdl:contract ... >
<ssdl:messages ....>
   <ssdl:message name="PurchaseOrderMsg">
       <ssdl:body ref="tns:PurchaseOrderDescription"/>
  </ssdl:message>
  ....
 <ssdl:protocol >
  <rls:rules>
  .....
  <rls:rule>
  <rls:rulemsgref ref="PaymentMsg" direction="in"  />
    <rls:condition>
       <rls:rulemsgref ref="InvoiceMsg" direction="out" />
    </rls:condition>
  </rls:rule>
  <rls:rule>
         .......
  </rls:rules>
</ssdl:protocol>
  </ssdl:protocols>
</ssdl:contract>
```

Figure 5. Message exchanges for merchant and customer in an e-procurement scenario: (a) unexpected payment reminder message and (b) deadlock condition

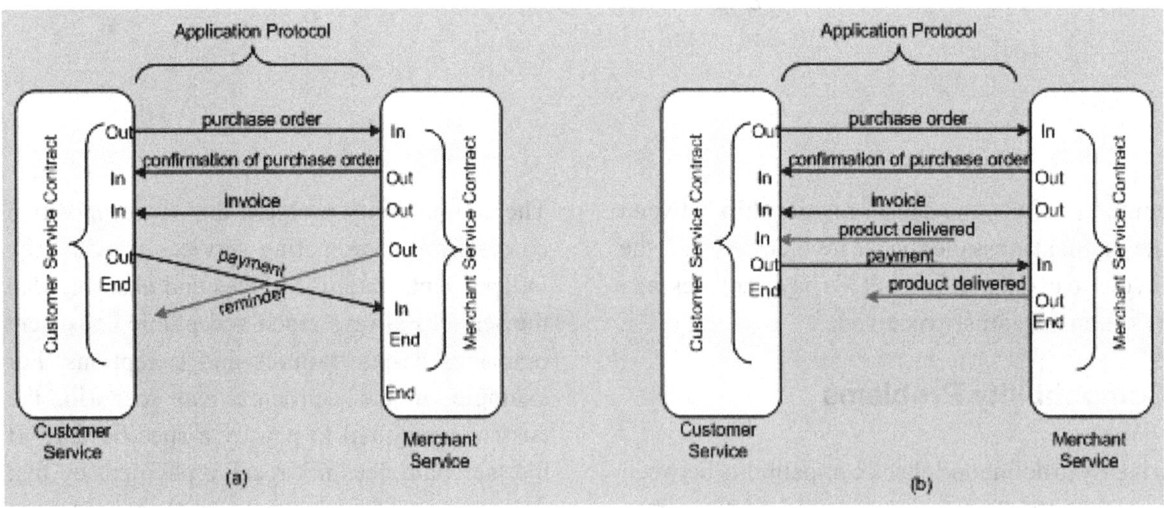

two contracts cannot be composed as they stand, as they cannot deal with this interaction.

The interaction between services may never reach termination due to deadlocks and starvation. A deadlock situation arises if both merchant and customer are waiting for messages from each other, as shown in Figure 5 (b). For example, a deadlock occurs when the merchant is waiting for the payment to deliver the goods and the customer is waiting for the delivery of goods to make the payment. A merchant service application may starve and never reach the termination if it is waiting for the message that will never arrive. For example, the merchant is waiting for an acknowledgement of the received goods from the customer, but the customer never sends an acknowledgement because it is not a specified behavior in its contract.

The termination of interacting service applications needs to be coordinated in such a way that there are no messages left unprocessed. For example, the merchant may terminate its service after the goods have been delivered while the goods returned by the customer are still in transit, leaving the returned goods unhandled. This unprocessed message leaves the application in inconsistent states, where the merchant remains in the state of successful sale and the customer in the state of unsuccessful sale.

Summarizing, the incompatibility between two service contracts is highlighted through their composition. The resulting system yields different behaviors to that of the normal situation illustrated in Figure 2. Referring back to the abstract diagram in Figure 1, the composed contracts from the merchant and customer have a larger set of behaviors possible than left hand side of the "arrow", (the abstract behavior of both) which is incorrect.

Compatibility Criteria

We say that a set of service contracts are compatible (i.e., composable) if all interactions defined by their contracts always reach one of the acceptable consistent termination states. Acceptable consistent termination states not only include the successful outcomes such as "paid in full", but also agreed unsuccessful outcomes such as "error". Note that it is natural that some acceptable consistent states such as "paid in full" are preferred to others such as "error".

The compatibility definition does not exclude service contracts that do not provide even a single path for the preferred outcomes. That is, two service contracts are compatible even if all possible interactions resulting from their application behaviors always reach an acceptable "error" state. Though these two contracts are compatible, the resulting composition of these contracts is not particularly useful, as it does not end in a "naturally preferred" state. As another example to illustrate this, consider that the merchant and customer services support different types of payment methods. The merchant service contract supports both cash and credit payment and the customer service contract only supports check payment. Naturally, when the customer sends the check, the merchant refuses to accept. Further, both agree to end the interaction in an "error" state. The fact that these two may be composed is clear, however, are the contracts compatible? From a simplistic point of view, these contracts are compatible as the composition reached an agreed outcome, but in this case, compatibility is not meaningful except that both parties agreed that there was an error.

We further extend our example and assume that the customer service now supports two types of payment methods: credit and check. When the customer sends the check, the merchant refuses to accept and both agreed to end the interaction in the acceptable "error" state as before. If the customer instead chooses to use a credit payment, the interaction terminates in "paid in full" state. If we insist that we always prefer to avoid "error" states, then compatibility between contracts must define at least one path in the application protocol that leads the interaction away from this undesirable termination state and towards one of the preferred states. For example, the merchant and customer service applications can coordinate payment activity to the most favorable state "paid in full" if they support at least one common payment method.

The contracts can be used to define a pattern in the application protocol to negotiate the paths. For example, the customer may choose to negotiate the method of payment with the merchant before initiating the payment. The negotiation pattern always favors the path in the protocol that leads to the most favorable agreed outcomes. In our example, the customer service negotiates with the merchant service for the payment method which results in the credit payment method, as this is the only method that provides the most favorable outcome. Note that this outcome is possible under the assumptions that nothing goes wrong while using the credit method for the payment.

Exception and failures may cause the deviations from the path that may provide the most favorable outcome. Example events that cause deviation from the successful credit payment include over credit limit, insufficient funds and expiry date exceeded. Each of these events pushes the interaction away from the favorable outcome path. However, there are protocol patterns that handle such deviations and bring the interaction back to the path leading to the possible most favorable outcome.

After considering these points, we elaborate our compatibility definition as follows. The composition of two (or more) contracts is referred to as *compatible* if

- The participating services can work together and achieve at least one outcome from a set of mutually agreed and pre-determined favorable consistent termination outcomes. For example, the merchant and customer services can coordinate payment activity to the most favorable outcome if they support at least one common payment method.
- The defined application protocol must deal with exceptional events that push the processing away from the path leading to one of the preferred consistent outcomes.
- The defined application protocol must support the minimum paths demanded by the business requirements. For example, the customer may like to cancel the order at any time during the processing. If the merchant service does not support this feature, then the two service contracts are incompatible. On the other hand, the customer may not like to cancel the order. If the merchant service contract supports the cancellation, then the two service contracts are compatible.

Though we discuss various issues in relation to the contract compatibility, our discussion in the rest of the section is limited to exact matching. By exact matching, we mean that if a service contract has an outgoing message, there must be another participating service contract with the incoming message and vice versa. This covers all possible outcomes. Note that the concepts and solutions proposed in this article are not limited to this definition and can be extended to cover non-trivial cases discussed above.

Our Approach

This sub-section describes our approach on how service-oriented applications can check the compatibility of service contracts at design time so that their contracts always reach one of the acceptable consistent states at termination. We propose methods of specifying: (a) termination patterns so that developers can check that services always terminate and (b) acceptable consistent states without violating the opaqueness and autonomy of services.

In summary, we hypothesize that these requirements are necessary and sufficient for ensuring compatibility under contract composition. We illustrate the principles behind our methodology here in terms of the SSDL protocol framework (SSDL, 2005). Although, the proof of this hypothesis is the subject of a forthcoming paper, empirically the approach has proven to be of value in constructing sound systems.

We use the SSDL rule-based protocol framework to illustrate our concepts, but it is applicable to other service contract languages such as MEP, WSDL and WSCI (Parastatidis et al, 2006). As with these languages, the currently available SSDL rule-based framework cannot be used to define compatibility properties. We therefore extend the current SSDL rule-based framework in two aspects: (a) specification of termination protocol and (b) specification of acceptable consistent states. Similar extensions are possible to other languages.

Termination Protocols

Without standard guidelines and support, application programmers have to write a termination protocol for each application they develop, but termination of complex business applications needs the coordination of participating business processes. The current set of Web service specifications that defines coordination protocols includes WS-Coordination (WS-Coord, 2005), WS-AtomicTransaction (WS-AT, 2005) and WS-BusinessActivity (WS-BA, 2005). WS-Coord is an extensible framework for providing protocols that coordinate the actions of distributed applications. Such coordination protocols are used to support a number of applications, including those that need to reach consistent agreement on the outcome of distributed activities. WS-AT allows the definition of atomic transaction coordination types that are used with the extensible framework described in the WS-Coord. It defines three specific agreement coordination protocols for the atomic transaction coordination type: completion, volatile two-phase commit, and durable two-phase commit. Developers can use any or all of these protocols when building applications that require consistent agreement on the outcome of short-lived distributed activities that have the all-or-nothing property. However, this protocol is not applicable to loosely coupled distributed application. On the other hand, WS-BA is intended for loosely coupled distributed environments and is suitable for coordinating interaction termination in service-oriented applications. The remainder of this section explains in detail the WS-BA specification and how it is used in coordinating services at termination.

WS-BA defines a set of message types and an ordering relationship between messages, as shown in Figure 6. For example, an ordering relation says that *Cancel* must be followed by *Cancelled*. The semantics of these messages is not defined in the

Figure 6. Business agreement with participant completion abstract state diagram

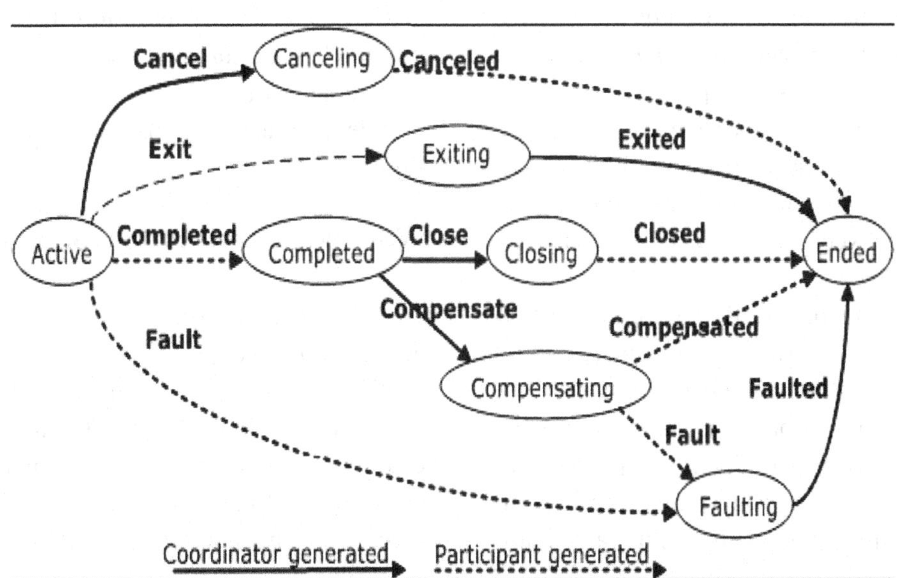

Figure 7. WS-BusinessActivity states

```
<xsd:simpleType name="BAStateType">
    <xsd:restriction base="xsd:QName">
        <xsd:enumeration value="Active"/>
        <xsd:enumeration value="Completing"/>
        <xsd:enumeration value="Completed"/>
        <xsd:enumeration value="Closing"/>
        <xsd:enumeration value="Ended"/>
        <xsd:enumeration value="Compensating"/>
        <xsd:enumeration value="Exiting"/>
        <xsd:enumeration value="Canceling"/>
        <xsd:enumeration value="Faulting"/>
    </xsd:restriction>
</xsd:simpleType>
```

standard, as application programmers may use these to define termination in their application protocols with appropriate meanings attached to them. For example, a message *Cancel* can be used in an application to abort the current activities done by it. In this way, message types and their priority-based ordering relationships define a possible set of allowable message exchanges when one party initiates a termination. These ordering relationships may be used to enforce a particular set of message interleaving and are usually defined by assigning priorities to messages. For example, when the participant generates *Completed* message and the coordinator generates *Cancel* message, one of these messages gets priority over other message. This property guarantees that possible race conditions at termination may be handled, which is one of the problems in reaching agreed termination between two parties using asynchronous messaging.

WS-BA protocols are defined between two entities: one is referred to as the coordinator while the other is referred to as the participant. WS-BA defines two completion coordination protocols between these two: participant completion and coordinator completion. The abstract state diagram for the business agreement with participant completion protocol is shown in Figure 6. We omit the discussion on the coordination completion protocol here due to the limitation of space, but the same concept applies to it.

The state diagrams only show the transitions occur in normal case and do not show the transitions due to race conditions. All possible transitions are given in the state transition table in the specification document (WS-BA, 2005).

We first extend the WS-BA extensible markup language (XML) schema and include definitions for states, paths, transitions, state conditions, and protocols, as the current schema definition provided by the standard does not cover all these definitions. We next describe them with examples. The detailed descriptions are omitted due to the limitation of space.

WS-States and State Conditions

We first define the nine possible states in WS-BA, as shown in Figure 7.

We then define the required condition for the services to be in each state. Figure 8 shows an example of a *Canceling* state. It can be seen that a service is at the *Canceling* state if it has sent *Cancel* message, but has not received *Canceled*,

Figure 8. Condition for cancelling state

```
<wsba:currentstate name="Canceling">
 <wsba:condition>
  <wsba:and>
   <wsba:rulemsgref ref="Cancel" direction="out" />
    <wsba:not>
        <wsba:rulemsgref ref="Canceled" direction="in" />
        <wsba:rulemsgref ref="Exit" direction="in" />
        <wsba:rulemsgref ref="Completed" direction="in" />
        <wsba:rulemsgref ref="Fault" direction="in" />
    </wsba:not>
  </wsba:and>
 </wsba:condition>
</wsba:currentstate>
```

Figure 9. WS-BusinessActivity path types

```
<xsd:simpleType name="PathType">
    <xsd:restriction base="xsd:QName">
        <xsd:enumeration value="wsba:Cancel-Canceled"/>
        <xsd:enumeration value="wsba:Exit-Exited"/>
        <xsd:enumeration value="wsba:Completed-Closed"/>
        <xsd:enumeration value="wsba:Completed-Compensated"/>
        <xsd:enumeration value="wsba:Completed-Faulted"/>
        <xsd:enumeration value="wsba:Fault-Faulted"/>
        <xsd:enumeration value="wsba:Complete-Closed"/>
        <xsd:enumeration value="wsba:Complete-Cancel-Canceled"/>
        <xsd:enumeration value="wsba:Complete-Exit-Exited"/>
        <xsd:enumeration value="wsba:Complete-Fault-Faulted"/>
        <xsd:enumeration value="wsba:Complete-Compensated"/>
        <xsd:enumeration value="wsba:Complete-Faulted"/>
    </xsd:restriction>
</xsd:simpleType>
```

Figure 10. An example description of Completed-Closed path

```
<wsba:path name="wsba:Completed-Closed">
    <wsba:statetransitions>
      <wsba:statetransition name="Active"    msg="Completed" direction="in" />
      <wsba:statetransition name="Completed"   msg="Close" direction="out" />
      <wsba:statetransition name="Closing"   msg="Closed" direction="in" />
    </wsba:statetransitions>
</wsba:path>
```

Exit, *Completed*, or *Fault* message. That means when *Canceled, Exit, Completed* or *Fault* is received, the service will be transitioned to the next state rather than remain at the *Canceling* state (note that there are rules defined to cover race conditions as well).

WS-BA State Transitions and Paths

We define the path types for WS-BA protocol covering all possible transitions in the state diagrams of both types of coordination protocol, as shown in Figure 9. An example description for *Completed-Closed* path is shown in Figure 10.

This means that an interaction follows the *Completed-Closed* path if the service receives the *Completed* message in the *Active* state, followed by sending the *Close* message in the *Completed* state, followed by receiving the *Closed* message in the *Closing* state.

WS-BA Termination Protocols

We next extend the contract definition language (SSDL rule-based protocol framework in our case) by incorporating the termination protocol from WS-BA. Figure 11 shows the XML code for the termination protocol part of extended SSDL contract.

The WS-BA contract extension specifies two important concepts. The first part specifies the WS-BA protocol types of (1) coordinator completion or (2) participant completion. The above termination protocol example shows that this particular service supports the coordinator completion protocol. The second part specifies the service type, that is, coordinator or participant, again referring to the example that the service is participating in the interaction as a participant. Figure 12 shows a part of SSDL merchant contract with a termination pattern for the payment activity.

A message that is declared with a path attribute is called a final message (e.g., *ReceiptMsg* in the above example). After this message is sent or received, a service follows the path specified by the path attributes to terminate its interaction. This means that an interaction follows the *Complete-Closed* path for termination when the merchant sends out a receipt message if it has already sent out an invoice and received the payment, but has not yet accepted the cancellation.

Guidelines for Using the Termination Protocol

Interaction boundaries: A lengthy pairwise interaction between two parties in a distributed application can often be naturally decomposed into a smaller set of pairwise interactions (or activities). Each such interaction can then use WS-BusinessActivity for coordinating agreed termination. It is therefore important for developers to find such boundaries in the interactions in an application. In our e-procurement example shown in Figure 2, there are three "natural" activities: (1) placing an order, (2) payment, and (3) delivery.

Figure 11. Definition of termination protocol in SSDL

```
<ssdl:protocol targetNamespace=
      http://example.org/service/termination                    xmlns:wsba="urn:wsba">
<wsba:Protocol>wsba:BusinessAgreementWithCoordinatorCompletion</wsba:Protocol>
   <wsba:Service>wsba:Participant</wsba:Service>
</ssdl:protocol>
```

Figure 12. A part of merchant service in SSDL

```
<rls:rule>
  <rls:rulemsgref ref="ReceiptMsg" direction="out"
                  path="wsba:Complete-Closed" />
   <rls:condition>
    <rls:and>
      <rls:rulemsgref ref="PaymentMsg" direction="in" />
       <rls:rulemsgref ref="InvoiceMsg" direction="out" />
      <rls:not>
 <rls:rulemsgref ref="CancelAcceptedMsg" direction="out" />
       </rls:not>
    </rls:and>
   </rls:condition>
</rls:rule>
```

Roles of interacting parties: Parties involved in a pairwise interaction can play two different roles: coordinator and participant. One party must act as a coordinator and the other as a participant. It is therefore important for developers to determine the role played by each party. The coordinator creates the context for the interaction and passes it to the participant, along with an application message, as an invitation to participate in an activity. The party that initiates the interaction and sends the first application message therefore becomes a natural candidate for the coordinator. In our e-procurement example in Figure 2, the customer becomes coordinator for placing an order activity and the merchant becomes coordinator for payment and delivery activities.

Coordination types: WS-BA defines two coordination types depending on which of the interacting service initiates termination. Developers need to decide which coordination type is most appropriate in their applications. In general, this is determined by which party initiates termination. Coordinator completion is the appropriate one if the coordinator initiates termination; otherwise, participant completion protocol type should be used. In our e-procurement example, the merchant is the coordinator and initiates the termination of the payment activity and thus uses coordinator completion type.

Paths in the protocol: The coordination type participant completion defines six possible paths from the active to ended state and coordinator completion defines nine possible paths. A pairwise interaction between two parties does not need to support all possible paths. It is therefore important for the developers to decide paths supported for an interaction.

The exiting path is natural to model situations where, once an activity finishes, the participant is no longer needs to participate in the distributed application. Referring to Figure 6, the paths through the completing state are natural to model cases where a party can perform post-activity actions once the activity has finished. The path through the closing state typically represents normal termination. The path through compensating state typically represents abnormal termination which may be requiring parties to undo the completed activity.

Acceptable Consistent State

The compatibility requirement of a distributed application is that all participating services must eventually terminate in an acceptable consistent state in all possible situations. The acceptable consistent states for the distributed application can be defined as global **consistency** constraints on application states of participating services. However, such constraints violate the fundamental principle of service-oriented systems. By the definition of service-oriented systems, services are opaque; their internal states are not accessible by other service applications. This makes it impossible for developers to define global consistency constraints based on (internal) application states. The question then arises: How do we define such constraints without accessing application states of participating services?

Messages represent the data external to the service whereas the application states represent the data inside the service (Helland, 2005). When the customer receives the message receipt, it reflects the value of the merchant's application state "paid in full" when the message was sent. However, the value of the application state may not be valid when the customer receives the message, as each participating service application can independently change its own internal state, and that state may or may not be causally related to the message. Consider now the following example based on the assumption that an interaction specific state never changes its value and remains stable. Suppose that the merchant sends a "receipt" message when it receives the full payment. The value of application state "paid in full" never changes once the receipt is sent. If there is an over payment, the merchant will refund the over paid amount. Hence, we could propose a definition of a mechanism of specifying global consistency constraints based on message-related states operating under the assumption that an interaction specific state never changes its value and remains stable. The question remains, however, as to who defines these global consistency constraints as each service is defined and developed by an independent application developer?

If we can map the global consistency constraints to local consistency constraints of all participants, then the consistency checking at termination is equivalent to proving that all participants are locally consistent at termination. Let $S_1, S_2, \ldots, S_N$ be N participating services in a distributed application. Let G denote a global set of integrity constraints expressed using internal states of participating services, and $L_1, L_2, \ldots, L_N$ be local consistency constraints in each service defined based on messages exchanged between services such that:

$$G = L_1 \wedge L_2 \wedge \ldots \wedge L_N$$

Each service application programmer then can define this local set of consistency constraints. This is possible under the realistic assumption of reliable messaging. Further discussion on this assumption is omitted here due to the limitation of available space.

We extend the SSDL rule-based framework so that a service can express their local consistency constraints. An example constraint specification in a merchant service contract for a payment activity in our e-procurement scenario is shown in Figure 13. It has two acceptable termination states: *PaidInFull* and *PaymentError*. The service reaches the *PaidInFull* state if it receives the payment message and sends the receipt message. Similarly, the service reaches the *PaymentError* state when it receives the payment message, but sends out fault payment message.

Guidelines for Defining Acceptable States

Message-related states: Not all states can be used in defining acceptable termination states in contracts. As service contracts express external behaviors, only message-related states are used in constraints since the external behavior of a service is expressed using messages sent and received by

Figure 13. An example acceptable termination states in service contracts

```
<rls:constraints>
   <rls:state> PaidInFull</rls:state>
         <rls:constraint>
 <rls:and>
   <rls:rulemsgref ref="PaymentMsg" direction="in" />
   <rls:rulemsgref ref="ReceiptMsg" direction="out" />
              </rls:and>
          </rls:constraint>
    <rls:state> PaymentError </rls:state>
        <rls:constraint>
              <rls:and>
<rls:rulemsgref ref="PaymentMsg" direction="in" />
<rls:rulemsgref ref="FaultPaymentMsg" direction="out" />
            </rls:and>
        </rls:constraint>
</rls:constraints>
```

the service. It is also important to note that not all message-related states are important for defining the termination states (e.g., the payment reminder message in the payment activity). This message will be either followed by receipt or payment fault message that is much more significant in terms of the outcomes of the payment interaction.

State coverage: It is important that all possible acceptable termination states for a service are specified. However, it is not obvious for an application developer to list them from a large pool of message-related states. This problem is partly addressed in this article by extending the contract definition framework with definitions of suitable termination patterns. Based on our observations, we found that the minimum set of message-related states, which must be used while defining the acceptable states, are driven by termination protocol patterns. If a message is followed by a termination protocol (such as receipt message in the payment activity), then its state must be included in the definition of acceptable termination states.

PROTOTYPE COMPOSABILITY CHECKING TOOL

This section briefly describes the tool we have developed to demonstrate the feasibility of our approach described in the earlier section. The tool takes two service contracts as inputs and checks whether applications defined by their contracts always reach one of the acceptable consistent states at termination. Figure 14 presents an overview of how the tool works. The SSDL contracts are converted into the process or protocol meta language (PROMELA) by translating each rule of the contract in turn. The semantics of SSDL and PROMELA are very similar, both being based on communicating sequential processes (CSP) (Hoare, 1985). Both have processes, data objects, and channels that allow messages to pass between processes, and allow a variety of parallel and sequential composition of processes. We use the SPIN model checker (Holzmann, 2003), but the concept can be easily carried into other model checking tools. Figure 15 shows a screenshot of a tool with the simulated view of payment interaction between the customer and merchant services.

Figure 14. The steps in compatibility checking tool

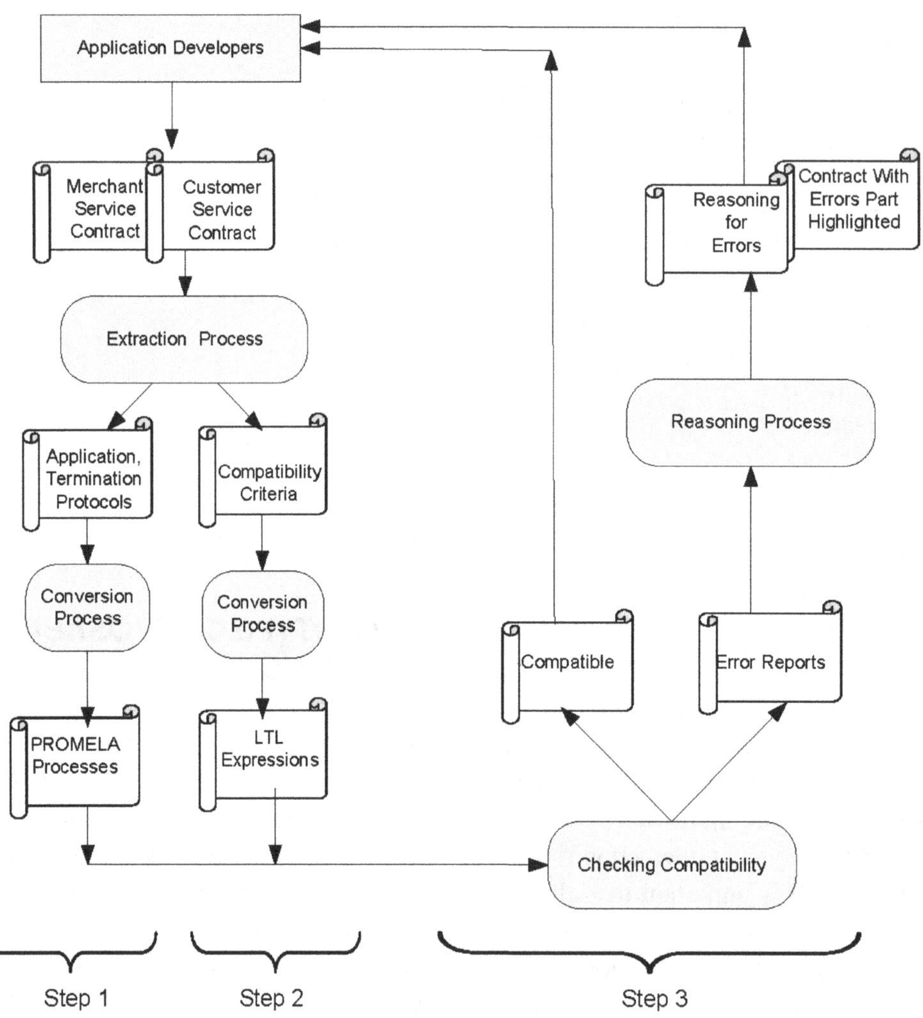

When a user submits contracts for the compatibility check, the tool does the following three steps.

1. The external behavior of the service expressed through service contracts are converted into PROMELA processes. Similarly, WS-BA protocol patterns expressed in service contracts are also converted into PROMELA processes.
2. Compatibility criteria are extracted from the service contracts and expressed as Linear Temporal Logic (LTL) expressions.
3. The SPIN model checker is then run to check the compatibility. Incompatibility errors are detected and presented to the user with appropriate reasoning. The user corrects the service contracts and submits to the tool. This process is repeated until we get the correct service contracts.

Figure 15. A screenshot of the compatibility checking tool with a simulated view of payment interaction

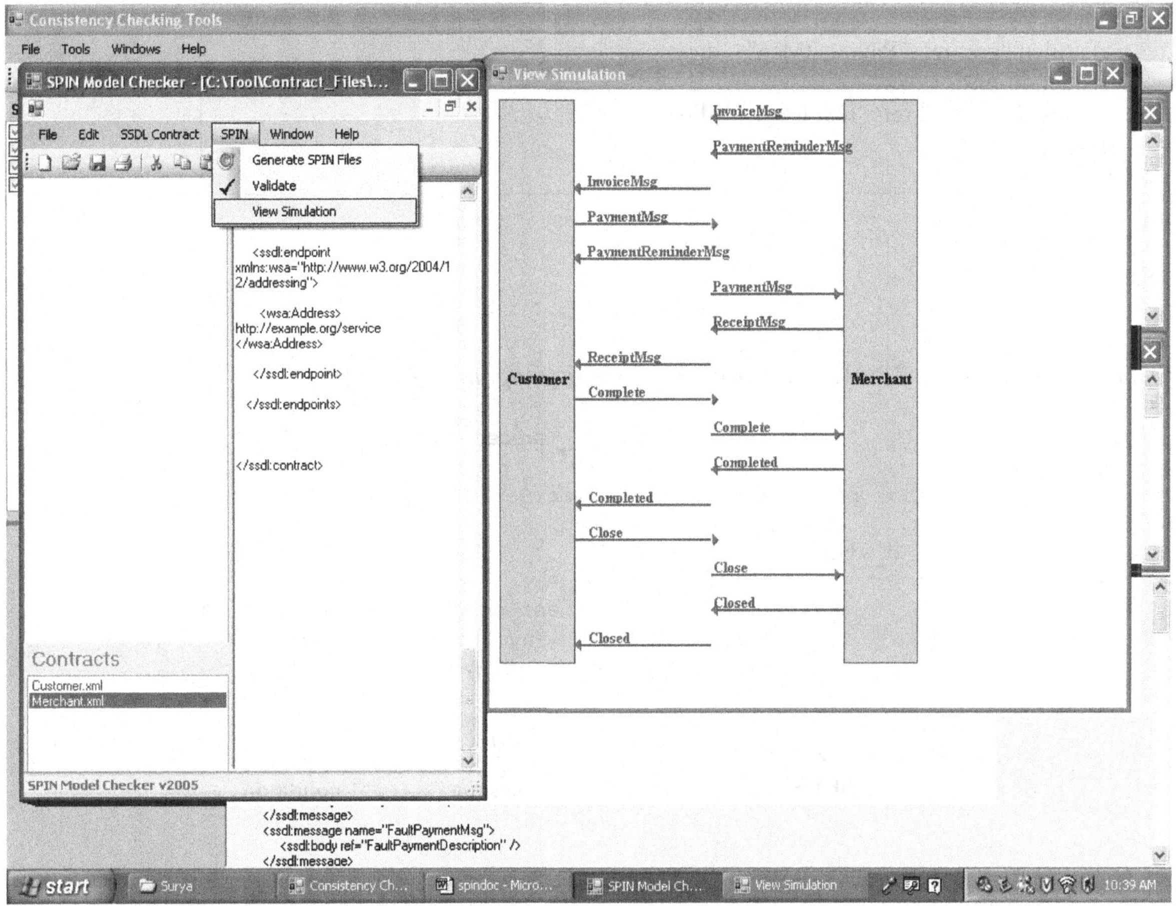

We further elaborate these steps below.

Conversion of the External Behaviors and Termination Protocols

Note that there are two kinds of messages: non-BusinessActivity (non-BA) and BusinessActivity (BA). All messages related to application are non-BA messages, whereas messages from WS-BA protocols are BA messages.

There are two types of rules in SSDL contracts. The first deals with sending outgoing messages, and the second with receiving incoming messages. For example, the extract, shown in Figure 16, from a customer service contract is a rule that is related to sending a payment to the merchant service.

The rule specifies that *PaymentMsg* is only sent if the *InvoiceMsg* has been received. Figure 17 and Figure 18 illustrate PROMELA statements for sending outgoing messages and receiving incoming messages, respectively.

A sending process has the following components recorded in the PROMELA d_step block:

- The current (WS-BA) state of the service when the message is sent. For nonBA messages, the state is set to Active.
- The condition for sending the message, considered as a PROMELA guard expression, and is converted from the SSDL rule condition. It controls the order in which messages are exchanged.

Figure 16. A rule for sending payment message

```
<rls:rule>
   <rls:rulemsgref ref="PaymentMsg"   direction="out" />
   <rls:condition>
      <rls:rulemsgref ref="InvoiceMsg" direction="in" />
   </rls:condition>
</rls:rule>
```

Figure 17. An example PROMELA process for sending outgoing messages

process name

```
active proctype paymentCustomerCoordPaymentMsgProc () {
end:
    d_step {
        (paymentCoordActive &&
         paymentCustomerPaymentCoordRecInvoiceMsg ) ->
        paymentMerchantChan !PaymentMsg, nonBA;
        paymentCustomerCoordSentPaymentMsg = true;
        }
}
```

state

channel

message

condition

Figure 18. PROMELA process for receiving incoming messages

```
active proctype paymentCustomerCoordPaymentMsgProc   () {
end:
   d_step {
            paymentCustomerChan ?ReceiptMsg , nonBA;
            assert (paymentCustomerCoordSentPaymentMsg   &&
            paymentCustomerCoordRecInvoiceMsg  );
            assert (paymentCoordActive  ||
                   paymentCoordCanceling  ||
                   paymentCoordCompleting );
           paymentCustomerCoordRecReceiptMsg   = true;
    }
}
```

Figure 19. A rule for receiving receipt message

```
<rls:rule>
<rls:rulemsgref ref="ReceiptMsg" direction="in"
                path="wsba:Complete-Closed" />
 <rls:condition>
  <rls:and>
  <rls:rulemsgref ref="PaymentMsg" direction="out" />
   <rls:rulemsgref ref="InvoiceMsg" direction="in" />
    </rls:and>
   </rls:condition>
</rls:rule>
```

- The message itself that is sent with its type set as nonBA.
- The statement that records that the message has been sent, that is, assignment of the message Boolean state variable to true. For example, bool "sentPaymentMsg" = true.

Figure 19 shown an example rule extracted from a customer service contract related to receiving a receipt from the merchant.

This rule states that *InvoiceMsg* must be received and *PaymentMsg* must be sent before receiving *ReceiptMsg*. We convert such rules to PROMELA process, as shown in Figure 18.

A receiving process has similar elements to a sending process except that there is no explicit condition required for receiving a message. Rather, there are two assert statements that verify the condition and state that the service as a whole must satisfy and are derived from the SSDL rules. The assertion for a state is a collection of all possible states that the service can be at when the message is received. Since WS-BA is used as a termination protocol, the states may include WS-BA states. A service receives a non-BA message at WS-BA state if it has already followed a BA path. The above process is from a customer coordinator service using a business agreement with coordinator completion protocol. Note that the customer may reach one of three states: (1) *Canceling*, by sending the *Cancel* message (2) *Completing*, by sending the *Complete* message or (3) remain in an *Active* state when it receives the *Receipt* message. Once formulated in PROMELA, the SPIN model checker (Holzmann, 2003) is used to detect any statements that violate these assertions.

WS-BA process generation follows the same rule except that they follow the sequence of states based on WS-BA messages exchanged. The termination of service interaction is reached if both participating services are at the WS-BA Ended state.

Conversion of Compatibility Criteria

Linear temporal logic (LTL) is a logic that has been widely applied to the verification of asynchronous systems. We use LTL to express the requirement that services must reach agreed outcomes at termination, and that the SPIN model checker (Holzmann, 2003) must perform a validation of the specified requirements. SPIN converts LTL formula into "never" claims with acceptance labels to allow detection of acceptance errors. Table 1 shows the usual temporal logic notation used with appropriate substitutions.

For the e-procurement scenario, our first compatibility requirement is that both services terminate at the end of a business transaction. This may be expressed in LTL using the eventually clause. This is expressed for our example as:

Table 1. Temporal logic notations and interpretations

<table>
<tr><th>Formula</th><th>ASCII representation</th><th>English Interpretation</th></tr>
<tr><td>□ p</td><td>[] p</td><td>p is invariantly true</td></tr>
<tr><td>◊ p</td><td><> p</td><td>p eventually becomes true</td></tr>
<tr><td>□ (p → q)</td><td>p && q</td><td>p always implies q</td></tr>
<tr><td>$p \wedge q$</td><td>p&q</td><td>logical conjunction of p and q</td></tr>
<tr><td>$p \vee q$</td><td>p || q</td><td>logical disjunction of p and q</td></tr>
<tr><td>$\neg p$</td><td>!p</td><td>logical negation of p</td></tr>
</table>

Table 2. List of SPIN error notification and interpretation

SPIN Error Notification	Reasons
"assertion violated"	Race conditions or incompatible path
"acceptance cycle"	Non-termination
"claim violated"	Consistency constraints are not satisfied
"undeclared variable"	Condition that is never satisfied in the contract

<>custEnded && <>merchEnded

This means both customer and merchant processes must eventually reach the WS-BA Ended states at termination. The second compatibility property implies that there are no unprocessed messages left in the channel. This may be checked by turning on appropriate run-time options in SPIN. For example,

spin –p –v payment.pml

The final compatibility requirement states that agreed outcomes must be reached at termination for both services. It is equivalent to saying that in the end, participating services are always at one of the specific states declared in the contracts. As an example, a customer and merchant service must always reach either *PaidInFull* or *PaymentError* state in the e-procurement payment activity, which is written as:

([](custEnded→(custPaidInFull || custError)))&&

([](merchEnded→(merchPaidInFull || merchError)))

Error Detection and Reporting

Basic assertions and never claims statements are used to detect errors in SPIN processes. Basic assertions check whether the process state or conditional requirements are violated and race conditions are identified as assertion violations. Never claims are generated from the compatibility requirements that a system must satisfy, termination and agreed outcomes. Table 2 summarizes the error reporting process.

Assertion violation: Incompatible path errors are caused by incompatible use of WS-BA paths. For example, the *Complete-Closed* WS-BA path is defined at the payment message in the customer contract while the *Complete-Closed* WS-BA path is defined at the receipt message, assuming the customer and merchant terminate the process when the customer sends a payment and the merchant sends a receipt message after the payment is received. The customer sends a *Complete* message immediately after sending the payment message but before receiving a receipt. The customer rule is equivalent to the receiving of the *Complete* message before sending the receipt at the merchant side, which violates the rule in the merchant contract. This will cause the generation of an 'assertion violated' error.

Race conditions may occur due to the asynchronous nature of the message transmission. The merchant sends a payment reminder if it does not receive a payment from the customer. This payment reminder may be sent at the same time as the payment from the customer. Therefore, the customer receives a payment reminder although it has sent a payment.

Acceptance error: Acceptance errors are due to the non-termination of either or both services. A message is sent but never received at the other side, leaving both services with no further progress as the message blocks the transmission channel. For example, sending out of a *PaymentWrong* message may be added to the customer contract while the merchant contract does not specify receiving of this message and so the *PaymentWrong* message will not be received (or recognized) by the merchant service. A consequence of this may be that not all the messages sent from the customer side subsequent to the *PaymentWrong* message can be received.

Incompatible WS-BA paths can also lead to the non-termination of the services. The *Cancel-Canceled* path attribute to the *PaymentMsg* rule in the customer service but not to the *PaymentMsg* rule in the merchant service results in the non-termination of the *Cancel-Canceled* path.

Errors in the contracts such as deadlocks, starvation, or a condition requirement that cannot be satisfied also cause services to be non-terminated

Claim violation: A claim is violated when the consistency constraints are not satisfied, which occurs when either or both services do not reach one of the expected states. For example, consistency constraints for the merchant service specifies to receive *PaymentMsg* but not to send out *ReceiptMsg*. However, consistency constraints for the customer service specify that both the *PaymentMsg ReceiptMsg* must be performed, and yet the merchant never sends out a *ReceiptMsg*. Therefore, the claim the customer consistency constraints to receive the *ReceiptMsg* is violated.

Undeclared variables: Boolean variables are declared based on the message set obtained from all the messages sent and received. An undeclared variable occurs when the condition for a particular rule is the sending or receiving of a message that does not belong to this message set. As a result, this condition may never be satisfied. For example, the customer contract may define the sending out of a *PaymentMsg* if both *InvoiceMsg* and *PaymentWrong* messages are received. However, the merchant may only send out *InvoiceMsg* without the *PaymentWrong* message (as it is not part of its contract), causing the *PaymentMsg* message never to be sent by the customer, resulting in an error as it is waiting for the *PaymentWrong* message to be received.

CONFORMANCE PROBLEM

This section focuses on the second category of compatibility problems that occur between a service contract and its implementation, which we define as a *conformance problem*. One of the main sources of incompatibility in service-oriented applications is the non-conformance between business processes and their external behaviors, expressed through service contracts. That is, the external behavior of the services is not implemented correctly (according to a contract) or the external behavior of the service does not reflect the internal behavior of a business process. This section addresses this problem by describing the relationship between the business process workflows and Web service contracts. Though the concepts discussed in the following sections are generic and applicable to any languages used for defining business processes such as BPEL and their service contract, we illustrate the concepts through a guard-action-trigger (GAT) model (Nepal, Fekete, Greenfield, Jang, Kuo & Shi, 2005) and SSDL (SSDL, 2005).

Conformance Criteria

Before proceeding to the development of a conformance checking tool, it is imperative to specify what is meant by *conformance* and the conformance criteria. For a defined set of messages, a business process conforms to a service contract if and only if all of the following hold:

1. All incoming messages specified in the service contract must be handled by the corresponding business process implementation and vice versa. In the GAT model, business processes communicate with each other and external parties through events. In a SSDL contract, communication between two services is achieved through message exchanges. Regardless of how business processes and contracts communicate, the incoming communication messages must convey the same transaction state and all messages/events must be handled; no messages or events are left unhandled in both service contract and the corresponding business process. For example, if an incoming message payment is defined in the contract, but there is no business process that handles this message, then a non-conformance is said to occur.
2. The business process must handle all outgoing messages specified in its contract and the service contract must handle all outgoing events in the business process.
3. The causal relationships between incoming and outgoing messages must be maintained when generating a business process from a service contract and vice versa. The causal relationships must be traceable and semantically identical in both business process and service contract. For example, if the merchant business process delivers goods only when the payment is received from the customer, the merchant's service contract must reflect this relationship between *GoodsDelivered* and *Payment* messages.
4. The service contract must reflect all acceptable termination states of a business process and vice versa. Similarly, the termination patterns in both business processes and service contracts must match.

It should be noted that it is possible and acceptable for a business process to contain more incoming and/or outgoing messages than that are captured in a service contract. Typically, these messages would be outside the set of messages dealt with by the service contract. For example, a merchant payment business process may support more than one type of payment method (e.g., cash, EFTPOS, credit, etc.). However, the service contract for this process may only cover the transaction states for only cash payments. Therefore, a service provider/consumer's business process must capture all possible transaction states; the service contract may only capture all or a subset of these transaction states. However, the same cannot be said for a service contract – a service contract is said to be non-conformant with its business process if the contract contains more incoming or outgoing messages than the business process.

The first three criteria are easy to check for a trivial normal case scenario. However, concurrency and composition add complexity, as the sequences of message replies representing possible responses to a message becomes very complex (and may allow different possible interleaved message sequences that may have unexpected results). For example, in response to a payment message, the merchant service may send *receipt* or "*late fee notification*" and *receipt* or "*payment error*". When the payment activity runs concurrently with the delivery, all messages related to delivery activities such as "*delay delivery notification*", "*in-transit notification*", and "*delivery cancellation*" could potentially interleave with those payment messages.

The most important and difficult part is to ensure that business processes and contracts reflect the same acceptable consistent states and termination patterns so that one service can be combined with other services to build a large distributed application. We have already described earlier on how to capture the acceptable states and termination patterns in a service contract using SSDL rule-based protocol. We next describe a way of capturing them in business processes using GAT. We then show how these criteria are used in the development of a conformance checking tool.

Our Approach

This section reviews the GAT model (Nepal et al., 2005) developed to specify business processes along with a proposed extension for the specification of compatibility requirements. The GAT model follows the fundamental correctness properties that a process must always terminate in an acceptable state, even if there are concurrent processes executing, and regardless of the outcomes of any activities within the process. The GAT model makes no distinctions between failure and successful states; all states are valid and properly dealt with at any stage of the execution. Instead of rolling back, GAT processes constantly move forward in any state. Once a process has begun, the process always terminates in an acceptable termination state and all states are explicit. The process itself must also be complete. In other words, it should be able to handle all messages received under all possible circumstances. These correctness properties ensure that all incoming and outgoing messages are handled appropriately and business transactions result in one of mutually defined acceptable state.

The existing GAT programming model (Nepal et al., 2005) does not allow the specification of termination protocols and consistency constraints (Bhuiya, Nepal & Zic, 2006). Hence, the GAT model has been extended in this chapter to accommodate termination and consistency constraints by including WS-BA protocol as a framework for coordinating the termination of a pair-wise interaction between two processes. For the purpose of illustrating the extension, only the Merchant's payment process (from the e-procurement scenario outlined previously) is used as an example throughout this section. The explanation of the GAT syntax and GAT specification for the payment process is shown in Figure 20.

A GAT specification for a business process consists of two sections: the *initialization* and the *body*. The termination protocol and consistency constraints specifications are enclosed within the initialization part (between INIT and /INIT tags). A termination protocol is a business activity protocol that coordinates activities in running business processes and permits business logic to handle business logic exceptions. Termination protocols describe the role of each participant involved in a business transaction (service type) and the type of WS-BA coordination protocol used by the business process.

In the GAT snippet in Figure 20, the merchant payment is a coordinator service and the termination protocol type used is coordination completion. Using this protocol, the participant (customer) relies on its coordinator (the merchant) to notify it when it has received all requests to do work within a business transaction. The messages participate in a termination protocol indicated by the tag [path]; for example, [path: fault-faulted] specifies a fault message be defined by the coordinator (merchant) to indicate that the participant (customer) has failed from the active or compensating state. For the next protocol message, the merchant will send a faulted message. When customer process receives this message, it knows that the merchant is aware of a fault and no further action is required from the customer.

For each of the acceptable termination states (defined by consistency constraints), the GAT specifies the associated termination protocol notifications, that is, a path in the BA protocol always gives a unique outcome. As such the *PaidInFull*

Figure 20. A GAT merchant payment process

```
INIT
TERMINATION PROTOCOL:
SERVICE TYPE: COORDINATOR
PROTOCOL TYPE: WSBAWithCoordinationCompletion

CONSISTENCY CONSTRAINTS:
PaidInFull: <OUT> Invoice AND <IN> PAYMENT AND <OUT> Receipt
FaultPayment: <OUT> Invoice AND <OUT>Reminder
/INIT
......
IN_EVENT: Payment
GROUP: RecievePayment
ACTIVITY: ProcessFullPayment
GUARD: FullPayment(payment) & <OUT>Invoice(invoice)<AND> <NOT><OUT>CancelAccepted(cancel)
ACTION: UpdateInvoice(payment)
TRIGGERS: {true} <INT>PaidInFull(payment)
........
ACTIVITY: processOverPayment
GUARD: OverPayment(payment) & <OUT>Invoice(invoice)<AND> <NOT><OUT>CancelAccepted(cancel)
ACTION: UpdateInvoice(payment)
TRIGGERS: {true} <INT>OverPayment(payment)
{true} <INT>PaidInFull(payment)
ACTIVITY: processFaultPayment
GUARD: <NOT> <OUT>Invoice(invoice)<AND> <NOT><OUT>CancelAccepted(cancel)
ACTION: PrepareFaultPaymentMsg(payment)
TRIGGERS:{true} <OUT>CustomerService.FaultPayment(payment) [path: Fault-Faulted]
ACTIVITY: AcceptCancelRequest
GUARD: <OUT>Invoice(invoice)<AND> <OUT>CancelAccepted(cancel)
ACTION: MerchantCancellation.AcceptCancel(cancelrequest)
TRIGGERS: none
.......
```

constraint follows the [path: Complete-Closed] path after the receipt message is sent. Upon the receipt of the *complete* message, the customer knows that it will receive no new requests from the merchant within the business activity. The customer process completes the application processing and then transmits *completed* message to the merchant. The merchant then sends *close* message to terminate the interaction. The *closed* notification then informs the merchant process that the customer process has finished successfully.

Consistency constraints define the conditions that need to be met before the business transactions can terminate, with and without fault. In Figure 20, *PaidInFull* is the state to be reached if the merchant completes payment process without a fault. In the event of a fault, the state to be reached is the FaultPayment. For each of these termination states, the consistency constraints are described in terms of the messages that must be sent/received before reaching the respective termination states.

The body part (after the /INIT tag) contains the business process specification. A process is defined by a set of activity groups, where each group handles an event (an arriving message). We have shown an activity group in Figure 20. Each activity group contains a set of activities.

Each Activity represents one possible response to its event. Each activity consists of a guard, an action and a set of trigger groups.

Guards are Boolean expressions that refer to parameters associated with an event and the current system state. Guards control whether their corresponding action should execute as part of the response to the event. The guard expressions in any one activity group are *closed*; that is, in an activity group, when an event is received, the Boolean expression of only one of the activities must be true and all the other Boolean expressions must be false. This property lets us guarantee that we always deterministically take some action every time an event is received.

An *action* is code that performs business logic in a circumstance evaluated by the guard expression. A trigger group is a set of *triggers*. A *trigger* consists of a *condition* and a *trigger expression*. When an action completes, the trigger condition is evaluated to determine whether a particular trigger should be set off as a result of the action.

Like Guards, the trigger expressions in each trigger group are also closed. That is, in a single trigger group, exactly one trigger expression must be true and only events in that trigger expression will be raised as a result. Activities can have multiple independent trigger groups, each corresponding to a different and parallel possible course of actions. Final messages invoked by the trigger have a WS-BA path tag, which specifies whether it was a normal completion, fault or other deviations from normal operations.

Figure 20 shows an example activity group for the payment process with four activities. Each of these activities represents one possible response to its event and consists of a guard, an action and a set of triggers groups. When an activity group receives an event, the activity group evaluates the guards and determines which activity to execute. The action part of an activity is written like conventional code to handle the incoming event under the precise circumstances specified by the guards. In the *RecievePayment* activity group, an update of invoice can occur only after full payment has been received and an invoice has been sent out to the customer. The trigger part of GAT consists of a condition and a set of events (messages). Each of the trigger conditions expressions are evaluated in turn and the corresponding events are only sent if the condition is true. For example, in the *RecievePayment* activity group above, if full payment has been made then the *PaidinFull* event is triggered. If *PaidinFull* event is set to true, then a receipt message is sent out to the customer. The events in the trigger can be fired immediately or can be deferred for a specified period.

PROTOTYPE CONFORMANCE CHECKING TOOL

This section describes a tool we have developed for checking conformance between a business process and its respective service contract. The tool provides the following functionalities.

- A GAT to SSDL generator, which takes a business workflow defined in GAT language and generates a SSDL contract that satisfies the conformance criteria.
- A SSDL contract validation tool that checks whether the generated SSDL contract (in XML) is syntactically correct. It is also used to validate any independently written SSDL contracts.
- A SSDL to GAT compatibility checker, which validates whether a contract is compatible with a relevant GAT process as per conformance criteria described earlier.
- A GAT template generator takes a pre-existing SSDL contract and generates a GAT skeleton. Figure 21 shows a screenshot of the tool.

GAT to SSDL generator: The GAT to SSDL generator is used to convert business processes described in GAT to corresponding SSDL contracts. The generated contracts satisfy all the conformance criteria. In our prototype tool, we use the e-procurement scenario involving one

Figure 21. A screenshot of conformance checking tool in operation

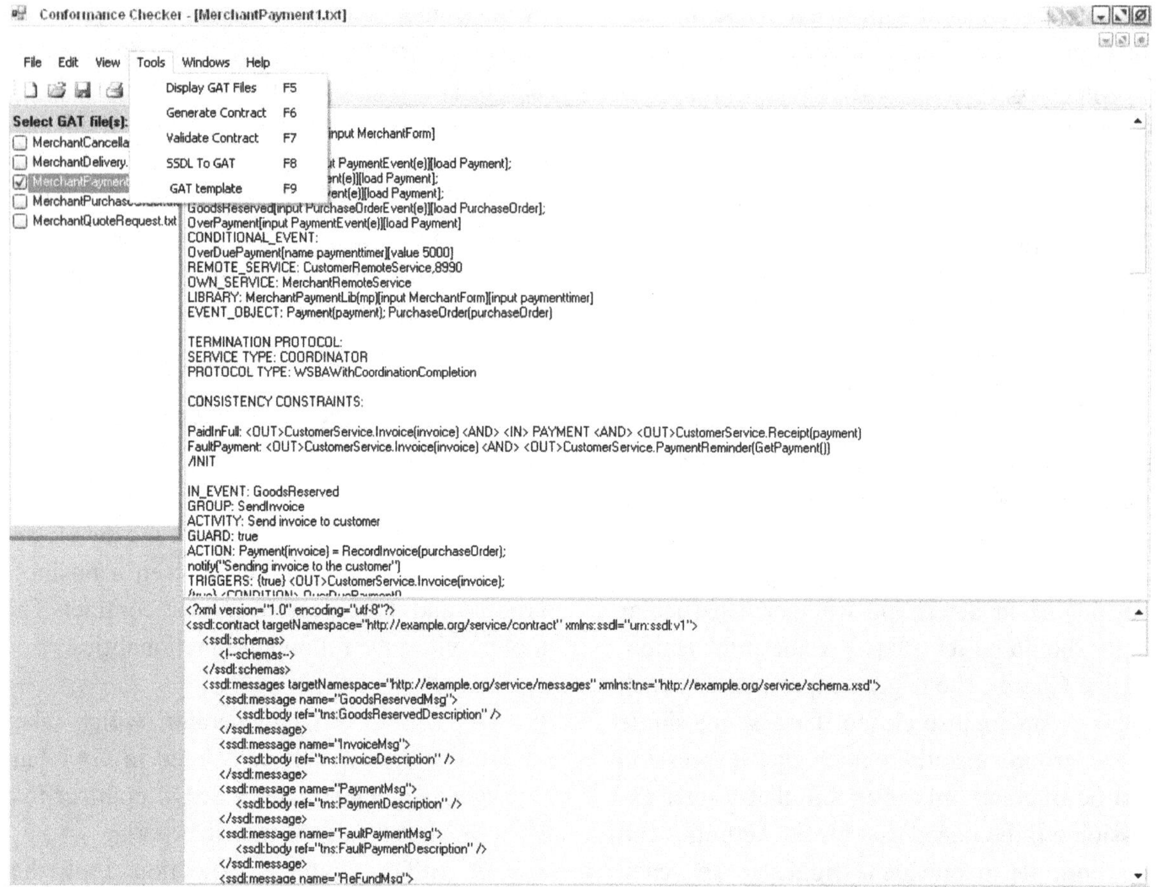

merchant, one customer and one shipper service. This generator parses the GAT files provided by the user and extracts the message choreography, i.e., the sequence of incoming and outgoing messages, their associated guard and trigger conditions. The generator also maps the termination protocols and consistency constraints to the message choreography. The generator then stores the message mappings in a persistent store for later use. From these message maps, the generator then produces a corresponding SSDL contract in XML. The GAT engine checks the validity and well formedness of a GAT process.

Contract validation tool: After contracts have been generated, a validation is performed to check whether the generated XML document is well formed with respect to the corresponding rule-based SSDL contract schema. This validation is done at the application level; it provides feedback to the user via the graphical user interface (GUI) about successful validations as well as failed validations such as the failing nodes or elements in the contract.

GAT template generator: The SSDL rule-based protocol framework is an independent language that allows architects to specify messaging behaviors of a service. A programmer needs to write a complete business process that is in conformance with the given SSDL contract. The GAT template generator can be used to create a GAT process that is semantically equivalent to the contract. The template generator parses the contract to extract message choreography, termination protocols and consistent constraints. The GAT syntax used by the generator has been implemented at the application level. Based on the parsing results, it then produces a GAT template, containing the guards, actions, trigger parameters as well as termination protocols and consistency constraints. The developers then use the template to build a complete business process that is in conformance with the given contract.

Conformance checker: As mentioned above, an architect may develop a service contract independently of the business process created by other personnel, say business analysts, and the conformance checker can be used to check conformance of a contract to the business process. When the user first uploads a SSDL contract, the conformance checker uses the contract validation tool to check the validity of the contract. The tool then checks the conformance between the business process and service contract. The checker takes a user specified contract and a GAT process as inputs, and performs parsing operations on them to extract their respective message choreography and the associated termination protocol and consistency constraints. The generator treats the GAT process as the benchmark and compares the contract's message choreography, termination protocols and consistency constraints with respect to that of GAT's to see if they conform to each other. The users are notified of any discrepancy along with suggestions on how to rectify the non-conformance. A built-in editor lets the user modify and save changes made to a SSDL contract. If there are no discrepancies, the user is notified of the successful conformance. We further discuss two important concepts within this tool.

Composition rules: It is easy to see how the conformance tool works in the payment activity. Our e-procurement example consists of three processes: placing an order, payment and delivery. The process of creating a merchant contract by combining these three business processes is quite complex. The composition rule defines a logic used by conformance checker tool to generate a composite SSDL contract from a service provider/consumer's component business processes. Specifically, it defines how to extract related incoming and outgoing messages and differentiate between internal message calls used to communicate between component merchant processes and messages that are received from or sent to external parties such as a customer. In a GAT process, outgoing message calls from a service to another have a service name prefix (e.g., *MerchantPayment.GoodsReserved*). An incoming message can be of either *EVENT* type or *IN_EVENT* type. *EVENT* type messages are actually message calls from other GAT processes. *IN_EVENT* messages are those that are generated by external business partners. As the conformance checker tool parses GAT processes one at a time, say GAT process A1, it looks at the guard and trigger conditions for all incoming messages and maps these conditions to all outgoing messages found in the trigger, be it internal messages or messages to a customer. When the parser reaches the GAT message block in another process, say A2, where the message name found in EVENT is identical to the internal message call it mapped earlier, the parser replaces the internal message call found in A1 with the outgoing message found in the trigger of A2. The parser keeps traversing the GAT tree, until all internal message calls in the GAT mapping have been replaced by outgoing message calls triggered because of invoking these message calls. This new GAT mapping is then used to generate a composite service contract.

Consistency constraints and termination protocols: Consistency constraints have been implemented at the application level. Hence, the agreed termination states are application specific, with the business analyst/developer being responsible for coding the constraints in both GAT business processes and SSDL contracts. The conformance checking tool ensures that the termination protocols and consistency constraints still hold when GAT business processes are translated to SSDL contracts and vice versa.

RELATED WORK

A major barrier to widespread adoption of SOA and supporting Web services technologies is the issue of maintaining consistency across long running business processes in the presence of failures and concurrent activities, given the autonomous, stateful nature of services (Greenfield et al., 2005). The definition of consistency in the SOA domain states that when the distributed applications finish, all participating services must terminate in an agreed set of acceptable consistent distributed final states. Traditional transactional models, such as Sagas (Garcia-Molina, & Salem, 1987), and Sagas-based standards such as WSDL (WSDL, 2001), business process execution language for Web services (BPEL4WS, 2002)) and Web services choreography interface (WSCI, 2002) were developed and used in developing service-oriented applications. However, these models and languages are inadequate for service-oriented applications, as such applications do not execute within a single trust domain. They only offer a partial solution to the consistency problem. We next elaborate four key issues we have encountered in our case studies of an e-procurement example, and discuss the relevant literature, including compatibility between Web Services contracts participating in a distributed application.

First, the Web services standards for defining business processes such as BPEL4WS use existing ideas from the database community, including workflow descriptions based on graph-like arrangements of the steps, and advanced transaction models with compensators and failure-handlers for nested scopes. Defining a normal behavior in a process is easy and straightforward using these standard graph-based languages. However, the same cannot be said for the exceptions and failures. The main reason is that exceptions are treated as failures, which make it difficult to describe exception paths in the process. This may cause inconsistency in data as well as status of the activities. Alternative models have been proposed such as the guard-action-trigger model (Nepal et al., 2005; Jang, Fekete, Greenfield, & Nepal, 2006), and extensions to BPEL4WS (such as BPEL4People and BPEL-SPE).

Second, the Web service contract also plays a part in the compatibility problem. There are a number of proposals from the SOA community such as WSCI and abstract BPEL4WS. These alternatives to contract languages have either insufficient expressiveness or that they become too verbose and tedious to use even for the simplest, straightforward business processes (Kuo, Fekete, Greenfield, Nepal, Zic, Parastitidis, & Webber, 2006). This lack of expressiveness is one of the main causes of inconsistency in long running Web transactions. Alternative approaches such as SSDL with a rule-based protocol framework (Parastatidis et al., 2006) have been proposed to address this inadequacy.

Third, one of the main sources of inconsistency is the compatibility of business processes and their corresponding contracts. A body of work has been done on applying formal methods and model checking in compatibility of service-oriented applications (Bultan et al., 2003; Nakajima, 2002; Nararaynan & Mcllraith, 2002;). Compatibility issue is studied in two broad categories: (a) between a service contract and its implementation (Nakajima, 2002) and (b) between contracts of different services (Bultan et al., 2003; Foster et al., 2004; Greenfield et al., 2005; Nararaynan & Mcllraith, 2002;).

The first category includes tools that have been developed to check the compatibility between a Web service contract and its implementation. A model based verification tool has been proposed by Foster, Uchitel, Kramer, & Magee (2003) to check the conformity of Web service implementation to its design specification. Designers specify the requirements of a Web service in UML in the form of message sequence charts (MSC). This MSC then gets translated into the domain independent notation of finite state process (FSP) specification. Developers on the other hand can develop the Web service in BPEL4WS and then convert that into FSP. A check is performed on the MSC FSP and the BPEL4WS FSP to check whether they are equivalent. Other conformance checking tools have also been developed, using DAML+OIL and Petri Nets instead of BPEL4WS and FSP (Nararaynan & Mcllraith, 2002). One of the shortcomings of these approaches is that they work with contracts and business processes expressed in notations that do not deal with consistency constraints and do not facilitate simple ways to check service termination. Bhuiyan, Nepal, & Zic (2006) propose a way to overcome some of the limitations of these approaches and presented an easier way of modeling application specific constraints within GAT (Nepal et al., 2005). They also developed a tool to check conformance of business processes defined in GAT with a corresponding service contract defined in SSDL rule-based framework (Kuo et al., 2006).

The second category includes tools that have been developed to check the compatibility of Web service contracts (Benatallah et al., 2004; Bultan et al., 2003; Cheng et al., 2002; Foster et al., 2004; Gao, Liu, Song, & Chen, 2006; Greenfield et al., 2005; Martens, Moser, Gerhardt & Funk, 2006; Nararaynan & Mcllraith, 2002; Shi, Zhang, Liu, Lin & Shi;2005). Foster et al. (2004) proposed a method for checking compatibility of service contracts, where the communication between services is modeled using synchronous message passing using a BPEL port as a communication channel. This is an extension of their earlier work presented in (i.e., Foster, Uchitel, Kramer, & Magee, 2003). Participating service activities as well as communication channels (BPEL ports) are modeled into a labeled transition system. The LTSA tool is then used to check standard correctness properties (e.g., that all messages sent are received, deadlock freeness, and eventual termination). Similar techniques were proposed by Fu, Bultan, and Su (2004) and Nakajima (2002). Instead of BPEL4WS and FSP, Nakajima (2002) uses WSFL and Promela, Fu, Bultan, & Su (2004) use BPEL4WS, guarded automata and PROMELA and Kuo et al. (2006) use SSDL rule and PROMELA. The SPIN model checker is then used to check standard correctness properties expressed in LTL. Bultan et al. (2003) define a conversational protocol and use it to model and verify Web services composition. One of the shortcomings of these approaches is that these solutions do not guarantee that compatible contracts always terminate in an acceptable state. Our observations and case studies show that the main reason for not being able to deal with it is that they do not support mechanisms for graceful termination.

Finally, a large body of work has been done in designing algorithms for distributed termination detection, but they can not be used at design time as they are mainly developed for run-time scenarios (Mattern, 1987). None of the standards defined for describing service contracts such as BPEL4WS (BPEL4WS, 2002), WSCI (WSCI, 2002), WSDL (WSDL, 2001) and SSDL (SSDL, 2005), allow specification of termination protocols. We propose a way of describing termination patterns in service contracts using WS-BusinessActivity (WS-BA) (WS-BA, 2005). Our approach that enables application programmers specify termination patterns and check the "termination" criterion at design time.

Recently, the problem of compatibility of contracts has attracted much attention in the research community. Castagna, Gesbert, & Padovani (2009) devise a theory of contracts that formalizes the compatibility of a client with a service, and the safe replacement of a service with another service. The purpose of the theory is to statically verify that all possible interactions between the client and service successfully terminate. They use the concept of filter. It enables service reuse or redefinition by introducing the concept of subcontracting. Davulcu, Kifer, & Ramakrishnan (2004) proposed a logic based formalism, called CTR-S, for modeling dynamic contracts for semantic Web services. They use the logic based formalism for modeling and reasoning about Web service contracts. Carpinet, Castagna, Laneve, & Padovani (2006) defined a formal contract language and provided a mechanism of checking its compliance with underlying business processes. The process algebra has also been used to formalize Web services contracts (Meredith & Bjorg, 2003; Shu, Qing, & Jing, 2008). Tan, Fan, & Zhou (2009) have used a Petri Net based method to check the composability aspect of Web services contract. Their method checks whether there exists any message mediator so that their composition does not violate the constraints imposed by participating services. Zhang, Sun, Yin, & Xu (2008) have also proposed a Petri Net based approach for checking behavioral compatibility (composability) of Web services. Martens et al. (2006) have also used the Petri Nets to analyze compatibility of BPEL processes.

This paper deals a composability problem at the contract syntax level and it is performed using exact matching of the messages. The problem of composability has been studied at two levels: *syntactic* and *semantics*. The popularity of the semantic Web has attracted by researchers to look the probem of composability at the level of semanctics. Medjahed, Bouguettaya, & Elmagarmid (2003) defined an algorithm for checking composability in semantic Web. In this paper, we deal with the problem of compatibility at the design time. The problems could occur at run time as well as described in (Bordeaux, Salaün, Berardi, & Mecella, 2005). The compatibility problems occur at run time due to the changes in either service contracts or businesses processes that are participating in the composition. Orriëns & Yang (2005) have looked at the compatibility problem for design time, specifically on collaborative business processes. They studied the compatibility along perspective and aspect. However, the study was limited to prescription and has not provided practical algorithms/protocols. Recently, Borovskiy, Mueller, Schapranow, & Zeier (2009) have looked at the compatibility problem from a practical point of view. The basic idea behind their work is to maintain Web service backward compatible. In particular, the authors suggest a new interface design technique called generic Web services that allows service providers to add new features to Web services without breaking compatibility with existing clients. Zhou, Ning, Bhiri, Vasiliu, Shu, & Hauswirth (2008) have looked at the compatibility issues from the point of view of information flow. They argued that the focus of the most of the works was on control-flow and the data-flow aspect of the compatibility issues has been largely ignored. They proposed an approach that takes both control and data flow aspects of the service into consideration. Yan, Aït-Bachir, Chen, & Zhang (2010) have taken a similar approach to address the composability aspect of compatibility. Their approach is to change the incompatible service and replace with a compatible one. They have used the finite state machine to model both data and control flow of the participating services.

CONCLUSION

We have designed and developed a framework for checking the compatibility of interacting services in service-oriented applications. We have looked at the compatibility problem from two aspects: *composability* and *conformance*. The composability deals with the compatibility between Web service contracts, whereas the conformance deals with the compatibility issues between a service contract and its implementation.

We first defined compatibility properties, that is, services always terminate in acceptable states. We then proposed a way of defining it in service contracts along with a set of guidelines for SOA application programmers and system designers. We proposed a method of specifying termination patterns along with acceptable consistent states. This is achieved by extending the existing Web services contract definition languages for specifying termination patterns and a set of constraints that need to be satisfied at termination. Our approach uses WS-BusinessActivity patterns as termination patterns and a form of rule-based language for defining termination constraints. The constraints are defined using states related to received and sent messages. This approach has an obvious limitation that not all types of constraints can be expressed using message-related states. However, the benefits of keeping services autonomous and opaque outweigh this limitation. Similarly, we showed a feasibility of extending business process language to specify acceptable consistent states.

Our discussion in this book chapter on composability is limited to exactly matching contracts, and we plan to examine partial matching contracts in our future work. Furthermore, the current work defines checking compatibility of Web service contracts only at design time. Due to the dynamic nature of business processes, the contracts may change and need to adapt to the changing business environment. Such changes may invalidate the contracts checked at design time. We need to have a mechanism of checking contracts at runtime as well. We plan to extend the framework so that compatibility properties can be checked dynamically at runtime. Our future work also includes a framework for extension of contract definition languages and definition of coordination logics in WS-BA termination patterns for multi-party interactions.

ACKNOWLEDGMENT

The authors would like to acknowledge that Thi Chau is one of the original authors of the article (Nepal, Zic, & Chau, 2009) upon which this article is based. The authors would also like to thank Paul Greenfield, Alan Fekete, Dean Kuo and Julian Jang for their comments and discussions, and Jenny Bhuiya and Thi Chau for the implementations of tools.

REFERENCES

Abrial, J.-R. (1996). *The B-nook: Assigning programs to meanings*. Cambridge University Press. doi:10.1017/CBO9780511624162

Benatallah, B., Casati, F., Grigori, D., Nezhad, H. R. M., & Touami, F. (2005). Developing adapters for Web Services integration. In *Proceedings of the International Conference on Advanced Information Systems Engineering (CAiSE)*, Porto, Portugal.

Benatallah, B., Casati, F., & Toumani, F. (2004, January). Web services conversation modeling: The cornerstone for e-business automation. *IEEE Internet Computing*, *8*(1), 46–54. doi:10.1109/MIC.2004.1260703

Bhuiyan, J., Nepal, S., & Zic, J. (2006, April). Checking conformance between business processes and web service contract in service oriented applications. In *Proceedings of the Australian Software Engineering Conference* (ASWEC 2006), Sydney, Australia (pp. 80-89).

Bordeaux, L., Salaün, G., Berardi, D., & Mecella, M. (2005). When are two web services compatible? In *Technologies for E-Services* (pp. 15–28). Berlin, Germany: Springer. doi:10.1007/978-3-540-31811-8_2

Borovskiy, V., Mueller, J., Schapranow, M., & Zeier, A. (2009). Ensuring service backwards compatibility with generic web services. In Proceedings of the 2009 *ICSE Workshop on Principles of Engineering Service Oriented Systems* (pp. 95-98).

BPEL4WS. (2002). Retrieved January 18, 2009, from http://www-128.ibm.com/developerworks/library/ specification/ ws-bpel/

Brogi, A., Canal, C., Pimentel, E., & Vallecillo, A. (2004). Formalizing Web service choreographies. In *Proceedings of the First International Workshop on Web Services and Formal Methods* (pp. 73-94).

Bultan, T., Fu, X., Hall, R., & Su, J. (2003, May). Conversation specification: A new approach to design and analysis of e-service composition. In *World Wide Web*, (pp. 403-410).

Carpinet, S., Castagna, G., Laneve, C., & Padovani, L. (2006). A formal account of contracts for Web services. In *Proceedings of 3rd International Workshop on Web Services and Formal Methods* (pp. 148-168)

Castagna, G., Gesbert, N., & Padovani, L. (2009, June). A theory of contracts for Web services. *ACM Trans. Program. Lang. Syst.*, *31*(5), 1–61. doi:10.1145/1538917.1538920

Cheng, Z., Singh, M. P., & Vouk, M. A. (2002). Verifying constraints on web service compositions. In Kashyap, V., & Shklar, L. (Eds.), *Real world semantic web applications*.

Davulcu, H., Kifer, M., & Ramakrishnan, I. V. (May 2004). CTR-S: A logic for specifying contracts in semantic web services. In *Proceedings of the 13th International World Wide Web Conference*, New York, NY, USA (pp. 144-153).

Elmagarmid, A. (1992). *Database transaction models for advanced applications*. Morgan Kaufmann.

Foster, H., Uchitel, S., Kramer, J., & Magee, J. (2003, October). Model-based verification of web service compositions. In *Proceedings of IEEE International Conference on Automated Software Engineering (ASE) Conference*, Montreal, Canada (pp. 95-99).

Foster, H., Uchitel, S., Kramer, J., & Magee, J. (2004, July). Compatibility verification for Web Service choreography. In *Proceedings of International Conference on Web Services (ICWS)*, San Diego (pp. 738-741).

Fu, X., Bultan, T., & Su, J. (2003). Conversation protocols: A formalism for specification and verification of reactive electronic services. In *Proceedings of 8th International Conferences on Implementation and Application of Automata (CIAA)* (vol. 2759, pp. 188-200).

Fu, X., Bultan, T., & Su, J. (2004, May). Analysis of interacting BPEL Web services. In *Proceedings of WWW*, New York (pp. 621-630).

Gao, C., Liu, R., Song, Y., & Chen, H. (2006). A model checking tool embedded into services composition environment. In *Proceedings of International Conference on Grid and Cooperative Computing* (pp. 355-362).

Garcia-Molina, H., & Salem, K. (1987). Sagas. In *Proceedings of ACM International Conference on Management of Data (SIGMOD)*, (pp. 249-259).

Gray, J., & Reuter, A. (1992). *Transaction processing: Concepts and techniques*. Morgan Kaufmann 1992.

Greenfield, P., Kuo, D., Nepal, S., & Fekete, A. (2005). Consistency for Web services applications. In *Proceedings of VLDB*, Trondheim, Norway (pp. 1199-1203).

Helland, P. (2005, January). Data on the outside versus data on the inside. In *Proceedings of Second Biennial Conference on Innovative Data Systems Research*, Asilomar, CA.

Hoare, C. A. R. (1985). *Communicating sequential processes*. Prentice-Hall International Series in Computer Science.

Holzmann, G. (2003). *The spin model checker: Primer and reference manual*. Addison-Wesley.

Jang, J., Fekete, A., Greenfield, P., & Nepal, S. (2006, October). An event-driven workflow engine for service-based business systems. In *Proceedings of International Enterprise Distributed Object Systems Conference (EDOC'06)*, Hong Kong, China, (pp. 233-242).

Kuo, D., Fekete, A., Greenfield, P., Nepal, S., Zic, J., Parastitidis, S., & Webber, J. (2006, September). Expressing and reasoning about service contracts in service-oriented computing. In *Proceedings of International Conference on Web Services (ICWS)*, Chicago, Illinois USA (pp. 915-918).

Martens, A., Moser, S., Gerhardt, A., & Funk, K. (2006). Analyzing compatibility of BPEL processes. In *Proceedings of the Advanced International Conference on Telecommunications and International Conference on Internet and Web Applications and Services*.

Mattern, F. (1987). Algorithms for distributed termination detection. *Distributed Computing*, *2*, 161–175. doi:10.1007/BF01782776

Medjahed, B., Bouguettaya, A., & Elmagarmid, A. (2003, Nov). Composing Web services on the Semantic Web. *The VLDB Journal*, *12*(4), 333–351. doi:10.1007/s00778-003-0101-5

Meredith, L. G., & Bjorg, S. (2003). Contracts and types. *Communications of the ACM*, *46*(10), 41–47. doi:10.1145/944217.944236

Milanovic, N., & Malek, M. (2004, Nov./Dec.). Current solutions for web service composition. *IEEE Internet Computing*, *8*(6), 51–59. doi:10.1109/MIC.2004.58

Milner, R. (1989). *Communication and concurrency*. Prentice-Hall International Series in Computer Science.

Nakajima, S. (2002). Model-checking verification for reliable web service. In *Proceedings of OOPSLA 2002 Workshop on Object-oriented Web Services*, Seattle, Washington.

Nararaynan, S., & Mcllraith, S. A. (2002, May). Simulation, verification and automated composition of web services. In *Proceedings of WWW*, Honolulu, Hawaii (pp. 77-88).

Nepal, S., Fekete, A., Greenfield, P., Jang, J., Kuo, D., & Shi, T. (2005). A service-oriented workflow language for robust interacting applications. In *Proceedings of CoopIS* (LNCS 3760, pp. 40-58, 2005).

Nepal, S., Zic, J., & Chau, T. (2006, September). Compatibility of service contracts in service-oriented applications. In *Proceedings of IEEE SCC*, Chicago (pp. 28-35).

Nepal, S., Zic, J., & Chau, T. (2009). An approach to checking compatibility of service contracts in service-oriented applications. *International Journal of Web Services Research*, *6*(2), 42–65. doi:10.4018/jwsr.2009040103

Orriëns, B., & Yang, J. (2005). Establishing and maintaining compatibility in service oriented business collaboration. In *Proceedings of the 7th international Conference on Electronic Commerce* ICEC '05, (pp. 446-453).

Parastatidis, S., Woodman, S., Webber, J., Kuo, D., & Greenfield, P. (2006). Asynchronous messaging between Web services using SSDL. *IEEE Internet Computing*, *10*(1), 26–39. doi:10.1109/MIC.2006.3

Shi, Y., Zhang, L., Liu, F., Lin, L., & Shi, B. (2005). Compatibility analysis of Web Services. In *Proceedings of the 2005 IEEE/WIC/ACM International Conference on Web intelligence* (pp. 483-486).

Shu, C., Qing, W. G., & Jing, X. (2008). A process algebra approach for the compatibility analysis of web services. In *Proceedings of the 2008 Second International Conference on Future Generation Communication and Networking* (pp. 305-308).

SSDL. (2005). *SOAP service description languages* (SSDL). Retrieved January 18, 2009, from www.ssdl.org

Tan, W., Fan, Y., & Zhou, M. (2009). A petri net-based method for compatibility analysis and composition of web services in business process execution language. *IEEE Transactions on Automation Science and Engineering*, *6*(1), 94–106. doi:10.1109/TASE.2008.916747

WS-AT. (2005). *WS-AtomicTransaction*. Retrieved January 18, 2009, from http://msdn.microsoft.com/ library/ en-us/ dnglobspec/ html/ WS-AtomicTransaction.pdf

WS-BA. (2005). *WS-BusinessActivity*. Retrieved January 18, 2009, from http://msdn.microsoft.com/ library/ en-us/ dnglobspec/ html/ WS-BusinessActivity.pdf

WS-Coord. (2005). *WS-Coordination*. Retrieved January 18, 2009, from http://msdn.microsoft.com/ library/ en-us/ dnglobspec/ html/ WS-Coordination.pdf

WSCI. (2002). *Web service choreography interface* (WSCI) 1.0. Retrieved January 18, 2009, from http://www.w3.org/ TR/ wsci/

WSDL. (2001). *Web services description language* (WSDL) 1.1. Retrieved January 18, 2009, from http://www.w3.org/ TR/ wsdl

Yan, Y., Aït-Bachir, A., Chen, M., & Zhang, K. (2010). Compatibility and reparation of web service processes. In *Proceedings of the 2010 IEEE International Conference on Web Services* (pp. 634-637).

Zhang, S., Sun, J., Yin, K., & Xu, B. (2008). Petri net based web service interactive behavior compatibility analysis. In *Proceedings of International Seminar on Business and Information Management* (pp. 473-476).

Zhou, Z., Ning, K., Bhiri, S., Vasiliu, L., Shu, L., & Hauswirth, M. (2008). Behavioral analysis of web services for supporting mediated service interoperations. In *Proceedings of the 10th International Conference on Electronic Commerce* (pp. 1-10).

Chapter 9
High Performance Approach for Server Side SOAP Processing

Lei Li
University of Science & Technology of China, China & The Chinese Academy of Sciences, China

Chunlei Niu
The Chinese Academy of Sciences, China

Ningjiang Chen
Guangxi University, China

Jun Wei
The Chinese Academy of Sciences, China

Tao Huang
University of Science & Technology of China, China & The Chinese Academy of Sciences, China

ABSTRACT

Web services, with an emphasis on open standards and flexibility, can provide benefits over existing capital markets' integration practices. However, Web services must first meet certain technical requirements, including performance, security, and so on. Based on extensible markup language (XML), Web services inherit not only the advantages of XML, but its relatively poor performance, which makes it a poor choice for many high-performance applications. In this article, a new approach is proposed to improve Web services performance. Focusing on avoiding traditional XML parsing and Java reflection at runtime, this article presents a service-specific simple object access protocol (SOAP) processor to accelerate the execution of Web services. Moreover, the SOAP processor embeds several cache implementations and uses a novel adaptive cache mechanism, which can choose an optimized cache implementation dynamically. Through the experiments in this article, it is to be observed that the proposed approach can achieve a significant performance gain by incorporating the SOAP processor into the SOAP engine.

DOI: 10.4018/978-1-61350-104-7.ch009

INTRODUCTION

Currently, there has been a tremendous development in the area of Web services and the simple object access protocol (SOAP) is a dominant enabling technology in it. Over the last few years, a lot of works (e.g., Bustamante, 2000; Chiu, Govindaraju, & Bramley, 2002; Elfwing, Paulsson, & Lundberg, 2002; Kohlhoff & Steele, 2003) have been carried out in comparing SOAP with binary protocols, such as Java RMI and CORBA. These researches show that there is a dramatic difference in the amount of encoding necessary for data transmission, when extensible markup language (XML) is compared with the binary encoding style followed in CORBA, and all these researches have proven that SOAP, because of its reliance on XML, is inefficient compared with its peers in distributed computing.

Although the performance of Web services has been adequate for many important purposes, processing speed unfortunately remains a problem in more performance-sensitive applications, especially when the SOAP engine is built in Java. Existing researches indicate that the performance of those systems built in Java cannot be compared to the system built in C/C++. This is because the C++ compiler translates source code into an executable file, which can be executed by a operation system directly, while Java source code is interpreted into bytecode by Java virtual machine. Eckel (2003) indicates that interpreted Java runs in the range of 20 times slower than C. Hence, the Java-based systems need to improve performance, particularly.

Many performance problems of Web services are inherent in core features of XML: it is text based, flexible in format, and carries redundant information. Let us simply describe the message processing flow in the SOAP engine in general. First, when the SOAP engine receives the message, it uses XML parser to parse the message. Second, it translates the parsed XML elements into Java objects by using deserializing operations. And then, it invokes service business logic with those objects. After that, it gets the results and translates them into a response message by using serializing operations. Finally, the response message will be sent to the user. Davis and Parashar (2002) indicate that in the overall processing flow, the XML parsing and Java reflection at runtime is exactly the performance bottleneck of Web services. Obviously, if we can avoid the time-consuming operation in the runtime, the performance may be greatly improved. There are two intuitive ways to solve this problem, one is to use a cache mechanism to avoid time-consuming operations, and the other is to deal with them before runtime.

Aiming at the problems, this article proposes a novel approach to improve the performance of Web services by optimizing SOAP processing. The SOAP engine presented in the article maintains specific SOAP processors for each Web service. The SOAP processor is generated by using the information from WSDL and service's classes during system startup or service hot-deployment. In essence, the SOAP processor is a composition of SOAP parser and deserializer. It can identify the SOAP messages related to a specific Web service. Moreover, the SOAP processor embeds several cache implementations and uses an adaptive mechanism to choose the optimized caching strategy dynamically. When receiving a message, the SOAP processor first uses an adaptive caching mechanism to choose the best cache implementation to handle the message. If the cache fails, it uses XML a preparsing framework and predeserializing templates to complete the processing. Using a service-specific SOAP processor we can avoid traditional XML parsing and Java reflection at runtime. Moreover, because the SOAP processor scans a SOAP message only once, the performance is improved remarkably. Our method supports the WSDL document/literal style, which is the direction where the industry is headed; in addition, it is the most consistent model from a Web services architecture perspective (Curbera, Duftler, & Khalaf, 2005). The evaluation presented in this article shows our approach is effective in both speed and memory usage aspects.

The main contributions of this article are as follows: (1) a novel approach to preparse and predeserialize the SOAP message; (2) an adaptive caching mechanism to dynamically choose an optimized cache implementation at runtime; (3) a novel service-specific SOAP processor based on the combination of above two approaches, which can help the SOAP engine to accelerate message processing.

The rest of the article is organized as follows: First, we survey the related works in the following section. We then analyze the performance problem. The forth section describes the preparsing and predeserializing approach and in the fifth section we present the hit ratio-based adaptive caching mechanism and introduce the implementation. The sixth section shows the results of experiments and finally, we conclude the article and introduce our future work in the last section.

RELATED WORKS

The growth of XML-based Web services is increasing the interest of high performance end-users in these technologies. Efficiency issues with XML and with the SOAP protocol that relies on it, however, have inhibited technology adoption. A variety of approaches have been proposed to optimize Web services performance.

Data Binding

Data binding means the mapping between XML text and Java object, and it can be divided into two types: late data binding and early data binding (Wei, Hua, & Niu, 2006). Late binding uses a Java reflection mechanism to do the mapping, but Java reflection is not efficient, and makes late binding the performance bottleneck of Web services. Early data binding creates template classes that record Java object properties and method information before runtime, and uses these template classes to do the mapping. Early data binding can avoid Java reflection at runtime, so it is more efficient than late data binding. Based on early data binding, this article embeds the template classes to the SOAP processor. When a SOAP message flows in, the SOAP processor uses these template classes to create a Java object.

JiBX is a very famous framework for binding XML data to Java objects. JiBX uses a byte code enhancing technique which is the most important cause for its extra performance. Current data binding tools all engage code generation techniques to enhance performance. This needs accessorial class to do the binding. However, JiBX generates data binding related codes and plants them directly into the object class. In this way, there is no extra class loading time and the planted generation logic can directly access the object data. The basic architecture of JiBX is very different from those of other XML data binding frameworks for Java applications. This leads to both advantages and drawbacks when comparing JiBX with other frameworks. On the plus side, JiBX gains the advantages of a very fast operation, a compact runtime, and greater isolation between XML document formats and Java language object structures. On the minus side, it is based on a relatively unproven parser technology and does not support the validation flexibility provided by some of the alternatives (especially JAXB). Some of the other differences between JiBX and alternative frameworks are less clear-cut. For instance, JiBX's technique of class file enhancement offers the advantage of keeping your source code clean. The binding code is added after you compile, so you never need to deal with it directly, but at the cost of an added step in the building process and potential confusion in tracking problems in your code accessed during marshalling or unmarshalling.

Just like JiBX, the SOAP processor also does not need accessorial class to do the binding. When doing the deserializing operation, the SOAP processor already knows the class type and loads it directly. Moreover, JiBX is a data binding tool, so it does not optimize the XML parsing, which is a very time-consuming operation in SOAP processing. Our approach optimizes the XML parsing and deserialization process. Actually, our approach can integrate the idea of serialization operation of JiBX to the SOAP processor to achieve further performance gain.

XML Parsing Optimization

XML schema is to define a class of XML documents. Chiu and Lu (2003) propose a finite-state parsing technique, which considers merging all aspects of low-level parsing and validation by constructing a single push-down automaton. This is a viable approach to high-performance XML parsing. Kotoulas, Matsa, and Mendelsohn (2006) present an integrated approach to high performance XML parsing, validation, and deserialization. A prototype called XML screamer is implemented to compile customized validating XML parsers from an XML schema. XML screamer demonstrates the importance of integrating deserialization with scanning, parsing, and validation, and of providing compiled optimizations particular to each XML API.

Takase, Miyashita, and Suzumura (2005) describe a system in which invariant output is discovered heuristically at runtime. As multiple similar input documents are parsed, common substrings are noted and used to build a deterministic finite automaton (DFA) against which subsequent input is validated. Kotoulas et al. (2006) indicate that Takase et al.'s system seems to have advantages particularly in situations where no schema is available, since it works on any series of structurally similar XML documents. Furthermore, this method is based on pure text matching, which has many restrictions. First, different clients have their own styles to encode a SOAP request, so although these requests are same in semantics, they are different in message text. This XML parser cannot detect this difference. Suzumura, Takase, and Tatsubori (2005) propose a new deserializing mechanism based on Takase et al.'s (2005) work. This approach reuses the existing deserialized Java objects last deserialized and can improve performance efficiently if the parameters of Web services do not change frequently.

Non-XML Data Representation

JSON is another data exchangeable format like XML, but it is more lightweight and easily readable. It is based on a subset of JavaScript language. The strengths and weaknesses of the formats are clear-cut. If you are transporting documents or are aiming for a wide range of extensibility, then you should be using XML. If you have control over both ends of the wire, for example, talking to your own Web server from hyper text markup language (HTML) pages served from that same server, then you should be using JSON. JSON has several benefits over XML: it is concise, which means a smaller message size to transport and correspondingly less time to process both at the server and client side, thus improving the application performance; and it is direct for JavaScript developers to consume, making it a good choice to work with AJAX-based applications. However, JSON has lots of drawbacks: no support for formal grammar definition, hence interface contracts are hard to communicate and enforce; no namespace support, hence poor extensibility; limited development tools support; and support by Web services product has just emerged. Moreover, the message with the format of JSON also needs to be parsed and deserialized before it can be consumed by the server, which are time-consuming operations. Our approach is not compatible to JSON style messages, but can provide some valuable reference to optimize JSON processing.

Caching Mechanism

Cache is a classic but effective approach to improve the round-trip time for request-response exchanges and reduce recurring computation in distributed systems. Especially for Web services, cache mechanisms contribute considerably to faster response time and higher throughput. Communication overhead does not affect the overall service throughput anymore with effective client-side cache. Takase and Tatsubori (2004) present an efficient response cache by selecting optimal data representation. Three optimization methods have been proposed to improve the performance, which reduce the overhead of XML processing or object copying. Devaram and Andresen (2003) present an optimized design utilizing a caching mechanism at the client side for SOAP messages and this approach achieves dramatically better performance (800%) over the original code. The above advantages make client-side cache very popular in mobile devices. However, client-side cache has some inherent drawbacks, for example, a low hit ratio and it is difficult to manage consistently, which make it infeasible in some situations. At present, most of the researches use time–to-live (TTL) to manage client-side cache consistency, but TTL has obvious defects. Compared to client-side cache, server-side cache has a higher hit ratio and is easier to manage consistently.

Server-side cache can shorten the response time and enhance the throughput efficiently. Takase (2002) proposes a solution for eliminating the critical cache busting behavior of SOAP requests by use of canonicalization. Request matches are determined by use of an XML canonicalization template. Gu and Li (2005) design a new virtual service cache model based on service gateway, which can shorten the average response time of service invocation efficiently. These are reverse proxy cache, which save the response message for the following requests. However, the cache key is associated with parameter values, so the hit ratio is very low for some Web services. Cache can avoid the repeated processing, but that only works if requests are completely unchanged and it fails if they are even slightly modified. Andresen, Devaram, and Ranganath (2004) present an approach to leverage multiple levels of caching and template-based customized response generation in a SOAP server. This approach is very efficient and has significant performance advantages over response-proxy cache in many scenarios. IBM (2002) indicates that about 35% of total time is spent in XML parsing. XML parsing and deserializing is exactly the performance bottleneck of Web services.

PROBLEM ANALYSIS

This section will first analyze the SOAP message processing flow on the server side in order to find and validate the performance bottlenecks.

Analyzing the Performance of Web Services

We use Apache Axis 1.2 as the analyzing object. Apache Axis works as a Web application hosted on a Web container, which handles the sending/receiving of a SOAP request/response message through HTTP protocol. Though the hyper text transfer protocol (HTTP) itself may be a possible performance bottleneck, we will not discuss this issue in the article.

A SOAP message processing could be decomposed of five stages, as shown in Figure 1 and discussed below:

1. **XML Parsing Stage.** A XML request message is parsed by a XML parser. Axis1.2 uses the SAX parser.
2. **Deserialization Stage.** The parsed XML data is deserialized to Java objects as parameters delivered to applications. Axis1.2 replays the recorded SAX events and notifies the deserializer of SAX events to finish their works.
3. **Application Invocation Stage.** Application invocation is finished in this stage. The time

Figure 1. SOAP message processing flow

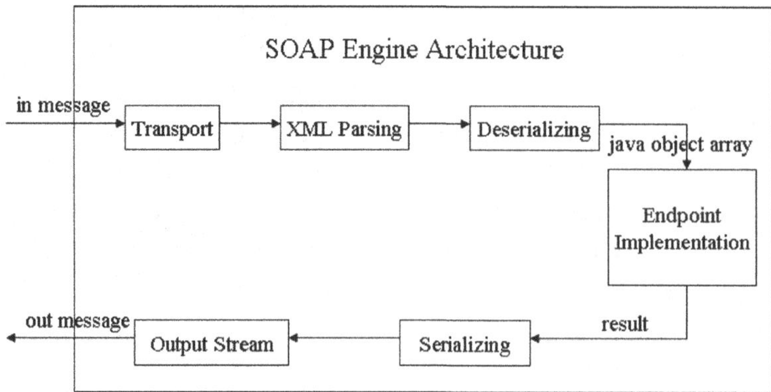

consumption is related with the complexity of business logic of application.

4. **Serialization Stage.** The results of application invocation. Java objects are serialized to XML data. In Axis1.2, the XML data are written into a memory buffer.
5. **Output Stream Stage.** The buffered response XML data are written into the output stream. Then the output stream is prepared as a HTTP response object.

During the five stages, the XML parsing and deserialization stages care about the mapping from XML data to Java data, and the serialization and output stream stages care about the transformation from Java data to XML data. We choose the WS Test 1.0 suite (Sun Microsystems, 2005) to test the time spent on each stage in the SOAP message process. And several kinds of test cases are designed to measure the performance of various types of Web services call, such as:

- **echoVoid:** Send/receive a message with an empty body.
- **echoStruct:** Send/receive an array of size 20; each element is a complex data type composed of three elements: an integer, a float, and a string.
- **echoList:** Send/receive a linked list of size 20; each element of the list is a Struct defined in *echoStruct*.

The experimental settings are as follows: CPU Pentium-4.1 2.80 GHz, 512 MB RAM, Windows XP Professional SP2, J2SK 1.4.2; Apache AXIS 1.2 as Web services runtime, Tomcat 5.0 Web container, and Apache Xerces-J 2.6.2 as XML Parser. The Web service client performs 10,000 iterations for each Web service call, and the client load is 5 hits per second. The XML payload is 4 KB. Figure 2(a) shows the average time spent on each stage for the three test cases. By experiments, we know that the three components in the SOAP processing mainly impact the performance of XML parsing and deserializing.

From the figure we can find that XML parsing and deserializing is exactly the performance bottleneck of Web services.

Analysis of Time Consuming Operations

Current implementations of XML parsers use a variety of different APIs, including DOM, SAX, and, especially in the Web services world, custom-generated object trees, such as JAX-RPC. That some heavyweight APIs, such as DOM, may have a significant impact on performance is qualitatively well known. Perkins, Kostoulas, and Heifets (2005) indicate that the computation specifically required to process XML documents includes tolerance for various character encodings, variable length of data, ignorable white spaces, line

Figure 2.

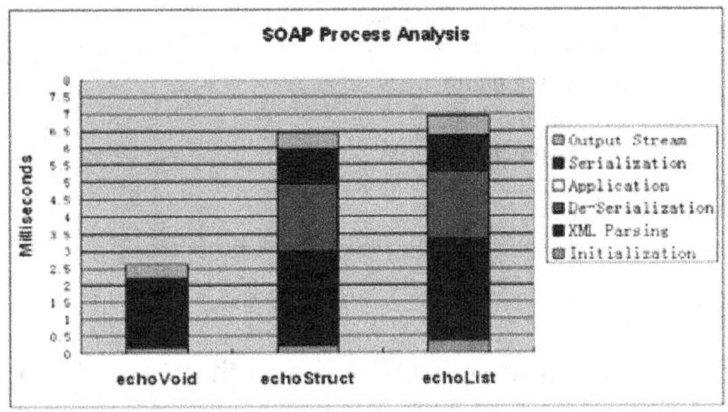

(a) Performance analysis

Processing Phase	XML Parsing	Deserializing	Serializing
echoVoid	80%	0	0
echoStruct	39%	33%	19%
echoList	38%	32%	18%

(b) Performance analysis

break normalization, handling of namespaces, and the creation of parsed result objects. The whole parsing can be divided into two steps. First, an XML parser needs to convert the character encodings, since the external encoding, the encoding format in which XML documents are encoded, may be different from the internal encoding and the encoding format used in a program. Second, an XML parser needs to construct parsed result objects so that it can pass them to its users through an API like SAX.

Perkins et al. (2005) explore the performance characteristics of XML APIs and show that transcoding and object creation are the bottleneck of XML parsing. The syntax of XML is specified in Unicode. XML documents, however, are stored and transferred in an encoded form. Similarly, data are passed to the application in some encoded form. In practice, these two encodings are often not the same one. This means that APIs that pass character data to the application must often transcode this data. Transcoding is a relatively expensive operation, and may be expected to contribute significantly to the cost of text-oriented APIs like SAX and DOM. In addition to transcoding, API production can incur overhead in object creation. This includes the cost of memory allocation and data structure population. For tree-based APIs such as DOM and JAX-RPC, object creation is significant, and the performance of these APIs suffers accordingly. Moreover, all of them require twice traversals of XML data.

Similar to XML parsing, deserializing is another performance bottleneck of Web services. Suzumura et al. (2005) indicate that deserializing is the process of reconstructing the object from the XML data. The serialization and deserialization mechanics in JAX-RPC rests on the availability of type mapping systems defined in a registry. When the SOAP engine reads a particular piece of XML and comes across a given element of a given schema type, it can locate an appropriate deserializer in order to convert the XML elements into Java objects. The SOAP engine usually has a registry that maintains a set of required type mappings. Generally, deserializing an XML message into Java objects involves the following steps:

- Get the XML element that represents the object;
- Recursively deserialize each of the object's members, which are encoded as subelements, after locating an appropriate deserializer from a type mapping system;
- Create a new instance of the Java type, initializing it with the deserialized members; and
- Return the new object.

Java reflection is generally used in the processing, and provides a very versatile way of dynamically linking program components. It allows program to create and manipulate objects of any classes (subject to security restrictions) without the need to hardcode the target classes ahead of time. These features make reflection especially useful for creating libraries that work with objects in very general ways. For example, reflection is often used in frameworks that persist objects to databases, XML, or other external formats.

Reflection is a powerful tool, but suffers from a few drawbacks. One of the main drawbacks is the effect on performance. Sosnoski (2005) indicates that using reflection is basically an interpreted operation, where you tell the JVM what you want to do and it does it for you. This type of operation is always going to be slower than just doing the same operation directly, and makes reflection much slower than direct code when used for field and method access. The performance issues will become a serious concern if reflection is used in the core logic of performance-critical applications.

Basic Idea of Our Approach

If we can avoid the time consuming operations in the runtime, we will achieve efficient performance gain. The basic idea of our approach is to avoid the above time consuming operations, such as XML parsing and Java reflection. We designed a component called SOAP processor and embedded it into a SOAP engine. We will introduce the background and the theoretical fundamental of our research in this section.

For the document/literal style SOAP messages, their XML tags obey the rules of WSDL schema, so the XML tags of SOAP messages must be identical if they call the same operation. For example, there is a Web service called EmployeeService, which has an operation called setPersonInfo(Person person). Person class is a JavaBean and its definition is shown in Table 1.

Table 2 shows the description of Person class in WSDL schema.

When the client desires to invoke the Web service, the Web service will generate a SOAP message according to WSDL schema information. Table 3 shows the SOAP message segment generated by the client to call the Web service.

From the above analysis, we can find that SOAP messages, with document/literal style, used

Table 1. Person class

```
public class Person{
String name;
int age;
String[] child;
......
}
```

to call the same operation, have the same XML tags. So, we can create a preparsing framework to avoid XML parsing in the runtime according to schema-specific parsing mechanism. Based on the preparsing framework, we can design a pre-deserializing approach by generating template classes that record Java object properties and method information in the framework. Using this framework, we can avoid time consuming operations in the runtime.

Furthermore, caching is a general approach in many areas and maybe the most widely used technique for dealing with poor performance. Recently, lots of researche on server-side cache implementation for Web services have been presented, which help a server to obtain a huge performance gain. However, each of these studies has its own limitations and no one is the best in all situations. For example, reverse-proxy cache saves the response message, which has the distinguished advantages and disadvantages. It has the shortest response time with cache hits, but unfortunately the hit ratio is very low because it is associated with parameter values. To improve the hit ratio of the cache, one way is to decrease the granularity of the cached content, which means application objects or other fine-grained content should be cached instead of the response message. But actually, caching application objects is not always better than caching the response message. If we can choose a better cache implementation for the special situation, we will get more performance improvement.

With the consideration above, this article constructs a special SOAP processor for each Web

Table 2. Person class description in WSDL schema

```
<complexType name="Person">
<sequence>
<element name="name" nillable="true" type="xsd:string"/>
<element name="age" type="xsd:int"/>
<element name="child" nillable="true" type="impl:ArrayOf_xsd_string"/>
</sequence>
</complexType>
```

Table 3. SOAP message segment

```
<soapenv:Envelope xmlns="....">
<soapenv:Body>
<setPersonInfo soapenv:encodingStyle="......">
<person>
    <name>Mike</name>
    <age>26</age>
    <child>
      <Item>Tom</Item>
      <Item>Jerry</Item>
    </child>
   </person>
</setPersonInfo>
</soapenv:Body>
</soapenv:Envelope>
```

service. When receiving a message, the SOAP processor first chooses the best cache implementation to handle the message. If the cache fails, it will use the XML preparsing framework and deserializing template to complete the processing. Using this service-specific SOAP processor we can avoid traditional XML parsing and Java reflection at runtime, and because the SOAP processor scans the SOAP message only once, the performance is improved remarkably.

PREPARSING AND PREDESERIALIZING

The basic function of the SOAP processor is to analyze a SOAP message. Different from the traditional XML parser, the SOAP processor has complete knowledge of the message structure and tag information before analyzing it. So, the SOAP processor only needs to match the XML tag to validate whether or not the message is valid and well-formed. In this article, a XML document is considered well-formed if it satisfies both of the requirements below:

- It conforms to the syntax production rules defined in the XML specification.
- It meets all the well-formed constraints given in the specification.

In the section below, we will introduce how the SOAP processor does the preparsing and pre deserializing.

Tag Recognition

Tag recognition is the first stage of processing a SOAP message. Based on the DFA theory (Linz, 2001), we designed a tag matching machine. Automaton is a mathematical model with a discrete input/output system. DFA has been widely used in lots of research areas (e.g., multipattern string matching, network intrusion detection, etc.) XML grammar uses extended Backus-Naur form (EBNF) notations and some symbols are written with an initial capital letter if they are the start symbol of a regular language; so a DFA can be built to recognize them (Ren, Cao, & Jin, 2005).

Definition 1 (Tag Matching DFA): *A tag matching DFA is a 5-tuple,* $TDFA=(S,U,\delta, q, F)$. *S is a nonempty set of states, U is an input alphabet, δ is a transition function, q is the initial state, and F is the final state.*

Table 4. Definition of special character

& [\t\v\n\f\r] white space $ deterministic and legal input character set * complement of $

Table 5. Syntax of start tag

StartTag ::= ' < ' *Name* (*S Attribute*)* *S* ? ' > ' *Attribute* ::= *Name Eq AttValue* *Name* ::= (*Letter* | '_' | ' : ') (*NameChar*)* *AttValue* ::= ' " ' ([^< &"] | *Reference*)* ' " ' | " ' " ([^< &'] | *Reference*)* " ' "

Table 4 defines the meaning of characters used in the following article. *&* represents white space. Each state has its own *$*, which denotes that if the next input character belongs to *$*, the state will transfer to deterministic and legal state. ADdfferent character of *$* is mapped to a different state. * denotes the complement of *$*, that is, *= *U-$*.

TDFA can be divided into two types: start tag matching DFA and end tag matching DFA.

Definition 2 (Start Tag Matching DFA): *STDFA is a TDFA, used to match the start tag of a XML element. The syntax of the start tag is shown in Table 5:*

According to the syntax of the start tag, we can design the start tag matching DFA. The fundamental character set of a XML start tag is US={'<', '>', '"', '/', ':', *} and the state set is $S' = \{ s_<, s_>, s_{"}, s_{*1}, s_{*2}, s_:, s_/ \}$. If the tag name is N=$s_0\ s_1 \dots s_{n-1}\ s_n$, the state set is $S'' = \bigcup_{0 \le i \le n} \{s_i\}$. Then, the state set of STDFA is $S_s = S' \cup S''$. $s_<$ is the start state, $s_>$ is the final state, and the definition of δfunctions is shown in Table 6.

If the input character does not conform to the transition function in Table 6, then the state will transfer to error state, which denotes that the start tag of XML element is not valid. Figure 3 shows the sketch map of STDFA.

Table 6. Definition of δ function

$$
\begin{aligned}
&\delta(s_<, \&) \rightarrow s_<, \delta(s_<, \text{`}s_0\text{'}) \rightarrow s_0, \delta(s_{"}, *) \rightarrow s_{"} \\
&\delta(s_<, *) \rightarrow s_{*1}, \delta(s_{*1}, *) \rightarrow s_{*1}, \delta(s_{*1}, \text{`:'}) \rightarrow s_: \\
&\delta(s_:, \text{`}s_0\text{'}) \rightarrow s_0, \delta(s_0, *) \rightarrow s_{*1}, \delta(s_{*2}, \text{`>'}) \rightarrow s_> \\
&\delta(s_i, \text{`}s_{i+1}\text{'}) \rightarrow s_{i+1}\ (0 \le i \le n-1), \delta(s_n, \text{`>'}) \rightarrow s_> \\
&\delta(s_{"}, \text{`"'}) \rightarrow s_{*2}, \delta(s_{"}, *) \rightarrow s_{"}, \delta(s_{*2}, \text{`"'}) \rightarrow s_{"} \\
&\delta(s_n, \&) \rightarrow s_n, \delta(s_n, *) \rightarrow s_{*2}, \delta(s_n, \text{`/'}) \rightarrow s_/ \\
&\delta(s_{*2}, *) \rightarrow s_{*2}, \delta(s_{"}, \text{`/'}) \rightarrow s_/
\end{aligned}
$$

Let us give a simple example to illustrate the work process of STDFA. Assume <name> is a start tag of a subelement in a SOAP body. The STDFA of <name> is shown in Figure 4.

When the SOAP processor detects the character '<', it transmits the control to the STDFA. After that, the STDFA begins to receive the input characters. If the next input character is 'n,' the state will transmit to state S_n, otherwise the state will transmit to state S_{*1}. At S_n; if the input is 'a,' the state will transmit to state S_a. Analogically, the state will transmit to the next state according to the input stream. Finally, the state will transmit to $S_>$ if the start tag is valid. This process is very simple and fast. An XML document may use namespaces to avoid collisions among tag names or attribute names, so XML namespaces and xsi:type are significant challenges for a high performance XML processing. Thus, the simplest approaches to start tag validation involve at least two passes: one to determine namespace prefix associations and xsi:type attributions, and the second to validate the element name and attribute content. Kotoulas (2006) introduces an efficient approach to validate the namespace, and in this article, we use this approach. The SOAP processor prepares its initial scanning data structures that support efficient validity checking. The possible local names of all attributes usable in an

Figure 3. Sketch map of STDFA

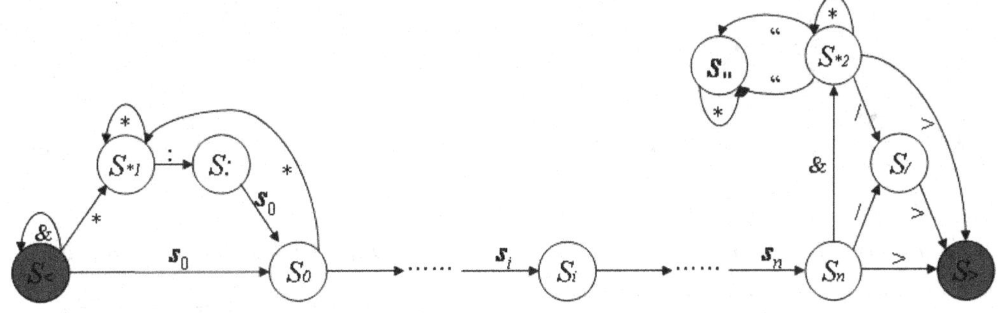

Figure 4. STDFA of <name>

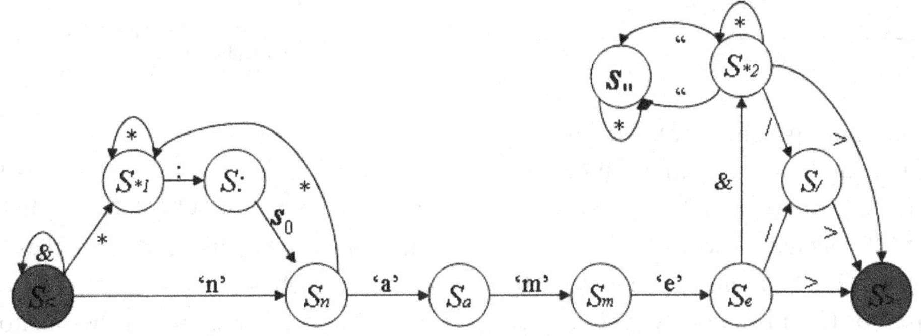

XML vocabulary are for the most part known from the schema, and each such name is assigned an offset in a bit vector. During scanning, the corresponding bit is turned on as each attribute of a given name is encountered. At the end of start tag scanning, after the type of the element has been reliably determined, simple bitmap comparisons are used to ensure that all required attributes are present, and that no disallowed attributes have been provided.

Definition 3 (End Tag Matching DFA): *ETDFA is a TDFA, which is used to match the end tag of a XML element. Similar to STDFA, the fundamental character set of a XML end tag is UE={'<', '/', '>', ':', *} and its relative state set is* $S^{'} = \{ s_{<}, s_{>}, s_{*}, s_{:}, s_{/} \}$. *If the tag name is* $N = s_0\ s_1 \ldots\ s_{n-1}\ s_n$, *the state set is* $S^{''} = \bigcup_{0 \le i \le n} \{s_i\}$. *Then, the state set of ETDFA is* $S_E = S^{'} \cup S^{''}$. $s_<$ *is the start state,* $s_>$ *is the final state, and definition of δfunction is shown in Table 7:*

Figure 5 shows the sketch map of ETDFA.

As we mentioned above, transcoding and object creation are the bottleneck of XML parsing. Using the tag matching DFA, we can avoid the time consuming operations. In essence, TDFA is a XML preparsing framework, which embeds the structure information of the incoming SOAP message. Because TDFA only needs to match the tag, it can improve the performance efficiently.

Object Generator

After tag recognition, the SOAP processor needs to generate Java objects to invoke service business logic. To this end, an object generator is created by using code generate technology. In our work, we use Javassist as the code generating tool. Ac-

Figure 5. Sketch map of ETDFA

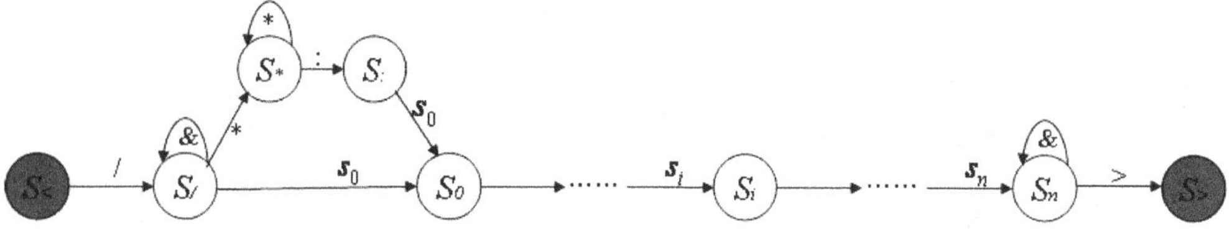

Table 7. Definition of δ function

$\delta(s_<, \text{‘/’}) \rightarrow s_/, \delta(s_/, \&) \rightarrow s_/$
$\delta(s_i, \text{‘}\, s_{i+1} \text{‘}) \rightarrow s_{i+1}\ (0 \leq i \leq n-1)$
$\delta(s_/, \text{‘}\, s_0 \text{‘}) \rightarrow s_0, \delta(s_n, \text{‘>‘}) \rightarrow s_>, \delta(s_n, \&) \rightarrow s_n$
$\delta(s_/, *) \rightarrow s_*, \delta(s_*, *) \rightarrow s_*, \delta(s_*, *) \rightarrow s_:, \delta(s_:, \text{‘}\, s_0 \text{‘}) \rightarrow s_0$

Table 8. Pseudo code of function logic

```
s ← new string
while next char ≠ '<' do
begin
s.append(next char)
end
int obj ← Integer.parseInt(s)
push obj to stack
```

cording to Java class type, there are three different object generators and each of them is embedded into the XML element processor. First, let' usintroduce the XML element processor.

Definition 4 (XML Element Processor): XML element processor (XP) is a component used to process the XML elements in a SOAP body and to extract Java objects for service business logic invoking. It is a 4-tuple: XP=(STDFA, Σ, G, ETDFA), where STDFA and ETDFA are defined above. Σ represents a set of child XML element processors, Σ= $\bigcup_{0 \leq i \leq n} \{childXP_i\}$. Each of the child XML element process is connected in series and embedded in a parent *XP*. G is an object generator. A XML element processor can be divided into the types: simple type *XP*, complex type *XP*, and operation *XP*.

(1) Simple Type XP Generation

Simple type XP is used to handle a simple type XML element, which is defined as sXP = (STDFA, ϕ, GS, ETDFA). For a simple type XP, the set of child processors is empty. Let us suppose the simple type XML element <N>T</N>, which is processed by the simple type XP. Here, N= $s_0\ s_1 \ldots\ s_{n-1}\ s_n$, T= $t_0\ t_1 \ldots t_{m-1}\ t_m$. When the control is transferred to GS, the first character input to GS is t_0. GS extracts characters until meeting the character '<'. After that, GS maps these characters into a Java object using the deserialization code generated in advance and pushes it into the object stack. The object stack is designed to store the intermediate results produced in processing. Before runtime, the tag name and Java type information can be obtained from the XML schema and service class. Using this information, function logic is created for GS by code generation technology. Next, we give an example to explain the function logic of GS.

Example 1. *Schema <element name="age" type="xsd:int"/>. This element corresponds to the simple Java type int and the pseudo code of its function logic is shown in Table 8.*

(2) Complex Type *XP* Generation

Complex type XP is used to handle a complex type XML element, which is defined as *cXP*=(STDFA, Σ, Gc, ETDFA, >). Σ= $\bigcup_{0 \leq i \leq m} \{childXP_i\}$. The child *XP* can be simple type *XP* or complex type *XP*. It is a recursive process

Table 9. Pseudo code of function logic

```
Person person ← new Person
person.setChild(pop())
person.setAge(pop())
person.setName(pop())
push person to stack
```

to construct *cXP*. First, a child *XP* is created and connected in series by their sequence in the complex type. Second, an object generator is created by code generation technology. Finally, each part is connected together in their sequence. Object generator of complex type *XP* is used to generate a complex Java object. When the control is transferred to Gc, the former n elements of the object stack are the objects pushed by child *XP*. At this time, Gc creates complex object, pops the n elements out of the stack, uses these elements to update the complex object fields, and pushes the complex object to the stack.

Example 2. *Schema element Person in Table 2 represents the complex Java type. Table 9 shows the pseudo code of its function logic generated for the object generator of its XP.*

It is necessary to point out that an array type is a special complex type. The number of child elements cannot be determined before runtime. So an array type element processor has only one child *XP* and the child *XP* is executed circularly until all child elements are completely handled.

(3) Operation *XP* Generation

Operation *XP* is used to handle the operation element. Operation *XP* is defined as *oXP*=(STDFA, Σ, Go, ETDFA, >), where $\Sigma = \bigcup_{0 \le i \le n} \{childXP_i\}$. Similar to complex type *XP*, child *XP* can be a simple type *XP* or a complex type *XP*. When the control is transferred to Go, the former n elements of the object stack are the objects pushed by the child *XP*. At this time, Go creates an object array, pops the n elements out of the stack, sets these elements to the array and pushes the array to the stack. Table 10 shows the pseudo code of function logic generated for Go.

Table 10. Pseudo code of function logic

```
Object [] objs ← new Object[1]
objs[0] ← pop()
return objs
```

Table 10 shows that object array can be obtained when the control flows out of Go. The object generator has many template classes that record Java object properties and method information before runtime. In the runtime the object generator uses these template classes to do the mapping so the SOAP processor can avoid Java reflection. It must be mentioned that the SOAP processor does not support the set and enumeration class currently, and we will fix it up in the future.

Structure Syntax of SOAP Processor

Definition 5 (SOAP Processor)*: *The SOAP processor is a 3-tuple, SP = (STDFA, XP, ETDFA), where STDFA and ETDFA are used to recognize the start tag and end tag, respectively. XP is a processor used to handle the subelement. The structure syntax of the SOAP processor is defined below:

The symbols used in Table 11 are defined above. According to the structure syntax and the above subcomponent, we can create an instance of the SOAP processor for each Web service.

Dynamic Execution Flow

When the SOAP message in Table 3 arrives, the SOAP engine dispatches it to its specific SOAP processor. At this time, the processor matches the message tag and creates a Java object. Figure 5 shows the execution flow.

Table 11. Structure syntax of SOAP processor

$$
\begin{array}{ll}
XP & ::= STDFA \cdot \chi \cdot G \cdot ETDFA \\
\chi & ::= S_x \mid C_x \mid Array_x \mid Op_x \\
S_x & ::= STDFA \cdot string \cdot G_s \cdot ETDFA \\
C_x & ::= ((C_x)^*(S_x)^*(Array_x)^*)^+ \\
Array_x & ::= (C_x)^* \mid (S_x)^* \\
Op_x & ::= ((C_x)^*(S_x)^*(Array_x)^*)^* \\
oXP & ::= STDFA \cdot Op_x \cdot G_o \cdot ETDFA \\
SP & ::= STDFA \cdot oXP \cdot ETDFA
\end{array}
$$

1. When the SOAP message processor gets the message, it matches the envelope and body tag to validate whether the message accords with the SOAP specification. After that, it passes the SOAP message stream to the operation processor.
2. The operation processor matches the operation tag and passes the message to its child processor directly. The child processor is a complex type *XP* corresponding to the person class, which has three child processors.
3. The first child processor of the complex type processor is a simple *XP*. The simple *XP* extracts the text between the start tag and the end tag, maps text to the Java object, and pushes the object into the stack. Figure 7(2) shows the status of the object stack at this time. When the process is completed, the message stream is passed to the second child processor. The executing process course of the second child processor is just as the first one. The status of the object stack is shown in Figure 7(3). The third child processor is an array type processor and Figure 7(4, 5, and 6) show the status of the stack after its execution.
4. When the processing of the three child processors is completed, the message stream is passed to the object generator of the complex type processor. The object generator initializes an instance of person class and updates the instance's fields with the value in the object stack. After that, the object is pushed down to the stack. At this time, the stack status is shown in Figure 7(7).
5. Then the message stream is passed to the operation processor. The processor generates an object array, pops the object out of stack to set the object array, and returns the array.
6. The SOAP processor matches the end tags and terminates processing.

According to the analysis above, after the message traverses the SOAP message processor, we can get the objects for the service business logic to invoke. The processing avoids traditional XML parsing and Java reflection in the runtime, and the whole message is scanned and processed only once, so the performance is highly improved.

HIT RATIO BASED ADAPTIVE CACHING MECHANISM

As we mentioned above, different caching implementation has its own limitations and no one is the best in all situations. If we can choose a better cache implementation for the special situation, we will get more performance improvement. In this section, we will introduce a hit ratio based adaptive caching mechanism used in SOAP Processor. First, we analyze the performance of the reverse proxy cache and the application objects cache.

Performance Analysis

As we all known, the reverse-proxy cache has the fastest response speed when cache hits, however, because the cache key is associated with parameter values, the hit ratio of the cache is very low. To improve the hit ratio of the cache, the only way is to decrease the granularity of the cached content, which means application objects or other fine-grained content should be cached instead of the response message. Now, we will compare the

Figure 6. Dynamic execution flow of SOAP processor

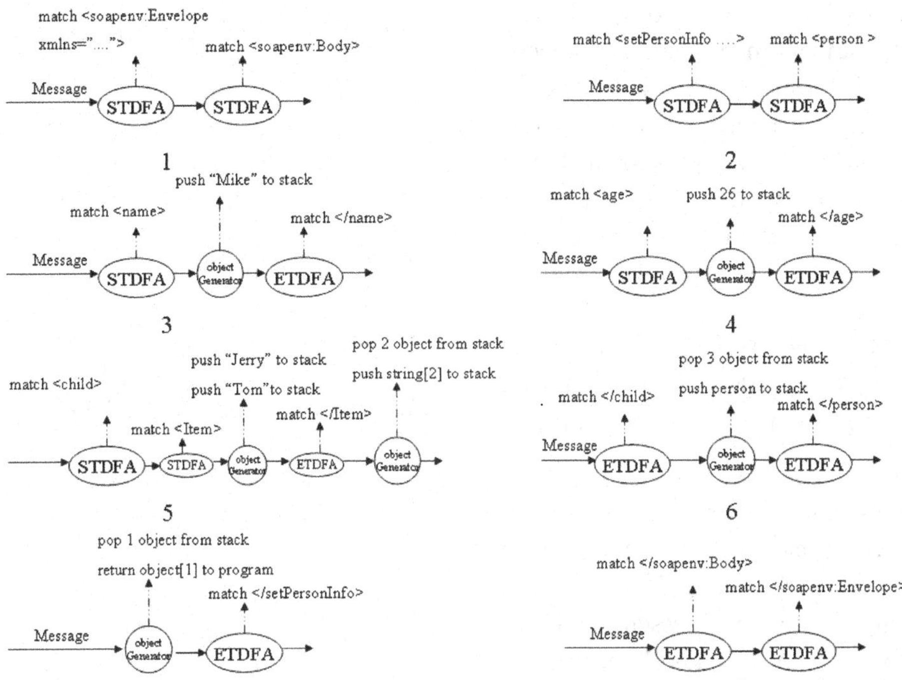

reverse-proxy cache and application objects cache to find which methods can get better performance improvement in a special scenario.

Let us consider the follow operation: Oper(param0, param1,...., paramn-1). Assume that the probabilities of the parameter reappearing are: $p_0, p_1 ..., p_{n-1}$. For reverse-proxy cache, the hit ratio of this operation is $P = \prod_{i=0}^{n-1} p_i$. If reverse-proxy cache can save *T* time when cache hits and consume more *t* time when cache misses, then as a whole, we can save:

$$PT - (1 - P)t \quad (1)$$

Compare to *T*, *t* is very tiny, so we ignore it and simplify Formula (1) to PT. Next, let us consider application objects cache. If we save the application objects as the cache content, when cache hits, we can save t_i. So totally, we can economize $\sum_{i=0}^{n-1} p_i t_i$, where p_i is the hit ratio of the object. We define the following function $f(n, p_0, ..., p_{n-1}, t_0 ... t_{n-1})$:

$$f(n, p_0, ..., p_{n-1}, t_0 ... t_{n-1}) = \frac{\sum_{i=0}^{n-1} p_i t_i}{\prod_{i=0}^{n-1} p_i} \quad (2)$$

When T> $f(n, p_0, ..., p_{n-1}, t_0 ... t_{n-1})$, choosing a response message cache is better than application objects cache, otherwise caching application objects will get more performance improvement. From Formula (2) we can find that $f(n, p_0, ..., p_{n-1}, t_0 ... t_{n-1})$ is monotonically increasing to variable n and t_i, and is monotonically decreasing with variable p_i. Different Web services have different parameter values and the probability of appearance. So, it is better for some Web services to use the reverse-proxy cache and for the others to use the cached application objects.

From the above analysis, we can see that reverse proxy cache has the faster response speed and lower hit ratio, while the application objects cache has the lower response speed and higher hit ratio. The two cache implementations have different advantages and are suitable to the different services.

In our SOAP engine implementation, we first run the system to get the values of T and $f(n, p_0, \ldots, p_{n-1}, t_0 \ldots t_{n-1})$ for each Web services (Although T and $f(n, p_0, \ldots, p_{n-1}, t_0 \ldots t_{n-1})$ are not changeless, they fluctuate within a very small range, so we can evaluate a value for each of them.), and then use these results to choose a better cache implementation. In essence, this approach tries to find a good trade-off between response speed and hit ratio.

Design Considerations

To design an adaptive caching mechanism, there are many problems to be considered. White spaces, tabs, new lines, and carriage returns are allowed in many places. It means that there are a variety of ways to express a tag with the same meaning. Moreover, different cache clients may generate a SOAP request message in several ways even if the message has the exact identical semantics. Takase (2002) proposes a solution for eliminating the critical cache busting behavior of SOAP requests by use of canonicalization. Request matching is determined by use of an XML canonicalization template. However, this is not an efficient method to generate a cache key, because canonicalization operation is very time-consuming, moreover, this method is likely to save many identical cache contents, which will waste a lot of memory. Although the semantically identical XML elements have different text representations, the object value that they represent are the identical. Based on this characteristic, we design a cache key generated mechanism to solve the problem.

Figure 7. Parameter object stack

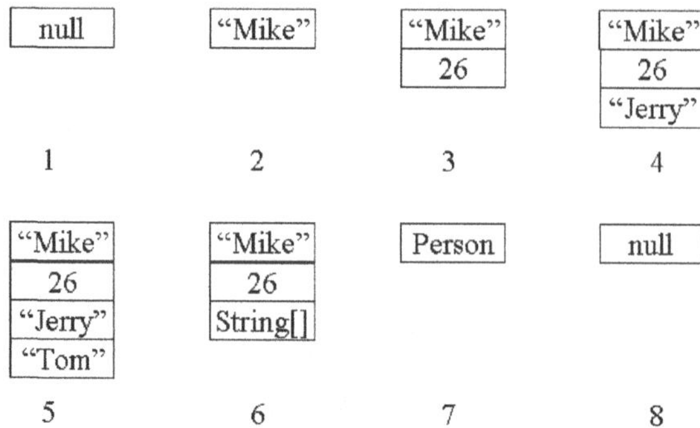

Figure 8. Structure of SOAP body

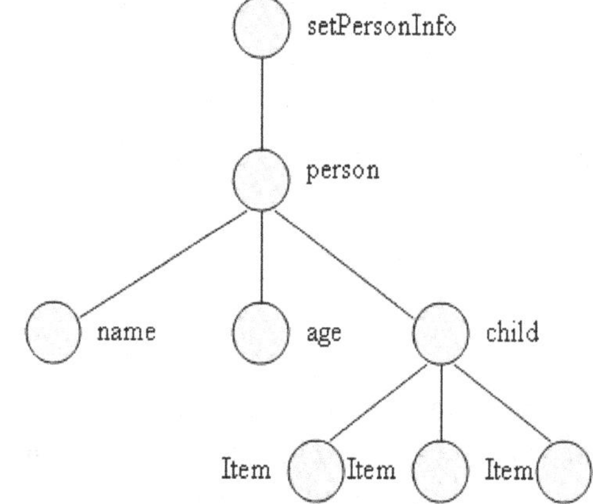

When the ACSII text format message comes into the SOAP processor, the processor matches the XML tag of the message, extracts the parameter values, and creates the Java object. Before creating the Java object, we can use the parameter values as the cache key. As we all know, the structure of XML can be described as a tree. Figure 7 shows the structure of the SOAP body in Table 3.

From Figure 7, we can see that all the real values are stored in the leaf node. Generally, a leaf node is simple type class. The SOAP processor scans the XML just like depth-first search. When the SOAP processor scans a leaf node, it extracts the parameter value. Before translated into Java object, the parameter value can be used as a part of the key. The structure of the key for the reverse proxy cache is: *ServiceName* + *OperName* + [*paramName* + *Value*]*. For example, the key generated for the SOAP message in Table 3 is EmployeeService + setPersonInfo + person + name + Mike + age + 26 + child + Item + Tom + Item + Jerry.

For application objects, the situation is more complicated. You cannot simply reuse the object because there could be some situations in which an application object is modified by applications. Therefore the issue is how an application object can be reused without any side effect while fulfilling the requirement that redundant object copying is avoided.

According to the direction of the transmission, a parameter can be divided into three types:

- **In type.** Only in a request message and used to transport parameter value. In this article, we assume this type parameter is read-only. (There could be some situations in which an application object is modified by applications. For these situations, we need to use clone operation to get a new object. In this article, we assume that all the in type objects are read-only.).
- **In-Out type**. Both in a request message and response message. The application objects will be modified by applications. So clone operation must be used first to create a new object before sending it to application.
- **Out type.** Never appears in request message and our approach does not take this type into consideration.

Only in-type object can be cached for reuse. We can find which parameter is in-type from WSDL.

Each of the XML elements in a SOAP body, except for the operation element, represents an application object. These elements may be a complex type or a simple type. A complex type object has many property fields, so even though the complex type object cannot be reused, its fields may be reused by the application. The syntax of the key for the cached object is shown as *ServiceName* + *OperName* + [*Depth* + *ParamName*]* + *Value*. Square brackets mean this item is optional and the star character indicates that this item can appear one time or more. The depth describes the nesting level of the element. For the name element in Table 3, the key will be EmployeeService+setPersonInfo+0+person+1+name+Mike.

SOAP express implement the hit ratio-based adaptive caching mechanism. This approach can utilize the predominance and avoid the drawback of each cache methods. It is worth mentioning that the adaptive caching mechanism is different from the multilevel caching mechanism. The adaptive caching mechanism only chooses one cache implementation no matter what cache hits or fails.

Implementation

A prototype of the SOAP processor has been implemented on the SOAP Express[1], which is a high performance SOAP engine developed by the Institute of Software, the Chinese Academy of Sciences. Figure 9 shows the SOAP engine architecture.

From the figure we can see that there are two cache databases: cache1 and cache2. Cache1 saves the response messages while cache2 saves the application objects. When a service is being deployed, the SOAP processor evaluates $f(n, p_0,\dots, p_{n-1}, t_0 \dots t_{n-1})$ (as Formula 2 shown). Although $f(n, p_0,\dots, p_{n-1}, t_0 \dots t_{n-1})$ are not changeless, they fluctuate within a very small range, so we can evaluate a value for each of them. After that, the SOAP processor uses $f(n, p_0,\dots, p_{n-1}, t_0 \dots t_{n-1})$ to decide whether to choose a response messages cache or application objects cache. The SOAP processor can choose the better cache implementation dynamically in the runtime. After a preset time slot, the SOAP processor reevaluates the above two values and

Figure 9. SOAP express architecture

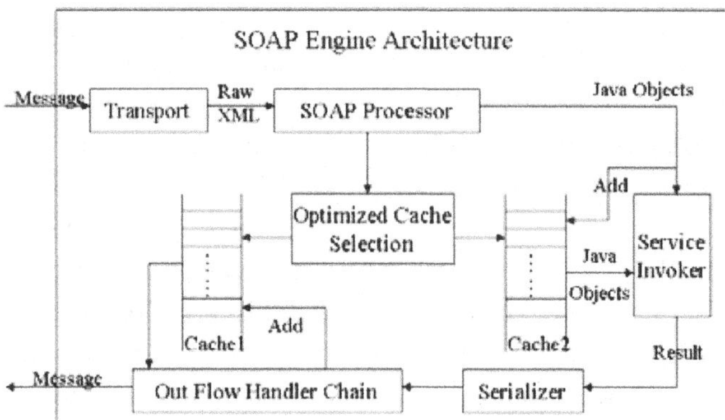

decides which cache implementation is the better one for the following request.

Moreover, except for Web service, the adaptive cache mechanism can be used in other applications, as long as the application has the following characteristics: (1) request-response pattern; (2) the processing can be divided into many independent phases; (3) each phase has its own processing result; (4) these result can be cached for reuse.

EVALUATION

In this section, we will introduce the experiments and evaluate the results. The experimental environment used Sun J2SK 1.4.2 as the Java virtual machine. The hardware and software of the server and client are the same: Pentium IV 2.8G CPU and 512M RAM, and two machines are connected via a 100Mb Ethernet; the operation system is Windows XP SP2 and OnceAS (Zhang, Yang, & Jin, 2004) is the application server. We compare the performance using two implementations: SOAP Express with no modification and SOAP Express with SOAP processor (we call it Delta SOAP Express hereafter). Finally, we compared Delta SOAP Express with Axis 1.2.

Evaluation of Preparsing and Predeserializing Mechanism

(1) Average Server Processing Time

In this group of tests, the influence of the network latency is not considered. We only calculate processing time of the server, which is the time between receiving the message and finishing sending the response. For the client, we use LoadRunner (Mercury, 2002) to simulate 100 concurrent users sending requests to a server for 20 minutes, and we calculate the processing time for each request at the server. Four Web services were used in this test. The parameters of the services are as follows: null, simple type, array type (contains 20 simple type children elements), and complex type (contains 20 simple type fields).

From Figure 10, we can find that the average processing time of Delta SOAP Express is much lower than SOAP Express; and when the input type is ComplexType, the performance of the server is improved about 175%. At the same time we can find that the more complex the data structure is, the higher performance improvement we can achieve.

Figure 10. Average server processing time

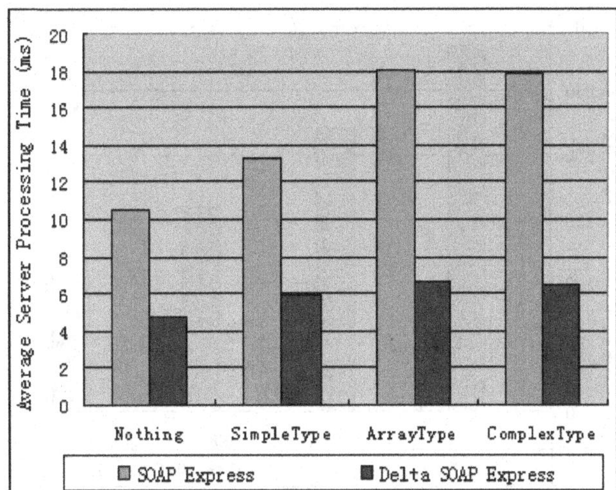

Figure 11. Transactions per seconds

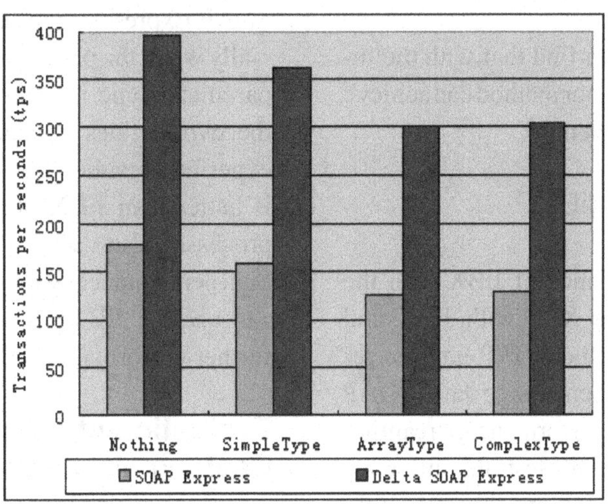

(2) Transactions per Seconds

In this group, we test the throughput of the server, which is defined as the number of transactions per second. At client side, we use LoadRunner to simulate 100 concurrent users sending 100,000 requests to server. The results are presented in Figure 11:

From the figure we can see that Delta SOAP Express can obtain about triple the throughput of SOAP Express; for array type, Delta SOAP Express can achieve 138% more throughput than SOAP Express.

(3) Message Size Influence

In this group, we test the influence of different sizes of messages to Axis and Delta SOAP Express separately. The input SOAP messages size varies between 1 KB, 2 KB, 5 KB, and 10 KB.

Figure 12. Transactions per seconds

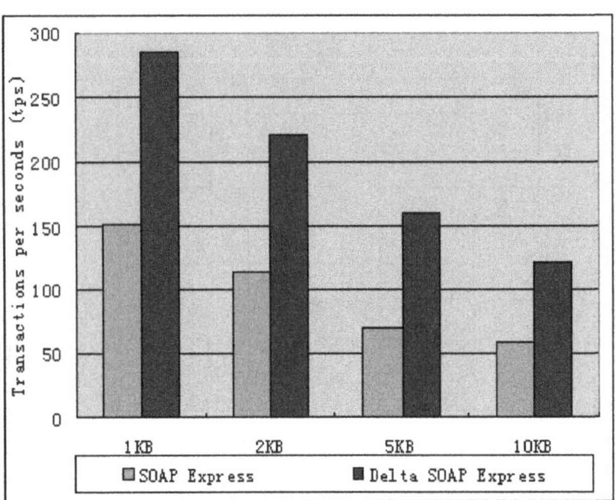

For each kind of message, we simulate 100,000 requests to the server.

From Figure 12 we can find that with the increase of a message's size, our method can achieve more performance improvement.

(4) Comparison with JiBX

We compare the performance of JiBX with the SOAP processor. We use XFirewith JiBX and Delta SOAP Express as the SOAP engine, respectively. XFire is an open source Java SOAP framework built on a high performance, streaming XML model. In this group of test, the influence of the network latency is not considered. We only calculate processing time between receiving the message and finishing sending the response. At the client, we use LoadRunner (Mercury, 2002) to simulate 100 concurrent users sending requests to the server for 20 minutes, and we calculate the processing time for each request at the server. Four Web services were used in this test. The parameters of the services are as follows: null, simple type, array type (contains 20 simple type children elements), and complex type (contains 20 simple type fields).

From the figure we can find that the Delta SOAP Express is a little faster than XFire, especially when the parameter type is array. When the parameter type is complex, the performance of the two engines is nearly equal. Although this experiment cannot prove that the SOAP processor is better than JiBX, it indicates that the SOAP processor also can help the server to achieve a high performance. Moreover, the SOAP processor can use the JiBX's serializing approach to get further performance gain.

Evaluation of Adaptive Caching Mechanism

In this group test, we gather the performance of response cache, application object cache, and no cache, respectively. The Web service with a complex type parameter (contains 20 simple type fields) was deployed to run the test. We set the probability of each object reappearing from 0% to 100%, respectively. Fifty concurrent users were simulated by LoadRunner to send requests to the server for 20 minutes, and we gathered the average response time and transactions per second of the server. Figure 14(a) and (b) show the results of the experiment.

Figure 13. Average server processing time

Figure 14. Performance of adaptive caching mechanism

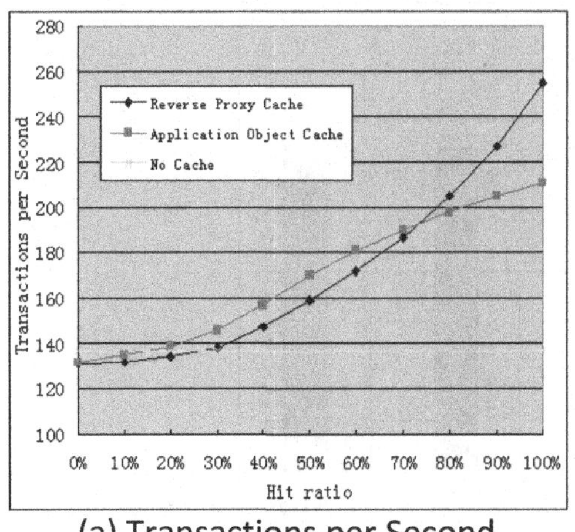

(a) Transactions per Second

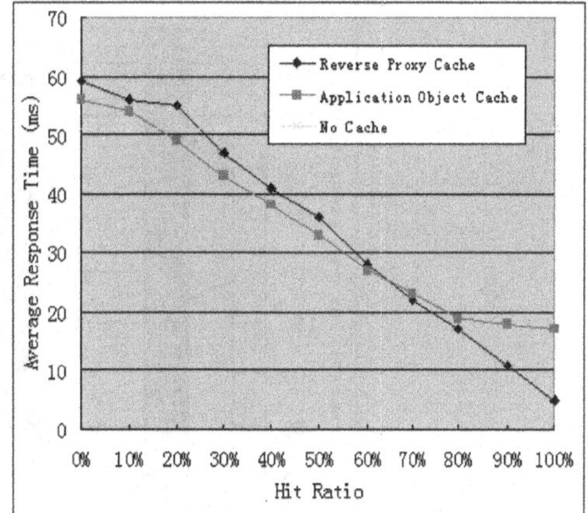

(b) Average Response Time

From the figure we can see that when the hit ratio is greater than 70% (approximately), the reverse proxy cache is the best, and in other situations, the application object cache is the best. The experiment results illustrate that there does not exist a cache implementation which is best in all scenarios. The hit ratio determines which one is better. Using an adaptive cache mechanism, we can get the best cache implementation for every SOAP request.

Evaluation of Overall Performance

This section will evaluate the overall performance of Delta SOAP Express. The results will be compared with Apache Axis 1.2.

(1) Average Server Processing Time

Similar to the test in 6.1, in this group of tests, the influence of the network latency isn't considered. We only calculate processing time of the server.

Figure 15. Average server processing time

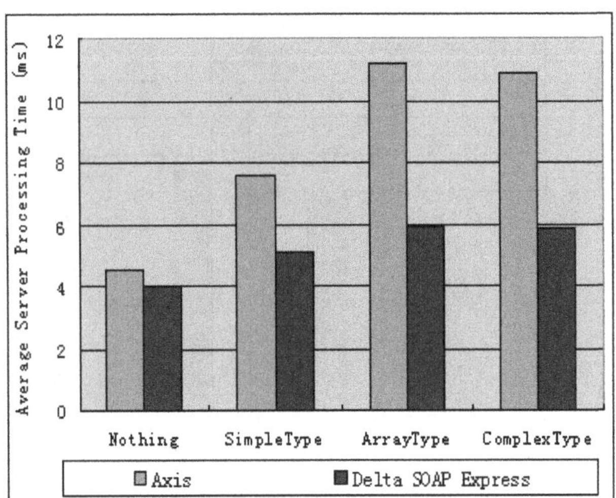

Figure 16. Transactions per seconds

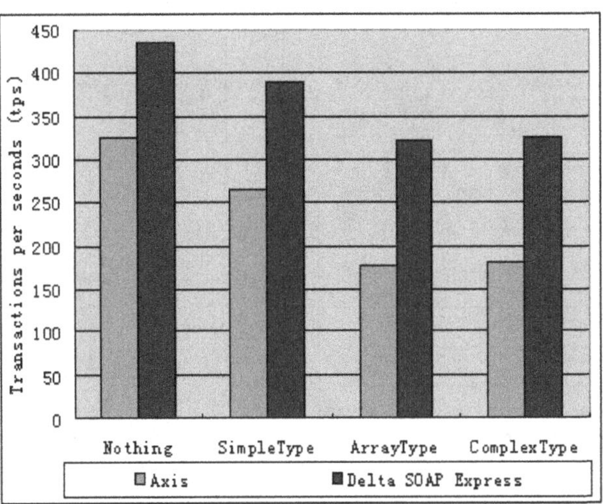

For the client, we use LoadRunner to simulate 100 concurrent users sending requests to the server for 20 minutes, and we calculate the processing time for each request at the server. Four Web services were used in this test. The parameters of the services are as follows: null, simple type, array type (contains 20 simple type children elements), and complex type (contains 20 simple type fields).

From Figure 15, we find that the average processing time of Delta SOAP Express is much lower than Axis1.2, and when the input type is array type, the performance of the server is improved about 89%.

(2) Transactions per Seconds

In this group, we test the throughput of the server, which is defined as the number of transactions per second. We use LoadRunner to simulate 100 concurrent users sending 100,000 requests to server. The results are presented in Figure 16:

Figure 17. Memory usage

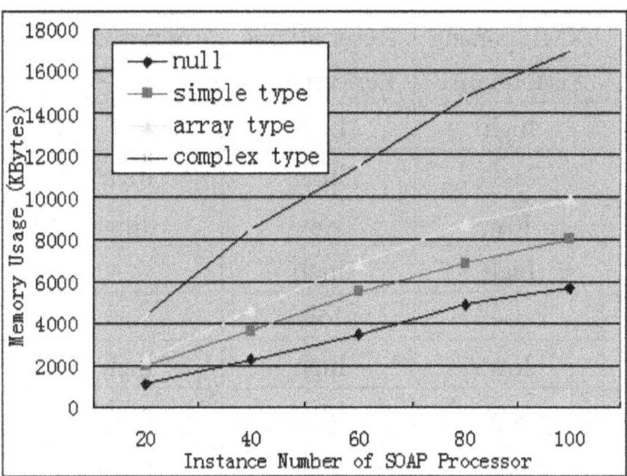

From the figure we can see that Delta SOAP Express obtained about triple the throughput of SOAP Express, and for array type, Delta SOAP Express recorded 81% more throughput than SOAP Express.

Discussion

When a SOAP message arrives, the SOAP processor already knows its structure, so the processor does not need to analyze the message to get the message semantics, but needs to match the XML tag to validate the legality of message, which will save a lot of time. The SOAP processor has some deserialization template class, which can create a Java object directly. So the processor can avoid Java reflection in the runtime and only scan the SOAP message for one time.

Without a preparsing and predeserializing mechanism, the total time of handling the SOAP message at server side is T1=Tother+Tp+Tde, where Tp is the time used to parse XML element, Tde is the time to do deserialization, and Tother is the other processing time. When we introduce the SOAP processor to the SOAP engine, the total time to handle the SOAP message is T2=Tother+TSP, where TSP is the time used by the SOAP processor. We use R to represent the ratio between T1 and T2:

$R = \frac{T_1}{T_2}$, which is $R = \frac{T_{other} + T_p + T_{de}}{T_{other} + T_{SP}}$

We set $\alpha = \frac{T_p + T_{de}}{T_{other}}$, $\beta = \frac{T_{SP}}{T_{other}}$, then

$$R = \frac{1+\alpha}{1+\beta} \tag{3}$$

From IBM (2002) and our experiments we can find that the SOAP engine takes 50% to 80% of the total time for deserialization and XML parsing. Therefore, $\alpha \in [1, 4]$. In our experiments, the SOAP processor consumes 20% to 40% of the total time, so $\beta \in [0.25, 0.67]$. Thus, $R \in [1.2, 4]$, which indicates that the preparsing and predeserializing mechanism can obtain about 20% to 300% performance gain.

The memory usage of the SOAP processor is related to a schema's complexity. We gathered the data of memory usage in the experiments. As in experiment in Section 5.1, we use four Web services and the parameters of the services are as follows: null, simple type, array type (contains 20 simple type children elements), and complex type (contains 20 simple type fields). Figure 17 shows the memory usage with various instance numbers of the SOAP processor.

The X- and Y-axes denote the instance number of the SOAP processor and the memory usage,

Figure 18. Comparisons of the related works

Related Approach	XML parsing Performance	Deserializing Performance	Serializing Performance	Caching
SOAP Processor	high	high	---	Yes
JIBX	---	high	high	---
Axis	low	low	low	No
Suzumura	high	high	---	---
JAXB	---	low	low	---
XMLBeans	low	high	high	No
XFire	low	high	high	No
.Net	high	high	high	Yes

respectively. We can find that the memory usage of the SOAP processor can be totally acceptable. It is worth mentioning that the memory used by cache is not concluding in the above result.

The experiment results also show that using the adaptive cache mechanism can help the SOAP processor to choose the best cache implementation for a special situation in the runtime. Therefore this mechanism can help the server to get the most performance improvement. So the adaptive cache mechanism is efficient and feasible. Moreover, the adaptive cache mechanism can be used in other applications as long as the application has the characteristics that we listed in Section 5.3.

Comparisons

A variety of approaches have been proposed to optimize Web services performance. Most of these approaches are focus on the performance of databinding (marshalling or unmarshalling), XML parsing, data representation, and caching mechanism. In this article, we proposed a service-specific SOAP processor to accelerate the speed of SOAP processing. The SOAP processor is integrated with the XML parsing, databinding, and caching mechanism, which can process a SOAP message with high performance. Different to the related works, the main framework of the SOAP processor is a DFA, which can avoid the traditional XML parsing and directly create a Java object. Moreover, the SOAP processor embeds several cache implementations and uses an adaptive caching mechanism to choose the optimized one dynamically. We compare the SOAP processor with the main stream SOAP engine and with some famous approaches.

From the figure we find that the SOAP processor has high performance on XML parsing and deserializing. Although the SOAP processor does not optimize the serializing operation, it can use the JiBX's idea to achieve the further performance gain. JiBX is efficient in deserializing and serializing. XFire use JiBX as the databinding tools, so it inherits the feature of JiBX. Axis1.0 has poor performance on the time-consuming operations, while Axis2.0 uses several mechanisms to improve the performance (e.g., XOM model)..NET has the most efficient SOAP engine. The main reason is that.NET is development by C and it implements a very efficient cache to accelerate the processing. All the above approaches have their own advantages and disadvantages and are suitable to different situations. The SOAP processor is a new SOAP processing framework, on which we can design many useful approaches.

CONCLUSION AND FUTURE WORK

As a standard for data representation and data exchange, XML is widely used in the domains of document processing, database, and Web services. In some scenarios such as applications in Web services, when the XML-based messages are delivered intensively and the system concurrency is at a high level, processing XML becomes a performance bottleneck of the system. So it is very important to improve the performance of XML processing.

In this article, we have presented an approach to create a service-specific SOAP processor to process a SOAP message. The SOAP processor is a composition of SOAP parser and deserializer, which can only identify the SOAP messages related to a specific Web service. Moreover, the SOAP processor embeds several cache implementations and uses adaptive caching mechanism to choose the optimized one dynamically. In balance, the SOAP processor can help the SOAP engine to accelerate message processing. Our experiments have shown the performance improvement with this strategy.

The system described here is a prototype. Although many of the most challenging SOAP specifications are fully supported, some others are not. For example, if the request message concludes nonfunction information, such as security, reliability, transaction, and so on, the SOAP processor cannot handle it because the structure of the SOAP header does not comply with the WSDL. In this situation, traditional XML parsing is required. This is the main drawback of the SOAP processor. In our SOAP engine implementation, when the engine finds that request message has nonfunction information, it will use the general way to process the message. In the future, we will ameliorate the SOAP processor to make it optimize the serializing operation and support the full SOAP specification.

ACKNOWLEDGMENT

We are grateful to the anonymous reviewers for their helpful comments on the preliminary version of the article. This work is supported by the National High-Tech Research and Development Plan of China under Grant No.2005AA112030; the National Natural Science Foundation of China under Grant No. 60573126; the National Grand Fundamental Research 973 Program of China under Grant No.2002CB312005.

REFERENCES

Andresen, D., Devaram, K., & Ranganath, V. P. (2004). LYE: A high-performance caching SOAP implementation. In *Proceedings of the 2004 International Conference on Parallel Processing* (pp. 143-150).

Bustamante, F., Eisenhauer, G., & Schwan, K. (2000). Efficient wire formats for high performance computing. In *Proceedings of the 2000 Conference on Supercomputing* (pp. 29-39).

Chiu, K., Govindaraju, M., & Bramley, R. (2002). Investigating the limits of SOAP performance for scientific computing. In *Proceedings of the 11th IEEE International Symposium on High Performance Distributed Computing HPDC-11 2002* (pp. 246-253).

Chiu, K., & Lu, W. (2003). *A compiler-based approach to schema-specific XML parsing* (Computer Science Technical Report 592). Indiana University.

Curbera, F., Duftler, M. J., & Khalaf, R. (2005). Colombo: Lightweight middleware for service-oriented computing. *IBM Systems Journal*, *44*(4). doi:10.1147/sj.444.0799

Davis, D., & Parashar, M. (2002). Latency performance of SOAP implementations. In *Proceedings of the 2nd IEEE/ACM International Symposium on Cluster Computing and the Grid* (pp. 407-412).

Devaram, K., & Andresen, D. (2003). SOAP optimization via client-side Caching. In *Proceedings of the First International Conference on Web Services* (pp. 520-524).

Developerworks, I. B. M. (2002). *Performance best practices for using WAS Web services.* Retrieved January 19, 2009, from http://websphere.sys-con.com/read/43436.htm

Eckel, B. (2003). *Thinking in Java* (3rd ed.). Prentice Hall.

Elbashir, K., & Deters, R. (2005). Transparent caching for nomadic WS clients. In *Proceedings of the IEEE International Conference on Web Services* (pp. 177-184).

Elfwing, R., Paulsson, U., & Lundberg, L. (2002). Performance of SOAP in Web service environment compared to CORBA. In *Proceedings of the Ninth Asia-Pacific Software Engineering Conferenece* (pp. 84-91).

Gu, L., & Li, S. L. (2005, April). Research and application of service gateway based virtual service cache model. *Chinese Journal of Computers, 28*(4).

Kohlhoff, C., & Steele, R. (2003). *Evaluating SOAP for high performance business applications: Real-time trading systems.* Paper presented at the World Wide Web Conference.

Kotoulas, M. G., Matsa, M., & Mendelsohn, N. (2006). XML screamer: An integrated approach to high performance XML parsing, validation and deserialization. In *Proceedings of the World Wide Web Conference* (pp. 93-102).

Linz, P. (2001). *An introduction to formal languages and automata.* Jones & Bartlett Publishers.

Mercury Interactive Corporation. (2002). *LoadRunner.* Retrieved January 19, 2009, from http://www.mercury.com/us/products/ performance-center/LoadRunner/

Perkins, E., Kostoulas, M., & Heifets, A. (2005). Performance analysis of XML APIs. XML 2005 Conference proceeding by RenderX, page 1-15.

Ren, X., Cao, D. L., & Jin, B. H. (2005). An efficient StAX based XML parser. In *Proceedings of the Joint International Computer Conference* (pp. 203-207).

Sosnoski, D. (2005). *Java programming dynamics, part 2: Introducing reflection.* Retrieved January 19, 2009, from http://www-128.ibm.com/developerworks/java/library/j-dyn0603/

Sun Microsystems. (2005). *WS Test 1.0.* Retrieved January 19, 2009, from http://java.sun.com/performance/reference/whitepapers/ WS_Test-1_0.pdf

Suzumura, T., Takase, T., & Tatsubori, M. (2005). Optimizing Web services performance by differential deserialization. In *Proceedings of the International Conference on Web Services* (pp. 185-192).

Takase, T. (2002). *A Web services cache architecture based on XML canonicalization.* Paper presented at the Eleventh International World Wide Web Conference.

Takase, T., Miyashita, H., & Suzumura, T. (2005). An adaptive, fast, and safe XML parser based on byte sequences memorization. In *Proceedings of the International World Wide Web Conference* (pp. 692-701).

Takase, T., & Tatsubori, M. (2004). Efficient Web services response caching by selecting optimal data representation. In *Proceedings of the 24th International Conference on Distributed Computing Systems* (pp. 188-197).

Wei, J., Hua, L., & Niu, C. L. (2006). Speed-up SOAP processing by data mapping template. In *Proceedings of the 2006 International Workshop on Service Oriented Software Engineering* (pp. 40-46).

Zhang, W. B., Yang, B., & Jin, B. H. (2004). Performance tuning for application server OnceAS. In *Proceedings of the Parallel and Distributed Processing and Applications* (pp. 451-462).

ENDNOTE

1 You can get the information of SOAPExpress at http://www.once.org.cn

This work was previously published in International Journal of Web Services Research, Volume 6, Issue 2, edited by Liang-Jie Zhang, pp. 66-93, copyright 2009 by IGI Publishing (an imprint of IGI Global).

Chapter 10
A Framework and Protocols for Service Contract Agreements Based on International Contract Law

Michael Parkin
The University of Manchester, UK

Dean Kuo
The University of Manchester, UK

John Brooke
The University of Manchester, UK

ABSTRACT

Current protocols to agree to Web/Grid service usage do not have the capability to form negotiated agreements, nor do they take into account the legal requirements of the agreement process. This article presents a framework and a domain-independent negotiation protocol for creating legally binding contracts for service usage in a distributed, asynchronous service-oriented architecture. The negotiation protocol, which builds on a simple agreement protocol to form a multiround "symmetric" negotiation protocol, is based on an internationally recognized contract law convention. By basing our protocol on this convention and taking into account the limitations of an asynchronous messaging environment, we can form contracts between autonomous services across national and juridical boundaries, necessary in a loosely coupled, widely geographically distributed environment such as the Grid.

DOI: 10.4018/978-1-61350-104-7.ch010

INTRODUCTION

An impediment in realizing a market of Web and Grid service consumers and providers trading resources is the lack of a standard mechanism by which formal, binding relationships can be made in a distributed, service-oriented architecture (SOA). These formalized relationships are necessary as mutual guarantees of service quality and availability are required when services are hosted in separate administrative domains, or virtual organizations (Foster, Kesselman, & Tuecke, 2001) and where there may be little or no trust between the service consumer and provider. In order to solve this problem, the obligations of each party, together with information regarding compensation if either party fails to carry out its commitments, can be gathered together in a legally binding contract.[1]

A contract serves to build trust between the two parties in a service provider-consumer relationship as it provides binding guarantees for both sides: service consumers have a guarantee of service quality through a service-level agreement, whilst providers have a guarantee of recompense from consumers for the use of their service(s). If either side breaks (or "breaches") their side of the contract, the other party has the legal right to receive or pursue compensation. Thus, trust is built around the contents of the agreed contract.

With the Grid community adopting SOA (Foster, Kesselman, Nick, & Tuecke, 2002; Foster et al., 2005) where the consumer/provider relationship will be based on well-defined contracts for service provision, a need exists for flexible, explicit, unambiguous, and standard protocols such as those presented here to establish trust through legally binding relationships that can be upheld in, and disputes resolved by, the courts of law if necessary.

Contract Law

This article is interested in the mechanisms and requirements for the negotiated formation of the contracts described. Contract law, which is "concerned with the transactions under which obligations are assumed" between two parties (Stone, 2000, p. 7), specifies these mechanisms and therefore the agreement and negotiation model we will use in this article follows the contract law model of a pair-wise process between a service provider and consumer. Later sections will present the rules of contract law in more detail, but it is enough to say here that these transactions effectively define a "protocol" for contract creation. We take the implicit protocol specified by an international contract law convention and make it explicit in order that it may be formally verified and, eventually, implemented between Web and Grid services (though this article does not discuss any implementation of these protocols).

Basing a contract agreement mechanism on existing contract law has many advantages. These include the fact that contract law specifies the mechanism for general, domain-independent contract creation and semantics of the "messages" in the contract formation process—that is, the content of the messages is orthogonal to the process and we can, therefore, use contract law to negotiate for *any* service, provided through a Web service or otherwise. Furthermore, we feel that using contract law will have a greater chance of being accepted by the wider (i.e., non-Web services) community as a process whereby contracts are created, and are understandable and accessible to many people outside our immediate community—crucial if a Grid SOA is to create a working market economy, Finally, in using contract law as a model for contract creation it will avoid the unnecessary re-creation of existing processes.

However, basing a protocol on contract law is not enough; in a distributed asynchronous messaging environment as in an SOA we must take into account additional factors, such as "[the] network losing messages, networks retrying messages [and] those … retries actually being delivered" (Helland, 2004) when developing our protocol. It is for this reason that we have investigated in detail cases where messages "overlap" in the conversation due to message delay, and checked each participant terminates in a consistent state by running the protocol through a model checker.

The creation of agreements like we have described is the premise of recent work within the Open Grid Forum's[2] (OGF) Grid Resource Allocation Agreement Protocol Working Group[3] that has resulted in the emerging WS-Agreement standard (Andrieux et al., 2006) that allows agreements to be formed between service consumers and service providers. However, for reasons discussed later in the Related Work section, WS-Agreement is not satisfactory since it has taken the approach of creating a new model to specify how these agreements should be created. This work takes the opposite approach by reusing an existing model, that of contract law, in order that the knowledge and experience gained by others in that field can be reused: contracts are the building blocks of business, ubiquitous in everyday life and their general principles of formation are understandable to those outside the Grid computing community—an advantage if Grid services are to be sold to businesses who may have a basic grasp of law but who are not specialists in the interpretation of WS-* standards.

Additionally, the process WS-Agreement and the Contract Net Interaction Protocol (FIPA, 2002; Smith, 1980), an agreement protocol developed by the agent community use to reach an agreement are basic: agreements are presented on a "take-it-or-leave-it" basis with no capability of reaching an agreement through negotiation. In certain situations, such as booking a time-limited resource, this behavior is required since the requirements of a service consumer may never exactly match times the resource is free and an agreement never reached. Negotiation, possibly through many rounds, provides consumer and provider with an opportunity to compromise through a dialog and reach a negotiated agreement. Thus, in the Agreement Through Negotiation section of this article a protocol to reach negotiated agreements is presented.

Summary

The uniqueness of this work is twofold: one, it brings together work from two separate areas (that of distributed computing and law) in order to explicitly describe a contract formation protocol; two, the framework and protocols presented in this article will not stand or fall on their technical specification—the messages sent and received are because of the demands of the "general law of contracts," which we now discuss.

CONTRACT LAW

This article presents a framework and protocols for the process of legally binding contract agreement using contract law as a model. This section describes the fundamental principles of contract law.

A legally binding contract is an agreement describing a set of obligations (or promises) between two or more parties and contract law defines the principles that govern, regulate, and enforce these voluntary, but binding, transactions. The same rules of the "general law of contracts" apply to all contracts regardless of their nature; buying short-lived, online services are subject to the same statutes as long-lived multimillion pound transactions (Stone, 2000, pp. 7).

In contract law an *offer* forms the basis for the creation of a contract. The *offeror* makes the offer to the *offeree*, and in doing so is legally bound to fulfill the consideration[4] in the offer if it is accepted. A general rule is that offers can be withdrawn, or revoked, by the offeror at any time before the offeror accepts the offer. However, withdrawal of an offer must be communicated to the offeree unless it has lapsed after a specified or reasonable period of time. The offeree may or may not decide to take up the offer made to them. In accepting the offer by communicating their acceptance to the offeror, they are legally bound to fulfill their obligations in the contract, formed in the point in time and space where the acceptance is received by the offeror.

However, before the offer-accept stage is reached, the offeree can make enquiries to the offeror into whether they are interested in entering into a contract. These enquiries, which can be thought of as a "quote for services," are known in contract law as *invitations to treat* (also known as *invitations to bargain* in the United States). Invites can be seen as attempts at discovering if another party is interested in entering into a contract and are not the basis for creating a contract and, therefore, invitations are legally nonbinding. Thus when an invite is sent it does not have to be explicitly withdrawn, unlike a legally binding offer.

An important point to note is how contract law does not prescribe the offeror and offeree being the producer and consumer of services; a producer *or* consumer can make and receive invitations to treat or make and receive offers, that is, have the role of offeror as well as offeree. This has a significant outcome. Upon receipt of an offer contract law allows for an offeree to issue an offer of its own, known as a "counter offer" (an offer based on the previous offer received that extinguishes any previous offer made) and, therefore, the roles of offeror and offeree can switch during the contract agreement process, facilitating negotiation where a dialog between the participants can take place.

Contracts also have various types. What has been described above is known as a bilateral contract, that is, when each participant of the contract has agreed on an obligation to another participant (for example, when money is exchanged for goods or services). Many other forms of contract exist, such as unilateral, option, complete, and incomplete. However, the various types of contracts other than bilateral are not specifically considered in this work as it is easiest to establish how and when a bilateral contract is formed, though the framework presented here does not prohibit the use of these other forms of contract.

Applicability of Existing Contract Law to Distributed Services

Generally, law works by analogy and therefore any legal contract agreement framework between services connected via the Internet and which uses routed electronic messages is subject to the same law that governs contracts established via more "conventional" means, allowing us to reapply existing contract law to this problem.

However, as we have described in a previous paper (Parkin, Kuo, & Brooke, 2006), an impediment to such contract formation in this environment is the fact that a network of Grid services operates over public and private networks between services and their consumers are distributed geographically over national and juridical boundaries. Thus, we cannot use a single county's contract law as a basis for an agreement protocol; we must use internationally agreed conventions in order that services can be used across these boundaries. In this case the appropriate law to use is the United Nations Convention on the International Sale of Goods (CISG) (Unicital, 1980). The CISG is "a treaty offering a uniform international sales law that is accepted by countries that account for two-thirds of all world trade" (Pace, 2006) and describes how a contact should be formed. Thus, although legal systems across the world differ, and each jurisdiction has its own definition of how and when a contract is formed, the mechanism of contract formation for services is assumed to be uniform so long as this convention is adhered to.

Figure 1. The high-level state machine for all participants of the contract session

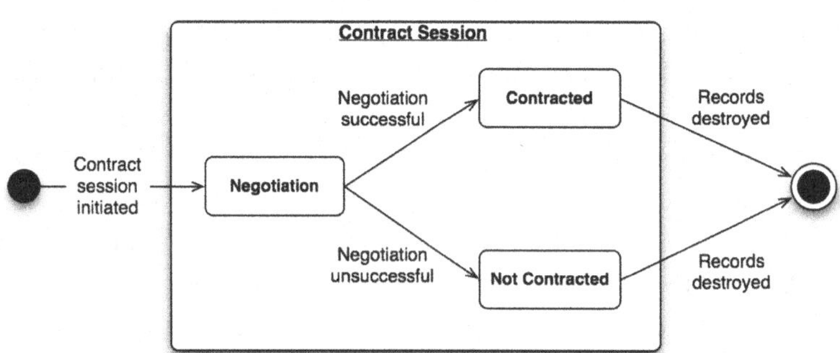

An Example Scenario

From this brief explanation of contract law, it can be seen how the principles developed for existing e-commerce applications can be applied to Grid services. An example is as follows: adverts of a services' capability can be made in response to a consumer's enquiry, or via a third-party (e.g., a yellow pages directory or a resource broker). These adverts are the invitations to treat, as they are nonbinding. Consumers can then send an offer based on the adverts to the service provider, and the service provider can decide if they wish to accept the offer. In accordance with contract law, if the consumer wishes to withdraw its offer before receiving the acceptance then it must do so by communicating this to the provider. If the offer is accepted, an acceptance is sent from the provider to the consumer and the contract is formed when the consumer receives the acceptance message.

Summary

International contract law defines a sequence of messages—a protocol—that must be exchanged that determine how and when a binding contract is formed between participants. The finite state machines necessary for the implementation of this protocol are now described.

THE FINITE STATE MACHINES

Having discussed the principles of contract law, the framework and protocols for contract creation are presented as finite state machines. We also provide a discussion on the formal verification of the protocols to conclude this section.

Framework and High-Level States

The high-level finite state machine of each participant in the contract process is shown in Figure 1. A contract session models a contract's formation and management lifecycle and provides a context for each pair-wise interaction between the parties in the agreement process. A unique instance of a contract session is created by each participant for each attempt to agree to a contract and then either manage a contract (if a contract is successfully agreed on) or handle a failed attempt at creating a contract. Thus, when instantiated, the contract session immediately enters the negotiation state. Within this state, a contract (it is not prescribed if this is unilateral, bilateral, complete, or incomplete) may or may not be established between the participants using a process compliant with contract law.

If a contract is not agreed within the negotiation state, each participant's contract session moves to the not contracted state. Depending on the participant's policies and procedures, the records of the failed agreement process can be kept available, archived for reference, or destroyed as there is no legal requirement on maintaining records of failed attempts at creating a contract.

If a contract is successfully established in the negotiation state, the contract session moves to the contracted state. As with a failed negotiation attempt, records of how the contract was agreed are subject to the internal policies and procedures of each participant as, again, there are no legal requirements for maintaining them. The termination of a session that achieves the contracted state is dependent on the contract agreed and the country the contract was agreed in. There are legal requirements on keeping records of contracts for a specified amount of time (known as the "limitation period" in law) that vary country-by-country (for example, in the United Kingdom the requirement is that a record of a completed contract is kept for 6 years).

The high-level states of negotiation, contracted and not contracted, shown in Figure 1 should be seen as a set of non-prescriptive "building blocks" that can be used together to complete a contract session the implementation of which can be manifold and use different protocols or procedures to achieve the completion of that state. For example, the negotiation state may be completed using a bi- or multilateral negotiation or English or Dutch auction procedures depending on the supported and preferred agreement processes of the participants. Similarly, the management of an agreed contract in the contracted state may be implemented in many different ways and use a variety of contract management processes and procedures, such as those described in Molina-Jimenez, Shrivastava, Solaiman, and Warne (2003, 2004).

The following subsections describe complex state machines necessary to complete each of the abstract high-level states of negotiation, contracted and not contracted, by detailing the substates passed through and state transitions made.

The Negotiation State

The negotiation state is where a contact is agreed or not agreed between participants. As described, contract law has basic requirements that determine if, and when, a contract is established (i.e., offer with acceptance with consideration). This most basic agreement type is presented here as the simple agreement scenario and equivalent to the level of complexity the WS-Agreement and Contract Net protocols support.

Building on the simple agreement scenario, state machines for protocols that achieve an agreement through a simple agreement with an invitation to treat and a multiround negotiation process are also presented and described.

A Simple Agreement Protocol

The negotiation state in Figure 1 is expanded into two state machines in Figure 2 that show the states of the offeror (the party making the offer) and offeree (the party receiving the offer). The simplest contract agreement process valid under the CISG is as follows: an offeror sends an offer, the offeree receives the offer and sends an acceptance to the offeror. At the point in time and space where the accept message is received, a contract is formed and the offeror and offeree are both in the contracted state; they are both contracted to the consideration stated in the offer.

This exchange of messages relies on the assumption made throughout all these state machines that all messages sent are received at some point in time. In practice this can be achieved by basing any implementation on top of existing reliable messaging standards or middleware that can guarantee eventual message delivery such as WS-ReliableMessaging (Bilorusets et al., 2005), Microsoft's Message Queuing (MSMQ) middleware, IBM's WebSphere MQ, or Java Message Services (JMS).

However, in a distributed, asynchronous environment there are multiple sequences of messages

Figure 2. Simple agreement

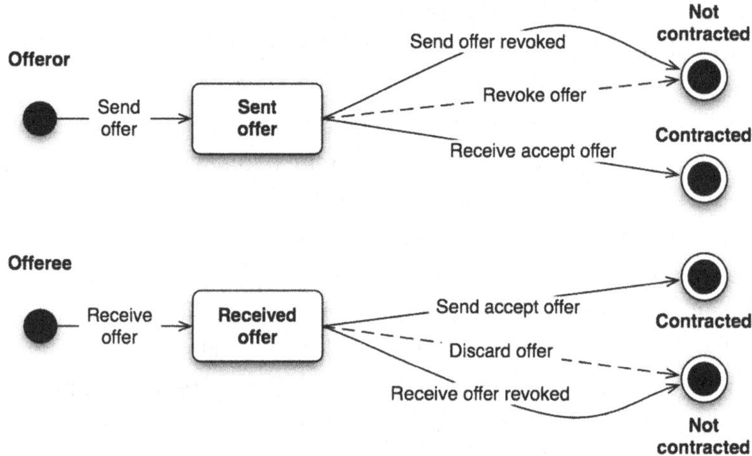

Figure 3. Handling the simple agreement protocol's first race condition

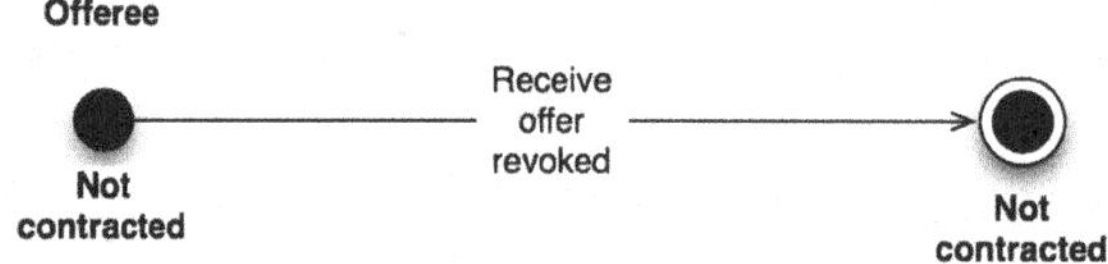

that could be sent. For example, after sending the offer the offeror can withdraw the offer it made by sending a message revoking the offer to the offeree and moving to the not contracted state. The offeree receives the revoke offer message and it too moves to the not contracted state.

Another sequence is also allowed: upon receipt of the offer, the offeree may discard it and move to the not contracted state.[5] This is the path shown by the discard offer state transition in the offere's state machine in Figure 2.[6] Hence the offeror never receives a reply to his offer and at some point withdraws the offer, moving to the not contracted state, either by sending a revoke offer message to the offeree or by making the internal revoke offer state transition. In allowing this behavior, an unhandled situation or "race condition" is introduced, that is, when the offeree is in the not contracted state and receives a message from the offeror revoking the offer. How this is handled is shown in the trivial state machine in Figure 3 where the offeree ignores the message and remains in the not contracted state.

Having to account for race conditions such as these, where the offeror and offeree may be out of sync and messages may be received out-of-order, is a disadvantage of including internal state transitions in these state machines. However, the advantage of including internal state transitions is that they reflect the manner in which this process operates in practice (offers are often not replied to or withdrawn due to the costs involved in transmitting the information to every interested party) and the nature of an asynchronous messaging environment. Thus, by allowing the revoke offer state transition, this model is more efficient as the offeror does not have to communicate this to all interested parties and offers do not have to be kept alive and available indefinitely by the offeror until it receives a response from the offeree and more accurately represents how this process operates in practice.

Figure 4. Handling the simple agreement protocol's second race condition

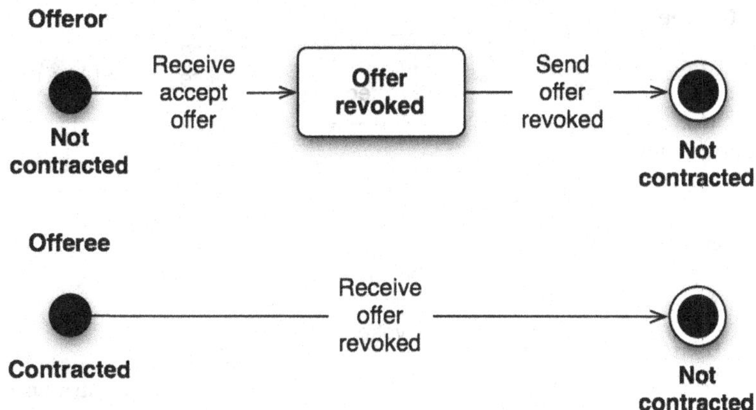

Figure 5. Simple agreement with invite to treat

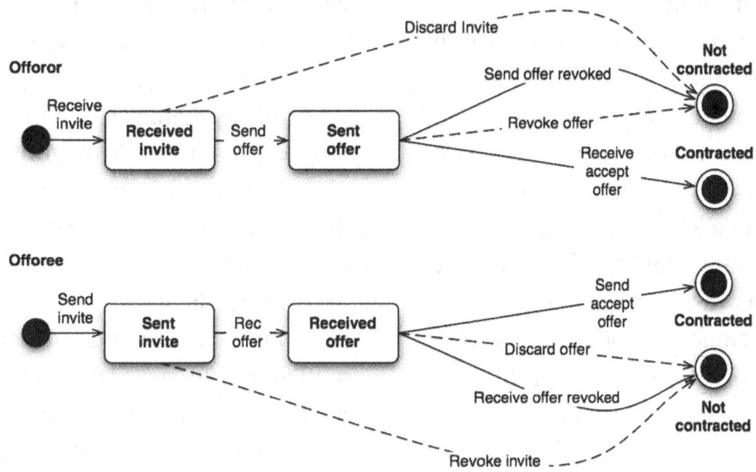

The final sequence allowed by the state machines occurs when the offeror has revoked the offer, and the offeree is not aware of this and sends the accept offer message to the offeror. This results in another race condition. How this is dealt with by the offeror is shown as the final pair of state machines in Figure 4; the offeror returns a message indicating the offer has been revoked. This results in the final, correct, outcome of both offeror and offeree being in the not contracted state.

Simple Agreement with Invite to Treat

An extension of the simple agreement case, and again an expansion of the negotiation state in Figure 1, is to add the sending of an initial, nonbinding invitation to treat by the offeree to the offeror. This protocol is shown in Figure 5. In this case, the offeror may choose to ignore the invitation and move to the not contracted state, the offeree's invitation lapses or is revoked at some point, and they too move to the not contracted state. Note that, unlike a potentially binding offer, the revocation of an invitation does not have to be

Figure 6. Additional race conditions

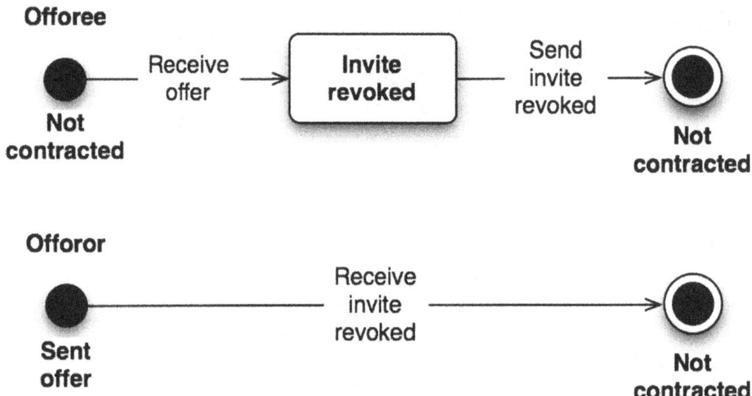

communicated by the party who made it (again, as the invitation is nonbinding).

If the invitation is accepted by the offeror, the acceptance response is sent to the offeree and the remainder of the process completes as in the previously described simple agreement state machine (Figure 2). However, a new race condition is introduced in addition to those shown in Figures 3 and 4; the case when the offeree receives an offer after it has revoked its invitation. The necessary state machine to handle this situation is shown in Figure 6, resulting in all participants finishing in the not contracted state.

Agreement Through Negotiation

Negotiation is "a discussion…with another (or others) aimed at reaching an agreement" (Oxford English Dictionary, 2006). In this context, a discussion can be introduced into the agreement process by allowing counter offers, that is, an offer based on the previous offer received that extinguishes any previous offer made.

The expansion of the negotiation state for this situation is shown in Figure 7, the state machine for each participant in the negotiation process being identical and the capabilities of each party being symmetrical. Consequently, we call this a symmetrical negotiation protocol. This state machine combines the capabilities of the previously described scenarios and also adds the ability for a participant to request an invitation to treat or offer and to synchronously send and receive multiple offers (i.e., counter offers).

As in any dialog, each participant must be able to break free from the negotiation, without penalty, if an agreement has not been reached. We incorporate this behavior by allowing the offeree to terminate the negotiation by sending a reject message to the offeror, or by an offeror explicitly revoking (withdrawing) an offer. Alternatively, a participant can end the negotiation without informing the other party by discarding an invitation to treat or offer, or by internally revoking an invitation or offer.

The result is a powerful domain-independent protocol where, through each party switching between roles of offeror, a bilateral contract can be formed as the participants send and receive offers as the rounds of the negotiation progress. This process also follows the principles of contract law as there is no restriction on which participant (i.e., the service provider or consumer) in the negotiation is the offeror or offeree.

In more detail, when an invitation is sent, the sender can then either wait until an offer or rejection is received or revoke the invitation internally and move to the not contracted state. The complementary behavior when an invitation is received is as follows: the receiver of the message can

Figure 7. Contract formation through negotiation

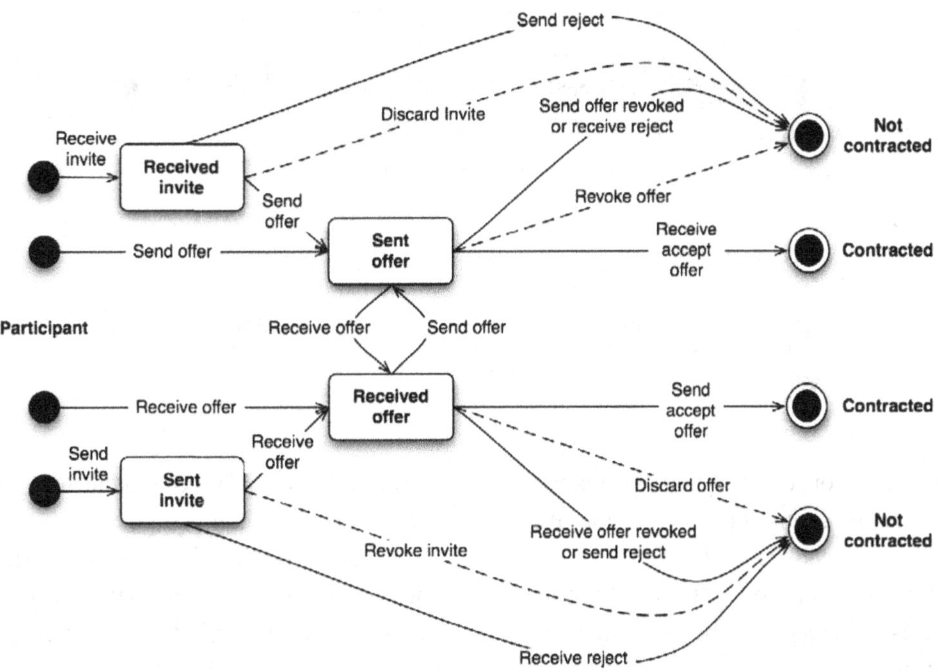

either make an offer based on the invitation, send notification that the participant is not interested by sending a reject message, or discard the invitation and move to the not contracted state.

When an offer is received and its contents are considered reasonable and satisfactory to a participant, they send an accept offer message to the offeror. Upon receipt of the accept message, if the offer is still valid, the offeror is legally bound to make the contract and the contract is formed.

However, in the intervening period between the offeror sending the offer and receiving an acceptance, the offer may have been revoked and the offeror moved into the not contracted state. When the acceptance is received the result is a race condition. How this behavior is dealt with is discussed in a later section of this article (see Handling Terminated Negotiations).

In summary, the complete implementation of this protocol by each participant allows each party to act as a peer in the negotiation process; a participant can act as both an offeror (receiving invitations and/or issuing offers) or offeree (issuing invites to treat and/or receiving offers) as is consistent with contract law. However, it could be that a noncomplete implementation of this state machine may not include all of the features described. For example, the facility to receive offer requests or invitations may be removed. However, as long as the principles of contract law are met, the state machine can be implemented in any appropriate way.

The Contracted State

As shown in Figure 1, following the agreement of a contract the contract session moves into the contracted state, the expansion of which is shown in Figure 8. The contract is immediately active and binding upon entering the active substate even if the contract is not due to be executed until some point in the future. Under contract law, only when the participants have carried out their contractual obligations does the contracted state (and therefore the contract session) move to the completed substate. When in the completed state, the contract

Figure 8. Expansion of the contracted substate

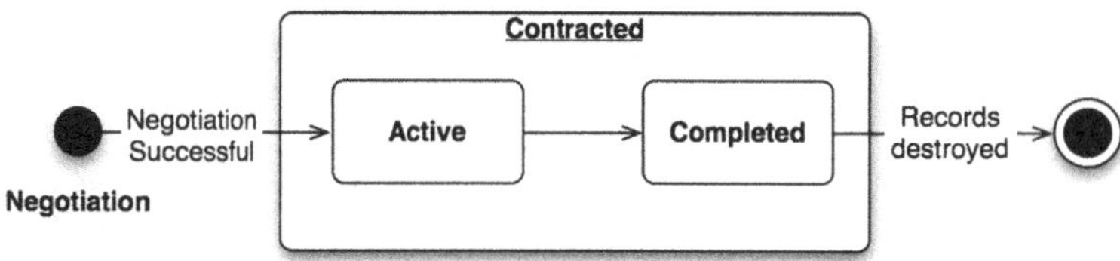

Figure 9. The not contracted state

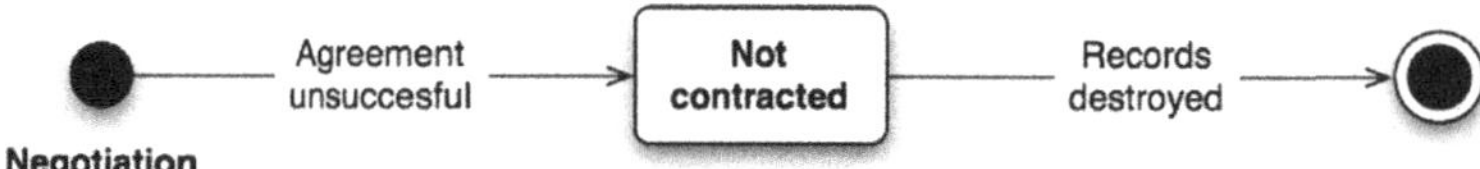

is made available for reference, again under the terms agreed in the contract (e.g., duration of the record, if it is made public). Only when the record of the contract is destroyed (after the limitation period expires, or later) does the contract session finally terminate.

The contracted state machine (Figure 8) deliberately lacks further detail other than the two substates shown as it is anticipated that the dynamic monitoring and management of the active state could be carried out in many ways. For example, through Really Simple Syndication (RSS) feeds, WS-Notification (Graham et al., 2004), or WS-Polling (Brown, Davis, Ferris, & Nadalin, 2005) events, the monitoring aspects of WS-Agreement, or the approaches described in work such as Molina-Jimenez et al. (2003, 2004), any combination of which could be used to accomplish this task.

The Not Contracted State

If a contract is not settled upon in the negotiation state, the contract session moves to the not contracted state (Figure 9). There are several possible paths into the not contracted state from the negotiation state; sending or receiving a rejection of an invitation to treat or offer, sending or receiving a message revoking an invitation or offer, discarding an invitation or offer, not receiving a response to an invitation or offer within a specified time, and revoking the invitation or offer without sending a message.

As described earlier, the final termination of the not contracted state (and therefore the contract session) can be carried out whenever is seen fit by the host of the session.

Handling Terminated Negotiations

The race conditions described for the two previous scenarios (Figures 3, 4, and 6) also apply to transitions made into the not contracted state. However, the extra functionality in the negotiation process introduces further race conditions, that is, if a participant decides to discontinue the negotiation after sending an invitation to treat or offer and before it receives an accept or reject message, then the sender may receive an offer or a message accepting an offer. The solution to this race condition is shown as the first state machine in Figure 10.

Thus, when a participant moves to the not contracted state after sending an invitation to treat (through the revoke invite internal state transition in Figure 7) and an offer message is received when in the not contracted state, an offer-revoked message is returned. The offeror receives this message and moves to the not contracted state.

A second race condition can occur when a participant decides to withdraw the offer it has made and perform the revoke offer state transi-

Figure 10. Handling terminated negotiations

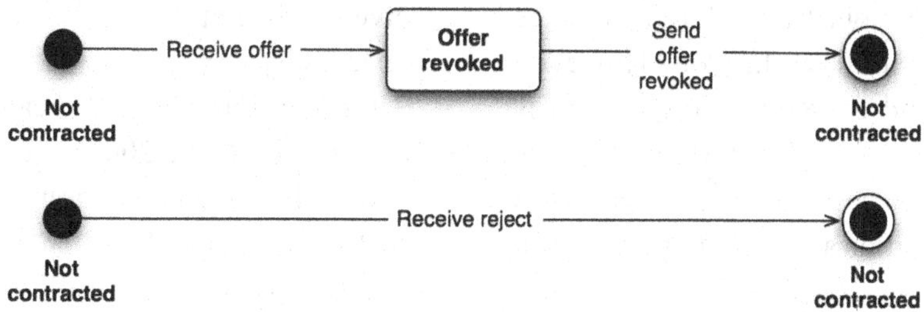

tion in Figure 7, that is, after a participant has made an offer and before receiving a response to that offer. As shown in the first state transition in Figure 10, if a subsequent offer, or a message accepting the offer, is received the participant returns an offer revoked message. As before, the participant who sent the offer or accept offer message receives the message and moves to the not contracted state itself.

Finally, a reject message can also be received when the offeror is in the not contracted state. How this is handed is shown in the second state machine in Figure 10. In this situation, the offeror does nothing; a response message is unnecessary, as it is understood that when a reject message is received, the sender is in the not contracted state.

Formal Verification of the State Machines

The description and discussions regarding the negotiation protocol presented above highlight the general difficulties in the design and specification of protocols for distributed computing and "service-oriented systems" (Helland, 2004). Without great care and experience, race conditions and deadlocks can easily be introduced into a protocol with ambiguous and incomplete specifications. Therefore, as an integral part of this work, we formally modeled and verified the negotiation protocol using the SPIN model checker (Holzmann, 2003) by encoding the protocol[7] in SPIN's input language (PROMELA). The protocol was then verified under the assumption that a service provider and service consumer will make at most a finite number of counter offers.

In our use of SPIN, the correctness properties—termination in consistent states and being deadlock free—are expressed declaratively in linear temporal logic (LTL). The model checker enumerates all possible message exchanges between the service provider and service consumer and ensures that the correctness properties are never violated. The benefits of modeling the protocol using a model checker and verifying the correctness of the protocol is significant as it identifies, in the design phase, potential race conditions, deadlocks and ambiguity in the initial specification. The resulting, final specification presented above can then be assured of correctness.

Under the condition that termination should be achieved in a finite number of steps, the model checker gave showed that negotiation protocol presented above would always terminate in a consistent state. This means that either both services are in the contracted state or in the not contracted state. Also, the SPIN verification shows that the protocol is deadlock free. Both the consistent termination and absence of deadlocks show that the protocol is free from race conditions.

RELATED WORK

Recent work by the OGF has produced an emerging standard to form agreements between Web services (i.e., WS-Agreement) and describe the contents of the messages exchanged during that process. Work on the representation of contracts has also been carried out by the UK E-Science GOLD Project (Periorellis et al., 2006). However, message content and contract representation is orthogonal to our work that concentrates on the framework and sequence of message exchanged to achieve contract creation and complete a contract, not on the messages themselves.

Prior to this work, and that of the Grid community in general, a great deal of work on reaching agreements has been carried out by the software agent community, which has many years of experience in negotiation protocols such as the Contract Net Interaction Protocol. However, it is felt that there are limitations with the WS-Agreement and Contract Net protocols, which are discussed further below.

The Contract Net Protocol

The Contract Net Interaction Protocol (Smith, 1980) describes a flow of messages between an initiator and one or more participants in an agreement process; an initiator makes a call for proposals to *n* participants, who return proposals or rejections within a deadline imposed by the initiator. The rejections are discarded by the initiator who informs the participants that returned a proposal if it accepts or rejects their proposal. The participants whose proposals were accepted finally return the agreement status to the initiator.

The protocol mandates a request/response message pattern between the initiator and participants. However, it is felt that this model of request/response does not reflect a real-life distributed agreement process; a participant may receive frequent calls for proposals from many initiators, all of which it have to be responded to. If the analogy of a "call for tenders" is used, it is understood that a response it not required from anyone not interested in that tender. This behavior, compared to the Contract Net approach, leads to the process being more efficient; those who are busy can discard calls they are not interested in without replying and the initiator does not receive and have to deal with more messages than is necessary.

Furthermore, the specification of the protocol contained in (FIPA, 2002) is described in the form of a UML sequence diagram showing a simple, ideal scenario and does not specify how all possible cases of message receipt/response should be dealt with. As such, this protocol specification is incomplete and does not, for instance, describe how race conditions arising from message delays should be handled and what *state* all participants should be left in.

Finally, although advertised as incorporating negotiation, the Contract Net specification does not allow for any form of negotiation to take place within the process; a proposal is presented in a "take-it-or-leave-it" manner. A negotiation protocol should incorporate an exchange of (multiple) counter offers between participants in order to reach an agreement.

The WS-Agreement Specification

"The objective of the WS-Agreement specification is to define a language and a protocol for advertising the capabilities of service providers and creating agreements based on creational offers, and for monitoring agreement compliance at runtime" (Andrieux, 2005, pp. 4-5).

WS-Agreement has recently completed its public comment phase of the Open Grid Forum's ratification process. Generally, it was felt that WS-Agreement is too broad in scope and tries to achieve too much in one specification; advertising, agreement creation, and agreement monitoring could be split into separate specifications, allowing a more modular approach like the one described in this article (and shown in Figure 1). The agent and automated negotiation community have also presented a critique of WS-Agreement (Paurobally & Wooldridge, 2005) which points out that, like the Contract Net protocol, the WS-Agreement agreement process is very simple, only allowing for an agreement proposal to be accepted or rejected, and does not allow negotiation.

Another important factor, particularly if the Grid community is to implement an economic market in computational services, is whether agreements made with WS-Agreement are legally binding; the specification does not make it clear if such agreements are valid in a court of law and it is notable that within the document no mention of terms such as "legal," "contract," or "responsibility" is made.

CONCLUSION AND FUTURE WORK

Initially this article introduced an abstract, simple, modular, high-level framework which models the contract lifecycle and that can be completed using different agreement processes and existing contract monitoring and management processes. The negotiation substate of this framework has been expanded and protocols for the creation of contracts using a simple agreement process, a simple agreement with an invitation to treat and a negotiation process—not achievable in current specifications such as WS-Agreement—have been developed and described incrementally. We have achieved this by building on the simple agreement process specified within the United Nations Convention on Contracts for the International Sale of Goods (CISG) convention and extending it to achieve negotiation thorough the use of counteroffers. The result is a protocol that allows a contract formation process not dissimilar to "bartering"—where offers are traded until one party either accepts or rejects the others.

The development of the negotiation protocol presented here had two primary motivations: one, existing protocols for agreement formation, standards, such as WS-Agreement, do not include the capability to negotiate an agreement; two, the distributed computing community has ignored the legal aspect of agreement formation between service consumer and provider and with the advent of business-oriented Web Services and Grids that will sell services to customers for guaranteed qualities of service. This, we feel, is a fundamental requirement to their operation. By extension, contracts must be established using a contract law compliant process in order that the contract itself is valid.

However, because of the nature of a geographically distributed computing environment, these negotiated contracts may be formed across national and juridical boundaries. We cannot specify protocols based on a single country's law, as these would, obviously, only be valid in that country. Therefore, have derived the agreement and symmetrical negotiation protocols presented in this article from the internationally recognized CISG. This work takes the implicit protocol within that convention and makes it explicit so that it can be formally proven to terminate in consistent state and, therefore, used safely between autonomous distributed services. Furthermore, and again because of the distributed nature of an SOA, messages exchanged between participants in the protocol can be lost or delayed. This has required us to investigate and describe the "unhandled situations" in the protocol and provide a course of action that must be taken in the event of them happening.

This work is unique insofar as it marries the work of the legal community with the restrictions and problems of service-based, distributed computing that operates through asynchronous messaging. This, we feel, is a reflection of our general methodology which is to always to seek to re-use existing, proven models of working, often from areas outside computer science, and re-apply them to the problems we face in distributed computing rather than creating completely new models of working.

As well as specifying a legally-compliant agreement and negotiation protocols, this work has the advantage that the processes used to achieve contract formation are understood by those outside the Grid and Web services community, essential if a market in distributed services is to be used by business, as the agreements made are binding and enforceable, guaranteeing service quality for the consumer and recompense for the service provider and, therefore, building a trust relationship between them.

Future Work

Having specified the negotiation protocol, we are in the process of implementing it for deployment on the UK's NW-Grid, a large-scale commodity compute Grid in the northwest of England, to facilitate scheduling and co-allocation of computational resources. However, a challenge with specifying a protocol in this manner and then implementing it is carrying out the translation from abstract finite state machines into code with no errors.

Future research will concentrate on developing further state machines based on those presented here that implement different forms of contract law compliant agreement processes (e.g., English auction) and formally describing a model that uses multiple instances of the negotiation protocol for the purposes of co-allocation of resources across administrative domains.

ACKNOWLEDGMENT

Michael Parkin's work is supported under the RealityGrid DTA program funded by the UK Engineering and Physical Sciences Research Council (RealityGrid EPSRC GR67699/01 and GR67699/02).

REFERENCES

Andrieux, A., Czajkowski, K., Dan, A., Keahey, K., Ludwig, H., & Nakata, T. (2006). *Web services agreement specification (WS-Agreement)*. Open Grid Forum Proposed Recommendation.

Bilorusets, R., Box, D., Cabrera, L. F., Davis, D., Ferguson, D., & Ferris, C. (2005). *Web services reliable messaging protocol (WS-ReliableMessaging). Organization for the Advancement of Structured Information Standards (OASIS) Web Services Reliable Messaging (WS-RX)*. Technical Committee.

Brown, K., Davis, D., Ferris, C., & Nadalin, A. (2005). *Web services polling (WS-Polling)*. W3C Member Submission. Retrieved March 17, 2009, from http://www.w3.org/Submission/ws-polling/

Foster, I., Kesselman, C., Nick, J. M., & Tuecke, S. (2002). *The physiology of the grid. An open grid services architecture for distributed systems integration*. Open Grid Service Infrastructure Working Group, Open Grid Forum.

Foster, I., Kesselman, C., & Tuecke, S. (2001). The anatomy of the grid: Enabling scalable virtual organizations. *The International Journal of Supercomputer Applications*, *15*(3).

Foster, I., Kishimoto, H., Savva, A., Berry, D., Djaoui, A., & Grimshaw, A. (2005). *The open grid services architecture version 1.0*. Open Grid Forum Informational Document.

Foundation for Intelligent Physical Agents (FIPA). (2002). *Contract net interaction protocol specification*. FIPA Document SC00029H.

Graham, S., Niblett, P., Chappell, D., Lewis, A., Nagaratnam, N., & Parikh, J. (2004). *Web services notification (WS-Notification). Organization for the Advancement of Structured Information Standards (OASIS) Web Services Notification (WSN)*. Technical Committee.

Helland, P. (2004). *Data on the outside vs. data on the inside: An examination of the impact of service. Oriented Architectures on Data*. Microsoft Corporation MSDN Technical Article.

Holzmann, G. J. (2003). *The SPIN model checker*. Addison-Wesley Publishing.

Molina-Jimenez, C., Shrivastava, S., Solaiman, E., & Warne, J. (2003). Contract representation for run-time monitoring and enforcement. In *2003 IEEE International Conference on E-Commerce Technology (CEC'03)* (pp. 113-120).

Molina-Jimenez, C., Shrivastava, S., Solaiman, E., & Warne, J. (2004). Run-time monitoring and enforcement of electronic contracts. *Electronic Commerce Research and Applications, 3*(2). doi:10.1016/j.elerap.2004.02.003

Pace Law School Institute of International Commercial Law. (2006). Electronic Library on International Commercial Law and the CISG. Retrieved March 17, 2009, from http://cisgw3.law.pace.edu/

Parkin, M., Kuo, D., & Brooke, J. (2006). Challenges in EU grid contracts. In *Proceedings of eChallenges e-2006 Conference* (pp. 67-75).

Paurobally, S., & Wooldridge, M. (2005). *A critical analysis of the WS-agreement specification (Tech. Rep.)*. Department of Computer Science, University of Liverpool.

Periorellis, P., Cook, N., Hiden, H., Conlin, A., Hamilton, M. D., Wu, J., et al. (2006). GOLD infrastructure for virtual organizations. In *Proceedings of the 5th UK All Hands Meeting (AHM2006)*. Retrieved March 17, 2009, from http://www.allhands.org.uk/2006/

Smith, R. G. (1980). The contract net protocol: High-level communication and control in a distributed problem solver. *IEEE Transactions on Computers, 29*(12), 1104–1113. doi:10.1109/TC.1980.1675516

Stone, R. (2000). *Principles of contract law*. Routledge Cavendish Publishing.

United Nations Commission on International Trade Law (Unicitral) Secretariat. (1980). *Convention on Contracts for the International Sale of Goods*.

ENDNOTES

1 Note that in this article we use the word "contract" to mean "a mutual agreement between two or more parties that something shall be done" (Oxford English Dictionary, 2006), not the SOA meaning of "message sequences allowed in and out of the service" (Helland, 2004) or the description of a software interface (e.g., as in Eiffel).

2 http://www.ogf.org

3 https://forge.gridforum.org/projects/graap-wg

4 "What each party to an agreement is giving, or promising, in exchange for what is being given or promised" (Stone, 2000, p. 49).

5 A reasonable comment here would be that the offeree could have sent a message to the offeror rejecting the offer. In contract law, these reject messages are optional and should be seen as a courtesy rather than a requirement of the agreement process. In our later state machines rejection messages are used, but in the simple agreement protocol, and the simple agreement with invite to treat protocols (described in the next section) they are deliberately omitted.

6 In the state machine diagrams in this article, a convention is used that internal state transitions, that is, those that are unobservable to external parties, are represented as dashed lines.

7 The negotiation protocol's SPIN input files can be downloaded from http://www.cs.man.ac.uk/~dkuo/spin/negotiation_protocol.tar.gz

This work was previously published in International Journal of Web Services Research, Volume 6, Issue 3, edited by Liang-Jie Zhang, pp. 1-17, copyright 2009 by IGI Publishing (an imprint of IGI Global).

Chapter 11
XML Data Binding for C++ Using Metadata

Szabolcs Payrits
Eötvös Loránd University, Hungary

Péter Dornbach
Nokia Research Center, USA

István Zólyomi
Eötvös Loránd University, Hungary

ABSTRACT

Mapping XML document schemas and Web Service interfaces to programming languages has an important role in effective creation of quality Web Service implementations. The authors present a novel way to map XML data to the C++ programming language. The proposed solution offers more flexibility and more compact code that makes it ideal for embedded environments. The article describes the concept and the architecture of the solution and compares it with existing solutions. This article is an extended version of the paper from ICWS 2006. The authors include a broader comparison with existing tools on Symbian and Linux platforms and evaluate the code size and performance.

INTRODUCTION

Web Service technology builds on simple foundations, like HTTP (Fielding et al., 1999), XML (Bray, Paoli, Sperberg-McQueen, Maler, & Yergeau, 2004), and SOAP (Gudgin, Hadley, Mendelsohn, Moreau, & Nielsen, 2003); yet such systems can easily become quite complex. Hence, most Web Service consumer and provider implementers prefer to use a toolkit that helps the implementation. In fact, good Web Service tools can decrease the implementation effort significantly so that application developers are able to concentrate on the real work (business logic).

A Web service toolkit typically provides a mapping of the Web service interface *types* and *operations* to the application development environment and programming language. Web service interfaces are commonly described in WSDL (Christensen, Curbera, Meredith, & Weerawarana, 2001), which also implies that XML data types are described in an XML Schema Description (XSD,

DOI: 10.4018/978-1-61350-104-7.ch011

Biron & Malhotra, 2004; Thompson, Beech, Maloney, & Mendelsohn, 2004). Such a mapping can simplify the work of developers enormously: it provides structures in a well-known language so that developers do not have to understand WSDL and XSD and it eliminates the need to manipulate XML documents directly and enforces conformance to the schema automatically (White, Kolpackov, Natarajan, & Schmidt, 2005).

Some development environments have a standard mapping. For example, Java defines the Java XML Binding (JAXB, Fialli & Vajjhala, 2003) that is well-supported in the Java environment. Microsoft.NET and, more recently, Windows Communication Foundation (Microsoft, 2006) defines a similar binding that hides XML data completely in most cases. These environments usually exploit the complete type reflection mechanism provided by the underlying virtual machine.

However, there are cases where the use of a virtual machine is inappropriate; this is often the case in mobile and embedded systems where small binary code size and memory footprint is crucial. The C++ programming language is widely used in such environments, for example in the Symbian smartphone platform and in Linux-based devices. This article focuses on creating an efficient and compact binding in C++. The proposed toolkit is ideal for mobile devices and may offer advantages in other C++ environments as well.

The remainder of the article is organized as follows: The next section explains the motivation of this work and investigates related tools. We then describe the concept of the proposed binding; and explain the architecture in detail. Remaining sections take a look at compatibility issues and compare the tool with existing solutions, including XML Schema conformance, code size, and performance.

This article is an extended version of the paper with the same title by Payrits, Dornbach, and Zólyomi (2006). Since the original paper, the tool has been improved significantly to handle more complicated XML Schema constructs. Besides the existing Symbian version, a standard C++ version was created that can be compared more deeply with a wider variety of tools. The "Results" section describes the new code size and performance results on Linux on Symbian.

Motivation

There are many open source and proprietary XML data binding tools available for C++ but they vary in principles and architecture. Our main goal was to create a layered architecture where the C++ mapping of data types is separated from the underlying XML InfoSet implementation as much as possible.

Another important goal was that we preferred data members in generated C++ structures, because use of accessor methods would have meant a significant increase in code size. In correlation with this, we wanted to minimize the amount of mapping-specific code and move as much logic to a mapping-independent library as possible.

Finally, we also desired our architecture to be independent from the underlying C++ type system as much as possible in order to be able to support multiple mobile application development environments relatively easily, for example Symbian and Linux.

RELATED WORK

According to Sourceforge (2006), gSOAP is an open source XML Schema and WSDL mapping implementation for C and C++. It is specifically advised to be used in embedded and mobile devices (van Engelen, 2004) because of its compact code size and standard-compliance. C code generated by gSOAP can be used in a wide variety of embedded environments including Symbian and PalmOS; gSOAP uses value objects to represent XML data but its serialization architecture is not layered as it is coupled with its own parser and XML InfoSet representation. In fact, gSOAP is the only tool that can be compared directly with the solution proposed in this article.

Apache Axis C++ (Apache Software Foundation, 2006) is another open source XML and WSDL binding implementation. In contrast with gSOAP, it provides a layered architecture that is able to support multiple XML InfoSet implementations by introducing an intermediate wrapper layer. Axis maps to polymorphic accessors in the mapped C++ classes so it is less suitable for comparison.

Liquid XML 2006 (Liquid Technologies, 2006) is a proprietary XML data binding tool from Liquid Technologies. It maps XML Schema (and other schema languages) to C++ (and other target languages), but has no support for mapping WSDL operations. It generates polymorphic accessors and does not provide a layered architecture on its external interfaces.

Unlike the previous tools, Microsoft Windows Communications Foundation (WCF, Microsoft 2006) is based on a CLR environment and does support managed C++ only; therefore it cannot be compared directly to the previous solutions. WCF is also optimized for the opposite direction, that is, mapping from supported languages (like C#) to XML Schema and hence cannot support arbitrary XML Schemas easily.

MXDB Solution

The authors have implemented a new tool for XML Schema type and WSDL operation mapping that we call Metadata-based XML Data Binding (MXDB). There are two implementations:

- The *MXDB Symbian implementation* conforms to the Symbian C++ conventions and class libraries. It uses Symbian strings, arrays, exception handling, and Symbian naming and memory management conventions. MXDB is built in into the Nokia WSDL-to-C++ Wizard (Nokia, 2006) that is available as a free download on Forum Nokia. The code was tested on devices based on the ARMv5 instruction set (ARM Ltd., 2006).
- The *MXDB standard C++ implementation* uses the standard template library (STL), standard C++ memory management streams and exceptions. The tool uses the same algorithms but uses an entirely different code base. This version was tested on Linux with an x86-family microprocessor.

MXDB supports both XML Schema and WSDL description of XML types and Web service interfaces. XML Schema is not the only and not the simplest (Lee & Chu, 2000) language to describe the schema of an XML document but it is the most widely used and its support is required by the WSDL standard.

In MXDB, the description of *types* is clearly separated from the mapping of *operations*. Type mapping depends on the programming language and its supported types; it can be used universally in a specific language environment to represent XML data as programming language structures. On the other hand, operation mapping depends on the communications infrastructure available in terms of TCP, HTTP, and SOAP support and service containers. It is possible to have multiple mappings for different underlying libraries.

Mapping Toolset

MXDB provides tools to transform WSDL and XML Schema descriptions to C++ code and provides a typed C++ API to manipulate the data. Similar tools are usually implemented as executable programs and are to be compiled and packaged for every supported development environment. The MXDB code generation back-end is implemented in XSLT 2.0 (Kay et al. 2006) and can be integrated with every development platform.

The tool supports the following front-ends:

Figure 1. MXDB layered architecture

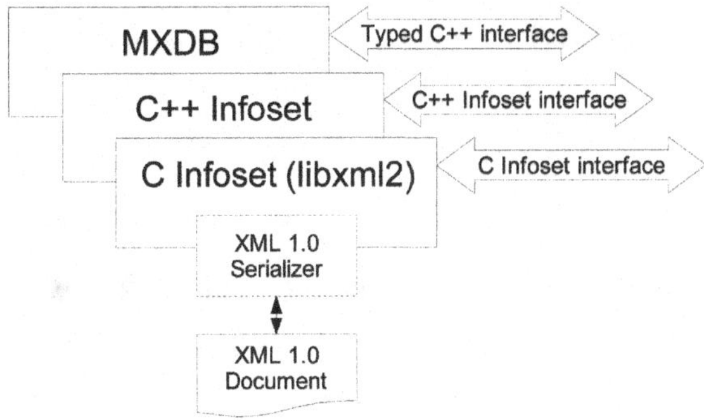

- Command-line front-end using the *Saxon* (Sourceforge, 2006) XSLT 2.0 processor running on J2SE 1.4
- Microsoft Visual Studio plug-in using the *Saxon.NET* (Sourceforge, 2006) XSLT 2.0 processor

Layering

MXDB is a layer on top of an XML InfoSet library that is a C++ wrapper over the *libxml2* (Veillard, 2006) open-source XML parser, as shown in Figure 1. Some environments like the Microsoft Windows Communication Framework (Microsoft, 2006) or Axis (Apache Software Foundation, 2006) do similar layering; other tools like gSOAP (Sourceforge, 2006) are vertical, monolithic.

Invoking the data binding library does not *serialize* the code into XML text immediately but *inserts* the data into an InfoSet; it does not deserialize from string, but *extracts* it from an InfoSet (see Figure 2).

With layered data binding architecture it is possible:

- to replace the textual XML serialization mechanism with other serialization techniques, like wire-optimized binary XML serialization.
- to even replace the DOM-based InfoSet layer with other storage mechanism, like an XML Schema-based database.

Metadada-Based XML Data Binding

The main purpose for MXDB is to support a Service Oriented Architecture implementation based on Web Service standards, thus we use this name. The proposed way of XML-based development starts with an XML Schema syntax description as shown by Gudgin et al. (2003). The mapping toolset generates *value objects* and associated *meta-information*.

We reuse the term *value object* that is a well-known pattern in distributed systems, to denote our typed C++ structures. As described by Brown and Johnston (2002), service-oriented interfaces are usually built around *value objects* to represent state across services. The practical output of code generation is a C++ header (.h) file defining user types for value objects. Usage of such value objects is described in Section "Value Interface" and Section "Raw Data Interface."

MetaInfo contains a binary mapping of the XML Schema syntax and some additional information on how the XML Schema elements are bound to the generated value object. *MetaInfo* is described in detail in Section "MetaInfo Interface." It is important to note that the meta-information is tightly bound to the *value object*, and they need to be generated together.

The MXDB runtime inserts the value objects into or extracts objects from an InfoSet or even textual XML as described in Section "MXDB Interface."

Value Interface

The value interface generated by the tool is to be used by the application programmer to access the *value objects*. In our targeted environment, this is a C++ struct. It resembles a plain old data (POD) except for implementing the TypedXmlData interface (see the section on MetaInfo Interface). We generate these structures for XML Schema types to support both XML elements and attributes, and we use the term *value object* to refer to them.

Figure 2. Conversion between programming language data and XML InfoSet

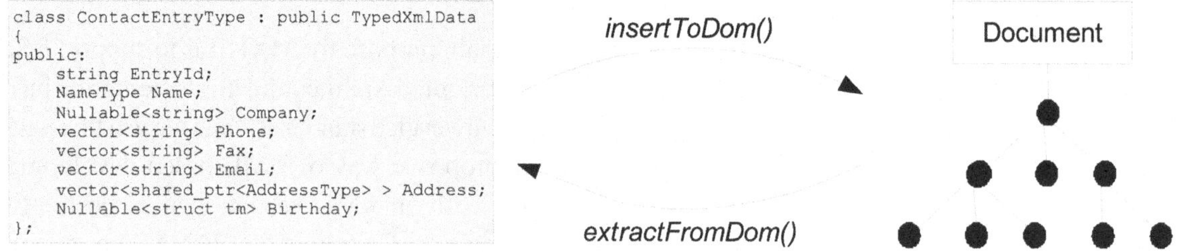

Figure 3. MXDB tools and interfaces

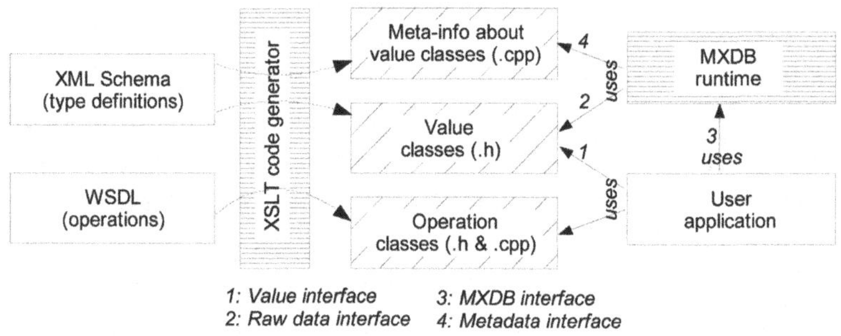

Note that we create *value objects* for all the XML Schema types, both for global and local types.

XML Schema elements and attributes inside XML Schema types are mapped to data members. XML Schema complexType has more expressive power than the simple enumeration of data members of a C++ class, therefore the mapping between XML elements and C++ members is not straightforward.

Conventionally, special XML Schema constructs are supported by object-oriented *polymorphism*, whereas the elements are behind *accessors*. Even a more heavy-weight polymorphic component architecture may be deployed as we see in JavaBeans (Fialli & Vajjhala, 2003).

We chose another path: *generic programming* is used to bridge the gap between expressiveness of XML Schema and C++ class members. A number of C++ templates help to achieve this goal. Given a child element or attribute with type of T, we define the XML Schema structure mapping as follows:

- elements with default cardinality and mandatory attributes are mapped to C++ data members with type T.
- optional attributes and elements with minOccurs=0 and maxOccurs=1 are mapped to Nullable<T>.
- simpleType lists and elements with maxOccurs>1 are mapped to std::vector<T>, equivalent of a vector.

This constitutes the API that the application developer sees. Exhibit 1 shows how an appointment could look like in an imaginary calendar interface.

The Exhibit 2 shows an actual *value interface* generated from the above schema.

The usage of this class is straightforward. After the class is instantiated, the member variables can be set directly and the object can be *inserted* into the XML tree. (see Exhibit 3)

Exhibit 1.

```
<xs:complexType name="ContactEntryType">
 <xs:sequence>
    <xs:element name="EntryId" type="xs:string"/>
    <xs:element name="Name" type="ct:NameType"/>
    <xs:element name="Company" type="xs:string"
               minOccurs="0"/>
   <xs:element name="Phone" type="xs:string"
               minOccurs="0" maxOccurs="unbounded"/>
   <xs:element name="Fax" type="xs:string"
               minOccurs="0" maxOccurs="unbounded"/>
   <xs:element name="Email" type="xs:string"
               minOccurs="0" maxOccurs="unbounded"/>
   <xs:element name="Address" type="ct:AddressType"
               minOccurs="0" maxOccurs="unbounded"/>
   <xs:element name="Birthday" type="xs:date"
               minOccurs="0"/>
 </xs:sequence>
</xs:complexType>
```

Exhibit 2.

```
class ContactEntryType: public esso::TypedXmlData
{
public:
    const esso::MetaType& MetaInfo() const;
    ContactEntryType();
    std::string EntryId;
    NameType Name;
    esso::Nullable<std::string> Company;
    std::vector<std::string> Phone;
    std::vector<std::string> Fax;
    std::vector<std::string> Email;
    std::vector<shared_ptr<AddressType> > Address;
    esso::Nullable<struct tm> Birthday;
};
```

Exhibit 3.

```
ContactEntryType contactEntry;
contactEntry.EntryId = "1234-ABCD";
contactEntry.Name.FirstName = "Joe";
contactEntry.Address.push_back(new AddressType());
contactEntry.Address[0]->City="Helsinki";
```

Exhibit 4.

```
void insertToDom(const esso::TypedXmlData& object, XmlElement toNode);
void extractFromDom(esso::TypedXmlData& object, XmlElement fromNode);
```

Raw Data Interface

We distinguish the raw data interface from the value interface above. Although in the current C++ implementations both are based on "POD-like" C++ struct definitions, they exploit different aspects of the C++ structures.

Raw data interface is used by the MXDB runtime to directly access the data layout of the value objects. As one of our explicit goal is to handle XML elements as value objects, we do not use polymorphic accessors, we use generative programming instead (code generator) to simulate a simple C++ class reflection. However, because of restricting ourselves to non-virtual C++ structures with data members only, we do not have to implement a generic C++ reflection, but the following methods suffice:

- Data member *type* information is neglected and substituted completely by the information gathered via the *MetaInfo* interface.
- Data member value is retrieved by direct memory access relying on raw object pointers and member offsets. These offsets are calculated from the by the C++ compiler when compiling the generated meta-information.

The following example explains the usage of the raw data interface with build-in types:

```
int val = *reinterpret_cast<const
int*>(objectAddress + offset);
```

Note that with other development platforms (programming languages) a different mechanism might be used to retrieve raw data from value objects.

MXDB Interface

MXDB interface is used by the application developer to insert value objects into an XML InfoSet and extract value objects from it. In our implementation, we use the DOM, the most widely accepted XML interface to handle InfoSets.

Serialization requires an object with readable meta-information (conforming to the *MetaInfo* interface) and an element from the XML document to hold the serialized representation of the

Exhibit 5.

```
std::string serialize(const esso::TypedXmlData &object,
                      const std::string &rootName = "",
                      const std::string &rootNsUri = "");
void deserialize(const std::string& xmlDocStr,
                 esso::TypedXmlData& toObject);
```

object. Deserialization is done analogously. (see Exhibit 4)

Additionally, there is an interface to serialize to strings and deserialize from strings directly. (see Exhibit 5)

MetaInfo Interface

The *MetaInfo* class hierarchy contains a representation of the XML Schema in the C++ language, and acts as the glue between the XML Schema and value objects. This glue consists of two parts:

- The dynamic part of this glue is the offset of data members in the memory representation of value objects, providing runtime type information about the internal structure of data members in the object. This feature is already present in many scripting languages interpreters and virtual machines referred to as reflection. The offset information is associated with every XML Schema element and attribute metadata.
- The other part describes the static XML Schema information. Since classic reflection is limited in expressiveness, our *MetaInfo* interface provides XML Schema-specific metadata beyond the capabilities of reflection of scripting and managed languages.

To represent metadata, we use simple data structures and initialize them with static initializer lists to gain smaller and more efficient code. Additionally, some platforms—like EKA1-based versions of Symbian operating system—do not support writable static data in dynamically loadable libraries. However, all target platforms support compile-time initialized C/C++ data structures. The C++ standard places additional restrictions: it is not possible to use static initializer lists on nontrivial classes, only on POD structures. Therefore, we had to simulate a class hierarchy like, for example, the libxml2 tree module (Veillard, 2006) and GTK. We use the type selector EnumDerivedType to specify the dynamic type of the metadata object:

```
struct MetaInfo
{
  EnumDerivedType type;
  unsigned int version;
};
```

In the base class *MetaInfo* we use an enumeration data member representing the actual derived type to simulate the virtual table of an object. This is necessary to avoid the use of writeable static data—a real virtual table would require a constructor. The version data member allows interoperability between binaries compiled with different versions of *MetaInfo* representations. Derived classes do not actually inherit from this class; only simulate inheritance, like in the case of the *MetaNamed* class representing any XML Schema construct with a qualified name:

```
struct MetaNamed  // ---: public
MetaInfo - should inherit from this
class
```

Figure 4. MetaInfo hierarchy

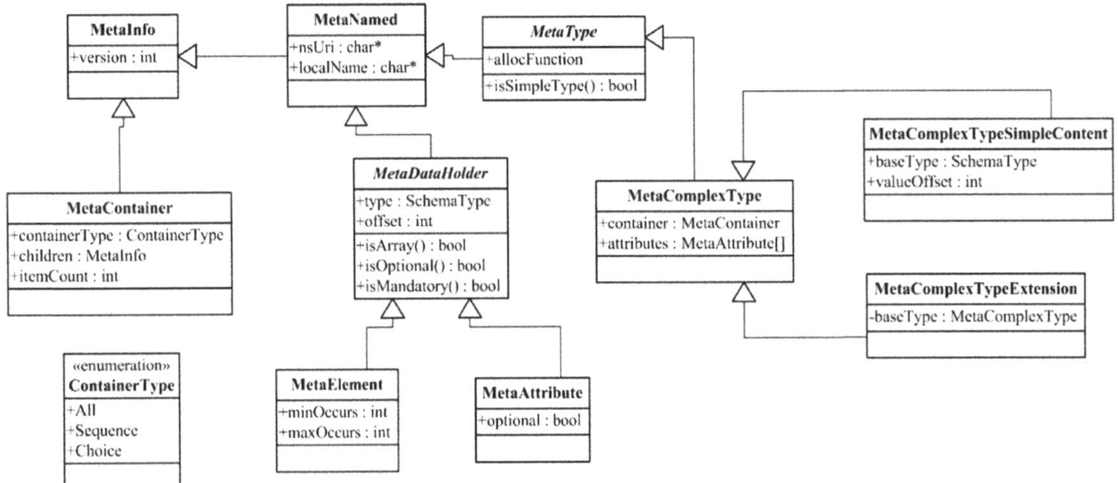


```
{
  EnumDerivedType construct;
  unsigned int version;
  const char *nsUri;
  const char *localName;
};
```

Figure 4 depicts the UML diagram of the *MetaInfo* hierarchy—without the XML Schema simpleType constructs for the sake of simplicity. Note that Figure 4 shows the real inharitance relationships instead of the EnumDerivedType members.

TypedXmlData is the basic interface for all value objects:

```
struct TypedXmlData
{
 virtual const MetaType& MetaInfo()
const = 0;
 virtual ~TypedXmlData() {}
};
```

Note that the provided information is not only of base type *MetaInfo*. It is known that a type provides a description derived from *MetaType*.

XML Schema Conformance

XML Schema can define really complex grammars with the combined use of complexType <sequence>, <all>, <choice> and simpleType <restriction>, <list> and <union> constructs. This is much more expressive than generic XML InfoSet and more expressive than the simple listing of *value object* members.

Schema Validation

During conversion of the XML data, the following error cases can emerge:

- Error during extraction of value objects from an InfoSet tree. This is the classic validation against the XML Schema.
- Error during the insertion of value objects into InfoSet tree. This is a novel problem and specific to typed XML data bindings.

The Windows Communications Framework (Microsoft, 2006), for example, solves this problem with restricting the usable XML Schema.

MXDB architecture enables the separation of the generation and the use of metadata during the serialization process. The generated metadata contains all the syntax of the XML Schema; it is up to the runtime, how strictly it enforces the schema syntax. Current MXDB runtime performs a full top-down validation against all XML Schema constructs during both extraction and insertion. However, if performance requires, it is possible to find subsets of XML Schema (like in WCF) where the mapping between InfoSet and value objects can be done without full top-down validation. This is a future work to be done.

The advantage of our architecture is that such optimizations are believed to be possible to do dynamically and transparently to the application developer with a backward-compatible change of the runtime.

Schema Features

We compared the support of various XML Schema constructs in MXDB with the gSOAP and Axis C++. The following conformance comparison shows how MXDB and the other tools support XML Schema features.

The main architectural element providing flexibility is the MXDB *MetaInfo* interface that is the runtime counterpart of the XML Schema type description. The *MetaInfo* interface binds the tool-generated meta-information and the MXDB runtime. A big benefit of this approach is that it is possible to develop further the features of the MXDB code generator and the MXDB code library independently. This has a big value as the XML schema is very feature-rich and a full implementation of the XML Schema specification may take a long time.

In Table 1, we record for every feature to what extent it is supported by MXDB:

- I Feature is reflected in the *MetaInfo* interface only. In this case it is possible to extend the code generator with new features while retaining backward-compatibility with existing core library.
- G Feature is supported by the code generator, so it is possible to extend the core library later with new schema validation features. There will be no need to rerun the code generation and there will be no need to recompile and redeploy the already used third party applications, what can be an important benefit for real-world software-distribution scenarios.
- ✓ Feature is supported by the runtime code library. Thus serialization/deserialiation and validation of the XML Schema feature will actually happen.

A feature is fully supported if it is supported by both the code generator and the code library. As Table 1 shows, MXDB library fully supports more XML Schema features than the competing tools. Moreover, the metadata based approach means that less (or not) supported features can be added with considerably less effort than with the conventional tools, potentially without recompilation and redistribution of existing applications.

The biggest immediate differentiating factor of the MXDB architecture is the correct handling of model group combinations. While both Axis and gSOAP are capable of limited, single-level handling of choice, all and sequence model groups, the classic code generation makes it hard to support multilevel syntax trees with combination of model groups. Therefore, neither of the tools is capable of processing combinations of more than one model group correctly. However, with the runtime metadata MXDB, it is possible to use a generic algorithm that is able to handle and validate arbitrary number of nested model groups—without any code size increase.

Operation Binding

In this section, we outline WSDL operation mapping that is based on the meta-information-based type-mapping infrastructure discussed before.

The operation binding follows the conventional practice—operations of a service are mapped to

Table 1. Summary of Web services tools and supported XML Schema features

	Axis	gSOAP	MXDB
Complex type complex content restriction	-[1]	✓	✓
Complex type complex content extension	✓[2]	✓	✓
Complex type simple content extension	✓	✓	✓
Element Declaration			
minOccurs = 0 (optional)	✓	✓	✓
minOccurs > 1	-	✓	✓
maxOccurs = 1	✓	✓	✓
maxOccurs > 1	-	✓	✓
maxOccurs = unbounded (array)	✓	✓	✓
Element substitution	-	-	-
Element group	-[3]	✓	-[4]
Attribute declaration			
required	✓	✓	✓
fixed	-	-	G
default	-	-	G
Attribute groups	-	-[5]	-[6]
Model groups			
all	✓	✓	✓
sequence	✓[7]	✓[7]	✓
choice	✓	✓	✓
multi-level combination of model groups	-	-	✓
Simple type restriction facets			
length, minLength, maxLength	-	-	✓
minInclusive, minExclusive, maxInclusive, maxExclusive	-	-	✓
totalDigits, fractionDigits	-	-	✓
whiteSpace	-	-	✓
enumeration	-	✓	✓
pattern	-	-	G
Simple type union	-	-	G
Simple type list	-	-	I

- : No support I : MXDB MetaInfo interface support only

✓ : Full support G : MXDB MetaInfo and code generator support

method calls in C++. Parts of a WSDL request *message* can be mapped to method arguments, while the response message of an operation is mapped to the return value of the method. Arguments and return values are *value objects* as previously introduced. Thus, communication details can be hidden from the user and the service invocation may be indistinguishable from a local method call. This concept is usually referenced as a stub or proxy.

We have already implemented an XSLT code generator that creates such stubs for services. The actual on-wire communication is based on the

Exhibit 6.

```
<message name="AddEntriesRequest">
  <part name="input" element="ct:AddEntriesRequest"/>
</message>
<message name="AddEntriesResponse">
  <part name="output" element="ct:AddEntriesResponse"/>
</message>
...
<portType name="ContactsPort">
  <operation name="AddEntries">
    <input message="cw:AddEntriesRequest"/>
    <output message="cw:AddEntriesResponse"/>
  </operation>
</portType>
```

HTTP protocol. For each operation, we generate several signatures to enable multiple choices for the convenience of the user. We differentiate synchronous and asynchronous calls and provide callbacks for the user to process the response in case of the latter. A detailed discussion on the operation mapping is outside the scope of this article; we show only an example for the synchronous case.

Assume having the WSDL description for our calendar service as shown in Exhibit 6.

The signature of the generated synchronous function:

```
std::auto_ptr<_AddEntriesResponse>
sendReceiveAddEntries(
    ContactEntrySequenceType &re-
quest,
  const esso::Url &target);
```

In case of a SOAP fault, a C++ exception is thrown. In the Symbian implementation, a different signature is required because Symbian conventions do not allow C++ exceptions, only integer leave codes. The Symbian implementation contains a signature that includes an optional outgoing SOAP fault argument.

Compatibility

Most XML Schema-based data binding tools generate code. A consequence of this approach is that it makes the development of WSDL/XML Schema tools vulnerable to development environment incompatibilities, as both the development and the target environment must be supported by the data binding tool.

The latest update in the Symbian operating system was a major one, with fundamental changes in the security architecture and even the kernel version changed from EKA1 to EKA2. MXDB aims to ease the incompatibility problems on both axes:

- **Target platform** incompatibility is minimized by the separation of the runtime from the metadata generation. The code library needs to be maintained and updated for minor target platform changes or for porting between platforms, with small or no changes of the code generator and development environments.
- **Development environment** incompatibility is minimized by the same separation and by extracting the code generator back-end into a pure, cross-platform XSLT transformation.

Table 2. Development environments and target platforms

Target platform / Development environment	Symbian EKA1	Symbian EKA2	Linux (STL)
Windows command line	✓	✓	✓
Linux command line	✓	✓	✓
Carbide.C++ (Eclipse-based)		✓	
Cardibe.vs (VS.NET-based)		✓	
MetroWerks CodeWarrior	×		
Visual Studio 6.0		×	

By separating the two incompatibility axis, MXDB needs to be tested against $N+M$ aspects instead of $N*M$, where N is the number of supported development platforms and M is the number of supported target platforms.

Results

We evaluated various characteristics of the Symbian and standard C++ MXDB implementation against the most popular Web service frameworks available for C++: gSOAP and Axis C++. Although MXDB can be used as an XML Schema tool without SOAP and WSDL, this comparison evaluates MXDB as a Web Services toolkit.

A toolkit for using Web Services with C and C++ is gSOAP (Sourceforge, 2006). It contains a code generator that parses the WSDL interface description and generates source files that can be used to consume and provide the service and access the XML data as C or C++ language structures (with or without STL). In gSOAP, both the code generator and the runtime are written entirely in C. When using the C language output, the generated sources can be compiled on a wide variety of platforms, including Symbian. The runtime comes as a separate source file "stdsoap2.c". Throughout this evaluation, we always compiled the runtime part as a separate library that is not included into the binary code size. We used gSOAP version 2.7.8c because that was the latest stable version when we started the comparison.

Axis C++ (Apache Software Foundation, 2006) is a Web services toolkit for C++. It is also able to generate C++ source files from WSDL for client and server mode as well as code to access the XML data. The generator is written in Java and the target language is C++. However, Axis C++ does not support the C++ standard template library. Axis C++ is more modular than gSOAP and supports more sophisticated concepts, like being able to use handlers when processing outgoing or incoming messages and support for different XML parsers. We used Axis C++ 1.6beta because it is a significant improvement over older versions. Unfortunately, the Axis 2 branch did not suit our purposes because it is C only and does not yet have any code generation tools.

MXDB is responsible for mapping XML Schema types and WSDL operations to C++, but it also needs a generic SOAP framework that takes care of transport and other issues. On Symbian, we used the Nokia Web Services Framework that is part of the Nokia S60 platform third edition and later releases. With the standard C++ implementation, we used the currently Nokia internal ESSO framework that is similar to Axis C++: it is a generic SOAP framework, supports an external XML parser and handlers to process messages.

We evaluated the binary code size of the generated code size with both MXDB implementations and the performance of the standard C++ implementation.

Figure 5. UML representation of the XML types in the Contacts.wsdl synthetic test

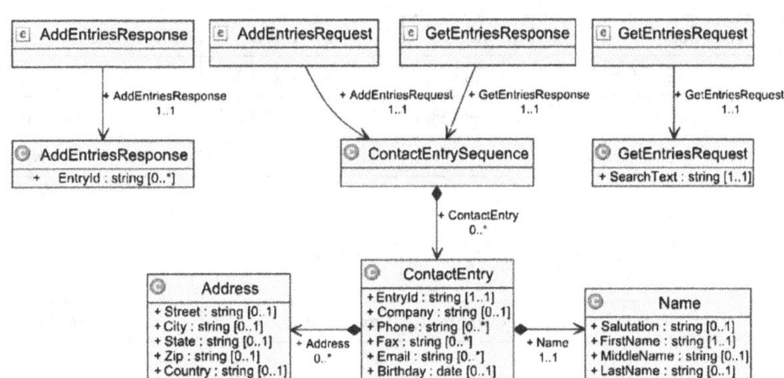

Table 3. Characteristics of WSDL files in the comparison

Number of:	Contacts	MapPoint	PayPal	Amazon	EBay
Bytes	5 309	83 858	236 433	111 189	1 492 534
Complex types	7	136	74	171	424
Elements	24	369	523	1 062	1 838
Messages	4	84	31	38	189
Operations	2	42	15	19	94

Test Cases

In our comparison, we used two different test cases:

- Contacts.wsdl is a synthetic test that we created for the sake of the comparison. It contains two operations: AddEntries and GetEntries and simple XML types that are understood by all toolkits. The XML types are shown in an UML diagram generated by the hyperModel XML modeling tool on Figure 5.
- In real-world test, we used WSDL files from real-world Web services: the MapPoint service, the PayPal service, the Amazon e-commerce service and the EBay Web service.

Standard C++ Tests

We tested the standard C++ implementation of MXDB against gSOAP and Axis C++ on Linux. In our tests, we generated code for the x86 instructions set and executed the code on an Intel CPU.

In the real world comparison, we generated the code from the source WSDL files and linked it to a source files that contained an empty main() function. The purpose of this comparison is to see the amount of generated binary code.

Table 4 shows the size of executables generated from the WSDL descriptions. Table 4 shows that MXDB generates clearly smaller code than both gSOAP and Axis. Depending on the case, code generated by MXDB was 45%-70% smaller than the code generated by gSOAP. Unfortunately, Axis C++ could not compile any of the real world cases because either the code generation failed or the generated code did not compile or contained other defects. Based on the only case that was compiled

Table 4. x86 binary size of executable generated from WSDL

Toolkit	Contacts	MapPoint	PayPal	Amazon	EBay
MXDB	23 800	248 760	299 192	536 856	1 042 008
gSOAP	73 732	649 908	879 252	946 164	3 049 140
Axis C++	31 412	N/A	N/A	N/A	N/A

Table 5. x86 binary size of the synthetic test implementations

Toolkit	Contacts client executable	Contacts server shared object
MXDB	49 784	90 972
gSOAP	115 620	187 496
Axis C++	37 716	64 280

Table 6. x86 execution time of the synthetic test implementations

Toolkit	user	sys	user+sys	real
MXDB	1.016s	0.180s	1.196s	2.624s
gSOAP	0.508s	0.184s	0.692s	1.067s
Axis C++	2.360s	0.152s	2,512s	4.224s

with Axis, it seems that MXDB generates smaller code than Axis C++.

In the synthetic comparison, we implemented a working service based on the code generated from Contacts.wsdl. We implemented the client and server part with all frameworks. Both the client and the server contain a method that fills in the SOAP messages with fake contact data that is sent to the other endpoint. We cross-tested all three implementations with each other. Even though we tried to keep Contacts.wsdl simple, the generated Axis service code used a faulty namespace for one element that prevented it from working with the MXDB and gSOAP clients. Axis also leaked one heap cell per invocation in the client and server implementation. All other combinations worked fine.

Table 5 shows the comparison of the binary code size. As one can see, the MXDB code is signficiantly smaller than gSOAP but larger than Axis. Our findings indicate that this is due to that MXDB uses templates extensively, including STL vector, shared_ptr and the implementation of nullable elements.

We also compared the runtime performance of the implementations. We did 100 invocations and each invocation transferred 100 contact entries with 16 details each (including name, e-mail, street address, etc.). We measured the time elapsed in the client when using the server implemented with the same toolkit. We used the Linux time program to measure execution time. We did not profile the MXDB implementation and did not optimize it for execution time.

Table 6 shows the execution time of the synthetic test implementation. We can conclude that MXDB falls between gSOAP and Axis. This means that gSOAP has advantage in runtime performance, but the metadata-based approach is not inherently slower than any code-based serialization/deserialization approach.

Table 7. ARMv5 binary size of generated code + data (bytes)

Toolkit	Contacts	MapPoint	PayPal	Amazon	EBay
MXDB	7 268	155 575	173 595	281 289	507 297
gSOAP	15 578	177 382	257 722	275 301	967 883
MXDB (% of gSOAP)	46.6%	87.7%	67,3%	102.2%	52.4%

Symbian Tests

On Symbian, we compared the size of the binary code generated for the ARMv5 instruction set that is quite popular in smartphones and other embedded devices. We used the third edition of the S60 platform provided by Nokia that is based on the Symbian operating system version 9.1. We used the RealView compiler (ARM Ltd., 2006) version 2.2. The data presented in Table 6 is the size of the code and data reported by the compiler when used from the CodeWarrior IDE.

Support for standard C and C++ in S60 is quite limited, MXDB being the only tool that fully supports the Symbian environment. Optimized for embedded devices (van Engelen, 2004), gSOAP, which is the only toolkit besides MXDB that is, is able to generate code that compiles on Symbian, hence the only tool where we could make a one-to-one comparison. On Symbian, we used gSOAP to generate pure C code.

Table 7 shows the binary size of the code and data generated from XML Schema types and WSDL operations. We can see that MXDB typically generates smaller binary code than gSOAP. Depending on the WSDL file, binary code can be 50% smaller. This does not seem to depend on the size of the WSDL—this works for small and large WSDL files. We can also see that in the worst case with the Amazon WSDL MXDB generates slightly larger code than gSOAP.

CONCLUSION

MXDB is a novel XML solution optimized for easy and efficient use of Web Services in C++ environment. The benefits of MXDB over existing solutions are:

- The representation of XML Schema as metadata instead of code means MXDB can support complicated schema constructs better (e.g., the multilevel mix of sequence, choice and all).
- Separation of XML Schema-based metadata and runtime potentially enables easier support for different development environment, target platforms, and even programming languages.
- The same separation enables smart syntax checking based on XML Schema.
- Layered architecture provides for different XML serialization techniques without the need to utilize intermediate wrapper layers.
- Smaller binary code is an important advantage in storage-constrained mobile platforms.

ACKNOWLEDGMENT

The authors would like to acknowledge the support of Nokia colleagues, especially Norbert Leser, Timo Skyttä, and John Kemp at the Web Services Technologies team at Nokia. We would like to acknowledge the support of Zoltán Papp at Nokia Research Center Budapest.

REFERENCES

Apache Software Foundation. (2006). *Apache Axis*. Retrieved March 17, 2009, from http://ws.apache.org/axis/

Biron, P. V., & Malhotra, A. (2004). XML schema Part 2: Datatypes (2nd ed.). In *World Wide Web Consortium (W3C)*. Retrieved March 17, 2009, from http://www.w3.org/TR/xmlschema-2/

Bray, T., Paoli, J., Sperberg-McQueen, C. M., Maler, E., & Yergeau, F. (2004). Extensible markup language (XML) 1.0 (3rd ed.). In *World Wide Web Consortium (W3C)*. Retrieved March 17, 2009, from http://www.w3.org/TR/2004/REC-xml-20040204/

Brown, A. W., & Johnston, S. (2002). *Using service-oriented architecture and component-based development to build Web service applications*. Rational Software White Paper TP032. Retrieved March 17, 2009, from http://www.alanbrown.net/files/SOA-paper.pdf

Christensen, E., Curbera, F., Meredith, G., & Weerawarana, S. (2001). Web services description language (WSDL) 1.1. *World Wide Web Consortium (W3C)*. Retrieved March 17, 2009, from http://www.w3.org/TR/wsdl

E-Bay. (2006). *SOAP API WSDL*. Retrieved March 17, 2009, from http://developer.ebay.com/soap/

Fialli, J., & Vajjhala, S. (2003). *The Java architecture for XML binding (JAXB), V1.0*. Sun Microsystems, Santa Clara, CA, USA. Retrieved March 17, 2009, from http://java.sun.com/xml/downloads/jaxb.html

Fielding, R., Gettys, J., Mogul, J., Frystyk, H., Masinter, L., Leach, P., et al. (1999). *Hypertext Transfer Protocol – HTTP/1.1*. Internet Engineering Task Force (IETF). Retrieved March 17, 2009, from http://www.ietf.org/rfc/rfc2616.txt

Gudgin, M., Hadley, M., Mendelsohn, N., Moreau, J.-J., & Nielsen, H. F. (2003). *SOAP Version 1.2 Part 1: Messaging framework*. World Wide Web Consortium (W3C). Retrieved March 17, 2009, from http://www.w3.org/TR/soap12-part1/

Kay, M. (2005). *XSL transformations (XSLT) Version 2.0*. World Wide Web Consortium (W3C). Retrieved March 17, 2009, from http://www.w3.org/TR/xslt20/

Lee, D., & Chu, W. W. (2000). Comparative analysis of six XML schema languages (pp. 76-87). *ACM SIGMOD Record*. New York: ACM Press.

Liquid Technologies. (2006). *Liquid XML 2006*. Retrieved March 17, 2009, from http://www.liquid-technologies.com/

Ltd, A. R. M. (2006). *ARM RealView development tools*. Retrieved March 17, 2009, from http://www.arm.com/products/DevTools/

Microsoft. (2006). *Windows communication foundation*. Retrieved March 17, 2009, from http://msdn.microsoft.com/windowsvista/connected/

Nokia. (2006). *Nokia WSDL-to-C++ Wizard for S60*. Forum Nokia. Retrieved March 17, 2009, from http://forum.nokia.com/info/sw.nokia.com/id/5ddeb939-c4e4-4e64-8f25-282e1e86afed/Nokia_WSDL_to_Cpp_Wizard_for_S60.html

Payrits, S., Dornbach, P., & Zólyomi, I. (2006). Metadata-based XML serialization for embedded C++. In *Proceedings of the IEEE International Conference on Web Services* (pp. 347-356). Washington, DC: IEEE Computer Society.

Sourceforge. (2006a). *gSOAP: C/C++ Web services and clients*. Retrieved March 17, 2009, from http://gsoap2.sourceforge.net/

Sourceforge. (2006b). *Saxon.NET*. Retrieved March 17, 2009, from http://sourceforge.net/projects/saxondotnet/

Thompson, H. S., Beech, D., Maloney, M., & Mendelsohn, N. (2004). *XML schema part 1: Structures* (2nd ed.). World Wide Web Consortium (W3C). Retrieved March 17, 2009, from http://www.w3.org/TR/xmlschema-1/

van Engelen, R. (2004). Code generation techniques for developing light-weight XML Web services for embedded devices. In *Proceedings of the 9th ACM Symposium on Applied Computing SAC 2004* (pp. 854-861). New York: ACM Press.

Veillard, D. (2006). *The XML C parser and toolkit of Gnome: libxml.* Retrieved March 17, 2009, from http://xmlsoft.org/

White, J., Kolpackov, B., Natarajan, B., & Schmidt, D. C. (2005). Reducing application code complexity with vocabulary-specific XML language binding. In *Proceedings of the 43rd Annual Southeast Regional Conference*. New York: ACM Press.

ENDNOTES

1. Axis crashed with null pointer exception during generation
2. Complex type extension is not mapped to object-oriented inheritence in AXIS
3. Axis handles element groups incorrectly as normal elements
4. No explicit support, but can be added to MXDB code generator without changing the code library
5. gSOAP crashes with segmentation fault during generation
6. No explicit support, but can be added to MXDB code generator without changing the code library
7. With incoming XML, both Axis and gSOAP handles *sequence* model groups are handled as if they were *all*s

This work was previously published in International Journal of Web Services Research, Volume 6, Issue 3, edited by Liang-Jie Zhang, pp. 18-34, copyright 2009 by IGI Publishing (an imprint of IGI Global).

Chapter 12
The Assurance Point Model for Consistency and Recovery in Service Composition

Susan D. Urban
Texas Tech University, USA

Le Gao
Texas Tech University, USA

Rajiv Shrestha
Texas Tech University, USA

Yang Xiao
Arizona State University, USA

Zev Friedman
Texas Tech University, USA

Jonathan Rodriguez
Texas Tech University, USA

ABSTRACT

This research has defined an abstract execution model for establishing user-defined correctness and recovery in a service composition environment. The service composition model defines a hierarchical service composition structure, where a service is composed of atomic and/or composite groups. The model provides multi-level protection against service execution failure by using compensation and contingency at different composition granularity levels. The model is enhanced with the concept of assurance points (APS) and integration rules, where APs serve as logical and physical checkpoints for user-defined consistency checking, invoking integration rules that check pre and post conditions at different points in the execution process. The unique aspect of APs is that they provide intermediate rollback points when failures occur, thus allowing a process to be compensated to a specific AP for the purpose of rechecking pre-conditions before retry attempts. APs also support a dynamic backward recovery process, known as cascaded contingency, for hierarchically nested processes in an attempt to recover to a previous AP that can be used to invoke contingent procedures or alternate execution paths for failure of a nested process. As a result, the assurance point approach provides flexibility with respect to the combined use of backward and forward recovery options. Petri Nets have been used to define the semantics of the assurance point approach to service composition and recovery. A comparison to the BPEL fault handler is also provided.

DOI: 10.4018/978-1-61350-104-7.ch012

INTRODUCTION

In a service-based architecture, a process is composed of a series of calls to distributed Web services and Grid services that collectively provide some specific functionality of interest to an application (Singh & Huhns, 2005). In a traditional, data-oriented, distributed computing environment, a distributed transaction is used to provide certain correctness guarantees about the execution of a transaction over distributed data sources. In particular, a traditional, distributed transaction provides all-or-nothing behavior by using the two-phase commit protocol to support atomicity, consistency, isolation, and durability (ACID) properties (Kifer, Bernstein, & Lewis, 2006). A process in a service-oriented architecture, however, is not a traditional ACID transaction due to the loosely-coupled, autonomous, and heterogeneous nature of the execution environment. When a process invokes a service, the service performs its function and then terminates, without regard for the successful termination of the global process that invoked the service. If the process fails, reliable techniques are needed to either 1) restore the process to a consistent state or 2) correct critical data values and continue running.

Techniques such as compensation and contingency have been used as a form of recovery in past work with transactional workflows (e.g., Worah & Sheth, 1997) and have also been introduced into recent languages for service composition (e.g., Lin & Chang, 2005). In the absence of a global log file, compensation provides a form of backward recovery, executing a procedure that will "logically undo" the affects of completed and/or partially executed operations. Contingency is a form of forward recovery, providing an alternate execution path that will allow a process to continue execution. Some form of compensation may be needed, however, before the execution of contingency plans. Furthermore, nested service composition specifications can complicate the use of compensating and contingent procedures. To provide a reliable service composition mechanism, it is important to fully understand the semantics and complementary usage of compensation and contingency, as well as how they can be used together with local and global database recovery techniques and nested service composition specifications. Service composition models also need to be enhanced with features that allow processes to assess their execution status to support more dynamic ways of responding to failures, while at the same time validating correctness conditions for process execution.

This research has defined an abstract execution model for establishing user-defined correctness and recovery in a service composition environment. The research was originally conducted in the context of the DeltaGrid project, which focused on building a semantically-robust execution environment for processes that execute over Grid Services (Xiao, 2006; Xiao, Urban, & Dietrich, 2006; Xiao, Urban, & Liao, 2006; Xiao & Urban, 2008). The service composition model defines a hierarchical service composition structure, where a service is composed of atomic and/or composite groups. An atomic group is a service execution with optional compensation and contingency procedures. A composite group is composed of two or more atomic and/or composite groups and can also have optional compensation and contingency procedures. A unique aspect of the model is the provision for multi-level protection against service execution failure by using compensation and contingency at different composition granularity levels, thus maximizing the potential for forward recovery of a process when failure occurs. The work in (Xiao and Urban, 2009) presents the full specification of the model using state diagrams and algorithms to define the semantics of compensation and contingency in the recovery process.

Our more recent work has extended the DeltaGrid service composition and recovery model in (Xiao et al., 2009) with the concept of *Assurance Points* (APs) and *integration rules* to provide a more flexible way of checking constraints and responding to execution failures. An AP is a combined logical and physical checkpoint. As a physical checkpoint, an AP provides a way to store data at critical points in the execution of a process. Unlike past work with checkpointing, such as that of (Dialini, Miles, Moreau, Roure & Luck, 2002; Luo, 2000) where checkpoints are used to port an execution to a different platform as part of fault tolerant architectures, our work focuses on the use of APs for user-defined consistency checking and rollback points that can be used to maximize forward recovery options when failures occur. In particular, an AP provides an execution milestone that interacts with integration rules. The data stored at an AP is passed as parameters to integration rules that are used to check pre-conditions, post-conditions, and other application conditions. Failure of a pre or post-condition or the failure of a service execution can invoke several different forms of recovery, including backward recovery of the entire process, retry attempts, or execution of contingent procedures. The unique aspect of APs is that they provide intermediate rollback points when failures occur that allow a process to be compensated to a specific AP for the purpose of rechecking pre-conditions before retry attempts. APs also support a dynamic backward recovery process, known as cascaded contingency, for hierarchically nested processes in an attempt to recover to a previous AP that can be used to invoke contingent procedures or alternate execution paths for failure of a nested process.

After presenting related work, this chapter first reviews the basic features of the hierarchical service composition model presented in (Xiao et al., 2009), together with an on-line shopping case study and a summary of an evaluation framework that was developed to demonstrate the functionality of the recovery algorithms. An understanding of these basic features is a precursor to a description of the extended model. The AP and integration rule extensions to the model are then presented, with a focus on the different forms of recovery actions as defined in (Shrestha, 2010). Petri Nets are then used to formalize the semantics of the extended model, including atomic and composite groups with shallow and deep compensation integrated with assurance points as well as rollback, retry, and cascaded contingency recovery activities. After discussing a prototype implementation of an execution engine for the model, a comparison of the approach to the fault handling and recovery procedures of BPEL is presented, demonstrating that the approach presented in this chapter provides a cleaner, hierarchical approach to compensation order rather than the "zigzag" behavior of BPEL as described in (Khalaf, Roller, & Leymann, 2009). The primary contribution of this research is found in the enhancements that assurance points and integration rules lend to the service composition and recovery process. In particular, the assurance point approach provides explicit support for user-defined constraints with rule-driven recovery actions for compensation, retry, and contingency procedures that support flexibility with respect to the combined use of backward and forward recovery options.

This chapter concludes with a summary and discussion of future research.

RELATED WORK

The traditional notion of transactions with ACID properties is too restrictive for the types of complex transactional activities that occur in distributed applications, primarily because locking resources during the entire execution period is not applicable for Long Running Transactions (LRTs) that require relaxed atomicity and isolation (Cichocki, 1998). Advanced transaction models (ATMs) have been proposed to better support LRTs in a distributed environment (deBy, Klas, & Veijalainen, 1998; Elmagarmid, 1992), including the Nested Transaction Model, the Open Nested Transaction Model, Sagas, the Multi-level Transaction Model and the Flexible Transaction Model. These advanced transaction models relax the ACID properties of traditional transaction models to better support LRTs and to provide a theoretical basis for further study of complex distributed transaction issues, such as failure atomicity, consistency, and concurrency control. These models have primarily been studied from a research perspective and have not adequately addressed recovery issues for transaction failure dependencies in loosely-coupled distributed applications.

Transactional workflows contain the coordinated execution of multiple related tasks that support access to heterogeneous, autonomous, and distributed data through the use of selected transactional properties (Worah et al., 1997). Transactional workflows require externalizing intermediate results, while at the same time providing concurrency control, consistency guarantees, and a failure recovery mechanism for a multi-user, multi-workflow environment. Concepts such as rollback, compensation, forward recovery, and logging have been used to achieve workflow failure recovery in projects such as the ConTract Model (Wachter & Reuter, 1992), the Workflow Activity Model (Eder & Liebhart, 1995), the CREW Project (Kamath & Ramamritham, 1998), the METEOR Project (Worah et al., 1997), and Units of Work (Bennett et al., 2000). These projects expose the weaknesses of using ATM techniques alone to support reliable transactional workflow execution, mainly due to the complexity of workflows. Previous work also shows the weakness of ATMs in support of the isolation, failure atomicity, timed constraints, and liveness requirements of distributed transactional workflows (Kuo, Fekete, Greenfield & Jang, 2002). Similar concerns are voiced in papers addressing transactional issues for traditional workflow systems (Alonso, Hagen, Schek, & Tresh, 1997; Kamath and Ramamritham 1996; Kamath et al.,1998) as well as workflow for loosely-coupled distributed sources such as Web Services (Fekete, Greenfield, Kuo, & Jang, 2002; Kuo et al. 2002). More comprehensive solutions are needed to meet the requirements of transactional workflows (Worah et al. 1997).

In the Web Services platform, WS-Coordination (2005) and WS-Transaction (2005) are two specifications that enable the transaction semantics and coordination of Web Service composition using Atomic Transactions for ACID transactions and Business Activity for long running business processes. The Web Services Transaction Framework (WSTx) (Mikalsen, Tai, & Rouvellou, 2002) introduces *Transactional Attitudes*, where service providers and clients declare their individual transaction capabilities and semantics. Web Service Composition Action (WSCA) (Tartanoglu, 2003) allows a participant to specify actions to be performed when other Web Services in the WSCA signal an exception. An agent based transaction model (Jin & Goshnick, 2003) integrates agent technologies in coordinating Web Services to form a transaction. Tentative holding is used in (Limthanmaphon & Zhang, 2004) to achieve a tentative commit state for transactions over Web Services. Acceptable Termination States (Bhiri, Perrin, & Godart, 2005) are used to ensure user-defined failure atomicity of composite services, where application designers specify the global composition structure of a composite service and the acceptable termination states.

More recently, events and rules have been used to dynamically specify control flow and data flow in a process by using Event Condition Action (ECA) rules (Paton & Diaz, 1999). ECA rules have also been successfully implemented for exception handling in work such as (Brambilla, Ceri, Comai, & Tziviskou, 2005; Liu, Li, Huang, & Xiao, 2007). The work in Liu et al. (2007) uses ECA rules to generate reliable and fault-tolerant BPEL processes to overcome the limited fault handling capability of BPEL. Our work with assurance points also supports the use of rules that separate fault handling from normal business logic. Combined with assurance points, integration rules are used to integrate user-defined consistency constraints with the recovery process.

Several efforts have been made to enhance the BPEL fault and exception handling capabilities.

BPEL4Job (Tan, Fong, & Bobroff, 2007) addresses fault-handling design for job flow management with the ability to migrate flow instances. The work in (Modafferi & Conforti, 2006) proposes mechanisms like external variable setting, future alternative behavior, rollback and conditional re-execution of the Flow, timeout, and redo mechanisms for enabling recovery actions using BPEL. The work in (Modafferi, Mussi, & Pernici, 2006) presents the architecture of the SH-BPEL engine, a Self-Healing plug-in for WS-BPEL engines that augments the fault recovery capabilities in WS-BPEL with mechanisms such as annotation, pre-processing, and extended recovery. The Dynamo (Baresi, Guiea, & Pasquale, 2007) framework for the dynamic monitoring of WS-BPEL processes weaves rules such as pre/post conditions and invariants into the BPEL process. Most of these projects do not fully integrate constraint checking with a variety of recovery actions as in our work to support more dynamic and flexible ways of reacting to failures. Our research demonstrates the viability of variegated recovery approaches within a BPEL-like execution environment.

In checkpointing systems, consistent execution states are saved during the process flow. During failures and exceptions, the activity can be rolled back to the closest consistent checkpoint to move the execution to an alternative platform (Dialini et al. 2002; Luo, 2000]. The AP concept presented in this chapter also stores critical execution data, but uses the data as parameters to rules that perform constraint checking and invoke different types of recovery actions.

Aspect-oriented programming (AOP) is another way of modularizing and adding flexibility to service composition through dynamic and autonomic composition and runtime recovery. In AOP, aspects are weaved into the execution of a program using join points to provide alternative execution paths (Charfi & Mezini, 2007). The work in (Charfi & Mezini, 2006) illustrates the application of aspect-oriented software development concepts to workflow languages to provide flexible and adaptable workflows. AO4BPEL (Charfi et al., 2007) is an aspect-oriented extension to BPEL that uses AspectJ to provide control flow adaptations (Kiczales et al., 2001). Business rules can also be used to provide more flexibility during service composition. APs as described in this chapter are similar to join points, with a novel focus on using APs to access process history data in support of constraint checking as well as flexible and dynamic recovery techniques.

Due to the distributed nature of services, service composition is often inflexible and highly vulnerable to errors. Even BPEL, the de-facto standard for composing Web services, still lacks sophistication with respect to handling faults and events. Our research is different than related work by providing a hierarchical composition structure with support for user-defined constraints with the use of rules for pre and post conditions. In addition, the AP model integrates the rules with different recovery actions as well as user-defined compensation and contingency. Thus, our AP model attempts to provide more flexible recovery process semantics with a focus on user-defined constraints, which is a combination of features that are not available in past research.

OVERVIEW OF THE DELTAGRID SERVICE COMPOSITION AND RECOVERY MODEL

Before describing the use of APs and integration rules, this section first outlines the basic features of the model in the context of the DeltaGrid project. This section first elaborates on atomic and composite group recovery issues and then presents a case study to illustrate the basic concepts of the model.

Hierarchical Service Composition and Recovery

In the DeltaGrid environment, a process is hierarchically composed of different types of execution entities. Table 1 shows seven execution entities defined in the service composition model. Figure 1 uses a UML class diagram to graphically illustrate the composition relationship among these execution entities. A process is a top-level execution entity that contains other execution entities. A process is denoted as p_i, where p represents a process and the subscript i represents a unique identifier of the process. An Operation represents a service invocation, denoted as $op_{i,j}$, such that op is an operation, i identifies the enclosing process p_i, and j represents the unique identifier of the operation within p_i. Compensation (denoted as $cop_{i,j}$) is an operation intended for backward recovery, while contingency (denoted as $top_{i,j}$) is an operation used for forward recovery.

An atomic group and a composite group are logical execution units that enable the specification of processes with complex control structure, facilitating service execution failure recovery by adding scopes within the context of a process execution. An atomic group contains an operation, an optional compensation, and an optional contingency. A composite group may contain multiple atomic groups, and/or multiple composite groups that execute sequentially or in parallel. A composite group can have its own compensation and contingency as optional elements. A process is essentially a top level composite group.

An atomic group is denoted as $ag_{i,j}$, while a composite group is denoted as $cg_{i,k}$. The subscripts in the atomic group and composite group notation indicate the nesting levels of an atomic group or composite group within the context of a process. For example, a process p_1 is a top-level composite group denoted as cg_1. Assume cg_1 contains two composite groups and an atomic group. The enclosed composite groups are denoted as $cg_{1,1}$ and $cg_{1,2}$, and the atomic group is denoted as $ag_{1,3}$. Assume $cg_{1,1}$ contains two atomic groups. These atomic groups are denoted as $ag_{1,1,1}$ and $ag_{1,1,2}$, respectively.

The only execution entity not shown in Figure 1 is the *DE-rollback* entity. DE-rollback is a system-initiated operation that is unique to the DeltaGrid environment. Services in the DeltaGrid environment, referred to as *Delta-Enabled Grid Services (DEGS)*, are extended with the capability of recording incremental data changes, known as *deltas* (Blake, 2005; Urban, Xiao, Blake, & Dietrich, 2009). Deltas are extracted from service executions and externalized by streaming data changes out of the database to a Process History

Table 1. Execution entities

Entity Name	Definition
Operation	A service invocation, denoted as $op_{i,j}$
Compensation	An operation that is used to undo the effect of a committed operation, denoted as $cop_{i,j}$
Contingency	An operation that is used as an alternative of a failed operation ($op_{i,j}$), denoted as $top_{i,j}$
Atomic Group	An execution entity that is composed of a primary operation ($op_{i,j}$), an optional compensation ($cop_{i,j}$), and an optional contingency operation ($top_{i,j}$), denoted as $ag_{i,j} = <op_{i,j}\ [,cop_{i,j}]\ [,top_{i,j}]>$
Composite Group	An execution entity that is composed of multiple atomic groups or other composite groups. A composite group can also have an optional compensation and an optional contingency, denoted as $cg_{i,k} = <(ag_{i,k,m} \mid cg_{i,k,n})^+\ [,cop_{i,k}]\ [,top_{i,k}])>$
Process	A top level composite group, denoted as p_i
DE-rollback	An action of undoing the effect of an operation by reversing the data values that have been changed by the operation to their before images, denoted as $dop_{i,j}$

Figure 1. Service composition structure

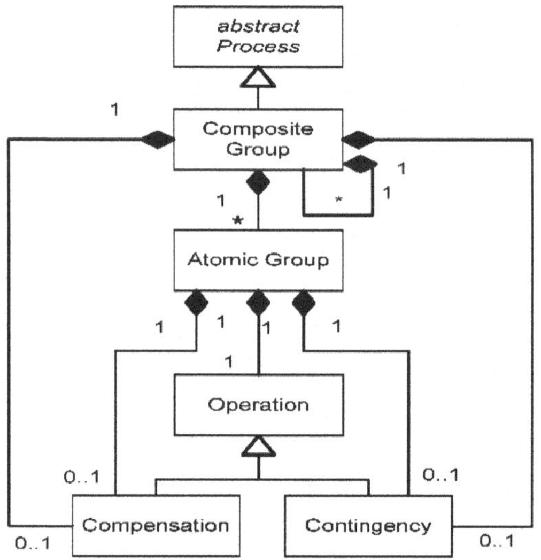

Capture System (PHCS) (Xiao et al., 2006). The PHCS merges deltas from distributed sources into a time-ordered schedule of the data changes associated with concurrently executing processes. Deltas can then be used to backward recover an operation through a process known as *Delta-Enabled Rollback (DE-Rollback)* (Xiao, 2006). DE-rollback can only be used, however, if certain recoverability conditions are satisfied, with the PHCS. The merged schedule of deltas providing the basis for determining the applicability of DE-rollback based on data dependencies among concurrently executing processes. A recoverable schedule requires that, at the time when each transaction t_i commits, every other transaction t_j that wrote values read by t_i has already committed (Kifer et al., 2006). Thus a recoverable schedule does not allow dirty writes to occur. In a recoverable schedule, a transaction t_1 cannot be rolled back if another transaction t_2 reads or writes data items that have been written by t_1, since this may cause lost updates. When interleaved access to the same data item disables the applicability of DE-rollback on an operation, compensation can be used to semantically undo the effect of the operation.

Figure 2 shows an abstract view of a sample process definition based on the DeltaGrid service composition structure. A process p_1 is the top level composite group cg_1. The process p_1 is composed of two composite groups $cg_{1,1}$ and $cg_{1,2}$, and an atomic group $ag_{1,3}$. Similarly, $cg_{1,1}$ and $cg_{1,2}$ are composite groups that contain atomic groups. Each atomic/composite group can have an optional compensation plan and/or contingency plan. Operation execution failure can occur on an operation at any level of nesting. The purpose of the DeltaGrid service composition model is to automatically resolve operation execution failure using compensation, contingency, and DE- rollback at different composition levels.

Atomic Group Execution and Recovery

When the execution of an atomic group fails, pre-commit recovery activities are applied locally to clean up the failed operation execution before the operation terminates and communicates its terminated status to the process execution environment.

Definition 1 (Pre-commit Recoverability): Pre-commit recoverability specifies how an atomic group should be locally recovered when an execution failure occurs before the operation as an execution unit commits.

Table 2 presents pre-commit recovery options for an atomic group. Ideally, an ag operation's pre-commit recoverability is *automatic rollback* for an ACID operation, or *pre-commit-compensation* for a non-ACID operation. With the delta capture capability of the DeltaGrid environment, an ag can also reverse the effect of the original operation through *DE-rollback* if the recoverability conditions are satisfied. If DE-rollback cannot be applied due to the violation of the semantic conditions for DE-rollback, the service composition model requires the use of a *service reset* function. The service reset function cleans up the effect of a failed

Figure 2. An abstract view of a sample process

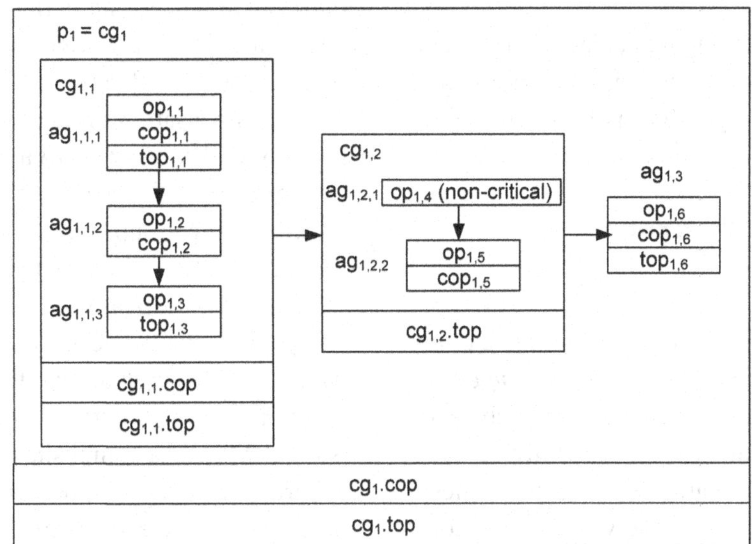

operation and prepares the execution environment for the next service invocation. A service reset typically requires a special program or a human agent to resolve the failed operation execution.

After an atomic group has been locally recovered, the failed execution transmits its terminated status to the process execution environment. In the context of the global process, an ag maximizes the success of an operation execution by providing an optional contingency plan that is executed as an alternative path if the original service execution of the ag fails.

In contrast to pre-commit recoverability, which defines how to locally clean up a failed operation execution, *post-commit recoverability* specifies how the process execution environment can semantically undo the effect of a successfully terminated atomic group due to another operation's execution failure.

Definition 2 (Post-commit Recoverability): Post-commit recoverability specifies how an operation's effect can be semantically undone after the operation has successfully terminated.

Post-commit recoverability is considered when a completed operation inside of a composite group needs to be undone due to runtime failure of another operation. Table 3 defines three post-commit recoverability options: *reversible* (through DE-rollback), *compensatable*, or *dismissible*. Post-commit recovery is only applicable in the context of composite group execution. Furthermore, the dismissable option indicates that a process execution can be application-dependent and might not require every operation to be successfully executed. The DeltaGrid service composition model offers the flexibility of marking execution entities with a *criticality* decorator when failure does not affect the execution of the enclosing composite group. By default, an operation's post-commit recoverability is compensatable.

Definition 3 (Criticality): An atomic group is *critical* if its successful execution is mandatory for the enclosing composite group. A *non-critical* group indicates that the failure of this group will not impact the state of the enclosing composite group, and the composite group can continue execution. When runtime execution failure occurs, contingency must be executed for critical groups, while contingency is not necessary for a non-critical group. By default, a group is critical.

As an example, in Figure 2, if $ag_{1,2,1}$ fails, $cg_{1,2}$ will continue executing since $ag_{1,2,1}$ is non-critical. Thus in the specification, there is no need to define a compensation and contingency plan for $ag_{1,2,1}$.

Composite Group Execution and Recovery

The recoverability of a composite group can be defined using the concepts of *shallow compensation* and *deep compensation*. The terms shallow and deep compensation were originally defined in (Leymann, 1995). Our research extends these concepts for use with nested service composition.

Definition 4 (Shallow Compensation): Assume a composite group $cg_{i,k}$ is defined as $cg_{i,k} = <(ag_{i,k,m} \mid cg_{i,k,n})^{+}, cop_{i,k} [,top_{i,k}]>$. Shallow compensation of $cg_{i,k}$ is the invocation of the compensation operation defined for the composite group $cg_{i,k}$, which is $cop_{i,k}$.

Definition 5 (Deep Compensation): Assume a composite group $cg_{i,k}$ is defined as $cg_{i,k} = <(ag_{i,k,m} \mid cg_{i,k,n})^{+}, cop_{i,k} [,top_{i,k}]>$. Within the context of a composite group $cg_{i,k}$, a subgroup is either an atomic group defined as $ag_{i,k,m} = <op_{i,j}, cop_{i,j} [,top_{i,j}]>$, or a composite group defined as $cg_{i,k,n} = <(ag_{i,k,n,x} \mid cg_{i,k,n,y})^{+}, cop_{i,k,n} [,top_{i,k,n}]>$. Deep compensation of $cg_{i,k}$ is the invocation of post-commit recovery activity (compensation or DE-rollback) for each executed subgroup within the composite group, such as $cop_{i,j}$ for an atomic group, and $cop_{i,k,n}$ for a nested composite group.

Shallow compensation is invoked when a composite group successfully terminates but needs a semantic undo due to the failure of another operation execution. A deep compensation is invoked if: 1) a composite group fails due to a subgroup execution failure, and needs to trigger the post-commit recovery of executed subgroups, or 2) a composite group successfully terminates, but no shallow compensation is defined for the composite group.

As a backward recovery mechanism for a successfully executed composite group, shallow compensation has higher priority than deep compensation. For example, in Figure 2, the failure of a critical subgroup $ag_{1,3}$ (both $op_{1,6}$ and $top_{1,6}$ fail) within the enclosing composite group cg_1

Table 2. Atomic group pre-commit recoverability options

Option	Meaning
Automatic rollback	The failed service execution can be automatically rolled back by a service provider
Pre-Commit-Compensation	A pre-commit-compensation is invoked by a service provider to backward recover a failed operation.
DE-rollback	A failed operation can be reversed by executing DE-rollback
Service Reset	The service provider offers a service reset function to clean up the service execution environment.

Table 3. DEGS post-commit recoverability options

Option	Meaning
Reversible (DE-rollback)	A completed operation can be undone by reversing the data values that have been modified by the operation execution.
Compensatable	A completed operation can be semantically undone by executing another operation, referred to as post-execution compensation.
Dismissible	A completed operation does not need any cleanup activities.

causes the two executed composite groups $cg_{1,1}$ and $cg_{1,2}$ to be compensated. Since $cg_{1,1}$ has a pre-defined shallow compensation, the shallow compensation $cg_{1,1}$.cop will be executed. $cg_{1,2}$'s deep compensation will be invoked since $cg_{1,2}$ does not have shallow compensation.

An Online Shopping Case Study

This section introduces an online shopping case study to illustrate the use of the service composition and recovery model. The online shopping application contains typical business processes that describe the activities conducted by shoppers, the store and vendors. For example, the process placeClientOrder is responsible for invoking services that place client orders and decrease the inventory quantity. The process placeVendorOrder checks the inventory, calculates restocking need, and generates vendor orders. The process replenishInventory invokes services that increase the inventory quantity when vendor orders are received.

Figure 3 presents a graphical view of the placeClientOrder process using the same notation as the abstract process example presented in Figure 2. As shown in Figure 3, the process placeClientOrder is hierarchically composed of composite groups and atomic groups. An atomic group has an operation, an optional post-commit compensation (cop) and contingency (top).

The placeClientOrder process starts when a client submits a client order by invoking a DEGS operation receiveClientOrder. The next operation creditCheck verifies if the client has a good credit standing to pay for the order. If the client passes the creditCheck, the inventory will be checked to see if there are sufficient inventory items to fill the order by executing checkInventory. If the client does not pass the credit check, the order will be rejected. If there are sufficient inventory items, the operation chargeCreditCard is to be executed to charge the client's credit card, and the operation decInventory is executed to decrease inventory. These two operations are grouped into a composite group indicating that both operations should be successfully executed as a unit. Then the order will be packed through operation packorder and shipped through operation upsShipOrder. If the inventory is not sufficient to fill the order, the order will be marked as a backorder through operation addBackorder, and the client will be charged the full amount.

When there is a service execution failure during process execution, the process will be recovered based on the recovery specification embedded in the process definition, such as compensation and contingency, as well as the recovery semantics of the service composition and recovery model. For example, if operation upsShipOrder fails, the contingency fedexShipOrder will be invoked, sending the order package through Fedex instead of UPS. If a client requests to cancel the

Figure 3. placeClientOrder process definition

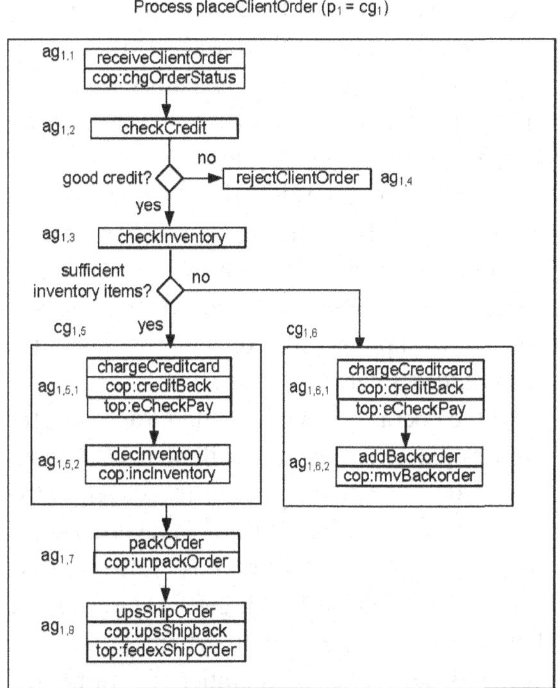

order after the operation packOrder but before upsShipOrder, each executed operation will be backward recovered in the reverse execution order using the following list of recovery commands: [cop:unpackOrder, cop:incInventory, cop:creditBack, DE-rollback:checkInventory, DE-rollback:checkcredit, cop:chgOrderStatus]. DE-rollback is to be performed on operations checkInventory and checkCredit since these two operations do not have pre-defined compensation and no other concurrently executing processes are write dependent on these two operations. Furthermore, since these two operations do not modify any data, no recovery actions will be performed for these two operations. Thus the final recovery commands for cancellation of an order is: [cop:unpackOrder, cop:incInventory, cop:creditBack, cop:chgOrderStatus].

Figure 4 gives a graphical view of the process placeVendorOrder. The process first invokes the operation getLowInventoryItems which goes through all the inventory items to create an entry for each inventory item whose quantity falls below a specified threshold. The operation getBackOrderItems goes through backorderList, adding items in the backorder list to the items to be ordered from the operation getLowInventoryItems. The process proceeds with the operation confirmPrice, which confirms the unit price of a product with each vendor. Then the operation genVendorOrder will generate vendor orders for different suppliers. After reviewVendorOrder which performs a final check on the vendor orders, these vendor orders are sent to suppliers by executing the operation sendVendorOrder.

If the operation reviewVendorOrder fails, the process placeVendorOrder will be backward recovered by executing post-commit recovery activity for each executed operation in reverse execution order: [cop:chgVOStatus, DE-rollback: confirmPrice, DE-rollback:getBackOrderItems, DE-rollback:getLowInventoryItems]. DE-rollback will be invoked on operations confirmPrice, getBackOrderItems and getLowInventoryItems since these operations do not have pre-defined compensation.

Figure 5 presents the replenishInventory process which is invoked when a vendor order package is received from a supplier. The process first verifies if there is any missing item by performing operation verifyVOItem. If there is any missing item, the relevant vendor will be contacted through operation contactVendor. Otherwise, received items are entered into the inventory and the operation incInventory is executed to update quantity for each received inventory item. The operation packBackorder iterates through the backorder list and pack backorders for shipment. After packBackorder, inventory will be decreased through operation decInventory to deduct the backorder quantity from the inventory. At last, operation sendBackorder dispatches backorders to customers.

As in the processes placeClientOrder and placeVendorOrder, the recovery procedure of process replenishInventory also conforms to the semantics defined in the service composition and recovery model. For example, if the vendor recalls

Figure 4. placeVendorOrder process definition

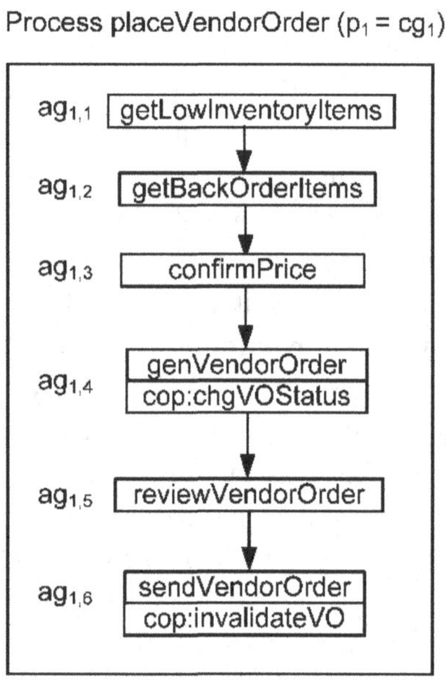

Process placeVendorOrder ($p_1 = cg_1$)

$ag_{1,1}$ getLowInventoryItems

$ag_{1,2}$ getBackOrderItems

$ag_{1,3}$ confirmPrice

$ag_{1,4}$ genVendorOrder / cop:chgVOStatus

$ag_{1,5}$ reviewVendorOrder

$ag_{1,6}$ sendVendorOrder / cop:invalidateVO

Figure 5. replenishInventory process definition

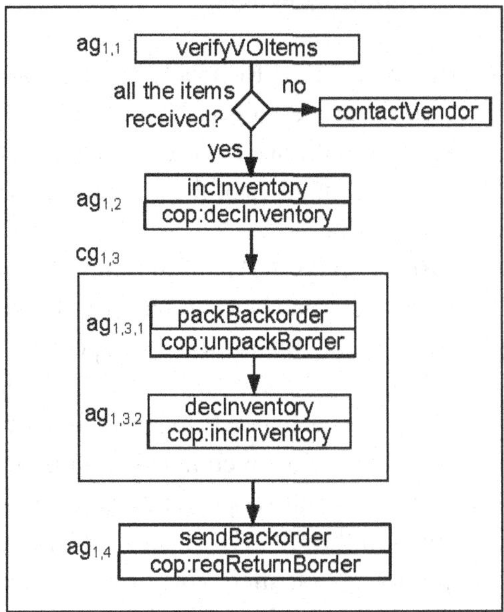

deficient items when the process finishes the execution of the operation decInventory, the process replenishInventory needs a backward recovery followed by sending the deficient items back to the vendor for a replacement. The backward recovery of the process will execute the compensation of every executed operation in reverse execution order: [cop:incInventory, cop:unpackBorder, cop:decInventory]. The operation verifyVOItems will not be recovered since verifyVOItems does not modify any data.

Simulation and Evaluation Framework

The original version of the DeltaGrid service composition and recovery model as described in this section has been formally presented in (Xiao et al., 2009; Xiao, 2006). The presentation includes state diagrams and algorithms that define the semantics of applying compensation and contingency when failure occurs. The work in (Xiao et al., 2009) also includes the description of a DeltaGrid simulation framework using the DEVSJAVA discrete event simulation tool (Zeigler & Sarjoughian 2004), as well as a performance evaluation of some of the implemented components of the simulation environment. Interested readers should refer to (Xiao et al., 2009) for further details on the formalization, simulation, and evaluation of the original model. In the remainder of this chapter, we describe an extension of the model to more completely address data consistency issues during execution and to also provide a means for partial rollback together with increased options for forward recovery. The concepts presented in this section are formalized together with the extended features using Petri Nets in the following sections of this chapter.

ASSURANCE POINTS AND INTEGRATION RULES FOR ENHANCING CONSISTENCY AND RECOVERY

The model described in the previous section has been extended with the concept of *Assurance Points (APs)* (Shrestha, 2010; Urban, Gao, Shrestha, & Courter, 2010a; Urban, Gao, Shrestha, and Courter, 2010b). An AP is a process execution correctness guard as well as a potential rollback point during the recovery process. Given that concurrent processes do not execute as traditional transactions in a service-oriented environment, inserting APs at critical points in a process is important for checking consistency constraints and potentially reducing the risk of failure or inconsistent data. An AP also serves as a milestone for backward and forward recovery activities. When failures occur, APs can be used as rollback points for backward recovery, rechecking pre-conditions relevant to forward recovery. In the current version of the model, it is assumed that APs are placed at points in a process where they are only executed once, and not embedded in iterative control structures. The version described in this chapter also does not address the use of APs in parallel execution structures, such as the <flowgroup> activity of BPEL, although a prototype execution engine supports this capability. An elaboration of these issues is beyond the scope of the current chapter and is addressed at the end of the chapter as part of future research.

An AP is defined as: AP = <apId, apParameters*, IR_{pre}?, IR_{post}?, IR_{cond}*>, where:

- apID is the unique identifier of the AP
- apParameters is a list of critical data items to be stored as part of the AP,
- IR_{pre} is an integration rule defining a pre-condition,
- IR_{post} is an integration rule defining a post-condition,
- IR_{cond} is an integration rule defining additional application rules.

In the above notation, * indicates 0 or more occurrences, while ? indicates zero or one optional occurrences.

IR_{pre}, IR_{post}, and IR_{cond} are expressed as Event-Condition-Action (ECA) rules using the format shown in Figure 6, which is based on previous work with using integration rules to interconnect software components (Jin, 2004; Urban, Dietrich, Na, Jin, Sundermier, & Saxena, 2001). An IR is triggered by a process that reaches a specific AP during execution. Upon reaching an AP, the condition of an IR is evaluated. The action specification is executed if the condition evaluates to true. For IR_{pre} and IR_{post}, a constraint C is always expressed in a negative form (not(C)). The action (action 1) is invoked if the pre or post condition is not true, invoking a recovery action or an alternative execution path. If the specified action is a retry activity, then there is a possibility for the process to execute through the same pre or post condition a second time, where action 2 is invoked rather than action 1. In general, any number of actions can be specified.

When pre and post conditions fail (not(C) = True), recovery actions are invoked. In its most basic form, a recovery action simply invokes an alternative process. Recovery actions can also be one of the following actions:

- **APRollback:** APRollback is used when the entire process needs to compensate its way back to the start of the process according to the semantics of the service compensation model.
- **APRetry:** APRetry is used when the running process needs to be backward recovered using compensation to a specific AP. By default, the backward recovery process will go to the first AP reached as part of the shallow or deep compensation process within the same scope. The pre-condition defined in the AP is re-checked. If the pre-condition is satisfied, the process execution is resumed from that AP by re-trying the recovered operations. Otherwise, the action of the pre-condition rule is executed. The APRetry command can optionally specify a parameter indicating the AP that is the target of the backward recovery process.
- **APCascadedContingency (APCC):** APCC is a backward recovery process that searches backwards through the hierarchical nesting of composite groups to find a possible contingent procedure for a failed composite group. During the APCC backward recovery process, when an AP is reached, the pre-condition defined in the AP will be re-checked before invok-

Figure 6. Integration rule structure

```
CREATE RULE    ruleName::{pre | post | cond}
EVENT          apId(apParameters)
CONDITION      rule condition specification
ACTION         action 1
[ON RETRY      action 2]
```

ing any contingent procedures for forward recovery.

The most basic use of an AP together with integration rules is shown in Figure 7, which shows a process with three composite groups and an AP between each composite group. The shaded box shows the functionality of an AP using AP2 as an example. Each AP serves as a checkpoint facility, storing execution status data in a checkpoint database (denoted as AP data in Figure 7). When the execution reaches AP2, IRs associated with the AP are invoked. The condition of an IR_{post} is evaluated first to validate the execution of cg_2. If the post-condition is violated, the action invoked can be one of the pre-defined recovery actions as described above. If the post-condition is not violated, then an IR_{pre} rule is evaluated to check the pre-condition for the next service execution. If the pre-condition is violated, one of the pre-defined recovery actions will be invoked. If the pre-condition is satisfied, the AP will check for any additional, conditional rules (IR_{cond}) that may have been expressed. IR_{cond} rules do not affect the normal flow of execution but provide a way to invoke additional parallel activity based on application requirements. Note that the expression of a pre-condition, post-condition or any additional condition is optional.

Assurance Point and Integration Rule Example

This section provides an example of assurance points, integration rules, and conditional rules in Figure 8 using a revised version of the online shopping application. All atomic and composite groups are shown in the solid line rectangles, while optional compensations and contingencies are shown in dashed line rectangles, denoted as cop and top, respectively. APs are shown as ovals between composite and/or atomic groups, where the AP identifiers and parameters are OrderPlaced(orderId), CreditCardCharged(orderId, cardnumber, amount), UPSShipped(orderId, UPSShippingDate), USPSShipped(orderId), Delivered(orderId, shippingMethod, deliveryDate).

Table 4 shows the integration rules and conditional rules associated with the APs in Figure 8. The components of an assurance point are explained below using the APs in Figure 8 and the rules in Table 4.

Component 1 (AP Identifiers and Parameters): An AP identifier defines the current execution status of a process instance. Each AP may optionally specify parameters that store data when the process execution reaches the AP. The data can then be examined in the conditions of rules associated with the AP. For example, the first AP is orderPlaced, which reflects that the customer has finished placing the shopping order. The parameter orderId is used in the rules associated with the AP.

Component 2 (Integration Rules): An integration rule is optionally used as a transition between logical components of a process to check pre and post conditions. In Table 4, the orderPlaced AP has a pre-condition that guarantees that the store must have enough goods in stock. Otherwise, the process invokes the backOrderPurchase process.

Figure 7. Basic use of AP and integration rules

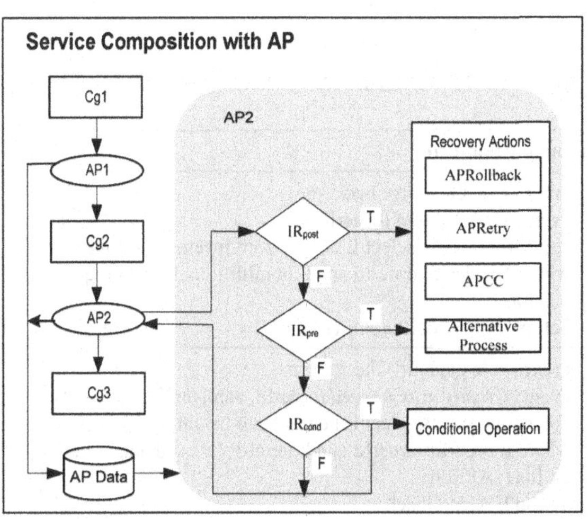

Figure 8. Online shopping process with APs

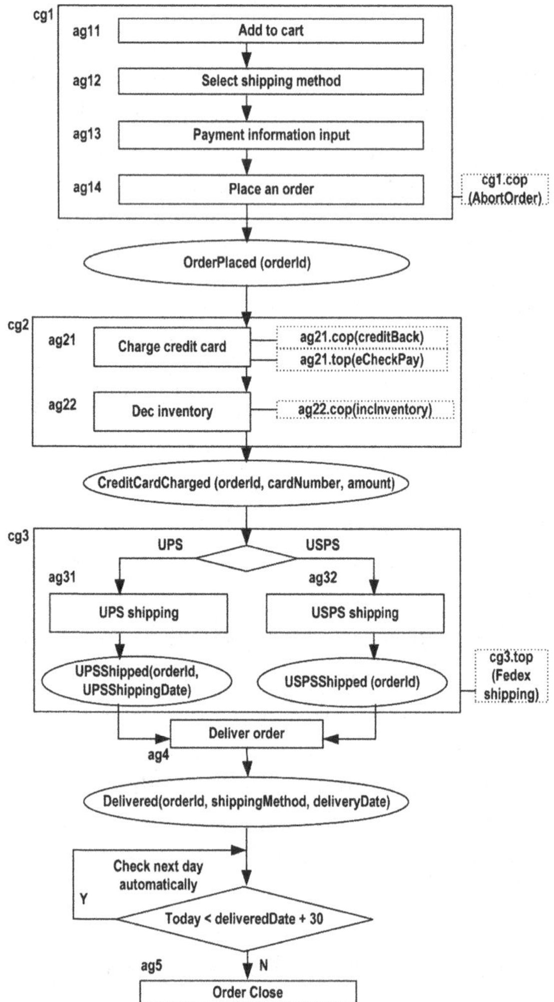

The CreditCardCharged AP has a post-condition that further guarantees the in-stock quantity must be in a reasonable status after the decInventory operation.

Component 3 (Conditional Rule): In Table 4, the CreditCardCharged AP has a conditional rule that sends a message notification for large charges. Since no pre or post condition is specified for the Delivered AP, only the conditional rule shippingRefund is evaluated. Assume the delivery method was overnight through UPS with an extra shipping fee. If UPS has delivered the item on time, then the Delivered AP is complete and execution continues. Otherwise, refundUPSShippingCharge is invoked to refund the extra fee while the main process execution continues. If backward recovery with retry takes place, it is possible that the process will execute the same conditional rule a second time. The action of the rule will only be executed during the retry process if the action was not executed the first time through.

A Closer Look at Recovery Actions

This section provides an informal illustration of the semantics of the APRollback, APRetry, and APCC recovery actions using the generic sample process in Figure 9 as well as the Online Shopping example in Figure 8. The remainder of this chapter does not elaborate on the use of conditional rules.

Table 4. AP rules in the online shopping process

Integration Rule	Conditional Rule
create rule QuantityCheck::pre **event:** ***OrderPlaced*** (orderId) **condition:** exists(select L.itemId from Inventory I, LineItem L where L.orderId=orderId and L.itemId=I.itemId and L.quantity>I.quantity) **action:** backOrderPurchase(orderId)	**create rule** Notice::cond **event:** ***CreditCardCharged*** (orderId, cardNumber, amount) **condition:** amount > $1000 **action:** highExpenseNotice(cardNumber)
create rule QuantityCheck::post **event:** ***CreditCardCharged*** (orderId, cardNumber, amount) **condition:** exists(select L.itemId from Inventory I, LineItem L where L.orderId=orderId and L.itemId=I.itemId and I.quantity<0) **action1**: APRetry **action2:** APRollback	**create rule** ShippingRefund::cond **event**: ***Delivered*** (orderId, shippingMethod, deliveryDate) **condition:** shippingMethod = UPS && deliveryDate != UPS-Shipped.UPSShippingDate+1 **action:** refundUPSShippingCharge(orderId)

Further details on conditional rules can be found in (Jin, 2004).

The process (cg_0) in Figure 9 is successively composed of composite groups cg_{01}, cg_{02} and cg_{03}, as well as atomic groups ag_{04} and ag_{05}. The assurance points AP1, AP2 and AP4 are inserted in the cg_0 scope following cg_{01}, cg_{02} and ag_{04}, respectively. AP3 is inserted in the cg_{03} scope after ag_{031}. As a result, AP3 is at a more deeply nested level than the other assurance points. In the following, assume that each AP in Figure 9 has an IR_{pre} and an IR_{post} rule. Recovery actions for failed pre and post conditions are considered first, followed by recovery actions for execution errors.

APRollback. Recall that APRollback is used to logically reverse the current state of the entire process using shallow and deep compensation.

Scenario 1 (APRollback): Assume that the post-condition fails at AP4 in Figure 9 and that the action of IR_{post} is APRollback. Since APRollback is invoked, the process compensates all completed atomic and/or composite groups. The APRollback execution sequence is numbered in Figure 9. First the process invokes ag_{04}.cop to compensate ag_{04}. Second, the APRollback process will deep compensate ag_{031} by invoking ag_{031}.cop since 1) there is no shallow compensation for cg_{03} and 2) ag_{032} is non-critical and therefore has no compensating procedure. Finally, APRollback invokes shallow compensation cg_{02}.cop and cg01.cop.

The APRollback procedure is a standard way of using compensation in past work. The originality of the rollback process in this work is the way in which it is used together with APs in the retry and cascaded contingency process to support partial rollback together with forward recovery options.

APRetry. APRetry is used to recover to a specific AP and then retry the recovered atomic and/or composite groups. If the AP has an IR_{pre}, then the pre-condition will be re-examined. If the pre-condition fails, the action of the rule is executed, which either invokes an alternate execution path for forward recovery or a recovery procedure for backward recovery. By default APRetry will go to the most recent AP. APRetry can also include a parameter to indicate the AP that is the target of the recovery process.

Scenario 2 (APRetry-default): Assume that the post-condition fails at AP4 in Figure 10 and that the action of IR_{post} is APRetry. This action compensates to the most recent AP within the same scope by default. In Figure 10, APRetry first invokes ag_{04}.cop to compensate ag_{04} at step 1. The process then deep compensates cg_{03} by executing ag_{031}.cop at

Figure 9. Generic process: Scenario 1 (APRollback)

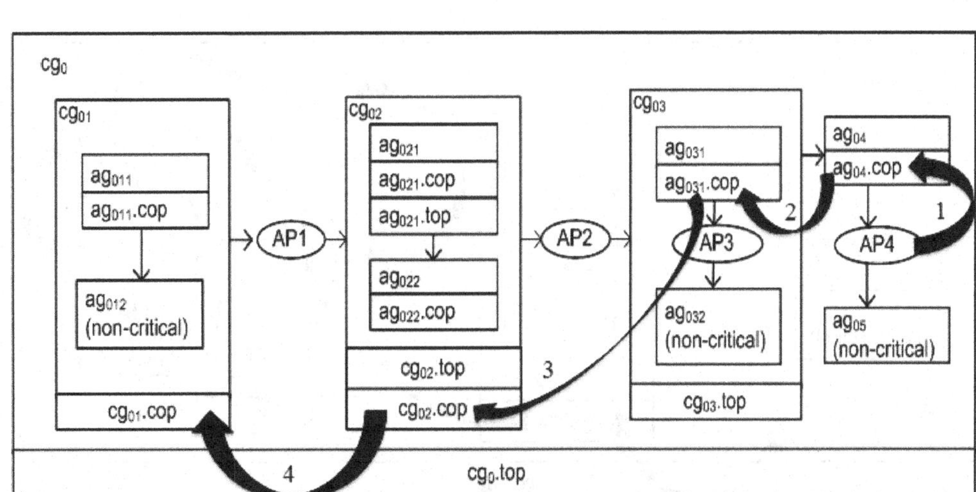

step 2. At this point, AP2 is reached and the pre-condition of IR_{pre} is re-evaluated shown as step 3. If the pre-condition fails, the process executes the recovery action of IR_{pre}. If the pre-condition is satisfied or if there is no IR_{pre}, then execution will resume again from cg_{03}. In this case, the process will reach AP4 a second time through steps 4, 5 and 6, where the post-condition is checked once more. If failure occurs for the second time, the second action defined on the rule is executed rather than the first action. If a second action is not specified, the default action will be APRollback as steps 7 through 10.

Scenario 3 (APRetry-parameterized): As shown in Figure 11, now assume that the action of the pre-condition for AP4 is parameterized as APRetry(AP1), indicating that the retry activity should rollback to AP1. The process will first compensate the procedure back to the point of AP1 through steps 1, 2, 3 and 4, ignoring all APs in between. The process then resumes execution from AP1 at step 5.

APCascadedContingency (APCC). The APCC process provides a way of searching for contingent procedures in a nested composition structure, searching backwards through the hierarchical process structure. When a pre or post condition fails in a nested composite group, APCC will compensate its way to the next outer layer of the nested structure. If the compensated composite group has a contingent procedure, it will be executed. Furthermore, if there is an AP with a pre-condition before the composite group, the pre-condition will be evaluated before executing the contingency. If the pre-condition fails, the recovery action of IR_{pre} will be executed instead of executing the contingency. If there is no contingency or if the contingency fails, APCC continues by compensating the current composite group back to the next outer layer of the nested structure and repeating the process described above.

Scenario 4 (APCC): Assume that the post-condition fails at AP4 in Figure 9 and that the IR_{post} action is APCC. The process starts compensating until it reaches the parent layer. In this case, the process will reach the beginning of cg_0 after compensating the entire process through deep or shallow compensation through the same steps as shown in Figure 9. Since there is no AP before cg_0, cg_0.top is invoked.

Scenario 5 (APCC): Assume that the post-condition fails at AP3 in Figure 12 and that the IR_{post} action is APCC. Since AP3 is in cg_{03}, which is nested in cg_0, the APCC process will compensate back to the beginning of cg_{03}, executing ag_{031}.

Figure 10. Scenario 2 (APRetry-default)

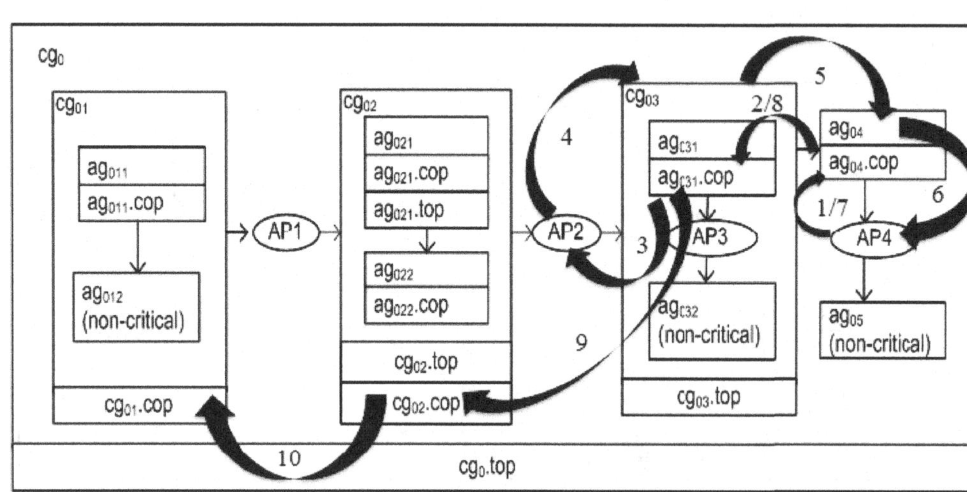

cop at step 1. The APCC process finds AP2 with an IR_{pre} rule for cg_{03} at step 2. As a result, the pre-condition will be evaluated before trying the contingency for cg_{03}. If there is no pre-condition or if the pre-condition is satisfied, then cg_{03}.top is executed at step 3 and the process continues, shown as step 4. Otherwise, the recovery action of IR_{pre} for AP2 will be executed and the process quits APCC mode. If cg_{03}.top fails at step 3 then the process will still be under APCC mode, where the process will keep compensating through steps 5 and 6 until it reaches the cg_0 layer, where cg_0.top is executed at step 7.

When process execution encounters an internal error, the running operation first tries the most immediate contingency. If the contingency succeeds, the recovery is complete and the execution continues. If the contingency fails or if there is no immediate contingency, then APCC mode is invoked.

Scenario 6 (Online Shopping Example - Failure at ChargeCreditCard): Returning to the Online Shopping Example of Figure 8, assume the process fails while executing chargeCreditCard. The process then executes the contingency ag_{21}.top (eCheckPay). If ag_{21}.top fails, then APCC process begins, during which the process reaches the orderPlaced AP, where the pre-condition of the AP is re-checked (rule QuantityCheck in Table 1). If the pre-condition is violated, the action backOrder is invoked, which means there are not enough goods in stock.

Scenario 7 (Online Shopping Example – Failure at UPShipping): From Figure 8, assume the process fails on the operation UPSShipping. Since there is no immediate contingency, the process invokes the APCC process, rolling back to the CreditCardCharged AP at the outer level. Since there is no pre-condition defined at the CreditCardCharged AP, the contingency cg_3.top (FedexShipping) will be executed. If cg_3.top fails, the process will be still under APCC mode, compensating its way back to the beginning of the transaction.

PETRI NET FORMALIZATION OF SERVICE COMPOSITION WITH ASSURANCE POINTS AND RECOVERY ACTIONS

In this section, the formal execution semantics of the web service composition and recovery model with assurance points and integration rules is presented using Petri Nets. Petri Nets have been useful for modeling systems that demonstrate

Figure 11. Scenario 3 (APRetry-parameterized)

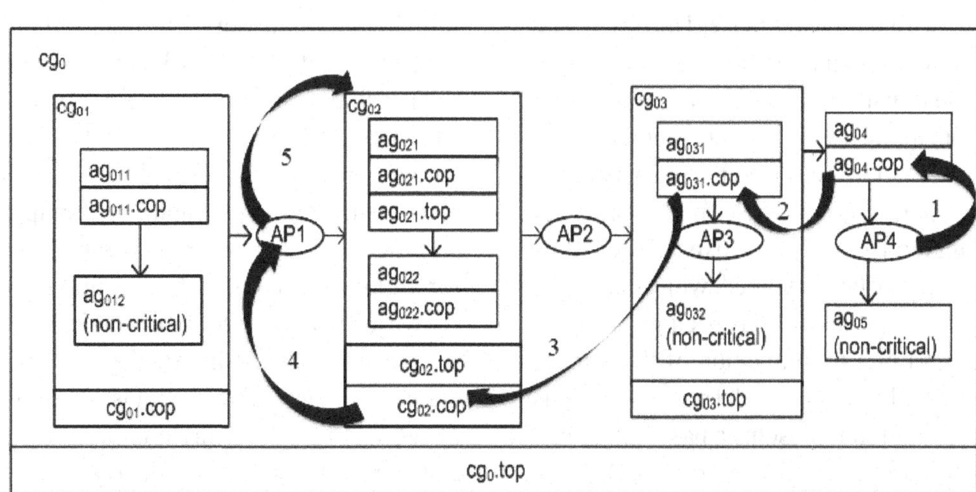

Figure 12. Scenario 5 (APCC)

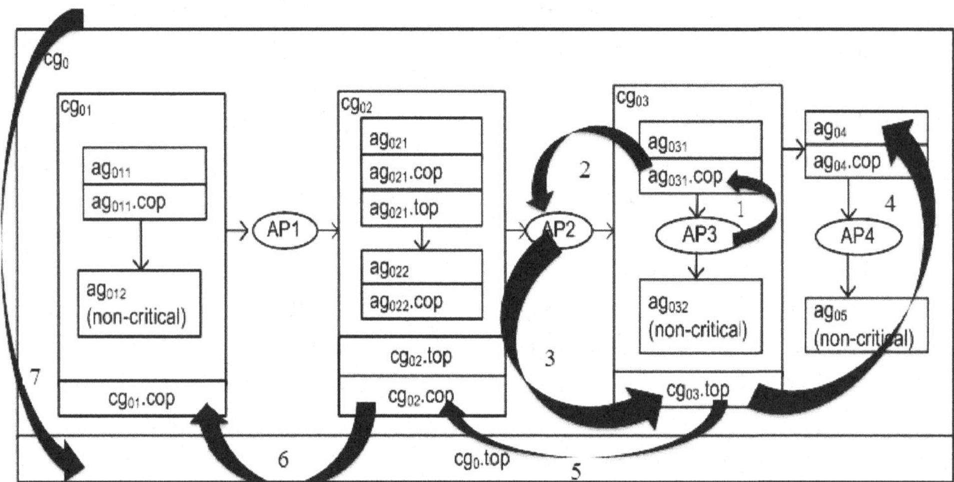

control flow behavior (Peterson, 1981). Van der Aalst (1998) was one of the first to use Petri Nets to represent workflow management systems. Desel (2005) discusses process modeling with Petri Nets. Stahl (2005) also gives the complete Petri Net semantics for the Business Process Execution Language for Web Services (BPEL).

General Approach

A Petri Net (Murata, 2002) is a directed, connected, and bipartite graph in which nodes represent places and transitions, and tokens occupy places. A directed arc in a Petri Net connects a place to a transition or a transition to a place. The places that have arcs running to a transition are called input places of the transition. The places that have arcs coming from a transition are called output places of the transition. A transition is enabled when each of its input places has at least one token. After firing a transition, exactly one token at each of its input places has been consumed, while one token at each of its output places has been generated.

In the Petri Net formalization of the service composition and recovery model presented in this chapter, a transition represents a basic task, such as invoking an operation of a process. A place represents an execution status, a condition, or a resource. A token at the place of an execution status corresponds to the thread of control in the flow. A token at the place of a condition indicates that some condition regarding the current status of a process instance is true. A token at the place of a resource indicates that the resource is (or in some cases is not) available. For example, in the service composition model, compensation is a resource associated with an atomic or composite group within a process, so resource places are used to indicate whether compensation is or is not available for a given group.

Before discussing the details of the Petri Net formalization, the notation used in the Petri Net diagrams is introduced. All transitions are labeled as Tn inside a transition node. Each place in a Petri Net has a short phrase beside the place node. Short phrases are used to label places due to limited room in the Petri Net graph. The complete set of all places that appear in the graphs that follow for atomic and composite execution groups are shown in Table 5, while Table 6 indicates the places that are associated with graphs for APs. The left column of each table contains the short phrase of each place. The middle column contains the actual meaning of places. The right-most column

Table 5. Places in an execution group Petri net

SHORT PHRASE	MEANING	TYPE
A	Activate	Status
S	Group executes successfully	Status
US	Group executes unsuccessfully	Status
AP_CC	AP_Cascaded Contingency	Status
AP_RB	AP_Rollback	Status
AP_RT	AP_Retry	Status
C_A	Compensation activates	Status
Running	Operation executing	Status
Aborted	Operation aborted	Status
T_Running	Contingency executing	Status
C_Running	Shallow compensation executing	Status
C_Error	Shallow compensation failed	Status
C_S	Compensation succeeds	Status
Critical	Critical atomic group	Resource
N_ Critical	Non-critical atomic group	Resource
T	Contingency exists	Resource
N_T	Contingency does not exist	Resource
Shallow_C	Shallow compensation exists	Resource
N_ Shallow_C	Shallow compensation does not exist	Resource

indicates the type of the place, which is specified as status, condition, or resource.

Atomic Group

An Atomic group is the most basic executable unit in the model. An atomic group contains an operation, an optional compensation, and an optional contingency. Figure 13 depicts the execution semantics for an atomic group as a Petri Net. All places standing on the lines of the box around a Petri Net represent the execution status, conditions, and resources of the atomic group.

An atomic group is activated when a token appears at place A. By firing transition T1, the operation of the atomic group is invoked, indicated by the place labeled Running. If the operation succeeds, the atomic group is finished successfully by marking place S through transition T2. Otherwise, the operation execution fails and must be aborted to place Aborted by transition T3. If an execution error occurs, the process will first try the immediate contingency if it is available. Places T and N_T are two resource places that represent the availability or non-availability, respectively, of an immediate contingency. If place T and aborted are marked, transition T4 is enabled, which means the immediate contingency is available. By firing T4, the immediate contingency is running. Note that place T is a resource place, therefore after firing T4, a token must be returned to place T. If the immediate contingency succeeds, transition T7 fires and then place S (successful) is marked. If the immediate contingency fails or does not exist, the APCC mode is triggered to cascade the search for contingencies to outer levels of the process. Transition T5 depicts contingency failure by marking places AP_CC (cas-

Table 6. Places in an AP Petri net

SHORT PHRASE	MEANING	TYPE
A	Activate	Status
P	AP Passed	Status
ALT	Alternative Process	Status
AP_CC	AP_Cascaded Contingency	Status
AP_RB	AP_Rollback	Status
AP_RT	AP_Retry	Status
APCC_PRE	Pre-condition re-check (AP-CC)	Status
APCC_P	Pre-condition re-check passed (AP-CC)	Status
APRT_PRE	Pre-condition re-check (AP-Retry)	Status
APRT_P	Pre-condition re-check passed (AP-Retry)	Status
POST_VIO_F	First time post-condition violation	Condition
PRE_VIO_F	First time pre-condition violation	Condition
POST_VIO_S	Second time post-condition violation	Condition
PRE_VIO_S	Second time pre-condition violation	Condition
POST	Post condition exists	Resource
N_POST	Post condition does not exist	Resource
PRE	Pre condition exists	Resource
N_PRE	Pre condition does not exist	Resource
POST-Checking	Checking post condition	Status
PRE-Checking	Checking pre condition	Status
POST-Passed	Post condition passed	Status
Pre-Passed	Pre condition passed	Status
POST-Violated	Post condition violated	Status
Pre-Violated	Pre condition violated	Status

caded contingency) and US (unsuccessful). Similarly, if places N_T and aborted are marked, transition T6 is enabled which represents the case that the immediate contingency does not exist.

The discussion above represents the normal atomic group invocation semantics. The normal atomic group invocation starts from place A and ends at either place S or places US and AP_CC. Now consider the compensation semantics of an atomic group. In Figure 13, if place C_A (compensation activity) is marked, the atomic group needs to be compensated. Here, four resource places are introduced. Place Critical represents that the atomic group is critical, whereas place N-Critical indicates that the atomic group is not critical. Place Shallow-C represents that the pre-defined compensation procedure is available, whereas place N-Shallow-C indicates that compensation is not available. There are four different atomic compensation cases in Figure 13:

- **Compensation is available and the atomic group is critical:** Transition T8 fires. After invoking compensation, two different situations may exist:
    - **Compensation succeeds:** Transition T9 fires and then place C_S is

Figure 13. Petri net of atomic group

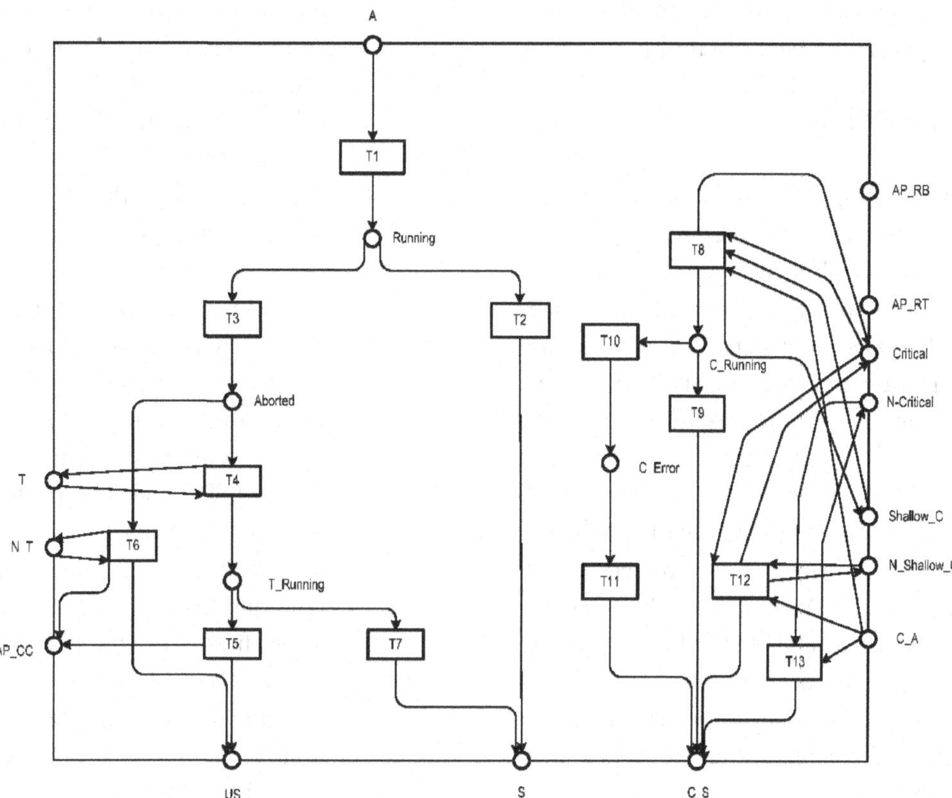

marked, indicating that compensation is successful.

- ◦ **Compensation fails:** Transitions T10 fires marking the C_Error status, indicating that compensation has failed. Then transition T11 fires which represents invoking DE-Rollback or service reset (involving human activity) to reset the error. Finally, place C_S is marked.

- **Compensation is unavailable and the atomic group is critical:** Transition T12 fires, which represents invoking DE-Rollback or service reset. Then place C_S is marked.
- **The atomic group is non-critical:** If the atomic group is non-critical, the process just ignores the compensation request by firing transition T13 and marking place C_S.

To preserve the group condition consistency, if a token at a resource place is consumed after firing a transition, a new token must be returned to the resource place immediately after the transition. For example, in Figure 13, firing transition T8 consumes three tokens at places C_A, Shallow_C and Critical respectively. After T8, two new tokens are generated back to places Shallow_C and Critical, respectively, as they are resource places. One might question the situation that a token appears at place C_A before the atomic group finishes successfully. Such a situation will never happen, however, since the compensation of a completed group can only be caused by an error that occurs in the remainder of the process. Therefore, the place C_A can only be marked by transitions after the completion of the current group. The section below on Deep and Shallow Compensation will discuss compensation issues for multiple groups.

Assurance Points

Before describing the semantics of a composite group, this section first describes the semantics of APs. Figure 14 gives the Petri Net for AP execution semantics. There are four resource places. Places POST and N_POST represent the presence and absence of a post-condition respectively. Similarly, places PRE and N_PRE represent the presence and absence of a pre-condition, respectively. In addition, places POST_VIO_F and PRE_VIO_F are condition places indicating that the post and pre conditions have never been violated before. Thus, places POST_VIO_F and PRE_VIO_F each must have a default token before execution. In the same manner, places POST_VIO_S and PRE_VIO_S are the conditions indicating that the post and pre conditions have been violated once, respectively.

A token at place A activates the AP. Depending on the status of the condition and resource places, different execution cases exist:

- **Post and pre conditions both exist:**
    - **Post and pre conditions are both satisfied:** Firing transition T1 and T2 represents that the post-condition is satisfied. Firing transition T4 and T6 similarly indicates that the pre-condition is satisfied. Finally, transition T8 fires and place P is marked, indicating that the AP was successfully executed (passed) with all relevant conditions satisfied.
    - **Post condition violated:** Transition T1 fires to check the post-condition. If the post-condition is violated, transition T3 is fired to mark the status place Post-Violated. If place POST_VIO_F is marked, indicating that this is the first time to execute the post condition, then either transition T11, T12, T13 or T14 will be fired to invoke the first action of the rule, depending on the rule action specification. POST_VIO_S is then marked. If place POST_VIO_S is already marked, indicating that this is the second time to execute the post condition, then either transition T15 or T16 will be fired to execute the second action defined in the rule.
    - **Post condition passed and pre condition violated:** Firing transition T1 and T2 that the post-condition is satisfied. Then transition T4 fires to check the pre-condition. If the pre-condition is violated, transition T7 is fired to mark the status place Pre-Violated. If place PRE_VIO_F is marked, indicating that this is the first violation of the pre-condition, then either transition T17, T18, T19 or T20 will be fired to invoke the first action of the rule and PRE_VIO_S is marked. If place PRE_VIO_S is already marked, indicating that this is the second violation of the pre-condition, then either transition T21 or T22 will be fired depending on the second action defined in the rule.
- **Only post condition exists:** Firing transition T1 checks the post-condition.
    - **Post condition is satisfied:** If the post-condition is satisfied, transition T2 fires and status place Post-Passed is marked. Because of the absence of a pre-condition, transition T9 fires and then place P is marked.
    - **Post condition is violated:** Transition T1 fires to check the post-condition. If the post-condition is violated, transition T3 is fired to mark the status place Post-Violated. If place

Figure 14. Petri net of assurance point

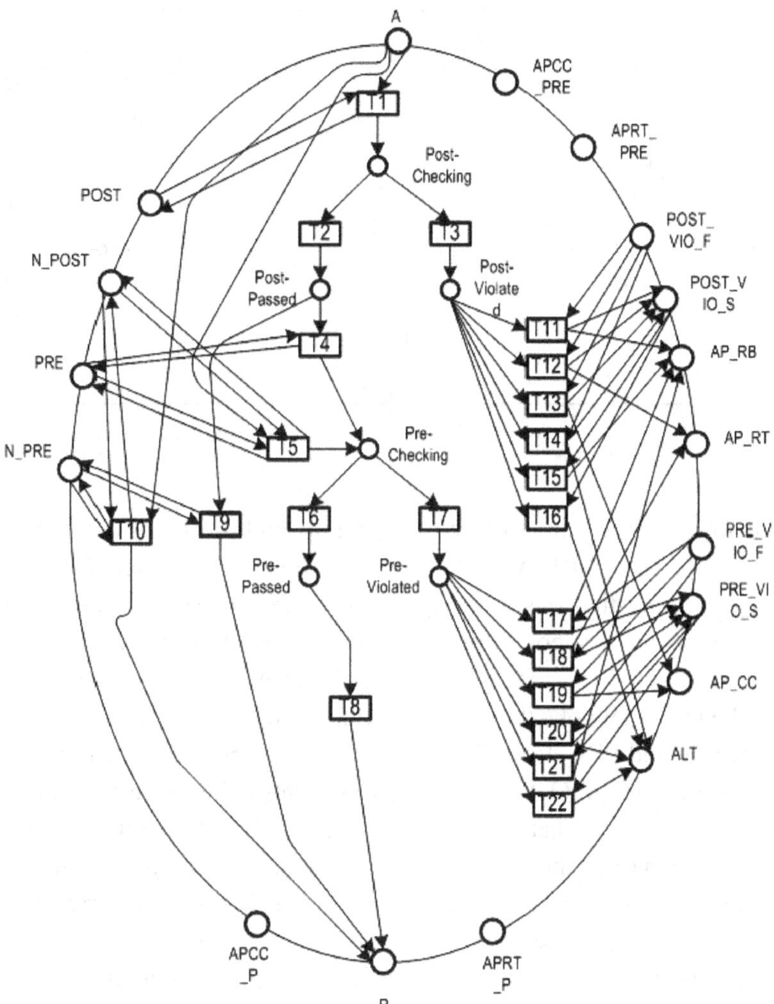

POST_VIO_F is marked, indicating that this is the first time to execute the post condition, then either transition T11, T12, T13 or T14 will be fired to invoke the first action of the rule, depending on the rule action specification. POST_VIO_S is then marked. If place POST_VIO_S is already marked, indicating that this is the second time to execute the post condition, then either transition T15 or T16 will be fired to execute the second action defined in the rule.

- **Only pre condition exists:** Because of the absence of the post-condition, when the AP is activated, transition T5 will be fired to check the pre-condition directly.
    - **Pre condition is satisfied**: If the pre-condition is satisfied, transitions T6 and T8 will be fired successively. Finally, place P is marked.
    - **Pre condition is violated:** If the pre-condition is violated, transition

Figure 15. Petri net of composite group with APs

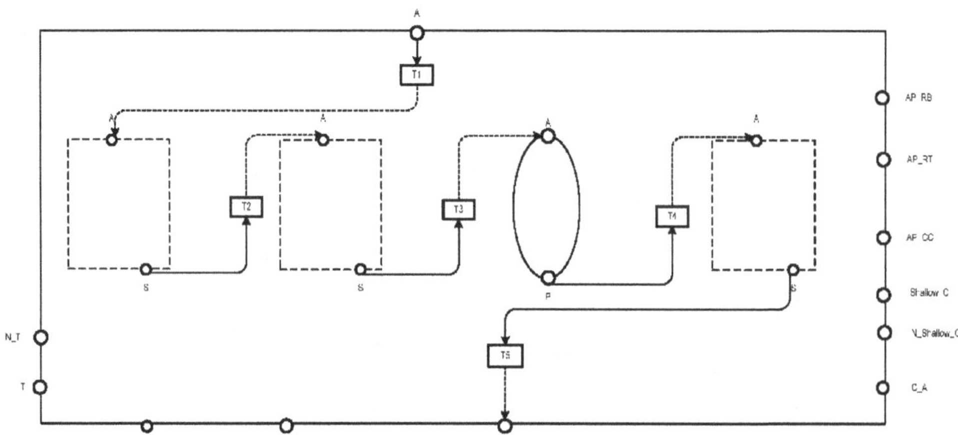

T7 is fired to mark the status place Pre-Violated. If place PRE_VIO_F is marked, indicating that this is the first violation of the pre-condition, then either transition T17, T18, T19 or T20 will be fired to invoke the first action of the rule and PRE_VIO_S is marked. If place PRE_VIO_S is already marked, indicating that this is the second violation of the pre-condition, then either transition T21 or T22 will be fired depending on the second action defined in the rule.

- **Post and pre condition do not exist:** After place A is marked, transition T10 fires and then place P is marked.

Note that there are four unlinked status places in Figure 14: APCC_PRE, APRT_PRE, APCC_P and APRT_P. These status places are relevant to the semantics of cascaded contingency and retry actions, which will be addressed in following sections.

Hierarchical Process Composition

In the service composition and recovery model, a composite group is composed of two or more atomic and/or composite groups and can also have optional compensation and contingency procedures. Clearly, a process under this model may contain multiple groups that are embedded at different levels. To represent the hierarchical model, a hierarchical approach is taken to the use of Petri Nets. Specifically, a dashed-line quadrilateral represents either an atomic or a composite group. A dashed-arc connecting a transition and a place represents repeating the same token movement pattern described at the current level. Furthermore, all dashed-line atomic and composite groups have the same places standing on the lines as introduced in Figure 13 and in Figure 15. However, to make the graphs concise, the unlinked places are omitted in hierarchical representations. APs that appear in hierarchical representations also omit unlinked places. Finally, to easily explain the semantics of the hierarchical organization of the diagrams, two group levels are defined. L_n is the outer level defined by a solid-line. L_{n+1} is the level of the inner dashed-line groups. For example, in Figure 15, the outer solid-line group is at level L_n and all inner dashed-line groups, as well as the inner AP, are at level L_{n+1}.

Figure 16. Petri net of deep compensation

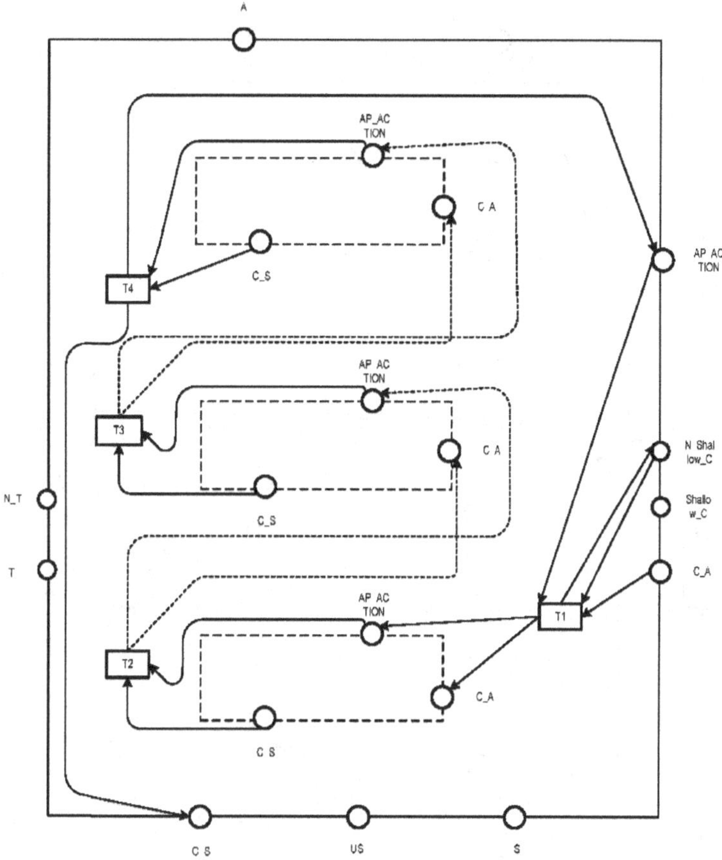

Composite Group with Assurance Points

The Petri Net for normal execution semantics of a composite group with APs is shown in Figure 15. A composite group may contain multiple groups and APs. All activities in a composite group are executed sequentially. Therefore, the normal execution semantics expressed in Figure 15 are straightforward. When a token appears at place A at level L_n, transition T1 fires to activate the first activity at the inner level L_{n+1}. Upon completion of the first inner activity, a transition T2 fires and the next activity is activated. In Figure 15, an AP is invoked after one of the atomic (or composite) groups. When place P at the AP at level L_{n+1} is marked, the AP is passed and the inner execution continues. Finally, after the last inner activity finishes, a transition fires and then place S at level L_n is marked. It is important to emphasize that in Figure 15, the Petri Net only shows the token movement pattern of the normal execution semantics of a composite group. The first activity in a composite group can be either an AP, an atomic group, or a composite group. However, no matter what activities a composite group contains, the activities are executed sequentially.

Shallow and Deep Compensation

The semantics of deep and shallow compensation are shown in Figure 16 and Figure 17, respec-

Figure 17. Petri net of shallow compensation

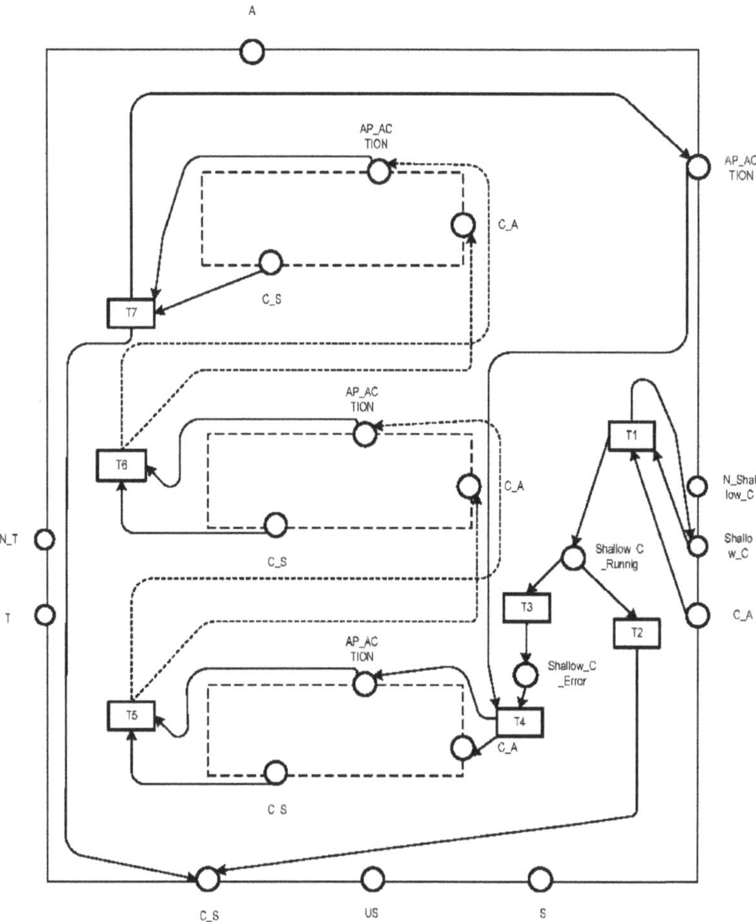

tively. The special place AP_ACTION is also introduced as a short hand notation for recovery actions. Because compensation is invoked under either AP-RB (rollback), AP-RT (retry), or AP-CC (cascaded contingency) mode, we introduce place AP_ACTION in Figures 16 and 17, representing either place AP_RB, AP_RT or AP_CC, since a process instance can only be under one of these recovery modes at any given time. So in Figures 16 and 17, places AP_ACTION at level L_n and L_{n+1} must represent the same mode status. For example, if in one scenario, place AP_ACTION represents AP_RB in Figure 16 at level L_n, all places AP_ACTION at level L_{n+1} must also represent AP_RB.

First consider deep compensation. Deep compensation is invoked directly when a composite group has no shallow compensation. The invocation of deep compensation is indicated by firing transition T1 in Figure 16. After firing T1, the token at the resource place N_Shallow_C at level L_n is consumed but also immediately returned. Also, the token at place AP_ACTION at level L_n is consumed and the places AP_ACTION and C_A at last inner group at level L_{n+1} are marked. Afterward, all groups at level L_{n+1} are backward compensated one by one through transitions T2 and T3. After place C_S at the first inner group at level L_{n+1} is marked, transition T4 is enabled to finish the compensation of the current level.

The deep compensation ends when places C_S and AP_ACTION at level L_n are marked.

In Figure 17, the semantics of shallow compensation is presented. Shallow compensation invokes a pre-defined procedure to compensate the entire composite group rather than executing compensation for each group within the composite group. However, if shallow compensation fails, deep compensation is initiated. Firing transition T1 indicates the invocation of the shallow compensation procedure. If the execution of shallow compensation succeeds, place C_S at level L_n is marked by firing transition T2. Then the shallow compensation ends. Otherwise, transition T3 fires and the status place Shallow_C_Error is marked. To complete the compensation, deep compensation takes place by firing transition T4. Through transitions T5, T6 and T7, the deep compensation semantics is performed. Finally, places C_S and AP_ACTION at level L_n are marked.

Note that during either shallow or deep compensation, APs are ignored. Also, if the dashed-line quadrilateral represents an atomic group, compensation semantics defined in Figure 13 takes effect. If the dashed-line quadrilateral represents a composite group, either shallow or deep compensation invokes depending on the availability of the shallow compensation procedure.

AP-Rollback

AP-Rollback mode is triggered when a status place AP_RB at an AP is marked. As shown in Figure 18, transition T1 fires to begin the AP-Rollback mode at level L_{n+1}. The purpose of AP-Rollback is to recover the overall process. Thus, all completed groups need to be compensated under AP-Rollback mode. Through transitions T2 and T3, all completed groups at level L_{n+1} are compensated. When the first group at level L_{n+1} is compensated, transition T4 fires and the AP-Rollback mode is propagated to level L_n by marking the status places AP_RB and C_S at level L_n. Then, the same AP-Rollback semantics executed at level L_{n+1} will take effect at level L_n to further rollback the overall process. Note that during the backward recovery, the status place AP_RB at a completed group is marked when the group is compensating.

AP-Retry

When a status place AP_RT at an AP is marked, AP-Retry mode is triggered. Figure 19 presents the semantics of the default AP-Retry mode, which recovers the process back to the most recent AP and checks the pre-condition before the re-execution. In Figure 19, transition T1 fires to start the recovery. Similar to AP-Rollback, the status place

Figure 18. Petri net of AP-rollback

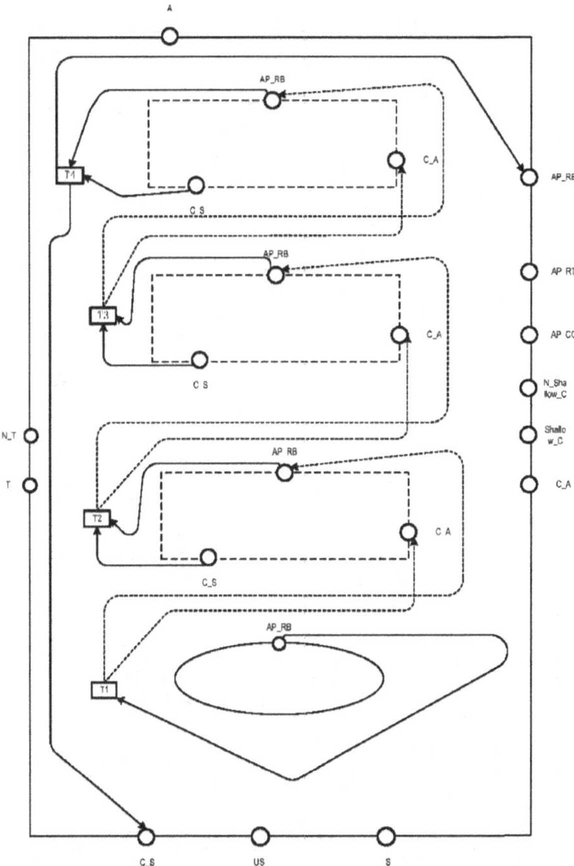

AP_RT at a completed group is marked when the group is compensating. When the group just after the most recent AP is compensated, transition T3 fires and the place APRT_PRE at the most recent AP is marked. Then the pre-condition defined at the most recent AP is re-checked. If the pre-condition is satisfied, the status place APRT_P is marked and transition T4 is enabled to start the retry process. If the pre-condition fails, another action will take place depending on the action specified in the rule.

Figure 20 presents the semantics of re-checking the pre-condition under AP-Retry mode. In Figure 20, if the pre-condition exists, transition T1 fires. If the pre-condition is satisfied, the APRT_P is marked through transitions T2 and T3. If pre-condition is violated, transition T4 fires to mark the status place Pre-Violated. At this point, two different situations can occur. If the place PRE_VIO_F is marked, either transition T5, T6, T7 or T8 is fired to invoke the first action and then PRE_VIO_S is marked. If the place PRE_VIO_S is already marked, either transition T9 or T10 will be fired depending on the second action defined in the rule. In both cases, the process quits AP-Retry mode and enters a new mode that depends on the rule action.

Figure 19. Petri net of AP-retry (default)

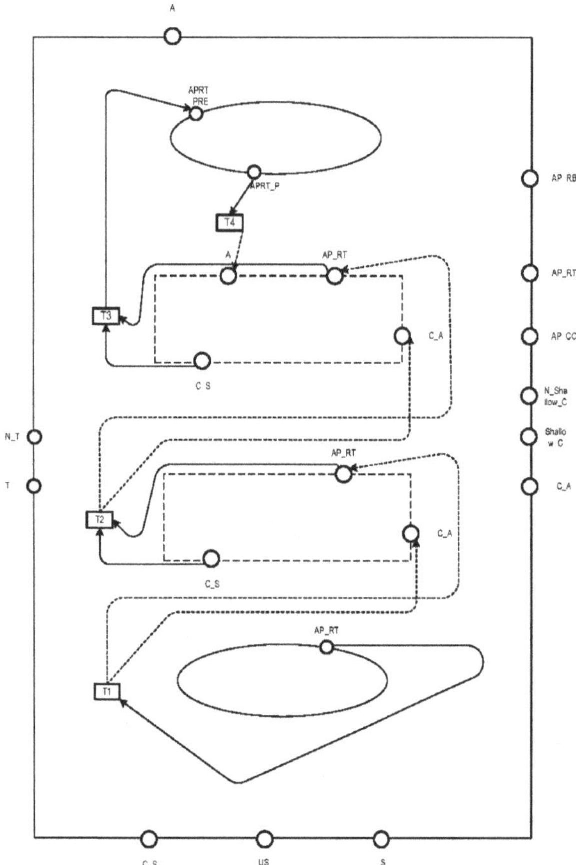

Recall that the recovery process only allows AP-Retry to occur within one composite group. For example, AP-Retry only affects level L_{n+1} in Figure 19 and does not extend to level L_n. For the Petri Net of the parameterized AP-Retry, refer to (Gao, L. & Urban, S., 2010).

AP-Cascaded Contingency

Two situations will trigger the AP-CC mode. One is when the process encounters an execution error. The other is when a post or pre condition violation invokes the AP-CC action. Furthermore, if there is an AP just before the failed group, then the pre-condition will be checked before executing the contingency. As a result, there are several different execution scenarios for AP-CC mode. Only one case is shown in Figure 21. All other cases have similar Petri Nets, which can be found in (Gao, L. et al., 2010).

Figure 21 presents the semantics of the AP-CC mode triggered by an execution error. An AP exists just before the failed group. If any error happens in a group at level L_{n+1}, the places US and AP_CC at the failed group are marked. This means the failed group has already tried the possible contingency at level L_{n+1}, but failed. To maximize forward recovery, the process attempts to execute the contingency at the outer level. First, transitions T1 and T2 fire to compensate all completed groups before the failed group at level L_{n+1}. After the first completed group at level L_{n+1} is finally compen-

Figure 20. Petri net of re-checking pre-condition (AP-Retry)

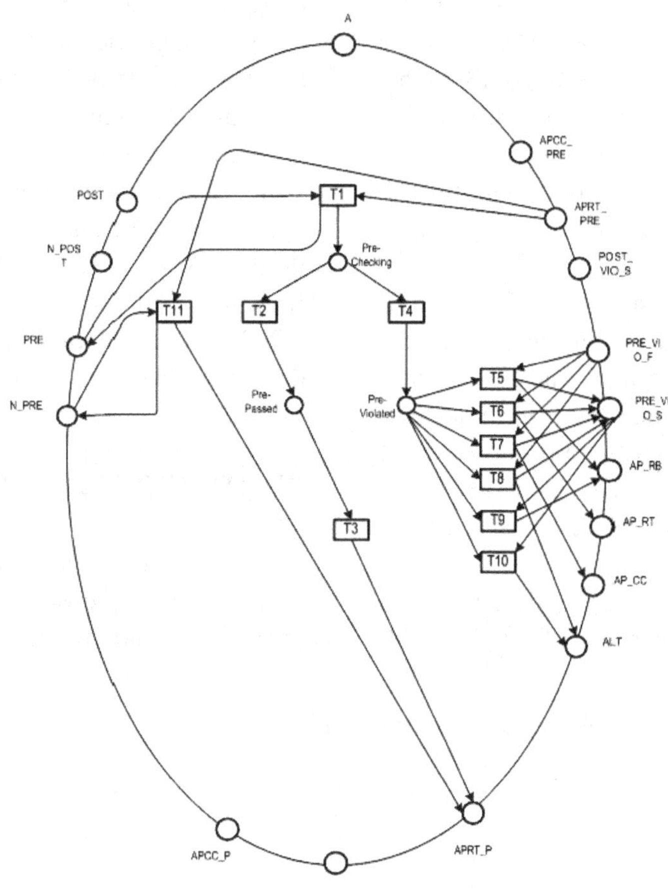

Figure 21. Petri net of AP-CC (AP exists before group)

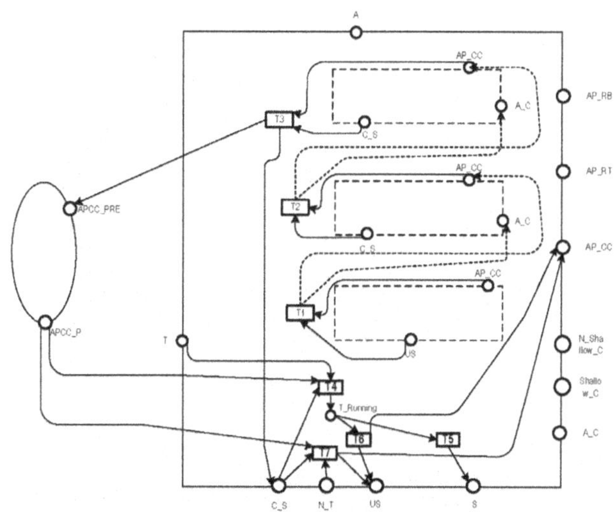

sated, transition T3 fires and the place C_S is marked. Since there is an AP before the compensated group at level L_n, the place APCC_PRE at the AP is marked as well after firing T3 so that the pre-condition is re-evaluated before trying the contingency at level L_n. If the pre-condition is satisfied, either transition T4 or T7 will fire depending on the availability of the contingency at level L_n.

If the contingency exists, there are two possible cases to consider. If the contingent procedure is successful, transition T5 fires. The process quits AP-CC mode by marking the place S at level L_n. If the contingent procedure is unsuccessful, transition T6 fires. The process is still under AP-CC mode by marking the places US and AP_CC at level L_n.

If the contingency at level L_n does not exist, transition T7 fires and the places US and AP_CC at level L_n are marked directly. The unsuccessful result will cause the process to search and execute other contingencies at the outer levels following the same semantics described in Figure 21.

Figure 22 presents the semantics of re-checking the pre-condition under AP-CC mode. This is the same semantics as in Figure 20, except that the AP logic starts at the place APCC_PRE and ends at the place APCC_P if the pre-condition is satisfied. If the pre-condition is violated, the process quits AP-CC mode and enters a new recovery mode depending on the action of the pre-condition rule.

PROTOTYPE IMPLEMENTATION

A prototype execution environment has been developed to demonstrate the extended service composition and recovery model with APs and

Figure 22. Petri net of re-checking pre-condition (AP-CC)

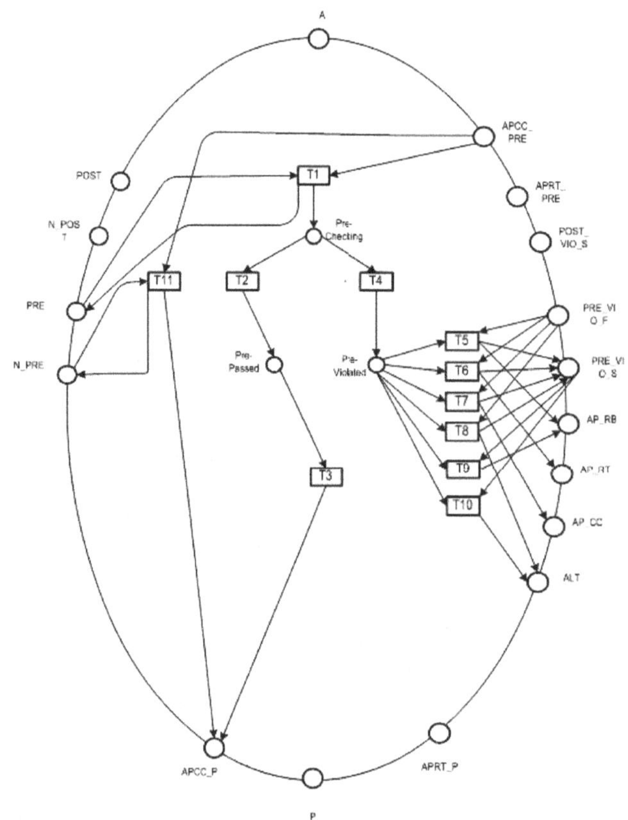

integration rules. The execution environment does not directly use BPEL since the broader scope of the research is addressing techniques for decentralized data dependency analysis among distributed Process Execution Agents (PEXAs) (Urban, Liu & Gao, 2009). Existing BPEL engines do not provide the flexibility needed to experiment with this form of decentralized communication among process execution engines. BPEL also has limitations with respect to demonstrating the functionality described in this chapter as outlined in the following section that addresses a comparison of the assurance point concept to the BPEL fault handler. The process specification framework, however, is based on BPEL using previous work with the Process Modeling Language (PML) described in (Ma, Urban, Xiao, & Dietrich, 2005).

The process specification framework uses a minimal set of activities, such as assign, invoke, and switch to illustrate the functionality of APs and the different forms of recovery. Figure 23 shows a sample process in XML to illustrate the syntax for defining atomic (<ag ...>) and composite (<cg ...>) groups with compensating (<cop ...>) and contingent (<top ...>) procedures. The syntax for APs and their parameters is also illustrated (<ap ...>). Integration rules are also specified using an XML format as shown in Figure 24

The parser for the XML Java binding process has been implemented in the execution engine using XMLBeans. For each activity defined in a process, a wrapper class has been developed that implements the semantics of the activity. AP data is stored in a db40 object-oriented database. The functionality described in this chapter has been fully developed to test and demonstrate all algorithms associated with the creation and use of APs, rules, and recovery procedures. The execution engine has also integrated the use of APs and recovery procedures into the <flowgroup> activity of BPEL to demonstrate how APs are used in the context of parallel execution threads. Discussion of the use of APs with the <flowgroup> activity, however, is beyond the scope of the current chapter.

Figure 23. PML activity syntax

```
<cg name= "cg0">
  :
  <ap name= "OrderPlacedAP">
     <apDataIn variable="orderId" />
  </ap>
  <cg name="cg2">
    <ag name = "ag21"
       <invoke name="chargeCreditCard" serviceName="chargeCreditCard"
        portType="cc:CreditCardPortType" operation="chargeCreditCard"
        inputVariable = "chargeCardInput"
        outputVariable = "chargeCardtOutput" />
      <top name="top21">
          <invoke name="eCheckPay" serviceName="eCheckPay"
          portType="cc:CreditCardPortType" operation="eCheckPay"
          inputVariable = "makePaymentInput"
          outputVariable = "makePaymentOutput" />
      </top>
      <cop name="cop21">
          <invoke name="creditBack" serviceName="creditBack"
          portType="cc:CreditCardPortType" operation=" creditBack"
          inputVariable = "makePaymentInput"
          outputVariable = "makeRefundOutput" />
      </cop>
    </ag>
    .
    .
    .
  </cg>
  <ap name= "creditCardChargedAP">
     <apDataIn variable="orderId" />
     <apDataIn variable="cardNumber" />
     <apDataIn variable="amount" />
  </ap>
  :
</cg>
```

COMPARISON TO THE BPEL FAULT HANDLER

This research has included a comparison of the AP model with the BPEL fault and compensation handlers. In BPEL, when a fault occurs, the fault handler attached to a scope catches the fault. The aim of the fault handler is to continue the process execution, which might require undoing certain actions already completed in the current scope. Since the compensation handler defines the semantics of undoing such changes, the fault handler

Figure 24. Integration rule syntax

```
<rules>
  :
<event ap="orderPlacedAP">
  <pre>
    <ecaRule>
      <condition name="QuantityCheck"
        <invoke name="checkQuantity" serviceName="ruleConditions"
          portType="rule:ruleConditionsPortType" operation="checkQuantity1"
          inputVariable="quantity" outputVariable="result" />
      </condition>

      <actions>
        <action name="backOrderPurchase">
          <invoke name="backOrderPurchase" serviceName="shopping"
          portType="sho:ShoppingPortType" operation="BackOrderPurchase"
          inputVariable="orderId" outputVariable="result" />
        </action>
      </actions>
    </ecaRule>
  </pre>
</event>
  :
</rules>
```

may start the compensation handler (Khalaf et al., 2009). Similar to our approach of deep and shallow compensation, the <compensate> activity does the compensation of the completed activities in the nested scopes, whereas, the <compensateScope> activity causes compensation of one single completed scope. If any of the handlers are not specified, then the default handler is assigned to each scope. Default compensation invokes the installed compensation handlers for all the inner scopes. When the default compensation is applied to a scope, the compensation handlers are executed in reverse order of completion of the scopes.

The work in (Khalaf et al., 2009) highlights two main problems with the fault and compensation mechanism in the current BPEL standard. In particular, compensation order can violate control link dependencies if control links cross the scope boundaries. In addition, high complexity of default compensation order can result due to default handler behavior. Like BPEL, the AP model also honors control links between peer-scopes. Unlike BPEL, however, the order of compensation is clear since the AP approach does not support control links between non-peer scopes, making the semantics of compensation in the AP approach unambiguous. In addition, the AP model supports a hierarchical structure during compensation as promoted in (Khalaf et al., 2009).

In general, the notion of compensation should also be capable of handling constraint violations (Coleman, 2005). Since BPEL's compensation handling mechanism through the <compensate> activity can only be called inside a fault handler, this limits the ability to call compensation outside of a fault handler. Thus, a fault has to occur to invoke a compensation procedure. In the case of the AP model, compensation can be invoked during normal execution (no error has yet occurred) when integration rules are not satisfied. This allows a flexible way to recover the process through compensation in response to constraint violations.

BPEL does not explicitly support a contingency feature other than fault, exception, and termination handlers. The designer is also responsible for complex fault handling logic, which, as pointed out in (Coleman, 2005; Khalaf et al., 2009), has the potential to increase complexity and create unexpected errors. The AP model provides explicit contingency activities so that forward recovery is possible. Compared to BPEL, the AP logic allows designers to have a clearer notion of how recovery actions take place and at the same time provide flexibility through different recovery actions depending upon the status of execution and user-defined integration rule conditions.

SUMMARY AND FUTURE DIRECTIONS

This research has defined a hierarchical service composition model that provides multi-level protection against service execution failure by using compensation and contingency at different composition granularity levels. The model has been enhanced with the concept of assurance points and integration rules to provide a flexible way of checking constraints and responding to execution failures. As a combined logical and physical checkpoint, an AP is used for user-defined consistency checking, invoking integration rules that check pre and post conditions at different points in the execution process. The unique aspect of APs is that they provide intermediate rollback points when failures occur that allow a process to be compensated to a specific AP for the purpose of rechecking pre-conditions before retry attempts. APs also support a dynamic backward recovery process, known as cascaded contingency, for hierarchically nested processes in an attempt to recover to a previous AP that can be used to invoke contingent procedures or alternate execution paths for failure of a nested process. As a result, the assurance point approach provides flexibility with respect to the combined use of backward and forward recovery options. Petri Nets have been used to define the semantics of the assurance point approach to service composition and recovery.

There are several directions for future research. As described in the implementation section, assurance points and the recovery actions described in this chapter have already been extended to support parallel execution threads within a process. We are currently in the process of extending the Petri Net formalization to describe the behavior of APs and recovery actions for parallel execution groups. We are also evaluating other high-level Petri Net theories, such as colored Petri Nets (Jensen, 1987), timed Petri Nets (Ramchandani, 1973), and the Workflow Net approach of Van Del Aalst (2005) to provide a more concise approach to description of the model.

Our research is also extending the concept of integration rules in several ways. One extension involves the use of invariant rules. Invariants provide a way to monitor the status of a condition in between two different APs to provide a more optimistic way for concurrent processes to access the same data. When a condition is violated, a process can be interrupted to invoke recovery procedures. Our initial results with the use of invariants are described in (Courter, 2010; Urban, Courter, Gao, and Shuman, 2011). We are also extending integration rules to the concept of application exception rules (AERs). AERs allow a process to be interrupted by an external event and to respond to the event depending on the execution status of the process as determined by the most recent AP that has been executed. We are also integrating the use of AERs with the data dependency analysis algorithms in (Urban, Liu, and Gao, 2009; Urban, Liu, and Gao, 2011) so that the recovery process can identify data dependencies among concurrently executing processes and use AERs as a means to communicate with the dependent processes of a recovered process about the need to check consistency constraints and possibly invoke recovery procedures.

ACKNOWLEDGMENT

This research has been partially supported by NSF Grant CCF-0820152. Opinions, findings, conclusions or recommendations expressed in this chapter are those of the author(s) and do not necessarily reflect the views of NSF.

REFERENCES

Alonso, G., Hagen, C., Schek, H.-J., & Tresh, M. (1997). Towards a platform for distributed application development. In Dogac, A., Kalinichenko, L., Ozsu, M., & Sheth, A. (Eds.), *Workflow management systems and interoperability*. Springer Verlag.

Baresi, L., Guinea, S., & Pasquale, L. (2007). Self-healing BPEL processes with dynamo and the JBoss rule engine. *ACM Int. Workshop on Eng. of Software Services for Pervasive Environments*, (pp. 11-20). New York, NY: ACM.

Bennett, B., Hahm, B., Leff, A., Mikalsen, T., Rasmus, K., Rayfield, J., & Rouvellou, I. (2000). A distributed object-oriented framework to offer transactional support for long running business processes. *Proc. of Int. Conf. on Distributed Systems Platforms Middleware.*

Bhiri, S., Perrin, O., & Godart, C. (2005). Ensuring required failure atomicity of composite web services. *Proc. of the 14th Int. Conf. on the World Wide Web.*

Blake, L. (2005). *Design and implementation of delta-enabled grid services*. MS Thesis, Department of Computer Science and Engineering, Arizona State University.

Brambilla, M., Ceri, S., Comai, S., & Tziviskou, C. (2005). Exception handling in workflow-driven web applications. *Proc. of the14th Int. Conf. on World Wide Web*, (pp. 170-179). New York: ACM.

Charfi, A., & Mezini, M. (2006). Aspect-oriented workflow languages. *Lecture Notes in Computer Science*, *4275*, 183. doi:10.1007/11914853_12

Charfi, A., & Mezini, M. (2007). AO4BPEL: An aspect-oriented extension to BPEL. *WWW Journal: Recent Advances on Web Services, March*, 309-344.

Cichocki, A., Helal, S., Rusinkiewicz, M., & Woelk, D. (1998). *Workflow and process automation concepts and technology*. Kluwer Academic Publishers.

Coleman, J. (2005). *Examining BPEL's compensation construct*. Workshop on Rigorous Eng. of Fault-Tolerant Systems.

Courter, A. (2010). *Supporting data consistency in concurrent process execution with assurance points and invariants.* M.S. Thesis, Texas Tech University, Department of Computer Science.

de By, R., Klas, W., & Veijalainen, J. (1998). *Transaction management support for cooperative applications*. Kluwer Academic Publishers.

Desel, J. (2005). Process modeling using petri nets. *Process-Aware Information Systems: Bridging People and Software through Process Technology*, (pp. 147-177).

Dialani, V., Miles, S., Moreau, L., De Roure, D., & Luck, M. (2002). Transparent fault tolerance for web services based architectures. *Lecture Notes in Computer Science*, , 889–898. doi:10.1007/3-540-45706-2_126

Eder, J., & Liebhart, W. (1995). The workflow activity model WAMO. *Proc. of the the 3rd Int. Conference on Cooperative Information Systems (CoopIs).*

Elmagarmid, A. (1992). *Database transaction models for advanced applications*. Morgan Kaufmann.

Fekete, A., Greenfield, P., Kuo, D., & Jang, J. (2002). Transactions in loosely coupled distributed systems. *Proceedings of Australia Database Conference* (ADC2003).

Gao, L., & Urban, S. (2010). A formal representation of the assurance point service composition and recovery model using Petri nets. Technical Report. Texas Tech University, Department of Computer Science, 2010.

Jensen, K. (1987). Coloured Petri nets. *Petri nets: Central models and their properties*, (pp. 248-299).

Jin, T., & Goschnick, S. (2003). Utilizing web services in an agent based transaction model (ABT), *Proc. of the 1st Int. Workshop on Web Services and Agent-based Engineering.*

Jin, Y. (2004). *An architecture and execution environment for component integration rules*. Ph.D. Diss., Arizona State University.

Jin, Y., Urban, S., & Dietrich, S. (2007). A concurrent rule scheduling algorithm for active rules. *Data & Knowledge Engineering, 60*(1), 530–546. doi:10.1016/j.datak.2006.02.007

Jin, Y., Urban, S., Dietrich, S., & Sundermier, A. (2006). An integration rule processing algorithm and execution environment for distributed component integration. *Informatica, 30*, 193–212.

Kamath, M., & Ramamritham, K. (1996). Correctness issues in workflow management. *Distributed Systems Engineering, 3*(4), 213–221. doi:10.1088/0967-1846/3/4/002

Kamath, M., & Ramamritham, K. (1998). Failure handling and coordinated execution of concurrent workflows. *Proc. of the IEEE Int. Conference on Data Engineering.*

Khalaf, R., Roller, D., & Leymann, F. (2009). Revisiting the behavior of fault and compensation handlers in WS-BPEL. *On the Move to Meaningful Internet Systems. OTM, 2009*, 286–303.

Kiczales, G., Hilsdale, E., Hugunin, J., Kersten, M., Palm, J., & Griswold, W. G. (2001). An overview of AspectJ. *Lecture Notes in Computer Science*, , 327–353. doi:10.1007/3-540-45337-7_18

Kifer, M., Bernstein, A., & Lewis, P. (2006). *Database systems: An application-oriented approach* (2nd ed.). Pearson.

Kuo, D., Fekete, A., Greenfield, P., & Jang, J. (2002). Towards a framework for capturing transactional requirements of real workflows. *Proceedings of the 2nd Int. Workshop on Cooperative Internet Computing*, Hong Kong.

Leymann, F. (1995). Supporting business transactions via partial backward recovery in workflow management. *Proc. of the GI-Fachtagung für Datenbanksysteme in Business, Technologie und Web (BTW'95).*

Limthanmaphon, B., & Zhang, Y. (2004). Web service composition transaction management. *Proc. of the 15th Australasian Database Conf.*

Lin, F., & Chang, H. (2005). B2B e-commerce and enterprise integration: The development and evaluation of exception handling mechanisms for order fulfillment process based on BPEL4WS. *Proc. of the 7th IEEE Int. Conference on Electronic Commerce.*

Liu, A., Li, Q., Huang, L., & Xiao, M. (2007). A declarative approach to enhancing the reliability of BPEL processes. *Proc. Of the Int. Conf. on Web Services*, pp. 272-279.

Luo, Z. W. (2000). Checkpointing for workflow recovery. *Proc. of the 38th Annual Southeast Regional Conf.*, (pp. 79-80). New York, NY: ACM.

Ma, H., Urban, S. D., Xiao, Y., & Dietrich, S. W. (2005). GridPML: A process modeling language and history capture system for grid service composition. *Proceedings of the International Conference on e-Business Engineering*, Beijing, China.

Mikalsen, T., Tai, S., & Rouvellou, I. (2002). Transactional attitudes: Reliable composition of autonomous web services. *Proc. of the Workshop on Dependable Middleware-based Systems (WDMS), Int. Conference on Dependable Systems and Networks (DSN)*.

Modafferi, S., & Conforti, E. (2006). Methods for enabling recovery actions in WS-BPEL. *Lecture Notes in Computer Science*, *4275*, 219. doi:10.1007/11914853_14

Modafferi, S., Mussi, E., & Pernici, B. (2006). SH-BPEL: A self-healing plug-in for WS-BPEL engines. *Proc. of the 1st Workshop on Middleware for Service-Oriented Computing*, (pp. 48-53). New York, NY: ACM.

Murata, T. (2002). Petri nets: Properties, analysis and applications. *Proceedings of the IEEE*, *77*(4), 541–580. doi:10.1109/5.24143

Paton, N. W., & Díaz, O. (1999). Active database systems. *ACM Computing Surveys*, 31.

Peterson, J. L. (1981). *Petri net theory and the modeling of systems*. Upper Saddle River, NJ: Prentice Hall PTR.

Ramchandani, C. (1973). *Analysis of asynchronous concurrent systems by timed Petri nets*. Massachusetts Institute of Technology.

Shrestha, R. (2010). *Using assurance points, events, and rules for recovery in service composition*. M.S. Thesis, Texas Tech University.

Singh, M., & Huhns, M. (2005). *Service-oriented computing: Semantics, processes, and agents*, J. Wiley & Sons, 2005.

Stahl, C. (2005). *A Petri net semantics for BPEL*. Technical Report 188, Humboldt-Universitat zu Berlin.

Tan, W., Fong, L., & Bobroff, N. (2007). Bpel4job: A fault-handling design for job flow management. *Lecture Notes in Computer Science*, *4749*, 27. doi:10.1007/978-3-540-74974-5_3

Tartanoglu, F., Issarny, V., Romanovsky, A., & Levy, N. (2003). Dependability in the web services architecture. *Proc. of Architecting Dependable Systems, LNCS 2677*.

Urban, S. D., Courter, A., Gao, L., & Shuman, M. (2011) Supporting data consistency in concurrent process execution with assurance points and invariants," to appear in *Rule-Based Modeling and Computing on the Semantic Web*, F. Olken, M. Palmirani, D. Sottara (Eds.): RuleML 2011 - America, *Lecture Notes in Computer Science 7018*. Springer.

Urban, S. D., Dietrich, S. W., Na, Y., Jin, Y., Sundermier, A., & Saxena, A. (2001). The IRules project: Using active rules for the integration of distributed software components. *Proc. of the 9th IFIP Working Conf. on Database Semantics: Semantic Issues in E-Commerce Systems*, (pp. 265-286).

Urban, S. D., Gao, L., Shrestha, R., & Courter, A. (2010a). Achieving recovery in service composition with assurance points and integration rules. *Proceedings of the Cooperative Information Systems Conference* (Crete, Greece) as part of *On the Move (OTM) 2010, Part 1* [Heidelberg, Germany: Springer.]. *Lecture Notes in Computer Science*, *6426*, 428–437. doi:10.1007/978-3-642-16934-2_31

Urban, S. D., Gao, L., Shrestha, R., & Courter, A. (2010b). The dynamics of process modeling: New directions for the use of events and rules in service-oriented computing. In Kaschek, R., & Delcambre, L. (Eds.), *The evolution of conceptual modeling, Lecture Notes in Computer Science 6520* (pp. 205–224). Heidelberg, Germany: Springer.

Urban, S. D., Liu, Z., & Gao, L. (2009). Decentralized data dependency analysis for concurrent process execution. *Proceedings of the 13th Enterprise Distributed Object Computing Conference Workshops* (EDOCW 2009) (pp. 74-83).

Urban, S. D., Liu, Z., & Gao, L. (2011) Decentralized communication for data dependency analysis among process execution agents, to appear in *International Journal of Web Services Research.*

Urban, S. D., Xiao, Y., Blake, L., & Dietrich, S. (2009). Monitoring data dependencies in concurrent process execution through delta-enabled grid services. *International Journal of Web and Grid Services, 5*(1), 35–66. doi:10.1504/IJWGS.2009.023870

Van der Aalst, W. (1995). *A class of Petri nets for modeling and analyzing business processes. (Computing Science Reports 95/26)*. Eindhoven: Eindhoven University of Technology.

Van der Aalst, W. M. P. (1998). The application of Petri nets to workflow management. *Journal of Circuits Systems and Computers, 8*, 21–66. doi:10.1142/S0218126698000043

Wachter, H., & Reuter, A. (1992). The conTract model. In Elmagarmid, A. (Ed.), *Database transaction models for advanced applications.*

Worah, D., & Sheth, A. (1997). Transactions in transactional workflows. In S. Jajodia & L. Kershberg *Advanced transaction models and architectures*. Springer.

WS-Coordination. (2005). *Web services coordination.* Retrieved from http://www-106.ibm.com/developerworks/ library/ ws-coor/

WS-Transaction. (2005). *Web services transaction.* Retrieved from http://www.ibm.com/developerworks/library/ws-transpec/

Xiao, Y. (2006). *Using deltas to support semantic correctness of concurrent process execution.* PhD Dissertation, Department of Computer Science and Engineering, Arizona State University.

Xiao, Y., & Urban, S. D. (2008). Process dependencies and process interference rules for analyzing the impact of failure in a service composition environment. *Journal of Information Science and Technology, 5*(2), 21–45.

Xiao, Y., & Urban, S. D. (2009). The DeltaGrid service composition and recovery model. *International Journal of Web Services Research, 6*(3), 35–66. doi:10.4018/jwsr.2009070103

Xiao, Y., Urban, S. D., & Dietrich, S. W. (2006). A process history capture system for analysis of data dependencies in concurrent process execution. *Proc. Second Int. Workshop on Data Engineering in E-Commerce and Services*, San Francisco, California, (pp. 152-166).

Xiao, Y., Urban, S. D., & Liao, N. (2006). The DeltaGrid abstract execution model: Service composition and process interference handling. *Proc. of the Int. Conf. on Conceptual Modeling (ER 2006),* (pp. 40-53).

Zeigler, B. P., & Sarjoughian, H. S. (2004). *DEVSJAVA*. Retrieved from http://acims.eas.asu.edu/ SOFTWARE/ software.shtml# DEVSJAVA

Chapter 13
Early Capacity Testing of an Enterprise Service Bus

Ken Ueno
IBM Research, Japan

Michiaki Tatsubori
IBM Research, Japan

ABSTRACT

An enterprise service-oriented architecture is typically done with a messaging infrastructure called an Enterprise Service Bus (ESB). An ESB is a bus which delivers messages from service requesters to service providers. Since it sits between the service requesters and providers, it is not appropriate to use any of the existing capacity planning methodologies for servers, such as modeling, to estimate the capacity of an ESB. There are programs that run on an ESB called mediation modules. Their functionalities vary and depend on how people use the ESB. This creates difficulties for capacity planning and performance evaluation. This article proposes a capacity planning methodology and performance evaluation techniques for ESBs, to be used in the early stages of the system development life cycle. The authors actually run the ESB on a real machine while providing a pseudo-environment around it. In order to simplify setting up the environment we provide ultra-light service requestors and service providers for the ESB under test. They show that the proposed mock environment can be set up with practical hardware resources available at the time of hardware resource assessment. Our experimental results showed that the testing results with our mock environment correspond well with the results in the real environment.

DOI: 10.4018/978-1-61350-104-7.ch013

INTRODUCTION

An enterprise service bus (ESB) is part of an infrastructure, a messaging bus based on Web Service standards (Leymann, 2005; Luo, Goldshlager, & Zhang, 2005; Weerawarana, Curbera, Leymann, Storey, & Ferguson, 2005). It is a platform for Web Service intermediaries [5], and fills a core infrastructural role in a service-oriented architecture (SOA), which is a collection of services communicating with each other Alonso & Casati, 2005; Patrick, 2005). The first middleware providing ESB functionality was introduced in 2004. One of the unique features of an ESB is the use of component programs called mediation modules. These are programs that run on an ESB. There are various kinds, depending on how the ESB is used. Even though the technical concept of an ESB is not completely new, the increased adoption of SOA in industry raises new engineering challenges for research. Performance estimation of an ESB is one such challenge.

Predicting the performance of an ESB is different from predictions for traditional application servers, for which many studies have been done (Avritzer & Weyuker, 2004; Avritzer, Kondek, Liu, & Weyuker, 2002; Litoiu, 2004; Mos & Murphy, 2002). This is because an ESB plays not just a server role but also plays a client role for multiple service providers. That also means that the methods used for a J2EE server's performance evaluation (Cecchet, Marguerite, & Zwaenepoel, 2002) aren't suitable for an ESB. The mediation functionalities also cause some differences in how ESB performance is evaluated compared to evaluating simple intermediaries like TCP/IP network routers. Nevertheless, performance estimation of the ESB in the capacity planning phase, which happens at a very early stage in the project lifecycle, is critical to a successful project. If the capacity of an ESB used for a system is overestimated, we might need significant changes in the architecture, a large effort for system performance tuning during development or deployment, and/or extra funding for additional hardware. If the capacity is underestimated, we might overestimate costs or seek unneeded compromises from the system stakeholders.

The goal of the work presented in this article is to provide a practical solution for IT architects assessing the capacity of an ESB. Though many researchers have addressed this issue through model-based approaches (Balsamo, Marco, Inverardi,& Simeoni, 2004Litoiu, Krishnamurthy, & Rolia, 2002), they often require elemental performance measurements and sophisticated modeling of the entire system, which is usually not feasible for complex systems. In an ESB, modeling involves intermediate components called mediation modules that provide functions such as routing and protocol conversion, and configurations can vary for each system. This complexity makes it difficult to estimate the performance of an ESB with a model-based approach.

In this article, we propose a capacity testing methodology for ESBs during the phase of capacity planning, which is conducted very early in a project's lifetime. Our approach is to allow performance testing of an ESB by using a lightweight experimental environment. This enables testing of the ESB with an actual hardware equivalent to that used in the production environment, while greatly reducing the hardware resources required to set up the testing environment. With the proposed technique, designers can evaluate the ESB capacity with a small hardware environment consisting of Web Service requesters and providers without having the server-class systems for the testing environment in the early stage of the system development project. In contrast to most capacity planning techniques, the results of this capacity testing can reveal the actual maximum capacity of the ESB server on the specific platform.

For our technique, we designed and implemented a novel framework for a lightweight Web Service provider and a lightweight Web Service client. In the framework, the lightweight service provider is implemented based on our mock environment technologies, while the lightweight Web Service client is implemented based on a common HTTP load generator. The framework can avoid the large processing overhead of Web Service handling and reduce the hardware resources required for constructing an experimental environment, which means that it allows us to measure the potential capacity of an ESB accurately with inexpensive hardware.

We built this kind of lightweight environment for a banking application example and evaluated the validity of our approach. As a result of our experiments, we observed that the measured results with our lightweight environment are almost identical to those with the real environment.

The rest of the article is organized as follows: First, we introduce the ESB concept and focus on the problems of an ordinary project using an ESB for a distributed system. Then we propose an ESB capacity testing approach for the capacity planning phase in a lightweight service provider environment. The fourth section describes the detailed implementation techniques for the proposed lightweight ESB environment and the fifth section shows the experimental results with our implementation. After discussing related work and several aspects of the applicability of our approach, we conclude the article.

CAPACITY PLANNING OF AN ESB

In this section, we discuss the motivating background of our research. First, we introduce and explain the notion of an Enterprise Service Bus (ESB) and the components of typical ESBs. Then we highlight a problematic part of development in a scenario involving system development with an ESB.

Enterprise Service Bus

An ESB refers to a software architecture construct implemented by using technologies found in a category of middleware infrastructure products usually based on Web Service (WS) standards. It provides foundational services for a more complex Service-Oriented Architecture (SOA) via an XML-based messaging engine (the bus), and thus provides an abstraction layer on top of an enterprise messaging system that allows integration architects to exploit the messaging without writing code.

The technical concept of an ESB is not especially new, but it is coming to play a significant role in the enterprise computing world as SOA is becoming widely adopted. In addition to the standardization efforts for the technologies around SOA, a reason for its importance to practitioners is that it allows faster and cheaper accommodation of existing systems and also scales from point solutions to enterprise-wide deployments. Also, it provides increased flexibility in changing systems as requirements change.

Since an ESB is a bus, it is topologically located at an intermediary position between two types of SOA participants: service requestors and service providers. These are usually WS clients and WS servers, respectively, usually using SOAP over HTTP.

From the seven-layer stack perspective of OSI, the presentation layer is provided by SOAP headers and SOAP bodies embedded in SOAP envelopes. An ESB recognizes the layer for protocol and data conversions, and for transport-independent policies such as routing, caching and security.

Typical Components around an ESB

The typical topology of a distributed system involving an ESB consists of five tiers. Figure 1 depicts the topology and participating components in the distributed system. Though various software vendors provide various ESB products with different capabilities, the basic architectural form of a distributed system with an ESB is in this typical topology. This belief is based on a large number of real ESB customer experiences, and we believe that customers currently accept this scenario as typical.

Figure 1. A typical topology of a distributed system with an ESB

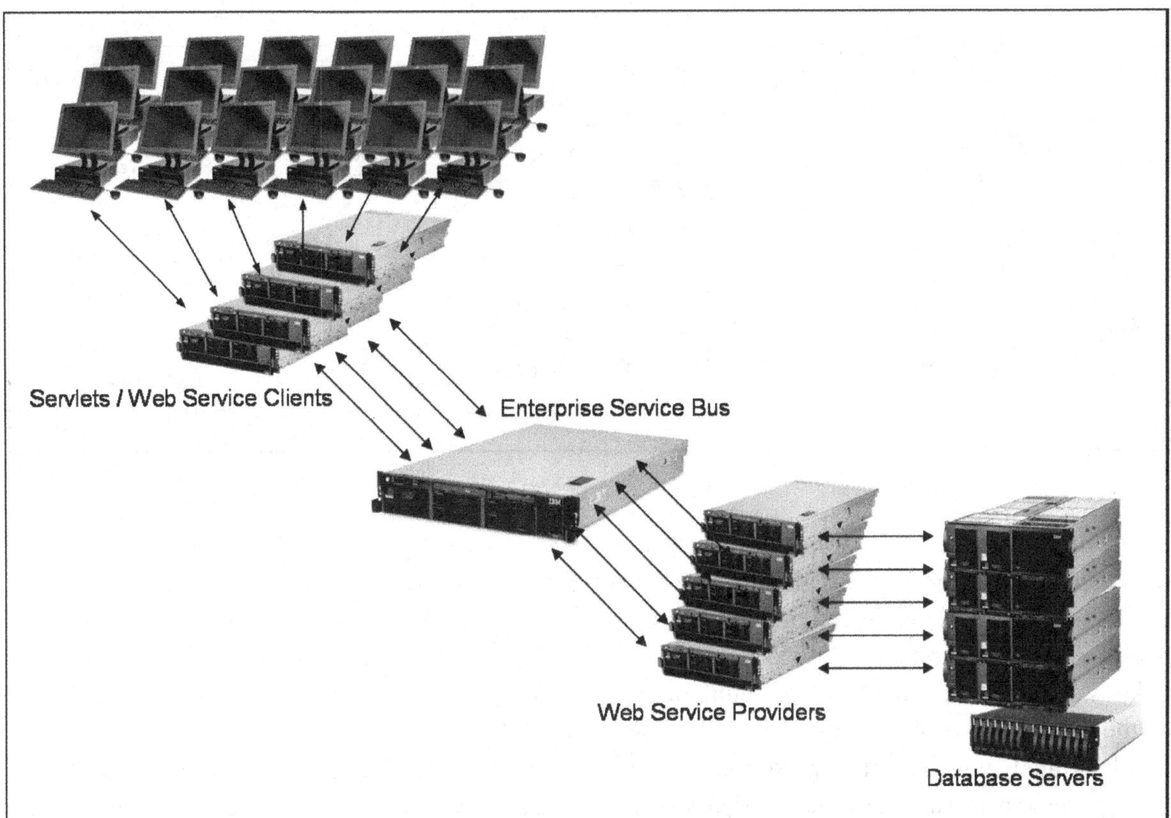

Most customers have been using Web browsers as their user interfaces, which is the first tier of the five tiers in Figure 1, while the last tier is provided by databases. First of all, when using a Web browser, each end user accesses Web application servers that dynamically generate webpages. A server running a Web application, the second tier, is typically implemented with a framework like JSP or servlets and is often built using an enterprise application container such as Apache Geronimo, JBoss Application Server, IBM WebSphere, or Microsoft ASP.NET. When the second tier is accessed, it invokes the Web Services by generating SOAP requests. The generated SOAP requests are typically sent using the HTTP. With an ESB, that request will be sent to the third-tier intermediary, which is an ESB. Then the ESB will perform some processing (if required) and forward the request to the target service provider, the fourth-tier of the topology. This tier is also provided by Web application servers. After the target service provider receives the request, it does any required operations, such as accessing an external database (in the fifth-tier) and processing any required business logic.

Capacity Planning

Among the various problems in developing a distributed system with an ESB, the problem we address in this article is capacity planning. The objective of capacity planning is to determine what hardware to buy to meet cost, performance, and scalability requirements. In a system development project, this happens at a very early stage of the project lifecycle (Denaro, Polini, & Emmerich, 2004) as shown in Figure 2. In many cases, we need to finalize the investment budget for a new project

Figure 2. Capacity estimation in early development cycle

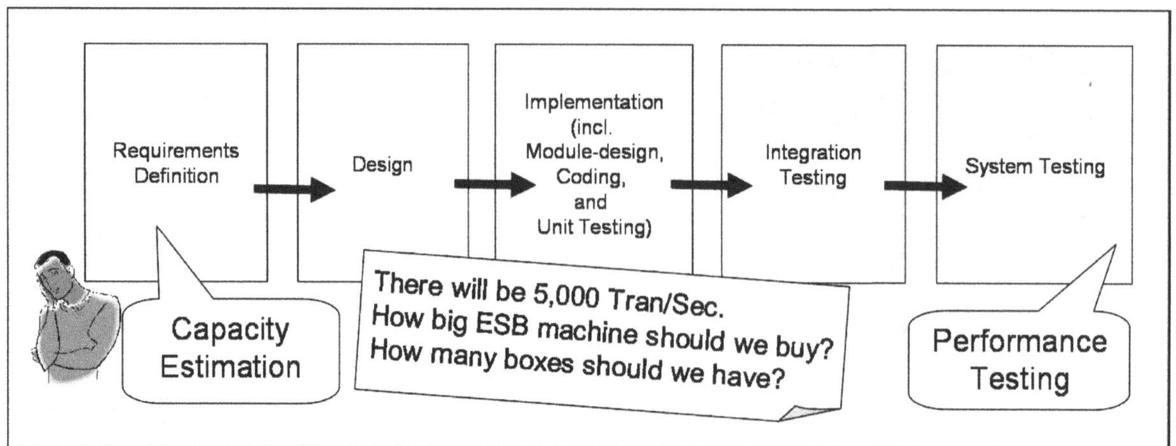

at that time. Usually this is in the abstract architecting phase of the project, just after the requirements analysis. When architecting a system, we need to evaluate the to-be-developed architecture to know whether or not it meets the requirements of the system stakeholders. Such an evaluation involves analyzing expected performance for the candidate hardware platforms. Based on the evaluated cost-performance of an architected system, an architect may need to negotiate with stakeholders for compromises on requirements or may proceed by refining the architecture to start detailed design and implementation as long as the design meets the requirements.

In a typical capacity-planning methodology (Menasce & Almeida, 2001), the simplest method for capacity planning is trend analysis. We collect data on current (and any past) system utilization and use it to estimate future utilization. The following are typical steps for capacity planning:

- Identify workload patterns
- Measure performance with the current configuration (infrastructure)
- Analyze trends and estimate growth trends and performance targets (Weyuker & Avritzer, 2002)
- Model the software and hardware infrastructure

In ESB capacity planning, however, there is a problem in the second step, the step of measuring the performance on the current configuration (Weyuker & Vokolos, 2000). Since an ESB is a relatively new infrastructure category, most of the projects that need capacity planning will not have any ESB in the existing configuration. Therefore, most new ESB systems will be purchased without prior experience. In addition, the configuration of an ESB varies for each project because of the intermediate components called mediation modules, which provide functionalities to customize the behavior of the bus, such as routing and protocol conversion.

Failure of capacity estimation can lead to disaster for a project. If the capacity of an ESB for a system is overestimated, it might cause a significant change of the architecture, increased work in system performance tuning during development or deployment, and/or the purchase of extra hardware. If the capacity is underestimated, we might overprice the project or request unneeded compromises from the system stakeholders.

EARLY CAPACITY TESTING WITH A LIGHTWEIGHT ENVIRONMENT

In this section, we will discuss early capacity testing for an ESB. We will also discuss requirements for capacity testing by using a typical misconfiguration of an ESB in a testing environment. Then we will discuss our mock environment and finally describe the parameters that we can configure with our lightweight environment.

Early Capacity Testing

What we are proposing here is a method for early capacity testing. Though capacity testing is usually conducted at a very late phase of a project, we strongly suggest that it should be conducted during an early phase, specifically during the capacity planning phase of the project. Capacity testing only reveals the ultimate limits of the servers that are used for the capacity testing rather than the capabilities of the production system. Such a test determines the capacity of a specific system rather than the entire production system infrastructure. We should do proper capacity testing during capacity planning as part of making the investment decisions.

Requirements for ESB Capacity Testing

When we evaluate the ESB performance capacity, the most important factor is that the ESB has to be under high load. Then we can saturate the ESB system (or approach saturation) to determine its maximum performance. While evaluating the ESB performance, the Web Service clients need to send and receive enormous numbers of messages through the ESB. We need to have Web Service clients and service providers that can handle such heavy message traffic.

Based on our actual experiences with ESB customers, we realized that the typical topology of many ESB-based systems consists of five tiers: Web browsers, Servlets (Web Service requestors), the ESB, Web Service providers, and backend servers such as database servers. The main reason why many customers have this topology is that the roles of both the end user tier and the backend tier are the same as a typical Web application (J2EE) topology. The significant differences lie in the middle tiers.

We need to be careful about the differences between a real production system environment and a performance evaluation system in a lab. In a real production system environment, there are usually multiple large service providers as well as Web Service clients. Compared to a real production environment, a typical performance evaluation lab system has a relatively small machine, such as a single-CPU server with a very small cache. If either the Web Service client or the Web Service provider can only handle very low workloads, then it is unlikely that the ESB will become a bottleneck. This is the common misconfiguration that we observed in some performance verification labs as shown in Figure 3.

Lightweight Mock Environment

With our approach we use an authentic ESB product and mediation modules on a realistic and large server. We configure the ESB middleware with a real WSDL (Leymann, 2005). Also, if necessary, we install mediation modules that can be used in the production system. Then we have an ESB server that is configured in a way that is very similar to the production system.

As we described before, in a real Web Service the clients are usually invoked by servlets instead of by the end users, who are typically using Web browsers. We need to remove any potential bottlenecks from the Web Service clients in the ESB performance evaluation environment. Therefore, we should use lightweight Web Service clients. With our approach, we use an HTTP workload simulator that emulates multiple virtual Web browsers (Joines, Willenborg, & Hygh, 2002). Since the Web Service clients of this article send SOAP messages using HTTP, an HTTP workload

Figure 3. Bottlenecks in a misconfigured ESB test environment

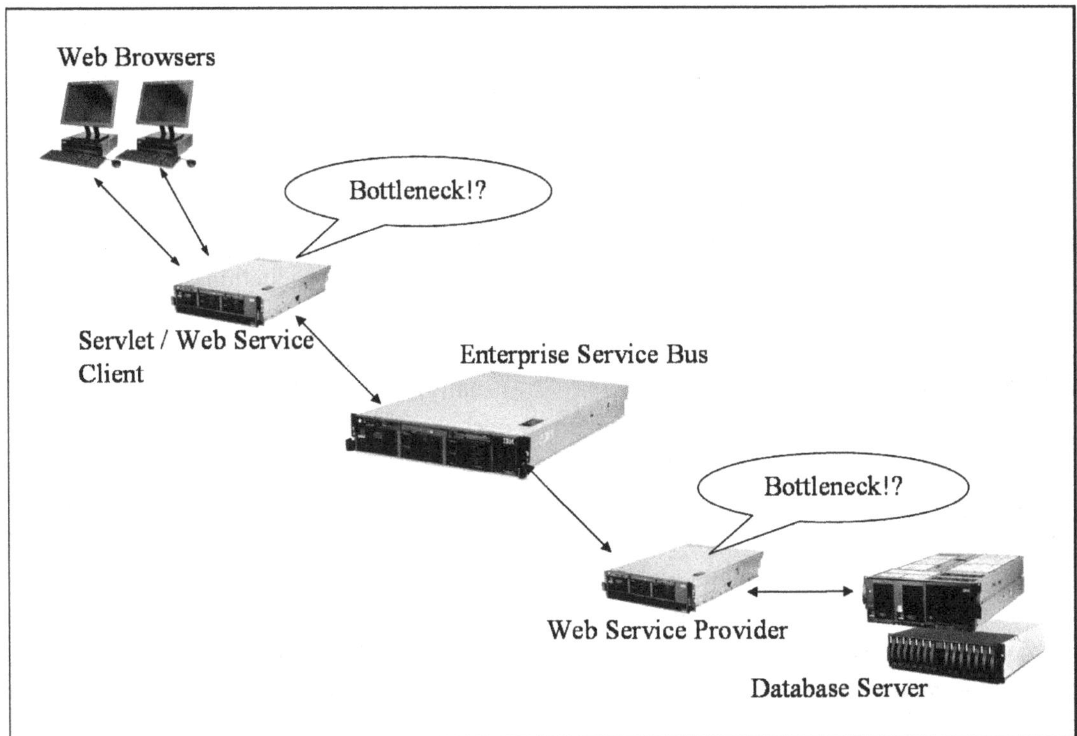

simulator is appropriate for creating the mock Web Service clients. The SOAP messages that the HTTP workload simulator sends should be the same as the messages that will be used in the production system. Then the ESB that we configure for the evaluation can handle those service requests as proper messages.

We also need to have a Web Service provider layer that can receive and respond to thousands of messages per second in order to load the ESB. We propose a method to create such an environment without setting up a real service provider environment such as a large server configuration. We call this a lightweight service provider. The lightweight service provider can receive messages from an ESB and respond with appropriate messages sent back to the ESB. Therefore the ESB cannot know whether or not the responses are from real service providers. The lightweight service provider is not a real Web Service provider. In the following section, we will discuss it in detail. The lightweight service provider may emulate delays such as those due to waiting for responses from backend database servers. Like the mock Web Service client we described earlier, the lightweight service provider should return the same SOAP messages that will be used in the production system. Therefore, in our ESB evaluation environment, the messages being passed around are the same as those the production system will use.

Configurable Parameters of a Lightweight Provider

Our lightweight mock provider supports the following configurable parameters in order to emulate the configurations of the production systems of service providers:

1) Multiple IP addresses with a single NIC
2) HTTP Keep Alive option

3) Number of threads
4) Response time within a mock provider

Since there will be multiple Web Services on multiple server nodes in a production environment, our mock provider should be able to handle several Web Services on a single system. The first parameter on the list will be used to support this.

The rest of the parameters will directly affect the results of the capacity tests, and the values set should be similar to those of a production environment. For example, the second parameter has several options, such as whether or not HTTP Keep Alive is allowed, the number of requests per connection using HTTP Keep Alive, and the maximum number of seconds to wait for the next request.

The third parameter controls the number of threads of the lightweight provider. With this option, we are able to control the minimum and maximum numbers of threads that can concurrently running on the provider to handle requests from an ESB. This will also affect the number of connections between the ESB and the mock providers.

The last option allows for emulating the response delay on the provider and/or the delays between the provider and the backend servers. In some cases, the response delays between the providers and backend database servers can affect the ESB performance, and it is possible to examine such situations with our approach.

IMPLEMENTATION OF THE MOCK ENVIRONMENT

There are seven components that we needed to prepare for the implementation of an experimental proof of our approach: the WSDL, the ESB, Web Service clients, Web Service providers, the mediation modules, the request SOAP messages, and the response SOAP messages, as depicted in Figure 4.

The following paragraphs describe each component. In general, we need to import a WSDL file from the Web Service into the ESB to configure it properly. Therefore, we need to have an appropriate WSDL file for our experiment.

For the second component, the ESB itself, we prepared the hardware, middleware (ESB software), and the mediation modules that we will use in the production system to assess the performance capacity of the specific hardware used in the ESB system. Since we are doing capacity testing, it is necessary to have appropriate hardware for the ESB.

The third component, the Web Service clients, calls for preparing lightweight Web Service clients. With our approach, we use an HTTP workload simulator that emulates multiple virtual Web browsers. Since our Web Service clients send SOAP messages using HTTP, an HTTP workload simulator is appropriate for the mock Web Service clients. There are many commercial and public domain HTTP workload simulators. Since they have been used in many projects, they are quite mature and require very few resources. If needed, we could alternately use many small machines and easily avoid performance bottlenecks.

The next component is a lightweight Web Service provider. With our approach, we don't require a large server machine which hosts a lightweight provider. Instead, we use a small system. We also need to prepare a lightweight Web Service to emulate the actual service provider. There are several ways to implement this. The simplest one is to make a servlet that can receive SOAP requests from the ESB as shown in Figure 5. In the WSDL that we imported into the ESB, there is a line that points to a real Web Service endpoint, such as http://host:80/service/Banking. In this example, we simply deploy the lightweight Web Service servlet to link to the URI. In the lightweight Web Service servlet, we implement logic that responds to the SOAP response messages that were prepared in advance to be sent via the ESB. This can be implemented

Figure 4. Components of mock environment for ESB capacity testing

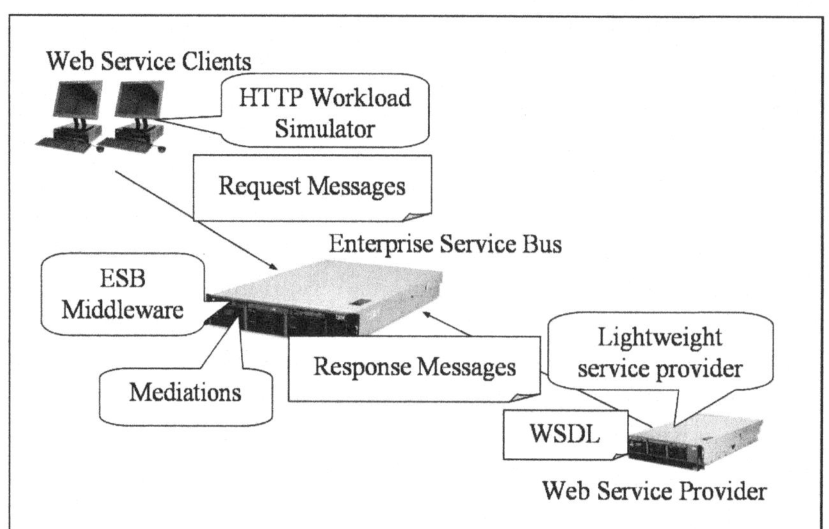

Figure 5. An Example of Lightweight Service Provider Implementation

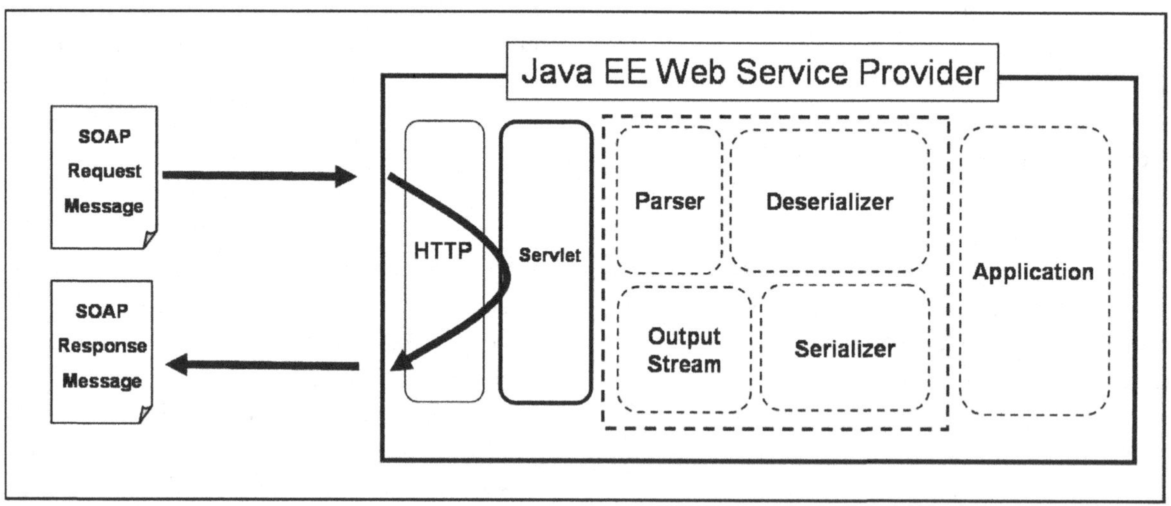

using the doPost() method. With Apache Axis as the Web Service engine, it is easy to implement this approach by modifying the org.apache.axis.transport.http.AxisServlet class. Of course we need to have a Web Service (J2EE) infrastructure to serve the lightweight Web Service servlet. The configurable parameters which we discussed earlier should be supported by either a Web Service infrastructure or a lightweight service provider.

The fifth type of components are request SOAP messages. The Web Service clients that form the HTTP workload simulator in our usage send these messages to the ESB using HTTP POST.

The last type of component consists of the response SOAP messages from the Web Service provider. In the lightweight Web Service servlet we described before, these messages are sent back to the ESB as response messages.

It is important to note that it should be very easy to set up this test environment and should be relatively simple to execute on a variety of different systems since we need to have this test environment in the very early phase of the project. To configure this system easy, we can use several existing open source programs and/or commercial products for generating WSDL, SOAP request messages, and SOAP response message. With such software, there's no need to create Web Service client and server programs to generate SOAP messages. If these programs are already in use, their SOAP messages can simply be captured on the wire by using a message monitoring tool.

EXPERIMENTAL RESULTS

We performed some experiments with the approach discussed in the last two sections. Based on the results, we determined that our approach is feasible. We explain our evaluation environment in the next few paragraphs.

Configuration

We used the following software and hardware for our experiments. For the Web Service client system, the ESB system, and the large Web Service provider system, an Intel Xeon MP 3.0 GHz 4-way server (4 MB L3 cache, 8 GB RAM) was used. For a small Web Service provider system, an Intel Pentium-M 1.7 GHz system (2 GB RAM) was used. We used gigabit Ethernet for a private network with a Cisco Catalyst 3750G 24T-E switch. For the authentic Web Service infrastructure and its ESB, IBM's middleware was used as the server software.

Through all the experiments, we used a realistic ESB system that is used in production environments. In this article, we focus on evaluating the server-side mock environment. We used an HTTP workload simulator on a rather large system to emulate the Web Service clients. Thus there is no bottleneck in the Web Service client layer in our evaluation system. However, that does not mean that we needed a large machine for the client-side test environment. In fact, the client machine could have been replaced with a much smaller one if necessary.

We provide three ESB test scenarios:

- No ESB,
- ESB without mediation, and
- ESB with mediation.

The first scenario doesn't have any ESB. The second scenario uses an ESB with no mediation modules. Since there are no mediation modules, the ESB receives the messages from the Web Service clients and simply forwards them to the service providers. The third scenario uses the ESB with mediation modules. These mediation modules route requests to ports defined for the service destinations. The mediation modules will route requests to one of four destinations depending on a specific value in the SOAP header in the request message.

For each scenario, we tested three types of service provider environments (see Figure 6):

- Real Web Service providers on a small server (Naïve Test System)—representing a naively configured test environment,
- Lightweight Web Service providers on a small server (Lightweight Test System)—representing the lightweight test environment proposed in this article, and
- Real Web Service providers on a large server (Production System)—representing the production environment.

In the following Sections, we show the experimental results for each scenario: no ESB, ESB without mediation, and ESB with mediation, respectively.

Figure 6. Performance evaluation system configuration

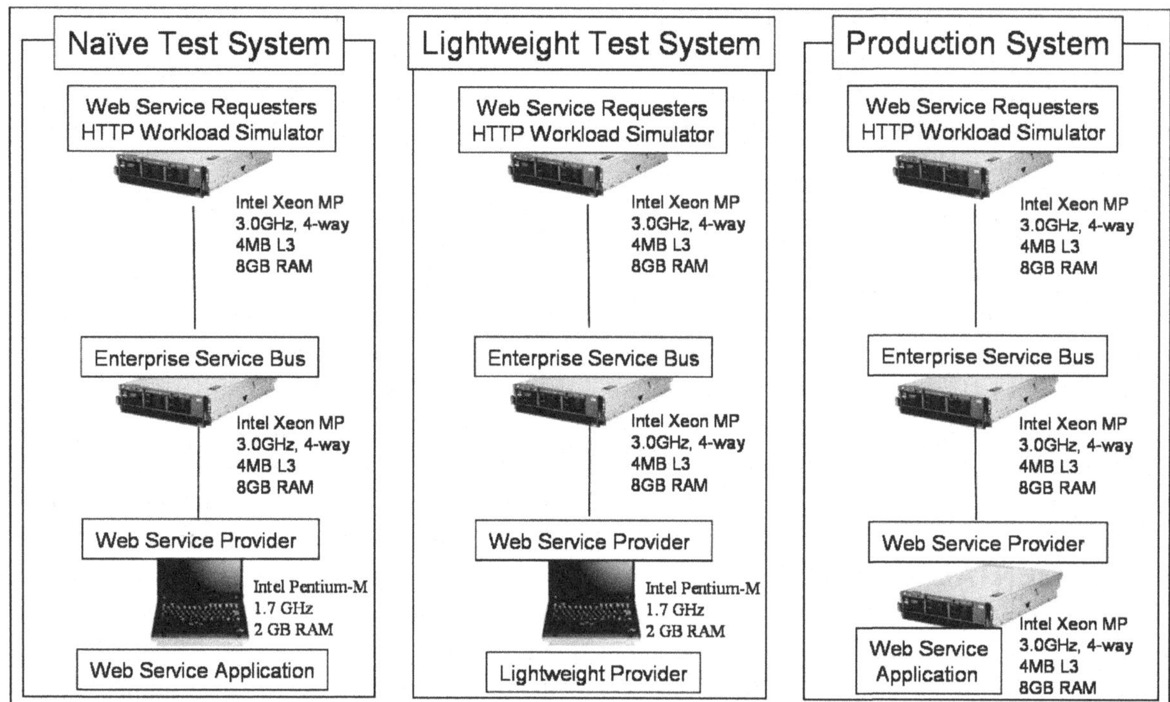

Service Provider Performance Comparison

An HTTP workload simulator sent requests directly to these service providers and we used these numbers as our baseline shown in Figure 7. Note that in all of the cases, the server CPU usage is 100 percent and the client CPU usage is only 1 to 6 percent. The results of these measurements tell us the maximum capacity of the service providers.

The Production System served 4,901 requests per second. Since this transaction rate is high enough to emulate large Web Services environments in the real world, we decided to continue using a single SMP system as our high volume service provider. Running as a Naïve Test System, it handled 513 requests per second, which is about 10% of the large server's throughput.

On the other hand, with our lightweight service provider, the small server recorded 2,028 requests per second. This shows that the lightweight service provider gave us a fourfold performance improvement.

Note that in all three cases the client CPU usage was very low (in case of the Production System which is the highest volume configuration, it was only 6%) and it was not a bottleneck. Therefore, we will mention only the ESB and Service Provider CPU usage in the following subsections.

ESB Performance Comparison

With the three different service provider environments, we measured the ESB performance without the mediation modules. This topology is a 3-tier configuration as shown in Figure 8.

With the Naïve Test System, the maximum throughput was 475 requests per second. With the Lightweight Test System and with the Production System, the maximum throughputs are 1,260 and

Figure 7. Service provider performance comparison

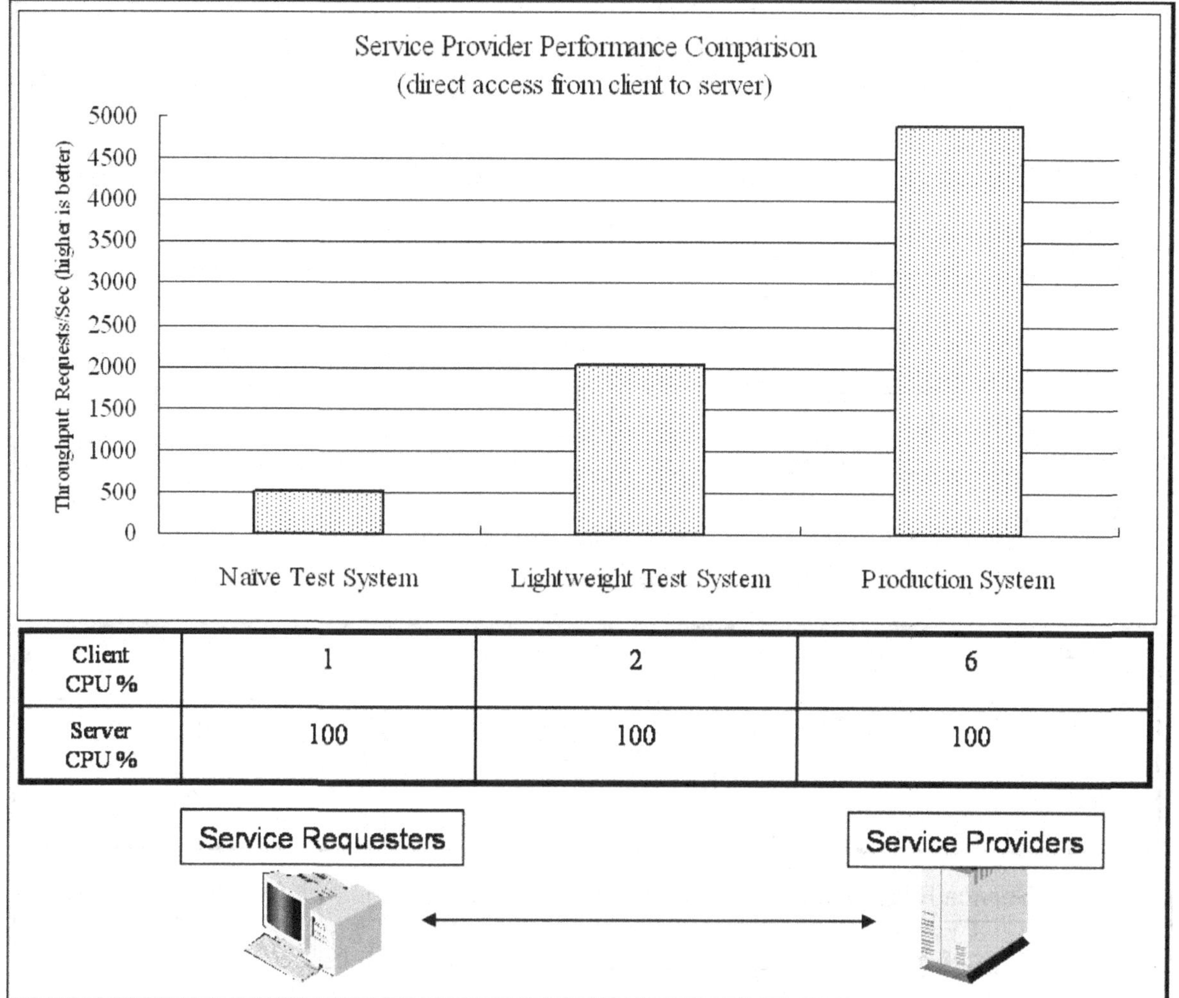

Client CPU %	1	2	6
Server CPU %	100	100	100

1,272 requests per second, respectively. The performance difference between these two cases is less than one percent.

If we look at the CPU usage on the service providers, it shows that the Naïve Test System was completely overloaded, but the other two systems were not. In comparison, if you took a look at the ESB's CPU usage, the Naïve Test System was using 37% and the other two cases were saturating it at 100%.

ESB Performance Comparison with Mediations

With a port routing mediation module with a 3-tier configuration (see Figure 9), we saw a similar trend as in the no-mediation scenario. With the Naïve Test System, the CPU usage of the server was 100% and the ESB's CPU usage was 63% which is not high enough to evaluate its maximum capacity. The throughput of this scenario was 397 requests per second. With the other two service provider scenarios, we completely maxed out

Figure 8. ESB performance comparison

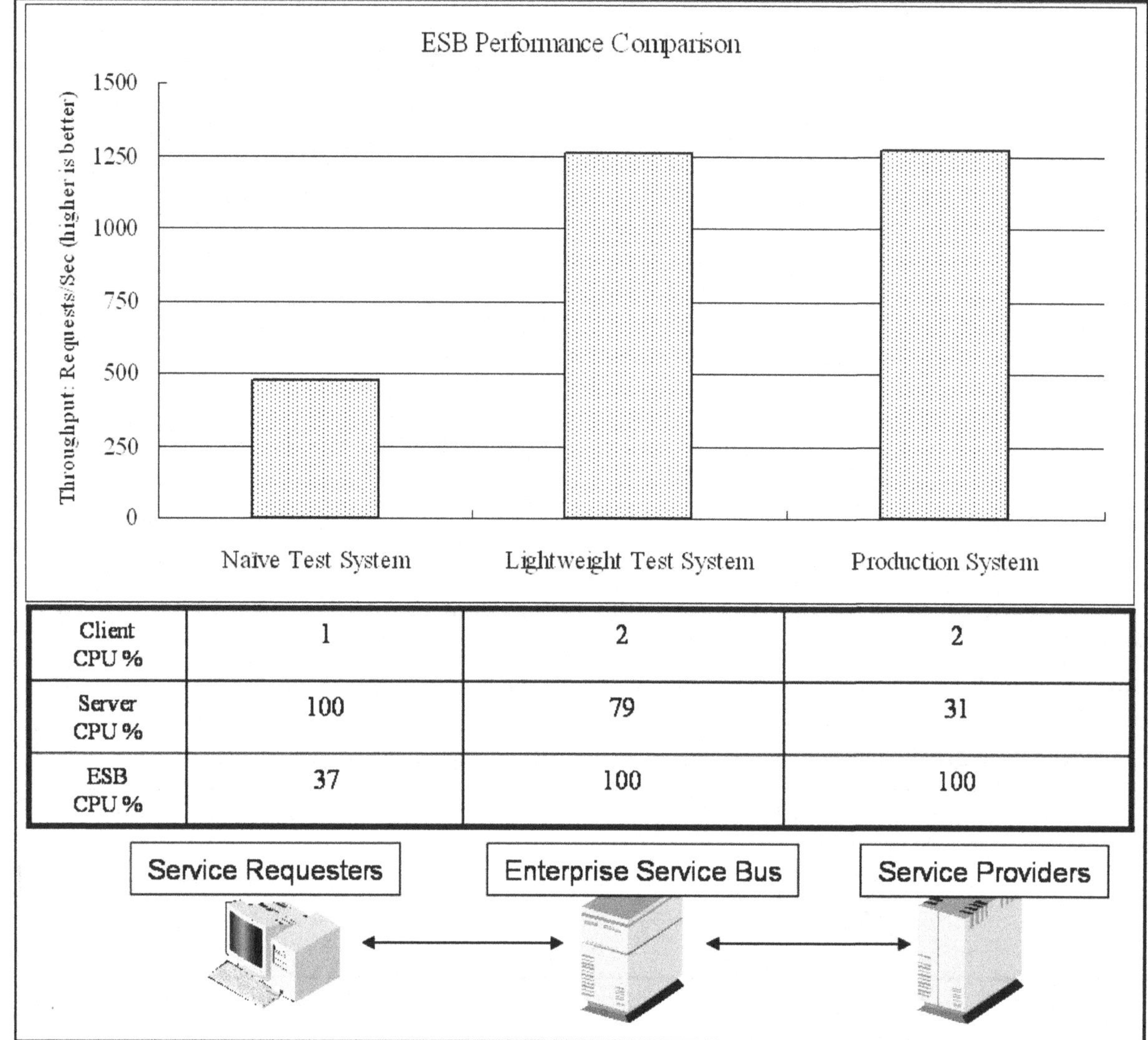

	Naïve Test System	Lightweight Test System	Production System
Client CPU %	1	2	2
Server CPU %	100	79	31
ESB CPU %	37	100	100

the ESB system, as shown in Figure 9. With the Lightweight Test System, the small server's CPU usage was 51% and the large server's usage was 14% with the Production System.

The throughput of these cases was 601 requests per second and 610 requests per seconds, respectively. The performance difference of these two environments was only one percent.

Performance Analyses

In theory, the ESB CPU usage should be close to one hundred percent to find the maximum performance of the system. In addition, it is important that both the Web Service client layer and the Web Service provider layer should not be highly loaded.

With the small server (Naïve Test System), there is not much performance difference with and without the ESB (see Figures 7 and 8). These small-system results are misleading. Without

Figure 9. ESB with mediations performance comparison

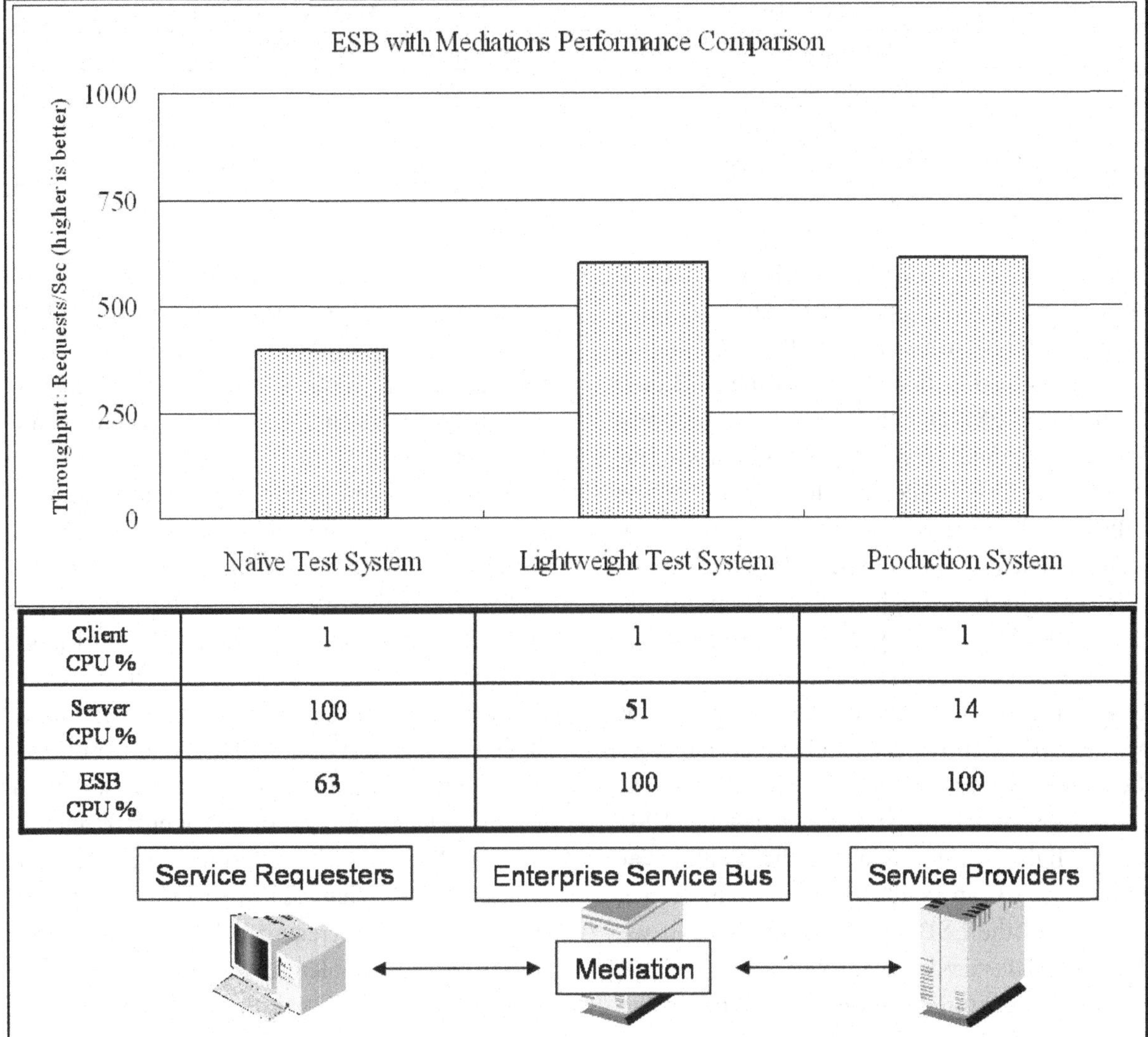

	Naïve Test System	Lightweight Test System	Production System
Client CPU %	1	1	1
Server CPU %	100	51	14
ESB CPU %	63	100	100

further analysis of these results, a designer might believe that this ESB system would be large enough for a production system. That might be true if the service provider in the production system is relatively small, as in our single-processor system. In this scenario, the bottleneck is in the server due to the system resource limitation on computing power. Since there is a lack of CPU cycles in the service provider, the service provider cannot send messages back to the ESB quickly enough to saturate it.

With the large server (Production System), there is a huge performance gap between the cases with and without the ESB (see Figures 7 and 8). In this scenario, unlike the small server (Naïve Test System) case, the ESB is a bottleneck. Since we have a powerful service provider system, the provider layer is no longer the bottleneck, but the ESB layer becomes the new chokepoint. With this scenario, we can measure the maximum capacity of this ESB system with a real Web server application on the service provider.

Table 1. Response time comparison: large server vs. lightweight service provider

Scenario	Response Time (seconds/request)
Large server via ESB	0.039
Lightweight service provider via ESB	0.039
Large server via ESB with mediation	0.081
Lightweight service provider via ESB with mediation	0.082

In the last test scenarios, which are using the lightweight provider on a small server (Lightweight Test System), we also see the performance gaps in the tests with and without the ESB (see Figures 7 and 8). Due to the limited computing power of the small server, the throughput without the ESB is much smaller than for the large server with a real Web Service application scenario. This is understandable and an expected result. The key point is that the lightweight provider using the ESB can handle almost exactly the same throughput as the large server with a real application scenario as depicted in Figure 8 and 9. This indicates that our lightweight provider can effectively simulate the large server environment. Since both the real application on the large server using the ESB and the lightweight provider on the small server using the ESB can handle thousands of messages per second, the ESB was fully utilized and we determined the maximum throughput of the ESB.

We also captured response times during the capacity testing. As shown in Table 1, the response times with the lightweight service provider and the large server are very similar, and this provides additional evidence of the validity of our approach.

RELATED WORK

In this section, we discuss the previous research on performance testing of distributed systems. As we have already discussed the alternative approaches for estimating capacity of ESBs in the introduction section, we here focus on actual testing with real machines for the systems under test. Specifically, we discuss the existing performance testing technologies, which can be used for capacity testing purposes. Since there are various techniques and products for testing performance of distributed systems, we can discuss only some representatives.

In the Grid computing research area, several performance testing tools have been proposed, since performance is one of the most critical issues addressed in this area. In a Grid environment, the research issues arise from the situation of large numbers of various types of nodes in the environment. The issues addressed are, for example, clock synchronization for a large number of testing machines to control performance estimation accuracy, heterogeneity of WAN environments, and coordination of large resource pools (Raicu, Dumitrescu, Ripeanu, & Foster, 2006). However, researchers have not regarded the lack of resources for testing as a problem in this area.

For the performance testing of Web application servers, many tools are available as products and are widely used by practitioners. For example, Mercury's Road Runner, Compuware's QALoad, Microsoft's Application Center Test, and IBM's Rational Performance Tester are the commercial products most widely used for Web application development. Their features are mainly differentiated by flexibility in customization of possible load scenarios and usability supported by the automation of testing. Unfortunately, their functionality is basically limited to load generation since their testing target is Web servers. In fact, their functionality can be regarded as a subset of the proposed testing environment in this article.

Figure 10. Mock environment for BPEL engine capacity testing

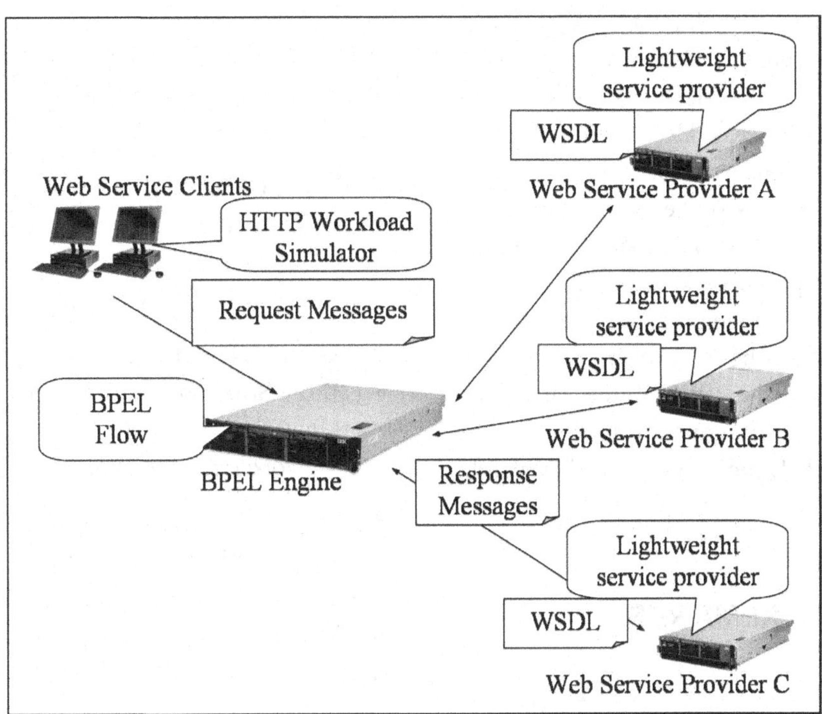

Emulating the backend servers is a natural approach to setting up a testing environment. An example of an application of this approach can be found in the SPECweb2005 benchmark environment. In the SPECweb2005 benchmark kit, a back-end simulator called BeSim is provided to set up the testing environment behind the Web server under test. BeSim is intended to emulate a back-end application server that the Web server must communicate with in order to retrieve specific information needed to complete an HTTP response (customer data, for example). BeSim exists in order to emulate this type of communication between a Web server and a back-end server.

The mock server used in the proposed testing approach is topologically the same as the BeSim server. However, since BeSim is designed for SPECweb2005, the messages to and from BeSim are predefined for this specific benchmark. Unlike the BeSim, our proposed mock server can receive and replay any messages that are required for the ESB capacity testing.

DISCUSSION

As mentioned, there are several kinds of mediation modules that we can run on an ESB. In previous sections, we use routing mediation as an example. There are a few mediation modules that might not work with our approach. For example, if mediation requires external resources such as database access, we need to have another system that emulates the database. We focused on Web Services, particularly SOAP over HTTP. For future work, we will study SOAP over JMS and other protocols.

In this article, we focused on an ESB which is one of the most important components for the SOA infrastructure. However, our lightweight service provider works not only with an ESB but also with the BPEL engine which is another important component for the SOA infrastructure as depicted in Figure 10. The BPEL engine is a runtime which hosts business processes written in the Business Process Execution Language (BPEL) (Andrews, Cubera, Dholakia et al., 2003) and for BPEL business processes. In particular, the BPEL engine orchestrates the Web services. Since Service Requesters talk to the BPEL engine instead of Service Providers, the Service Requesters don't know about the response messages from Service Providers to the BPEL engine. Therefore, our approach for early capacity testing can be applied to the BPEL engine with our lightweight service provider.

CONCLUDING REMARKS

In this article, we proposed a capacity testing method for an ESB that can be used during the phase of capacity planning. With our proposed capacity testing, designers can assess the ESB server capacity using a very small hardware environment by using lightweight service providers and an HTTP workload simulator as lightweight Web Service clients. Our proposed capacity testing requires very limited preparation time to configure a test environment. Unlike most other capacity planning methods, the results of this capacity testing can reveal the actual maximum capacity of an ESB server on a specific platform.

ACKNOWLEDGMENT

The authors would like to thank the member of the IBM Tokyo Research Laboratory including Yuichi Nakamura, Toshiro Takase, and Naohiko Uramoto for their comments on an earlier draft of this article.

REFERENCES

Alonso, G., & Casati, F. (2005). Web Services and Service-Oriented Architectures. *International Conference on Data Engineering, 1147.*

Andrews, T., Cubera, F., Dholakia, H., et al. (2003). *Business Process Execution Language for Web Services version 1.1.* ftp://www6.software.ibm.com/ software/ developer/ library/ ws-bpel.pdf

Avritzer, A., Kondek, J., Liu, D., & Weyuker, E. J. (2002). Software performance testing based on workload characterization. *Workshop on Software and Performance* (pp. 17-24).

Avritzer, A., & Weyuker, E. J. (2004). The Role of Modeling in the Performance Testing of E-Commerce Applications. *IEEE Transactions on Software Engineering, 30*(12), 1072–1083. doi:10.1109/TSE.2004.107

Balsamo, S., Marco, A. D., Inverardi, P., & Simeoni, M. (2004). Model-Based Performance Prediction in Software Development: A survey. *IEEE Transactions on Software Engineering, 30*(5), 295–310. doi:10.1109/TSE.2004.9

Cecchet, E., Marguerite, J., & Zwaenepoel, W. (2002). Performance and Scalability of EJB Applications. *Proceedings of the 17th ACM SIGPLAN conference on Object-oriented programming, systems, languages, and applications* (pp. 246–261).

Compuware QALoad. http://www.compuware.com/

Denaro, G., Polini, A., & Emmerich, W. (2004). Early Performance Testing of Distributed Software Applications. *Proceedings of the Fourth International Workshop on Software and Performance* (pp. 94-103).

Dikaiakos, M. D. (2004). Intermediary infrastructures for the World Wide Web. *Computer Networks, 45*(4), 421–447. doi:10.1016/j.comnet.2004.02.008

Joines, S., Willenborg, R., & Hygh, K. (2002). *Performance Analysis for Java Websites*. Massachusetts: Addison-Wesley Longman Publishing Co., Inc.

Leymann, F. (2005). The (Service) Bus: Services Penetrate Everyday Life. *ICSOC, 2005*, 12–20.

Litoiu, M. (2004). Migrating to Web services: a performance engineering approach. *Journal of Software Maintenance and Evolution: Research and Practice*, *16*(1-2), 51–70. doi:10.1002/smr.285

Litoiu, M., Krishnamurthy, D., & Rolia, J. A. (2002). Performance Stress Vectors and Capacity Planning for E-Commerce Applications. [Springer.]. *International Journal on Digital Libraries*, *3*(4), 309–315. doi:10.1007/s007990100045

Luo, M., Goldshlager, B., & Zhang, L. (2005). Designing and implementing Enterprise Service Bus (ESB) and SOA solutions. *Tutorial, IEEE International Conference on Services Computing, xiv.* Menasce, D.A., & Almeida, V. (2001). *Capacity Planning for Web Services: metrics, models, and methods*. New Jersey: Prentice Hall PTR.

Mercury Load Runner. http://www.mercury.com/

Microsoft Application Center Test. http://www.microsoft.com/

Mos, A., & Murphy, J. (2002). Performance Management in Component-Oriented Systems Using a Model Driven Architecture Approach. *Proceedings of the 6th International Enterprise Distributed Object Computing Conference* (pp. 227–237). IEEE Computer Society.

Patrick, P. (2005). Impact of SOA on enterprise information architectures. *Proceedings of the 2005 ACMSIGMOD international conference on Management of Data* (pp. 844–848).

Raicu, I., Dumitrescu, C., Ripeanu, M., & Foster, I. (2006). The Design, Performance, and Use of DiPerF: An automated Distributed PERformance evaluation Framework. [Springer.]. *Journal of Grid Computing*, *4*(3), 287–309. doi:10.1007/s10723-006-9037-5

Rational Performance TesterI. B. M.http://www.ibm.com/

Standard Performance Evaluation Corporation (SPEC). http://www.spec.org/

Weerawarana, S., Curbera, F., Leymann, F., Storey, T., & Ferguson, D. F. (2005). *Web Services Platform Architecture*. New Jersey: Prentice Hall.

Weyuker, E. J., & Avritzer, A. (2002). A metric for predicting the performance of an application. under a growing workload. *IBM Systems Journal*, *41*(1), 45–54.

Weyuker, E. J., & Vokolos, F. I. (2000). Experience with Performance Testing of Software Systems: Issues, an Approach, and Case Study. *IEEE Transactions on Software Engineering*, *26*(12), 1147–1156. doi:10.1109/32.888628

This work was previously published in International Journal of Web Services Research, Volume 6, Issue 4, edited by Liang-Jie Zhang, pp. 30-47, copyright 2009 by IGI Publishing (an imprint of IGI Global).

Chapter 14
An Integrated Framework for Web Services Orchestration

C. Boutrous Saab
Université Paris Dauphine, France

D. Coulibaly
Université Paris Dauphine, France

S. Haddad
LSV, ENS Cachan, CNRS, France

T. Melliti
Université d'Evry, France

P. Moreaux
Université de Savoie, France

S. Rampacek
Université de Bourgogne, France

ABSTRACT

Currently, Web services give place to active research and this is due both to industrial and theoretical factors. On one hand, Web services are essential as the design model of applications dedicated to the electronic business. On the other hand, this model aims to become one of the major formalisms for the design of distributed and cooperative applications in an open environment (the Internet). In this article, the authors will focus on two features of Web services. The first one concerns the interaction problem: given the interaction protocol of a Web service described in BPEL, how to generate the appropriate client? Their approach is based on a formal semantics for BPEL via process algebra and yields an algorithm which decides whether such a client exists and synthetize the description of this client as a (timed) automaton. The second one concerns the design process of a service. They propose a method which proceeds by two successive refinements: first the service is described via UML, then refined in a BPEL model and finally enlarged with JAVA code using JCSWL, a new language that we introduce here. Their solutions are integrated in a service development framework that will be presented in a synthetic way.

DOI: 10.4018/978-1-61350-104-7.ch014

INTRODUCTION

At the hour of fusions, reorganizations of companies, Information Systems (IS) must have the capacity to take into account these economic constraints. What results is a need for flexibility, adaptability, opening and even for interoperability between remote and/or heterogeneous IS, i.e. based on different technical bases. Interoperability supposes that the applications are able to be located, to be identified, to expose the functionalities (services) which they offer, and finally, to exchange data. The Web services arise today as the most suitable solution in order to connect remote IS, eventually heterogeneous ones.

Indeed, Service Oriented Architectures Services (SOA), initially based on the components and their capacity to communicate through their interfaces, quickly showed their limits in terms of weak coupling (necessary to meet the needs for flexibility and adaptability) and of interoperability. The Web services bring these properties to the SOA which were precisely lacking with the component based architectures. The Web services lie on standards for the information exchange as well as on protocols for their transport.

Web services are "self contained, self-describing modular applications that can be published, located, and invoked across the Web" (Tidwell, 2000). They are based on a set of independent open platform standards to reach a high level of acceptance. Web services framework is divided into three areas - communication protocol, service description, and service discovery - and specifications are being developed for each one: the "Simple Object Access Protocol" (SOAP) (Gudgin, 2000), which enables communication among Web Services, the "Universal Description, Discovery and Integration" (UDDI) (Bellwood, 2002), which is a registry of Web Services descriptions and the "Web Services Description Language" (WSDL) (Christensen, 2001), which provides a formal, computer-readable description of Web services. The latter describes such software components by an interface listing the collection of operations that are network accessible through standard XML messaging. This description contains all information that an application needs to invoke such as the message structure, the response structure and some binding information like the transport protocol, the port address, etc.

However, simple operation invocation is not sufficient for some kind of composite services. They also require a long-running interaction derived by an explicit process model. This kind of services may often be encountered in two cases. First, when a Web service is developed as an agent, it is composed of a set of accessible operations and a process model which schedules the invocation to a correct use of the service. Secondly, facing to the capability limits of Web services, composite services may be obtained by aggregating existing Web services in order to create more sophisticated services (and this in a recursive way).

In order to deal with the behavioural aspects of complex services, some industrial and academic specifications languages have been introduced. Among them, *Business Process Execution Language for Web Services* (BPEL4WS or more succinctly BPEL) has been proposed by leading actors of industry (BEA, IBM, and Microsoft) and has quickly become a standard (Alves, 2007). BPEL supports two different types of business processes (Juric, 2005). (i) *Executable processes* specify the exact details of business processes. They can be executed by an orchestration engine. (ii) *Abstract business protocols* specify the public message exchange between the client and the service. They do not include the internal details of process flows but are required in order, for the client, to correctly interact with the service.

Given the description of an executable process, its associated abstract protocol is obtained by an abstraction mechanism (which masks all the internal operations of the service). However, the issues raised by these two types of processes are very different. On the one hand, the specification of an executable process is close to the definition of a program and naturally yields the expressivity problem: how generic, rich and concise are the constructions of the language? On the other hand, the specification of an interaction protocol mainly raises the synthesis problem: how to synthesize a client which will correctly handle the interaction with the service?

The Expressivity Problem

Whereas BPEL is appropriate for composing Web services into business processes, it does not have all the features of a programming language like Java. Therefore, different works aim at extending BPEL by combining it with Java. The two prominent approaches are *BPELJ for Java* (BPELJ) (Blow, 2004) and the *Web Services Invocation Framework* (WSIF) (Duftler, 2001). BPELJ provides the possibility to include Java code (which is called Java snippets) in BPEL process definitions. WSIF follows another idea: use the same syntax in BPEL to invoke any resource (or service) and describe it using WSDL even if it is a Java resource that does not communicate through SOAP (the applicative communication protocol of Web services). With both approaches, the design of a service is a two-step process: first one models the service with a BPEL program, then one refines it by developing Java code for the local treatments and exchanging values between the Java and the BPEL parts. However, due to the verbose and declarative style of BPEL, when the logic of the application is complex, this process leads to a program which is almost impossible to manage. In order to design a composite service whose application logics is the main complexity factor, we propose an alternative solution: enhancing Java with BPEL features. So, our first contribution is the definition of the language Java Complex Web Service Language (JCWSL). Furthermore, starting from a JCSWL program, we automatically produce both the associated BPEL interaction protocol and a code which can be invoked through a Web server.

The Synthesis Problem

By construction, the external behaviour of a service is non deterministic due to its internal choices. It is then *a priori* unclear whether a client, *i.e.* a deterministic program, can be designed to interact with it. Furthermore, the specification often includes timing constraints (e.g. implicit detection of the withdrawal of an interaction by the client) implying that these timing constraints must also be taken into account by the client. However, since no semantics of the interaction process is given for BPEL (not to be confused with the semantics of the service execution), this problem could not be formally stated. Thus, we have addressed this problem and proposed a solution based on a formal semantics (Melliti, 2003; Haddad, 2004).

First, we specify what an external behaviour is, i.e. we give an operational semantics to an abstract BPEL specification in terms of a timed transition system. The semantics is obtained by a set of rules in a modular way. Given a constructor of the language and the behaviour of some components, a rule specifies a possible transition of a service built via this constructor applied on these components. As previously discussed, the transition system is generally non deterministic.

Then, we define a relation between two communicating systems which formalizes the concept of a correct interaction. There are standard relations between dynamic systems like the language equivalence and the bisimulation equivalence but none of them matches our needs. Thus, we introduce the interaction relation which can be viewed as a bisimulation relation modified in order to capture the nature of the events (i.e. the sending of a message is an action whereas the reception is a reaction).

Afterwards, we focus on the synthesis of a client which is in an interaction relation with the transition system corresponding to the system. The client we look for must be implementable, in other words it should be a deterministic automaton. It has appeared that some BPEL specifications do not admit such a client i.e. they are inherently ambiguous. Thus, the algorithm we have developed either detects the ambiguity of the Web service or generates a deterministic automaton satisfying the interaction relation. The core of our algorithm is a kind of determinisation of the transition system of the service.

This article is organized as follows. "Web Services" section points out the principles of the Web services and details the BPEL constructions. Then, in the "client synthesis" section, we propose a formal semantics of this language, we define the interoperability between a client and a service and we describe the client synthesis algorithm. We introduce JCSWL, our extension of BPEL in section "JCWSL: a design language for Web services". In the "Web service design framework"section, we give an overview of the architecture of our environment. Finally, in "related work" section, we review related work before concluding.

WEB SERVICES

The Web services are an instantiation model of software architecture called service oriented architecture. We first describe the intrinsic characteristics of this model. Then, we detail the Web services principles while insisting on the dynamic aspects. Finally, we present BPEL and its major syntactic constructions, the design language of Web services Web (the current standard).

Service Oriented Architecture Characteristics

A service oriented architecture consists in structuring an application, an applicative block even an Information System (IS), in contracted services in order to answer the following stakes: (i) the implementation of global services between applicative blocksby an interoperability policy ; (ii) the seek of re-using inside an applicative block or an application, in particular on the service infrastructure level or the business service unit, by a re-use policy.

The re-use takes all its importance especially at two levels. (1) On the service infrastructure level, which are without a business value but that each application must inevitably implement for its own needs (safety, exchanges, etc). (2) On the fine granularity business service level, that it is of the re-use of software components within an application (for example, a software layer of common services for the "batch" chains) or about the invocation of a transverse Web Service of "adress validation" type. The re-use of such services avoids the duplication of code between the applications or the modules of an application. On the other hand, for the business service coarse grain, which exposes the value of an information system outside its borders, the stake relates more to the capacity of these services to interoperate with other IS blocks being its clients.

A service oriented architecture must guarantee technological neutrality, weak coupling, transparency with respect to their accessibility, message orientation, composition and autonomy. Today, Web services are the best technological solution adapted to answer these objectives.

From Service Oriented Applications to Web Services

Web service is a specific type of service identified by a URI and showing the following characteristics: (i) it exposes its functionalities through Internet using standards and Internet protocols ; (ii) it is implemented via a self-descriptive interface based on an Internet standard.

The concept of Web Service is currently articulated around the following three acronyms: (i) SOAP ("Simple Object Access Protocol") is an exchange protocol between independent applications of any platform, based on the XML language ; (ii) WSDL ("Web Services Description Language") gives a Web service description in a XML format while specifying the called methods, their signature and the access point (URL, port, etc); (iii) UDDI ("Universal Description, Discovery and Integration") standardizes a solution of distributed Web service directory, allowing simultaneously the publication and the exploration. UDDI behaves as a Web service where its methods are called via the SOAP protocol. The Web service provider publishes its service interface in WSDL format. The client searches the Web service according to a set of characteristics defined by the UDDI directory. The directory finds the service and sends the localization of the server hosting the service. The client asks the server for the suggested contract of the service. The server replies with a call format in WSDL. The client invokes the service with a SOAP message and the server replies by providing a result.

Current standardization around Web services is a vast work that aims to define a true distributed infrastructure, which is able to satisfy the application's needs, as well as in term of exchange standardization as in term of transverse services. These standards were specified by an organization gathering the industrialists, major actors of the market: the WS-I (http://www.ws-i.org/).

BPEL

BPEL primarily lies on WSDL to deal with the information relating to the localization of the service and the data format of the messages. Here, we limit the presentation to the business process components while breaking them up into two catégories: elementary operations and constructors. We do not take into account the exact (verbose) BPEL syntax in this part. BPEL makes it possible to handle variables and types. Notice that we mask some important features of BPEL as the compensation mechanism which do not have significant impact on the interoperability.

Elementary Operations

- the receive primitive *receive* corresponds the reception of a message (coming from a client or another service). BPEL offers the possibility of synchronous or asynchronous communication. We chose to study only the asynchronous mode because it is easy to simulate a synchronous communication using this mode, whereas opposite simulation requires the creation of some auxiliary processes. Moreover, in the composite service framework, the asynchronous mode is more suitable for the long transactions and the weak coupling.
- the primitive *invoke* relates to the sending of a message (to a client or another service). Contrary to the reception of a message which suspends the service if the required message is not present in the buffer, the process continues its activity after the emission.
- the primitive *raiseproc* makes it possible for a process to give up an execution context while signaling a fault. The corresponding fault is treated by the current context or is transmitted to the global context. If the fault is not cached by any context, it causes the end of the process.
- the primitive *terminate* makes it possible for a process to stop the service. One can compare it to an untreated fault; we will study it only in the case of a process which completes normally its treatment.

The introduced constructors can be seen as processes built from sub-processes and elementary operations.

Constructors

- Process *empty* (as its name indicates it) does nothing. It is introduced into BPEL to specify the lack of treatment in some branches of a conditional execution.
- Process *sequence* executes sequentially the corresponding processes.
- Process *switch* consists of sub-processes where their execution is conditioned by a Boolean expression of internal variables (thus unknown of the client) and executes the first branch of which the condition is satisfied. In an optional way, the last branch can not be conditioned by a test.
- Process *while* carries out repeatedly a sub-process as long as a Boolean expression (similar to those appearing in *switchproc*) is satisfied.
- Process *scope* defines an execution context of a sub-process in the following way. This process can be given up on reception of a message whose type belongs to a given set, on reaching a deadline which begins with context activation or on a fault signal. In all cases, a process is linked to each one of these events.
- Process *pick* waits for a message whose type belongs to a given set in order to execute a process corresponding to each message type. In an optional way, a delay can control this waiting. It is easy to simulate a *pickproc* process using a *contextproc* process. Again we will not study it explicitly.
- Process *flow* begins a parallel execution of the corresponding processes and finishes when all these processes finish. These processes can be synchronized in the execution. Since this synchronization is not perceived by the client of the service, we will not model it. It is obviously a simplification which we will remove in a future work.

CLIENT SYNTHESIS

One of the contributions of the Web services is that potential clients discover, *at the time of invocation*, the service specification. However, that raises for the client the problem of leading, in a correct way, the interaction with the service given the flow of exchanged messages. In this section, we develop a formal approach which provides a client synthesis, *i.e.*, an implementable description of an entity interacting with the Web service defined with BPEL (named "the service" in the sequel). The method breaks up into three levels.

We initially define the formal semantics of a BPEL (abstract) process. Since time is explicit in the BPEL language, this semantics is given by a (dense) Timed Automaton (TA). Due to the BPEL language itself, we use a Process Algebra like approach to build the TA associated with every BPEL process.

We then define a suitable interaction relation between a service and its potential client. Since this relation must take into account the various timed behaviours of the processes, it should be based on the timed executions of the service and its client. So, we define the interaction relation in the context of Timed (labelled) Transition Systems (TTS), the standard semantics of TA.

Finally, and this the most difficult step, we build when this is feasible, a deterministic client TA, by means of a specific synthesis algorithm. This TA interacts with the server automaton underlying the service process according to the interaction relation.

A Semantic Approach for Web Service Behaviour

To be able to generate and run a dynamically built composed service from Web services described with BPEL, it is first necessary to give a precise semantics to BPEL. BPEL provides a set of operators describing in a modular way the observable behaviour of an abstract process. As

Figure 1. A timed automaton with two clocks

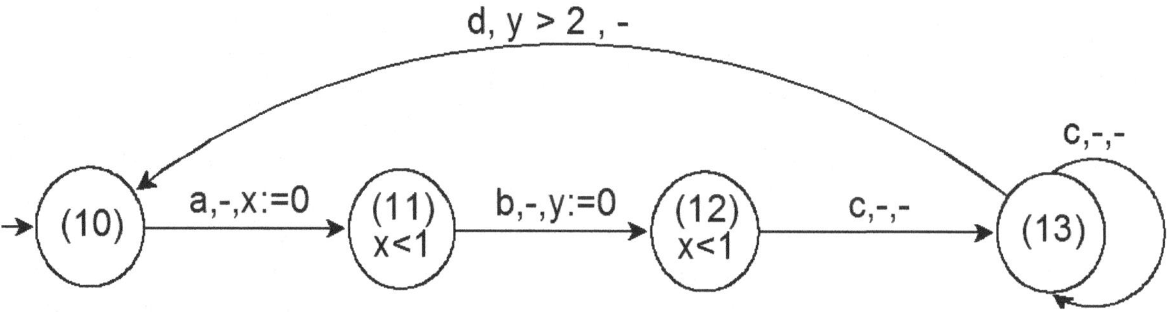

shown in (Staab, 2003), this kind of process description is close to the Process Algebra paradigm illustrated for instance by CCS (Milner, 1989), CSP (Hoare, 1985) and ACP (Bergstra, 1984). A Process Algebra is a model of behaviours of active entities called processes. Each process may execute elementary actions belonging to a given set. Processes may also be combined by means of a set of operators, like sequencing, parallel execution, choice between several processes, etc. With a set of elementary actions and a set of operators, we can describe more complex processes, and new operators as we do in the mathematical framework of algebraic structures (groups, rings, etc.). Since time is explicitly present in some of the BPEL constructors (the operators of a Process Algebra), we must extend the standard Process Algebra semantics with time. Several models have been defined for Timed Process Algebras (see (Nicollin, 1991) for underlying problems), like (Baeten, 1991) for timed ACP, (Nicollin, 1994) for ATP, (Schneider, 1995; Leonard, 1997) for timed CSP and timed LOTOS. However, as we try to *construct* the timed model of an adapted executable client of a BPEL service, we associate directly a Timed Automaton with a BPEL process.

So, we define the semantics of a BPEL process in two steps: first we review how the constructors of the BPEL language can evolve (operational rules) when executing actions; then we construct a TA for each BPEL process.

Timed Automata

A Timed Automaton is an automaton extended with time specification. Time is introduced through *clocks*, invariants, guards and clock reset(see Figure 1). Let us denote by *C(X)* the set of constraints over a set *X* of variables, conjunctions of elementary constraints $x \trianglelefteq c$ with $x \in X, c \in Q_{\geq 0}$ and $\leq \ \in \{\leq, <, >, \geq\}$.

Definition 3.1 (Timed Automaton (Alur, 1994)) *A Timed Automaton (TA) is a tuple* $(L, A_\tau, X, E, I, L_0, L_f)$ *where:*

- *L is the set of* locations;
- $A_\tau = A\{\tau\}$ *is the set of* actions and $\tau \notin A$ *is the* silent action;
- *X is the set of positive real-valued* clocks;
- $E \subseteq L \times C(X) \times A_\tau \times P(X) \times L$ *is the set of* edges: *an edge e is a tuple (s,g,a,R,d) with s the source location, g a guard, a an action, R a subset of clocks to reset and d the destination location.*
- $I \in C(X)^L$ *assigns an* invariant *to any location. Elementary constraint operators in invariants are restricted to* < and ≤.
- L_0 *is the set of* initial locations.

An execution of a TA is a sequence of transitions and time elapsing between states of the TA. A state is composed of a location of the wautomaton and a value *v(x)* per clock *x* (called

Figure 2. TA of process ?Start;scope(while[!Question];!End,[{(?Evt, !Evt)}, (H1:2, !TimeOut), {}]))

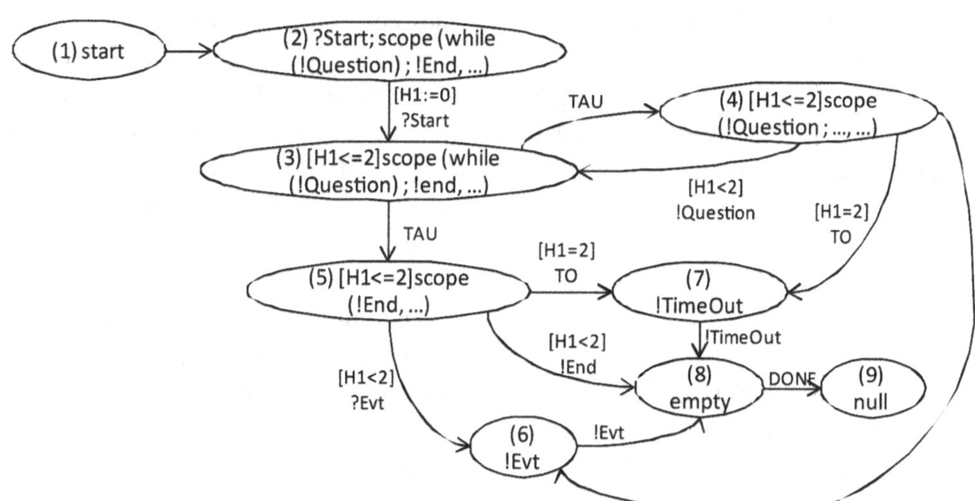

the clock valuation). Transitions are either continuous (time passing) or discrete (actions from A_τ). A continuous transition is $(l,v) \xrightarrow{t} (l',v')$ with $l' = l$ and $v' = v + t$ (where this sum means that t is added to the valuation of every clock) provided that $\forall 0 \leq t' \leq t, I(l)(v+t') = true$ (l invariant remains true). A discrete transition is $(l,v) \xrightarrow{a} \{a\}\ (l',v')$ ifwf $\exists\ (l,g,a,R,l') \in E$ such that $g(v)=true$ (guard), $v'(x)=v(x)\ x \notin R$, and $v'(x)=0$ for $x \in R$ (clocks reset). For instance, a possible execution of the TA given in Figure 2 is: $(l_0, 0, 0) \xrightarrow{1.2} (l_0, 1.2, 1.2) \xrightarrow{a} (l_1, 0, 1.2) \xrightarrow{0.7} (l_1, 0.7, 1.9) \xrightarrow{b} (l_2, 0.7, 0) \xrightarrow{0.1} (l_2, 0.8, 0.1) \xrightarrow{0.1} (l_2, 0.9, 0.2)$.

Let us explain how we build the TA of a BPEL process *P*. Locations of the TA are exactly the processes derived from *P*: these processes correspond to the possible evolutions of *P* when executing BPEL operators. Evolutions are given by a set of so called semantics rules, in the line of Structured Operational Semantics (Plotkin, 1981) for Process Algebras. A rule defines partially a set of edges in the TA. Actions of the TA model the activities of the processes. Each edge is complemented with timing annotations (guard and clocks to reset). Finally, invariants are added to locations based on the time semantics of the BPEL operators (like *scope*). We successively describe actions of the TA, rules of the BPEL language, handling of the clocks and definition of the guards and invariants of a BPEL process. As usual, we denote by 0 the "process" which does nothing, corresponding to the final state of a previously active process.

Actions

From the definition of BPEL, four kinds of actions are possible:

- Immediate actions correspond to logical actions such as selection of an alternative or throwing an exception. They are not visible to the client and are denoted by τ, the silent action. We denote by E_x the set of exceptions which appear in the semantic rules.
- Expiration of a delay is denoted by *to*.
- Reception and sending of messages are basic Web service interactions. Note that we do not model the timing of message transfers. The set of message types is noted by *M*. A sending is denoted by *!m* and a recep-

tion by $?m$ with $m \in M$. We also introduce $!M= \{!m|m\in M\}$ and $?M=\{?m|m\in M\}$. Finally, the generic character * represents either ! or ?.

- In order to check that the client detects the end of the service, we introduce √, the termination event. This action simplifies the definition of some rules.

Rules

For each constructor *op* of BPEL involving processes P_i for $i \in I$, a rule describes the possible transformations of the process $P= op(P_1, P_2,...)$ according to the actions executed by the processes P_i. A generic rule, presented in a standard form has the following structure ($\{u_i\}$ stands for $\{u_i|i\in I\}$):

$$op: \frac{B(\{P_i \xrightarrow{\alpha_i} P_i'\})}{P \xrightarrow{L(\{\alpha_i\})} N(P,\{P_i'\})} \text{if } G(\{\alpha_i\})$$

The components of a rule are:

- a Boolean expression relative to the potential transitions of some components of P: $B(\{P_i \xrightarrow{\alpha_i} P_i'\})$;
- this condition is supplemented by a second condition, called the guard of the rule, on the labels appearing in the transitions, denoted by $G(\{\alpha_i\})$.
- If the two conditions are met, then a transition is possible for P whose label $L(\{\alpha_i\})$ is an expression depending on the transition labels of the subprocesses. If there is no B nor G expression, the upper part and the line in the rule are omitted.
- the new process is an expression $N(P, \{P'_i\})$ which depends of the running process and the new subprocesses.

Note that if the processes P_i and *op* do not involve immediate actions, time passing is not explicitly modelled in the rules. We present below rules corresponding to each BPEL constructor, beginning with the elementary processes *empty*, ?o{m}, !o{m} and *throw*. Observe also that since the invoke process calls a subprocess operation, corresponding message exchanges are "silent" actions from the point of view of the client; hence we do not need to model this constructor in our perspective of server-client interaction.

The empty *process*: empty is a basic element, which can only terminate; hence, it is the last action that a process can execute:

$$\text{empty} \xrightarrow{\surd} 0.$$

The ?o{m} and !o{m} processes: the process ?o{m}, which corresponds to the input operation of WSDL, consists in receiving a message of type *m*. The process !o{m} (the notification operation of WSDL), consists in sending a message of type *m*:

$$*\text{o}\{\text{m}\} \xrightarrow{*m} \text{empty } *\in\{?, \backslash\}.$$

The throw process: the throw process r[e] simply raises an exception e which must be handled in some way (see below the scope process):

$$\forall e \in E, r[e] \xrightarrow{e} 0.$$

The sequence process (;): the process $P;Q$ executes the process P then the process Q. Since the operator ";" is associative, we safely restrict the number of operands to two processes. The sequence process acts as its first subprocess as long as this process does not indicate its termination. In the latter case, the sequance process becomes the second process in a silent way:

$$\forall a \neq \surd, \frac{P \xrightarrow{a} P'}{P;Q \longrightarrow P';Q} \text{ and } \forall a,$$

$$\frac{P \xrightarrow{\surd} \text{ and } Q \xrightarrow{a} Q'}{P;Q \xrightarrow{a} Q'}$$

Note that if there is an action $a \neq \pi$ such that $P \xrightarrow{a} P'$, then $P \xrightarrow{\surd}$ cannot arise.

The switch process: the process switch[$\{P_i \mid i \in I\}$] chooses to behave as one process among the set $\{P_i\}$. Each branch of its execution is guarded by an *internal* condition. Conditions are evaluated w.r.t. the order of their appearance in the description. However since the client has no way to predict the choice of the service, this order is irrelevant. The main consequence is that from the point of view of the client, *this choice is non deterministic.* The switch process becomes one of its subprocesses in a silent way. Let us note that we have implicitly supposed that at least one condition is fulfilled. In the other case, it is enough to add the process empty as one of the subprocesses:

$\forall i \in I$, switch[$\{P_i \mid i \in I\}$] $\xrightarrow{\tau} P_i$.

The while process: the process while[P] iterates an inner process as long as an *internal* condition is satisfied. Like switch, while evaluates in a silent way its condition (because it's an internal choice of the process, we do not know what appends exactly). Thus we have two rules depending on this internal evaluation.

while[P] $\xrightarrow{\tau} P$; while[P] and while[P] $\xrightarrow{\tau}$ empty

The flow process: the process flow[$\{P_i \mid i \in I\}$] simultaneously activates a set of processes $\{P_i\}$. In the present work, we do not model synchronization primitives associated with flow introduced in BPEL4WS and not defined in XLANG.

This parallel execution is similar to a "fork-join" in the sense that the combined process ends its interaction when all subprocesses have completed their execution. Subprocesses of a flow process act independently except for one action: they simultaneously indicate their termination.

- Individual actions

Immediate actions of any process P_i occurs without delay, and the flow process is maintained between new subprocesses:

$\forall$ a $\in E_x \cup \{\tau\}$,

$$\frac{\exists j \in I, P_j \xrightarrow{a} P_j'}{flow[\{P_i \mid i \in I\}] \xrightarrow{a} flow[\{P_i \mid i \in I \setminus \{j\}\} \cup \{P_j'\}]}$$

Message exchanges are proceeded by the processes P_i and the flow process is maintained between new subprocesses:

$\forall$ $m \in M$,

$$\frac{\exists j \in I, P_j \xrightarrow{*m} P_j' \; and \; \forall i \neq j, \; \forall a \in E_x \cup \{\tau\}, \; not \exists \; i \in I, (P_i \xrightarrow{a})}{flow[\{P_i \mid i \in I\}] \xrightarrow{*m} flow[\{P_i \mid i \in I \setminus \{j\}\} \cup \{P_j'\}]}$$

- Common timeout

The rule about *to* describes the case where a subset J of processes execute simultaneously a *to* action:

$$\frac{\exists j \subseteq I, \forall j \in J, P_j \xrightarrow{to} P_j'}{flow[\{P_i \mid i \in I\}] \xrightarrow{a} flow[\{P_i \mid i \in I \setminus J\} \cup \{P_j' \mid j \in J\}]}$$

- Common termination

When all processes terminate, the flow process becomes the null process:

$$\frac{\forall i \in I, P_i \xrightarrow{\surd} 0}{flow[\{P_i \mid i \in I\}] \xrightarrow{\surd} 0}$$

The scope process: scope(P,E) with

$E =_{def} [\{(m_i,P_i) \mid i \in I\}, (d,Q), \{(e_j,R_j) \mid j \in J\}]$

may evolve due to P evolution, reception of a message m_i, expiration of the timeout with duration d or occurrence of an exception e_j. We define $M_I=\{m_i \mid i \in I\}$ and $E_J=\{e_j \mid j \in J\}$.

- P actions

If P ends then scope also ends. If P may execute an action a (but not the termination nor an exception handling nor a m_i message receiving) then scope executes a:

$$\frac{P \xrightarrow{\surd}}{scope(P,E) \xrightarrow{\surd} 0}$$

and $\forall a \notin \{\pi\} \cup E_x \cup M_I$

$$\frac{P \xrightarrow{a} P'}{scope(P,E) \xrightarrow{a} scope(P',E)},$$

- Receiving a message m_i

If a m_i message is received, then scope(P,E) becomes P_i:

$$\forall i \in I, \frac{\forall a \in E_x \cup \{\tau, \surd\}, \text{ not } (P \xrightarrow{a})}{scope(P,E) \xrightarrow{?m_i} P_i}$$

- Timeout occurrence

If P does not end, nor handle an exception nor execute a silent action, then the process scope may ends with a timeout:

$\forall a \in \{\tau,\pi\} \cup E_x$,

$$\frac{\text{not } (P \xrightarrow{a})}{scope(P,E) \xrightarrow{to} Q}$$

- Exception handling

Expected exceptions e_j lead to associated processes R_j whereas other exceptions are transmitted to the upper level. This last derivation allows detection of an exception e never cached at any level including the topmost one, which is an erroneous service definition:

$$\forall j \in J, \frac{P \xrightarrow{e_j}}{scope(P,E) \xrightarrow{\tau} R_j}$$

and

$$\forall e \notin E_J, \frac{P \xrightarrow{e}}{scope(P,E) \xrightarrow{e} 0}$$

The pick process: pick is a special case of the scope process: a scope with a main process P being empty:

pick[E] = scope(empty,E).

Locations of the Timed Automaton

Initially, there is only one location (the initial location) corresponding to the studied process. After the construction of a new edge from the automaton, using a semantic rule, a new process is computed. If this process does not already label a location of the automaton, a new location is created. Because of the definition of the semantic rules described above, the number of derived processes is finite (and consequently the number of the automaton locations). Each location is completed with an invariant (see below).

Clocks, Guards and Invariants of the Timed Automaton

We associate a clock with each subprocess scope of the process and a particular clock (x_{im}) to manage immediate actions. Given a process, we determine by a downward analysis which clocks are active, *i.e.* which subprocesses scope are in the course of execution.

The invariant of a location depends on the possibility of an immediate action. In such a case, the invariant is $x_{im}=0$; if this is not the case, the invariant is the conjunction of elementary conditions $x \leq d$ with x, an active clock and d the time defined in the subprocess corresponding to x.

For a given edge, the clocks to reset are the inactive clocks of the source process which become active in the destination process. x_{im} is always reset.

From each location which contains active clocks, we apply the common timeout rule to every subset of active clocks which may reach their temporal bound, giving a set of edges. For such an edge, the guard specifies that the clocks of the subset reached their limit while the other active clocks did not. Edges outgoing from locations without active clocks have a *true* guard.

Construction of the Timed Automaton

The algorithm building the TA of a BPEL process can be summarized as follows:

- It maintains a set of processes to be examined and a partially built automaton. It starts with the process and an automaton reduced to only one location.
- When analyzing a process, it initially builds the edges corresponding to the semantic rules and it inserts each destination process, not yet present in the automaton, in the set of the processes to be examined.
- Then, it determines the set of active clocks of the process. From this information and already built edges, it deduces the location invariant. Finally, it generates the timeout edges.
- The Computation of the subset of clocks to reset on an edge is carried out either at the construction time of the edge if the destination process was already examined, or during the (later) examination of this process.

Example of the Timed Automaton of a BPEL Process

Let us apply our algorithm to the process

?Start;scope(while[!Question];!End,[{(?Evt, !Evt)}, (H1:2, !TimeOut), {}])

This server process receives a *Start* message, then it starts a scope process associated with a *timeout* event (this *timeout* can occur after 2 units of time) and also associated with a reception event called here *Evt*. The core of this scope process is a loop while that can send *Question* zero, one or more times. When the loop terminates, the server sends a message *End* and derives on the 0 (null) process. Our algorithm builds the TA of Figure 3.

Client-Service Interaction Relation

Clearly, the built TA is a compact representation of the observable behaviour of a BPEL abstract process. However, since we try to construct a model of a client adapted to a given service we must study the interaction between these processes at the level of their timed executions. Timed executions define exactly the semantics of a TA. The formal model of the set of these executions and their relations is a Timed (labelled) Transition System (TTS). A TTS is a tuple $(S, S_0, A, \rightarrow)$ with S the set of states, $S_0 \subseteq S$ the set of initial states, A a finite set of actions and $\rightarrow \subseteq S \times (A \cup R_{\geq 0}) \times S$ the set of transitions. We also write $q \xrightarrow{e} q'$ if $(q, e, q') \in \rightarrow$. A transition $q \xrightarrow{t} q'$ with $t \in R_{\geq 0}$ corresponds to t units time passing. The

Figure 3. Subset of service locations (left) -- associated client location (right)

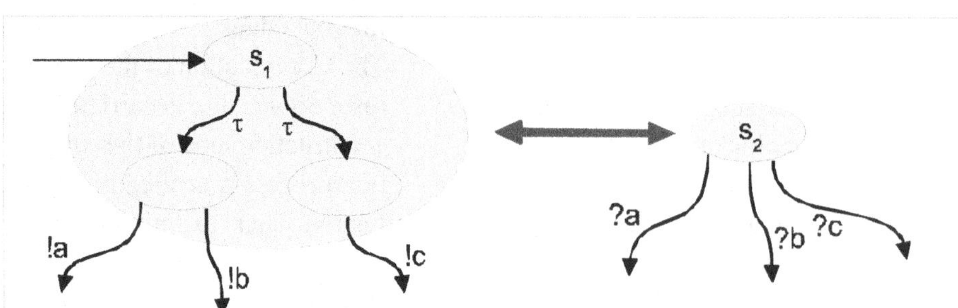

states of a TTS associated with a TA are naturally its states (pairs (l,v)) and the transitions of the TTS are either the discrete transitions ($e \in A_\tau$) or time passing in a location.

First of all, we describe, in an informal way, what should be a correct interaction between two TTS. It is defined as a relation between states of the TTS, like the classical bisimulation relation between Labelled Transition Systems (LTS). Obviously, pairs of initial states must belong to the relation.

Moreover, a pair of related states must have a coherent vision of the forthcoming interaction. This implies that the relation must take into account mutually observable transitions only, *i.e.*, discarding τ actions. Hence, we define the observable transitions of a TTS by $s \overset{a}{\Rightarrow} s'$ iff $s \xrightarrow{\tau^* a \tau^*} s'$, $s \overset{\varepsilon}{\Rightarrow} s'$ iff $s \xrightarrow{\tau^*} s'$ and $s \overset{d}{\Rightarrow} s'$ iff $s \xrightarrow{d_1 \tau \ldots \tau d_n} s'$ with $\sum d_i = d$.

Then, we could require that (in a similar way to bisimulation), when a state s of a pair (s,s') can evolve by an observable transition to a state s_1, s' should have a transition with the same label leading to a state s'_1 composing with s_1 another pair of consistent states.

However, we must be careful. First, if a TTS sends a message then the other TTS must be able to receive it. So, it is necessary to introduce the concept of complementary actions $\overline{?m} = !m$, $\overline{?m} = ?m$ and $\forall a \notin \{!m\}_{m \in M} \cup \{?m\}_{m \in M} \ \bar{a} = a$ and to require that the "synchronized" evolution be carried out by complementary actions.

But such a definition is too strong because it does not distinguish between the different nature of sending and receiving messages: sending a message is an action whereas receiving a message is a *reaction* and cannot spontaneously occur. Consequently, in a more suitable way, the interaction relation requires that, if in a state s of a pair (s,s'), a TTS can receive a message m, then (1) there is a state s'' of the other TTS not distinguishable of s' from the observable transitions point of view which can send m and, (2) in s' the other TTS can send a message (possibly different from m). The first condition reflects the fact that the first TTS is not over-specified while the second implies that it will not indefinitely wait a message.

These considerations lead to the following definition.

Definition 2 *(Interaction relation) Let $T_1 = (S, \{s_{01}\}, A, \rightarrow_1)$ and $T_2 = (S, \{s_{02}\}, A, \rightarrow_2)$ be two TTS. Then T_1 and T_2 interact correctly iff $\exists \sim \subseteq S_1 \times S_2$ such that $s_{01} \sim s_{02}$ and $\forall (s_1, s_2)$ such that $s_1 \sim s_2$:*

Let $a \notin \{?m \mid m \in M\}$:

o *if* $\exists\ s_1 \overset{\alpha}{\Rightarrow}_1 s'_1$, *then* $\exists\ s_2 \overset{\bar{\alpha}}{\Rightarrow}_2 s'_2$ *with* $s'_1 \sim s'_2$ *and*

o *if* $\exists\ s_2 \overset{\alpha}{\Rightarrow}_2 s'_2$, *then* $\exists\ s_1 \overset{\bar{\alpha}}{\Rightarrow}_1 s'_1$ *with* $s'_1 \sim s'_2$

Let $m \in M$: *if* $s_1 \overset{?\mu}{\Rightarrow}_1 s_1'$ *then*

o $\exists\ s_{\bar{2}} \overset{\omega}{\Rightarrow}_2 s_{2'}$, $\exists\ s_{\bar{2}} \overset{\omega}{\Rightarrow}_2 s_2^+$, $\exists\, s_2^+ \overset{!\mu}{\Rightarrow}_2 s_2'$ *with* $s_1 \sim s_2^+$ *and* $s_1' \sim s_2'$ where w is a word on $A\backslash\{\tau\}$;

o $\exists\, s_{\bar{2}} \overset{!\mu'}{\Rightarrow}_2 s_2'$

Let $m \in M$: *if* $s_2 \overset{?\mu}{\Rightarrow}_2 s_2'$ *then*

o $\exists\ s_{\bar{1}} \overset{\omega}{\Rightarrow}_1 s_1$, $\exists\ s_{\bar{1}} \overset{\omega}{\Rightarrow}_1 s_1^+$, $\exists\, s_1^+ \overset{!\mu}{\Rightarrow}_1 s_1'$ *with* $s_1^+ \sim s_2$ *and* $s_1' \sim s_2'$ where w is a word on $A\backslash\{\tau\}$;

o $\exists\, s_{\bar{1}} \overset{!\mu'}{\Rightarrow}_1 s_1'$

Synthesis Algorithm

We are now in position to present the synthesis algorithm of the client. First of all, the client must be implementable, which means that its behaviour must be deterministic. In addition, since it must take into account the *clocks* of the service, and has to interact with the service as explained above, its behaviour must be expressed with a TTS. This leads us to construct a client's model as a deterministic TA having an interaction relation with the service automaton.

Before describing this algorithm, let us notice that some BPEL processes do not admit a client able to correctly interact with them. For example, the process switch[?*o*[*m*],?*o*[*m'*]] chooses, in an internal way, to receive either a message *m* or a message *m'*. Hence a deterministic client must send either *m*, or *m'*. However, once its choice is carried out, the service waits only for one of the two messages. In other words, the corresponding two states of the TTS cannot be in an interaction relation. Note that, in contrast, the process switch[!*o*[*m*],!*o*[*m'*]] admits a deterministic interacting client which waits for either the message *m* or the message *m'*. The same problem arises with the service process *while*{!*a*} since a client does not know how many messages to receive before leaving the loop. Clocks are another cause of ambiguity (temporal ambiguity) which will be explained latter. We say that a process is *ambiguous* if it does not admit a deterministic TA which is in interaction relation with him.

The general approach of our algorithm is similar to a determinization procedure: a location of a client TA corresponds to a subset of locations of the service TA linked with edges labelled with τ (Figure 4). However, determinization of TA is known to be undecidable in the general case (Alur, 1994). So, similarly to approaches which determinize subclasses of TAb(Alur, 1999), our algorithm seeks a TA with the same clocks only as the service TA.

The algorithm builds the client automaton A_C, processing potential client locations it has previously defined and pushed on a stack. Building of A_C stops either when an ambiguity is detected (returning "fail") or when the stack is empty, returning the client automaton. Let us detail the algorithm for a given client potential location l_C.

A Step of the Algorithm

Let $L_S(l_C)$ be the set of service locations temporary associated with l_C (the initial location $l_{0,C}$ is associated with the initial location of the service automaton A_S. We have the following steps:

- Creation of a new client location: we compute the ε-closure of $L_S(l_C)$, *i.e.* all reachable locations from $L_S(l_C)$ by sequences of τ L_S-actions. If this subset (say $L'_S(l_C)$) is already associated with a location l'_C of the client, then edges of the client TA which have generated l_C (*i.e* with destination l_C) are redirected to l'_C and we are done with the step. Otherwise, a new client location is created.
- Check for temporal ambiguity: we compute the subset $L''_S(l_C)$ of $L'_S(l_C)$ with no τ labelled outgoing edge and we check if all

Figure 4. Client timed automaton for the server timed automaton of Figure 3

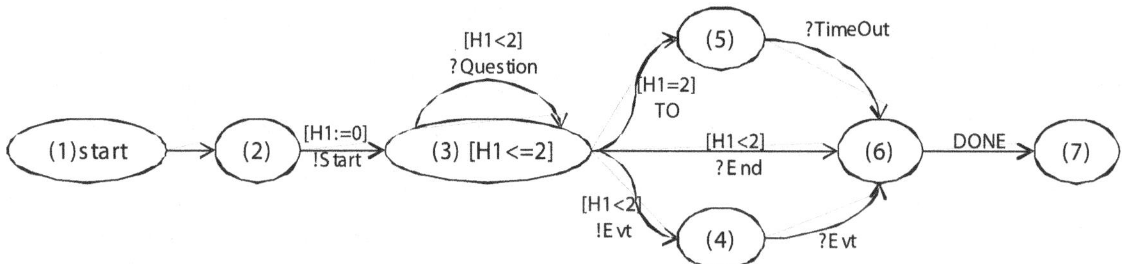

locations of $L''_S(l_C)$ have the same set of clocks. If this is not the case we say that the service is temporally ambiguous and the algorithm returns fail.

- Check for interaction relation: we verify that the interaction between l_S and l_C is satisfied (see below). The algorithm returns fail if this is not true.
- Creation of new edges and new potential client locations: each outgoing edge of $L'_S(l_C)$ not labelled with τ (visible service actions) gives rise to an outgoing edge from l_C (the associated client action) labelled with its complementary action. Destination locations of these edges provide new potential client locations, pushed on the stack.
- Guards and invariants definition: we copy to A_C, clock guards of the edges and clock invariants of the locations of A_S.

Interaction Verification

To verify the interaction relation, we compute and then analyze the Terminal Strongly Connected Components (TSCC) of the server locations set $L'_S(l_C)$ with respect to τ actions. Client and server interact correctly iff the following properties hold:

- If one of the TSCC does not send any message, then none of the server locations can send a message,
- otherwise, each TSCC must send a message. The set of messages sent by the server locations is the set of messages sent by all the TSCC.
- The set of messages received by the server locations must exactly be the same as the set of messages received by any of the TSCC.
- If any TSCC may execute √ (termination) then any TSCC must also be able to perform it, and so the server locations set can do it.

Example

Figure 5 gives the synthetis client TA of the server TA ?*Start*; scope(while [!*Question*]; !*End*, [{(?*Evt*, !*Evt*)}, (*H*1:2, !*TimeOut*), {}]) shown in Figure 3. Observe that some locations are "merged" in the client TA. Location labelled (2) in the server is present in the client with the same label (2) but its outgoing edge receives the message *Start*, whereas the client sends this message. Location (3) in the client is more involved. The ε-closure $L'_S(3)$ of $L_S(3)$ is the set {(3), (4), (5)} of server locations. Although these locations are important in the server behaviour, the client could not know whether the server is in location (3), (4) or (5). Hence, the algorithm "merges" these three locations in the client location (3). The different outgoing edges of $L'_S(3)$ are adapted to the client merging. Other locations are generated in nearly the same way as the client location (2).

Figure 5. False ambiguity detection for process switch(!o[c],scope(!o[a],[{(b,empty)},(4,empty),{}])

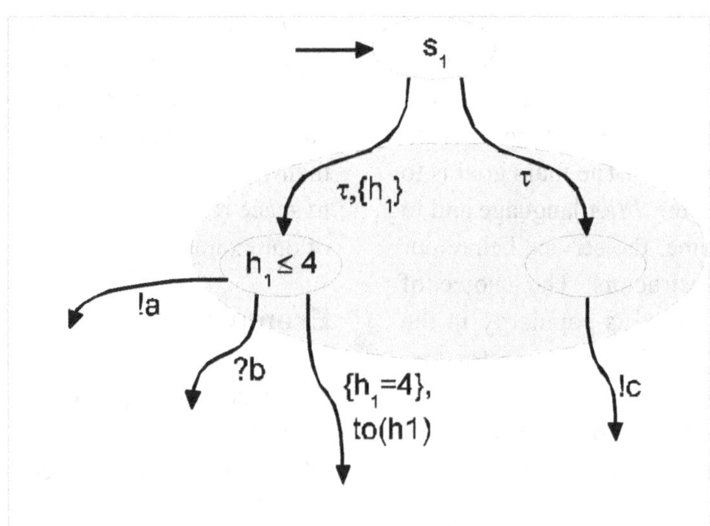

Dense vs. Discrete Time

We have chosen a dense time model for our formal semantics of BPEL process behaviours. In a previous work (Haddad, 1994), the discrete time semantics was preferred for simplicity reasons.

The discrete time approach has the following drawbacks. First, the passing of a unit of time is modelled by an explicit transition (χ) in the transition system which means that the compact representation of timing constraints by values is now hidden in the model by their combination with logical transitions. In other words, whereas handling correctly the interaction with the service, the client automaton is hardly understandable by a user. Moreover if two timing constraints are not of the same order, the time unit must be chosen w.r.t. the shorter one leading to a combinatory explosion of the automaton due to the "translation" of the longer one.

Conversely, the derivation of the client TA from the operational rules is more intricate than in the discrete time context since, on the one hand, the values of the timing constraints are handled symbolically with the help of clocks and, on the other hand, given some expression, we must determine which clocks are active and how they govern the guards of the edges. Moreover, our algorithm tries to synthetize a client TA with the same clocks as the server TA. This restriction, due to the fact that non deterministic TA are strictly more expressive than the deterministic ones may lead to false ambiguity detection. For instance, consider the process (Figure 6) switch: one branch of this switch starts with a scope process and another branch does not activate a timing constraint. Our algorithm detects this process as an ambiguous service although it may be that a client TA (with a different set of clocks) exists: in one branch there is an active clock whereas in the other one there is none and the client cannot decide which edge to follow. In a discrete time framework, the previous (complete) method produces a client. We implicitly work at a (discrete) TTS level. In the dense time framework, we work at a higher level (the TA one). This incompleteness of the algorithm is the price to pay in order to obtain a more compact representation of the client but we consider that this restriction on the clocks is reasonable because such false temporal ambiguity detections correspond to unrealistic BPEL processes.

JCWSL: A DESIGN LANGUAGE FOR WEB SERVICES

JAVA Complex Web Service Language (JCWSL) is a *JAVA* script language extended with the BPEL4WS constructors. The main goal is to design the CWS using the *JAVA* language and to define, in the same time, the service behaviour using BPEL4WS constructors. The choice of *JAVA* is essentially due to its popularity in the Web services community. The BPEL constructors are defined and implemented with respect to the semantics defined by the description language.

JCWSL offers the following properties:

- **High expressivity level**: It supports *JAVA* language, and therefore offers a high level of expressivity in order to define and design a complex Web service.
- **Transparency**: Local and/or distant Web services orchestration is integrated in the language in a transparent way.
- **Flexibility**: It offers two types of operation's invocation: visible or invisible invocation. A visible invocation appears in the service behaviour, while an invisible one executes the invocation without appearing in the service behaviour.
- **Strong coupling**: JCWSL extends in an elegant and natural way the *JAVA* language. Thus, the operations and messages manipulation are visible and accessible in both parts of the program *i.e.* the implementation (*JAVA*) and the behaviour (BPEL) parts.

UML Modeling

The Unified Model Language (UML) is widely used in the development of object oriented software and has also been used for business process modelling and system design. In the literature, there is different works that propose to map UML modelling to BPEL (Baresi, 2003; Skogan, 2004; Gronmo, 2006; Gardner, 2003; Cambronero 2007}. Among all this papers, Cambronero 2007 seems to be, in our sense, the most exhaustive since it proposes different stereotypes and covers the main orchestration constructors essentially those concerning time constraints. In the sequel, we use their profile in order to model our example. Due to space reasons, we restrict our UML modeling of our example to the sequence diagram.

Example

We present, in this section, the development in JCWSL of a CWS (*Example 1*) implementing an advanced quiz game based on an existing BWS. The BWS, located at www.hlrs.de/quiz/quiz.wsdl, implements a simple quiz game consisting of the invocation of a set of questions with different difficulty levels, and checking the correctness of the answer. This example presents a new game where the goal is to answer a fixed number of questions within a fixed delay. The difficulty level of any question can be chosen randomly or specified by the player. Here are the different steps of the application:

- The player requests to start the game by specifying the number of questions (*nbQuestion*).
- The player asks for a question with a given difficulty level or a random one.
- The player has to answer *nbQuestion* questions.
- The player must answer within a fixed delay otherwise the service skip to the next question.
- At the end, the final score, computed according to the number of correct answers and their difficulty level, is sent to the player.

The Sequence diagram of the example is presented in the Figure 7. Note that we use only The <<RTAction>> stereotype form (Cambronero 2007) to model the time out on the player answer.

Figure 6. The sequence diagram of the composite quiz service

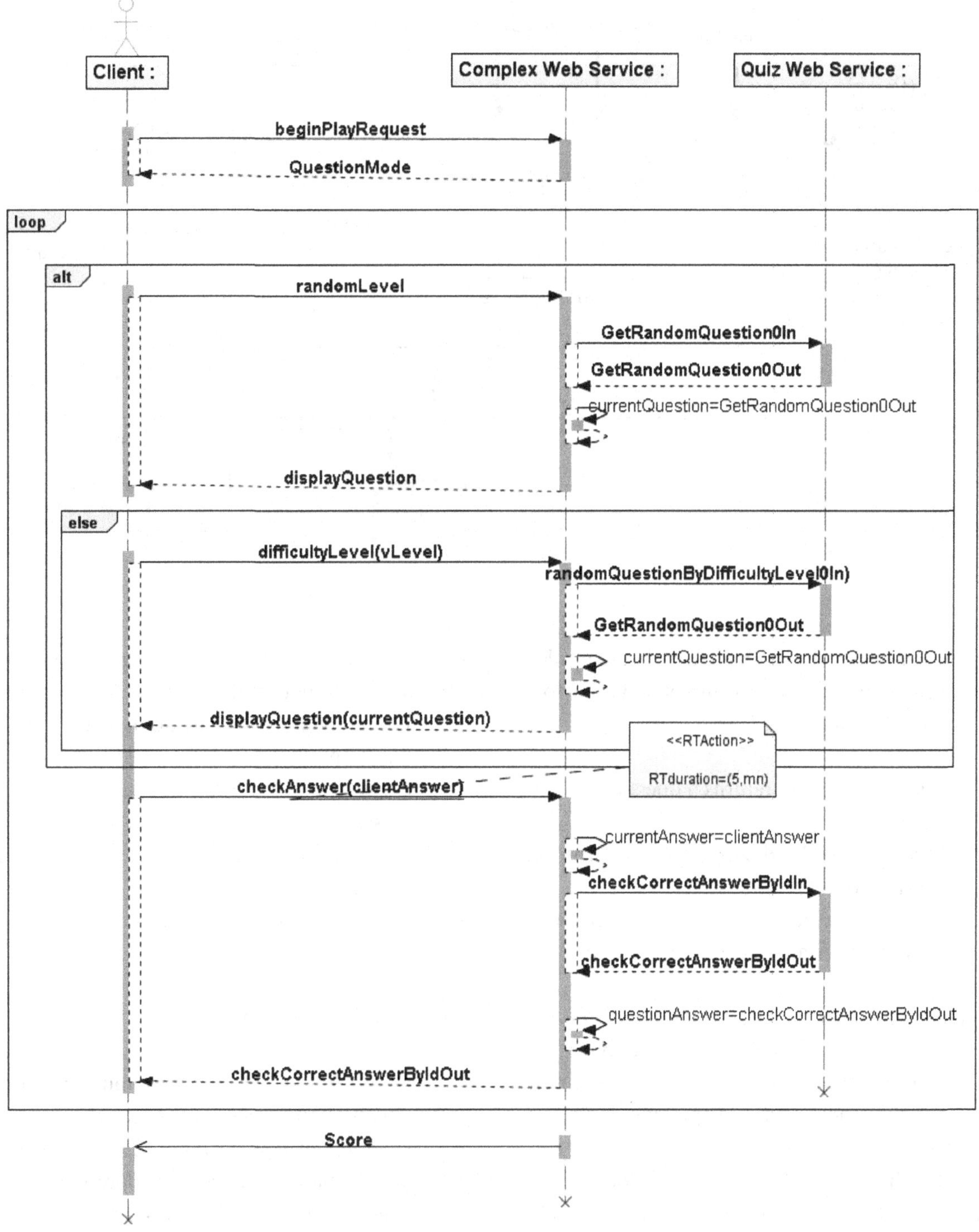

Figure 7. Platform architecture

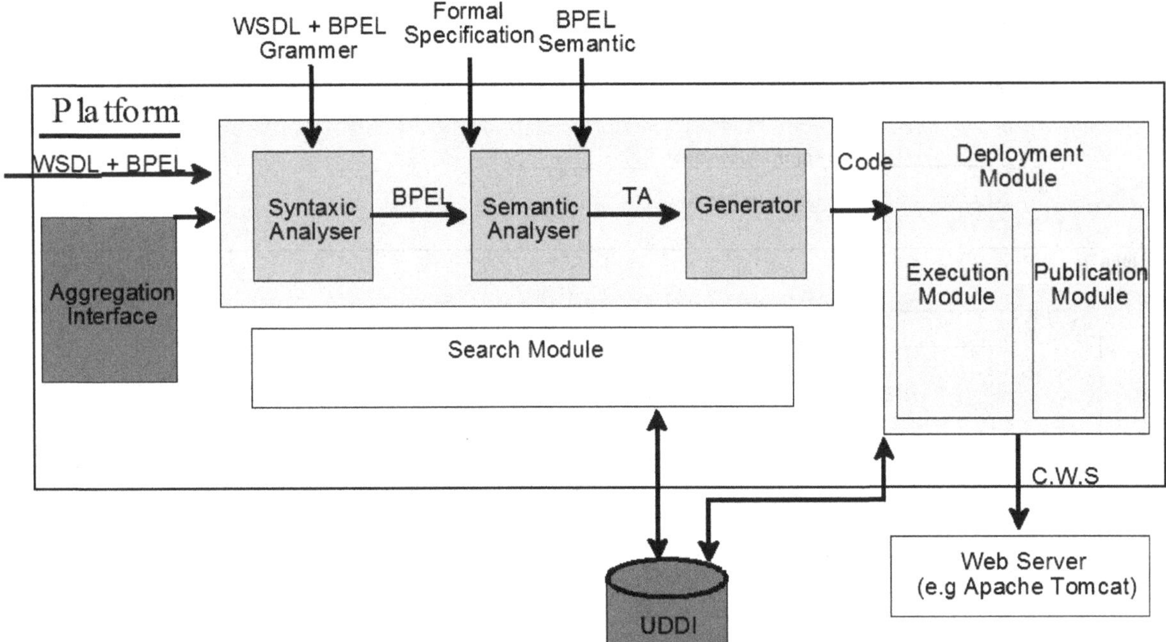

The CWS uses the BWS cited earlier to implement this game. The BWS implements the following operations:

- ***randomQuestion*** returns a question of any level;
- ***randomQuestionByDifficulty*** returns a question of a specified level;
- ***checkCorrectAnswer*** checks the correctness of a user answer for a given question.

Thus, the CWS includes in the *import block*, the importation of the BWS to be able to invoke its operations. It also needs to include the input/output *JAVA* package for displaying purposes (lines 3 and 4).

After the *import block*, the *definition block* includes a declaration block and a main block. In the declaration block, operations and messages used later must be declared here. Here, five types of messages are defined (lines 9 to 30):

- *Answer*: is the answer on a given question and it includes the question and its answer;
- *Level*: defines the difficulty level of a question;
- *ChoiceMode*: represents a notification message;
- *Questions*: represents the number of questions;
- *Score*: represents the final score;

and the following operations:

- *beginPlay:* is an input output operation which allows to begin the game;
- *randomLevel*: is an input operation which allows player to choose random level;
- *checkAnswer*: is an input operation which receives the answer on a specified question;
- *difficultyLevel*: is an input operation which allows player to choose a difficulty level;

- *getScore*: is an input operation which allows to get the score;
- *finalScore*: is an output operation which sends the final score;
- *displayQuestion*: is an input operation which allows to display a question;

Several messages and operations defined earlier are instantiated. There are either defined from the imported BWS ''squiz" types or in the CWS (lines 35 to 45).

The implementation of the CWS begins with the main method (line 34). In addition to the instantition of messages, the main method is composed of a *behaviour block* identified by one of the BPEL constructors and/or an *implementation block* identified by the *JAVACODE* keyword. These two blocs may be nested and, all the variables declared in the *JAVACODE* section can be accessed by the BPEL constructors.

In this example, we first define the CWS behaviour using the different BPEL constructors. The *sequence* constructor specifies that the execution of the following instructions must be performed sequentially.

The definition of this example in JCWSL is as follows:

There are two types of function for calling an operation: execute or invoke. Both functions allow the assignment of an input, output or input/output messages. The main difference between these two functions is the external visibility. In this example, we call the invoke function which takes an input and output messages ("modeChoice" and "mode" respectively) and which is visible for the outside (*i.e.* it is part of the CWS behaviour).

The *pick* constructor is then used to wait, a given time, for a player's answer. The CWS switches then according to the chosen mode in order to send a question of the appropriate level. After sending a question, the service will also use the pick constructor to implement a deadline after which it will go to the next question. In fact, it waits for 5 units of time the reception of the answer before going to the next question. At the end, the CWS returns the final score computed according to the received answers (line 95).

JCWSL Description

The development of a CWS with JCWSL is divided into two sections: an importation block **importBlock** and a definition block **defBloc**. The definition block represents the body of the complex service.

CWSLanguage::≡ (<importBloc> <defBloc>)+

Importation block: importBlock: is composed of two importation types, *JAVA* packages and Web service importations. Since our language is an extension of the *JAVA* language, JAVA packages needed by a CWS are imported exactly as in any JAVA program.

importBloc::≡ ("importBWS" <ID> = <STRING>";"| "import" <ID> (.<ID>)* ";")*

Web service importation allows to include in the complex Web service the required Web services. An imported Web service is identified by a unique name mapped with its URL, and which acts as a namespace for the service. Inside the definition block, a service data structure can be accessed exactly the same way as any *JAVA* package. In fact, an imported service is considered as a package composed of a set of classes representing the messages, the operations and the types declared in the WSDL file. Each service library is composed of a set of classes: a class for each complex type defined in the *types* section in the WSDL file, a class per message and a set of *stub* classes representing a client for each binding type.

Stub classes have the same name as the binding element in the WSDL file and are composed of the list of service operations accessible via the link. **importBloc** may contain zero or several import instructions.

Example 1. Quiz game example

```
// Importation block
import java.io.*;
importBWS squiz = "http://www.hlrs.de/quiz/quiz.wsdl";

public CWSDefinition jeuxQuiz{

// Declaration block
public DefMessage Answer{String choice;}
public DefMessage Level{String l;}
public DefMessage ChoiceMode{String message;}
public DefMessage Questions {int nb;}
public DefMessage Score{int value;}
public DefOperation beginPlay(Input/Output: Questions q,ChoiceMode my-
choice) {
    JAVACODE{ mychoice.message="Choose a Mode (Random or
         specified level): ";
    return mychoice;}
public DefOperation randomLevel(Input: Level lv) {}
public DefOperation checkAnswer(Input: Answer a) {}
public DefOperation clientLevel(Input: Level lv) {}
public DefOperation getScore(Input: Score s) {}
public DefOperation finalScore(Output: Score s)
    {JAVACODE{return s;}}
public DefOperation displayQuestion(
    Output:squiz.GetRandomQuestion0Out m) { JAVACODE{return m;}}

// Main block

void main {
 Variables{
 Variable(vQuestions,Questions);
 Variable(vScore,Score);
 Variable(currentQuestion, squiz.GetRandomQuestion0Out);
 Variable(currentAnswer,squiz.CheckCorrectAnswerByIdIn);
 Variable(questionAnswer,squiz.CheckCorrectAnswerByIdOut);
 Variable(clientAnswer, Answer);
 Variable(vLevel, Level);
 }//Variables
 Sequence{
 JAVACODE{
  int nbQuestion=0;
```

continued on following page

Example 1. Continued

```
 vScore.value=0;
}//JAVACODE
Receive(beginPlay,vQuestions);
While{JAVACODE{nbQuestion<vQuestions.nb},
 Sequence{
 Pick{
  OnMessage(randomLevel,vLevel) {
  Sequence{
   Invoke(squiz.randomQuestion,, currentQuestion);
  }//Sequence
  }//OnMessage
  OnMessage(clientLevel, vLevel) {
  Sequence{
   Invoke(squiz.randomQuestionByDifficultyLevel,
      vLevel.l,currentQuestion);
  }//Sequence
  }//OnMessage
 }//pick
 Reply(displayQuestion,currentQuestion);
 Pick{
 OnMessage(checkAnswer,clientAnswer){
  JAVACODE{
   currentAnswer.setId(currentQuestion.getId());
   currentAnswer.setGuessedAnswer(clientAnswer.choice);
  }//JAVACODE
  Invoke(squiz.checkCorrectAnswerById,
      currentAnswer,questionAnswer);
JAVACODE{
    if((questionAnswer!=null)
     &&(questionAnswer.getResult()==true)) {
   vSore.value =
      vScore.value+currentQuestion.getDifficultyLevel();
 }//IF
}//JAVACODE
  }//OnMessage
  OnAlarm(For="5"){JAVACODE{;}
  }//Pick
 }//Sequence
 nbQuestion++;
 currentQuestion=null;
 currentAnswer=null;
```

continued on following page

Example 1. Continued

```
  questionAnswer=null;
  clientAnswer=null;
  } // end of sequence for while
 } // end of while
 Receive(getScore,vScore);
 Reply(finalScore, vScore);
 } // end sequence for main
 } // end of main
}// end of CWSDefinition
```

Definition block represents the body of the CWS. It contains the definition and the behaviour of the complex Web service. It is composed of two blocs: a declaration block **declaration** and a main block **main**.

defBlock::≡ "public" "CWSDefinition" <ID> (<declaration> <main>)+

Declaration block is composed of local operations declaration and/or messages declaration. This block is optional, no messages or operations needs to be declared.

declaration::≡ (<opdeclaration> | <messDeclaration>)*

An operation is identified by a name and one or two messages depending on its type. There are three types of operations: input, output, and input/output. The operations defined in this section are appended to those defined by the imported Web services. An operation may also include a body composed of *JAVA* code.

opDeclaration ((("public defOperation" <operationName>

"(" "input" ":" <messageType> <ID> | "output" ":" <messageType> <ID>

| "input" ":" <messageType> <ID> "," "output" ":" <messageType> <ID>

")" "{"<operationBody>"}"

operationBody is the main part of the operation. It is composed of either a set of JAVA instructions JAVAInstructions or the BPEL constructor execute, or both. JAVAInstructions is preceeded by the JAVACODE keyword.

operationBody ((((<java> | <execute>)* <java> ((("JAVACODE" {(<javaInstructions>)+}

A message is identified by its name and is composed of one or several variables. Message declaration does not contain methods. Automatically, while developing the CWS, a set of management methods are created. These methods have the following form: get<variableName> and set<variableName>.

messDeclaration (((“public defMessage” <messageName>

“{”(<variableType> <variableName>”;”)+”}”

Main block The second part of defBlock is the main block. It contains the definition and the behaviour of the CWS. It is composed of the service activities and of JAVA code. Service activities are defined using BPEL constructors, whereas the service definition is written in JAVA. Those two types are not overlapped in our language, but may be nested. However, the visibility of the JAVA variables is preserved outside the JAVACode bloc and can be used in the activity blocs. In the activity bloc, only constructors imbrication and operation invocation are allowed.

main::≡ “void” “main” “{”(<process>|<java>)* “}”

process represents CWS behaviour and is composed of the following constructors:

process::≡ <pick> | <switch> | <opCall> | <sequence> | <while> | <wait>

pick is an event handler to catch the cited events. An event is either the triggering of an alarm or a message reception. It suspends the execution until the occurrence of an event, and then executes the appropriate code.

<pick>::≡ “pick” “{” (<evt>)+ [<delayfor>] “}”

<evt>::≡ “eventhandler” “{” <invoke> “}” “{” (<process>)* “}”

<delayfor>::≡ “delayfor” “(” <integer_literal> “)” “{” (<process>)* “}”

switch is a conditional statment. It is used to perform different actions depending on the value of the associated condition.

switch::≡ Switch (“{” “JAVACODE” “{”<condExpr> “}” “}” “{ <process> “}”)

opCall allows to call an operation in a visible or invisible way. Therefore, it is composed of two constructors *invoke* and *execute*. In both cases, the operation type is either one way or request/reply. *invoke* and *execute* are executed exactly the same way, the only difference is the external visibility of the operation. **invoke** allows to invoke an operation in a transparent way. The invocation is visible from outside the CWS and is taken into consideration while defining the CWS behaviour. Whereas, **execute** allows to invoke an operation internally, *i.e.* the invocation is not visible from the outside and is not taken into account when defining the CWS behaviour. In both cases, *inputVariable* and *outputVariable* represent messages.

opCall::≡ (<invoke> | <execute>)

invoke::≡ “invoke” “(” <operationName> [,<inputVariable> |

(<inputVariable>, <outputVariable>)] “)”

execute::≡ “execute” “(” <operationName> [,<inputVariable>|

(<inputVariable>, <outputVariable>)] “)”

sequence defines a block of instructions to be executed sequentially.

sequence::≡ “sequence” “{” <process> “}”

while is a loop statement. It executes the block of instructions as long as the condition is satisfied.

while::≡ “while” “{” “JAVACODE” “{”<conditionalExpr> “}” “}” “{”<process>”}”

wait suspends the process execution for the specified duration or until the expiration of the deadline.

wait::≡ “Wait” (“for”=<duration-expr> | “until”=<deadline-expr>)

WEB SERVICE DESIGN FRAMEWORK

Platform Architecture

The platform allows to build CWS from BWS. It offers different modules in order to define, compile and deploy CWS. It is composed of four modules: search module, aggregation interface, compiler, and deployment module Figure 7 illustrates the different modules of the platform as well as their different interactions.

Search Module

This module is a UDDI client which allows to explore and search the UDDI registry in order to locate basic Web services. It is used by the generator to locate and upload BWS and consequently communicates with the UDDI registry.

Aggregation Interface

It is a CWS development environment. It allows to define CWS from BWS operation's aggregation. The environment is based on JCWSL.

Compiler Module

The generator takes in entry the description of the CWS written in JCWSL and generates the corresponding code and behaviour in BPEL. It is composed of an analyzer and a generator.

- The analyzer applies syntactic and semantic analysis.
  - During syntactic analysis, the analyzer checks the file conformity with the language grammar and the validity of each BWS, constructs for each BWS its library <<**package**>>, and generates the syntactic tree of the CWS.
  - The semantic analyzer ensures that the CWS fulfills some properties. In fact, giving the semantic tree and an abstraction algorithm, it generates the observable description of the service and its TA in order to check service ambiguity.
- The generator takes as input the TA and the syntactic tree generated earlier, and generates the CWS Java code.

Deployment Module

It generates the Web application which hosts the Web service. It also defines an implementation of the service communication model. In fact, information about the service communication is used in order to define the binding part of the service description.

Publication Module

It allows to publish, in a UDDI register, the BPEL4WS file of the service. The platform provides, in addition to the utilities necessary for the design and the development of complex services, a module named generic client, which generates a client for a complex service (see section Client Synthesis).

Client Module

It allows to generate automatically a client to interact correctly with the service if the service is not ambiguous, or an error otherwise. The generic customer is composed of two submodules:

a synthesis module and an execution module. The synthesis module recovers, from the UDDI directory, the service specifications in BPEL, analyses and then produces the corresponding timed automaton. The execution module is a middleware which, at the service invocation time, loads the corresponding timed automaton in order to manage the client/service interaction.

An Application Life Cycle

This section describes, in detail, the various stages of a complex Web service installation using our platform: the service design, automatic generation of the service including the publication and the deployment, and finally the generation of the corresponding client.

Complex Web Service Design

The developer has a framework in order to describe its complex Web service (CWS). A module, in relation with the UDDI registry, can be used to locate existing Web services. The description of the service is made using the JCWSL language which makes it possible to describe at the same time the observable behaviour of the service with BPEL constructors and the service implementation with the *JAVA* language.

CWS Generation, Publishing and Deployment

The second step deals with the deployment of the CWS and includes the CWS generation, the behaviour generation and publishing, and the CWS deployment. From the file ".jcwsl", the compiler generates the CWS behaviour in BPEL and the Web application in *JAVA*. The publication of the complex service is carried out exactly the same way as for a basic service. Then, the deployment of a complex service consists of the creation of a JAXM servlet which plays the role of a proxy between the client and the service. When the servlet receives a message corresponding to the activation of an object (the first message in the protocol of the service), it creates an instance of the corresponding class of the complex service, initializes the correlation attributes (according to the message value), adds it in the queue and carries out its behaviour (*i.e.* starts the corresponding thread). The servlet URI corresponds to the address of the complex service. Each received message is redirected towards the instance of the corresponding class according to the object and the attributes values of the correlation instance.

Service Invocation

The last stage is the client generation starting from the service description in order to allow a correct interaction with the service. It consists of the generation and the deployment of a JAXM servlet which acts as an input/output interface of the client instance of a given service. The servlet acts as a dispatcher which, at the reception of a SOAP message, redirects it towards the corresponding client instance. The initialization of an interaction creates a new automaton and links it to the servlet. The servlet URI address is used by all the clients.

Implementation

Parser Generation

The choice of *JAV*ACC (JAVA Compiler Compiler) to describe our language grammar is the natural choice since it extends *JAVA*. Once the description of the grammar is finished, it is written in a notation similar to BNF. In fact, *JAVACC* works with a.jj file. When the *JAVACC* is run against the.jj file, it generates a number of *JAVA* source files. One is the primary parsing code, Parser_1.*JAVA*, which you will invoke from your application when you have an expression to parse. *JAVACC* also creates six other auxiliary files that are used by the parser. Three files are specific to this particular grammar; the last four are generic helpers that are always generated no matter what the grammar looks like. Once *JAVACC* has generated these seven *JAVA* sources, they can be compiled and linked into a *JAVA* application. The new parser can be used to parse the description file for a CWS written in JCWSL. It produces a BPEL4WS describing the behaviour of the corresponding CWS.

Internal Structure

While parsing the CWS definition file, an internal representation is automatically created. This representation is a set of objects representing the different element of the service. Thus, an instance of the object called definition is created. Then, the other elements of the CWS are added *i.e.* the local messages, local operations, imported Web services. In order to do so, each time the parser meets an element of the service, it creates the corresponding element. An object called import containing the set of imported services is built. A CWS may declare local messages and operations. A message class is created for the set of local messages as well as an operation class is created for the set of local operations. A portype class is created in order to be able to invoke the declared operations. In a portType, it is possible to gather several operations. Operation class is always linked with the message class, since an operation handles messages (one or two). As for the behaviour block, it is represented as a set of activities which defines the behaviour orchestration of the CWS. Those activities are defined in the definition class. All the previously cited classes are designed using the *JAVA* API. *JAVA*, associated to XML allow a simple and rapid development of CWS. These classes are represented in XML format validated with XML Schema Language.

RELATED WORK

The composite Web service adds two dimensions by comparison to the simple ones; they are statefull and they obey to an operational behaviour (interaction protocol). This raises many theoretical and practical issues which are part of ongoing research (Nakajima, 2002). Due to the lack of a formal semantic to BPEL (its semantic is defined using English prose), it is hard to define formal tools and methods that can validate and verify behavioural properties by acting directly on BPEL expressions. The main approach, followed by most of the state-of-the-art works, is to translate a service behaviour (BPEL process) into a mathematically well-founded model, considering just the semantical elements that are relevant for the property to be verified. Then, model-checking methods can be applied to the formal representation of the composite service behaviour. There are three major formalisms which were successfully applied: finite state Machines (FSM), process algebras (PA) and Petri Nets (PN). A great number of works therein aims to verify specific properties of a BPEL process.

In (Breugel, 2005), the authors translate a given BPEL process into a process algebraic expression in order to verify its control flow. Based on this work, they provide an in-depth-analysis of BPELs Dead-Path-Elimination by formal means. In (Ferrara, 2004), a similar approach is given and which translates to LOTOS. In previous works, we give an operational semantic to Xlang (ancestor of BPEL) in order to verify the ambiguity (non usability) of a Web service behaviour (not deadlock-free) (Melliti, 2003; Haddad, 2004). In (Schlingloff, 2005) a similar work is done using Petri Net. In (Stahl, 2004; Ouyang, 2005; Hamadi, 2003) and (Schmidt, 2004), the authors propose a pattern-based translation of activities into Petri Nets, and then they use Petri Net properties to check properties.

Most of these works try to verify properties related to a single BPEL process (the coordinator). In this article, we begin by giving an observable operational semantic to abstract BPEL. We consider it as a grammar of timed process algebra and we define its operational semantic according to its informal definition. This step allows us to model the partners behaviour using a TTS (by applying operational rules) with regard to their interaction.

CONCLUSION

The approach developed in this article emphasizes a new interest of formal semantics. Traditionally, equipping a language of a formal semantics has two main goals: allowing the programmer to understand the language constructors in order to write correct applications and ensuring that the execution of a program is independent of the compiler and the target machine. In our case, the search of a semantic for complex Web services led us to raise an ignored problem of the experts: the service ambiguity.

Moreover, our approach (partially) answers to the service dynamicity since a client discovering a new service (or an existing but modified service) generates a timed automaton whose execution makes it possible to correctly interact with the service. Finally, this semantic decreases the cost of software development since the interface generation and the service deployment shares many components.

Our second contribution aims at unifying the design and the implementation process by providing a language that mixes BPEL with *JAVA*. In our environment, the designer starts from a UML description then transforms it in a BPEL specification and enlarges it (when necessary) in a JCSWL program that will translated in *JAVA* and deployed on the server.

Our future work will exploit this semantics in order to solve the service composition problem, namely how to guarantee that composed service does not block itself, never finishes, etc. In a complementary manner, we carry our efforts on the integration of the orientation aspect concepts in Web services. The *weaving* is obviously an activity related to the execution and thus lends itself naturally to our approach.

REFERENCES

Alur, R., & Dill, D. L. (1994). A Theory of Timed Automata. *Theoretical Computer Science, 126*(2), 183–235. doi:10.1016/0304-3975(94)90010-8

Alur, R., Fix, L., & Henzinger, T. A. (1999). Event-clock Automata: a Determinizable Class of Timed Automata. *Theoretical Computer Science, 211*(1–2), 253–273. doi:10.1016/S0304-3975(97)00173-4

Alves, A., Arkin, A., Askary, S., Barreto, C., Bloch, B., Curbera, F., et al. Van der Rijn, D., Yendluri, P., & Yiu, A. (2007). *Web Services Business Process Execution Language Version 2.0.* OASIS WSBPEL Technical Committee. http://docs.oasis-open.org/ wsbpel/ 2.0/ wsbpel-v2.0.pdf.

Baeten, J. C. M., & Bergstra, J. A. (1991). Real Time Process Algebra. *Formal Aspects of Computing, 3*(2), 142–188. doi:10.1007/BF01898401

Baresi, L., Heckel, R., Thöne, S., & Varrò, D. (2003). Modeling and Validation of Service-Oriented Architectures: Application vs. Style. *Proceedings of the 9th European software engineering conference held jointly with 11th ACM SIGSOFT international symposium on Foundations of software engineering* (pp. 68-77). New York, NY: ACM Press.

Bellwood, T., Clément, L., & von Riegen, C. (2002). *Universal Description, Discovery and Integration.* OASIS UDDI Specification Technical Committee. http://www.oasis-open.org/ cover/ uddi.html.

Bergstra, J. A., & Klop, J. W. (1984). Process Algebra for Synchronous Communication. *Information and Control*, *60*(1-3), 109–137. doi:10.1016/S0019-9958(84)80025-X

Blow, M., Goland, Y., Kloppmann, M., Leymann, F., Pfau, G., Roller, D., & Rowley, M. (2004). *BPELJ: BPEL for JAVA*. BEA and IBM. http://www-128.ibm.com/ developerworks/ library/ specification/ ws-bpelj/.

Cambronero, M.E., Pardo, J.J., Díaz, G., & Valero, V. (2007). Using RT-UML for modelling web services. *ACM symposium on Applied computing.*

Christensen, E., Curbera, F., Meredith, G., & Weerawarana, S. (2001). *Web Services Description Language (WSDL) 1.1.* World Wide Web Consortium. http://www.w3.org/ TR/ wsdl.

Duftler, M. J., Mukhi, N. K., Slominski, A., & Weerawarana, S. (2001). *Web Services Invocation Framework (WSIF).* The Apache Software Foundation. http://ws.apache.org/wsif/.

Ferrara, A. (2004). Web Services: a Process Algebra Approach. [ACM.]. *ICSOC*, *2004*, 242–251. doi:10.1145/1035167.1035202

Gardner, T. (2003). UML Modelling of Automated Business Processes with a Mapping to BPEL4WS. *First European Workshop on Object Orientation and Web Services* (pp. 21-25), Germany.

Gronmo, R., & Jaeger, M. C. (2006). Model-Driven Methodology for building QoS-Optimised Web Service Compositions. *WEWST06*, Zurich, Switzerland.

Gudgin, M., Hadley, M., Mendelsohn, N., Moreau, J., & Nielsen, H. (2000). *Simple Object Access Protocol (SOAP) 1.1.* World Wide Web Consortium. http://www.w3.org/ TR/ SOAP/.

Haddad, S., Melliti, T., Moreaux, P., & Rampacek, S. (2004). A Dense Time Semantics for Web Services Specifications Languages. *Proc. of the 1st Int. Conf. on Information & Communication Technologies: from Theory to Applications (ICTTA'04)* (pp. 647–648), Damascus, Syria.

Haddad, S., Melliti, T., Moreaux, P., & Rampacek, S. (2004). Modelling Web Services Interoperability. *Proceedings of the Sixth International Conference on Entreprise Information Systems* (pp. 287-295), Porto, Portugal.

Hamadi, R., & Benatallah, B. (2003). A Petri Net-based model for web service composition. In K-D. Schewe & X. Zhou (Eds.), *Fourteenth Australasian Database Conference (ADC2003)*, v(17) of *CRPIT* (pp. 191-200). ACS.

Hoare, C. A. R. (1985). *Communicating Sequential Processes*. Englewood Cliffs, NJ, USA: Prentice Hall.

Juric, M., Sarang, P., & Mathew, B. (2005). *Business Process Execution Language for Web Services*. Packt Publishing.

Léonard, L., & Leduc, G. (1997). An Introduction to ET-LOTOS for the Description of Timesensitive Systems. *Computer Networks and ISDN Systems*, *29*(3), 271–292. doi:10.1016/S0169-7552(96)00078-5

Melliti, T., & Haddad, S. (2003). Synthesis of Agents for Web Services Interaction. *Workshop Semantic Web Services for Enterprise Application Integration and E-Commerce of the Fifth International Conference on Electronic Commerce*, Pittsburgh, USA.

Milner, R. (1989). *Communication and Concurrency.* Englewood Cliffs, NJ, USA: Prentice-Hall.

Nakajima, S. (2002). Model-Checking Verification for Reliable Web Service. *Workshop on Object-Oriented Web Services*, Seattle, Washington.

Nicollin, X., & Sifakis, J. (1991). An Overview and Synthesis on Timed Process Algebras. In J. W. de Bakker, C. Huizing, W. P. de Roever, & G. Rozenberg (Eds.), *Proc. Real-Time: Theory in Practice, REXWorkshop*, v(600) of *LNCS* (pp. 526-548). Springer-Verlag.

Nicollin, X., & Sifakis, J. (1994). The Algebra of Timed Process, ATP: Theory and Application. *Information and Computation*, *114*(1), 131–178. doi:10.1006/inco.1994.1083

Ouyang, C., Verbeek, E., van der Aalst, W., Breutel, S., Dumas, M., & ter Hofstede, A. (2005). *Formal Semantics and Analysis of Control Flow in WS-BPEL*. BPM-05-13, Business Process Management Center.

Plotkin, G. D. (1981). A Structural Approach to Operational Semantics. Technical Report FN-19, DIAMI, CSD, U. of Aarhus, Aarhus, Denmark.

Schlingloff, B.-H., Martens, A., & Schmidt, K. (2005). Modeling and Model Checking Web Services. *Electronic Notes in Theoretical Computer Science*, *126*, 3–26. doi:10.1016/j.entcs.2004.11.011

Schmidt, K. &. Stahl, C. (2004). A Petri Net Semantic for BPEL4WS - Validation and Application. In E. Kindler (Ed.), *Workshop on Algorithms and Tools for Petri Nets (AWPN 04)* (pp. 1-6), Germany.

Schneider, S. A. (1995). An Operational Semantics for Timed CSP. *Information and Computation*, *116*(2), 193–213. doi:10.1006/inco.1995.1014

Skogan, D., Gronmo, R., & Solheim, I. (2004). Web Service Composition in UML. *EDOC '04: Proceedings of the Enterprise Distributed Object Computing Conference, Eighth IEEE International (EDOC '04)* (pp. 47-57), Washington, DC, USA: IEEE Computer Society.

Staab, S., van der Aalst, W., Benjamins, V. R., Sheth, A., Miller, J. A., & Bussler, C. (2003). Web Services: Been There, Done That? *IEEE Intelligent Systems*, *18*, 72–85. doi:10.1109/MIS.2003.1179197

Stahl, C. (2004). *A Petri Net Semantics for BPEL*. Technical report 10099, Humboldt-Universitäat zu Berlin.

Tidwell, D. (2000, November). Web Services - The Web's Next Revolution. *IBM developerWorks*.

van Breugel, F., & Koshinka, M. (2005). Dead-Path-Elimination in BPEL4WS. *5th International Conference on Application of Concurrency to System Design* (pp. 192-201). IEEE.

This work was previously published in International Journal of Web Services Research, Volume 6, Issue 4, edited by Liang-Jie Zhang, pp. 1-29, copyright 2009 by IGI Publishing (an imprint of IGI Global).

Chapter 15
Security for Web Services:
Standards and Research Issues

Lorenzo D. Martino
Purdue University, USA

Elisa Bertino
Purdue University, USA

ABSTRACT

This article discusses the main security requirements for Web services and it describes how such security requirements are addressed by standards for Web services security recently developed or under development by various standardizations bodies. Standards are reviewed according to a conceptual framework that groups them by the main functionalities they provide. Covered standards include most of the standards encompassed by the original Web Service Security roadmap proposed by Microsoft and IBM in 2002 (Microsoft and IBM 2002). They range from the ones geared toward message and conversation security and reliability to those developed for providing interoperable Single Sign On and Identity Management functions in federated organizations. The latter include Security Assertion Markup Language (SAML), WS-Policy, XACML, that is related to access control and has been recently extended with a profile for Web services access control; XKMS and WS-Trust; WS-Federation, LibertyAlliance and Shibboleth, that address the important problem of identity management in federated organizations. The article also discusses the issues related to the use of the standards and open research issues in the area of access control for Web services and innovative digital identity management techniques are outlined.

DOI: 10.4018/978-1-61350-104-7.ch015

INTRODUCTION

Today Web services are a fundamental component of agile e-business. Through the use of eXtensible Markup Language (XML), Simple Object Access Protocol (SOAP) (Gudgin, 2007), and related open standards deployed in Service Oriented Architectures (SOA), they allow data and applications to interact through dynamic and ad hoc connections. Web services technology can be implemented in a wide variety of architectures, can co-exist with other technologies and software design approaches, and can be adopted in an evolutionary manner without requiring major transformations to legacy applications and databases. Interoperability is a key requirement for Web services and, at the same time, it is the key objective and promise of the standardization effort. Web services enhance interoperability and are thus able to support business applications composed by chains of Web services. Interoperability is a key promise of Web service technology and therefore notions such as Web service composition and technologies like workflow systems are being investigated and developed.

The use of Web services, stand-alone or composed, must however provide strong security guarantees. Security is today a relevant requirement for any distributed application, and in particular for these enabled by the Web such as e-health, e-commerce, e-learning. Providing security guarantees in open dynamic environments characterized by heterogeneous platforms is however a major challenge. Web services security encompasses several requirements that can be described along the well known security dimensions:

- Integrity, whereby information can be modified only by users who have the right to do so, and only in authorized ways. In particular, message integrity requires that a message remain unaltered during transmission. Ensuring information integrity might also require that information is transferred only among intended users and in intended ways.
- Confidentiality, whereby information can be disclosed only to users authorized to access it. When applied to messages, it requires that the content of a message cannot be viewed while in transit, except by authorized services.
- Availability, whereby the use of the system cannot be denied to entitled users inadvertently or due to denial of service attacks by a malicious party.
- Accountability, whereby users are accountable for their security-relevant actions. A particular case of this is non-repudiation, where responsibility for an action cannot be denied.

Furthermore, each Web service must protect its own resources against unauthorized access. This in turn requires suitable means for: identification, whereby the recipient of a message must be able to identify the sender; authentication, whereby the recipient of a message needs to verify the claimed identity of the sender; authorization, whereby the recipient of a message applies access control policies to determine whether the sender has the right to use the required Web service and other protected resources. In a Web service environment it is however not enough to protect the service providers, it is also important to protect the parties requiring services. Since a key component of the Web service architectures is represented by the discovery of services, it is crucial to ensure that all information used by parties to this purpose be authentic and correct. Also we need approaches by which a service provider can prove its identity to the party requiring the service in order to avoid attacks, such as phishing attacks.

Within this context, the goal of securing Web services can be decomposed in three broad subsidiary goals:

- Providing mechanisms and tools for securing the integrity and confidentiality of messages as well as the guarantee of message delivery.
- Ensuring that the service acts only on message requests that comply with the policies associated with the services.
- Ensuring that all information required by a party in order to discover and use services is correct and authentic.

Different security mechanisms and tools, such as encryption algorithms and access control mechanisms, have been developed and deployed over time to this end. Such security mechanisms are provided at all levels, from the network and the operating system, up to database management systems and the Web applications themselves. The overall goal of Web services security standards is to make interoperable such different security mechanisms so as to provide end-to-end security guarantees and to reduce the cost of security management. To achieve this goal, Web services security standards have to provide standard "languages" to define security policies, standard ways to represent security meta-information and standard protocols to exchange security meta-information among all the involved software agents and Web applications. Furthermore, standards must be extensible in order to address new requirements and/or incorporate available security technologies.

The article is organized as follows. Section 2 introduces the different notions of standards. This classification gives indications about the maturity, the stability and the level of endorsement of a standard. Then a framework for the security standards is presented. In this framework, Web services security standards are conceptually grouped depending on the various aspects of Web services security they address. Then, for each security aspect of the framework, the related standards are briefly surveyed, describing their specific purpose, their main features and their current status. The section concludes with a brief discussion on the main issues concerning the adoption of such standards. Section 4 outlines recent research proposals and discuss open research issues. Section 5 outlines some conclusions.

A FRAMEWORK FOR WEB SERVICES SECURITY STANDARDS

In this section we present first the different notions of standards. We then present the conceptual framework for Web services security standards, and, for each level of this framework, we survey existing and proposed standards, their specific purpose, and their current status.

The Concept of Standard

The concept of "standard" covers different notions, ranging from a public specification issued by a set of companies, to a de-jure standard issued by a recognized standardization body. These different notions can provide to the potential users useful indications about the maturity, the stability and the level of endorsement of a given standard. The following "types" of standards can be distinguished:

1. **De-facto standard:** a technology that is used by a vast majority of the users of a function. Such function may for example be provided in a product from a single supplier that dominates the market; or it may be a patented technology that is used in a range of products under license. A de-facto standard may be endorsed by a standardization initiative, and eventually become a consortium recommendation, or a de-jure standard. The relevant requirements are that the standard is widely used, meets the needs for functionality, and supports interoperability
2. **De jure-standard:** standards defined by entities with a legal status in international or national law such the International

Table 1. Standardization organizations

Standardization Body	Date Established	Main Goal	Main Security Standards Issued
W3C	1994	To promote Web evolution by providing fundamental standards	- XML Encryption - XML Signature
OASIS	1993 as SGML Open 1998 as OASIS	To promote on line trade and commerce by providing specialized Web services standards	- XACML - WS-Security - WS-SecurityPolicy
WS-I	2002	To foster interoperability using Web services standards	- Basic Interoperability Profile - Basic Security Profile
The Liberty Alliance Project	2001	To establish open standards, guidelines and best practices for identity management	- ID-FF 1.2, the Identity Federation Framework - Identity Assurance Framework (IAF) 1.1 Specification - Identity Governance Framework (IGF) 1.0 Specifications

Organization for Standardization -ISO-, national standards bodies (e.g. the BSI British Standards in the UK, the American National Standards Institute -ANSI- in the US) or continental standards (e.g. European standards). These standards are relevant in "vertical" application areas such as the health and safety related areas, in business quality measures and in long term IT areas.

3. **Consortium recommendation:** a technology agreed on and recommended by a groups of companies in order to fulfill some functionality. Such consortia may vary in size from groups of a few large manufacturers (e.g. Microsoft, IBM and BEA) to much larger groups or organizations such as the Organization for the Advancement of Structured Information Standards (OASIS), the World Wide Web Consortium (W3C) and the Internet Engineering Task Force (IETF).

It is worth noting that standards are specifications that can be very complex. Standard specifications provide indications about how to represent security information and also about how an implementation of the standard should behave. Indications about the standard's implementation behavior can be mandatory or non mandatory. Whereas the former must be adhered to by a standard's implementation, the latter may not. Hence, the complexity of standard specifications and the presence of non mandatory indications may lead to non-interoperable implementation of the same standard specification. Thus, the need emerged of a further standardization effort in order to provide specific guidelines to guarantee, as far as possible, the interoperability of different implementation of a given standard specification. To help solving these problems, the Web Services - Interoperability organization (WS-I), an industry consortium whose primary goal is to promote Web Services interoperability across many technology substrates (platforms, OSs, languages, etc.) was established. The main standardization bodies relevant to Web services are listed in Table 1.

The definition of a standard and its issuance by a standardization body or by a consortium is a long lasting process which can take many years, and which is subject to formalized organizational procedures. For example, W3C takes 6 months to establish a working group on a technology, and then 18 months to 3 years to agree a

Recommendation. A W3C Recommendation is a specification or set of guidelines that, after extensive consensus-building, has received the endorsement of W3C Members and the Director. The Recommendation is only released if there are working interoperable implementations of all functions in the technology, and enough of the members of W3C support it. OASIS Standards must be approved within an OASIS Committee, submitted for public review, implemented by at least three organizations, and finally ratified by the Consortium's membership at-large.

De-facto standards, eventually promoted to the-jure standard by a subsequent endorsement by a standardization body, offer a higher guarantee of support for interoperability. Conversely, de-jure standards or consortia recommendations do not guarantee per se that a standard will be widely endorsed or the market availability of really interoperable implementations by multiple vendors.

The Framework

Web services security standards address a variety of aspects, ranging from the message level security to the identity management. In order to provide a structured and engineered approach to the development of the standards, an overall conceptual reference framework was needed. Such a reference framework is crucial in organizing the standards according to layers and in promoting the reuse of already developed specification. The first structured framework was proposed in April 2002, by Microsoft and IBM in the white paper: "Security in a Web Services World: A Proposed Architecture and Roadmap" (Microsoft and IBM, 2002). Such a roadmap describes a strategy for addressing security requirements in a Web services environment based on the development of a set of composable standard specifications. An integral part of the roadmap is the identification of a reference framework, driven by the following underpinning criteria:

- Web services security standards have to be independent of specific underlying technologies.
- Web services security standards have to be composable.
- Web services security standards have to be organized in layers, so that standards at an upper level could use and extend standards at a lower level.
- Web services security standards have to be extensible, to deal with new requirements and technologies.

As shown in Figure 1, the Web Services Security (WSS) specifications encompass different specifications, each addressing specific aspects of security.

According to the roadmap, WS-Security was to provide a message security model and the specification of mechanisms to attach signature and encryption headers to SOAP messages. WS-Policy was intended to describe: (1) the security policies, such as required security tokens and supported encryption algorithms, as well as more general policies adopted by a Web service; (2) the mechanisms by which trusted SOAP message exchanges could be built. WS-Trust was intended to define the model for establishing both direct and brokered trust relationships (including third parties and intermediaries) by means of primitives and extensions for security token exchange enabling the issuance and dissemination of credentials within different trust domains. WS-Privacy would have to define a model for embedding a privacy language into WS-Policy and for associating privacy claims with a message in WS-Security.

On top of such standards, further follow-on specifications were envisaged. WS-SecureConversation was introduced with the goal of extending the single message security provided by WS-Security to a conversation consisting of multiple message exchanges, whereas WS-Federation was introduced with the goal of describing how to

Figure 1. Web services security standards framework

WS-SecureConversation	WS-Federation	WS-Authorization
WS-Policy	WS-Trust	WS-Privacy
WS-Security		
SOAP Foundation		

manage and broker trust relationships in a heterogeneous federated environment. Finally, the goal of WS-Authorization was to provide a support for the specification of authorization policies and for managing authorization data.

It is worth noting that the specifications for WS-Authorization and WS-Privacy followed a different development with respect to the other standards of the roadmap. In particular, WS-Authorization was replaced by the specification of XACML, whereas WS-Privacy does not seem to have received the same level of effort, but rather it was addressed by manufacturer proposals such as the IBM Enterprise Privacy Authorization Language (EPAL) (IBM, 2003).

With respect to the original framework, we adopt a slightly different classification, as shown by Figure 2. This classification has been adopted in order to take into account in the discussion the standards below the SOAP layer and, most importantly, to group the standards by their main intended purpose rather than adopting a pure ``stack" view that emphasizes mainly how each specification is built on top of the other ones. In particular, we deem useful to separate message-level security specifications (the two groups labeled Message Security and Reliable Messaging) from the specifications addressing Policy and Access Control, Security Management, and Identity Management issues.

An Overview of Current Standards

This section provides an overview of the Web services security standards according to the revised framework previously described. The status of the reviewed standards is summarized in Table 2.

"Near the Wire" Security Standards

At the transport layer, the well known Secure Socket Layer and the Transport Layer Security (Dierks and Rescorla, 2008), collectively referred as SSL/TLS, are the de facto standards used to assure transport level security for Web services applications. SSL was originally developed by Netscape in 1996 and it served as the basis for IETF RFC 2246 Transport Layer Security (TLS) standard. SSL/TLS provides a fast, efficient and widely accepted protocol for: i) mutual authentication of end systems, by using certificates and public keys; ii) data confidentiality, by using symmetric cryptography for data encryption (e.g., DES, RC4 etc.); iii) data integrity, by using a Message

Figure 2. Refined classification of the standards

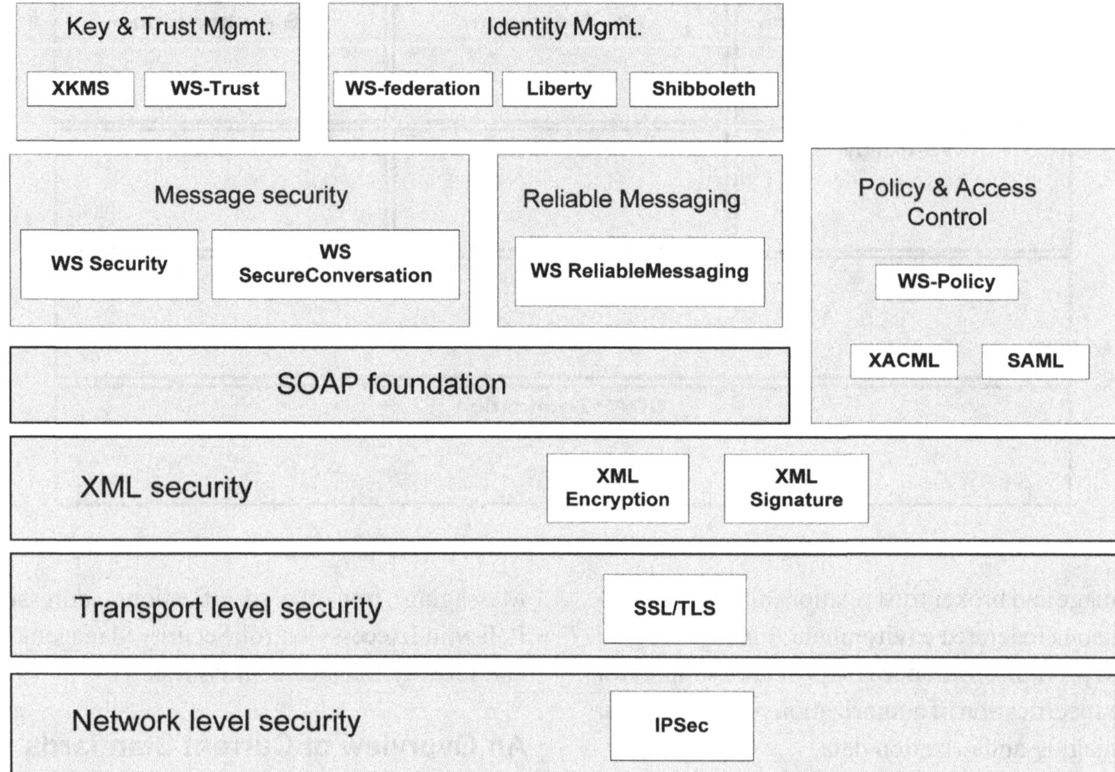

Authentication Code (MAC) generated through a secure hash function (MD5). With respect to SSL, TLS version 1.1 (Dierks and Allen, 1999), incorporates an optional session caching scheme to reduce the number of connections that need to be established from scratch. This optimization is intended to improve the performance of cryptographic operations, in particular those using public keys. TLS version 1.2 is a proposed standard that removes the protocol's dependency on the MD5 and SHA-1 digest algorithms, which have been either wholly or partially compromised by recent research. The proposed standard will also work on new authenticated encryption modes for TLS, including modes based on counter mode encryption (CTR) and combined encryption/authentication modes, and may define major new cipher suites for TLS for this purpose.

Encrypting the communication between a browser and a Web service is a fairly safe procedure because the connection is exclusive to the client browser and the Web server that acts as the gateway to internally hosted application logic. However, a message transmitted by a client, such as browser or an application, might be routed (and processed) by a number of intermediary services before reaching its destination, as in the case of SOAP intermediaries. SSL protects the message contents only while being transmitted between pair-wise intermediaries but it cannot protect the message end-to-end along the complete path of intermediaries up to the final receiver. Furthermore, because the message is decrypted before being delivered to the application layer, the intermediary application/service might then, inadvertently or maliciously, examine or even modify the message before transmitting it again to the next recipient.

Table 2. Web services security standards status

Standard	Issuing body	Status	Issuance date
SSL	Netscape	De facto standard	1996
TLS version 1.1	IETF	Standard	January 1999
TLS version 1.2	IETF	Proposed standard	RFC 5246, August 2008
XML Encryption	W3C	W3C Recommendation	10 December 2002
XML Signature (Second Edition)	W3C	W3C Recommendation	10 June 2008
Web Services Security v1.1 (WS-Security)	OASIS	OASIS Standard	Approved February 2006
WS-SecureConversation v1.3	OASIS	Consortium revised public draft release	Approved March 2007
SAML 2.0	OASIS	OASIS standard	Approved March 2005
XACML v2.0	OASIS	OASIS standard	Approved February 2005
Web Services Policy 1.5 – Framework (WS-Policy)	W3C	W3C Recommendation	04 September 2007
Web Services Policy 1.5	W3C	W3C Recommendation	04 September 2007
Web Services Policy Attachment (WS-PolicyAttachment)	W3C	W3C Member Submission See WS-Policy	25 April 2006
WS-SecurityPolicy v1.2	OASIS	OASIS standard	Approved July 2007
WS-ReliableMessaging v1.1	OASIS	OASIS standard	Approved July 2007
XKMS Version 2.0	W3C	W3C recommendation	28 June 2005
WS-Trust v1.3	OASIS	OASIS standard	Approved July 2007
WS-Federation V1.2	OASIS	Committee Draft 01	23 June 2008
Shibboleth	Intenet2 Consortium[1]		March 19 2008
Liberty Alliance Complete Specifications	Liberty Alliance Project	Final and Draft Specifications	2 October 2008

The other inadequacy of SSL/TLS is that it does not allow one to selectively encrypt parts of the data (payload) to be transmitted. At the network layer, IPSec is a de-jure standard for transport security that may become relevant for Web services. IPSec provides security services including access control, connectionless integrity, data origin authentication, protection against replays (a form of partial sequence integrity), confidentiality (encryption), and limited traffic flow confidentiality.

XML Payload Security

XML can be considered as one the technological pillars of the Web and as its "lingua franca". Web services too rely upon XML to encode the messages they exchange. Hence, securing XML data, that is ensuring XML payload confidentiality and integrity, is a key requirement. XML confidentiality and integrity are provided by using encryption and digital signatures. XML-Encryption (Eastlake and Reagle, 2002) and XML-Digital Signature (Eastlake, Reagle, and Solo 2002) standards were developed to represent in standard way all the information needed to represent the encrypted parts of XML payload and the digital signature information.

XML Encryption

The XML-Encryption specification (Eastlake and Reagle, 2002) contains a standard model for encrypting both binary and textual data, as well as a means of communicating information essential for recipients to decrypt the contents of received messages. The result of encrypting data is an XML Encryption EncryptedData element which contains (via one of its children's content) or identifies (via a URI reference) the cipher data. XML Encryption is a W3C Recommendation and it is the commonly accepted standard for XML encryption.

XML-Digital Signatures

XML-Digital Signatures (Eastlake, Reagle, and Solo 2002) specifies an XML syntax and the processing rules for creating and representing digital signatures. Digital signatures assure the recipient of the message that the message was in fact transmitted by the expected sender and that the message was not altered while in transit. They also support for non-repudiation so that the sender of the message can not deny of having sent it. XML Signatures can be applied to any digital content, not only to XML content, and to the content of one or more resources. In other words, through XML Signature it is possible to selectively sign parts of digital content, such as parts of the XML payload. XML Signature can be represented in the signed XML document itself; in this case the XML Signature can be the outermost element of the signed document or element (enveloping signature) or the document/element can contain the XML signature (enveloped signature). XML signature may also refer to data external to the signature itself (detached signatures). It is worth noting that, as described by the XML Signature specification document, the standard specifies a method for associating a key with referenced data. The standard does not specify how keys are associated with persons or institutions, nor the meaning of the data being referenced and signed. Consequently, XML Signature is not sufficient to address all application security/trust concerns, particularly with respect to using signed XML (or other data formats) as a basis of human-to-human communication and agreement.

WS-Security

SOAP Message Security ("WS-Security") (Nadalin et alii 2004) has been specified by OASIS and is the commonly accepted standard for message security in Web and Grid Services. WS-Security describes enhancements to SOAP messaging to provide single-message origin authentication and single-message confidentiality by using XML Encryption and XML Signature standards. At its most basics, WS-Security specifies how to attach and include security tokens within SOAP messages through a general-purpose mechanism. A (software) security token is a representation of security-related information (e.g. X.509 certificate, Kerberos tickets and authenticators, mobile device security tokens from SIM cards, username, and so forth). WS-Security specifies a general-purpose mechanism for associating security tokens with messages, without requiring the use of any specific type of security token. Various security token formats have been specified for use with WS-Security, including username/password, SAML assertions (Ragouzis, Hughes, Philpott 2005) by OASIS, XrML/REL tokens by OASIS, X.509 certificates by IETF and OASIS, Kerberos tickets by OASIS. For security tokens that are not encoded in XML, such as X.509 certificates and Kerberos tickets, WS-Security provides a mechanism for encoding binary security tokens. Due to the variety of supported security token formats, WS-Security is very flexible; moreover, it can be extended with profiles to support new security tokens. Message integrity is provided by using XML Signature in conjunction with security tokens (which may contain or imply key data). WS-Security supports multiple signatures, potentially by multiple actors, and it can be extended to support additional signature formats. The signatures may reference (i.e. point to) a security token.

WS-SecureConversations

The interactions between a client and a Web service or between two Web services typically consist of multiple message exchanges. Thus, it is important to secure not only a single message, but also a set of messages that are needed to complete a meaningful transaction. WS-SecureConversation (Nadalin, Goodner, Gudgin, 2007a) defines extensions, based on WS-Security and WS-Trust (Nadalin, A., Goodner, M., Gudgin 2007b), aimed at providing a secure session at the SOAP level between two communicating parties. These extensions are based on the establishment and sharing of a security context between the communicating parties and on the derivation of keys from the established security contexts. A security context is an abstract concept that refers to an established authentication state and it is represented by a Security Context Token. This specification defines three different ways of establishing a security context among the parties of a secure communication: the context initiator can request a Security Token Service, as defined by WS-Trust, to create a security context token, or a security context token can be created by one of the communication parties and propagated within a message; or a security context token can be created when needed through negotiation/exchanges among the participants. According to this strategy potentially more efficient keys or new key information can be exchanged, thereby increasing the overall performance and security of the subsequent message exchanges.

WS-ReliableMessaging

Guaranteeing the integrity and the confidentiality of the messages does not prevent messages from being lost, duplicated or reordered. Correct delivery of messages must also be assured. Delivery' guarantee is provided by several middleware components implementing the "store and forward" paradigm, such as Microsoft Message Queuing (MSMQ), IBM Messaging and Queuing (WebSphere, MQ), or Sun Java System Message Queue. WS-ReliableMessaging (Iwasa, 2004) defines a messaging protocol to identify, track, and manage the reliable delivery of messages between exactly two parties, a source and a destination endpoints (referred to as the Reliable Messaging – RM - Source and Reliable Messaging - RM - Destination, respectively), despite the presence of software component, system, or network failures. The protocol supports the communicating endpoints in providing delivery assurances. It is the responsibility of the RM Source and RM Destination to fulfill the delivery assurances, or raise an error. Endpoints can provide four basic delivery assurances:

- AtMostOnce assurance guarantees that messages will be delivered at most once without duplication, or that an error will be raised on at least one endpoint. It is possible that some messages in a sequence may not be delivered.
- AtLeastOnce assurance guarantees that every message sent will be delivered, or an error will be raised on at least one endpoint. Some messages may be delivered more than once.
- ExactlyOnce assurance guarantees that every message sent will be delivered without duplication, or an error will be raised on at least one endpoint.
- InOrder assurance guarantees that messages will be delivered in the order that they were sent. This delivery assurance may be combined with any of the above delivery assurances. It does not provide any assurance about message duplications or omissions.

The messaging protocol defined in this specification can be implemented using different network transport technologies. However, this specification defines a SOAP binding in order to support interoperable Web services.

Access Control Standards

We now briefly discuss the standards that have a key role in the specification and enforcement of access control policies.

Security Assertions Mark-up Language

The Security Assertions Mark-up Language (SAML) (Ragouzis, Hughes, Philpott 2005) is an XML based framework, developed by OASIS, to support the exchange of security information, also called trust assertions, between online business partners, such as vendors, suppliers, customers, over the Internet. The applications and the environments that can use SAML are quite varied, from simple browser-based applications to more complex n-tiered architecture web services. Security information takes the form of security assertions, where an assertion states certain facts (characteristics and attributes) about a subject. The current SAML framework supports three kinds of security assertions: Authentication, Attribute and Authorization decisions. An Authentication assertion states that the subject S was authenticated by means M at a certain time. It is issued by the party that successfully authenticated the subject. An Attribute assertion states that the subject S is associated with the set of attributes A with values B (for example, that Alice is associated with attribute "Company" with value "Hertz"). An Authorization decision assertion states which actions the subject S is entitled to execute on resource R (for example, that a user has been authorized to use a given service). An example of SAML authentication assertion, stating Alice was originally authenticated using a password mechanism at 2006-04-02T19:05:17 is shown in Figure 3.

Assertions are issued by SAML authorities, namely authentication authorities, attribute authorities or policy decision points. SAML can also be used to make assertions about credentials, however it does not provide mechanisms to check or revoke credentials. In order to exchange security assertions between involved parties, SAML defines a request and response protocol that consists of XML-based messages.. These messages can be bound to many different underlying communication and transport protocols. SAML also defines several profiles. Generally, a profile of SAML defines constraints and/or extensions of the core protocols and assertions in support of the usage of SAML for a particular application, by specifying how particular statements are communicated using appropriate protocol messages over specified bindings. For example, the Web Browser Single Sign-On (SSO) profile specifies how SAML authentication assertions are communicated using the Authentication Query and Response messages over a number of different bindings in order to enable Single Sign-On for a browser user. SAML assumes that the two or more endpoints of a SAML transaction are uncompromised, but the attacker has complete control over the communications channel. Moreover, SAML does not directly address two important security issues:

- **Initial Authentication:** authentication assertions convey information about an already happened authentication act. Consequently, such an assertion can be trusted by the party receiving the assertions as far as this party trusts the party/authority that made the assertion.
- **Trust Model:** the security of a SAML conversation will depend on the underlying key management infrastructure (shared key or asymmetric key) and hence it is secure as long as the keys used can be trusted. Undetected compromised keys or revoked certificates, for example, could result in security breaches.

As to security, the SAML protocol is susceptible to a denial of service (DOS) attack, as described in the SAML specification itself. As

Figure 3. An example of a SAML assertion


```
<saml:Assertion
  xmlns:saml="urn:oasis:names:tc:SAML:1.0:assertion"
  MajorVersion="1" MinorVersion="1"
  AssertionID="biuEZCGxcGiF4gIkL5PNltwU7duY1az"
  Issuer="www.it-authority.org"
  IssueInstant="2006-04-02T19:05:37">
  <saml:Conditions
   NotBefore="2006-04-02T19:00:37" NotOnOrAfter="2006-04-02T19:10:37"/>
  <saml:AuthenticationStatement
   AuthenticationMethod="urn:oasis:names:tc:SAML:1.0:am:password"
   AuthenticationInstant="2006-04-02T19:05:17">
  <saml:Subject>
   <saml:NameIdentifier
       NameQualifier= www.it-authority.org
              Format="http://www.customformat.com/">
              uid=alice
   </saml:NameIdentifier>
    <saml:SubjectConfirmation>
       <saml:ConfirmationMethod>
              urn:oasis:names:tc:SAML:1.0:cm:artifact-01
                 </saml:ConfirmationMethod>
          </saml:SubjectConfirmation>
  </saml:Subject>
 </saml:AuthenticationStatement>
</saml:Assertion>
```


to the performance of SAML implementations, handling a SAML request is potentially a very expensive operation, since it includes parsing the request message (typically involving construction of a DOM tree), database/assertion store lookup (potentially on an unindexed key), the construction of a response message, and potentially one or more digital signature operations.

eXtensible Access Control Markup Language –XACML

XACML (Moses, 2005) provides an extensible, XML-encoded language for managing authorization decisions. To this end, XACML language allows one to express access control policies and access requests/responses. XACML was conceived as one component of a distributed and inter-operable authorization framework, with the following underlying rationales:

- First, access control policies do not have to be embedded or tightly linked to the system they govern.
- Second, XACML policies can be applied to different heterogeneous resources, such as XML documents, relational databases, application servers, web services.
- Third, a standard policy exchange format allows different web services to exchange or share authorization policies, as well as to deploy the same policy to heterogeneous systems.

Figure 4. Non-normative model of XACML

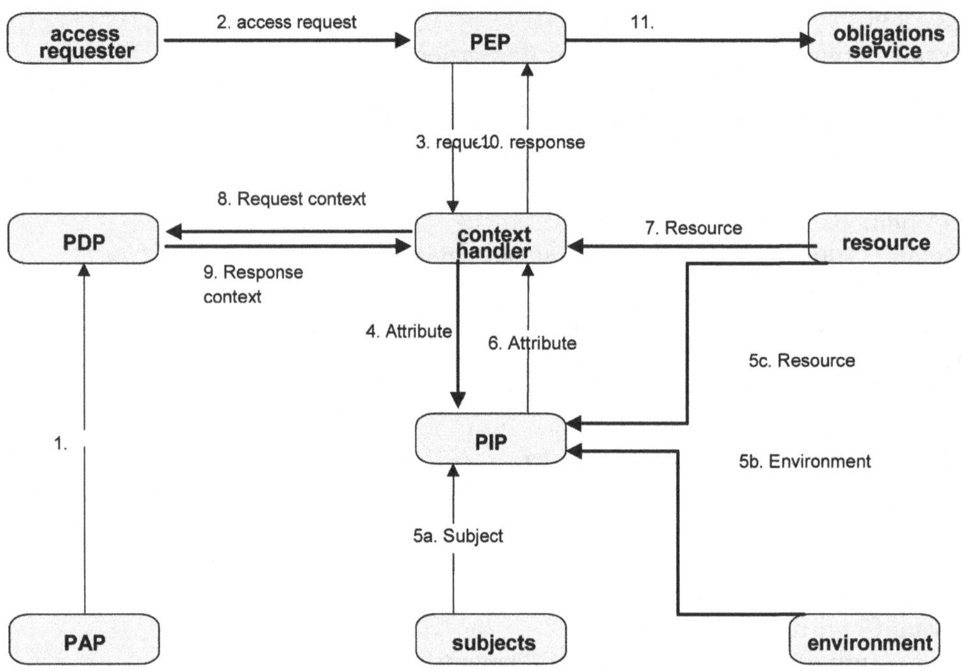

It is worth noting that XACML includes also a non-normative data flow model, reported in Figure 4 that describes the major parties involved in the processing of an access request. This model, which can be considered as an evolution of the ISO 10181-3 model (ISO), can be used as a reference model for the implementation of a XACML engine.

The components of such model are the following:

- The Policy Administration Point (PAP) creates security policies and stores these policies in the appropriate repository.
- The Policy Enforcement Point (PEP) performs access control by making decision requests and enforcing authorization decisions.
- The Policy Information Point (PIP) serves as the source of attribute values, or the data required for policy evaluation.
- The Policy Decision Point (PDP) evaluates the applicable policy and renders a response to the PEP containing the authorization decision. The possible response values are: Permit, Deny, Indeterminate (in case an error occurred or some required value was missing, so a decision cannot be made) or Not Applicable (the request cannot be answered by this service).

The PEP and PDP might both be co-located within the same application, or might be distributed across different servers.

In XACML, the access request is represented by the Request schema. It specifies the requesting Subject, the requested Object and the specific Action requested on the Object. The XACML policy language was designed to be general enough so as to describe general access control requirements. It is also extensible, by means of standard extension points, in order to accommodate the definition of new functions, data types, combining logic, and so forth. In XACML, a policy is the smallest element that the PDP can evaluate. A policy represents a single access control policy, expressed through a set of Rules. A Rule specifies the Target which it applies to and the effect of the rule, that is, Permit or Deny. The Target basically models the access request, by means of a set of simplified conditions for the Subject, Resource and Action that must be met, i.e. evaluate to true, for the Rule to apply to a given request. Any number of Rule elements may be used, each of which generates a true or false outcome. Combining these outcomes yields a single decision for the Policy, which may be "Permit", "Deny", "Indeterminate", or a "Not Applicable" decision.

As an example, consider the following policy: "MPEG movie for adults cannot be accessed by users with age less than 18 years". The movie is the resource the access to which must be controlled; it will be modeled by an element having an attribute "category". Similarly, the subject will have an attribute "age". In this case, the policy is composed by a single rule, that specifies the condition: "age less than 18" for the subject, the condition: category = "adult only" for the resource, the condition: download"' for the action, and the effect "Deny".

More than one rule (or more than one policy) may result applicable to a given access request; XACML defines a set of Combining Algorithms to reconcile multiple outcomes into a single decision, namely, Deny-overrides, Permit-overrides, First-applicable, Only-one-applicable.

In XACML a policy can have scopes of different granularity; actually, a policy can apply to all the operations provided by a Web service, or rather to a specific operation of the Web service. The same policy can be "reused" by different services by applying it to different ports. The OASIS XACML Profile for Web-Services (Anderson, 2007), hereafter referred to as XACML2, is a proposal for extending XACML to deal with the specific characteristics of Web services. It has two main extensions. The first one is the possibility of defining in a precise way the various aspects to which a security policy applies to, for example distinguishing the security policy that must be applied to the message level from the access control policy applied to a Web service or to an operation of the Web service. The second one is the use of the policy combination mechanisms defined in XACML in order to combine the preference/requirements policy of the Web service client with the access control policy of the Web service provider. XACML2 thus supports the specification of policies for the whole service (a WSDL port), for a Web service operation (a single WSDL operation), for a request message (WSDL message) or for a combination of these. The policies associated with a port are represented by a <PolicySet> element that in turn can include other <PolicySet> elements representing the policies for an operation or a message. Each <PolicySet> element contains several <Policy> elements, which are associated with a single aspect of an end-point policy where an aspect is an independent set of technical features and parameters associated with the use of the Web service (for example, data rate allocation). The <Target> sub-element of a <Policy> element identifies the set of conditions governing the aspect (referred to as objective) of the end-point policy. Further, a <Policy> element must contain a set of <Rule> elements that define acceptable alternative solutions for achieving the objective. A <Rule> element includes a set of <Apply> elements containing predicates expressing conditions on attributes. Attributes can be of three different types: unconstrained, constrained and authorized. An unconstrained attribute is such that its value can be set by the policy-user, like for instance the minimum time between retransmission of an unacknowledged message. The value of a constrained attribute, on the other hand, is out of the control of the policy-user. Examples of constrained attributes are environmental attributes like time, or subject's attributes the values of which are set by some an entity or user different

Figure 5. Normal form schema of a policy according to WS-Policy

```
<wsp:Policy ... >
 <wsp:ExactlyOne>
        [<wsp:All> [<Assertion ...> ... </Assertion> ]* </wsp:All> ]*
 </wsp:ExactlyOne>
</wsp:Policy>
```

from the policy-user (for instance, the status of the subject in a customer loyalty program). The value of an authorized attribute is asserted by an authority, like the policy-user's role. Another interesting feature of XACML2 is that it adopts the XACML mechanisms for combining either multiple policies or multiple rules in a single policy, to blend the policies of the service consumer, expressing the preference/requirements of the consumer about the service provision, and the policies of the service provider. The <PolicySet> element, resulting from the combination process, represents a solution to both the consumer and provider policy statements. A service invocation using this solution conforms to the policy of both the consumer and the provider. This paves the way for the introduction of negotiation capabilities between the client and the service provider that would ultimately increase the flexibility of the access control model. XACML2 is at the stage of a working draft.

Standards for Policy Specification

The Web Services Policy Framework (Vedamuthu et al., 2007) provides a framework that allows Web services to describe their policies to Web Service requestors. The main underlying concept is that a Web service provider might expose a policy to specify the conditions under which it provides the service, thus allowing the requestor to decide whether to use the service. The Policy Framework is supplemented by three other standards:

- WS-PolicyAssertions (Box, 2003), that specifies a few generic policy assertions.
- WS-Policy Attachment (Box at al., 2006), that defines how to associate a policy with a service, either by directly embedding it in the WSDL definition or by indirectly associating it through a UDDI.
- WS-SecurityPolicy (Nadalin et al., 2007), that defines the security policy assertions corresponding to the security claims defined by WS-Security: message integrity assertion, message confidentiality assertion, and message security token assertion.

WS-Policy provides an extensible model and a single grammar for expressing all types of domain-specific policy models: transport-level security, resource usage policy, QoS characteristics, or the end-to-end business-process level policy. In WS-Policy, a policy is a collection of policy alternatives, where an alternative is a collection of policy assertions. The model and the grammar specify a core set of constructs to indicate how choices and/or combinations of domain specific policy assertions apply in a Web service environment. The normal form schema of a policy according to Ws-Policy is shown in Figure 5. In this schema, * indicates 0 or more occurrences of an item, while [~] indicates that the contained items must be treated as a group.

The assertions used in a policy expression can be defined in public specifications, like WS-SecurityPolicy and WS-PolicyAssertion, or they can be defined by the entity owning the Web service. The assertions of the first type are named standard assertions and they are understandable potentially from any client. In particular, WS-SecurityPolicy specifies the security policy assertions

Figure 6. An example of a policy expressed in WS-Policy

```
<wsp:Policy xml:base=http://dico.unimi.it wsu:Id=MyPolicy>
  <wsp:ExactlyOne>
   <wsp:All>
    <wsse:SecurityToken>
      <wsse:TokenType>wsse:Kerberosv5TGT</wsse:TokenType>
    </wsse:SecurityToken>
   </wsp:All>
   <wsp:All>
    <wsse:SecurityToken>
     <wsse:TokenType>wsse:X509v3</wsse:TokenType>
    </wsse:SecurityToken>
   </wsp:All>
  </wsp:ExactlyOne>
</wsp:Policy>
```

that can be used in WS-Policy framework. The security policy assertions state requirements on the kind of security tokens used and whether or not a message has to be signed or encrypted. The assertions defined by the entity owning the Web service instead can be understood only by those clients to whom the entity has already released the specifications. The policy assertions standardized so far are those defined in WS-SecurityPolicy and WS-PolicyAssertions. WS-Policy is also able to incorporate other policy models such as SAML and XACML. Figure 6 reports an example of policy that adheres to WS-Policy specification. This example, taken from the WS-Policy specification, shows two policy alternatives, each composed by a single policy assertion. The policy has to be interpreted as follows: if the first alternative is selected, only the Kerberos token type is supported; conversely, if the second alternative is selected, only the X.509 token type is supported.

Defining the Web service policy is not however enough, if such a policy cannot made publicly available to the potential clients of the Web service when they try to discover the services they are potentially interested in. To this end, the WS-PolicyAttachment specifies mechanisms for using policy expressions with existing XML Web service technologies. In particular it defines how to associate policy expressions with WSDL (Christensen et alii, 2004) type definitions and UDDI (Clement, 2004) entities. It also defines how to associate implementation-specific policies with all or part of a WSDL portType when exposed from a specific implementation.

Key and Trust Management Standards

As described in the previous sections, cryptographic keys and digital certificates are essential to guarantee the security of the exchanged messages. In the same way as standards are needed in order to provide interoperability between client and Web services, and among Web services, standards are needed to assure interoperability between a Web service and the certification authorities that issue, distribute and verify asymmetric cryptographic keys and digital certificates. This is the goal of

XML Key Management Standard (XKMS) and WS-Trust standard.

XKMS - XML Key Management Standard

XKMS (Hallam-Baker & Mysore, 2005) specifies protocols for distributing and registering public keys, suitable for use in conjunction with the proposed standard for XML Signature and XML Encryption. XKMS comprises two services - the XML Key Information Service (X-KISS) and the XML Key Registration Service Specification (X-KRSS). X-KISS allows a client to delegate part or all of the tasks required to process XML Signature <ds:KeyInfo> elements to an XKMS service. A key objective of the protocol design is to minimize the complexity of applications using XML Signature. By becoming a client of the XKMS service, the application is relieved of the complexity and syntax of the underlying Public Key Infrastructure (PKI) used to establish trust relationships, which may be based upon a different specification such as X.509/PKIX, SPKI or PGP.X-KRSS describes a protocol for registration and subsequent management of public key information. A client of a conforming service may request that the registration service bind information to a public key. The bound information may include a name, an identifier or extended attributes defined by the implementation.

WS-Trust

WS-Trust (Nadalin, 2007b) defines extensions to WS-Security that all together provide a method and a protocol for requesting to a Security Token Service the issuance, the renewal, and the validation of security tokens. The main goal of WS-Trust is to enable the issuance and dissemination of credentials among different trust domains. It intends to solve three potential issues that the recipient of a WS-Security-protected SOAP message faces when processing the security token contained within the Security header, namely:

1. Format -- the format or syntax of the token is not known to the recipient.
2. Trust -- the recipient may be unable to build a chain-of-trust from its own trust anchors (e.g. its X.509 Certificate Authority, a local Kerberos KDC, or a SAML Authority) to the issuer or signer of the token
3. Namespace -- the recipient may be unable to directly comprehend the set of claims within the token because of syntactical differences

In WS-trust terminology, a security token represents a collection of claims, where a claim is a statement made about a client, service or other resource (e.g. name, identity, key, group, privilege, capability, etc.). In particular, a signed security token is a security token that is cryptographically endorsed by a specific authority (e.g. an X.509 certificate or a Kerberos ticket).

Identity Management Standards

Identity management (ID management) deals with identifying entities in a system (such as a country, a network, an enterprise, a Web service) and controlling their access to resources within that system. This is realized by associating rights and restrictions with the established identity. As an example, a Web service usually requests users to register, by asking name, address, and other information, and assigns them an account and a password. Then, to access the Web service the users must specify their identity, that is, their account and password; the Web service, in turn, uses these information to control the access to its resources. The management of identity-related information can be a costly process for Web service providers and might adversely impact both the security of the system and the users' experience, particularly when the same user accesses several Web services. The relevance of global identity management for the development of the Web and of the Web services, and the requirements to be addressed, were identified and discussed in a position paper by W3C, "Requirements for a Global

Identity Management Service" (OneName, 2001). The W3C position paper stipulates, among other things, that such a system that must be universally portable and interoperable; that it must support unlimited identity-related attributes; that it must provide adequate mechanisms for privacy and accountability; and that it must be overseen by an independent governing authority. One of the first applications of Identity Management is Single Sign On (SSO). Single sign-on technology enables users to perform a single action of authentication and allows them to authenticate themselves to all the services where they are eligible to, without the need to provide the same credential multiple times.

The other goal of ID management is to provide the means for building a federated identity infrastructure that enables cross-boundary single sign-on, dynamic user provisioning and identity attribute sharing. By providing for identity portability, identity federation affords end-users with increased simplicity and control over the movement of personal identity information while simultaneously enabling companies to extend their security perimeter to trusted partners. ID management is being investigated extensively in the corporate world and in standardization bodies and initiatives, such as W3C and Liberty Alliance. In what follows we describe the three major digital identity management initiatives.

WS-Federation

IBM/Microsoft WS-Federation (Lockhart, 2006) provides generic models for federated identity, attribute, authentication, and authorization management, built upon WS-Trust and WS-Policy. A federation consists of multiple Web services domains, each equipped with its own Security Token Service, and with its own security policy. WS-Federation describes how to manage and broker trust relationships in a heterogeneous federated environment including support for federated identities, attributes, and pseudonyms. WS-Federation specifies scenarios using WS-Trust for example to allow requesters from the one domain to obtain security tokens in the other domain and subsequently to get access to the services in the other domain. Additionally, it defines mechanisms for single sign-on and single sign-out, sharing of attributes based on authorization and privacy policies, and integrated processing of pseudonyms (aliases used at different sites/federations).

Shibboleth

Shibboleth (Shibboleth, 2005) is a project run by the Internet2 consortium in the USA. It is standard-based, open source middleware software which provides a federated SSO across or within organizational boundaries, by implementing OASIS SAML 1.1 specification. Shibboleth assumes that participating organizations have previously established a mutual trust relationship. It defines a protocol allowing users to access remote resources, where users are authenticated at their home site and authorized by a set of user attributes provided by their home site. The home site can use whatever type of authentication it likes e.g. username/password, Kerberos, digital signatures, and so forth. The users can be located at their home site, or anywhere else on the Internet. Under Shibboleth, the user's home site is equipped with an Identity Provider (IdP) service, which maintains users' credentials and attributes and that, upon request of relying parties, provides the relying parties with authentication or attribute assertions. Thus the IdP acts as an Authentication Authority. The remote Web site implements a Shibboleth Service Provider (SP) that manages the secured resources. When a user makes a request to access a remote Web site that does not know about him/her, the remote Web site redirects the user request to a Where Are You From (WAYF) service, which maintains the list of the organizations whose users may access the resource. The user can choose his/her own home organization and then he/she is redirected to his/her home Web site, where he/she is authenticated. Then the IdP service running at his/her home site generates a handle for him/her, associates the authentication assertion with it, and redirects the users request back to the remote Web site. The service provider at the remote Web site validates the assertions received and, eventually, asks the IdP of the user home site additional assertions. These assertions are then passed to the Web application that, based on its access control policy, decides whether the user's access is permitted or denied. Shibboleth preserves user privacy in that the IdP at the user home site, and the browser user can control what information is released to the service provider of the remote Web site. Thus, unless requested by the remote We site policy, users can remain anonymous and do not have to disclose sensitive identity information.

Liberty Alliance Project

The Liberty Alliance (Liberty Alliance, 2003) was formed in December 2001 to serve as an open standard organization for federated network identity management and identity-based services. The main concept of Liberty Alliance is to provide the specification of a federated identity infrastructure in which "individuals and businesses can more easily interact with one another, while respecting the privacy and security of shared identity information." (Liberty Alliance, 2003). Liberty Alliance is based on circle of trust concept. A circle of trust is constituted by service providers and IdP's. Service providers are organizations offering Web-based services to users. IdP's are service providers offering business incentives so that other service providers will affiliate with them. A circle of trust is created by establishing such relationships between service providers. Liberty Alliance architecture is organized around three building blocks: (1) the Federation Framework (ID-FF); (2) the Identity Web Services Framework (ID-WSF); (3) the Identity Services Interface Specifications (ID-SIS). ID-FF enables identity federation and management, and it supports, among the others, a simplified SSO and anonimity. ID-WSF is a foundational layer that uses ID-FF. Liberty ID-WSF defines a framework for creating, discovering, and consuming identity services. Identity Services Interface Specifications are a collection of specifications for interoperable services to be built on top of Liberty's ID-WSF. Liberty Alliance is based on SAML and provides open standards for SSO with decentralized authentication. In Liberty, a user authenticates via an identity provider, which may be any Internet service provider. As in Shibboleth, the actual method of authentication is not specified, and identity providers may use whatever authentication method they deem to be appropriate, for example username/password, X.509 public key certificates, Kerberos, one-time password schemes, and so forth. Identity federation is based on linking users' service provider and IdP accounts. Each user has a different login identity at each service provider site. These identities are linked together by the underlying identity federation, but at each site, the user still continues to use his/her site-specific login identity. Login identities are not exchanged among the sites; they are referenced by a Liberty user handle, an identifier known by both sites and unique within the circle of trust. A Liberty handle is created by performing a hash of the user's login identity and other information known only to the provider. Because the handle is at least 128 bits, it is virtually guaranteed to be unique. Note that each handle is only known by the two sites that are federated together and a service provider will use different handles for the same user with different service providers. The user is in charge of federating sites together, and new handles are created each time, so that multiple sites cannot exchange information about the same user by using one handle. A vulnerability of this approach is that if a malicious user successfully authenticates itself once with the identity provider, it can subsequently use any of the victim's information in the federation.

Issues in the Application of the Proposed Standards

Web services security standards raises three main broad questions. The first question is related to the specific security threats posed by XML itself and by the Web services security standards. The second one is related to the degree of interoperability that can be really achieved by the adoption of Web service security standards. The third one concerns the bandwidth and computational overhead that can be generated by the joint use of XML and of software packages implementing the Web services security standards.

With respect to the first issue, XML by itself introduces new security threats like SQL injection through XML payload, XPath Injection, unexpected attachments, malformed XML and so forth. As to the enhanced security achievable by the adoption of security standards, we can say that the framework and the syntax defined by each specific Web service security standard do not provide by themselves any guarantee of security; each standard specification contains a specific section (Security Considerations) that describes the security concerns that the adopter of the standards should be aware of. These security concerns vary depending on the purpose of the standard. For example, when adopting security standards for SOAP messages encryption and signature, it must be taken into account that the XML signature created to verify data integrity is often sent in plain text. The plain text signature could be used by an attacker to perform an offline guessing attack potentially allowing the attacker to guess the value of the body of the message. Thus attention must be paid to use the Ws-Security feature that encrypt also the SOAP signature.

As to the interoperability issue, the framework for security standard development identified in the security Roadmap by Microsoft and IBM (Microsoft and IBM, 2002) postulates a layered approach, such that every upper layer standard can re-use and extend the specification of lower-layer standards. However, the specifications of the standard at a given layer (for example WS-Trust) are sometimes developed by a standardization body different from that specifying the standard at the other layer (for example SAML). Thus, the two involved standard specifications are not always compatible. Such situation requires an activity of verification and alignment of the specifications that involves further iterations within each standardization body. Moreover, such an alignment might be further constrained by the fact that one of the standards involved is more stable and mature and is already implemented by some manufacturer.

A related issue concerns the real interoperability between the standard implementations by different manufactures. Although one of the main purposes of the standard is to guarantee the interoperability between different platforms, it might be necessary to test it on the field. This in turn might require a careful planning of the adoption and of the deployment of platforms implementing the standards.

As to the performance issue, the overhead induced by XML was addressed by the World Wide Web Consortium, that recently released three W3C Recommendations to improve Web services performance by standardizing the transmission of large binary data: XML-binary Optimized Packaging (XOP) (Gudgin, 2005a), SOAP Message Transmission Optimization Mechanism (MTOM) (Gudgin & Mendelsohn, 2005c), and Resource Representation SOAP Header Block (RRSHB) (W3C, 2005c). These recommendations are intended to provide ways to efficiently package and transmit binary data included or referenced in a SOAP 1.2 message. The performance overhead generated by the processing requirements of the software implementing Web services security standards lead to the development of the so-called XML appliances.

XML Appliances

XML messages processing can require a very large amount of bandwidth with respect to traditional binary messaging protocols. Moreover, the processing of WS-* security compliant messages requires encryption/decryption and eventually signature management capabilities. Many manufacturers provide specialized products, based on proprietary hardware and operating systems that have the goal of improving the performance of XML message processing and of providing an integrated management of XML-related security functions. Such products are commonly refereed to as XML appliances and include the XML accelerators and the XML firewalls. A XML accelerator appliance is a customized hardware and software where the following processing consuming tasks are performed: XML/SOAP parsing, XML schema validation, XPath processing and XSLT transformation functions. XML firewalls, also known as XML security gateways, are devices that, in addition to the functions of a XML accelerator, support the WS-Security standards and a range of security-related functions such as: content or metadata-based XML/SOAP filtering functions; XML messages encryption/decryption at the message or element level; XML signature verification and XML message signing according to XML Encryption standard; Authentication and authorization functions (that in some XML appliance can be based on local or on off-board repositories); Auditing and accounting functions.

RESEARCH PROPOSALS AND OPEN RESEARCH ISSUES

Despite such intense research and development efforts, current Web service technology does not yet provide the flexibility needed to "tailor" a Web service according to preferences of the requesting clients, thus failing to fulfill the mass-customization promises made at the beginning of the Web services era. At the same time, Web service providers demand enhanced adaptation capabilities in order to adapt the provisioning of a Web service to dynamic changes of the Web service environment according to their own policies. Altogether, these two requirements call for policy-driven access controls model and mechanisms, extended with negotiation capabilities. Models and languages to specify access and management control policies have been widely investigated in the area of distributed systems (Damianou et al., 2001). Standardization bodies have also proposed policy-driven standard access control models which we have surveyed in the previous section. The main goals of such models are to separate the access control mechanism from the applications and to make the access control mechanism itself easily configurable according to different, easy deployable access control policies. The characteristics of open Web environments, in which the interacting parties are mostly unknown each other, have lead to the development of the trust negotiation approach as a suitable access control model for this environment (Winslett, 2003), (Bertino et al., 2003). Trust negotiation has been extended with adaptive access control, in order to adapt the system to dynamically changing security conditions. Automated negotiation is also being actively investigated in different application domains, such as e-business and Grid computing. However, a common key requirement that has been highlighted is the need of a flexible negotiation approach that enables the system to dynamically adapt to changing conditions. In addition, the integration of trust negotiation techniques with Semantic Web technologies, such as semantic annotations and rule-oriented access control policies, has been proposed. In such approaches, the resource under the control of the access control policy is an item on the Semantic Web, with its salient properties represented as RDF properties. RDF metadata, managed as facts in logic programming, are associated with a resource and are used to determine which policies are applicable to the resource. When extending a Web service with negotiation capabilities, the invocation of a Web service has to be managed as the last step of a conversation between the client and the Web service itself. The rules for such a conversation are defined by the negotiation protocol itself. Such a negotiation protocol should be described and made publicly available in a similar way as a Web service operation is publicly described through WSDL declarations. An XML-based, machine-processable negotiation protocol description allows an electronic agent to automatically generate the messages needed to interact with the Web service. Of course, the client and the Web service must be equipped with a negotiation engine that evaluates the incoming messages, takes decisions and generated the outgoing messages according to the agreed upon protocol. The models already proposed for peer-to-peer negotiations assume that both parties are equipped with the same negotiation engine that implements the mutually understood negotiation protocol. This assumption might not, however, be realistic and may prevent the wide adoption of negotiation-enhanced access control model and mechanisms.

In the remainder of this section we present a short overview of a system, addressing those requirements, and then we discuss open research issues.

Ws-AC1: An Adaptive Access Control System for Web Services

In order to address the adaptation and negotiation requirements, that we have briefly outlined, a system has been recently proposed supporting a Web service access control model and an associated negotiation protocol (Bertino et al., 2006). The proposed model, referred to as Web service Access Control Version 1 (Ws-AC1, for short) is based on a declarative and highly expressive access control policy language. Such language allows one to specify authorizations containing conditions and constraints not only against the Web service parameters but also against the identity attributes of the party requesting the service and context parameters that can be bound, for example, to a monitor of the Web service operating environment. An additional distinguishing feature of Ws-AC1 is the range of object protection granularity it supports. Under Ws-AC1 the Web service security administrator can specify several access control policies for the same service, each one characterized by different constraints for the service parameters, or can specify a single policy that applies to all the services in a set; in order to support such granularity we introduce the notion of service class to group Web services. To the best of our knowledge Ws-AC1 is the first access control model developed specifically for Web services characterized by articulated negotiation capabilities. A model like Ws-AC1 has important applications, especially when dealing with privacy of identity information of users and with dynamic application environments. In order to represent the negotiation protocol, an extension to the Web Services Description Language (WSDL) standard has also been developed. The main reason of that choice is that, although the Web Services Choreography Description Language (WS-CDL) is the emerging standard for representing web services interactions, WS-CDL is oriented to support a more complex composition of Web services in the context of a business process involving multiple parties.

Ws-AC1 is an implementation-independent attribute based access control model for Web services, providing mechanisms for negotiation of service parameters. In Ws-AC1 the requesting agents (also referred to as subjects) are entities (human being or software agents) the requests by which have to be evaluated and to which authorizations (permissions or denials) can be granted. Subjects are identified by means of identity attributes qualifying them, such as name, birth date, credit card number, and passport number. Identity attributes are disclosed within access requests invoking the desired service. Access requests to a web service (also referred to as provider agent) are evaluated with respect to access control policies. Note that in its initial definition, Ws-AC1 does not distinguish between the Web service and the different operations it provides, that is, it assumes that a Web service provides just a single operation. Such model can be applied to the various operations provided by a Web service without any extension. Access control policies are defined in terms of the identity attributes of the requesting agent and the set of allowed service parameters values. Both identity attributes and service parameters are further differentiated in mandatory and optional ones. For privacy and security purposes, access control policies are not published along with the service description but are internal to the Ws-AC1 system. Ws-AC1 also allows one to specify multiple policies at different levels of granularity. It is possible to associate fine-grained policies with a specific service as well with several services. To this end, it is possible to group different services in one or more classes and to specify policies referring to a specific service class, thus reducing the number of policies that need to be specified by a policy administrator. A policy for a class of services is then applied to all the services of that class, unless policies associated with the specific service(s) are defined. Moreover, in order to adapt the provision of the service to dynamically changing conditions, the Ws-AC1 policy language allows one to specify constraints, dynamically evaluated, over a set of environment variables, referred to as context, as well as over service parameters. The context is associated with a specific service implementation and it might consist of monitored system variables, such as the system load. The access control process of Ws-AC1 is organized into two main sequential phases. The first phase deals with the identification of the subject requesting the service. The second phase, executed only if the identification succeeds, verifies the service parameters specified by the requesting agent against the authorized service parameters.

The identification phase is adaptive, in that the provider agent might eventually require the requesting agent to submit additional identity attributes in addition to those originally submitted. Such an approach allows the provider agent to adapt the service provisioning to dynamic situations: for example, after a security attack, the provider agent might require additional identity attributes to the requesting agents. In addition, to enhance the flexibility of access control, the service parameter verification phase can trigger a negotiation process. The purpose of this process is to drive the requesting agent toward the specification of an access request compliant to the service specification and policies. The negotiation consists in an exchange of messages between the two negotiating entities in order to limit, fix, or propose the authorized parameters the requesting agent may use. The negotiation of service parameters allows the provider agent to tailor the service provisioning to the requesting agent preferences or, at the opposite, to "enforce" its own preferred service provisioning conditions.

Open Research Issues

Even though Ws-Ac1 provides an initial solution to the problem of adaptive access control mechanisms for Web services, many issues need to be investigated. A first issue is related to the development of models and mechanisms supporting a comprehensive characterization of Web services that we refer to as Web service profiles. Such a characterization should be far more expressive that conventional approaches, like those based on UDDI registries or OWL. The use of such profiles would allow one to specify more expressive policies, taking into account various features on Web services, and to better support adaptation.

The second issue is related to taking into account the conversational nature of web services, according to which interacting with real world Web services involves generally a sequence of invocations of several of their operations, referred to as conversation. Most proposed approaches, like Ws-AC1, assume a single operation model where operations are independent from each other. Access control is either enforced at the level of the entire Web service or at the level of single operations. In the first approach, the Web service could ask, in advance, the client to provide all the credentials associated with all operations of that Web service. This approach guarantees that a subject will always arrive at the end of whichever conversation. However, it has the drawback that the subject will become aware of all policies on the base of which access control is enforced. In several cases, policies need to be maintained confidential and only disclosed upon some initial verification of the identity of the client has been made. Another drawback is that the client may have to submit more credentials than needed. An alternative strategy is to require only the credentials associated with the next operation that the client wants to perform. This strategy has the advantage of asking from the subject only the credentials necessary to gain access to the requested operation. However, the subject is continuously solicited to provide credentials for each transition. In addition, after several steps, the client may reach a state where it cannot progress because the lack of credentials. It is thus important to devise strategies to balance the confidentiality of the policies with the maximization of the service completion. A preliminary approach to such strategies has been recently developed (Mecella et al., 2006); the approach is based on the notion of k-trustworthiness, where k can be seen as the level of trust that a Web service has on a client at any point of their interaction. The greater the level of trust associated with a client, the greater is the amount of information about access control policies that can be disclosed to this client, thus allowing the client to determine early in the conversation process if it has all necessary credentials to satisfy the access control policies. Such approach needs however to be extended by integrating it with an exception-based mechanism tailored to support access control enforcement. In particular, in a step-by-step approach, whenever a client cannot complete a conversation because of the lack of authorization, some alternative actions and operations are taken by the Web service. A typical action would be to suspend the execution of the conversation, ask the user to acquire the missing credentials, and then resume the execution of the conversation; such a process would require investigating a number of issues, such as determining the state information that need to be maintained, and whether revalidation of previous authorizations is needed when resuming the execution. A different action would be to determine whether alternative operations can be performed to replace the operation that the user cannot execute because of the missing authorization. We would like to develop a language according to which one can express the proper handling of error situations arising from the lack of authorization.

The third issue is related to security in the context of composite services; in such case, a client may be willing to share its credentials or other sensitive information with a service but not with other services that can be invoked by the initial service. To handle such requirement different solutions may be adopted, such as declaring the possible services that may be invoked by the initial service or associating privacy policies with the service description, so that a client can specify its own privacy preferences.

Other relevant issues concern workflow systems. Such systems represent an important technology supporting the deployment of business processes consisting of several Web services and their security is thus crucial. Even though some initial solutions have been proposed, such as the extension of the WS-BPEL standards with role-based access control (Paci et al., 2008a), more comprehensive solutions are required, supporting adaptive access control and sophisticated access control constraints, including the notion of resiliency constraint (Paci at al., 2008b).

Finally the problem of secure access to all information needed to use services, such as information stored by UDDI registries, needs to be addressed. To date solutions have been developed to address the problem of integrity through the use of authenticated data structures (Bertino at al.,

2004). However further work is needed to address the problem of suitable access control techniques assuring the confidentiality and privacy of such information and thus supporting its selective sharing among multiple parties.

CONCLUDING REMARKS

In this article we have presented an overview of relevant standards concerning security for Web services. Such standards encompass a large number of security-related aspects, such as access control and digital identity management, and thus provide a solid basis for the deployment of Web service technology. We have also briefly outlined a more innovative approach that is the first proposing a negotiation-based access control model, able to provide support for adaptation, and we have discussed some open research issues.

ACKNOWLEDGMENT

The work reported here has been supported by the IBM OCR project "Privacy and Security Policy Management" and the NSF grant 0712846 "IPS: Security Services for Healthcare Applications".

REFERENCES

W3C (2005c). *W3C Resource Representation SOAP Header Block.* (W3C Recommendation 25 January 2005). Retrieved from http://www.w3.org/ TR/ 2005/ REC-soap12- rep- 20050125/

W3C XML-binary Optimized Packaging W3C Recommendation 25 January 2005. Retrieved August 10 2008 from http://www.w3.org/ TR/ 2005/ REC- xop10- 20050125/

Anderson, A. (Ed.). (2007). *Web Services Profile of XACML* (WS-XACML). Version 1.0. Working Draft 10 (OASIS, 10 August 2007) Retrieved September 15, 2008 from http://www.oasis-open.org/ committees/ download.php/ 24951/ xacml-3.0- profile- webservices- spec- v1- wd- 10-en.pdf

Bertino, E., Carminati, B., & Ferrari, E. (2004). Merkle Tree Authentication in UDDI Registries. *International Journal of Web Services Research, 1*(2), 37–57.

Bertino, E., Ferrari, E., & Squicciarini, A. C. (2003, June). X-TNL: An XML-based Language for Trust Negotiations. Bertino, E., Squicciarini, A.C., Martino, L., & Paci, F. (2006). An Adaptive Access Control Model for Web Services. *International Journal of Web Services Research, 3*(3), 27–60.

Box, D., et al. (2003, May). *Web Services Policy Assertions Language.* (WS-PolicyAssertions) Version 1.1Box, D. et al. (2006). *Web Services Policy 1.2 - Attachment* (WS-PolicyAttachment). (W3C Member Submission, 25 April 2006). Retrieved September 15, 2008 from http://www.w3.org/ Submission/ WS-PolicyAttachment/

Christensen, E., Curbera, F., Meredith, G., & Weerawarana, Clement, L., Hately, A., von Riegen, C., & Rogers, T. (Eds.) (2004). *UDDI Version 3.0.2 UDDI Spec Technical Committee Draft.* (OASIS, 2004-10-19). Retrieved September 15, 2008 from http://www.uddi.org/ pubs/ uddi_v3.htm

Damianou, N., Dulay, N., Lupu, E., & Sloman, M. (2001, June). The Ponder Policy Specification Language. *Proceedings of the 2nd IEEE International Workshop on Policies for Distributed Systems and Networks*, Bristol, UK.

Dierks, T., & Allen, C. (1999, January). *The TLS Protocol Version 1.0. IETF RFC 2246.* Retrieved September 12, 2007, from http://www.ietf.org/ rfc/ rfc2246.txt

Dierks, T., & Rescorla (2008, August). *E.: The Transport Layer Security (TLS) Protocol Version 1.2. IETF RFC 5246.* Retrieved September 15, 2008, from http://www.ietf.org/ rfc/ rfc5246.txt

Eastlake, D., & Reagle, J. (2002, December). *XML Encryption Syntax and Processing. W3C Recommendation.* Retrieved September 15, 2008 from http://www.w3.org/ TR/ xmlenc-core/

Eastlake, D., Reagle, J., & Solo, D. (Eds.). (2002, February). *XML-Signature Syntax and Processing.* Retrieved September 15, 2008 from http://www.w3.org/ TR/ xmldsig-core/

Gudgin, M. (2007, April). *SOAP Version 1.2 Part 1: Messaging Framework* (2nd ed.). Retrieved September 12, 2007, from http://www.w3.org/ TR/ 2007/ REC- soap12- part1-20070427/

Gudgin, M., Mendelsohn, N., Nottingham, M., & Ruellan, H. (Eds.). (2005a). *W3C XML-binary Optimized Packaging.* (W3C Recommendation, 25 January 2005). Retrieved September 15, 2008 from http://www.w3.org/ TR/ 2005/ REC- xop10-20050125/

Gudgin, M., Mendelsohn, N., Nottingham, M., & Ruellan, H. (Eds.). (2005b). *W3C SOAP Message Transmission Optimization Mechanism.* (W3C Recommendation 25 January 2005). Retrieved September 15, 2008 from http://www.w3.org/ TR/ 2005/ REC- soap12-mtom- 20050125/

Hallam-Baker, P., & Mysore, S. H. (Eds.). (2005) XML Key Management Specification (XKMS 2.0) Version 2.0. (W3C Recommendation, 28 June 2005). Retrieved September 15, 2008 from http:// www.w3.org / TR/ 2005/ REC- xkms2- 20050628/

IBM. (2003). *The Enterprise Privacy Authorization Language (EPAL 1.1) - Reader's Guide to the Documentation.* Retrieved September 15, 2008 from http://www.zurich.ibm.com/ security/ enterprise- privacy/epal

Iwasa, K. (Ed.). (2004). *Web Services Reliable Messaging TC WS-Reliability 1.1.* Liberty Alliance Project - Introduction to the Liberty Alliance Identity Architecture Revision 1.0 March, 2003.

Lockhart, H., et al. (2006). *Web Services Federation Language* (WSFederation) Version 1.1. Retrieved September 15, 2008 from http://download.boulder.ibm.com/ ibmdl/ pub/ software/ dw/ specs/ ws-fed/ WS-Federation- V1-1B.pdf?S_ TACT= 105AGX04&S_ CMP=LP

Mecella, M., Ouzzani, M., Paci, F., & Bertino, E. (2006, May 23-26). Access Control Enforcement for Conversation-based Web Services. *Proceedings of the 2006 WWW Conference*, Edinburgh, Scotland.

Microsoft and IBM (2002). *Security in a Web Services World: A Proposed Architecture and Roadmap.*

Moses, T. (2005). *Extensible Access Control Markup Language (XACML), Version 2.0.* (OASIS Standard, 2005). Retrieved September 15, 2008 from http://docs. oasis-open.org/ xacml/ 2.0/ access_control-xacml. 2.0-core-spec-os.pdf.

Nadalin, A., Goodner, M., Gudgin, M., Barbir, A., & Granqvist, H. (Eds.). (2007). *WS-SecurityPolicy 1.2 OASIS Standard.* (OASIS, 1 July 2007). Retrieved September 15, 2008 from http:// docs.oasis-open. org/ ws-sx/ ws-securitypolicy/ 200702/ ws-securitypolicy-1.2- spec-os.html

Nadalin, A., Goodner, M., Gudgin, M., Barbir, A., & Granqvist, H. (Eds.). (2007a). *WS-SecureConversation 1.3. (OASIS Standard, 1 March 2007).* Retrieved September 15, 2008 from http://docs. oasis-open.org/ ws-sx/ ws- secureconversation/ 200512/ ws-secureconversation- 1.3-os.html

Nadalin, A., Goodner, M., Gudgin, M., Barbir, A., & Granqvist, H. (Eds.). (2007b). *WS-Trust 1.3 OASIS Standard.* (OASIS, 19 March 2007). Retrieved September 15, 2008 from http://docs.oasis-open.org/ ws-sx/ ws-trust/ 200512/ ws-trust-1.3-os.html

Nadalin, A., Kaler, C., Hallam-Baker, P., & Monzillo, R. (Eds.). (2004). *Web Services Security: SOAP Message Security 1.0 (WS-Security 2004).* (OASIS Standard, March 2004). Retrieved September 15, 2008 from http://docs.oasis-open.org/ wss/ 2004/ 01/ oasis- 200401- wss- soap-message- security-1.0.pdf

OneName. (2001). *Requirements for a Global Identity Management Service.* A Position Paper from OneName Corporation for the W3C Workshop on Web Services, 11-12 April 2001, San Jose, CA USA

Paci, F., Bertino, E., & Crampton, J. (2008a). An Access-Control Framework for WS-BPEL. *International Journal of Web Services Research,* *5*(3), 20–43.

Paci, F., Ferrini, R., Sun, Y., & Bertino, E. (2008b, December). Authorization and User Failure Resiliency for WS-BPEL Business Processes. *Proceedings of 6th International Conference on Service Oriented Computing (ICSOC 2008),* Sydney, Australia.

Proceedings of the 4th IEEE International Workshop on Policies for Distributed Systems and Networks, *Como, Italy.*

Ragouzis, N., Hughes, J., Philpott, R., & Maler, E. (Eds.). (2005). *Security Assertion Markup Language (SAML) 2.0 Technical Overview - Working Draft 03.* (OASIS, 20 February 2005). Retrieved September 15, 2008 from http://www.oasis-open.org/ committees/ download. php/ 20645/ sstc-saml- tech- overview-2\ %200-draft-10.pdf

S. (2004). Web Services Description Language (WSDL) Version 1.1.

Shibboleth (2005). *Shibboleth Architecture Technical Overview.* Working Draft 02, 8 June 2005. Retrieved August 10 2008 from http://shibboleth.internet2.edu/ shibboleth-documents.html

Vedamuthu, A. S., Orchard, D., Hirsch, F., Hondo, M., Yendluri, P., Boubez, T., & Yalcinalp, U. (2007). *Web Services Policy 1.5 – Framework.* (W3C Proposed Recommendation 06 July 2007). Retrieved September 15, 2008 from http://www.w3.org/ TR/ 2007/ PR-ws-policy-20070706/

Winslett, M., Yu, T., & Seamons, K. (2003). Supporting Structured Credentials and Sensitive Policies through Interoperable Strategies for Automated Trust Negotiation. *ACM Transactions on Information and System Security, 6*(1), 20–45.

ENDNOTE

1 Internet2 or UCAID (University Corporation for Advanced Internet Development) is a non-profit consortium which develops and deploys advanced network applications and technologies, for education and high-speed data transfer purposes. It is led by over 200 universities and partners with many affiliate members and corporate members drawn from companies in the publishing, networking and other technology industries. "Internet2" is a registered trademark.

This work was previously published in International Journal of Web Services Research, Volume 6, Issue 4, edited by Liang-Jie Zhang, pp. 48-74, copyright 2009 by IGI Publishing (an imprint of IGI Global).

Chapter 16
Web Service Enabled Online Laboratory

Yuhong Yan
Concordia University, Canada

Yong Liang
National Research Council, Canada

Abhijeet Roy
University of New Brunswick, Canada

Xinge Du
University of New Brunswick, Canada

ABSTRACT

Online experimentation allows students from anywhere to operate remote instruments at any time. The current techniques constrain users to bind to products from one company and install client side software. We use Web services and Service Oriented Architecture to improve the interoperability and usability of the remote instruments. Under a service oriented architecture for online experiment system, a generic methodology to wrap commercial instruments using IVI and VISA standard as Web services is developed. We enhance the instrument Web services into stateful services so that they can manage user booking and persist experiment results. We also benchmark the performance of this system when SOAP is used as the wire format for communication and propose solutions to optimize performance. In order to avoid any installation at the client side, the authors develop Web 2.0 based techniques to display the virtual instrument panel and real time signals with just a standard Web browser. The technique developed in this article can be widely used for different real laboratories, such as microelectronics, chemical engineering, polymer crystallization, structural engineering, and signal processing.

DOI: 10.4018/978-1-61350-104-7.ch016

INTRODUCTION

In science and engineering education, experimentation plays a crucial role. The classic university science course entails lecture and lab: students' active participation in experiments enhances their understanding of the principles described in the lectures. However, not every educational institution can afford all the experimental equipment it would like. Moreover, colleges and universities increasingly offer distance-learning programs, allowing students to attend lectures and seminars and complete coursework using the Internet. In situations such as these, access to online laboratories or experiment systems can greatly enhance student learning - increasing the range of experiments available at an institution and giving the distance learners hands-on, real-time experience. Online laboratories, however, are not as mature as online courses. There is no matured software system to support online experimentation. Experimentation is also an important approach for scientific discovery. Sharing expensive equipment is a common practice in the scientific community. Some research facilities, e.g. synchrotrons and accelerators, are very expensive that a country normally invests to build one of the kind. These facilities are shared by the scientific community national wide and/or international wide. Currently, the scientists need to reserve a time slot in these facilitates and travel to the site to conduct the experiments. With the capacity of online experimentation, traveling cost can be saved. More importantly, online experimentation can allow the users to reserve shorter time slots, because the users do not need to finish an experiment during their travel. Therefore, the resource sharing can be more efficient.

Current online experiment systems fall into two categories (Naef, 2006): *virtual laboratories* provide a simulation environment in which students conduct experiments; and *remote laboratories*, with real instruments and equipments at the remote sites. The later is the scope of our research. The ultimate goal of our research is to provide IT techniques for remote experimentation over Internet. Our focus in this article is to let students use a Graphic User Interface (GUI) to operate actual instruments via remote control.

The difficulty with creating an effective laboratory operated by remote control is making scattered computational resources and instruments operable across platforms. Existing online experiment systems commonly use a classic client-sever architecture and off-the-shelf middleware for communication (Hardison, *et al.* 2005, Auer and Gallent, 2000, Latchman, *et al.* 1999). Normally, to ensure interoperability, these systems rely on instruments from a single company—such as National Instruments or Agilent—and Microsoft Windows as the common operating system. Users must then install additional software to operate the remote instruments. For a student using an old laptop or the computer at a public library, this could be difficult. So, online labs configured this way can't achieve the ultimate goals of sharing heterogeneous resources among online laboratories and easy access via the Web. Our solution to these shortcomings is to base online experiment systems on Web services, which are designed to support interoperable, machine to-machine interaction over a network and can also integrate heterogeneous resources. We have devised a service-oriented architecture for online experiment systems, enabled by Web service protocols, and a methodology for wrapping the operations of the instruments into Web services. Although these methods probably aren't suitable for time-critical missions or applications that need real-time control, such as robot operation, they do work for controlling standard commercial instruments over low-speed or unreliable communication networks—the types of networks available to many college students. Using this framework, we can create an online experiment system for students—or an online research lab for scientists—that incorporates a great variety of instruments and that users can access without installing special software.

This article is organized as follows: following the present of service oriented architecture for online experiment systems, we present the solution to wrap instruments as Web services and to display dynamic graphics for real time signals. Then we discuss the management of stateful instrumental Web services and benchmark the performance of Web services in this application and present the optimization methods to improve performance. At the last is the discussion and conclusions.

SERVICE ORIENTED ARCHITECTURE FOR ONLINE EXPERIMENT SYSTEMS

A Web service is a software system that typically relies on a set of W3C standards. Identified by a Uniform Resource Identifier (URI), a Web service has public interfaces and bindings defined and described in Extensible Markup Language (XML), specifically, the WSDL format (W3C, 2004a). Other software systems can discover the Web service definition—for example, via a registry server using Universal Description Discovery and Integration (UDDI) protocol (UDDI.org, 2004). These other systems can then interact with a Web service as its definition prescribes, using Simple Object Access Protocol (SOAP) (W3C, 2004b), an XML-based messages format, conveyed by Internet protocols such as Hypertext Transfer Protocol (HTTP).

An Online Experiment System (OES) uses the scattered computational resources and instruments on the networks for experiments. It is a Web-enabled distributed system: the user accesses an OES via the Web interface; and the heterogeneous resources and devices interoperate with each other using Web service protocols. Our major efforts in this study are the service oriented architecture for OES and the techniques to operate remote instruments wrapped as Web services.

Figure 1 diagrams our service oriented architecture for an OES. It combines two client-server architectures. The first client-server architecture mediates between the client's browser and the Web server associated with the online lab management system. The second client-server architecture mediates between the online lab management system and scattered resources wrapped as Web

Figure 1. Service oriented architecture for an online experiment system

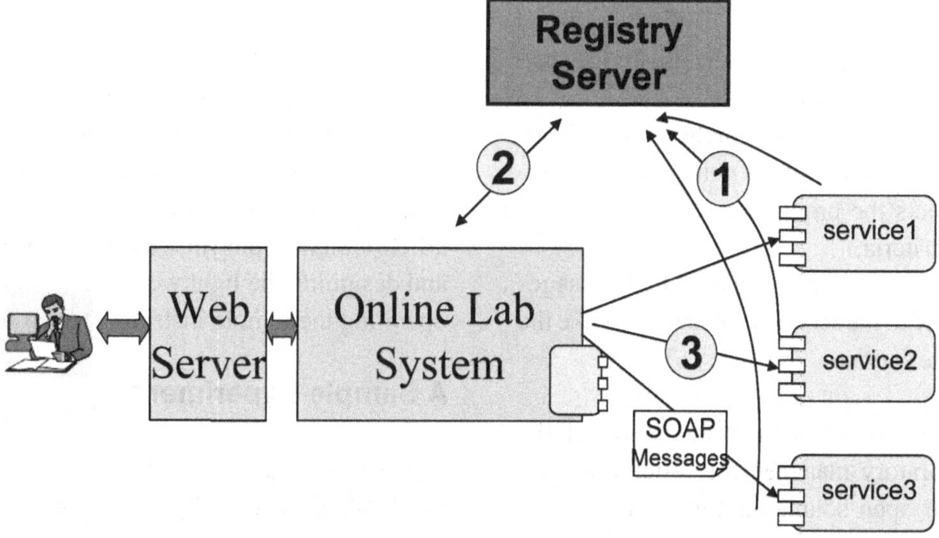

Figure 2. An implementation online laboratory management system

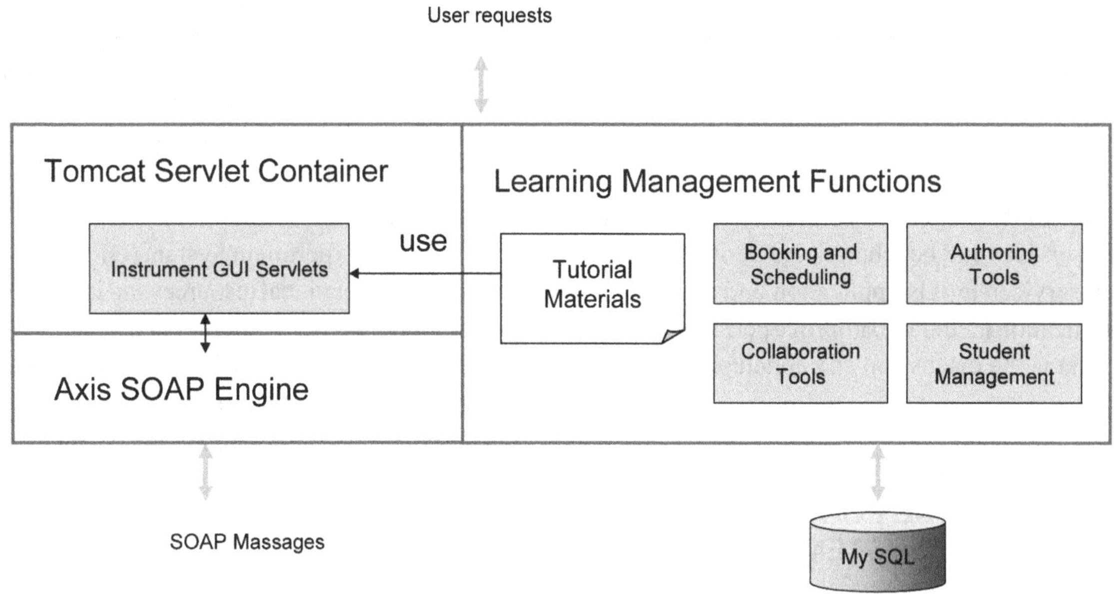

services. The online laboratory uses SOAP messages to communicate with the remote resources. The online lab management system is the key component in this architecture. It has standard learning management functions such as tutorial management, student management, and so on. The system uses service oriented architecture to invoke remote services. It works in a series of steps, indicated by the numbered green circles in Figure 1:

1. A service provider registers its services in a UDDI registry server.
2. A service requester searches the registry server and finds all the potential resources. It selects the proper services based on its own criteria.
3. The service requester sends SOAP messages directly to the service provider to invoke the remote service.

Figure 2 shows our implementation of the online laboratory management system. We use Moodle, an open source learning management system, to realize the learning management functions. These modules are an authoring tool to generate tutorials, quizzes, and homework; a student management system to manage the enrollment, marks and progresses of students; a booking and scheduling module to book timeslots for the experiments; and multiple collaboration tools, such as discussion forums, wikis, and chat rooms for students to communicate and work in group. The tutorial pages contain Instrument GUI for displaying instrument panels and real time signals. The students can press the buttons and enter inputs from the Web interface to operate the remote instruments. The GUI code is designed to be very light weight, and no particular installation is needed at the client side. Our major focus of this article is on wrapping instruments as Web services and designing the light weight GUI interface for operating the remote instrument Web services.

A Sample Experiment

Our research targets the online education at college level. We are especially interested in electronic

Figure 3. Common emitter amplifier

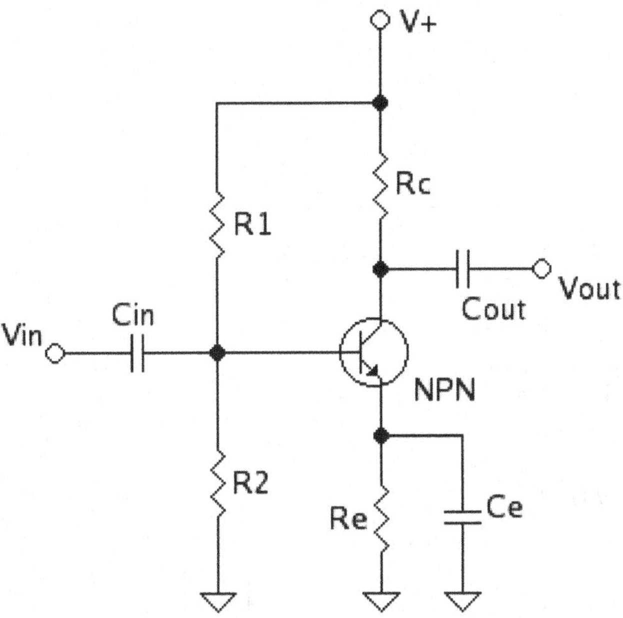

circuit experiments, because the instruments in this domain commonly have digitalized interface to computer. A sample experiment is common emitter NPN transistor amplifier. The circuit diagram is as in Figure 3. The common emitter circuit comprises the load resistor R_C and NPN transistor with the output connected as shown. The resistors R_1 and R_2 are chosen to ensure the base-emitter voltage is approximately 0.7 volts, which is the "on" voltage for a transistor. These resistors, along with R_E, also determine the quiescent current flowing through the transistor and therefore its gain. The input signal V_{in} is generated by a waveform generator. The amplified signal is the output V_{out}.

We use a waveform generator, Agilent 33220A, to generate the input signal V_{in}. And we use a data acquisition and switch unit, Agilent 34970A, to read in V_{in} and V_{out}. Please notice that in a real lab, people normally use an oscilloscope to observe the signals, but for online lab, everything has to be digitalized. Therefore, we need to use data acquisition devices. That means that we need to change the usual way to do experiment for putting an experiment online. In order to operate the instruments via GUI interface and via Web service protocols, we develop some techniques below to wrap the instruments into Web services and to display the instrument panels and the real time signals on Web pages.

WRAPPING INSTRUMENT OPERATIONS AS WEB SERVICES

A WSDL file contains the operations of the Web service and the arguments to invoke operations. When instrument functions are wrapped as Web services, the interface of the instrument Web service is described in a WSDL file. An instrument service needs to provide three kinds of information: 1) the input/output parameters to operate the instrument; 2) the information about rendering the GUI of the instrument panels; and, 3) the metadata

Figure 4. The relations of the instrument I/O standards

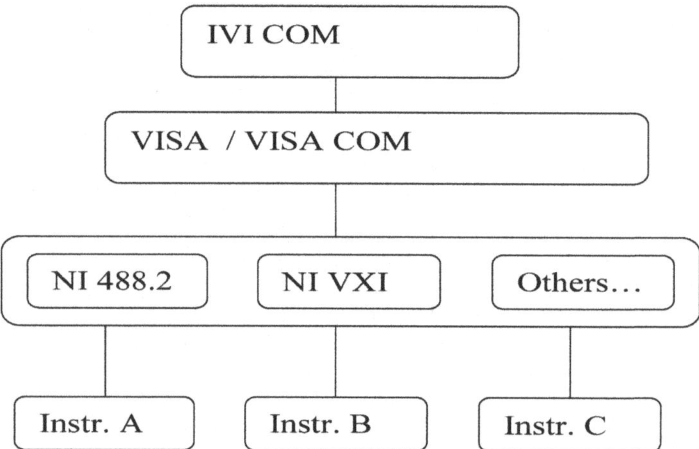

Figure 5. Sample code of IVI COM

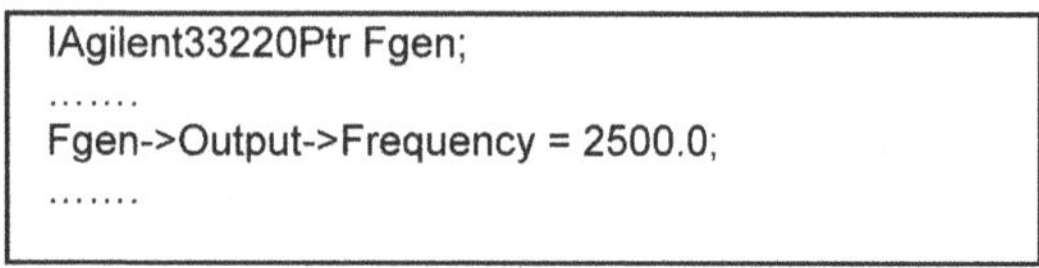

```
IAgilent33220Ptr Fgen;
.......
Fgen->Output->Frequency = 2500.0;
.......
```

Figure 6. Sample code of VISA COM

```
Fgen->WriteString("FREQuency 2500")
```

about the instruments. These issues are described individually below.

Generic Approach to Wrap Instrument Operations based on VISA standard

Instrument I/O is a well studied topic for which industrial standards have been established. Two methods to control instruments are by using an instrument driver or by making direct calls to the I/O library. If using an instrument driver, the user will call functions that cause the instrument to take some action. If using the I/O library, the user will control the instrument by sending an ASCII string to it and reading ASCII strings back from it. The commonly used languages to operate instruments are C, C# or Visual Basic. The commonly accepted industrial standards are Virtual Instrument System Architecture (VISA) and Interchangeable Virtual Instruments (IVI) (Aglient, 2005). Most commercial products follow these standards. The purpose of these standards is to enable interoperability of instruments, which means using common APIs of the instruments. Therefore, it is possible to generate generic WSDL interfaces for instruments based on these standards. The relationship between VISA and IVI is shown in Figure 4. The individual instruments – Instr. A, B and C – have their own drivers. These drivers are wrapped by VISA complaint drivers. The IVI compliant drivers are built still on the top of VISA standard.

Both VISA and IVI standards operate the instruments by reading and sending ASCII strings to the instruments. Compared with VISA, IVI can operate the instrument by referencing its properties. The IVI standard classifies the instruments into eight classes. Each class has basic properties that are shared by all the instruments in the same class, and extension properties that are unique to the individual instrument. As an example, Figure 5 shows the code to set the frequency of an

Figure 7. The snippet of WSDL to operate an instrument

```
<?xml version="1.0" encoding="UTF-8"?>
<wsdl:definitions ......>
   ......
 <!--define the response message -->
<wsdl:message name="writeStringResponse">
 <wsdl:part name="writeStringReturn" type="xsd:int"/>
</wsdl:message>
<!--define the request message -->
 <wsdl:message name="writeStringRequest">
  <wsdl:part name="in0" type="xsd:string"/>
 </wsdl:message>
 <!--define the operation -->
<wsdl:operation name="writeString" parameterOrder="in0">
  <wsdl:input message="intf:writeStringRequest" name="writeStringRequest"/>
  <wsdl:output message="intf:writeStringResponse" name="writeStringResponse"/>
      </wsdl:operation>
   ......
</wsdl:definitions>
```

Figure 8. Sinusoid waveform parameters in one string

```
"*RST;FUNCtion SINusoid;OUTPut:LOAD 50;FREQuency
2500;VOLTage 1.2;VOLTage:OFFSet 0.4;OUTPut ON";
```

Agilent Waveform Generator 33220A to 2500.0HZ, using IVI COM. Figure 6 is the code of VISA COM to implement the same function. Using VISA COM, people do not know the semantics of the parameters. That is to say, setting the Frequency or Voltage, people will use the same API.

We consider that using the VISA standard, the methodology of wrapping the instrument services can be generic to any of the instruments, which means that many instruments can share the same Web services interface. Indeed, using the VISA standard, we need only to define an operation *writeString* for sending commands or data to the instrument. The argument of this operation is always string, which is the same for any instrument. Figure 7 is the snippet of WSDL for defining the operation of *writeString*. Similarly, we can define an operation *readString* for getting status or data from the instrument, which is eliminated from Figure 7.

In the example in Figure 8, we demonstrate how to operate the waveform generator to generate a sinusoid waveform. The set of control parameters for the sinusoid waveform contains "instrument address", "wave shape", "impedance", "frequency", "amplitude", and "offset". In order to improve performance by reducing the time taken to send SOAP messages (ref Section 5), those parameters are put into one string. This means that only one SOAP message is transported to pass all the parameters from the client to the server. After the server gets the string from the client, it will parse the string according to the delimiter (here we use ";") and send the command to the instrument.

Although we prefer to use the VISA standard to wrap the instrument functions, it is also possible to use the IVI standard. The difference

Figure 9. LOM attributes for instruments

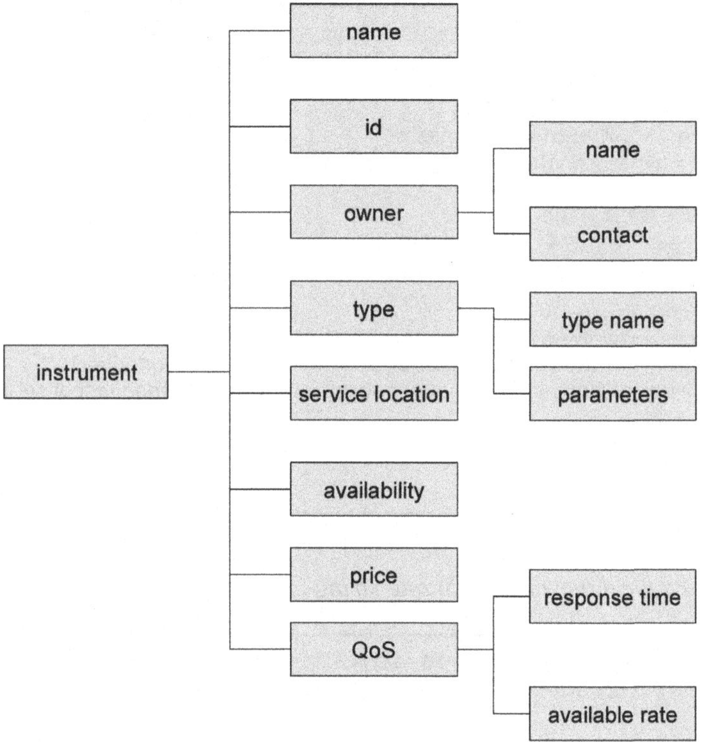

is that each instrument class will have a common WSDL file in which the operations for the basic properties of this instrument class are defined. For instruments having extension properties, the WSDL has to be generated separately to include the operations for the extension properties. Therefore, if using the IVI standard, the interoperability is satisfied if the instruments are in the same class and if they have the same extension properties.

Interfaces of Metadata

The IEEE Learning Object Metadata (LOM) standard defines metadata for a learning object (LTSC, 1999). Any entities which can be used, reused or referenced during technology supported learning are learning objects. Examples of learning objects include multimedia content, instructional content, learning objectives, instructional software and software tools, and persons, organizations, or events referenced during technology supported learning. The LOM standard focuses on the minimal set of attributes needed to allow these learning objects to be managed, located, and evaluated.

An online course is a most common learning object. Relevant attributes of LOM for online courses are author, owner, terms of distribution, language, teaching or interaction style, grade level, and prerequisites etc. A part of an online experiment is similar to an online course as it also has tutorial materials and pedagogical attributes. (Bagnasco, Chirico, and Scapolla, 2002) extended the LOM standard for experimentation context to include instrument attributes and assignments. In their work, instruments are a part of an entire experiment and the information about them are not sufficient for searching and booking. Our work studies how to share instruments and operate instruments in more detail. Therefore, we need

Figure 10. The operations to get metadata information in WSDL

```
<!--define the operation -->
<wsdl:operation name="getLOMMateData">
 <wsdl:output name="getLOMDataResponse">
 </wsdl:output>
<!--define the operation -->
<wsdl:operation name="getAvailabilityInfo">
 <wsdl:input name="getAvailabilityRequest">
 </wsdl:input>
 <wsdl:output name="getAvailabilityResponse">
 </wsdl:output>
<!--define the operation -->
<wsdl:operation name="getQoSInfo">
 <wsdl:output name="getQoSResponse">
 </wsdl:output>
```

to extend their LOM extension for instrument attributes. Figure 9 shows the extended LOM attributes for instruments.

The LOM metadata information is defined in an XML file. In the WSDL, we define the operation, *getLOMMetaData*, to download the information (c.f. Figure 10). The LOM information can be used to search, evaluate, and utilize the proper instrument for an experiment. The information about availability and Quality of Service (QoS) are especially useful for evaluating and booking the instrument service. Therefore, we generate two operations, *getAvailabilityInfo* and *getQoSInfo*, for the two attributes. From *getAvailabilityInfo*, we can get all the available timeslots during a time interval, or query if the instrument is available for a specific time period.

QoS information is accumulated from history and can become an important selling and differentiating point of Web services with similar functionality. We record the successful connecting rate to the instrument and the response time to the instrument. QoS information is used when selecting available instruments for an experiment. The higher QoS of the instrument service, the more likely the OES selects this instrument or recommends it to the user to use. The operation *getQoSInfo*, is designed for this.

LIGHTWEIGHT WEB GUI FOR INSTRUMENTS

The primary advantage of a Web application over a desktop application is universal access. The client side of a Web application, in the best case, does not require local installations other than a standard Web browser. Therefore, Web applications are highly portable and platform independent. The Web interface to remotely operate an instrument needs to be user friendly and interactive, and gives the user a similar look and feel as the real instruments. For efficient reason, we should also reduce the amount of data transferred from the server to the client. We have solved the following two problems using only JavaScript enabled Web browser at the client side: to display the instrument panel graphical; to display dynamic graphics for real time signals.

The Web GUI for Virtual Instrument Panels

The panel of a remote instrument should be displayed graphically on a Web browser. The user operates the GUI to control the instruments. The methodology to describe instrument panels is presented in (Fattouh and Saliah, 2004). The principle is to design an XML schema which defines the syntax of the panel of a kind of instruments.

Figure 11. A snippet of the XML to describe the panel of Agilent 34401A

```
<parentFrame parentFrameName="Frame Container">
 <parentFrameLayout> ... </parentFrameLayout>
</parentFrame>
<parentPanel parentPanelName="Parent Panel">
 <parentPanelLayout>GridBagLayout</parentPanelLayout>
<parentPanelDimension>...</parentPanelDimension>
</parentPanel>
<childPanel childPanelName =  "ExternalParametersChildPanel">
 <childPanelLayout> ... </childPanelLayout>
 <component className="jLabel">
   <componentName> ... </componentName>
   ...
 </component>
 ...
</childPanel>
```

An XML file compliant to the schema describes the panel of an individual instrument. Then the XML file can be parsed and rendered at the client side. We use the multimeter Agilent 34401A as an example. A snippet of the XML for its panel is in Figure 11.

One can see the container panel objects are the *parentFrame*, *parentPanel* and *childPanel*. A container object can contain other panel objects, such as labels and text boxes. A container object has a layout that describes how to render the objects inside the container. If one is familiar with java, one can see the objects can be mapped one by one to the classes in a java swing GUI package.

Figure 12 shows the principle to display the panel from its XML description. The XML schema for the Digital Multimeter is in DMM_GUI.xml. It validates the file DMM_Agilent_34401A_GUI.xml which defines the GUI for the Aglient 34401A. The JAXB is used to parse DMM_Agilent_34401A_GUI.xml. Then a java servlet is used to display the panel object on an HTML page. The generated GUI page is displayed on the right bottom section of Figure 12.

Display Real Time Signal on Web GUI

A large number of instruments display a coordinate diagram (graphs and charts) in a panel. A vital feature of the instrument Web interface is to display experiment results that closely resemble the output of the instrument itself. Displaying dynamic textual results in a browser is straightforward. However, displaying dynamic pictorial results is challenging due to the limited graphical capabilities of prevalent Web browsers.

AJAX, shorthand for "Asynchronous JavaScript and XML", is a development technique for creating interactive Web applications (Garrett, 2005). The main technologies used in an AJAX enabled web application are asynchronous data retrieval using XMLHttpRequest and dynamic manipulation and display of html elements based on the retrieved data using Document Object Model (DOM). The intent is to make Web pages feel more responsive by exchanging small amounts of data with the server behind the scenes, so that the entire Web page does not have to be reloaded each time the user requests a change. AJAX is a good solution for displaying and updating the real time signals. We can transfer just the discrete data points for the signals and update just part of the screen

Figure 12. The principle to display instrument panel from its XML description

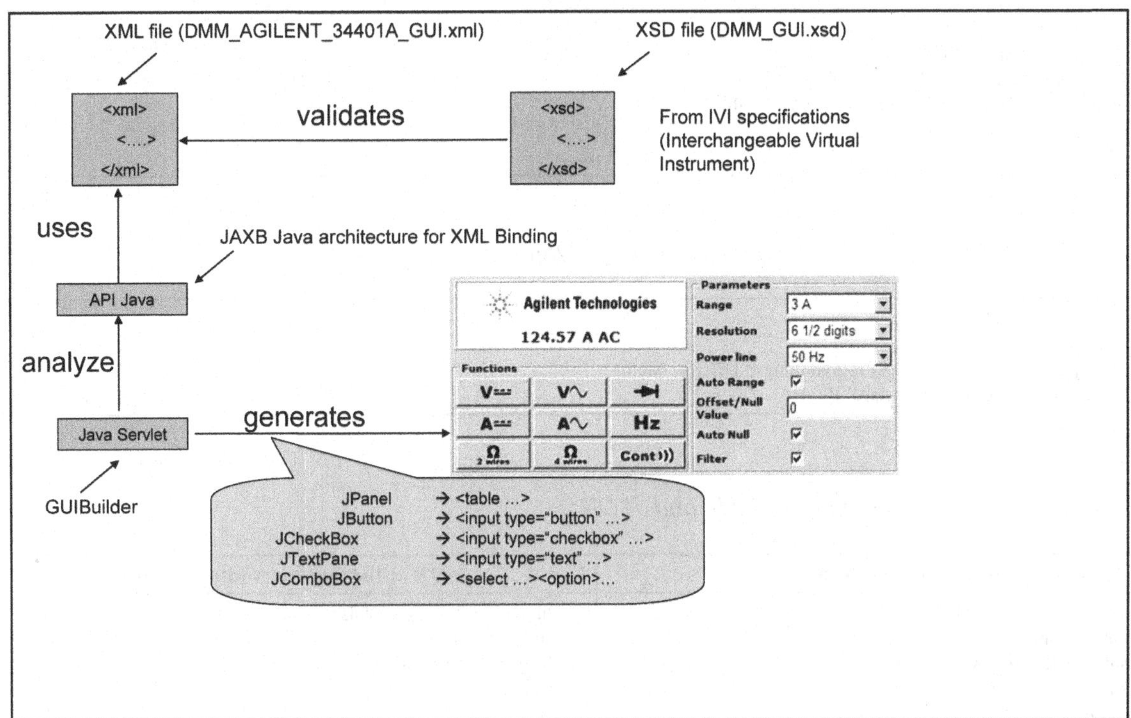

for displaying the data points. Then whole screen looks still and the signal is updating. Bandwidth requirement is reduced making Web pages load faster. This approach also allows keeping data independent of the presentation layer.

JavaScript Object Notation (JSON) is used for transferring the data points between the end user and the servlet. JSON is a text based data interchange format (JSON.org, 2007). What makes JSON rather useful is its inherent support within JavaScript. JavaScript, being the most widely supported scripting language for Web browsers, is very efficient in parsing JSON messages. JSON is not going to replace XML anytime soon, but it provides a viable alternative.

Parsing XML messages within a browser results in a Document Object Model (DOM) tree, which makes the code to manipulate it complicated. On the other hand, parsing JSON results in JavaScript objects and the code to manipulate it is straight forward. Table 1 shows a JSON text and Table 2 shows the equivalent JavaScript objects that can be obtained from parsing the above JSON text. In JSON, an object can be represented by a name value pair separated by a colon and surrounded by curly brackets. An array can be represented within square brackets, and values can be separated by a comma. The value of an object can be a string, an integer, another object, or arrays. In addition, the Boolean literals "true" and "false" are supported. The void concept of "null" is also supported. JavaScript "eval" function, which invokes the JavaScript compiler, can be used for parsing JSON text.

JSON can represent semi-structured data very efficiently compared to XML. Table 3 provides a comparison between XML and JSON representation that shows the similarity and differences between these two formats. XML is relatively verbose and would almost always require more characters to represent the same data. JSON has been touted as the "fat free alternative to xml".

Table 1. Code snippet: a JSON document

```
{
"name": "Jack Sullivan",
"student": true,
"subjects": ["Web Programming", "Discrete Math",
"Psychology", "Operating Systems"]
}
```

Table 2. Code snippet: JSON string to Java Script Object

```
var name = "Jack Sullivan";
var status = true;
var subjects = new Array("Web Programming","Discrete Math",
"Psychology", "Operating Systems");
```

Table 3. Code snippet: comparing XML and JSON

XML ... 146 characters without blanks	**JSON ... 103 characters without blanks**
<student fulltime="false"> <name>Wallace</name> <subject>Rabbit psyche</subject> <subject>Carrot care</subject> <subject>Cage building</subject> </student>	{ "student": { "fulltime": false, "name": "Wallace", "subjects": ["Rabbit psyche", "Carrot care", "Cage building"] } }

Figure 13 depicts the technique used for creating dynamic coordinate diagrams for the Web interface. As stated earlier, a browser is not an ideal platform to construct dynamic images. HTML 4.01 specifications recommended by the W3C does not even state the basic unit of graphics – the pixel as one of the HTML elements. Lutz Tautenhahn, a German software developer, has created a JavaScript library that can be used to display coordinate diagrams (Tautenhahn, 2005). The JavaScript Diagram Builder library is available as a freeware. In our solution we utilise this library to draw the coordinate space and to translate coordinates to positions within a Web page.

The div html element of 1px width and 2px height is used to mark a coordinate in the graph panel. The divs are placed within the Web page according to the translated coordinate. The AJAX engine as seen in Figure 13 is JavaScript method that creates XMLHttpRequest object binds it with a timer and fetches the data from the Servlet. AJAX technique is used to fetch the coordinates from the application server in JSON format and is dynamically displayed over the output panel. In order to mimic the constant output of a wave generator we continuously call the server periodically for new data. The final interface looks like in Figure 14. The demo can be found at our testing Web site http://flydragontech.com/prototypes/lms/oisee/OISEE.htm.

MANAGING STATEFUL INSTRUMENT WEB SERVICES

Instrument Web services involve remotely operating real devices in real time. Improper design of the Web services can cause damage to the instrument,

Figure 13. Web page dynamic graphics technique

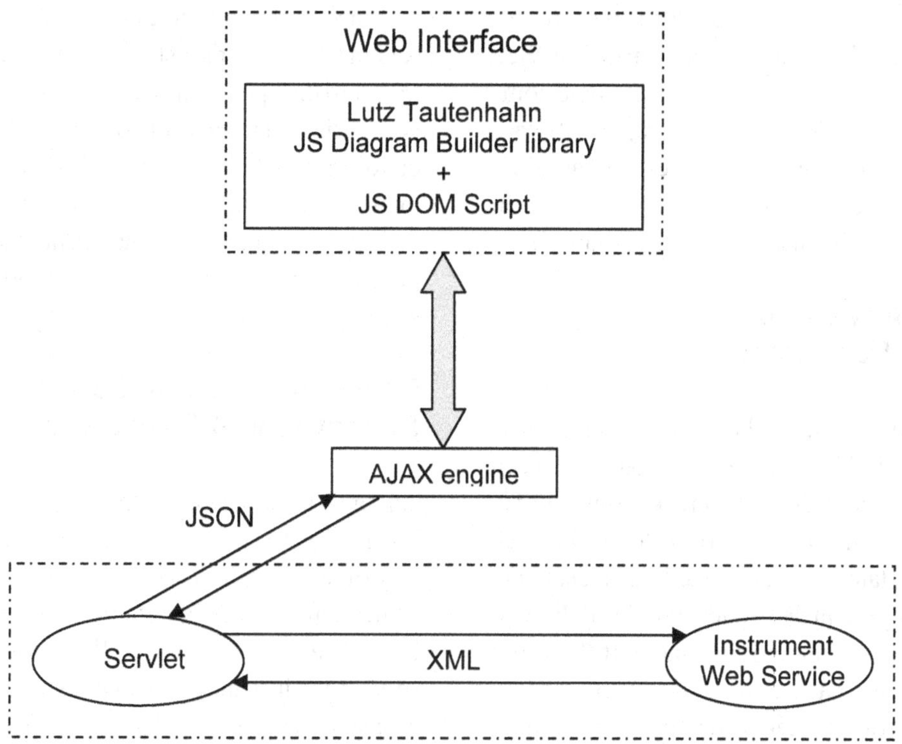

Figure 14. Display real time signal on Web GUI with AJAX and JSON

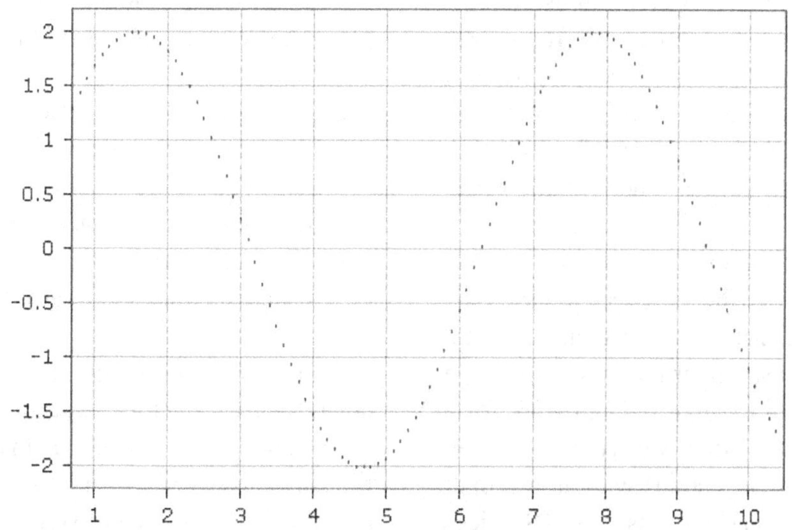

and can lead to false measurement and control, which in turn will result in failure of the online experiment. In (Yan, *et al.*, 2005), we present the special requirements for the instrument Web services, such as reliability mechanisms and communication strategies. By using proper software technologies, these requirements can be satisfied. In the following sub-sections, we will focus on how to manage the instruments as resources.

Stateful Service for Stateless Resources

It is well known that classic Web services is stateless, i.e. it does not maintain states between different clients or different invocations. HTTP, the commonly used transport protocol for Web services, is a stateless data-forwarding mechanism. There are no guarantees of packets being delivered to the destination and no guarantee of the order of the arriving packets. Classic Web services are suitable for services providing non-dynamic information. In this subsection, we discuss if additional effort is needed to manage the instrument Web services.

An instrument itself is a stateless resource. This is because an instrument itself does not record client information or invocations. Indeed, an instrument acts in a reactive way. It receives commands, executes them accordingly, and returns the results. If we say an instrument has "states", these are the parameters of its working mode, which have nothing to do with the states of a Web service.

An instrument can only be occupied by one user at a time. Unlike the resources in Grid Services, instruments can only accept one user at a time because an instrument needs to be set to a specific working mode before it can work for a certain experiment. Normally it is not possible to recover an instrument's status without a proper procedure, so many mechanisms in Grid Services are not useful in our application. The use of an instrument is booked by time slots. On some occasions, the tasks of an instrument can be managed by a queue (Hardison, *et al.*, 2005).

An instrument service needs to be stateful for several reasons. It must be stateful when it needs to record the operations from one user for payment accounting, or to support booking and scheduling, or to control how the user can use this instrument, or when the results need to be transported among several resources asynchronously. In the next subsection, we present a method to build the stateful instrument Web services.

Design the Stateful Service for Instrument Resources

As stated previously, we know that the instrument service has to identify clients and maintain a history of the operation. This kind of stateful service is different from the available stateful framework in Grid Services and WSRF. We design the stateful service for instrument resources as in Figure 15. The states are managed by the resource management layer. The client ID is transferred in SOAP to identify the states of the services. In detail:

(1) The client sends the request to the Web service. The request should contain the ID of the client to identify the session.
(2) The Web service returns the identifier of the reference.
(3) The client always contacts the service using the resource identifier.
(4) – (5) The online experiment is executed and the results are returned to the Web service.
(6) The Web service records the results in a proper manner and returns the results to the client.

Compared to Grid Services, our method does not use a service factory to create service instances for different users, because an instrument service is a single user service, thus no service instances are created. Compared to WSRF, the resource in our method itself remains stateless. We add a layer to manage the states.

Figure 15. The stateful service for instrument resources

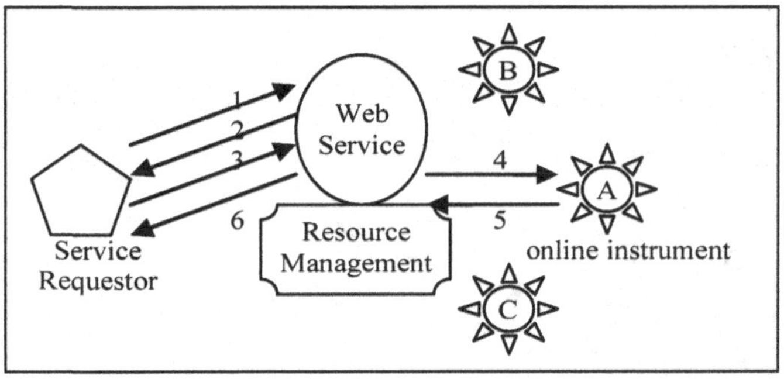

THE PERFORMANCE ISSUES FOR WEB SERVICES FOR ONLINE EXPERIMENT

Although Web services have strong advantages on interoperability, it has intrinsic weaknesses on latency and scalability because it uses more transport layers.

The trade-off of the high interoperability of Web services is its lower performance. Web services have intrinsic performance weaknesses for two main reasons: there are more transport layers than for middleware; and the overhead of using SOAP. Many researchers have analyzed the problem of SOAP efficiency and identified some factors that can affect the latency performance of Web services and SOAP (Chiu, Govindaraju and Bramley, 2002) (Litou, 2002) (van Engelen, 2003). For each factor that could cause the latency, there are some proposed methods to improve the performance. In this article, we benchmark the SOAP efficiency in this context and propose the solutions to improve performance.

Benchmark of Latency

This benchmark test is aimed at determining the time to transport a service request from the requester to the provider. The time involves marshalling the SOAP message and binding it to the HTTP protocol at the request side, and the transportation time and decoding time on the service side. This test takes place when the instrument Web service and the OES are on the same host, thus, the delay by the Internet is not considered. In above, we described that instruments accept ASCII strings as input according to VISA and IVI standards. Therefore we use ASCII strings for encoding a volume of the floating numbers in SOAP message. In our test, we assumed each of the floating numbers had 16 digits to provide adequate precision. Therefore the size of the strings for floating numbers is directly proportional to the number of digits. We measured the time delay starting before the call of the service and ending as the request reaches the service endpoint.

Figure 16 shows the relation of the delay time vs. the number of data points per message. One can see that the delay increases quasi-linearly as the data points increase. There is also a basic overhead for the transportation, which is primarily the time for setting up the TCP/IP connection.

Optimize the SOAP Efficiency

Latency of SOAP message is caused by the time of transportation, which is proportional to the size of SOAP, and the delay caused by the TCP/IP layer.

The most straightforward method of optimization is to reduce the SOAP message size by extracting the string out of the XML, compressing it into binary format (we use ZIP compression format here) and sending it as an attachment. The size of the payload is reduced to approximately

Figure 16. The delay vs. number of data point

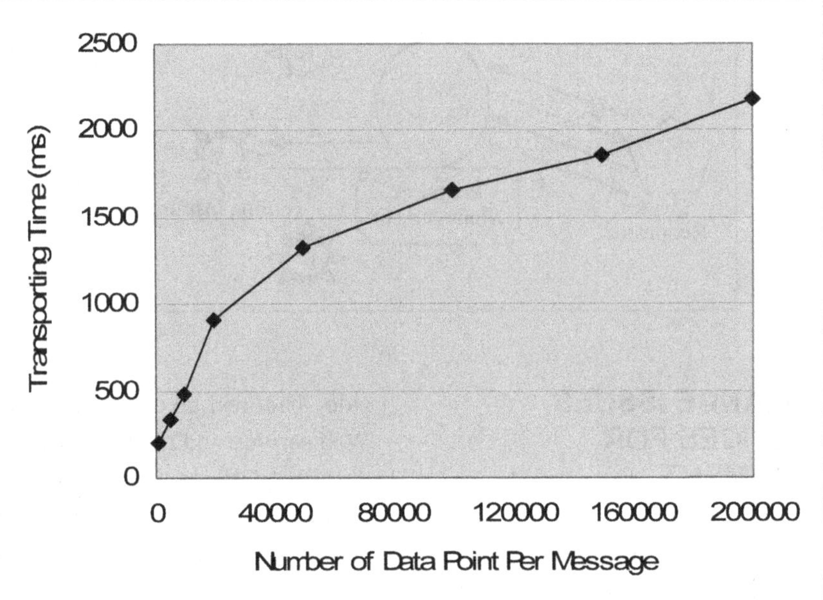

40 to 50 per cent of its original size. The SOAP messaging protocol supports Multipurpose Internet Mail Extensions (MIME) or Direct Internet Message Encapsulation (DIME) attachments. The difference is that MIME is designed to provide flexibility, while DIME is designed to be simpler and to provide more efficient message encapsulation. The results of applying different attachment approaches are shown in Figure 17. One can see that the transportation time can be reduced dramatically by compressing the SOAP content.

We can also optimize the underlying HTTP and TCP protocols for SOAP messaging. We present the possible methods below without testing results:

Persistent HTTP Connection

Persistent connection could "keep-alive" a connection and save the time needed to establish HTTP connection every time. For HTTP 1.0, the persistent connection works only if there is no proxy between the client and server. For HTTP1.1, the persistent connection can be used with more than one proxy between a client and a server.

Disable Nagle Algorithm and Remove TCP Delay ACK

The Nagle algorithm in combination with the TCP delayed ACK (the acknowledge response in TCP) are used to prevent network congestion (Litou, 2002), but they cause unnecessary delays when sending a SOAP message (Elfwing, R., Paulsson, U., and Lundberg, L., 2002). It is possible to disable Nagle on both the server and client side to get considerable improvement for the response time.

Better Pipelined Connection by Using HTTP 1.1

The use of HTTP inherits some of the TCP features such as the three-way handshake. This can cause delays. HTTP1.1 attempts to solve these problems. The result shows that HTTP1.1 can reduce the RTT (Round Trip Time) to half of HTTP1.0 implementation (Nielsen, *et al.*, 1997).

Figure 17. Different methods to send string data through SOAP

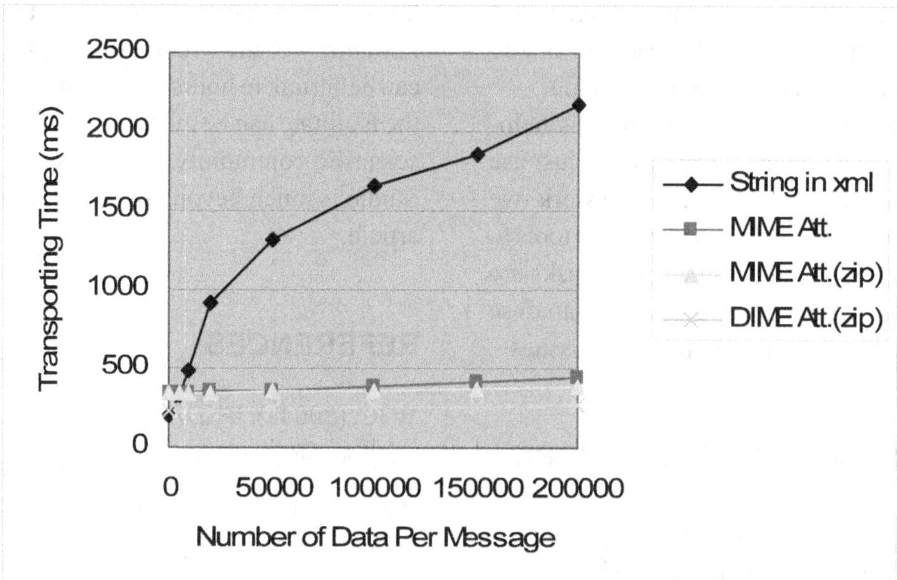

DISCUSSIONS

Service oriented architecture is the new technique to build distributed system. It has attracted attention for building online experiment systems as well. iLab at MIT adopts SOAP for communications between users and labs (Hardison, *et al.* 2005). Their architecture has three roles: lab server, end user and service broker. The service broker mediates the communication between the user and the lab server and provides storage and administrative services that are generic and can be shared by multiple labs within a signal university. Their focus is on providing such a kind of broker. In our architecture, the broker role is rather weak and not more than the function of registration. Our focus in this article is to study how to control a remote device via Web service protocol and how to design lightweight Web GUI for remote instruments using Web 2.0 techniques. We consider that the communication between the end user and the online lab should be very light that SOAP is too heavy to use. So far as we know, our work is unique in this domain.

During our study, we find that the current devices and the way of experiments are not completely suitable for online experiments. For example, the users have to do everything by sending command, not using their hands. In our sample experiment, the users cannot assemble the circuits, nor tune the resistor to change the amplitude. Therefore, we need to design a special circuit to allow the users to configure the circuit by sending commands. Technically it is possible in our experiment. But in some other cases, to achieve reconfiguration is not so straightforward. Moreover, in real lab, the input and output signals are observed by oscilloscopes. In this article, we digitalize the signals and display them on the Web site. We consider it is a cheaper way than using digital oscilloscopes. So people can see that we have different ways to do online experiments than real experiments. We have also found that not all the instruments can be shared online. For example, waveform generator produces analog signals which are not sharable without digitalization. Therefore, it is hard to say that it is useful to share a waveform generator online. Under current experiment devices and methods, it is commonly feasible to share a whole experiment or share a group of devices that has digital interface. We suppose more devices and experiment methods will be designed for online experiment and online engineering domain.

Collaborative working environment is helpful for online experiment. Currently, we just use the standard online tools. In the future work, we would use camera and video conferencing tools to enhance our environment. Other future tasks are to optimize the SOAP messaging and to analyse the resource description and integration issues.

CONCLUSION AND FUTHER WORK

Our vision is to share expensive equipment and educational materials associated with lab experiments as broadly as possible within higher education and beyond. In this article, we propose to wrap the remote instruments as Web services for online experiment systems. The advantage of Web services is its inter-operability across platforms and programming languages. Its trade-off is low efficiency caused by SOAP messaging. This article covers the essential issues to build instrument Web services, such as WSDL design, stateful service management and performance issues. This article also presents the lightweight Web GUI to display virtual instrument panels and real time signals using Web 2.0 techniques. The technique developed in this article can be widely used for different real laboratories, such as microelectronics, chemical engineering, polymer crystallization, structural engineering, and signal processing.

As the article is published, we have got a Canarie (http://www.canarie.ca/about/index.html) funded project called Science Studio for enabling remote experimentation with the synchrotron within Canada Light Source (CLS) (http://www.lightsource.ca/), a national science research laboratory. Currently the scientists who use the facilitate to do experiments need to travel to Winnipeg where the CLS is located and reserve the beamline time for 3 days as a minimum unit. With the capacity of remote experimentation, the scientists can save traveling time and cost. Furthermore, the occupy time of an experiment can be shrunk to hours instead of days. Therefore, the facilitate can be more efficiently shared in the scientific community. Our work within Science Studio is much beyond the topics touched in this article.

REFERENCES

W3C, (2004a). *WSDL Specification*. http://www.w3.org/ TR/ wsdl.

W3C, (2004b). *SOAP Specification*. http://www.w3.org/ TR/ soap12-part1/.

Agilent Inc. (2005). *About Instrument I/O.* http://adn.tm.agilent.com/ index.cgi? CONTENT_ID=239, retrieved in 2005.

Auer, M. E., & Gallent, W. (2000). The 'Remote Electronic Lab' as a Part of the Telelearning Concept at the Carinthia Tech Institute. *Proc. Interactive Computer-Aided Learning (ICL),* Kassel University Press.

Bagnasco, A., Chirico, M., & Scapolla, A. M. (2002). XML Technologies to Design Didactical Distributed Measurement Laboratories. *IEEE Instrument and Measurement Technology Conference (IMTC),* Anchorage, Alaska, USA.

Chiu, K., Govindaraju, M., & Bramley, R. (2002). Investigating the Limits of SOAP Performance for Scientific Computing. 11th *IEEE international Symposium on High Performance Distributed Computing* HPDC-11.

Elfwing, R., Paulsson, U., & Lundberg, L. (2002). Performance of SOAP in Web service Environment Compared to CORBA. *Proceedings of the Ninth Asia-Pacific Software Engineering Conference (APSE'02).* IEEE.

Fattouh, B., & Saliah, H. H. (2004). Model for a Distributed Telelaboratory Interface Generator. *Proceedings of Int. Conf. On Engineering* [), Czech Republic.]. *Education and Research,* (June): 27–30.

Garrett, J. J. (2005). *Ajax: A New Approach to Web Applications*. Available at http://adaptivepath.com/ publications/ essays/ archives/ 000385.php, last retrieved March 29 2007.

Hardison, J., Hardison, D. J., Zych, D., del Alamo, J. A., et al. (2005). The Microelectronics WebLab 6.0—An Implementation Using Web services and the iLab Shared Architecture. *Proc. Int'l Conf. Engineering Education and Research (iCEER2005), Int'l Network for Engineering Education and Research,* 2005. http://wwwmtl.mit.edu/ ~alamo/ pdf/ 2005/ RC-107% 20paper.pdf.

Hardison, J. D., Zych, J. A., & del Alamo, V. J. Harward, et al. (2005). *The Microelectronics WebLab 6.0 – An Implementation Using Web services and the iLab Shared Architecture. iCEER2005,* March, Tainan, Taiwan.

JSON.org. (2007). *Introducing JSON.* Available at: http://www.json.org/. Last retrieved in March 29 2007.

Latchman, H. A., Salzmann, Ch., Gillet, D., & Bouzekri, H. (1999, November). Information Technology Enhanced Learning in Distance and Conventional Education. *IEEE Transactions on Education*, 247–254. doi:10.1109/13.804528

Litou, M. (2002). Migrating to Web services – Latency and Scalability. *Proceedings of Fourth Int. Workshop on Web Site Evolution (WSE).* IEEE.

LTSC (IEEE Learning Technology Standards Committee). (1999). *IEEE 1484 Learning Objects Metadata (IEEE LOM).* http://www.ischool.washington. edu/ sasutton/ IEEE1484.html.

Naef, O. (2006). Real laboratory, virtual laboratory or remote laboratory: what is the most efficient way? *International Journal of Online Engineering, v2*(n3). http://www.i-joe.org/ ojs/ sitemap.php.

Nielsen, H., Gettys, J., Baird-Smith, A., Prud'hommeaux, E., Lie, H., & Lilley, C. (1997). *Network Performance Effects of HTTP/1.1, CSS1, and PNG.* http://www.w3.org/ Protocols/ HTTP/ Performance/ Pipeline.html, June 1997.

Salzmann, C., & Gillet, D. (2002). Real-time Interaction over the Internet, *Proceedings of IFAC2002. UDDI.org.* http://uddi.org/ pubs/ uddi_ v3.htm.

Tautenhahn, T. (2005). *JavaScript Diagram Builder 3.3.* http://www.lutanho.net/ diagram.

van Engelen, R. (2003). Pushing the SOAP Envelop With Web services for Scientific Computing. *Proceedings of the International Conference on Web services (ICWS)* (pp. 346-354).

Yan, Y., Liang, Y., Du, X., Saliah-Hassane, H., & Ghorbani, A. (2005). Design Instrumental Web services for Online Experiment Systems. *Ed-Media 2005*, Montreal, Canada.

This work was previously published in International Journal of Web Services Research, Volume 6, Issue 4, edited by Liang-Jie Zhang, pp. 75-93, copyright 2009 by IGI Publishing (an imprint of IGI Global).

Chapter 17
An Efficient Service Discovery Method and its Application

Shuiguang Deng
Zhejiang University, China

Zhaohui Wu
Zhejiang University, China

Jian Wu
Zhejiang University, China

ABSTRACT

To discover services efficiently has been regarded as one of important issues in the area of Service Oriented Computing (SOC). This article carries out a survey on the issue and points out the problems for the current semantic-based service discovery approaches. After that, an information model for registered services is proposed. Based on the model, it brings forward a two-phase semantic-based service discovery method which supports both the operation matchmaking and operation-composition matchmaking. Th authors import the bipartite graph matching to improve the efficiency of matchmaking. An implementation of the proposed method is presented. A series of experiments show that the method gains better performance on both discovery recall rate and precision than a traditional matchmaker and it also scales well with the number of services being accessed.

DOI: 10.4018/978-1-61350-104-7.ch017

INTRODUCTION

Background

Nowadays, as the Internet has become the main platform on which enterprises carry out businesses globally, the environment of enterprise applications will be characterized by frequently changing market demands, time-to-market pressure and fierce competition. Therefore, it requires that the enterprise business systems should provide more flexibility than present-day systems can afford. The key to tackle this challenge completely is to utilize a kind of novel software system architecture which is required to be distributed, loose-coupled and reconfigurable. Fortunately, these requirements can be best addressed by Service-oriented Architecture (SOA).

SOA is an architectural style whose goal is to achieve loose coupling among interacting services and to build software systems by composing services (Papazoglou & Georgakopoulos, 2003). It provides greater flexibility and agility while allowing business systems to use heterogeneous resources efficiently and effectively. Web services technology has been regarded as the preferred implementation vehicle for SOA. A Web service is a software entity that supports interoperable application-to-application interaction over Internet. At present, the accelerating creation and use of Web Services in enterprises informatics is a major trend (Kalogeras, Gialelis et al., 2006). Thus, more and more Web services are published in Internet by enterprises to accelerate the cooperation with their partners. For example, in the scenario of supply chain management, a manufacturer receives an order to deliver some merchandise to a retailer. In order to accomplish this business, the manufacture finds possible suppliers and selects the best available service provided by one supplier. However, due to the highly distributed and dynamic environment, Web services may be located at different enterprises and come and leave at any time without prior warning. In that context, no one is likely to have the detailed knowledge of all Web services in advance. As a result, one of great challenges is how to discover the suitable Web services accurately and quickly. Thus, service discovery, which aims at retrieving services advertised in a repository that match a user's goal, has allured much attention both from industry and academy.

Problem

Currently, there is a good body of work on service discovery. Among the work, the effort of semantic Web service from the semantic Web community has been regarded as the most promising way to retrieve services in an accurate and automatic way. Based on related ontology languages and inference engines, semantic Web services provide machine understandable descriptions of what services do and how they achieve their goals (McIlraith, Son et al., 2001). Semantic Web service discovery utilizes semantic matchmaking to check whether an advertised service satisfies a user's request by computing the similarity degree between the description for the service and the one for user's request. If the similarity degree exceeds some threshold value specified by the user, the service is returned as a candidate for the user. Due to the accurate and unambiguous description of a service's functionalities and a user's request both enhanced by semantics, semantic Web service discovery tends to get good recall rate and precision. However, they can achieve even better performance with the following two factors taken into consideration.

(1) Not all inputs are compulsory for each output

According to the most frequently cited semantic Web service matchmaking algorithm proposed by Paolucci, Kawamura et al. (2002), an advertised service matches a request if the request provides all the inputs (possibly more) needed by the service while the service generates all the outputs (possibly more) needed by the requester. In other words, a successful matching demands that the request provides all the inputs of the advertised service to get any output of the service. This requirement has been widely accepted by most semantic Web service matchmaking methods.

However, the successful matching criteria are too strict and may lead to some unwanted situations. Consider an abstract scenario between an advertised service *S* and a request *R*, where *S* has two inputs (*a* and *b*) and two outputs (*o* and *p*), and *R* specifies one input (*a*) and one output (*o*). According to the above successful matching criteria, *S* does not match *R* as *R* cannot provide the input *b*. But for *S*, maybe the input *b* is optional for the output *o*. In this case, *S* should be a candidate service for *R* but it is excluded. Consider a real weather report service (http://www.webservicex.com/globalweather.asmx?WSDL). It has an operation named *GetWeather* that returns *WeatherResult* on receiving a *CityName* and a *CountryName*. However, this operation also serves well if the inputs only include a *CityName*. Both the abstract and real cases show that to some extent, the recall rate can be improved with the interface dependency information (i.e., the dependency of outputs on inputs) considered.

(2) Operation compositions provide value-added functions

According to WSDL (Web Service Definition Language), the defacto standard service description language, a service is a collection of operations and each provides a function. For example, a stock service can provide both the stock query and exchange functions. At present, there are a large number of services described in WSDL and published in local or global repositories on Internet. We have implemented a program to query and download the WSDL files on Internet automatically by network programming with Google APIs. After collecting some statistics, we have two findings: One is that about 75% WSDL files contain more than two operations, about 30% contain more than five operations and about 5% contain more than ten operations; another significant finding is that there are more than 30% WSDL files, in which some outputs of an operation are the same as some inputs of others. For example, the service (http://www.ripedev.com/webservices/ZipCode.asmx?WSDL) has two different operations named *CityToZipCode* and *ZipCodeToTimeZone*, respectively. The former translates from a *CityName* to its *ZipCode* and the latter from a *ZipCode* to its corresponding *TimeZone*. As the output *ZipCode* of the first operation is the same as the input of the second one, it implies that the service has the function to translate indirectly from a *CityName* to its *TimeZone* through the concatenation of the two operations. This example shows that the operations within a service may be concatenated to provide value-added functions.

However, for the most current service discovery methods, they all regard a service as an operation or several isolated ones. While matchmaking between an advertised service and a request, they simply check whether there is such an operation that offers the requested function. If such an operation exists, the service will be selected as a candidate one; otherwise, it will be filtered. Accordingly, some deserved services that actually match the request by a composition of several operations are excluded. Thus, taking the composition of operations within a service into matchmaking can improve the recall rate.

Research Objective and Methodology

The above two factors has been discussed in our two pre-published papers (Deng, Wu et al., 2006a & 2006b), respectively. However, the service matchmaking algorithms proposed in these two papers are with high computing complexity. And moreover, these two factors are not taken into consideration together before. Thus, in this article we consider the above two factors in one discovery method and propose an efficient two-phase semantic service discovery mechanism (TSSD). Given an advertised service and a request, TSSD checks whether there is a single operation matching the request at the first phase, where the semantic matchmaking is carried out between each operation and the request, and the interface dependency of an operation is also considered. If no single operation matches the request, it performs operation-composition matchmaking to check whether there is such a composition of operations matching the request. Compared with our pre-published work, we import the concept of bipartite graph matching and proposed a new matchmaking algorithm based on it to improve the matchmaking efficiency. A series of evaluations in our implementation suggest that considering these two factors in TSSD offers better performance and TSSD scales well with the number of services being accessed.

The article is organized as follows. In the second section of this article, we give a literature survey on service discovery. Then, an information model for registered services is introduced in the third section. In the fourth section, we present the two-phase service discovery method. The implementation of TSSD and A series of evaluations are given in the fifth section. Finally, we conclude this article and give the future direction in the sixth section.

LITERATURE SURVEY

Service discovery is an active research area. It originates from the issue of software component reuse and discovery in software engineering, distributed computing and information retrieval in knowledge and data engineering. During the past few years, much effort was placed in the area of service discovery. In this section, we discuss some representative semantic-based approaches and classify them into the following categories according to the semantic service models used in discovery. Notice that besides OWL-S/DMAL-S (Ontology Web Language for Service/ DARPA Agent Markup Language for Service) and WSMO (Web Service Modeling Ontology), WSDL-S and SWSO (Semantic Web Service Ontology) are other two semantic service models. However, there is little literature on service discovery based on these two models at present.

OWL-S/DAML-S Based Semantic Service Discovery

OWL-S (formerly DAML-S) is an OWL-based Web service ontology. As the first effort towards semantic Web service, it provides a core set of concepts for describing the properties and capabilities of a Web service in an unambiguous and computer-interpretable way. It describes a service through three main parts: the service profile for advertising and discovering services; the process model, which gives details on how the service works; and the grounding, which provides the description on how to access the service.

Based on the service profile of DAML-S, Paolucci et al. (2002) firstly proposed an approach for semantic matchmaking of Web service capability. It considered the matching of input/output concepts defined in an ontology. After that, they augmented the UDDI (Universal Description, Discovery, and Integration) registry with a new module (Semantic Services Matchmaker), a search engine for Web services that enhanced the discovery facilities of UDDI to make use of semantic information described in a service profile (Kawamura, Blasio et al. 2003; Srinivasan, Paolucci et al., 2004). Luo et al. (2006) proposed a method to enable the syntax-based UDDI search engine behavior like a semantic matchmaker without requiring modification in the UDDI registries. During the service publication, they transformed OWL-S service profiles into a UDDI data model, resolved ontology concepts and indexed them. So UDDI registries performed semantic matchmaking like querying on UDDI data.

Due to the process model of OWL-S providing a far richer description of a service than the service profile, some researchers also utilized the process model in service matchmaking. Bansal and Vidal (2003) stored an OWL-S process model as a tree, in which the root of the model was the root of the tree; the composite processes were intermediary nodes; and atomic processes were leaves. They proposed a service matchmaking algorithm based on tree matching. As an improvement on Bansal and Vidal's work, Brogi and Corfini (2007) proposed a method named SAM (Service Aggregation Matchmaking) that determined whether a query could be satisfied by a service by the analysis of a dependency graph constructed according to the process model of the service. Unlike Bansal and Vidal's algorithm performing matchmaking at the level of entire services, SAM supported the matching both at the level of atomic processes and at the level of composition of their composition.

Besides the service profile and process model used in service discovery and matchmaking, the underlying logic basis of OWL-S—Description Logic (DL) had also attracted researchers' attention. Benatallah et al. (2005) proposed an approach in the context of description logics to automate the Web service discovery. They transformed a service discovery as the best covering problem and then formalized the problem in the framework of DL-based ontologies. Then, they presented a service matchmaking algorithm using a hypergraph-based algorithm to compute the best cover.

WSMO Based Semantic Service Discovery

WSMO is a conceptual model for semantically describing Web services and their specific properties. It depicts a semantic Web service through four elements: ontologies which provide the terminology for other elements; Web services which define a semantic description of services; goals which specify the users' requirements for a Web service; and mediators which resolve the heterogeneity problem (Roman, Lausen et al., 2005).

Keller et al. (2004) gave an in-depth analysis of the major conceptual issues involved in Web service discovery and proposed a conceptual model for the discovery in WSMO. They differentiated between service and Web service discovery and performed Web service discovery based on matching abstracted goal descriptions with semantic annotations of Web services. They utilized the set-based modeling approach to model Web services and goals; and based on set-theoretic criteria, proposed two conceptual semantic-based discovery approaches, namely discovery based on simple semantic descriptions of services and discovery based on rich semantic descriptions of services. Both of them differentiated between different types of matches such as exact-match, subsumes-match, plug-in-match and intersection match. Kifer et al. (2004) presented a logical framework to dynamically discover Web services in two stages, namely discovery and contracting, in the processes of searching for an appropriate service. They defined proof obligations that formalized the concepts of a match in these two stages based on the WSMO conceptual model. Stollberg et al. (2005) presented a partner and service discovery approach in their system for automated collaboration on the semantic Web by integrating agents, ontologies and Web services. They utilized WSML and the logic expression to model the action knowledge and object knowledge of a Web service, respectively; and then performed service discovery by the set-based object matchmaking using a theorem prover.

Miscellaneous Semantic Service Discovery Approaches

Besides the above two categories of semantic-based service discovery methods, there are many others. For example, Klein and Bernstein (2004) used process models to capture service semantics and proposed a pattern-matching algorithm to retrieve target services. Syeda-Mahmood et al. (2005) used domain-independent and domain-specific ontologies to find matching service descriptions. They combined the two cues to determine an overall semantic similarity score. In addition, they integrated semantic and ontological matching with attribute hashing to accelerate service retrieval. Osman et al. (2006) utilized the case based reasoning (CBR) methodology for modeling dynamic Web service discovery and matchmaking. In order to improve the accuracy of service discovery and matchmaking, they took into account the past matchmaking experiences and used ontology to describe both services and rules of CBR reasoning engine.

After a deep insight into the above representative methods, we find that they did not consider the interface dependency relation in a Web service while doing matchmaking. This is due to the absence of some information to describe interface dependency relations in a Web service registered in a registry. Moreover, most of them did not support the matchmaking at the operation composition level. Although there exist a few composition-oriented discovery approaches composing services on the fly for users (Aversano, Canfora et al., 2004; Liang, Chakarapani et al., 2004), they belong to the coarse-grain composition rather than fine-grain, namely operation-oriented composition as in our approach. Furthermore, compared with those approaches supporting service-oriented composition, our approach achieves efficiency by pre-computing off-line all the compositions for the later online matchmaking.

INFORMATION MODEL FOR SERVICE REGISTRATION

To enable Web services provided by different enterprises to be findable, accessible and reusable, they must be published and registered in a service repository. In fact, service discovery is carried out within such repositories by performing service matchmaking between a user's request and the registration information of services. As a de-facto standard registry for Web services, UDDI make use of a data structure tModel to represent the registered information of a service. However, Due to the fact that UDDI preserves the syntax information of services only, such as names, comments and descriptions, service discovery is key-word based and does not yield a satisfactory performance. To address this issue completely and also to make the aforementioned ignored factors be considered in service discovery, it is a key step to enrich the information for registered services in a repository. Thus, we extend the standard registered information of a service in UDDI in the following three aspects.

(1) Annotate inputs/outputs with semantic information

Semantic information can help machine understand the capability of services accurately and explicitly. This information can be gained by requesting a service provider to annotate each input/output with a concept (also called term or word) from a public domain-independent ontology such as WordNet (Miller, 1995) and HowNet (Dong & Dong, 2006) when he/she registers a service. For example, when the service provider advertises the aforementioned order-management service, he/she is required to specify a concept from a public ontology for each input message and output message. This extension enhances operations with semantics and enables matchmaking at the semantic level.

Notice that we do not use a domain-ontology for service annotation here. This is because of the following three reasons: 1) different services in a repository come from different domains. For many domains, no public ontology is available at present. It is a difficult and time-consuming project to establish a new and widely accepted one; 2) Multiple domain-ontology used by services brings much complexity to semantic service discovery, due to many open issues in the ontology research area such as ontology integration, ontology mapping and semantic similarity computing (Rodriguez & Egenhofer, 2003); 3) the design of public ontologies such as WordNet and HowNet is inspired by current psycholinguistic and computational theories of human lexical memory. They have enough concepts to annotate various services from different domains.

(2) Add interface dependencies between inputs and outputs

For each output of an operation, its interface dependency is used to find out inputs, on which the output depends on. Interface dependency can be declared by service providers who can specify the optional inputs for each output in an operation. For example, "*CountryName*" is required to be declared as optional for "*WeatherResult*" by the provider of the service mentioned before. The declaration indicates that *WeatherResult* depends on *CityName* only. This extension makes it possible to consider interface dependency in matchmaking.

(3) Add assignment relation into an advertised service

An assignment relation between an output of an operation and an input of another one indicates that the output can be fed into the input both at the syntactic and semantic level. As the inputs/outputs have been annotated with ontology concepts, assignment relations can be automatically generated by the semantic inference among concepts. In order to reduce the semantic differentia in an assignment, one ontology concept can be assigned to another only if both of them are the same or the former is a subclass of the latter. For an input, we can get outputs which can be fed to it directly using assignment relations. Thus, adding assignment relations into a service in advance can accelerate the process of composing operations to fulfill a request.

We present the formal definition for an operation and service as follows after the above three extensions are added. Notice that, we do not aim to propose a new service model different from existing models such as WSDL, OWL-S and WSMO. In fact, the information model for service registration can be regarded as a common abstraction from those service models which represents the necessary information in a repository used by service discovery.

Definition (*Operation*) *An operation p is a 4-tuple:* $p = \{n_p, I, O, f_p\}$ *where:*

1. n_p is the operation name.
2. $I = \{i_1, i_2, \ldots, i_n\}$ is the set of input names.
3. $O = \{o_1, o_2, \ldots, o_m\}$ is the set of output names.
4. $f_p : O \rightarrow P(I)$ is a mapping from the set O to the power set of I.

Notice that any element in I or O corresponds to a concept in a public domain-independent ontology. For an output $o \in O, f_p(o) = I'$ means that o depends on the input set I' (denoted as $o \propto I'$), i.e., all the inputs in I' must be provided for an invocation of this operation to get o.

Definition (*Fully-dependent/Partially-dependent Output*) *Given an operation* $p = \{n_p, I, O, f_p\}$ *and* $o \in O$, *if* $o \propto I$, *i.e.,* $f_p(o) = I$, *o is a fully-dependent output; otherwise, i.e.,* $f_p(o) \subset I$, *o is a partially-dependent output.*

This definition indicates that a fully-dependent output depends on all the inputs whereas a partially-dependent output depends on a part of the inputs.

Definition (*Service*) *A service s is a 3-tuple:* $s = (n_s, P, f_s)$ *where:*

Figure 1. An geography information service extended with interface dependency and assignment relations

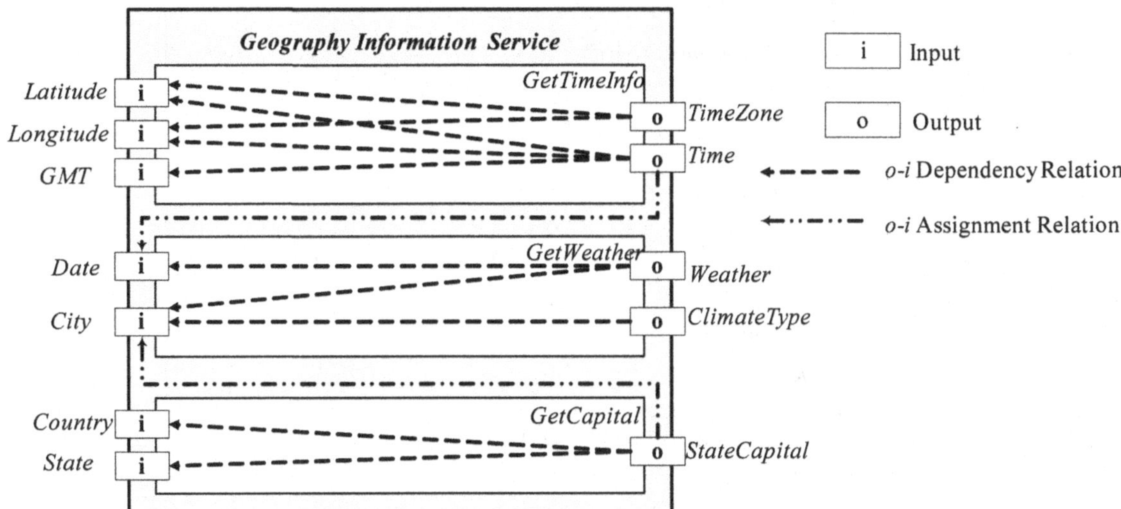

(1) n_s is the service name.
(2) $P = \{p_1, p_2, \ldots, p_m\}$ is the set of operations.
(3) $f_s : \bigcup_{1 \le i \le n} p_i.O \rightarrow P(\bigcup_{1 \le i \le n} p_i.I)$ is the mapping from all outputs to the power set of all inputs.

Notice that the service definition only includes the necessary information to be used for service matchmaking but ignores others, such as the information about the service provider and the service binding. It shows that a service is a collection of operations. For any output o of an operation, the function f_s returns those inputs of others that can be assigned with o. For example, three operations $p_i (i = 1,2,3)$ of a service, $p_1.O = \{o_1, o_2\}$, $p_2.I = \{i_1, i_2\}$ and $p_3.I = \{i_3, i_4, i_5\}$, the two assignment relations $f_s(o_1) = \{i_2, i_3\}$ and $f_s(o_2) = \{i_1, i_5\}$ mean that o_1 can be assigned to i_2 and i_3, while o_2 can be assigned to i_1 and i_5.

Consider the *Geography Information Service* shown in Figure 1. There are three operations named *GetTimeInfo*, *GetWeather* and *GetCapital*, respectively. Within the operations, a dashed line directed from an output to an input represents an *o-i Dependency Relation*, i.e., the input is compulsory for the invocation of the operation to get the output. A double dots line directed form an output to an input between two operations represents an *o-i Assignment Relation*, i.e., the output can be fed into the input.

According to the definitions of an operation and a service, we formalize the above service as shown in Exhibit 1.

TWO-PHASE SERVICE DISCOVERY

For a service request and a registered service, a semantic service discovery method carries out service matchmakings to evaluate to what extent the service's description satisfies the request's description by calculating the Semantic-Similarity Degree (SSD) between them. If the degree exceeds the threshold value specified by the requester, for example 80%, the service is returned. The higher the degree, the more the service matches the request. In general, a similarity degree ranges from "0" to "1". The value "1" means that the service matches the request completely whereas "0" means that the service doesn't match the request at all. A value between "0" and "1" means the service matches the request partially. While computing

Exhibit 1.

$$
\begin{aligned}
&s = (n_s, P, f_s), \; where: \\
&\quad n_s = \text{"Geography Information Service"} \\
&\quad P = \{p_1, p_2, p_3\} \\
&\quad\quad p_1 = \{n_{p_1}, I_1, O_1, f_{p_1}\} \\
&\quad\quad\quad n_{p_1} = \text{"GetTimeInfo"} \\
&\quad\quad\quad I_1 = \{Latitude, Longitude, GMT\} \\
&\quad\quad\quad O_1 = \{TimeZone, Time\} \\
&\quad\quad\quad f_{p_1}(TimeZone) = \{Latitude, Longitude\}; f_{p_1}(Time) = \{Latitude, Longitude, Date\} \\
&\quad\quad p_2 = \{n_{p_2}, I_2, O_2, f_{p_2}\} \\
&\quad\quad\quad n_{p_2} = \text{"GetWeather"} \\
&\quad\quad\quad I_2 = \{City, Date\} \\
&\quad\quad\quad O_2 = \{Weather, ClimateType\} \\
&\quad\quad\quad f_{p_2}(Weather) = \{Date, City\}; f_{p_2}(ClimateType) = \{City\} \\
&\quad\quad p_3 = \{n_{p_3}, I_3, O_3, f_{p_3}\} \\
&\quad\quad\quad n_{p_3} = \text{"GetCapital"} \\
&\quad\quad\quad I_3 = \{Country, State\} \\
&\quad\quad\quad O_3 = \{StateCapital\} \\
&\quad\quad\quad f_{p_3}(StateCapital) = \{Country, State\} \\
&\quad f_s(Time) = \{Date\}; \; f_s(StateCapital) = \{City\}
\end{aligned}
$$

the SSD, a semantic matchmaking method utilizes the semantic information in the descriptions of a service and a request, for example, the ontology concepts annotated with inputs and outputs.

Semantic Similarity Computing Between Concepts

The study of semantic similarity between ontology concepts has been a generic issue in the areas of natural language processing and information retrieval for many years. At present, a number of semantic similarity computing methods have been proposed and proven to be practicable in some specific applications. These methods can be classified into two categories: edge counting-based (or dictionary/thesaurus-based) methods and information theory-based (or corpus-based) methods (Li, Bandar et al., 2003).

The methods in the first category calculate the similarity between two concepts using the shortest path between concepts in the hierarchical structure of the shared ontology. In general, the longer the shortest path between two concepts is, the smaller the similarity between them. Besides shortest path, some methods also consider the depth of the two concepts in the hierarchical structure and the density of the sub-hierarchies of two concepts in the hierarchical structure. Methods in this category are intuitive, intelligible and easy to be implemented.

The methods in the second category calculate the similarity of two concepts by the amount of information shared by the two concepts. In general, the more information shared, the greater the similarity between them. The shared information can be defined as the maximum of the information content of the concept that subsumes the two concepts in the taxonomy hierarchy. And the information content of a concept can be evaluated by the probability of encountering an instance of the concept in a corpus (Resnik, 1999). As the information content is calculated from an application-dependent corpus, the methods in

Figure 2. A fragment of the semantic hierarchy of WordNet

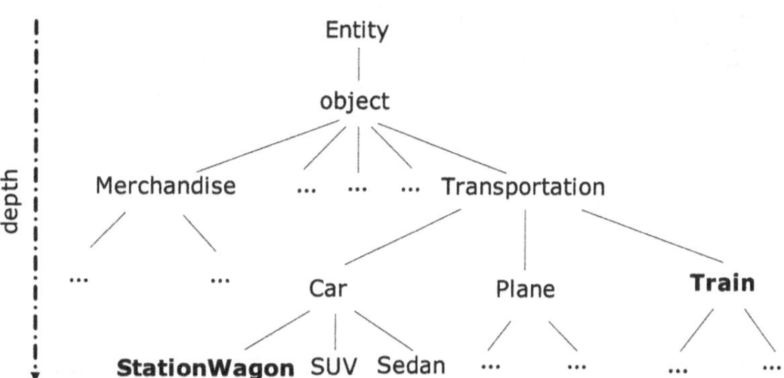

this category are not general and do not adapt to a domain-independent ontology well. Moreover, due to its reliance on the statistic on the occurrence frequency of a concept and its sub-concept in a generous corpus, the methods in this category, compared to those in the first category, are more complex and difficult to be implemented.

Thus, we prefer the methods of the first category. Since the method proposed by Li et al. (2003) considers both the shortest path and the depth and outperforms other methods significantly, we select it for the semantic similarity computing between two ontology concepts. The method calculates the similarity between two concepts C_1 and C_2 (denoted as $SimCC(C_1,C_2)$) according to formula (1).

$$SimCC(C_1,C_2)=\begin{cases} e^{-\alpha l}\cdot\dfrac{e^{\beta h}-e^{-\beta h}}{e^{\beta h}+e^{-\beta h}}, & if\ (C_1 \neq C_2) \\ 1, & if\ (C_1 = C_2) \end{cases} \quad (1)$$

where l is the length of the shortest path between them; h is the depth of the closest ancestor of both C_1 and C_2 in the hierarchical structure; and $\alpha,\beta\geq 0$ are parameters scaling the contribution of l and h, respectively. It shows that the similarity between two concepts is monotonically decreasing with respect to l and monotonically increasing with respect to h. According to the experiments proposed by Li et al, $\alpha = 0.2$ and $\beta = 0.6$ bring the optimal effect and they are used in this work.

Consider the similarity between two concepts (*StationWagon* and *Train*) in the fragment of the semantic hierarchy of WordNet shown in Figure 2, the shortest path between them is *StationWagon-Car-Transportation-Train* and the closest ancestor for both *StationWagon* and *Train* is *Transportation*. Thus $l = 3$, $h = 2$ and $SimCC(StationWagon,Train)=e^{-0.2\times 3}\cdot\dfrac{e^{0.6\times 2}-e^{-0.6\times 2}}{e^{0.6\times 2}+e^{-0.6\times 2}}=0.64$.

First Phase: Discovery Based on Operation Matchmaking

As different functions of a service are provided by its operations indeed, in TSSD, whether a service satisfies a request is whether there is such an operation or a composition of operations matching the request. In this section, we introduce how TSSD discovers services based on operation matchmaking.

Definition (*Service Request*) *A service request r is a 3-tuple: $r = (I^r,O^r,w)$ where:*

(1) *I^r is the set of inputs that a requester can provide to invoke a target service.*

Table 1. Algorithm: Discovery of best-matched-operations (DBMO)

```
Input: A service s = (n_s,P,f_s) and a service request r = (I^r,O^r,w)
Output: Best-Matched-Operations or null
---------------------------------------------------------------
Initiate MaxSim = 0 and SOP = ∅;
for each operation op∈P{
if(sim(op,r)==MaxSim){
sop.insert(op);
}else if(Sim(op,r)>MaxSim){
sop.clear();
sop.insert(op);
        MaxSim = sim(op,r);
}
 }
return (MaxSim≥w)?sop:null;
```

(2) *O^r is the set of outputs that the requester desires to get from the invocation of the service.*
(3) *$0 < w \leq 1$ is the threshold value specified by the requester to show to what extent the target service should match the request.*

Notice that, to simplify the problem at this stage so as to focus on the key points of the article, here we only concern the input/output requirements in a request description but ignore non-functional requirements such as QoS at present. All the inputs and outputs in a request are also annotated by a requester with ontology concepts in order to ensure the request to be also semantic-enhanced.

Definition (*Matched-Operation*) *For an operation p and a request $r = (I^r, O^r, w)$, p is a Matched-Operation for r if $SimPR(p,r) \geq w$, where SimPR(P,R) is the SSD between p and r.*

Definition (*Best-Matched-Operation*) *For a service s, one of its operation p and a request $r = (I^r, O^r, w)$, p is a Best-Matched-Operation for r if p is a Matched-Operation and $\forall p_i \in P$, $SimPR(p,r) \geq SimPR(p_i,r)$.*

For a service request $r = (I^r, O^r, w)$, and an service $s = (n_s, P, f_s)$, the goal of TSSD in the first phase is to find the *Best-Matched-Operation*. The algorithm DBMO shown below accepts a service and a request as inputs and returns the *Best-Matched-Operations* for the request. It computes the SSD represented by *sim(op, r)* between each operation and the request and chooses the operations with the highest SSD. Then it judges whether the SSD of the selected operations is higher than the threshold value *w*. If it is, the selected operations are returned as the *Best-Matched-Operations*; otherwise there is no operations matching the request (see Table 1).

For an operation $p = \{n_p, I, O, f_p\}$ and a request $r = (I^r, O^r, w)$, *sim(p,r)* is calculated through the algorithm *calSim* shown in below.

(1) Judge whether $|O^r| \leq |O|$ holds, i.e., check whether *p* can provide all the requested outputs. If it can, *calSim* goes on to the next step; otherwise, it terminates and returns *SimPR(p,r)* = 0.
(2) Find an injection *f* from O^r to *O*, i.e., $f: O^r \rightarrow O$, that makes $\sum_{o^r \in O^r} SimCC(o^r, f(o^r))$ reach its max. In fact, the goal of this step is to find a different matched output in *O* for each one in O^r and to ensure the sum of pairwise similarity to be the max. We denote the range of *f* as *O'*, i.e., $O' = \bigcup_{o^r \in O^r} f(o^r)$.
(3) Determine the input set that must be provided to invoke *p* to get all the outputs in *O'*. The

result set is $I' = \bigcup_{o \in O'} f_p(o)$ according to the interface dependency. Go on to the next step.

(4) Judge whether $|I'| \leq |I^r|$ holds, i.e., check whether I^r can provide all the necessary inputs. If I^r can, *calSim* goes on to the next step; otherwise, it terminates and returns $SimPR(p,r) = 0$.

(5) Find an injection g from I' to I^r, i.e., $g : I' \rightarrow I^r$, that makes $\sum_{i' \in I'} SimCC(i', g(i'))$ reach its max. In fact, the goal of this step is to find a different matched input in I^r for each one in I' and to ensure the sum of pairwise similarity to be the max.

Calculate *sim(p,r)* through the following formula.

$$sim(p,r) = \frac{\sum_{o^r \in O^r} \left[SimCC(o^r, f(o^r)) \times \sum_{i \in f_p(f(o^r))} SimCC(i, g(i)) \Big/ \left| f_p(f(o^r)) \right| \right]}{|O^r|} \quad (2)$$

It is easy to prove that *sim(p,r)* returned from *CalSim* ranges from 0 to 1. Step (2) and (5) are the keys in *calSim* and both of them can be described as follows. Given two sets of ontology concepts $X = \{x_1, x_2, \ldots x_m\}$ and $Y = \{y_1, y_2, \ldots, y_m\}$ where $n \leq m$, $\forall x_i (1 \leq i \leq n)$, y_i $(1 \leq i \leq m)$, $0 \leq SimCC(x_i, y_j) \leq 1$, the problem is to find an injection $f: X \rightarrow Y$ that ensures $\sum_{x \in X} SimCC(x, f(x))$ to be the max.

In fact, we can model the given conditions as a weighted bipartite graph $G = (X, Y, E)$ where X and Y are two sets of vertices corresponding to the given two sets of ontology concepts, respectively, and E is the set of weighted edges constructed according to the following rule. For $\forall x_i (1 \leq i \leq n)$, y_i $(1 \leq i \leq m)$, if $SimCC(x_i, y_j) > 0$, we draw an edge $< x_i, y_j >$ with a weight $W_{x_i y_j} = SimCC(x_i, y_j)$. After that, the problem is transformed to find an optimal matching from X to Y in G and ensure that the matching covers all the vertices in X. Thus, the optimal matching is the target injection $f : X \rightarrow Y$. We design a method named *IOMatch* based on the Kuhn-Munkres algorithm (Lovasz and Plummer, 1986) to find such a matching. Due to the constraint $n \leq m$, i.e., $|X| \leq |Y|$, specified in the problem, *IOMatch* considers the following two cases.

1) $|X| \leq |Y|$. In this case, we use the Kuhn-Munkres algorithm directly to find an optimal matching M for G. According to the algorithm, M is a perfect matching in G, i.e., M covers all the vertices in X and Y. Thus M is the target matching.
2) $|X| \leq |Y|$. In this case, we change G to G' by adding $|Y|-|X|$ vertices into X. Then, between each new added vertex and each vertex in Y, add a new edge with a weight 0. If the new added vertices set is denoted as $v = \{v_1, v_2, \ldots, v_k\}$, $k = |Y|-|X|$, we get $G' = (X \cup V, Y, E')$, where $E' = \cup \{<v_i, y_j>| 1 \leq i \leq k, 1 \leq j \leq m\ W_{v_i y_j} = 0\}$,. We also use the Kuhn-Munkres algorithm to find an optimal matching M for G'. Then we change M to M' by eliminating those edges which cover vertices in V. Because the sum of weight of the eliminated edges equals 0, M' is an optimal matching for G' and G. Due to M' covering all vertices in X, M' is the target matching.

As the complexity of the Kuhn-Munkres algorithm is $O(n^3)$, where $n = |Y| = |X|$, the complexity of *calSim* is $O(2m^3)$ where $m = |Y|$ and that of algorithm *DBMO* is $O(p \times 2q^3)$, also a polynomial complexity, where p is the number of the operations in a service and q is the biggest number of outputs of an operation. According to the aforementioned statistic result in Introduction, only 5% services contain more than ten operations. So the value of q is always less than 10. Moreover, p and m are always less than 5. Thus *calSim* and *DBMO* have an acceptable time complexity.

To introduce the bipartite graph matching and the Kuhn-Munkres algorithm is beyond the scope

Figure 3. A matchmaking example between an operation and a request

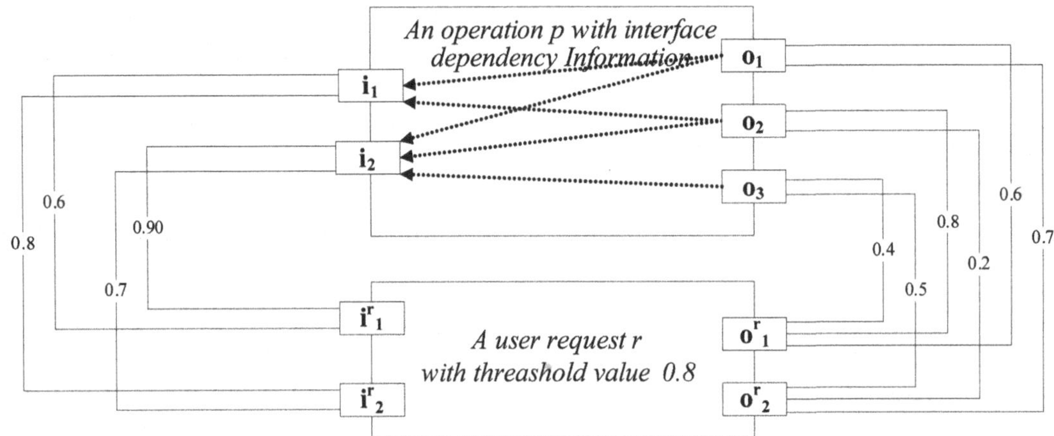

Figure 4. Use IOMatch to find optimal matching for a bipartite graph

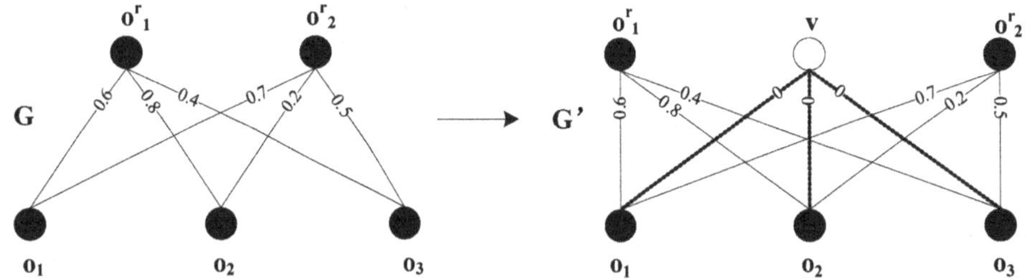

of this article. Here we show how *calSim* calculates *sim(p,r)* using the example illustrated in Figure 3. where the operation p has three outputs and two inputs, and the request r specifies two inputs and two outputs. The value on each connection between O_i and O^r_j $(1 \leq i \leq 3,\ 1 \leq j \leq 2)$, I_i and I^r_j $(1 \leq i,j \leq 2)$ I^r_j denotes the semantic similarity between the two concepts connected. Below is the process for the calculation of *sim(p,r)* according to *calSim*.

(1) As $(|O^r| = 2 \wedge |O| = 3 \Rightarrow |O^r| < |O|$, *calSim* continues.

(2) Use *IOMatch* to find an injection $f: O^r \rightarrow O$. We model the problem into the optimal matching problem from O^r to O in $G=(X,Y,E)$ shown in the left of Figure 4 where $X = \{o^r_1, o^r_2\}$, $Y = \{o_1, o_2, o_3\}$ and $E = \{<o^r_1, o_1>, <o^r_1, o_2>, <o^r_1, o_3>, <o^r_2, o_1>, <o^r_2, o_2>, <o^r_2, o_3>\}$. Since $|X|<|Y|$, *IOMatch* changes G to G' by adding one vertex named v into X and three 0-weighted edges $<v, o_1>$, $<v, o_2>$ and $<v, o_3>$ into E as shown in the right of Figure 4. Then it uses the Kuhn-Munkres algorithm to find an optimal matching M for G'. Thus, we get $M = \{<o^r_1, o_2>, <o^r_2, o_1>, <v, o_3>\}$ and the sum of the weight is 0.8+0.7+0=1.5. Then *IOMatch* changes M to $M' = \{<o^r_1, o_2>, <o^r_2, o_1>\}$ by eliminating the edge $<v, o_3>$. Accordingly, we get $f(o^r_1) = o_2$, $f(o^r_2) = o_1$ and $O' = \bigcup_{o^r \in O^r} f(o^r) = \{o_1, o_2\}$.

(3) Get

$$I' = \bigcup_{o \in O'} f_p(o) = f_p(o_1) \cup f_p(o_2) = \{i_1, i_2\} \cup \{i_2, i_3\} = \{i_1, i_2\}$$

(4) As $(|I'| = 2 \wedge |I^r| = 2) \Rightarrow |I'| = |I^r|$, *calSim* continues.

(5) Use *IOMatch* to find an injection g from I' to I^r, i.e., $g: I' \rightarrow I^r$. Since $|X| = |Y|$, *IOMatch* uses the Kuhn-Munkres algorithm directly to find the optimal matching $M = \{<i_1,i^r_2>,<i_2,i^r_1>\}$. Thus, we get $g(i_1) = i^r_2$ and $g(i_2) = i^r_1$.

Calculate *sim(p,r)* according to formula (2).

$$sim(p,r) = \frac{SimCC(o^r{}_1, o_2) \times (SimCC(i_1, i^r{}_2) + SimCC(i_2, i^r{}_1)) / 2}{2} + \frac{SimCC(o^r{}_2, o_1) \times (SimCC(i_1, i^r{}_2) + SimCC(i_2, i^r{}_1)) / 2}{2} = 0.6375$$

The value of *sim(p, r)* is less than the threshold value $w = 0.8$ specified in the request, it denotes that the operation doesn't satisfy the request. If none of the operations within a service can satisfy the request alone, it doesn't mean that the service should be ignored. In fact, a composition of operations within a service can bring value-added functions. Thus, in this case, TSSD goes on to its second phase.

Second Phase: Discovery Based on Composition Matchmaking

Operations can be connected by feeding one's output to the other's input in an orchestration way similar to an assembly line in a factory. Notice that there are such cases where the inputs of a service cannot be fed by all the outputs from only one service, but can be fed by the outputs from more than one service. At present, we only support the linear composition in which two services can be concatenated together only if all the inputs of the successive service are fed by the outputs of the preceding one. In this section, we introduce how TSSD performs service discovery based on the matchmaking of operation compositions.

Definition (*Operation-Concatenation*) *Given a service* $s = (n_s, P, f_s)$ *and its two operations* $p_1 = \{n_{p_1}, I_1, O_1, f_{p_1}\}$ *and* $p_2 = \{n_{p_2}, I_2, O_2, f_{p_2}\}$, p_2 *can be concatenated to* p_1 *(denoted as* $P_1 \cdot P_2$*) if and only if:*

(1) $|O_1| \geq |I_2|$, and
(2) For $\forall i_1, i_2 \in I_2$ and $i_1 \neq i_2$, $\exists o_1, o_2 \in O_1$, $o_1 \neq o_2$, $i_1 \in f_s(o_1)$ and $i_2 \in f_s(o_2)$

If an output o of p_1 is fed into an input i of p_2, they construct a Concatenation Point (denoted as a 2-tupe $cp = <o, i>$). $P_1 \cdot P_2$ is called an Operation-Concatenation and denoted as a 3-tupe: $oc = (p_1, p_2, CP)$ where $CP = \{cp_1, cp_2, \ldots, cp_k\}$ $(k = |O_2|)$ is the set of connection points.

This definition indicates the conditions under which two operations can be concatenated together. The first condition ensures that the input number of p_2 is not larger than the output number of p_1; and the second condition ensures that for any input of p_2 there is one different output of p_1 that can be assigned to the input. According to the assignment relations defined in a service, one output can be assigned to an input if both of them are the same concept or the output is a sub-class of the input. For an concatenation point $cp = <o, i>$, if the output and the input are of the sub-class-of relation, the semantic difference between them bring a semantic distance in an operation-concatenation. For an operation concatenation $oc = (p_1, p_2, CP)$, the semantic distance of the concatenation (denoted as $\varsigma(oc)$) is computed according to the formula (3).

$$\varsigma(oc) = 1 - \frac{\sum_{cp \in CP} SimCC(cp.o, cp.i)}{|CP|} \tag{3}$$

Definition (*Operation-Sequence*) *For a service* $s = (n_s, P, f_s)$ *and an ordered operation set* $os = <p_i, p_j, \ldots, p_k>$ $(1 \leq i, j, \ldots, k \leq n)$, *for any two neighboring elements* p_p *and* p_q *in os, if they construct an operation-concatenation, i.e., the relation* $p_p \cdot p_q$ *holds, os is called an operation-sequence for S.*

Figure 5. An operation-sequence example

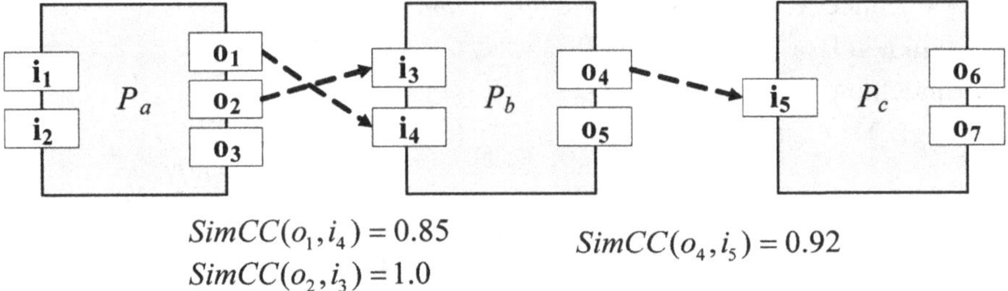

The number of the operations in s is called the length of the operation-sequence.

If two operations construct an operation-concatenation, they also construct an operation-sequence with the length of 2. In fact, every two neighboring operations in an operation-sequence form an operation-concatenation.

Definition (*Sequence-Distance*) *For an operation-sequence os = <p_1,p_2,...,p_n>, its Sequence Distance (denoted as $\zeta(os)$) is the weighed-sum of a Physical Distance (denoted as $\ell(os)$) and a Semantic Distance (denoted as $\hbar(os)$), where the parameter λ is a preference parameter specified by a service requester according to his/her preference.*

$$\zeta(os) = \lambda(1 - \frac{1}{\ell(os)}) + (1-\lambda)\hbar(os), \text{ where } 0 \leq \lambda \leq 1 \quad (4)$$

The Physical Distance of *os* is defined as the length of *os*, i.e, ℓ (os) = |os|. The Semantic Distance of an operation-sequence is computed according to the formula (5), where *oc* is an operation-concatenation constructed by two neighboring operations p*i* and pi_{+1}.

$$\hbar(os) = \frac{\sum_{1 \leq i \leq |os|-1} \varsigma(oc_i)}{|os| - 1} \quad (5)$$

For example, consider the operation-sequence composed by three operations named p_a, p_b and p_c, respectively, shown in Figure 5. The value of ℓ (os) is 3 and the value of $\hbar(os)$ is calculated as:

$$\hbar(os) = \frac{\varsigma(oc_1) + \varsigma(oc_2)}{2} = \frac{(1 - \frac{(0.85 + 1.0)}{2}) + (1 - 0.92)}{2} = 0.0775.$$

Thus, the Sequence Distance is $\zeta(os) = \lambda(1 - \frac{1}{3}) + (1-\lambda) \times 0.0775 = 0.0775 + 0.589\lambda$.

An operation-sequence can provide value-add functions for users. However, to compose operations together on-line for each new incoming request is time-consuming, especially when the number of operations within a service is large. In order to avoid the time consumption in the service discovery, we can transfer the composition process from the service discovery to the service registration. That means when a service is registered, we can find out all the possible operation-sequences in it and also compute their sequence-distances using a background program running on the service registry. After all the operation-sequences are constructed, they can be used for the service discovery based on composition matchmaking.

Figure 6. The architecture of service registration and discovery sub-system in DartFlow

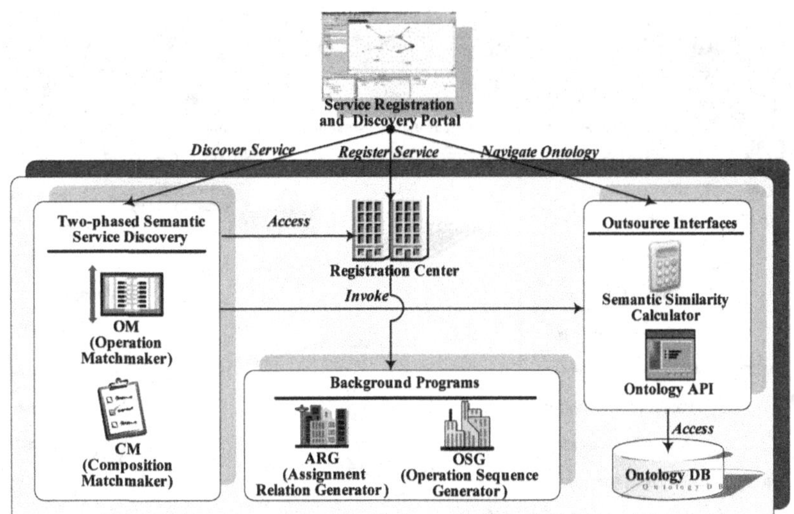

From the perspective of a user, an operation-sequence can be regarded as a pipe-line that accepts inputs from the beginning operation, generates outputs at the end and hides its inner details. Thus, an operation-sequence can be transformed into an operation extended with a sequence-distance attribute. In this operation, the input set is the input set of its first operation and the output set is the output set of its last operation. Thus, for an operation-sequence $os = <p_1,p_2,\ldots,p_n>$ and a service request $r = (I^r,O^r,w)$, we can follow the steps of the algorithm *calSim* to compute the similarity *Sim(os,r)* between them except that in step (5) we calculate the similarity using the new formula (6) instead of (2).

$$Sim(os,r)\frac{\sum_{o^r\in O^r}\left\{SimCC(o^r,f(o^r))\times\sum_{i\in f_p(f(o^r))}SimCC(i,g(i))\Big/\left|f_p(f(o^r))\right|\right\}}{\left|O^r\right|}\times(1-\zeta(os)) \quad (6)$$

If the value of *Sim(os,r)* is larger than the threshold value *w*, the sequence is returned; Otherwise, it is excluded. Notice that a user can adjust the value of *Sim(os,r)* by giving the parameter λ a different value.

IMPLEMENTATION AND EVALUATION

The aim of this section is to introduce the implementation of the proposed service discovery mechanism; and also to show the efficacy of the discovery method through a set of experiments.

Implementation of Service Discovery in DartFlow

The proposed service discovery mechanism have been implemented in DartFlow (Deng, Li et al. 2006c) which is a business process management platform for e-commerce. Its goal is to provide a convenient and efficient way to model and execute collaborative processes based on Web services across enterprises. The architecture of the service registration and discovery sub-system in DartFlow is shown in Figure 6. It can be divided into two sides: the client and server.

For the client, we have implemented a service registration and discovery portal based on Eclipse GEF as shown in Figure 7. With this portal, users can register and discover services. During the registration, a user provides a service's URL. Then

Figure 7. Service registration and discovery portal in DartFlow

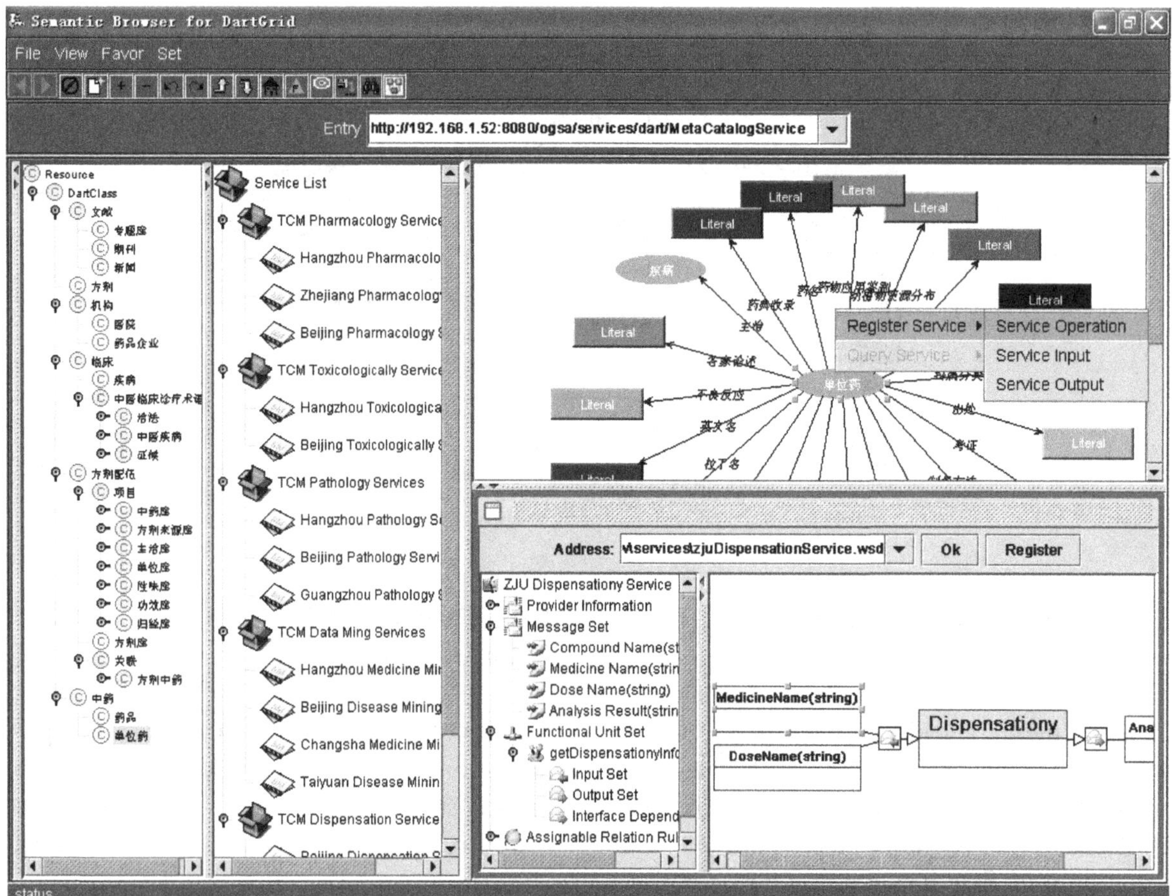

the portal parses the WSDL files and displays operations and interfaces using graphic elements as shown in the right-bottom of Figure 7. Then the user is required to annotate the service with ontology concepts shown in the top-right of Figure 7.

For the server, we have built a service registration center using Apache JUDDI (v0.9) and Oracle database (Oracle 9i). In order to support the extended-WSDL model in JUDDI, we have added additional tables in database to save semantic information, interface dependency, assignment relation and operation sequences for a registered service. Two programs named ARG (Assignment Relation Generator) and OSG (Operation Sequence Generator) are running on the background of registration center to generate assignment relations and operation sequences for a new registered service. In order to deal with both Chinese and English concepts, we use HowNet as the ontology resource—an common-sense knowledge base unveiling inter-conceptual relations and inter-attribute relations of concepts as connoting in lexicons of the Chinese and their English equivalents (Dong and Dong, 2006). The version used in the system is HowNet 2005 which has more than 80000 Chinese concepts and 70000 English concepts. We have implemented the algorithm proposed by Li et al. (2003) using JAVA to compute the semantic similarity between concepts from HowNet. For the two-phase semantic service discovery, we have implemented it through the combination of two algorithms named OM (Operation Matchmaker) and CM (Composition Matchmaker). Moreover, we also provide a simple version of Operation Matchmaker named SOM (Simple Operation Matchmaker) which doesn't consider the interface dependency. For CM, we use a backward-chaining method to retrieve all the operation sequences for a new registered service in advance.

Experiments and Evaluations

We evaluate the performance of the service discovery mechanism by using three well-recognized metrics, namely *service recall rate, precision rate,* and *scalability*. The recall rate is the proportion of relevant services that are retrieved. It can be calculated according to the formula (7). The precision rate is the proportion of retrieved services that are accurately matched which can be calculated according to the formula (8). Scalability refers to the computing complexity with respect to the growing number of services being accessed.

$$Recall\ Rate = \frac{|\{relevent\ services\} \cap \{retrieved\ services\}|}{|\{relevent\ services\}|} \quad (7)$$

$$Precision = \frac{|\{relevent\ services\} \cap \{retrieved\ services\}|}{|\{\ retrieved\ services\}|} \quad (8)$$

EXPERIMENTAL SETUP

In order to prepare the test set for the discovery experiments, we developed a tool based on the IBM XML Generator that enables one to generate random XML files based on schemas. With this tool, we generate 5 groups with 100 services for each as Table 2 shows. During the generation of each group, we ensure that the number of operations in this group is approximately in accordance with the statistics aforementioned in Introduction, i.e., 25% services has only 1 operation, 45% has 2-4 operations, 25% has 5-9 operations and 5% has 10-15 operations. Moreover, we make the proportion of partially-dependent outputs (PPDO) for the 5 groups is 0%, 20%, 60%, 80% and 100%, respectively. We select a sub-concept-tree with 200 concept-nodes from HowNet to be used for the annotation for inputs and outputs. When generating an operation of a service, the number of inputs or outputs is randomly selected from 1 to 5. And each input/output is annotated with a concept randomly selected from the sub-concept-tree.

Table 2. Test set preparation

Group	Service Number	Proportion of Partially-Dependent Outputs (PPDO)
G-1	100	0%
G-2	100	20%
G-3	100	60%
G-4	100	80%
G-5	100	100%

We carry out a series of service discoveries on each group. The discovery process is carried out automatically and the criteria for judging whether a service satisfies a request is to determine whether there is a matched operation or matched operation composition. Notice that we use a same service request which is randomly generated within the sub-concept-tree for all the service discoveries conducted in the experiments. We run the experiments on an IBM x260 server with a 2.0-GHz Intel Xeon MP processor and 1-GB of RAM, running a RedHat Linux operating system.

RECALL RATE AND PRECISION OF SERVICE DISCOVERY

Experiment A: *How the Partially-Dependent Outputs Influence the Recall Rate and Precision?*

In this experiment, we carry out twice service discovery using OM and SOM on each group. We

Figure 8. The influence of partially-dependent outputs on recall rate and precision

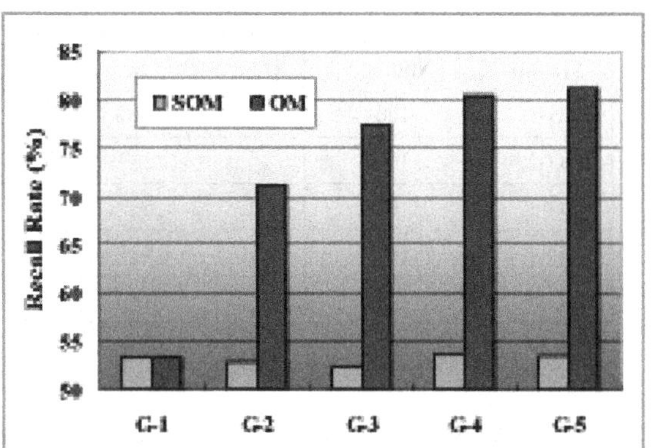

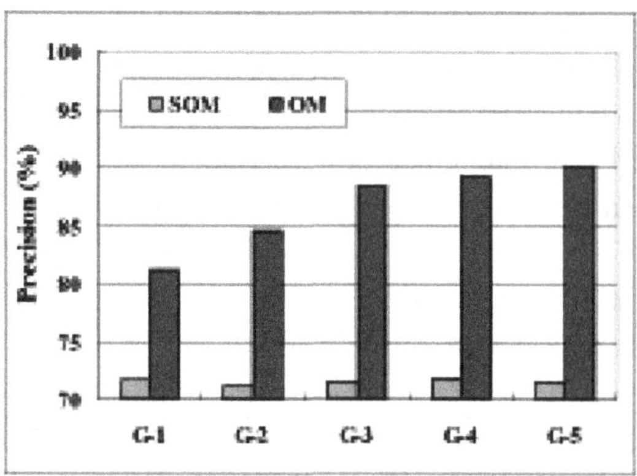

Figure 9. The influence of operation composition on recall rate and precision

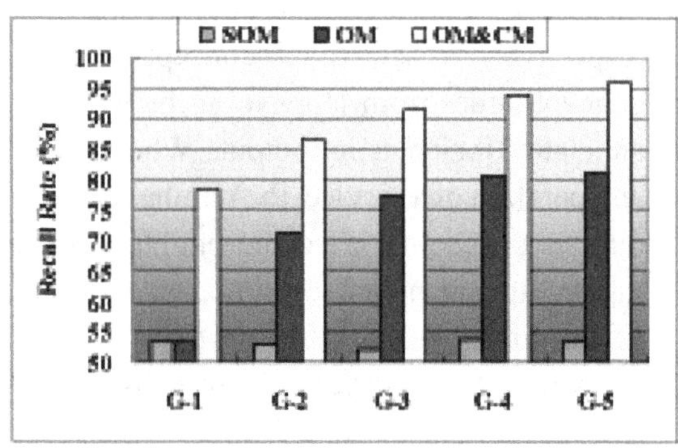

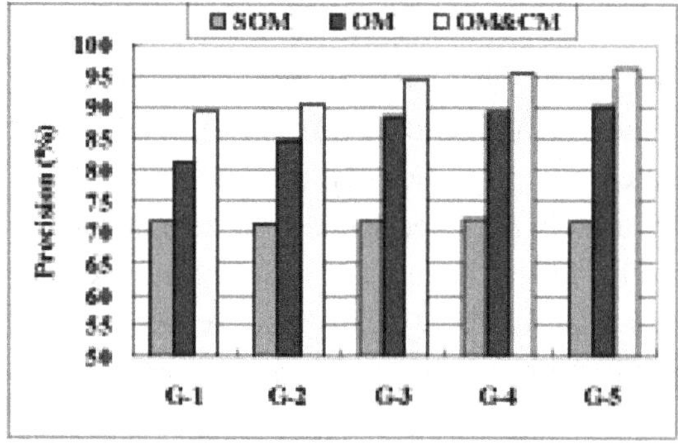

specify the threshold value in the request as w = 0.8. The experiment result is illustrated in Figure 8. For each group in the following two bar charts, the first bar represents the recall rate or precision from SOM whereas the second represents that from OM..

The experiment result illustrates that 1) both the recall rate and precision from SOM maintain almost stable with respect to the proportion of partially-dependent outputs. However, the recall rate from OM is increasing dramatically with respect to PPDO; the precision from OM is increasing slightly with respect to the proportion of partially-dependent outputs; 2) for each group besides G-1, the recall rate and precision from OM gain a distinct improvement on those from SOM; 3) the improvement from OM is increasing with respect to PPDO. The average improvement for recall rate and precision from G-2 to G-5 is about 24% and 15%, respectively; 4) for G-1, the result from OM and SOM are the same because there are no partially-dependent outputs in it.

The above four findings indicate that 1) taking interface dependency information into consideration can bring a better recall rate and precision; especially that it can improve the recall rate to a great extent; 2) the more the partially-dependent outputs in a set of services, the more significant the improvement of the recall rate and precision.

Experiment B: *How the Operation Composition Influence the Recall Rate and Precision?*

In this experiment, we carry out a service discovery using the combination of OM and CM on each group. We specify the threshold value in

Figure 10. The influence of parameter λ on composition matchmaking

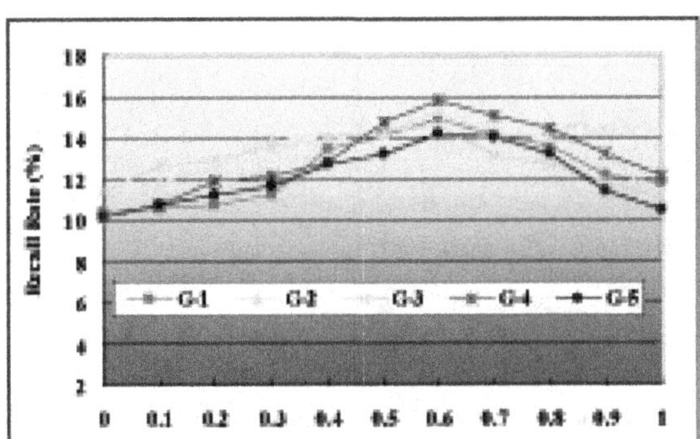

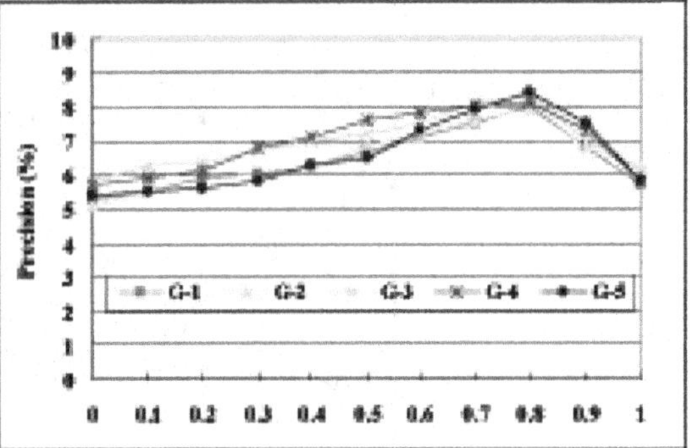

the request that $w = 0.8$ and the parameter $\lambda = 0.6$ for composition matchmaking. The comparison between the results of this experiment with those from Experiment A is illustrated in Figure 9.

The comparison illustration shows that 1) for each group, both the recall rate and the precision from OM&CM are better than those from SOM and OM; 2) Compared to SOM (or OM), OM&CM gain an average improvement of the recall rate and precision that are 37% (or 15%) and 21% (or 8%), respectively; the improvement of the recall rate from OM&CM is larger than that of the precision; 3) the improvement of the recall rate and the precision from OM&CM compared to OM maintains almost stable although the proportion of partially-dependent outputs is increasing from G-1 to G-5.

The above three findings indicate that taking the composition of operations into matchmaking can bring a better recall rate and precision. However, due to the ignorance of interface dependency information in composition matchmaking, the improvement is not affected by the proportion of partially-dependent outputs.

Experiment C: *How the Preference Parameter λ Influence the Composition Matchmaking?*

In this experiment, we carry out A series of service discovery using CM with the parameter λ from 0 to 1 with a 0.1 interval on each group. We specify the threshold value $w = 0.8$. The experiment is shown in Figure 10.

The experiment result shows that, for each group, the recall rate reaches the max when the parameter $\lambda = 0.6$ and the precision reaches the max value when the parameter $\lambda = 0.8$.

SCALABILITY OF SERVICE DISCOVERY

Experiment D: *How the scale of a service repository influence the response time?*

A good service discovery method should scale well as the number of services being accessed is increasing. After accepting a service discovery request, it must return the target services quickly even for a repository with a large number of services. We evaluate the discovery for different scale of service repositories. We generate 6 test sets with 100, 200, 400, 600, 800 and 1000 services and make the proportion of partially-dependent outputs in each set 20%. On each set, we conduct three discoveries using SOM, OM and OM&CM, respectively with the parameter $\lambda = 0.7$. The response time of each discovery is shown in Figure 11.

The experiment result illustrates that 1) the response times for SOM, OM and OM&CM are almost linearly increasing with respect to the

Figure 11. Scalability of service discovery with the increasing number of services accessed

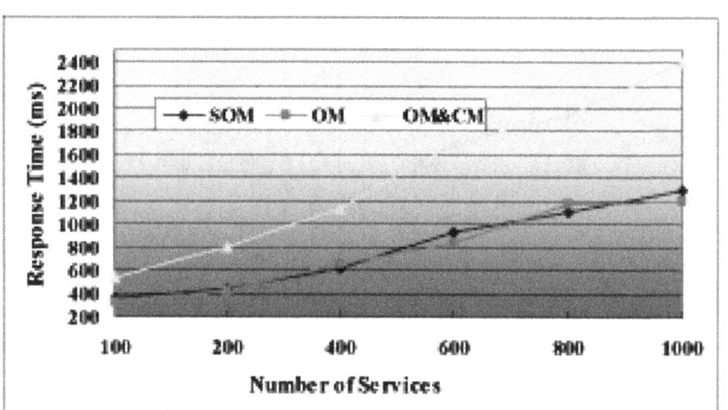

number of services[1]; 2) the response time of OM is almost the same to that of SOM; 3) the response time of OM&CM is about twice as much as that of SOM and OM. The findings indicate that the proposed discovery method scales well with the number of services in a repository. That is to say the proposed approach can return the result in a short time even the service repository has a large number of services.

CONCLUSION

This article proposes a two-phase semantic-based service discovery mechanism. The main contributions of this work are (1) it is the first time to point out the two shortcomings in the most current service matchmaking methods and find out that both of them lower the recall rate and the precision for discovery; (2) it proposes an information model for registered services in a repository with feasible and convenient mechanisms to describe operation relations and interface dependencies implied in a service; (3) it proposes a two-phase semantic-based service discovery method. Compared to other approaches, the new method has two salient characteristics: (a) it takes into account the interface dependencies and imports the bipartite graph matching to improve the efficiency of matchmaking; b) it supports two-level matchmaking, namely operation matchmaking and operation-composition matchmaking. A series of experiments demonstrate that the proposed mechanism has both a good recall rate and precision and also scales well with the number of services accessed.

However, the two-phase semantic-based service discovery mechanism, in the second phase, only supports matchmaking on the linear composition of operations. So, how to enhance its ability to support matchmaking on more complex composition is one of the future directions. Moreover, to simplify the problem at this stage so as to focus on the key points of the article, this work has not taken into account the QoS requirements for a service request at present, which is also one of our future direction.

ACKNOWLEDGMENT

This work is supported by the National Natural Science Foundation of China under Grant No. 60803004, 60873224 and 60873045; the National High-Tech Research and Development Plan of China under Grant 2007AA01Z124, 2008AA01Z141 and 2009AA01Z121.

A preliminary and shorter version of this article was published as a 2-page poster paper in the proceeding of 17th International Conference on

World Wide Web (WWW2008), Beijing, China, April 21-25, pp1189-1190.

REFERENCES

Aversano, L., Canfora, G., & Ciampi, A. (2004, July 6-9). An Algorithm for Web Service Discovery through Their Composition. *Proceedings of International Conference on Web Services* (pp. 332–341), San Diego, California, USA.

Bansal, S., & Vidal, J. (2003, July 14-18). Matchmaking of Web Services Based on the DAML-S Service Model. *Proceedings of International Joint Conference on Autonomous Agents* (pp. 926–927), Melbourne, Australia.

Benatallah, B., Hacid, M., Leger, A., Rey, C., & Toumani, F. (2005). On Automating Web Services Discovery. *The VLDB Journal*, *14*(1), 84–96. doi:10.1007/s00778-003-0117-x

Brogi, A., & Corfini, S. (2007). Behaviour Aware Discovery of Web Service Compositions. *International Journal of Web Services Research*, *4*(3), 1–25.

Deng, S. G., Li, Y., Xia, H. J., Wu, J., & Wu, Z. H. (2006c, September 3-7). Exploring the Flexible Workflow Technology to Automate Service Composition. *Proceedings of Asian Semantic Web Conference* (pp. 444-458), Beijing, China.

Deng, S. G., Wu, J., Li, Y., & Wu, Z. H. (2006a, June 17-19). Service Matchmaking Based on Semantics and Interface Dependencies. *Proceedings of International Conference on Advances in Web-Age Information Management* (pp. 240-251), Hong Kong, China.

Deng, S. G., Wu, J., Li, Y., & Wu, Z. H. (2006b). Consideration of Operation Composition in Semantic Service Matchmaking. *Proceedings of International Conference on Services Computing*, Illinois, USA, September 18-22, 240-251.

Dong, Z. D., & Dong, Q. (2006). *HowNet and the Computation of Meaning*. Singapore: World Scientific.

Kalogeras, A. P., Gialelis, J. V., Alexakos, C. E., Georgoudakis, M. J., & Koubias, S. A. (2006). Vertical Integration of Enterprise Industrial Systems Utilizing Web Services. *IEEE Transactions on Industrial Informatics*, *2*(2), 120–128. doi:10.1109/TII.2006.875507

Kawamura, T., Blasio, D., Hasegawa, T., Paolucci, M., & Sycara, K. (2003, December 15-18). Preliminary Report of Public Experiment of Semantic Service Matchmaker with UDDI Business Registry. *Proceedings of International Conference on Service-Oriented Computing* (pp. 208-224), Trento, Italy.

Keller, U., Lara, R., Polleres, A., Toma, I., Kifer, M., & Fensel, D. (2004). *WSMO Web Service Discovery*. Retrieved from http://www.wsmo.org/ 2004/ d5/ d5.1/ v0.1/ 20041112/ d5.1v0.1_20041112.pdf.

Kifer, M., Lara, R., Polleres, A., Zhao, C., Keller, U., Lausen, H., & Fensel, D. (2004). *A Logical Framework for Web Service Discovery*. Retrieved from http://www.ai.sri.com/ SWS2004/ final-versions/ SWS2004- Kifer-Final.pdf

Klein, M., & Bernstein, A. (2004). Toward High-Precision Service Retrieval. *IEEE Internet Computing*, *8*(1), 30–36. doi:10.1109/MIC.2004.1260701

Li, Y., Bandar, Z. A., & Mclean, D. (2003). An Approach for Measuring Semantic Similarity between Words Using Multiple Information Sources. *IEEE Transactions on Knowledge and Data Engineering*, *15*(4), 871–882. doi:10.1109/TKDE.2003.1209005

Liang, Q., Chakarapani, L. N., Su, S. Y. W., Chikkamagalur, R. N., & Lam, H. (2004). A Semi-Automatic Approach to Composite Web Services Discovery, Description and Invocation. *Journal of Web Services Research*, *1*(4), 64–89.

Lovasz, L., & Plummer, M. D. (1986). *Matching Theory*. Amsterdam: Elsevier Science Publishers...

Luo, J., Montrose, B., Kim, A., Khashnobish, A., & Kang, M. (2006, September 18-22). Adding OWL-S Support to the Existing UDDI Infrastructure. *Proceedings of International Conference on Web Service* (pp. 153-162), Chicago, Illinois, USA.

McIlraith, S. A., Son, T. C., & Zeng, H. L. (2001). Semantic Web Services. *IEEE Intelligent Systems, 16*(2), 46–53. doi:10.1109/5254.920599

Miller, G. A. (1995). WordNet: A Lexical Database for English. *Communications of the ACM, 38*(11), 39–41. doi:10.1145/219717.219748

Osman, T., Thakker, D., & Al-Dabass, D. (2006, September 18-22). Semantic-Driven Matchmaking of Web Services Using Case-Based Reasoning. *Proceedings of International Conference on Web Service* (pp. 29-36), Chicago, Illinois, USA.

Paolucci, M., Kawamura, T., Payne, T. R., & Sycara, K. (2002, June 9-12). Semantic Matching of Web Services Capabilities. *Proceedings of International Semantic Web Conference* (pp. 36-47), Sardinia, Italy.

Papazoglou, M. P., & Georgakopoulos, D. (2003). Service-Oriented Computing. *Communications of the ACM, 46*(10), 25–28. doi:10.1145/944217.944233

Resnik, P. (1999). Semantic Similarity in a Taxonomy: An Information-based Measure and Its Application to Problems of Ambiguity in Natural Language. *Journal of Artificial Intelligence Research, 11*(1), 95–130.

Rodriguez, M. A., & Egenfoher, M. J. (2003). Determining Semantic Similarity among Entity Classes from Different Ontologies. *IEEE Transactions on Knowledge and Data Engineering, 15*(2), 442–456. doi:10.1109/TKDE.2003.1185844

Roman, D., Lausen, H., & Keller, U. (2005). *Web Service Modeling Ontology (WSMO)*. Retrieved from www.wsmo.org/ TR/ d2/ v1.2/ D2v1-2_ 20050414.pdf.

Srinivasan, N., Paolucci, M., & Sycara, K. (2004, July 6). Adding OWL-S to UDDI, Implementation and Throughput. *Proceedings of International Workshop on Semantic Web Services and Web Process Composition* (pp. 5-21), San Diego, CA, USA.

Stollberg, M., Keller, U., & Fensel, D. (2005 July 11-15). Partner and Service Discovery for Collaboration Establishment with Semantic Web Services. *Proceedings of International Conference on Web Service* (pp. 473-480), Orlando, FL, USA.

Syeda-Mahmood, T., Shah, G., Akkiraju, R., Ivan, A.-A., & Goodwin, R. (2005 July 11-15). Searching Service Repositories by Combining Semantic and Ontological Matching. *Proceedings of International Conference on Web Service* (pp. 13-20), Orlando, FL, USA.

ENDNOTE

1. Notice that, for OM&CM, the time consumption doesn't include the time for composing operations on-the-fly. In fact, the process of composing is carried out during the service registration. All the possible compositions are prepared before discovery. Thus, the time for composing operations is excluded from the total discovery time. So, the time consumption of OM&CM increases linearly.

This work was previously published in International Journal of Web Services Research, Volume 6, Issue 4, edited by Liang-Jie Zhang, pp. 94-117, copyright 2009 by IGI Publishing (an imprint of IGI Global).

About the Contributors

Liang-Jie (L.J.) Zhang is Senior Vice President, Chief Scientist, & Director of Research at Kingdee International Software Group Company Limited, and director of The Open Group. Prior to joining Kingdee, he was a Research Staff Member at IBM Thomas J. Watson Research Center. Dr. Zhang has published more than 140 technical papers in journals, book chapters, and conference proceedings. He has 40 granted patents and more than 20 pending patent applications. Dr. Zhang received his Ph.D. on Pattern Recognition and Intelligent Control from Tsinghua University in 1996. He chaired the IEEE Computer Society's Technical Committee on Services Computing since 2003. He also chaired the Services Computing Professional Interest Community at IBM Research from 2004 to 2006. He was the lead IBM researcher on Service-Oriented Architecture (SOA) solutions, web services, and interactive media systems. Dr. Zhang has served as the Editor-in-Chief of the International Journal of Web Services Research since 2003 and is the founding Editor-in-Chief of IEEE Transactions on Services Computing. He was elected as a Fellow of the IEEE in 2011, and in the same year won the IEEE Technical Achievement Award "for pioneering contributions to Application Design Techniques in Services Computing". Dr. Zhang also chaired the 2010 IEEE 3rd International Conference on Cloud Computing (CLOUD 2010) and its sister conferences.

* * *

Ajay Bansal is a PhD candidate in the Department of Computer Science at the University of Texas at Dallas. He is also a research assistant in the Applied Logic Programming-Languages and Systems (ALPS) Lab. His research interests include logic programming, semantic Web, semantic description of Web services, Multi-agent systems, and Programming Languages. He received his BTech in computer science from Regional Engineering College, Warangal, India in 1999 and his MS in computer science from Texas Tech Univ. Lubbock in 2002. He has 3 years of industry experience. He worked as a software developer in Siemens (1999-2000) and Tyler Technologies (2001-2003).

John Brooke is the co-Director of the North-West eScience Centre (ESNW) and an Honorary Lecturer in the School of Computer Science, the University of Manchester. His main research interests are in grid computing, visualization and nonlinear problems in astrophysics. He is a co-Investigator on the EPSRC RealityGrid project, which pioneered the use of computational steering in very large simulations. This work won major awards at international supercomputing conferences in 2003, 2004 and 2005. ESNW acts as a focus to promote interdisciplinary collaboration between computational scientists, computer scientists and visualization experts

Ningjiang Chen received the PhD degree in computer science from the Institute of Software, Chinese Academy of Sciences in 2006. He is an associate professor with the Department of Computer Science at Guangxi University. His research interests are in the areas of Web services, distributed systems and Web application server.

Marie-Odile Cordier received a PhD degree in computer science in 1979 and an « Habilitation à Diriger des Recherches » in 1996, both from the University of Paris-Sud, Orsay, France. She was Associated Professor at University of Paris-Sud from 1973 and became full Professor at University of Rennes, France, in 1988, performing her research activity at IRISA-INRIA. She is currently the scientific leader of the DREAM Team (Diagnostic, Reasoning and Modeling). Her main research interests are in artificial intelligence, focusing in model-based diagnosis, on-line monitoring, model acquisition, using model checking techniques and Inductive Logic Programming, temporal abductive reasoning and diagnosability of discrete-event systems. She has been responsible for several industrial projects, published numerous papers in international conference proceedings and scientific journals, and served as Program Committee member and area chair of several conferences. She is an ECCAI fellow since 2001.

Demba Coulibay has obtained a master's degree of computer science at University of Kiev in 1992. He is currently both an engineer of University of Bamako and a PhD student under the supervision of C. Boutrous and S. Haddad. His main research interests concern Web services and software engineering.

Philippe Dague received the engineering degree from "Ecole Centrale de Paris" in 1972, and the PhD degree in theoretical physics from the University Paris 6 in 1976. He was a Mathematics assistant at the University of Poitiers, then at the University Paris 6, from 1976 to 1983. From 1983 to 1992, he was a research engineer in computer science at IBM Paris Scientific Center. He received the "Habilitation à Diriger des Recherches" degree in computer science in 1992 from the University Paris 6. From 1992 to 2005, he was professor of computer science at the University Paris-Nord 13, where he founded and led in 1999 the Artificial Learning, Diagnosis and Agents group of the "Laboratoire d'Informatique de Paris-Nord" (LIPN). From 2005, he is professor of computer science at the University Paris-Sud 11, adjunct director of the "Laboratoire de Recherche en Informatique" (LRI), member of the Arificial Intelligence and Inference Systems group, and director of the Computer Science department of the engineer school. His research activity from 1984 deals with Artificial Intelligence techniques for Engineering, in particular qualitative, causal and temporal modeling and reasoning, and model-based diagnosis (MBD) and supervision of complex systems. His active research topics from some years are: bridging the Control Engineering and the AI MBD approaches, building qualitative models from numeric design models or from specifications, distributed diagnosis for discrete-event systems, diagnosability analysis. He applied these techniques to various fields: diagnosis of electronic, automotive and spatial systems, supervision of telecommunication networks, monitoring of Web services. These applications were conducted through several partnerships with industrials, national and European projects. He has been member of the program committee of about 45 conferences and is the author of more than 60 papers in international or national conferences and journals, and of several books.

Peter Dornbach got his MSc at the Budapest University of Technology and Economics, Hungary in 1998 after being a visiting student at Heriot-Watt University in Edinburgh, Scotland in 1996-1997.

Since 2000, he works at Nokia Research Center and researches distributed technologies optimized for embedded devices. He is responsible for Web Services Research since 2004 and works as a Research Manager since 2006. His main interests are Web Services for mobile and embedded systems. He has several publications in this field.

Zev Friedman is a student at Texas Tech University in an integrated B.S and M.S. degree program in Computer Science and Mathematics. He is currently participating in an NSF-funded Research Experience for undergraduates program with research focused on service composition and recovery in service-oriented environments.

Le Gao received his B.S. degree in computer science in 2004 from Nanjing University of Aeronautics and Astronautics, China. He is currently a Ph.D. student in the Department of Computer Science at Texas Tech University. Before coming to Texas Tech University, he was a Database Engineer at China Mobile corporation from 2006-2007. He was also working at China Telecom Corporation as a Database Operator from 2004-2006.

Gopal Gupta is a professor and associate department head of computer science at UT Dallas. He also directs the Applied Logic and Programming Languages and Systems (ALPS) Laboratory. His research interests lie in programming languages, parallel processing, logic programming, Web/Web services, assistive technologies, and software engineering. He has published extensively in these areas in refereed journals and conferences. His research group has produced several research software systems, some of which have been publicly distributed. He has been awarded more than thirty research grants from agencies such as the National Science Foundation, the Environment Protection Agency, the Department of Education, the Department of Energy, the National Research Council, the North Atlantic Treaty Organization and the Japan Advanced Institute of Science and Technology. He is a member of the editorial board of the journal Theory and Practice of Logic Programming, Cambridge University Press, and an executive board member of the Association for Logic Programming. He also served in the board of the European Association on Programming Languages and Systems (2002-2006). He and his students have received several best paper awards, most recently at the 2nd European Conference on Web services in 2005.

Serge Haddad was formerly student at the Ecole Normale Supérieure de l'Enseignement Technique in Mathematics. He obtained his PhD in computer science in 1987. In 1993, he became a full professor at University Paris-Dauphine and he has recently moved to ENS Cachan. His research interests are focused on the design, the verification and the evaluation of cooperative and distributed applications.

Thomas Hite is responsible for Metallect's technology strategy. He brings 17 years of executive experience in both early-stage and publicly traded companies. Prior to co-founding Metallect, Hite was chief technical officer of AMX Corporation (Nasdaq: AMXC), where he led the development of a sophisticated software platform for home and business automation. Previously, Hite was VP of Software Development at AnswerSoft, Inc. prior to its acquisition by Concerto Software (Nasdaq: CRTO). Hite's experience also includes technical management positions at Micrografx, R&TH, Inc., and CADSI. Hite holds BS and MS degrees in mechanical engineering from the University of Iowa.

Tao Huang received the PhD degree in computer science from University of Science and Technology of China in 1994. He is a professor, PhD supervisor and director of the Institute of Software, Chinese Academy of Sciences. His research interests are in the areas of Web services, distributed systems, Web application server and software engineering. He has been a program committee member of several international conferences. He is a senior member of China Computer Federation.

Yeon-Seok Kim received the B.S. degree in Information Engineering from MyongJi University, YongIn, Korea, in 2003 and the M.S. degree in Computer Science from Yonsei University, Seoul, Korea, in 2005. Currently, he is working toward the Ph.D. degree in Computer Science at Yonsei University. His research interests include internet computing, service-oriented computing, and mobile Web services. He is a member of the Korean Institute of Information Scientists and Engineers.

Srividya Kona is a PhD candidate in the Department of Computer Science at the University of Texas at Dallas. She is also a research assistant in the Applied Logic Programming-Languages and Systems (ALPS) Lab. Her research interests include semantic Web, semantic description of Web services, secure querying of semantic Web, and logic programming. She received her BTech in computer science from Regional Engineering College, Warangal, India in 1999 and her MS in computer science from Texas Tech Univ. Lubbock in 2002. She has 5 years of industry experience. She worked as a software developer in SAP Labs (1999-2000) and Tyler Technologies (2001-2005).

Dean Kuo is Grid architect at the North-West eScience Centre (ESNW) and an Honorary Lecturer in the School of Computer Science, the University of Manchester. His current research focuses on architectures and technologies for building loosely-coupled distributed systems including service-oriented architectures, and the specification and correctness of service-oriented systems. He has a BSc and a PhD in computer science from the University of Sydney Australia.

Dongwon Lee has been an Associate Professor at the Pennsylvania State University, College of Information Sciences and Technology, since 2002. He earned a B.S. from Korea University (1993), an M.S. from Columbia University (1995), and a Ph.D. from UCLA (2002), all in Computer Science. His research interests include databases, XML and web analysis, and semantic web services.

Kyong-Ho Lee received his B.S., M.S., and Ph.D. degrees in Computer Science from Yonsei University, Seoul, Korea, in 1995, 1997, and 2001, respectively. Previously, he worked as a guest researcher in the IT Laboratories at NIST (National Institute of Standards and Technology), Maryland. Currently, he is an Associate Professor in the Department of Computer Science at Yonsei University. His research interests include Semantic Web and service-oriented computing. He is a member of the editorial board of the *Journal of Web Science, Journal of Information Processing Systems,* and *Journal of Korea Multimedia Society*.

Lei Li received the Bachelor degree in computer science from University of Science and Technology of China in 2002. He is a PhD candidate in the Institute of Software, Chinese Academy of Sciences. His research interests are in the areas of Web services and distributed systems.

Maozhen Li is a lecturer in School of Engineering and Design at Brunel University, UK. He received the PhD from Institute of Software, Chinese Academy of Sciences in 1997. He has published over 50 research papers in international journals and conferences. His research interests are in the areas of web services, service discovery and composition, semantic web, intelligent systems, grid computing. He co-authored a book on grid computing entitled The Grid: Core Technologies which was published by Wiley in April 2005. He has been serving as a TPC member for a number of conferences in this area, e.g. IEEE CCGrid'05, CCGrid'06, CCGrid'07, CCGrid'08, IEEE SKG'05, SKG'06, SKG'07, IEEE CSE'08. He is on the editorial boards of Encyclopedia of Grid Computing Technologies and Applications, and the International Journal of Grid and High Performance Computing.

Ajay Mallya is a PhD candidate in the Department of Computer Science at the University of Texas at Dallas. He is also a teaching assistant in the Department of Computer Science. His research interests include programming languages, formal methods and real-time systems. He received the degree of Bachelor's of Engineering (honors) in computer science from University of Mysore, India in 1999. He obtained his MS degree in computer science from the University of Texas at Dallas in December 2002. He worked as a software engineer in the industry for two years.

Tarek Melliti is, since 2006, an assistant professor at IBISC (Informatique biologie intégrative et systèmes complexes) laboratory located at University of Evry Val-Essonne (France). He obtained his PhD in Computer Science in 2004. His researches deal with formal methods applied to orchestrated and choreographed Web services Composition. Recently, his researches focused on model-based Web services Diagnosis and Diagnosability.

Patrice Moreaux is "professeur agrégé de mathématiques" and received his PhD in computer science in 1996. Since 2005, he is a full professor at University of Savoie. His research interests are focused on the modelling, the verification and the performance evaluation in automation, networks, distributed and parallel computer systems.

Surya Nepal is a Principal Research Scientist working on trust and security aspects of distributed systems at CSIRO ICT Centre. His main research interest is in the development and implementation of technologies in the area of distributed computing. He obtained his BE from Regional Engineering college, Surat, India, ME from Asian Institute of Technology, Bangkok, Thailand and PhD from RMIT University, Australia. At CSIRO Surya undertook research in the area of multimedia databases, web services and service oriented architectures, and security and trust in collaborative environment. He has also edited a book on "Managing Multimedia Semantics". He has several journal and conference papers in these areas to his credit.

Chunlei Niu received the master degree in computer science from the Institute of Software, Chinese Academy of Sciences in 2007. He is a senior programmer of Google China.

Seog-Chan Oh has been a Senior Researcher at General Motors R&D center since 2007. He earned a B.S. and an M.S. from Dongguk University (1993 and 1996, respectively), and a Ph.D. from the

Pennsylvania State University (2006). His research interests include web service composition and its applications to manufacturing field as well as ai, agent, and semantic web services.

Myung-Woo Park received his B.S. and M.S. degrees in Physics and Computer Science, respectively, from Yonsei University, Seoul, Korea, in 2004 and 2007. Currently, he is working as a researcher at LIG System. His research interests include service-oriented computing and mobile Web services. He is a member of the Korean Institute of Information Scientists and Engineers.

Michael Parkin is a third-year PhD student in the School of Computer Science at the University of Manchester. He graduated with a BSc in Physics from the University of Leicester in 1993 and spent 8 years in industry before returning to academia to gain a MSc in Computer Science from the Victoria University of Manchester in 2003. His current research interests are lightweight collaborative Grid environments, their formation, use, security models and scalability and their interactions with resource providers.

Szabolcs Payrits got his MSc at the Eötvös Loránd University Budapest, Hungary in 2004 after being a visiting student at the University of Paderborn in 1999. He works for Nokia since 2000 and joined Nokia Research Center in 2004. Since then, he was an active contributor to Nokia Web Services technologies and has a big role in developing the Nokia WSDL-to-C++ Wizard that is based on MXDB technology. He is a lecturer at Eötvös Loránd University and works currently for SAP Labs.

Yannick Pencolé is a CNRS research fellow at CNRS-LAAS, Université de Toulouse, France, since 2006. He obtained his Ph.D. degree in Computer Science at IRISA, University of Rennes, France, in 2002. From 2003 to 2006, he worked as a postdoctoral research fellow in the Computer Science Laboratory, at the Australian National University and in the Knowledge Representation and Reasoning group of NICTA (National ICT of Australia). He is working on model-based diagnosis, discrete event systems, prognostics and distributed artificial intelligence.

Man Qi is a lecturer in Department of Computing at Canterbury Christ Church University, UK. She was a research fellow in Dept. of Computer Science at University of Bath, UK from Jan. 2001 to Oct. 2003. Her research interests are in the areas of computer graphics, multimedia and Web services applications.

Sylvain Rampacek is an assistant professor at LE2I laboratory (UMR CNRS 5158) located at Université de Bourgogne (France). He obtained his PhD in computer science in 2006. His research is focused on formal methods applied to service oriented architecture. The results are implemented and mainly consist to help the development of secured and adapted software in this environment.

Jonathan Rodriguez is a student at Texas Tech University currently working towards a B.S. degree in Computer Science and B.A. in Mathematics. He is currently participating in an NSF-funded Research Experience for Undergraduates program with research focused on service composition and recovery in service-oriented environments. He is a member of the Association for Computing Machinery and Mathematical Association of America.

Céline Boutrous Saab is an assistant professor at LAMSADE (Laboratoire d'Analyse et Modélisation de Systèmes pour l'Aide à la Décision) located at the University of Paris-Dauphine since 2002. She obtained his PhD in computer science in 2000. Her research interests are focused on the design and the implementation of cooperative and distributed applications.

Vijay Sahota is currently a PhD student in school of engineering and design at Brunel University, UK. His research interests are in the areas of Web services modeling and monitoring, service discovery, scalable peer-to-peer networks, and grid computing.

Rajiv Shrestha received the M.S. degree in computer science from the Department of Computer Science at Texas Tech University in 2010. He is currently a Software Developer with Baker Hughes in Houston, Texas.

Luke Simon is a PhD candidate in the Department of Computer Science at the University of Texas at Dallas. He is also a research assistant in the Applied Logic Programming-Languages and Systems (ALPS) Lab. His research interests include Lambda-calculi, mobile-calculi, type theory, and logic category theory. He received his Bachelor's of Engineering degree in computer science from the UTD in 2001. Since then, he is pursuing PhD in computer science at UTD. He has extensive industry experience, and has worked at several companies as a software engineer including: DSC Communications (1996-1998), Mylex (Summer 1998), Alcatel (1998-1999), Multigen (1999-2000), and CVA Inc (2000-2001). He is also a Sun Certified Java Programmer, Developer, and Enterprise Architect.

Susan D. Urban is a Professor in the Department of Computer Science at Texas Tech University. She received the Ph.D. degree in Computer Science from the University of Louisiana at Lafayette in 1987. She is the co-author of *An Advanced Course in Database Systems: Beyond Relational Databases* (Upper Saddle River, NJ: Prentice Hall, 2005). Her research interests include active/reactive behaviour in data-centric distributed computing environments; event, rule, and transaction processing for grid/web service composition; integration of event and stream processing. Dr. Urban is a member of the Association for Computing Machinery, the IEEE Computer Society, and the Phi Kappa Phi Honour Society.

Alf Weaver received his Ph.D. in Computer Science from the University of Illinois in 1976. He was the founding Director of the Commonwealth of Virginia's Internet Technology Innovation Center, and he is the Director of the University of Virginia's Applied Research Institute. He was an ACM National Lecturer, gave keynote addresses at several leading conferences, held the Lucian Carr III endowed chair, and is a Fellow of the IEEE. He has authored or co-authored four books, six book chapters, over 140 refereed papers, and a patent. His research focus is secure, available, and reliable medical and e-business systems.

Jun Wei received the PhD degree in computer science from Wuhan University in 1997. He is a professor of the Institute of Software, Chinese Academy of Sciences. His research interests are in the areas of Web services, distributed systems and software engineering.

Zhengping Wu is an Assistant Professor of Computer Science and Engineering at the University of Bridgeport. He received his Ph.D. in Computer Science from the University of Virginia in 2008. He has authored or co-authored eight book chapters and over forty refereed papers. His research interests include information and network security, distributed systems, web services, cloud computing, operating systems, and medical informatics. He has served as reviewers for numerous conferences and journals, including *IEEE Transactions on Services Computing* and *International Journal of Web Services Research*. He has also served as committee members in numerous conferences including the International Conference on Services Computing. He is a member of IEEE.

Yang Xiao received the Ph.D. degree in Computer Science from Arizona State University in 2006. She is currently a software testing engineer at Microsoft, focusing on integrated development environment testing methodologies and practices. Her research interests include process failure recovery and application-dependent correctness in Grid/Web service composition environment.

Yuhong Yan is an assistant professor in the Department of Computer Science and Software Engineering in Concordia University, Montreal, Canada. She is also an adjunct professor at the Faculty of Computer Science of the University of New Brunswick. Before she joined Concordia in 2008, she was a research officer at the Institute of Information Technology at the National Research Council. She received her PhD from Tsinghua University (China) from a joint program between Tsinghua University and University of Leipzig (Germany) funded by a DAAD scholarship in 1999. She has worked at the University of Toronto and the University of Paris as a post-doc from 1999 to 2002. In 2004 and 2005 she worked briefly at INRIA (France) and the University of Paris as a visiting professor. Her current research interests are in the areas of Web services, e-business and e-science.

George O.M. Yee is a senior scientist in the Information Security Group, Institute for Information Technology, National Research Council Canada (NRC). Prior to joining the NRC in late 2001, he spent over 20 years at Bell-Northern Research and Nortel Networks. George received his PhD (electrical engineering) from Carleton University, Ottawa, Canada, where he is currently an adjunct research professor. He is a senior member of IEEE, and member of ACM and Professional Engineers Ontario. His research interests include security and privacy for e-services, using software agents to enhance reliability, security, and privacy, and engineering software for reliability, security, and performance.

Bin Yu received the PhD from school of engineering and design at Brunel University in April 2007. He is currently a system analyst in Levele Limited in Edinburgh. His research interests are in the areas of service oriented computing, grid computing and applications, service discovery and composition optimization.

John Zic is a Principal Research Scientist at CSIRO ICT Centre. He also holds a Visiting Associate Professor appointment in the School of Computer Science and Engineering, UNSW. He was previously a project leader of the "User Centred Identity Management Project" in the Smart Internet Technologies Collaborative Research Centre. Prior to that has held appointments at Motorola Australian Research Centre as a Principal Research Engineer in the area of home networking, and was at UNSW as a Senior Lecturer where he taught networking and concurrent computing for eight years. His current research interests are in trust, identity and security management; collaboration support via network and storage virtualization, and distributed, networked systems modeling and verification.

István Zólyomi got his MSc at the Eötvös Loránd University Budapest, Hungary in 2003, where he is finishing his PhD studies. He is researching the methodologies of programming and has a main interest in metaprogramming. He worked for several firms since 2000, contributed in designing and programming portal, business administration and service oriented systems, and is currently involved in developing computer games.

Index

A

B

C

D

E

F

G

H

I

J

L

M

N

O

P

Q

R

S

T

U

V

W

X